Taking SIDES

Clashing Views on Controversial Issues in American History, Volume II, Reconstruction to the Present

Eighth Edition

Edited, Selected, and with Introductions by

Larry Madaras
Howard Community College
and
James M. SoRelle
Baylor University

Dushkin/McGraw-Hill
A Division of The McGraw-Hill Companies

To Maggie and Cindy

Photo Acknowledgments

Cover image: © 2000 by PhotoDisc, Inc.

Cover Art Acknowledgment

Charles Vitelli

Library of Congress Cataloging-in-Publication Data

Main entry under title:
    Taking sides: clashing views on controversial issues in American history, volume II, reconstruction to the present/edited, selected, and with introductions by Larry Madaras and James M. SoRelle.—8th ed.
    Includes bibliographical references and index.
    1. United States—History—1865–. I. Madaras, Larry, *comp.* II. SoRelle, James M., *comp.*

                                               973

0-07-303162-3   ISSN: 1091-8833

Printed on Recycled Paper

PREFACE

The success of the past seven editions of *Taking Sides: Clashing Views on Controversial Issues in American History* has encouraged us to remain faithful to its original objectives, methods, and format. Our aim has been to create an effective instrument to enhance classroom learning and to foster critical thinking. Historical facts presented in a vacuum are of little value to the educational process. For students, whose search for historical truth often concentrates on *when* something happened rather than on *why*, and on specific events rather than on the *significance* of those events, *Taking Sides* is designed to offer an interesting and valuable departure. The understanding that the reader arrives at based on the evidence that emerges from the clash of views encourages the reader to view history as an *interpretive* discipline, not one of rote memorization.

As in previous editions, the issues are arranged in chronological order and can be easily incorporated into any American history survey course. Each issue has an issue *introduction*, which sets the stage for the debate that follows in the pro and con selections and provides historical and methodological background to the problem that the issue examines. Each issue concludes with a *postscript*, which ties the readings together, briefly mentions alternative interpretations, and supplies detailed *suggestions for further reading* for the student who wishes to pursue the topics raised in the issue. Also, Internet site addresses (URLs) have been provided on the *On the Internet* page that accompanies each part opener, which should prove useful as starting points for further research.

Changes to this edition   In this edition we have continued our efforts to maintain a balance between the traditional political, diplomatic, and cultural issues and the new social history, which depicts a society that benefited from the presence of African Americans, women, and workers of various racial and ethnic backgrounds. With this in mind, we present seven entirely new issues: *Was it Wrong to Impeach Andrew Johnson?* (Issue 1); *Was John D. Rockefeller a "Robber Baron"?* (Issue 2); *Did Nineteenth-Century Women of the West Fail to Overcome the Hardships of Living on the Great Plains?* (Issue 3); *Were American Workers in the Gilded Age Conservative Capitalists?* (Issue 4); *Did Yellow Journalism Cause the Spanish-American War?* (Issue 6); *Was the United States Responsible for the Cold War?* (Issue 12); and *Was America's Escalation of the War in Vietnam Inevitable?* (Issue 14). Also, for Issue 11, *Was Franklin Roosevelt a Reluctant Internationalist?* the NO side has been replaced to bring a fresh perspective to the debate. In all there are 15 new selections.

A word to the instructor   An *Instructor's Manual With Test Questions* (multiple-choice and essay) is available through the publisher for the instructor using *Taking Sides* in the classroom. A general guidebook, *Using Taking Sides in the Classroom*, which discusses methods and techniques for integrating the pro-con approach into any classroom setting, is also available. An online version of *Using Taking Sides in the Classroom* and a correspondence service for Taking Sides adopters can be found at http://www.dushkin.com/usingts/. For students, we offer a field guide to analyzing argumentative essays, *Analyzing Controversy: An Introductory Guide*, with exercises and techniques to help them to decipher genuine controversies.

   Taking Sides: Clashing Views on Controversial Issues in American History, Volume II is only one title in the Taking Sides series. If you are interested in seeing the table of contents for any of the other titles, please visit the Taking Sides Web site at http://www.dushkin.com/takingsides/.

Acknowledgments   Many individuals have contributed to the successful completion of this edition. We appreciate the evaluations submitted to Dushkin/McGraw-Hill by those who have used *Taking Sides* in the classroom. Special thanks to those who responded with specific suggestions for this edition:

Gary Best
University of Hawaii
   at Hilo

James D. Bolton
Coastline Community
   College

Mary Borg
University of Northern
   Colorado

John Whitney Evans
College of St. Scholastica

Gordon Lam
Sierra College

Andrew O'Shaugnessy
University of
   Wisconsin–Oshkosh

Elliot Pasternack
Middlesex County College

Robert M. Paterson
Armstrong State College

Ethan S. Rafuse
University of Missouri at
   Kansas City

John Reid
Ohio State University–Lima

Murray Rubinstein
CUNY Baruch College

Neil Sapper
Amarillo College

Preston Shea
Plymouth State College

   We are particularly indebted to Maggie Cullen, Cindy SoRelle, Barry A. Crouch, Virginia Kirk, Joseph and Helen Mitchell, and Jean Soto, who shared their ideas for changes, pointed us toward potentially useful historical works, and provided significant editorial assistance. Megan Arnold and Anne Markulis (Howard Community College) performed indispensable typing duties connected with this project. Susan E. Myers in the library at Howard Community College provided essential help in acquiring books and articles on interlibrary loan. Finally, we are sincerely grateful for the commitment, encouragement, and patience provided over the years by David Dean, former list manager for the Taking Sides series; David Brackley, senior developmental editor; and the entire staff of Dushkin/McGraw-Hill.

Larry Madaras
Howard Community College

James M. SoRelle
Baylor University

CONTENTS IN BRIEF

CONTENTS

Historian Irving Brant argues that President Andrew Johnson was the victim
of partisan Republican politics and that the articles of impeachment passed
by the House of Representatives violated the U.S. Constitution. Professor
of history Harold M. Hyman contends that Congress's decision to impeach
President Johnson was wholly justifiable on constitutional grounds in light
of Johnson's repeated defiance of national law.

Historian Matthew Josephson depicts John D. Rockefeller as an unconscionable manipulator who employed deception, bribery, and outright conspiracy to eliminate his competitors for control of the oil industry in the United
States. Business historians Ralph W. Hidy and Muriel E. Hidy argue that
Rockefeller and his associates were innovative representatives of corporate
capitalism who brought stability to the often chaotic petroleum industry.

Professor of history Christine Stansell contends that women on the Great Plains were separated from friends and relatives and consequently endured lonely lives and loveless marriages. Professor of history Glenda Riley argues that women on the Great Plains created rich and varied social lives through the development of strong support networks.

Professor of history Carl N. Degler maintains that the American labor movement accepted capitalism and reacted conservatively to the radical organizational changes brought about in the economic system by big business. Professor of history Herbert G. Gutman argues that from 1843 to 1893, American factory workers attempted to humanize the system through the maintenance of their traditional, artisan, preindustrial work habits.

Professor emeritus of history Alexander B. Callow, Jr., insists that William M. "Boss" Tweed and his infamous "ring" extracted enormous sums of ill-gotten money for their own benefit in post–Civil War New York. Professor of history Leo Hershkowitz argues that Tweed's reputation as the symbol for urban political corruption is grossly undeserved.

Journalist W. A. Swanberg argues that newspaper mogul William Randolph Hearst used the sensational and exploitative stories in his widely circulated *New York Journal* to stir up public opinion and to force President William McKinley to wage a war against Spain to free Cuba. Historian Richard Hofstadter maintains that the Spanish-American War was fought as an idealistic humanitarian crusade to liberate Cuba.

Professor of history Donald Spivey contends that Booker T. Washington alienated both students and faculty at Tuskegee Institute by establishing an authoritarian system that failed to provide an adequate academic curriculum to prepare students for the industrial workplace. Professor emeritus of history Louis R. Harlan portrays Washington as a political realist whose policies and actions were designed to benefit black society as a whole.

Professor of history Richard M. Abrams maintains that progressivism was a failure because it never seriously confronted the inequalities that still exist in American society. Professors of history Arthur S. Link and Richard L. McCormick argue that the Progressives were a diverse group of reformers who confronted and ameliorated the worst abuses that emerged in urban industrial America during the early 1900s.

History professor William E. Leuchtenburg argues that the growing secularization of American society and the hedonistic mood in the country in the 1920s produced a youth rebellion against the symbols of Victorian authority. Author David A. Shannon asserts that the social and cultural changes described by many as revolutionary were actually superficial elements whose significance to the 1920s has been exaggerated.

Professor of history Roger Biles contends that, in spite of its minimal reforms, the New Deal created a limited welfare state that implemented economic stabilizers to avert another depression. Professor of history Gary Dean Best argues that Roosevelt's regulatory programs retarded the nation's economic recovery from the Great Depression until World War II.

Diplomatic historian Robert A. Divine argues that even after France fell to Nazi Germany in June 1940, Franklin Roosevelt remained a reluctant internationalist who spoke belligerently but acted timidly because he sincerely hated war. Professor of history William E. Kinsella, Jr., argues that from the time Adolf Hitler came to power in 1933, Roosevelt viewed Hitler as an overbearing, aggressive, warlike German whose long-range goal was to conquer Europe and the United States.

Professor of history Thomas G. Paterson argues that the Truman administration exaggerated the Soviet threat after World War II because the United States had expansionist political and economic global needs. Professor of history John Lewis Gaddis argues that the power vacuum that existed in Europe at the end of World War II exaggerated and made almost inevitable a clash between the United States and the USSR.

Professor of history and sociology Melvyn Dubofsky and professor of history Athan Theoharis argue that throughout the 1950s, the U.S. economy dominated much of the globe and created a period of unprecedented growth and prosperity for the percentage of the American population that made it into the middle class. Professor of history Douglas T. Miller and journalist Marion Nowak argue that the 1950s were an era of conformity in which Americans feared the bomb, communists, crime, and the loss of a national purpose.

Professor of history Brian VanDeMark argues that President Lyndon Johnson failed to question the viability of increasing U.S. involvement in the Vietnam War because he was a prisoner of America's global containment policy. H. R. McMaster, an active-duty army tanker, maintains that the Vietnam disaster was not inevitable but a uniquely human failure whose responsibility was shared by President Johnson and his principal advisers.

Professor of history Robert Weisbrot describes the lasting achievements produced by the civil rights movement in the realm of school desegregation, the protection of voting rights for African Americans, and the deepening commitment to racial harmony. Political journalist Tom Wicker recognizes that legal segregation ended in the South in the 1960s but contends that in the 1970s and 1980s white animosity toward African American achievements drained momentum from the movement for true racial equality.

According to professor of history Joan Hoff-Wilson, the Nixon presidency reorganized the executive branch and implemented a number of domestic reforms, despite its limited foreign policy successes and the Watergate scandal. Professor and political commentator Stanley I. Kutler argues that President Nixon was a crass, cynical, narrow-minded politician who unnecessarily prolonged the Vietnam War to ensure his reelection.

Political analyst Kevin Phillips argues that President Ronald Reagan's tax reform bills in the 1980s widened the income gap by decreasing the tax burden on the rich and increasing the taxes paid by the middle-income and poor classes. Conservative economist Alan Reynolds asserts that all income groups experienced significant gains in income during the 1980s.

INTRODUCTION

The Study of History

Larry Madaras
James M. SoRelle

In a pluralistic society such as ours, the study of history is bound to be a complex process. How an event is interpreted depends not only on the existing evidence but also on the perspective of the interpreter. Consequently, understanding history presupposes the evaluation of information, a task that often leads to conflicting conclusions. An understanding of history, then, requires the acceptance of the idea of historical relativism. Relativism means that redefinition of our past is always possible and desirable. History shifts, changes, and grows with new and different evidence and interpretations. As is the case with the law and even with medicine, beliefs that were unquestioned 100 or 200 years ago have been discredited or discarded since.

Relativism, then, encourages revisionism. There is a maxim that "the past must remain useful to the present." Historian Carl Becker argued that every generation should examine history for itself, thus ensuring constant scrutiny of our collective experience through new perspectives. History, consequently, does not remain static, in part because historians cannot avoid being influenced by the times in which they live. Almost all historians commit themselves to revising the views of other historians, synthesizing theories into macrointerpretations, or revising the revisionists.

SCHOOLS OF THOUGHT

Three predominant schools of thought have emerged in American history since the first graduate seminars in history were given at the Johns Hopkins University in Baltimore in the 1870s. The *progressive* school dominated the professional field in the first half of the twentieth century. Influenced by the reform currents of Populism, progressivism, and the New Deal, these historians explored the social and economic forces that energized America. The progressive scholars tended to view the past in terms of conflicts between groups, and they sympathized with the underdog.

The post–World War II period witnessed the emergence of a new group of historians who viewed the conflict thesis as overly simplistic. Writing against the backdrop of the cold war, these *neoconservative* or *consensus* historians argued that Americans possess a shared set of values and that the areas of agreement within the nation's basic democratic and capitalistic framework were more important than the areas of disagreement.

In the 1960s, however, the civil rights movement, women's liberation, and the student rebellion (with its condemnation of the war in Vietnam) fragmented the consensus of values upon which historians and social scientists of the 1950s centered their interpretations. This turmoil set the stage for the emergence of another group of scholars. *New Left* historians began to reinterpret the past once again. They emphasized the significance of conflict in American history, and they resurrected interest in those groups ignored by the consensus school. In addition, New Left historians critiqued the expansionist policies of the United States and emphasized the difficulties confronted by Native Americans, African Americans, women, and urban workers in gaining full citizenship status.

Progressive, consensus, and New Left history is still being written. The most recent generation of scholars, however, focuses upon social history. Their primary concern is to discover what the lives of "ordinary Americans" were really like. These new social historians employ previously overlooked court and church documents, house deeds and tax records, letters and diaries, photographs, and census data to reconstruct the everyday lives of average Americans. Some employ new methodologies, such as quantification (enhanced by advancing computer technology) and oral history, while others borrow from the disciplines of political science, economics, sociology, anthropology, and psychology for their historical investigations.

The proliferation of historical approaches, which are reflected in the issues debated in this book, has had mixed results. On the one hand, historians have become so specialized in their respective time periods and methodological styles that it is difficult to synthesize the recent scholarship into a comprehensive text for the general reader. On the other hand, historians know more about the American past than at any other time in history. They dare to ask new questions or ones that previously were considered to be germane only to scholars in other social sciences. Although there is little agreement about the answers to these questions, the methods employed and issues explored make the "new history" a very exciting field to study.

The topics that follow represent a variety of perspectives and approaches. Each of these controversial issues can be studied for its individual importance to American history. Taken as a group, they interact with one another to illustrate larger historical themes. When grouped thematically, the issues reveal continuing motifs in the development of American history.

ECONOMIC QUESTIONS

Issue 2 explores the dynamics of the modern American economy through investigations of the nineteenth-century entrepreneurs. It evaluates the contributions of post–Civil War entrepreneurial giants. Were these industrial leaders robber barons, as portrayed by contemporary critics and many history texts? Or were they industrial statesmen and organizational geniuses? Matthew Josephson argues that John D. Rockefeller is a key example of a monopoly capitalist who utilized ruthless and violent methods in organizing the oil industry. More favorable and representative of the business historian approach is the interpretation of Ralph W. Hidy and Muriel E. Hidy. Rockefeller, they argue, possessed an extraordinary mind, a penchant for detail, foresight and vision, and an ability to make decisions. They conclude that Rockefeller was among the earliest organizational innovators and that he standardized production and procedures and created a large integrated industrial corporation.

POLITICAL REFORMS AND THE STATUS QUO

Issue 5 assesses the nature of urban government in the late nineteenth century. Focusing on the activities of William M. "Boss" Tweed in post–Civil War New York City, Alexander B. Callow, Jr., discusses corrupting influences on city and state governments and on big businesses. Leo Hershkowitz presents a contrasting viewpoint, emphasizing Tweed's services and benefits to the city. He rejects Tweed's reputation for corruption, suggesting that it is undeserved.

The Progressive movement is examined in Issue 8. Richard M. Abrams attributes the failure of the movement to its limited scope. He maintains that it imposed a uniform set of values on a diverse people and did not address the inequalities that prevail in American society. Arthur S. Link and Richard L. McCormick, however, emphasize the reforms introduced by the Progressives to check the abuses of industrialization and urbanization during the early 1900s.

One of the more timely issues in this book, which demonstrates that history can shed some light on a current political controversy, is Issue 1 on whether or not President Andrew Johnson should have been impeached. Irving Brant takes the traditional view and argues that Johnson treated the 11 defeated Confederate states as legal entities who never left the Union, not as conquered provinces. Johnson favored a more lenient Reconstruction program than his Republican congressional opponents, and he vetoed their policies. Furthermore, Brant maintains, passage of the Tenure of Office Act wrongly nullified the president's constitutional right to fire cabinet members without the approval of Congress. Harold M. Hyman, in response, argues that Johnson deserved to be impeached because he obstructed the Reconstruction policies passed by the congressional Republican majority. However, by the time of the Senate trial, notes Hyman, Johnson had changed some of his obstructionist ways by nominating a moderate as secretary of war and sending to the Senate for ratification the Reconstruction constitutions of South Carolina and Arkansas. Hyman reasons that these actions explain in part why seven moderate senators voted against convicting Johnson of the impeachment charges.

FROM DEPRESSION THROUGH PROSPERITY: 1930–1990

The Great Depression of the 1930s remains one of the most traumatic events in U.S. history. The characteristics of that decade are deeply etched in American folk memory, but the remedies that were applied to these social and economic ills—known collectively as the New Deal—are not easy to evaluate. In Issue 10, Roger Biles contends that the economic stabilizers created by New Deal programs prevented the recurrence of the Great Depression. Gary Dean Best, on the other hand, criticizes the New Deal from a 1990s conservative perspective. In his view, the Roosevelt administration prolonged the depression and retarded the recovery. Because New Deal agencies were antibusiness, they overregulated the economy and did not allow the free enterprise system to work out of the depression.

Issue 13 deals with the decade of the 1950s. Melvyn Dubofsky and Athan Theoharis stress the global superpower role of the United States and the prosperity of the middle class, which they feel made these years an era of happiness and optimism. Douglas T. Miller and Marion Nowak detect the underlying anxiety in the decade, with shadows of the cold war, communism, and the atomic bomb looming.

Because he was forced to resign the presidency to avoid impeachment proceedings resulting from his role in the Watergate scandal, President Richard Nixon remains a controversial political figure. How will Nixon, who died in 1994, be remembered? In Issue 16, Joan Hoff-Wilson downplays the significance of the Watergate scandal as well as foreign policy accomplishments in assessing Nixon's legacy. Instead, she argues, Nixon should be applauded for his domestic accomplishments, including reorganizing the executive branch of the federal government and implementing important civil rights, welfare, and economic planning programs. Stanley I. Kutler disagrees with these revisionist treatments of the former president, insisting that Nixon was a crass, cynical, narrow-minded politician who unnecessarily prolonged the Vietnam War to ensure his reelection and who implemented domestic reforms only to outflank his liberal opponents.

Following the economic upheavals of the 1970s, created by the Vietnam War and the oil crisis, President Ronald Reagan introduced economic policies based on supply-side economics. The success of these policies is the subject matter of Issue 17. Kevin Phillips focuses on the economic advantages that this approach brought to the wealthy. Alan Reynolds, on the other hand, uses statistics to show that all income groups experienced a rise in income levels during this decade.

THE OUTSIDERS: LABORERS, BLACKS, WOMEN, AND INTELLECTUALS

In the wake of industrialization during the late 1800s, the rapid pace of change created new working conditions for the laboring class. How did laborers react to these changes? Did they lose their autonomy in the large corporations? Did they accept or reject the wage system? Were they pawns of the economic cycles of boom and bust, to be hired and fired at will? Did they look for an alternative to capitalism by engaging in strikes, establishing labor unions, or creating a socialist movement? In Issue 4, Carl N. Degler maintains that American workers accepted capitalism and the changes that it brought forth. Degler argues that workers wanted to improve their livestyle with better workplace conditions, shorter hours, better pay, and more benefits. Herbert G. Gutman sees the workers responding to the changing capitalist system in a different manner than Degler does. In the years 1843–1893, says Gutman, American factory workers attempted to humanize the system by maintaining their traditional artisan values. By the beginning of the twentieth century, however, the organizational innovations of John D. Rockefeller and the assembly-line techniques pioneered by Henry Ford had revolutionized American capitalism.

One of the most controversial figures in American history was the early-twentieth-century African American leader Booker T. Washington. Was Washington too accommodating toward white values and goals and too accepting of the political disfranchisement and social segregation that took away the basic freedoms that African Americans earned after their emancipation from slavery? In Issue 7, Donald Spivey argues the case against Washington's ideology and policies, while Louis R. Harlan maintains that there were two Washingtons. Harlan argues that Washington, while publicly assuring whites that he accepted segregation, fought active and bitter battles behind the scenes to advance the political, economic, and educational opportunities for African Americans. Washington, then, was a political realist whose long-range goals of progress toward equality was a practical response to the climate of the times in which he lived.

Issue 15 evaluates the civil rights movement, which has brought many tangible opportunities to blacks and minorities, according to Robert Weisbrot. Tom Wicker, on the other hand, points out that racial equality has still not been achieved and that programs such as affirmative action have been the cause of bitterness and division among the races.

One of the less well known areas of American history is the impact of the frontier on the women who migrated west. In Issue 3, Christine Stansell maintains that women who migrated west in the late nineteenth century lost their networks of family and friends back east and that they were isolated and lonely and often endured loveless marriages on the Great Plains. Glenda Riley agrees that women faced many hardships on the frontier. However, she argues that women rebuilt friendships on the frontier through church gatherings and quilting bee sessions. Also, says Riley, it was no accident that western women were at the forefront of the women's suffrage movement.

The decade of the 1920s had a unique flavor. The role of intellectuals in protecting the values of the era is discussed in Issue 9. William E. Leuchtenburg views the era as one of social and cultural rebellion, whereas David A. Shannon sees these changes as superficial in comparison with the economic expansion that ushered in a culture of mass consumption.

THE UNITED STATES AND THE WORLD

As the United States developed a preeminent position in world affairs, the nation's politicians were forced to consider the proper relationship between their country and the rest of the world. To what extent, many asked, should the United States seek to expand its political, economic, or moral influence around the world?

This was a particularly intriguing question for a number of political, military, and intellectual leaders at the close of the nineteenth century, who pondered whether or not it was necessary to acquire an overseas empire to be considered one of the world's great powers. Many historians consider the Spanish-American war a turning point in American history. In Issue 6, W. A. Swanberg argues that newspaper mogul William Randolph Hearst used the sensational and exploitative stories in his widely circulated and nationally influential *New York Journal* to stir up public opinion and to push President William McKinley into a questionable war. Taking a broader view, Richard Hofstadter contends that the pressures of the 1980s—a major economic depression, labor violence, and Populist unrest—caused a "psychic crisis" in the nation that climaxed with the Spanish-American war.

The role of the United States in World War II is closely linked with President Franklin D. Roosevelt. In Issue 11, Robert A. Divine portrays Roosevelt as a leader whose words were tough but whose actions betrayed his hatred of war. In contrast, William E. Kinsella, Jr., argues that from the time Hitler came to power in 1933, Roosevelt viewed him as an overbearing, aggressive, warlike German whose goal of world conquest would have to be stopped by American military action at the appropriate time.

The United States had barely emerged victorious against Germany and Japan in 1945 when a cold war developed against its former ally, the Soviet Union. Issue 12 tackles the question of responsibility. Thomas G. Paterson blames the United States for exaggerating the Soviet threat to world peace. He argues that the United States, untouched physically by the war and having emerged as the world's greatest military and economic power, tried to reshape the world political and economic structures to meet the needs of American capitalism. John Lewis Gaddis, taking a different position, argues that the power vacuum that existed in Europe at the end of World War II exaggerated the countries' differences and made a clash between the democratic, capitalist United States and the totalitarian, communist USSR almost inevitable.

No discussion of American foreign policy is complete without some consideration of the Vietnam War. Was America's escalation of the war inevitable in 1965? In Issue 14, Brian VanDeMark argues that President Lyndon Johnson was a prisoner of America's global "containment" policy. He was afraid to pull out of Vietnam because he feared that his opponents would accuse him of being soft on communism and that they would also destroy his Great Society reforms. H. R. McMaster blames Johnson and his civilian and military advisers for failing to develop a coherent policy in Vietnam.

CONCLUSION

The process of historical study should rely more on thinking than on memorizing data. Once the basics of who, what, when, and where are determined, historical thinking shifts to a higher gear. Analysis, comparison and contrast, evaluation, and explanation take command. These skills not only increase our knowledge of the past but they also provide general tools for the comprehension of all the topics about which human beings think.

The diversity of a pluralistic society, however, creates some obstacles to comprehending the past. The spectrum of differing opinions on any particular subject eliminates the possibility of quick and easy answers. In the final analysis, conclusions are often built through a synthesis of several different interpretations, but even then they may be partial and tentative.

The study of history in a pluralistic society allows each citizen the opportunity to reach independent conclusions about the past. Since most, if not all, historical issues affect the present and future, understanding the past becomes necessary if society is to progress. Many of today's problems have a direct connection with the past. Additionally, other contemporary issues may lack obvious direct antecedents, but historical investigation can provide illuminating analogies. At first, it may appear confusing to read and to think about opposing historical views, but the survival of our democratic society depends on such critical thinking by acute and discerning minds.

On the Internet . . .

POTUS: Presidents of the United States

This page of the Internet Public Library offers some factual information on Andrew Johnson, the 17th U.S. president, and links to biographies of Johnson, related historical documents, and other resources on the Internet.
http://www.ipl.org/ref/POTUS/ajohnson.html

National Women's History Project

The National Women's History Project is a nonprofit corporation, founded in Sonoma County, California, in 1980. The organization provides numerous links to sites on women's history under such categories as The Women's Rights Movement, Politics, African-American Women, and War and Peace.
http://www.nwhp.org/links.html

John D. Rockefeller and the Standard Oil Company

This site, created by Swiss entrepreneur François Micheloud, provides a highly detailed history of the American oil industry, with John D. Rockefeller as a main focus. It includes the discovery of oil, the main players in the oil industry, the rise of the Standard Oil Company, the passing of the Sherman Antitrust Act, and the dismantling of Standard Oil, as well as both short and detailed chronologies of the company.
http://www.micheloud.com/FXM/SO/rock.htm

Gilded Age and Progressive Era Resources

This page of the Department of History at Tennessee Technological University offers over 100 links to sites on the Gilded Age and the Progressive era. Links include general resources, political leaders, transformation of the West, the rise of big business and American workers, and literary and cultural resources.
http://www.tntech.edu/www/acad/hist/gilprog.html

PART 1

Reconstruction, Immigration, and the Industrial Revolution

Deep and bitter wounds were left in the American nation as a result of the Civil War. Reconstruction was a period of further turmoil as the political institutions of the South were redesigned.

Economic expansion and the seemingly unlimited resources available in postbellum America offered great opportunity and created new political, social, and economic challenges. Political freedom and economic opportunity provided incentives for immigration to America. The need for cheap labor to run the machinery of the industrial revolution created an atmosphere for potential exploitation that was intensified by the concentration of wealth in the hands of a few capitalists. The labor movement took root, with some elements calling for an overthrow of the capitalist system, while others sought to establish political power within the existing system. Strains began to develop between immigrant and native-born workers as well as between workers and owners.

With the growth of industry, urban problems became more acute. Improvements in water and sewerage, street cleaning, housing, mass transit, and fire and crime prevention developed slowly because incredible population growth strained municipal services. Urban governments had limited powers, which often fell under the control of political bosses. Historians disagree as to whether or not attempts to remedy these problems were successful.

The westward movement served as a partial safety valve for the exploding population, but women experienced emotional difficulties in uprooting themselves from family ties.

■ Was It Wrong to Impeach Andrew Johnson?

■ Was John D. Rockefeller a "Robber Baron"?

■ Did Nineteenth-Century Women of the West Fail to Overcome the Hardships of Living on the Great Plains?

■ Were American Workers in the Gilded Age Conservative Capitalists?

■ Did William M. Tweed Corrupt Post–Civil War New York?

1

ISSUE 1

Was It Wrong to Impeach Andrew Johnson?

YES: Irving Brant, from *Impeachment: Trials and Errors* (Alfred A. Knopf, 1972)

NO: Harold M. Hyman, from *A More Perfect Union: The Impact of the Civil War and Reconstruction on the Constitution* (Alfred A. Knopf, 1973)

ISSUE SUMMARY

YES: Historian Irving Brant argues that President Andrew Johnson was the victim of partisan Republican politics and that the articles of impeachment passed by the House of Representatives constituted a bill of attainder in violation of the U.S. Constitution.

NO: Professor of history Harold M. Hyman contends that Congress's decision to impeach President Johnson was wholly justifiable on constitutional grounds in light of Johnson's repeated defiance of national law and his efforts to seize control of the army.

On December 19, 1998, the U.S. House of Representatives approved two articles of impeachment charging President Bill Clinton with committing "high crimes and misdemeanors" for allegedly thwarting an investigation of his personal relationship with White House intern Monica Lewinsky. As the case made its way to the Senate, media pundits and constitutional scholars across the nation provided the American people with a historical context for the first impeachment trial of an American president in 130 years. In doing so, they reminded their viewers and readers of the political drama played out in Washington, D.C., only three years after the end of the Civil War, when President Andrew Johnson escaped being removed from office by a single vote in the Senate.

Johnson, born into poverty in North Carolina in 1808, migrated to Tennessee at the age of 18 and, through a combination of ambition and hard work, made a name for himself in Democratic politics. As governor of the Volunteer State and the most prominent Southern politician to reject secession, Johnson attracted the attention of Abraham Lincoln, who offered him a spot as his vice presidential running mate on the Union party ticket in 1864. In April 1965, shortly after their electoral success, Lincoln was assassinated. As a result, Johnson became president within days of the end of the Civil War and was confronted with the enormous responsibilities associated with restoring the states of the former Confederacy to the Union.

For radical Republicans, Andrew Johnson initially seemed a preferable architect of postwar Reconstruction than the martyred Lincoln. After all, Johnson had openly expressed his desire to punish members of the planter aristocracy by prohibiting them from political participation until they had obtained a pardon from Johnson himself. In fact, Johnson envisioned a new political order in the South that would empower poor whites at the expense of the traditional political elite—the planters.

The honeymoon between congressional Republicans and the new president, however, was short-lived. Johnson adopted a Reconstruction policy that was similar to the lenient program outlined by Lincoln prior to his death, and he celebrated the rapidity with which the former Confederate states were restored to the Union. Radical Republicans were shocked when Johnson accepted the new Southern governments—many of whose elected leaders had been waging war against the United States only a few months earlier—into the national fold. They were dismayed by the president's acquiescence to the discriminatory "Black Codes" adopted by each of these states in place of the defunct slave statutes and by his refusal to seek congressional advice on the Reconstruction process. Relations further deteriorated when Johnson vetoed the Civil Rights Act of 1866 and a bill to extend the life of the Freedmen's Bureau. With the aid of moderate Republicans, the radicals succeeded in overriding these presidential vetoes, but the die had been cast. Johnson continued to resist the implementation of the Military Reconstruction Acts passed by Congress a year earlier, and he attempted to remove Secretary of War Edwin Stanton from office in apparent violation of the Tenure of Office Act. For these offenses, in 1868 the House of Representatives adopted 11 articles of impeachment against Johnson.

Were these actions justified? Had Johnson overstepped the constitutional bounds of his office? Had he threatened the sanctity of the Constitution of the United States? Was he guilty of "high crimes and misdemeanors," as charged by his congressional critics? These questions are addressed in the following selections by Irving Brant and Harold M. Hyman.

Brant agrees that Andrew Johnson did a great deal to incur the wrath of congressional Republicans. However, he argues that these actions did not warrant impeachment proceedings. In fact, Brant asserts, the Tenure of Office Act was patently unconstitutional, and the articles of impeachment adopted by the House amounted to a bill of attainder, the legality of which is rejected by the Constitution of the United States.

Hyman supports the decision to impeach Andrew Johnson. He argues that Johnson obstructed numerous congressional measures and directly violated the Tenure of Office Act. In the wake of this defiant behavior, says Hyman, the Republicans were fully within their constitutional rights to impeach the president.

3

YES
Irving Brant

THE JOHNSON TRIAL: ATTAINDER
BY IMPEACHMENT

The impeachment trial of President Andrew Johnson presented a strange phenomenon that has gone unnoticed in histories. Besides rebutting the specific charges against him, Johnson's counsel assailed the impeachment as a violation of the Constitution. By the nature of those charges, they contended, the proceeding violated the clause forbidding Congress to pass bills of attainder. Lawyer after lawyer hammered on that theme, but not once did a House Manager reply. The reason appears obvious: they regarded silence as a better strategy than unconvincing denials.

What is a bill of attainder? The Supreme Court defined it in the very year of the Johnson impeachment, when the Court struck down two laws passed at the close of the Civil War that required lawyers and clergymen to take loyalty oaths as a precondition to practicing their profession. Said the Court in *Cummings* v. *Missouri,* holding the oath for lawyers to be in violation of the Constitution:

"A bill of attainder is a legislative act which inflicts punishment without a judicial trial. If the punishment be less than death, the act is termed a bill of pains and penalties. Within the meaning of the Constitution, bills of attainder include bills of pains and penalties." ...

President Andrew Johnson did many things that invited the wrath of a Congress gripped by deep emotions after four years of civil war. Johnson, a Tennessee senator who opposed the secession of his state and adhered to the Union throughout the war, was given the vice presidential nomination in 1864 out of gratitude and party policy. The assassination of President Lincoln thrust him into the Presidency on April 15, 1865, at the moment of transition from war to peace, from preservation of the Union to the difficult and complex task of restoring national government and national unity.

The immediate question was: Should the eleven Confederate states be regarded as still legally part of the Union, and treated as if they never had left it? Or should they be regarded as conquered provinces, to be readmitted as states under such conditions as Congress should prescribe and they should agree to? President Johnson took the former view; Congress the latter. Each

From Irving Brant, *Impeachment: Trials and Errors* (Alfred A. Knopf, 1972). Copyright © 1972 by Irving Brant. Reprinted by permission of Alfred A. Knopf, Inc. Notes omitted.

4

side invoked the name of Abraham Lincoln, but Lincoln's final policies put him much closer to the views of his successor than to those of the Radical Republican leadership in Congress.

On the crucial issue of "rebel suffrage" there were three successive postwar policies. In reorganizing Arkansas, Louisiana, Tennessee, and Virginia, Lincoln as commander in chief disfranchised only Confederate leaders. President Johnson, ruling alone in the April–December 1865 absence of Congress, extended the disfranchisement to Confederate generals and men owning property worth more than $20,000. His object was to let poor whites govern the South and to break up the big plantations. The Radical Republicans in Congress demanded full enfranchisement of the former slaves who, under the Johnson plan already in effect, were being held close to their former status.

In the Congress that convened in December 1865, Representative Thaddeus Stevens of Pennsylvania rose swiftly to leadership of the radicals by virtue of his personal drive and the intensity of his convictions. In the Senate Charles Sumner of Massachusetts, a veteran abolitionist, gained similar preeminence. In swift succession, over the President's veto, Congress passed a series of Reconstruction Acts largely designed to protect the black population. From the Radical Republicans also came the historic Thirteenth, Fourteenth, and Fifteenth Amendments, which, as far as infringement by state action is concerned, now form the bedrock of liberty and equality under the law for all American citizens and particularly safeguard Negro rights. To enforce the Reconstruction laws, the states of the late confederacy were divided into military districts ruled by Union troops.

Trouble mounted between Johnson and Congress. In the Cabinet, Secretary of War Edwin Stanton vigorously opposed the President's Reconstruction policies. Word spread that Stanton was to be asked to resign. Congress quickly passed "an Act regulating the tenure of certain offices," which became law (again over Presidential veto) on March 2, 1867. By its terms the President could not remove any head of department without the prior consent of the Senate.

This law was patently unconstitutional. The President's power to remove such officers without consent of the Senate was debated at length in 1789 and thoroughly established by a declaratory act of Congress, not conferring that authority but worded to recognize its existence as an exclusive constitutional power....

Andrew Johnson thus had constitutional warrant for disregarding the Tenure of Office Act, but nearly a year went by with Secretary Stanton still in office. On January 30, 1868, an event occurred that revealed the Stevens faction's hair-trigger attitude toward impeachment and its sweeping concept of the power to impeach. Congressman Schofield of Pennsylvania took the floor in the House and read a short editorial from the Washington *Evening Express* of the previous day. The paper asserted that at a large social gathering one of the justices of the Supreme Court "declared in the most positive terms" that all the Reconstruction acts "were unconstitutional, and that the court would be sure to pronounce them so." Warned that such remarks were indiscreet, "he at once repeated his views in a more positive manner." The Baltimore *Gazette* named the speaker: Associate Justice Stephen J. Field, whom President Lincoln had appointed to office.

Schofield moved that the Judiciary Committee make an inquiry "and report whether the facts constituted such a misdemeanor in office as to require the House to present to the Senate articles of impeachment against the said justice of the Supreme Court." The motion was instantly approved, leaving no doubt that the Radical Republican majority regarded Justice Field's remarks as impeachable. Besides being an invasion of freedom of speech, the House action clearly meant that anything its members regarded as a "misdemeanor in office" was a constitutional ground of impeachment, even though it had not the faintest taint of criminality. Field's remark was an indiscretion, but no reasonable person could call it an impeachable misdemeanor. If the Constitution means what it says, both on impeachment and on attainder, nothing could more plainly stamp such an impeachment as a bill of attainder in disguise.

In three weeks, the impeachment move against Justice Field dropped out of sight and out of mind. For on February 21 President Johnson removed Secretary Stanton from office for undercutting Presidential policies. Three days later the House of Representatives, by a majority of 126 to 47, voted articles of impeachment against the President.

Eleven articles were presented, but ten related to the Stanton episode. Primarily, the House charged as a high crime and misdemeanor that on February 21 the President did unlawfully "issue an order in writing for the removal of Edwin M. Stanton from the office of Secretary for the Department of War... which order was unlawfully issued with intent then

and there to violate the act entitled 'An act regulating the tenure of certain civil offices,' passed March 2, 1867."

In the only unrelated article, the House charged that Andrew Johnson did, on August 18, 1866, "deliver with a loud voice certain intemperate, inflammatory, and scandalous harangues, and did therein utter loud threats and bitter menaces as well against Congress as the laws of the United States duly enacted thereby." These were the impeachable words of the President, cited by the House Managers:

"We have witnessed in one Department of the Government every endeavor, as it were, to prevent the restoration of peace, harmony and union... we have seen Congress pretend to be for the Union when every step they took was to perpetuate dissolution, and make disruption permanent. We have seen every step that has been taken, instead of bringing about reconciliation and harmony, has been legislation that took the character of penalties, retaliation and revenge."

The citing of such sharp but orderly political remarks as a ground of impeachment stamped the movement for what it was—a determination to oust President Johnson because of hostility to his policies, not for any impeachable misconduct.

Notable among the seven House Managers were General Benjamin F. Butler of Massachusetts, a famous orator who was embroiled in controversy throughout his life; John A. Bingham of Ohio, leading drafter and congressional expositor of the Fourteenth Amendment; George S. Boutwell of Massachusetts, later Secretary of the Treasury under President Grant; and Thaddeus Stevens. They were armed with a brief on impeachment precedents furnished by Representative William Lawrence of Ohio.

President Johnson's quintet of legal defenders included some of the outstanding lawyers of the United States. Henry Stanbury resigned as Attorney General to head the group, but illness disabled him except for the opening and closing addresses to the Senate. Benjamin R. Curtis had been appointed to the Supreme Court in 1851 at the age of forty-one, but had resigned six years later in protest against the Dred Scott decision, from which he and one other justice dissented. William M. Evarts, a recognized leader of the American bar for several decades, was also a diplomat without office: President Lincoln had sent him twice to England to dissuade the British government from aiding the Confederate navy. W. S. Groesbeck and Thomas A. R. Nelson completed the team.

The trial commenced in mid-March, three weeks after the impeachment, with General Butler opening for the Managers. He began adroitly by showing familiarity with and at the same time misrepresenting the famous trial of Warren Hastings in England:

"May it not have been that the trial then in progress [in 1787] was the determining cause why the framers of the Constitution left the description of offenses because of which the conduct of an officer might be inquired of to be defined by the laws and usages of Parliament as found in the precedents of the mother country, with which our fathers were as familiar as we are with our own?"

This question by its implications carried multiple distortions, both of the Hastings case itself and of the deductions to be drawn from it—distortions magnified by Hastings's acquittal. The seven-year Hastings trial was indeed cited by George Mason, but only as a reason for extending the grounds of impeachment beyond treason and bribery. Instead of supporting Butler's implication that the case carried impeachment beyond criminal misfeasance in office, the accusatory articles against Hastings piled crime on crime.

More subtle and even more misleading was Butler's equation of "high crimes and misdemeanors" with "the usages of Parliament as found in the precedents of the mother country." Those precedents included prosecutions forced on Parliament by omnipotent kings, prosecutions initiated by Parliaments snatching omnipotence away from the monarchs, and prosecutions that were mere outbursts of unreasoning passion. They reflected the violations more than the inclusions of the common law.

Later in the Johnson trial defense counsel Evarts exposed this perversion of history by showing that in the Hastings trial itself, British precedents on impeachment were repudiated. Lord Loughborough, said Evarts, sought "to demonstrate that the ordinary rules of proceedings in criminal cases did not apply to parliamentary impeachments, which could not be shackled by the forms observed in the Courts below" (that is, below the House of Lords). Evarts quoted the words by which Lord Thurlow overthrew this contention:

"My lords, with respect to the laws and usage of Parliament, I utterly disclaim all knowledge of such laws. It has no existence. True it is, in times of despotism and popular fury, when to impeach an individual was to crush him by the strong hand of power, of tumult, or of violence, the laws and usage of Parliament were quoted in order to justify the most iniquitous or atrocious acts. But in these days of light and constitutional government, I trust that no man will be tried except by the laws of the land, a system admirably calculated to protect innocence and to punish crime."

Thus whenever a representative or senator in Congress cites British precedent to justify going beyond the Constitution, he invokes "despotism and popular fury ... the strong hand of power, of tumult, or of violence." Was that what the framers intended when they limited the grounds of impeachment to "high crimes and misdemeanors"?

General Butler, of course, ignored Lord Thurlow's denunciation of historic British practices that destroyed them as valid precedents. Instead, he sought to buttress his position by extended examples, contained in the brief submitted by Representative Lawrence, which he placed at this point in the record of the trial.

Lawrence cited case after case, from Hallam and other legal historians, of great lords done to death by impeachment—and then undermined his cause by placing them in Hallam's context of history, which supported Thurlow. First employed by Edward III in 1376, the impeachment process was set to one side by Tudor kings who found bills of attainder more convenient. The House of Stuart brought impeachment back. Between 1620 and 1688, it was employed forty times by Stuart kings or by a Parliament in rebellion against those kings. Attainder and impeachment as described by Hallam (as well as by historian Thomas Erskine May) were used interchangeably to destroy political offenders, and almost by the same process. Impeachment permitted a defense before the House of Lords; attainder had no standards.

It is impossible that the framers of our Constitution, knowing this history, would have prohibited bills of attainder and yet allowed the same forbidden results, actuated by the same passion, to be put into effect by a power of impeachment modeled by silent implication on British precedent. The debate in the Constitutional Convention, the wording of the impeachment clauses, the wholehearted devotion of the framers to liberty and justice, combine to forbid such a thought. In portentous contrast, the spirit of attainder ran through the trial of President Andrew Johnson. With truth, candor and impassioned rhetoric, Senator Sumner revealed the political motive for the prosecution:

"Andrew Johnson is the impersonation of the tyrannical Slave Power. In him it lives again ... and he gathers about him ... partisans of slavery North and South.... With the President at their head, they are now entrenched in the Executive Mansion. Not to dislodge them is to leave the country a prey to one of the most hateful tyrannies of history."

It was in this manner that the entire prosecution of President Johnson was conducted—in the spirit and actuality of a bill of attainder, with Johnson's counsel calling it by that name. It was brought in the form of impeachment solely because the Constitution prohibits bills of attainder. The House Managers thinly cloaked this purpose in their interpretations of the impeachment power.

General Butler put heavy reliance on Madison's remark in supporting the exclusive constitutional power of a President to remove his appointees from office, that if he made "wanton removal of meritorious officers," he would be subject to impeachment. Butler omitted the qualifying statement that the motive for such an action "must be that he may fill the place with an unworthy creature of his own." The Manager saw clear proof in this that the Senate had power to convict President Johnson for removing Secretary Stanton, regardless of the validity or invalidity of the Tenure of Office Act.

Such an argument revealed at one stroke the twin errors of Madison's statement and of the deduction Butler drew from it. In August 1867, without removing Stanton as Secretary of War, President Johnson nominated General Ulysses S. Grant to that position. The Senate, as was expected, defeated confirmation. The stage was set for Grant to seek the post by court action, thus testing the constitutionality of the Tenure of Office Act. However, the General refused to make the challenge. The Secretaryship of War was then offered to General William T. Sherman, who declined; political war was a bit too hellish. The President then removed Stanton and nominated Lieutenant General Lorenzo Thomas. None of these three men could be termed an "unworthy creature." Manager Bingham disclaimed criticism of Thomas; the crime was removal of Stanton. Thus by Madison's own terms, the President's removal of "meritorious" Secretary Stanton offered no constitutional ground of impeachment. Butler's misuse of Madison's words for such a purpose revealed the fallacy in Madison's argument, which he had thought up on the moment to score a point in polemics. General Butler summed up the Managers' position by quoting and concurring in these words of Representative Lawrence:

"We define therefore an impeachable high crime or misdemeanor to be one in its nature or consequences subversive of some fundamental or essential principle of government or highly prejudicial to the public interest, and this may consist of a violation of the Constitution, of law, of an official oath, or of duty, by an act committed or omitted, or, without violating a positive law, by the abuse of discretionary powers from improper motives, or for any improper purpose."

In other words, an impeachable misdemeanor was any action which the Senate regarded as improper, and which in its opinion proceeded from an improper motive. Butler turned to England for support:

"It is but common learning that in the English precedents the words 'high crimes and misdemeanors' are universally used; but any malversation in office highly prejudicial to the public interest, or subversive of some fundamental principle of government by which the safety of a people may be in danger, is a high crime against the nation, as the term is used in parliamentary law."

This obsolete British definition (done to death by Lord Thurlow) was the same as saying that President Johnson's 1866 speech criticizing Congress, and his transfer of the War Department from Edwin M. Stanton to Lorenzo Thomas, were impeachable either as "highly prejudicial to the nation" or as dangerous to the safety of its people. The Butler-Lawrence interpretation of "high crimes and misdemeanors" can be boiled down to the single word "maladministration," which the framers refused to put in the Constitution as a ground of impeachment. House Manager Bingham heightened this perversion of the framers' intentions by saying that in determining such grounds, the Senate was "a law unto itself"—a remark that gave the trial the precise quality of a bill of attainder.

Counsel for President Johnson referred to the 1789 debate in Congress on the President's power to remove officers, proving conclusively from Madison's speech (and acts of Congress based on it) that this power was recognized to lie in the President alone, unalterable by legislative action. General Butler conceded that if Johnson, instead of sending "his defiant message to the Senate," had said he was acting to test the constitutionality of the Tenure of Office Act, the House of Representatives might not have impeached him. So, said defense counsel Benjamin Curtis, the ground of impeachment was "not the removal of Mr. Stanton but the manner in which the President communicated the fact of that removal to the Senate after it was made."

Logically, this exchange of remarks, combined with the invalidity of the Tenure of Office Act, demolished the only charge against President Johnson that could fall within the definition of a "high misdemeanor." Curtis then proceeded to his main argument (which was a bit too broad, as it excluded all violations of state laws):

"My first position is, that when the Constitution speaks of 'treason, bribery, and other high crimes and misdemeanors,' it refers to, and includes, only high criminal offenses against the United States, made so by some law of the United States existing when the acts complained of were done, and I say that this is plainly to be inferred from each and every provision of the Constitution on the subject of impeachment."

He quoted the various clauses referring to "offenses," "conviction," "crimes," etc., in connection with impeachment, and said that the argument on this point was "vastly strengthened" by the Constitution's direct prohibition of bills of attainder and *ex post facto* laws. Curtis said:

"What is a bill of attainder? It is a case before the Parliament where the Parliament make the law for the facts they find. Each legislator (for it is in their legislative capacity they act, not in a judicial one) is, to use the phrase of the honorable Managers [Bingham], 'a law unto himself'; and according to his discretion, his views of what is politic or proper under the circumstances, he frames a law to meet the case and enacts it or votes in its enactment."

Still dwelling on Bingham's maladroit remark, Curtis went on:

"According to the doctrine now advanced bills of attainder are not prohibited by this Constitution; they are only slightly modified. It is only necessary for the House of Representatives by a majority to vote an impeachment and send up certain articles and have two thirds of this body vote in favor of conviction, and there is an attainder; and it is done by the same process and depends on identically the same principles as a bill of attainder in the English Parliament. The individual wills of the legislators, instead of the conscientious discharge of the duty of the judges, settle the result.

"I submit, then, Senators, that this view of the honorable Managers of the duties and powers of this body cannot be maintained."

In conclusion, Curtis turned to the article impeaching the President for slander of Congress in a speech. This, he said, was not only an attempt to set up an *ex post facto* law where none existed "prior to the act to punish the act"; it was a case where Congress was expressly prohibited, by the First Amendment, from making any law whatever, even to punish subsequent speech.

What was this law on freedom of speech designed to be? Was it to be, "as the honorable Managers seem to think it should be, the sense of propriety of each Senator appealed to"? That was "the same freedom of speech, Senators, in consequence of which thousands of men went to the scaffold under the Tudors and the Stuarts.... Is that the freedom of speech intended to be secured by our Constitution?"

This trial, Curtis predicted, would live in history as the most conspicuous American example either of justice or of injustice. It would (to paraphrase Edmund Burke) either exemplify that justice which is the standing policy of all civilized states, or it would produce "that injustice which is sure to be discovered, and which makes even the wise man mad, and which, in the fixed and immutable order of God's providence, is certain to return to plague its inventors."

The House Managers continued to provide defense with openings to call the impeachment a bill of attainder. Later in the trial, defense counsel Groesbeck put some of these remarks together. Without naming the Managers, he said that one of them (it was Butler) had stated that in sitting as a court of impeachment, the Senate "knew no law, either statute or common, and consulted no precedents save those of parliamentary bodies." Another (it was Bingham) had claimed that the Senate "was a law unto itself; in a word, that its jurisdiction was without bounds; that it may impeach for any cause, and there is no appeal from its judgment." A third (John A. Logan) said much the same as Bingham. And it was argued by Butler that when the words "high crimes and misdemeanors" were used, "they are without signification and intended

merely to give solemnity to the charge." Under these interpretations "everything this tribunal may deem impeachable becomes so at once." Said Groesbeck, pursuing the issue of attainder:

"To sustain this extraordinary view of the character of this tribunal we have been referred to English precedents, and especially to early English precedents, when, according to my recollection, impeachment and attainder and bills of pains and penalties labored together in the work of murder and confiscation."

The Constitution, Groesbeck declared, placed limitations on the executive and judicial departments, and he had supposed the legislative was also limited. But according to the argument made in this trial, it was otherwise. The Senate "has in its service and at its command an institution [impeachment] that is above all law and acknowledges no restraint; an institution worse than a court martial, in that it has a broader and more dangerous jurisdiction."

The question of attainder was sharpened by a vitriolic attack on Johnson by Thaddeus Stevens, who asserted that the Senate had rendered final judgment against Johnson even before the House impeached him. It did so, he declared, in a resolution adopted on February 21 (three days before the House acted) declaring that the President had no power to remove Stanton. By that vote, Stevens maintained, the senators were committed to find him guilty. Exclaimed the fiery Radical Republican leader:

"And now this offspring of assassination turns upon the Senate... and bids them defiance. How can he escape the just vengeance of the law? Wretched man, standing at bay, surrounded by a cordon of living men, each with the ax of an executioner uplifted for his just punishment!"

Defense counsel Evarts seized on this as one more proof that the Managers were seeking to pass a bill of attainder. If, said he, judgment was rendered in that vote of February 21, "then you are here standing about the scaffold of execution." If so, of what service was the constitutional prohibition of bills of attainder? He asked, as had a fellow counsel:

"What is a bill of attainder; what is a bill of pains and penalties?... It is a proceeding by the legislature as a legislature to enact crime, sentence, punishment all in one.... [If you follow the Stevens rule] you are enacting a bill of pains and penalties upon the simple form that a majority of the House and two thirds of the Senate must concur, and the Constitution and the wisdom of our ancestors all pass for naught."

To emphasize the element of attainder, Evarts quoted the admission of House Manager Buchanan in the case of Judge Peck that to convict the judge of impeachable official misbehavior, "we are bound to prove that the respondent has violated the Constitution or some known law of the land." He endorsed the argument of his colleague Curtis, "upon the strict constitutional necessity, under the clause prohibiting *ex post facto* laws, and under the clause prohibiting bills of attainder," that articles of impeachment be confined to "what is crime against the Constitution and crime against the law."

Here was the clearest statement that to go beyond crimes against the laws and Constitution and give sanction to general ideas of misbehavior was to convert impeachment into both a bill of attainder and an *ex post facto* law. If the case of Warren Hastings was to be used

as a guide, Evarts declared, the standard of impeachable misconduct must meet the specifications laid down by Edmund Burke as manager of the Hastings trial. He quoted Burke's opening address to the House of Lords:

"We know, as we are to be served by men, that the persons who serve us must be tried as men, and with a very large allowance indeed to human infirmity and human error. This, my lords, we knew, and we weighed before we came before you. But the crimes which we charge in these articles are not lapses, defects, errors of common human frailty, which, as we know, and feel, we can allow for. We charge this offender with no crimes that have not arisen from passions which it is criminal to harbor; with no offenses that have not their root in avarice, rapacity, pride, insolence, ferocity, treachery, cruelty, malignity of temper; in short, in nothing that does not argue a total extinction of all moral principle, that does not manifest an inveterate blackness, dyed ingrain with malice, vitiated, corrupted, gangrened to the very core."

Evarts could have carried his case further. For at the close of that seven years' trial the Lords, passing on Burke's catalog of heinous accusations, found Hastings not guilty. They found that his conduct consisted, not of crimes in office, but of errors of judgment in performance of his duties as governor general of India. For these he could not properly be impeached. Thus prosecution and defense, in combination, narrowed the grounds of impeachment permissible under British precedents. Both sides cast aside the Tudor-Stuart concept of impeachment. The British reform went further: Public opinion in and out of Parliament discarded the entire institution of impeachment. Except for one trivial case a few years later, no impeachment has taken place in Great Britain from 1786 to the present. But members of Congress claim that the framers, without saying so, embodied British concepts of impeachment in the Constitution, and cite as their only evidence the fact that the Constitution was written during the Hastings impeachment—which put an end to the British system.

Evarts's quotation from Burke brought to a climax the fundamental defense of President Johnson: that the articles of impeachment brought against him constituted a bill of attainder. The argument was answered by total silence. Not once was the word "attainder" spoken by any House Manager, nor did any touch on the concept of attainder. Any attempt at rebuttal would have brought the issue fully before the Senate, and the weakness of the Managers' denials would have given their arguments a hollow ring. Even the admission that grounds of argument on attainder existed might have given a new aspect to the trial, producing in some senatorial minds an unwillingness to cast a vote for an unconstitutional conviction. Indeed, the one-sided discussion had that tendency, reducing the case against Johnson to two narrowly technical points— denial by the Managers that when the President removed Secretary Stanton, he intended to test the constitutionality of the Tenure of Office Act, and the question of criminal libel in Johnson's criticism of Congress.

The defense met the first of these arguments by putting General William Tecumseh Sherman on the stand. He testified that when the post of Secretary of War was being offered to him, the President said: "If we can bring the case to the courts it would not stand half an hour." Pursuing that line, defense counsel Nelson argued that the Tenure of Office Act was unconstitutional, but that in any case impeachment was unwarranted because "the President acted from laudable and honest motives, and is not, therefor[e] guilty of any crime or misdemeanor."

Manager Bingham brought the case against President Johnson to a close by defining freedom of speech in terms of the Sedition Act of 1798. This he linked with an 1806 set of Army regulations by Congress in which military officers and soldiers were made subject to court-martial for using "contemptuous or disrespectful words" against the President, Vice President, or Congress. If those two laws are constitutional, declared Bingham, seditious utterances "are indictable as misdemeanors, whether made by the President or anybody else, and especially in an official charged with the execution of the laws." Indeed, he continued, seditious utterances by an executive officer always were indictable at common law:

"But, say counsel, this is his guarantied right under the Constitution. The freedom of speech, says the gentleman, is not to be restricted by a law of Congress. How is that answered by this act of 1806, which subjects every soldier in your Army and every officer in your Army to court-martial for using disrespectful words of the President or of the Congress or of his superior officers? The freedom of speech guarantied by the Constitution to all the people of the United States, is that freedom of speech which respects, first, the right of the nation itself, which respects the supremacy of the nation's laws, and which finally respects the rights of every citizen of the Republic."

Thus an unconstitutional Sedition Act (so pronounced by the Supreme Court more than a century after it expired), and a military regulation laid down to maintain discipline in the Army, were to measure the right of the President of the United States to criticize Congress. What this meant was that the First Amendment was worthless without the enforcing strength of the Supreme Court. On the constitutional level, impeachment trials throughout American history have been prosecuted on the legal plane occupied by the Sedition Act of 1798. In every instance where the drive for impeachment has been politically motivated—the prosecutions of Judge Pickering, Justice Chase, and President Johnson, and the abortive moves against Justices Field and Douglas—the same passions that produced the Sedition Act of 1798 have inflamed and degraded the driving forces in Congress.

The ordeal of President Andrew Johnson ended on May 16, 1868, when, after a two-month trial, the Senate voted on the eleven articles of impeachment. The vote was the same on each: guilty, 35; not guilty, 19—only one short of the needed two thirds. Before the balloting began, Senator Lyman Trumbull of Illinois presented a written opinion in which he said:

"In view of the consequences likely to flow from this day's proceedings, should they result in conviction on what my judgment tells me are insufficient charges and proofs, I tremble for the future of my country."

The ferocity of the prosecution and closeness of the verdict combined to establish the Johnson impeachment as a menacing portent of the future. The failure of this case to serve as a permanent warning against perversion of the Constitution is more ominous still. Nevertheless, if the cogent and powerful arguments of the defense influenced a single senator—and they probably converted several—they prevented the deepest tragedy in American political history.

NO

Harold M. Hyman

HOW TO SET THE LAW IN MOTION

The Tenure law [Tenure of Office Act] provided that persons appointed by the President and confirmed by the Senate should not be removed without Senate concurrence. The President could suspend an official if the Senate was not in session, but must report the suspension to the Senate on its reassembly and ask its consent. Republican congressmen differed on the question of whether the Tenure bill embraced Lincoln holdovers such as War Secretary [Edwin M.] Stanton in Johnson's cabinet. But enough sentiment obtained to lock Stanton in to comfort those in and out of the Army who feared the quality of a Johnson-appointed successor, a pleasure increased by provisions in the Army Appropriations Act requiring Congress's assent to transfer orders directed to the commanding general from the President.

In unhappy chronological conjunction, ambitions and events transformed efforts during March 1867 at stability into nervous near crisis. All through spring and summer, the President and Attorney General Henry Stanbery interpreted the Reconstruction statutes to hamstring commanding generals. A central issue was a general's authority to remove from office provisional state civil officials who failed to enforce state and local laws when blacks and Unionists were the victims of illegality and violence. In late April, Mississippi resorted to the Supreme Court for a permanent injunction directed against the President and the Army commander in that state, to forbid enforcement there of the allegedly unconstitutional Reconstruction statute. But even Johnson and his Attorney General acknowledged that Mississippi's request was unprecedented and outrageous; no court could enjoin a President. Congress had required the President to execute a law constitutionally enacted with respect to procedure, Stanbery told the court. The Mississippi petition, without legal or historical merit, received no support in the Court.

Almost simultaneously, Georgia sought injunctions against enforcement of the Reconstruction statute in the state, naming the Secretary of War and generals from Grant down. Georgia's counsel stressed Congress's alleged obliteration of the state. Responding for the defendants, Stanbery insisted that the Court's jurisdiction ended at political matters, and the Congress's decision concerning Georgia's status was political. Accepting Stanbery's argument on May 13, 1867, the Supreme Court dismissed both petitions.

By denying the Georgia and Mississippi petitions, the Court avoided for its own convenience direct confrontation with Congress concerning the Reconstruction law's constitutionality. The jurists' grounds were historical and jurisprudentially proper; plaintiffs' counsel had misfired.

Congress's Reconstruction authorizations to the Army appeared to have passed all foreseeable constitutional and political obstacles that the provisional southern states and the President could raise and the Supreme Court would entertain. Despite partisan contrary assertion, no judicial decision yet issued questioned directly the Reconstruction law or the Army's derivative policies in the South. In substantial confidence and good humor, therefore, on July 19 Congress passed over Johnson's veto another supplement to the Reconstruction law. Directly contradicting the Attorney General's hamstringing efforts, it authorized Army commanders to follow Grant's precedent instructions and to remove provisional state and local officials who failed equally to enforce their states' civil and criminal statues. Retrospectively, along with the McCardle case and the impeachment, this amendment forms the context in which Reconstruction's beginning ended and in which Reconstruction's end began.

Under Congress's authorization and Grant's orders most Reconstruction commanders became involved in numerous details of life and labor including criminal-law enforcement, professional licensing, municipal police, and debt collections, without which more decent po-litical action, racially defined, was impossible, according to General [Daniel] Sickles in South Carolina. Sickles suspended execution of debt-collection judgments and debt-imprisonment sentences issuing from all courts, including national tribunals. He explained to Grant that under the 1789 Judiciary Act federal courts were required to employ the procedures of forum state courts. But it was precisely to reform state procedures that Congress had ordered the Army to Reconstruction duty. Therefore Sickles had suspended existing state laws and derivative judgments that in his view were unfair to citizens. But it was all fruitless if national courts, employing state procedures, substantively reinforced that state's unjust processes and results. Federal courts obeyed Congress's 1789 order to use state procedures. Should not national judges obey also Congress's 1867 laws that the southern states' constitutions, laws, and procedures become at least as decent as those of other states?

Though Grant and Stanton sustained Sickles and other generals, it was clear that Reconstruction matters had gone awry. Even [Supreme Court Chief Justice Salmon P.] Chase felt that however worthy the goals, Congress had given the Army too much latitude and had upset both power separation and national-state relationships. Whether Chase objected more to Sickles's intrusions into state and local commercial tax, debt, labor, and criminal matters, or into inferior national court procedures, is not known. But he believed fervently in the maintenance of state governments as the base of the federal union. Chase revered the national judiciary as the pacific links for Union, and he saw nothing amiss in the tradition that national judges use applicable state pleadings and procedures. The Army as servants for Congress and the national courts was one matter; the Army as master of federal court procedures was quite another.

Conservatives sniffed the shifting wind and discerned opportunity in the Army's intrusion into property and judicial matters. Lawyers and southern politicos picked up the theme that Reconstruction laws were unconstitutional not only as infringements on civil liberties but also as deprivations of property rights. "The [South's] only gleam of hope for the Constitution then was in the Supreme Court," recalled Alabama's conservative constitutionalist, Hilary Herbert.

But appropriate litigation in the sense of dramatic, politically compelling qualities did not come up every day. A Louisiana suit remained obscure in state courts even though it challenged the Army's power to set aside interest payments on a municipality's debt and despite plaintiff's argument that the suspension deprived good-faith bondholders of property in a manner the national Supreme Court had declared unconstitutional in the Gelpcke v. Dubuque decision.

Nationwide political attention turned instead to William McCardle's suit. He was a Vicksburg newspaper publisher whose editorials encouraged violent resistance to racial-equality provisions of the Reconstruction statutes. Arrested and awaiting a military commission trial, McCardle sought release by means of a habeas corpus writ from the United States Circuit Court. Its judge denied his petition and remanded him to Army jurisdiction.

Responding sensitively to growing civil-law concerns among lawyers, Jeremiah Black and David Dudley Field, McCardle's counsel, without abandoning the basic theme of the Reconstruction law's unconstitutionality, played down civil-military aspects. In order to get the case to the Supreme Court the appellants had to overcome the Vallandigham and Milligan precedents, which, taken together, suggested that no Supreme Court jurisdiction existed in appeals from military authority and that only wartime executive extensions of Army courts over civilians were unjustifiable. Instead McCardle's counsel seized on Congress's 1867 Habeas Corpus law and insisted that it gave adequate jurisdiction to the Supreme Court to protect McCardle.

Many elements made McCardle's case dramatic. Although the Attorney General had appeared very recently on behalf of the government and its officers in the Georgia and Mississippi injunction litigation, he refused to appear against McCardle. Grant obtained for the Army the services of Senators Lyman Trumbull and Matthew Carpenter. Only a week after denying itself competency to issue Georgia the requested injunction against the Reconstruction law, the Supreme Court accepted jurisdiction of McCardle's appeal. A decision was possible adverse to the congressional statutes now being militarily enforced. Further, events determined that judgment in McCardle's case must issue in the superheated politics of the nation's first impeachment, which in its unique way was also testing issues implicit in McCardle's case.

In short, McCardle kept the Supreme Court in the most exposed salient of Reconstruction politics. As Henry Dutton noted, McCardle's case involved the fates of the South's states and Negroes, of the President of the United States, and of the Army. Unique among the world's courts, the United States Supreme Court was to determine national policy, the destiny of races, and the quality and direction of a great society.

Aware of context and implications, the government's counsel chose to fight McCardle's appeal on his selected battlefield. Carpenter boasted confidently that in his brief he had "avoided all talk of the rights of conquest, a theme that is very unpalatable to that [Supreme] court... & placed [Congress's] right to pass the [Reconstruction] law upon entirely peace powers of the [national] government. This foundation is as solid as a rock, & if that Court decides the case upon judicial, not political, points, we have a sure thing."

Congress made a surer thing of it. Over somnambulistic Democratic resistance and a tepid presidential veto—the impeachment was under way, after all—on March 27 Congress repealed the provisions of the February 1867 law that provided it appellate jurisdiction in McCardle's case. In April the Court acquiesced and dropped consideration of McCardle's appeal.

But it dropped only that litigation. Accepting Congress's jurisdiction limitation, Chase stipulated carefully that "Counsel [for McCardle] seems to have supposed, if effect be given to the repealing act... that the whole appellate power of the court in cases in *habeas corpus* is denied. But this is an error." Instead McCardle meant only that quite constitutionally, Congress determined the Court's jurisdiction, which it elected now partially to excise.

While McCardle's appeal made its way to Washington, the President asserted his alleged right to independent control over the Army, i.e., to issue orders contrary to Congress's Reconstruction purposes. In August 1867, complying with the Tenure law, he suspended Stanton

and named Grant ad interim successor. The President relieved from command Sickles and other generals who had actively enforced Congress's Reconstruction statutes. Wearing two hats as commanding general and temporary War Secretary, Grant saw to it that the Army kept in motion Congress's basic Reconstruction directives involving redistricting, voter registration, and new state constitutional conventions. In December when Congress reassembled, as the Tenure law required, the President reported Stanton's suspension to the Senate. It refused approval. The President refused in turn to readmit Stanton to the Cabinet. Grant turned the War Office keys back to Stanton, who occupied the Secretaryship in defiance of the President.

Unable to reverse Reconstruction through appeals to voters, to standpat and retrograde congressmen, or to courts, the President, defying a national law, reached out for control over one of Reconstruction's two essential instruments, the Army. Therefore, despite the clear political hazards and ambiguities involved in the unprecedented move, the Republican center decided for impeachment, a wholly constitutional procedure.

Johnson's obstructive replacements of Reconstruction generals and rejection of Stanton were last straws calling impeachment into action.... Laws on confiscation, test oaths, Freedmen's Bureau courts, Civil Rights, and Military Reconstruction had suffered Johnson's nonenforcements, malforming interpretations, or outright obstructions. Yet his piecemeal impediments had kept impeachment only a minority dream. Fall elections in 1867 and a worrisome business recession had disposed many Republicans against further political unsettlements and made impeachment the more unlikely despite the President's now-open appointments of conservative generals to commands in the South. Nevertheless, in early 1868 Johnson managed to transform the Republicans' search for stability into an impeachment consensus.

It was easier to decide on the need for the act than to know confidently how to proceed or to anticipate the consequences of success. Since 1789 impeachments had been whistled up sporadically for Presidents, but never came to action. A very small number of lesser official fry had been impeached.

The Republican decision to impeach Johnson was hardly an expression of partisan contempt for the Presidency, as distinguished from the incumbent. M. L. Benedict, author of the best inquiry into the subject, concludes that the impeachment grew from Republicans' incapacity to be legislative despots or to conceive of Military Reconstruction without the Army's Commander-in-Chief commanding. In Benedict's judgment, "Historians should view the... impeachment for what it was,... one of the great legal cases of history in which American politicians demonstrated the strength of the nation's... institutions by attempting to... give a political officer a full and fair trial in a time of political crisis."

This moral victory would have been impossible had the Constitution's sparse impeachment clause failed to work. Impeachment became another instance in the Civil War and Reconstruction when politicians and legal scholars reviewed history in order for the first time actually to apply a dormant part of the Constitution.

Fortunately for congressmen a useful literature was available by early 1868 as a result of abortive efforts at impeachment in 1867. In this literature, attitudes about the law and politics of impeachment—and impeachment mixed characteristics of a trial at law and of a political contest—were sharply variant. A narrow view, insisted on throughout the trial by Democrats and conservative Republicans, was that English and American precedents applied which allowed impeachment of an official only if he had committed an indictable criminal act. The broad view, taken up by Republicans, insisted that English precedents were not wholly applicable. There the House of Lords could punish as well as try any offender, including officials. Here Congress could only remove officials. Therefore American precedents failed to sustain a need for indictable crime as a reason for removal.

History leans strongly toward the broad Republican position. "That an impeached official can be tried in a criminal court after his trial on impeachment does not imply [that] only those who can be tried in a criminal court can be impeached," Benedict concluded. "It means, rather, that where an officer *is* impeached for an indictable offense, the impeachment does not preclude a later indictment." The Constitution's framers and ratifiers had themselves carefully sidestepped their own double-jeopardy, jury-trial, and pardon provisions when dealing with impeachments, envisaging instead a special political process set to lawlike procedures.

Perhaps any strictly legalistic analyses would have assumed the Constitution's creators. As John Norton Pomeroy noted just before the Johnson impeachment got under way, the men of 1787 aimed actually to check unpredictable future power abuses at the highest political level, where discretion had to exist, else free government could not live. Therefore the framers wrote into the Constitution a brooding impeachment threat rather than a precise weapon.

Impeachment's adversary features gave the President's counsel ample scope to develop the narrow tradition that an indictable offense was necessary for conviction, that the Tenure law did not cover Stanton, that the President had equal right with Congress to determine if a law was unconstitutional, and that by violating the disputed law the President aimed at a court test. These lawyerlike arguments-in-the-alternative well suited the substantively political yet procedurally legal contours of the impeachment proceeding. Concerning Stanton's amenability to the Tenure law, Benedict's careful analysis convinces that by the final vote on its passage congressmen had "concluded [that] the bill protected Stanton after all," and that Johnson's retention of Stanton in the Cabinet "was ... a virtual reappointment" acquiring tenured status. On the matter of the President testing a law he thinks is unconstitutional by violating it, no evidence exists that Johnson actually tried for a court test. Benedict properly raises the derivative query, what if after violation a court or the Congress finds the law constitutional? As a defense, the President's argument raised endless abysses for the survival potential of American government.

This evaluation of the President's scattergun points suggests a need to re-evaluate also the Republicans' omnibus accusations against him. They too were equivalents to a lawyer's arguments-in-the-alternative aimed to sweep as wide horizons as possible. In terms of Republican intraparty factionalism in the House the impeachment articles sought to accommodate conservative and centrist waverers whose goals were won

with the President's mark-time response to impeachment, and who therefore felt little or no compulsion to proceed on the unmarked road to conviction.

Mixtures of politics and law featured also the Senate's maneuvers in committee and on the floor concerning rules of procedure for the impeachment trial. If the Senate proclaimed itself a court then the presiding officer stipulated in the Constitution, the Chief Justice of the United States, could "vote" as well as interpret points of evidence and law. But if the Senate retained its noncourt character, the Chief Justice could not claim a vote. Deciding that the Senate was not a court, senators determined also that they had the power to overturn Chase's rulings on disputed questions of law and evidence.

But senators' efforts not to be bound by Chase's unpredictable rulings on law collapsed in the trial's first days. As Chase administered oaths to senators to do impartial justice, Democrats insisted that Ben Wade should not sit, since he would succeed Johnson if the President were removed. Chase ruled that Wade should sit, since the Senate was a court and his status as president of the Senate was irrelevant. The Chief Justice implicitly resolved in his own favor the matter of his right to vote. It all meant that the trial would proceed far more slowly than Republicans wished. The conservatives won time for reaction to set in.

In constitutional terms, Edward S. Corwin concluded, "the impeachers had the better of the argument for all but the most urgent situations." And there was the heart of the matter. For conviction of Johnson involved the nation's most urgent situations, ranging from the unhappy prospects of Wade as President supporting agrarian monetary and tariff heresies, of continuing racial instability southward, of Negro suffrage issues in northern states, and of political corruption everywhere. Republican centrists impeached the President for refusing to execute their statutes. If the impeachment swerved his course, conviction became unnecessary.

While the trial was on Johnson made clear his intention to name a moderate general to be Secretary of War; forwarded to the Senate the Reconstruction constitutions of Arkansas and South Carolina, created by terms of Congress's Reconstruction laws which he said were unconstitutional, including ratification of the detested Fourteenth Amendment and provisions for blacks' voting; and ceased obstructing the progress of congressional Reconstruction in other provisional states by devious interpretations of the laws or other overt means. Politically, the seven recusant Republican senators who voted not to convict Johnson merely affirmed impeachment's victory. Little wonder that contrary to tradition, they did not suffer disastrously at the hands of their constituents or party. Little wonder also that history is redressing opinion concerning the senators who voted finally and unavailingly to convict. They were, Benedict concludes, "motivated by the same desire for impartial justice [or lack of it] that historians and partisans ascribed only to the recusants."

Between die-hard Democrats convinced of the need to acquit the President and Radical Republicans determined to convict him, senators in the center wrestled to come to decision on ambiguous technical points. Days, weeks, and months passed in complex skirmishes on the admissibility of evidence and on such technical legal points as estoppel and the President's independent power

of removal. An over-all review sustains Benedict's judgment: "After the events leading to impeachment... it is difficult to understand how anyone could have accepted at face value the moderate and reasonable interpretation Johnson's lawyers put on his activities." But because evidential disproofs of the President's inner intentions were impossible to evoke, because Republican senators wished to retain existing constitutional configurations, and because all senators wished to prevent the "Mexicanization" of the Presidency, Johnson benefited. He received the one vote needed to secure nonconviction; in mid-May the impeachment ended.

A kind of quiet returned to the Potomac. The President, smarting from his one-vote escape and his inability to win the Democratic party's 1868 nomination for a whole term, contented himself with giving a "little lecture on constitutional law" to such captive visitors as youthful political reporter Henry Adams. But the scholarly pose failed to conceal the stubborn activist. Immediately after the Senate vote, Johnson considered sliding in the detested [William] Seward as War Secretary, but, fortunately dissuaded, named conservative General John Schofield. The Senate consented "inasmuch as... Stanton has relinquished his place." Mutual ill-humor aside, the President's belated acquiescence in the impeachment's verdict indicated that at last he had learned the lesson which Republican congressmen had been trying for two years to teach him. Now Reconstruction would proceed as Congress had prescribed.

A profound psychological release, the impeachment was another of the proofs accumulating since early 1861 concerning the Constitution's tough workability. In terms of early 1868, it allowed a procedurally pacific institutional readjustment between the nation's governing branches, badly skewed in favor of the White House by reason of the War, another item in the South's debits. It was an article of Republican faith that Reconstruction of the South also involved improved equilibrium between the nation's branches, which helps to explain Congress's devotion to increasing the federal courts' jurisdictions and powers.

Contemporaries saw impeachment's nonviolent course and constructive outcome as proof of Reconstruction's terminal phase. From 1866–68 Congress had embodied in legislation the War's "logical results," according to publicist Samuel Bowles. Insuring the protection of these results without the second civil war which reasonable men feared, the impeachment began a two-year-long wrapping-up of the War's residuals. By 1870 Ignatius Donnelly believed that "not a single issue of the many which agitated us in the past remains alive today—slavery—reconstruction—rebellion—impartial suffrage—have all perished." However coarse, his perception required a view of impeachment as a constitutional process accompanied by enormous political hazards that had rasped the nation's tight nerves. Pressures increased on politicians to close off Reconstruction. These pressures played essential roles in determining impeachment's hair-breadth outcome, the 1868 presidential elections, the Fourteenth and Fifteenth Amendments' ratifications and enforcements, and the nature of certain Supreme Court judgments.

POSTSCRIPT

Was It Wrong to Impeach Andrew Johnson?

Authority for the impeachment and potential removal from office of federal officials is established in Article 1, Sections 2 and 3 of the Constitution of the United States, which delegate sole power to impeach to the House of Representatives and the power to try all impeachments to the Senate. This power, however, has been invoked only 16 times in 200 years and only twice —in the cases of Andrew Johnson and Bill Clinton—against a president of the United States. The other cases involved a U.S. senator (William Blount, 1798), a Supreme Court justice (Samuel Chase, 1804), a Cabinet officer (William Belknap, 1876), and 11 federal judges. Less than half of the cases have resulted in conviction and removal from office.

In *Federalist*, No. 65, Alexander Hamilton noted that impeachment was an instrument to be used when individuals engaged in misconduct that abused the public trust. Recognizing the political nature of such offenses, he warned,

> The prosecution of them . . . will seldom fail to agitate the passions of the whole community, and to divide it into parties more or less friendly or inimical to the accused. In many cases it will connect itself with the pre-existing factions, and will enlist all their animosities, partialities, influence, and interest on one side or on the other; and in such cases there will always be the greatest danger that the decision will be regulated more by the comparative strength of parties, than by the real demonstrations of innocence or guilt.

Such was undoubtedly true in the case of Andrew Johnson.

For historical studies of Johnson's impeachment, see Michael Les Benedict, *The Impeachment and Trial of Andrew Johnson* (W. W. Norton, 1973) and Hans L. Trefousse, *Impeachment of a President: Andrew Johnson, the Blacks, and Reconstruction* (University of Tennessee Press, 1975). Johnson's biographers also devote attention to the impeachment. See Albert Castel, *The Presidency of Andrew Johnson* (Regents Press of Kansas, 1979); James E. Sefton, *Andrew Johnson and the Uses of Constitutional Power* (Little, Brown, 1980); and Hans L. Trefousse, *Andrew Johnson: A Biography* (W. W. Norton, 1989).

For more general studies of impeachment, see William H. Rehnquist, *Grand Inquests: The Historic Impeachments of Justice Samuel Chase and President Andrew Johnson* (William Morrow, 1992) and Michael J. Gerhardt, *The Federal Impeachment Process: A Constitutional and Historical Analysis* (Princeton University Press, 1996).

ISSUE 2

Was John D. Rockefeller a "Robber Baron"?

YES: Matthew Josephson, from *The Robber Barons: The Great American Capitalists, 1861–1901* (Harcourt, Brace & World, 1962)

NO: Ralph W. Hidy and Muriel E. Hidy, from *History of Standard Oil Company (New Jersey), vol. 1: Pioneering in Big Business, 1882–1911* (Harper & Brothers, 1955)

ISSUE SUMMARY

YES: Historian Matthew Josephson depicts John D. Rockefeller as an unconscionable manipulator who employed deception, bribery, and outright conspiracy to restrain free trade in order to eliminate his competitors for control of the oil industry in the United States.

NO: Business historians Ralph W. Hidy and Muriel E. Hidy argue that although Rockefeller and his associates at Standard Oil occasionally used their power ruthlessly, they were innovative representatives of corporate capitalism who brought stability to the often chaotic petroleum industry and made a significant contribution to the rapid development of the national economy as a whole.

Between 1860 and 1914 the United States was transformed from a country of farms, small towns, and modest manufacturing concerns to a modern nation dominated by large cities and factories. During those years the population tripled, and the nation experienced astounding urban growth. A new proletariat emerged to provide the necessary labor for the country's developing factory system. Between the Civil War and World War I, the value of manufactured goods in the United States increased 12-fold, and the capital invested in industrial pursuits multiplied 22 times. In addition, the application of new machinery and scientific methods to agriculture produced abundant yields of wheat, corn, and other foodstuffs, despite the decline in the number of farmers.

Why did this industrial revolution occur in the United States during the last quarter of the nineteenth century? What factors contributed to the rapid pace of American industrialization? In answering these questions, historians often point to the first half of the 1800s and the significance of the "transportation revolution," which produced better roads, canals, and railroads to move people and goods more efficiently and cheaply from one point to another. Technological improvements such as the Bessemer process, refrigeration, electricity, and the telephone also made their mark in the nation's "machine age." Government cooperation with business, large-scale immigration from Europe and Asia, and the availability of foreign capital for industrial investments provided still other underpinnings for this industrial growth. Finally, American industrialization depended upon a number of individuals in the United States who were willing to organize and finance the nation's industrial base for the sake of anticipated profits. These, of course, were the entrepreneurs.

American public attitudes have reflected a schizophrenic quality with regard to the activities of the industrial leaders of the late nineteenth century. Were these entrepreneurs "robber barons" who employed any means necessary to enrich themselves at the expense of their competitors? Or were they "captains of industry" whose shrewd and innovative leadership brought order out of industrial chaos and generated great fortunes that enriched the public welfare through the workings of the various philanthropic agencies that these leaders established? Although the "robber baron" stereotype emerged as early as the 1870s, it probably gained its widest acceptance in the 1930s, when, in the midst of the Great Depression, many critics were proclaiming the apparent failure of American capitalism. Since the depression, however, some historians, including Allan Nevins, Alfred D. Chandler, Jr., and Maury Klein, have sought to revise the negative assessments offered by earlier generations of scholars. In the hands of these business historians, the late-nineteenth-century businessmen have become "industrial statesmen" who skillfully oversaw the process of raising the United States to a preeminent position among the nations of the world. The following selections reveal the divergence of scholarly opinion as it applies to one of the most notable of these American entrepreneurs—John D. Rockefeller, founder of the Standard Oil Company, who came to epitomize both the success and excess of corporate capitalism in the United States.

Matthew Josephson, whose 1934 attack on monopolistic capitalism became the model for the "robber baron" thesis for post-depression-era historians, characterizes Rockefeller as a parsimonious, deceptive, and conspiratorial businessman. Rockefeller's fortune, Josephson argues, was built upon a series of secret agreements that wrung concessions from America's leading railroad magnates and allowed Rockefeller to decimate his competitors through the establishment of the South Improvement Company and, subsequently, Standard Oil.

Ralph W. Hidy and Muriel E. Hidy, on the other hand, accentuate Rockefeller's positive accomplishments in their study of Standard Oil of New Jersey. Rockefeller could be ruthless in his business dealings, they admit, but he operated within the law and introduced innovations that stabilized the petroleum industry, produced a mass-marketing system, and spearheaded the nation's economic growth in the late nineteenth and early twentieth centuries.

YES   Matthew Josephson

THE ROBBER BARONS

John Rockefeller who grew up in Western New York and later near Cleveland, as one of a struggling family of five children, recalls with satisfaction the excellent practical training he had received and how quickly he put it to use. His childhood seemed to have been darkened by the misdeeds of his father, a wandering vendor of quack medicine who rarely supported his family, and was sometimes a fugitive from the law; yet the son invariably spoke of his parent's instructions with gratitude. He said:

> ... He himself trained me in practical ways. He was engaged in different enterprises; he used to tell me about these things ... and he taught me the principles and methods of business. ... I knew what a cord of good solid beech and maple wood was. My father told me to select only solid wood ... and not to put any limbs in it or any punky wood. That was a good training for me.

But the elder Rockefeller went further than this in his sage instructions, according to John T. Flynn, who attributes to him the statement:

> I cheat my boys every chance I get, I want to make 'em sharp. I trade with the boys and skin 'em and I just beat 'em every time I can. I want to make 'em sharp.

If at times the young Rockefeller absorbed a certain shiftiness and trading sharpness from his restless father, it was also true that his father was absent so often and so long as to cast shame and poverty upon his home. Thus he must have been subject far more often to the stern supervision of his mother, whom he has recalled in several stories. His mother would punish him, as he related, with a birch switch to "uphold the standard of the family when it showed a tendency to deteriorate." Once when she found out that she was punishing him for a misdeed at school of which he was innocent, she said, "Never mind, we have started in on this whipping and it will do for the next time." The normal outcome of such disciplinary cruelty would be deception and stealthiness in the boy, as a defense.

But his mother, who reared her children with the rigid piety of an Evangelist, also started him in his first business enterprise. When he was seven years old she encouraged him to raise turkeys, and gave him for this purpose

From Matthew Josephson, *The Robber Barons: The Great American Capitalists, 1861–1901* (Harcourt Brace, 1961). Copyright © 1934, renewed 1961, by Matthew Josephson. Reprinted by permission of Harcourt Brace & Company. Notes omitted.

the family's surplus milk curds. There are legends of Rockefeller as a boy stalking a turkey with the most patient stealth in order to seize her eggs.

This harshly disciplined boy, quiet, shy, reserved, serious, received but a few years' poor schooling, and worked for neighboring farmers in all his spare time. His whole youth suggests only abstinence, prudence and the growth of parsimony in his soul. The pennies he earned he would save steadily in a blue bowl that stood on a chest in his room, and accumulated until there was a small heap of gold coins. He would work, by his own account, hoeing potatoes for a neighboring farmer from morning to night for 37 cents a day. At a time when he was still very young he had fifty dollars saved, which upon invitation he one day loaned to the farmer who employed him.

"And as I was saving those little sums," he relates, "I soon learned that I could get as much interest for $50 loaned at seven per cent—then the legal rate of interest—as I could earn by digging potatoes for ten days." Thereafter, he tells us, he resolved that it was better "to let the money be my slave than to be the slave of money."

In Cleveland whither the family removed in 1854, Rockefeller went to the Central High School and studied bookkeeping for a year. This delighted him. Most of the conquering types in the coming order were to be men trained early in life in the calculations of the bookkeeper, Cooke, Huntington, Gould, Henry Frick and especially Rockefeller of whom it was said afterward: "He had the soul of a bookkeeper."

In his first position as bookkeeper to a produce merchant at the Cleveland docks, when he was sixteen, he distinguished himself by his composed orderly habits. Very carefully he examined each item on each bill before he approved it for payment. Out of a salary which began at $15 a month and advanced ultimately to $50 a month, he saved $800 in three years, the lion's share of his total earnings! This was fantastic parsimony.

He spent little money for clothing, though he was always neat; he never went to the theater, had no amusements, and few friends. But he attended his Baptist Church in Cleveland as devoutly as he attended to his accounts. And to the cause of the church alone, to its parish fund and mission funds, he demonstrated his only generosity by gifts that were large for him then—first of ten cents, then later of twenty-five cents at a time.

In the young Rockefeller the traits which his mother had bred in him, of piety and the economic virtue—worship of the "lean goddess of Abstinence" —were of one cloth. The pale, bony, small-eyed young Baptist served the Lord and pursued his own business unremittingly. His composed manner, which had a certain languor, hid a feverish calculation, a sleepy strength, cruel, intense, terribly alert.

As a schoolboy John Rockefeller had once announced to a companion, as they walked by a rich man's ample house along their way: "When I grow up I want to be worth $100,000. And I'm going to be too." In almost the same words, Rockefeller in Cleveland, Cooke in Philadelphia, Carnegie in Pittsburgh, or a James Hill in the Northwestern frontier could be found voicing the same hope. And Rockefeller, the bookkeeper, "not slothful in business ... serving the Lord," as John T. Flynn describes him, watched his chances closely, learned every detail of the produce business which engaged him, until finally in 1858 he made bold to open a business of his own in partnership with a young Englishman named Clark (who was destined to be left far behind). Rockefeller's grimly accumulated savings of $800, in addition to a loan from his father at the usurious rate of 10 per cent, yielded the capital which launched him, and he was soon "gathering gear" quietly. He knew the art of using loan credit to expand his operations. His first bank loan against warehouse receipts gave him a thrill of pleasure. He now bought grain and produce of all kinds in carload lots rather than in small consignments. Prosperous, he said nothing, but began to dress his part, wearing a high silk hat, frock coat and striped trousers like other merchants of the time. His head was handsome, his eyes small, birdlike; on his pale bony cheeks were the proverbial side-whiskers, reddish in color.

At night, in his room, he read the Bible, and retiring had the queer habit of talking to his pillow about his business adventures. In his autobiography he says that "these intimate conversations with myself had a great influence upon my life." He told himself "not to get puffed up with any foolish notions" and never to be deceived about actual conditions. "Look out or you will lose your head—go steady."

He was given to secrecy; he loathed all display. When he married, a few years afterward, he lost not a day from his business. His wife, Laura Spelman, proved an excellent mate. She encouraged his furtiveness, he relates, advising him always to be silent, to say as little as possible. His composure, his self-possession was excessive. Those Clevelanders to whom Miss Ida Tarbell addressed herself in her investigations of Rockefeller, told her that he was a hard man to best in a trade, that he rarely smiled, and almost never laughed, save when he struck a good bargain. Then he might clap his hands with delight, or he might even, if the occasion warranted, throw up his hat, kick his heels and hug his informer. One time he was so overjoyed at a favorable piece of news that he burst out: "I'm bound to be rich! *Bound to be rich!*" ...

The discovery of oil in the northwestern corner of Pennsylvania by [Edwin L.] Drake in 1859 was no isolated event, but part of the long overdue movement to exploit the subsoil of the country. When thousands rushed to scoop the silver and gold of Nevada, Colorado and Montana, the copper of Michigan, the iron ore of Pennsylvania and New York, technical knowledge at last interpreted the meaning of the greasy mineral substance which lay above ground near Titusville, Pennsylvania, and which had been used as a patent medicine ("Kier's Medicine") for twenty years. The rush and boom, out of which numerous speculators such as Andrew Carnegie had drawn quick profits and sold out—while so many others lost all they possessed—did not escape the attention of Rockefeller. The merchants of Cleveland, interested either in handling the new illuminating oil or investing in the industry itself, had sent the young Rockefeller to spy out the ground.

He had come probably in the spring of 1860 to the strange, blackened valleys of the Oil Regions where a forest of crude derricks, flimsy shacks and storehouses had been raised overnight. Here he had looked at the anarchy of the pioneer drillers or diggers of oil, the first frenzy of exploitation, with a deep disfavor that all conservative merchants of the time shared. There were continual fires, disasters and miracles; an oil well brought a fortune in a week, with the market price at twenty dollars a barrel; then as more wells came in the price fell to three and even two dollars a barrel before the next season! No one could tell at what price it was safe to buy oil, or oil acreage, and none knew how long the supply would last.

Returning to Cleveland, Rockefeller had counseled his merchant friends against investments in oil. At best the refining trade might be barely profitable if one could survive the mad dance of the market and if the supply of oil held out. Repugnance was strong in the infinitely cautious young merchant against the pioneering of the Oil Creek rabble. Two years were to pass before he approached the field again, while his accumulations increased with the fruitful wartime trade in provisions.

In 1862, when small refineries were rising everywhere, when more and more oil fields were being opened, the prospects of the new trade were immensely more favorable. A Clevelander named Samuel Andrews, owner of a small still, now came to the firm of Rockefeller & Clark with a proposal that they back him in setting up a sizable oil-refinery. The man Andrews was something of a technologist: he knew how to extract a high percentage of kerosene oil from the crude; he was one of the first to use the by-products developed in the refining process. Rockefeller and his partner, who appreciated the man's worth, invested $5,000 at the start with him. The affair flourished quickly, as demand widened for the new illuminant. Soon Rockefeller missed not a day from the refinery, where Andrews manufactured a kerosene better, purer than his competitors', and Rockefeller kept the books, conducted the purchasing of crude oil in his sharp fashion, and saved old iron, waste oils, made his own barrels, watched, spared, squirmed, for the smallest bargains.

In 1865, with uncanny judgment, Rockefeller chose between his produce business and the oil-refining trade. He sold his share in the house of Rockefeller & Clark, and purchased Clark's share in the oil-refinery, now called Rockefeller & Andrews. At this moment the values of all provisions were falling, while the oil trade was widening, spreading over all the world. Several great new wells had come in; supply was certain—10,000 barrels a day. Concentrating all his effort upon the new trade, he labored unremittingly to entrench himself in it, to be ready for all the hazards, which were great. He inaugurated ruthless economies; giving all his attention "to little details," he acquired a numerous clientele in the Western and Southern states; and opened an export selling agency in New York, headed by his brother William Rockefeller. "Low-voiced, soft-footed, humble, knowing every point in every man's business," Miss Tarbell relates, "he never tired until he got his wares at the lowest possible figures." "John always got the best of the bargain," the old men of Cleveland recall: "'savy fellow he was!" For all his fierce passion for money, he was utterly impassive in his bearing, save when some surprisingly good purchase of oil had been made at the creek. Then he could no longer restrain his shouts of joy. In the oil trade, John Rockefeller grew up in a hard school of struggle; he endured the merciless and unprincipled competition of rivals; and his own unpitying logic and coldly resolute methods were doubtless the consequence of the brutal free-for-all from which he emerged with certain crushing advantages.

While the producers of crude oil contended with each other in lawless fashion to drill the largest quantities, the refiners at different industrial centers who processed and reshipped the crude oil were also engaged in unresting trade conflicts, in which all measures were fair. And behind the rivalry of the producers and the refiners in different cities lay the secret struggles of the large railroad interests moving obscurely in the background. Drew's Erie, Vanderbilt's New York Central, Thomson and Scott's Pennsylvania, extending their lines to the Oil Regions, all hunted their fortune in the huge new traffic, pressing the interests of favored shipping and refining centers such as Cleveland or Pittsburgh or Buffalo to suit themselves. It would have been simplest possibly to have oil-refineries at the source of the crude material itself; but the purpose of the railroads forbade this; and there was no way of determining the outcome in this matter, as in any other phase of the organization of the country's new resources, whose manner of exploitation was determined only through pitched battles between the various gladiators, wherein the will of Providence was seen.

Rockefeller, who had no friends and no diversions, who was "all business," as John T. Flynn describes him, now gave himself to incessant planning, planning that would defeat chance itself. His company was but one of thirty oil-refiners located in Cleveland; in the Oil Regions, at Oil City and Titusville, there were numerous others, including the largest refineries of all, more favorably placed for shipping. But in 1867 Rockefeller invited into his firm as a partner, a business acquaintance of his, Henry M. Flagler, son-in-law of the rich whiskey distiller and salt-maker S. V. Harkness. Flagler, a bold and dashing fellow, was deeply attracted by the possibilities of the oil business.

Thanks to Harkness, he brought $70,000 into the business, which at once opened a second refinery in Cleveland. Within a year or two the firm of Rockefeller, Flagler & Andrews was the biggest refinery in Cleveland, producing 1,500 barrels a day, having its own warehouses, its export agency in New York, its own wooden tank cars, its own staff of chemists or experts who labored to improve or economize the manufacturing processes. The company moved steadily to the front of the field, surpassing its rivals in quality, and outselling them by a small, though not certain or decisive, margin. How was this done?

In the struggle for business, Rockefeller's instinct for conspiracy is already marked. The partnership with Flagler brought an access of fresh capital and even more credit. Then in a further step of collusion, this of profound importance, Rockefeller and Flagler approached the railroad which carried so many carloads of their oil toward the seaboard, and whose tariff figured heavily in the ultimate cost. They demanded from it concessions in freight rates that would enable them to meet the advantages of other refining centers such as Pittsburgh, Philadelphia and New York. Their company was now large enough to force the hand of the railroad, in this case, a branch of Vanderbilt's New York Central system; and they were granted their demands: a secret reduction or "rebate" on all their shipments of oil. "Such was the railroad's method," Rockefeller himself afterward admitted. He relates:

A public rate was made and collected by the railroad companies, but so far as my knowledge extends, was seldom retained in full; a portion of it was repaid to the shipper as a rebate. By this method the real rate of freight which any shipper paid was not known by his competitors, nor by other railroads, the amount being a matter of bargain with the carrying companies.

Once having gained an advantage Rockefeller pressed forward relentlessly. The volume of his business increased rapidly. Thanks to the collaboration of the railroad, he had placed his rivals in other cities and in Cleveland itself under a handicap, whose weight he endeavored to increase.

The railroads, as we see, possessed the strategic power, almost of life and death, to encourage one industrial group or cause another to languish. Their policy was based on the relative costs of handling small or large volume shipments. Thus as the Rockefeller company became the largest shipper of oil, its production rising in 1870 to 3,000 barrels a day, and offered to guarantee regular daily shipments of as much as sixty carloads, the railroads were impelled to accept further proposals for rebates. It was to their interest to do so in view of savings of several hundred thousand dollars a month in handling. On crude oil brought from the Oil Regions, Rockefeller paid perhaps 15 cents a barrel less than the open rate of 40 cents; on refined oil moving from Cleveland toward New York, he paid approximately 90 cents against the open rate of $1.30. These momentous agreements were maintained in utter secrecy, perhaps because of the persisting memory of their illegality, according to the common law ever since Queen Elizabeth's time, as a form of "conspiracy" in trade.

In January, 1870, Rockefeller, Flagler & Andrews were incorporated as a joint-stock company, a form increasingly popular, under the name of the Standard Oil Company of Ohio. At this time their worth was estimated at one million dollars; they employed over a thousand workers and were the largest refiners in the world. Despite deeply disturbed conditions in their trade during 1870, profits came to them in a mounting flood, while in the same year, it is noteworthy, four of their twenty-nine competitors in Cleveland gave up the ghost. The pious young man of thirty who feared only God, and thought of nothing but his business, gave not a sign of his greatly augmented wealth, which made him one of the leading personages of his city. His income was actually a fabulous one for the time. The Standard Oil Company from the beginning earned something like 100 per cent on its capital; and Rockefeller and his brother owned a full half-interest in it in 1870. But with an evangelistic fervor John Rockefeller was bent only upon further conquests, upon greater extensions of the power over industry which had come into the hands of the group he headed.

In the life of every conquering soul there is a "turning point," a moment when a deep understanding of the self coincides with an equally deep sense of one's immediate mission in the tangible world. For Rockefeller, brooding, secretive, uneasily scenting his fortune, this moment came but a few years after his entrance into the oil trade, and at the age of thirty. He had looked upon the disorganized conditions of the Pennsylvania oil fields, the only source then known, and found them not good: the guerilla fighting of drillers, or refining firms, of rival railroad lines, the mercurial changes in supply and market value—very alarming in 1870 —offended his orderly and methodical spirit. But one could see that petroleum was to be the light of the world. From the source, from the chaotic oil fields where thousands of drillers toiled, the grimy stream of the precious commodity, petroleum, flowed along many diverse channels to narrow into the hands of several hundred refineries, then to issue once more in a continuous stream to consumers throughout the world. Owner with Flagler and Harkness of the largest refining company in the country, Rockefeller had a strongly entrenched position at the narrows of this stream. Now what if the Standard Oil Company should by further steps of organization possess itself wholly of the narrows? In this period of anarchic individual competition, the idea of such a movement of rationalization must have come to Rockefeller forcibly, as it had recently come to others.

Even as early as 1868 the first plan of industrial combination in the shape of the pool had been originated in the Michigan Salt Association. Desiring to correct chaotic market conditions, declaring that "in union there is strength," the salt-producers of Saginaw Bay had banded together to control the output and sale of nearly all the salt in their region, a large part of the vital national supply. Secret agreements had been executed for each year, allotting the sales and fixing the price at almost twice what it had been immediately prior to the appearance of the pool. And though the inevitable greed and self-seeking of the individual salt-producers had tended to weaken the pool, the new economic invention was launched in its infantile form. Rockefeller's partners, Flagler and Harkness, had themselves participated in the historic Michigan Salt Association.

This grand idea of industrial rationalization owed its swift, ruthless, methodical execution no doubt to the firmness of character we sense in Rockefeller, who had the temper of a great, unconscionable military captain, combining audacity with thoroughness and shrewd judgment. His plan seemed to take account of no one's feelings in the matter. Indeed there was something revolutionary in it; it seemed to fly in the fact of human liberties and deep-rooted custom and common law. The notorious "South Improvement Company," with its strange charter, ingeniously instrumenting the scheme of combination, was to be unraveled amid profound secrecy. By conspiring with the railroads (which also hungered for economic order), it would be terribly armed with the power of the freight rebate which garrotted all opposition systematically. This plan of combination, this unifying conception Rockefeller took as his ruling idea; he breathed life into it, clung to it grimly in the face of the most menacing attacks of legislatures, courts, rival captains, and, at moments, even of rebellious mobs. His view of men and events justified him, and despite many official and innocent denials, he is believed to have said once in confidence, as Flynn relates:

I had our plan clearly in mind. It was right. I knew it as a matter of conscience. It was right between me and my God. If I had to do it tomorrow I would do it again in the same way—do it a hundred times.

The broad purpose was to control and direct the flow of crude petroleum into the hands of a narrowed group of refiners. The refiners would be supported by the combined railroad trunk lines which shipped the oil; while the producers' phase of the stream would be left unorganized—*but with power over their outlet to market* henceforth to be concentrated into the few hands of the refiners.

Saying nothing to others, bending over their maps of the industry, Rockefeller and Flagler first drew up a short list of the principal refining companies who were to be asked to combine with them. Then having banded together a sufficient number, they would persuade the railroads to give them special freight rates —on the ground of "evening" the traffic —guaranteeing equitable distribution of freight business; and this in turn would be a club to force other elements needed into union with them. They could control output, drive out competitors, and force all foreign countries throughout the world to buy their product from them at their own terms. They could finally dictate market prices on crude oil, stabilize the margin of profit at their own process, and do away at last with the dangerously speculative character of their business.

Their plans moved forward rapidly all through 1871. For a small sum of money the "conspirators" obtained the Pennsylvania charter of a defunct corporation, which had been authorized to engage in almost any kind of business under the sun. Those who were approached by the promoters, those whom they determined to use in their grand scheme, were compelled in a manner typical of all Rockefeller's projects to sign a written pledge of secrecy:

> I, ——— ———, do solemnly promise upon my honor and faith as a gentleman that I will keep secret all transactions which I may have with the corporation known as the South Improvement Company; that should I fail to complete any bargains with the said company, all the preliminary conversations shall be kept strictly private; and finally that I will not disclose the price for which I dispose of

any products or any other facts which may in any way bring to light the internal workings or organization of the company. All this I do freely promise.

At the same time, in confidential pourparlers with the officials of the Erie, the Pennsylvania and the New York Central Railroads, the men of the Standard Oil represented themselves as possessing secret control of the bulk of the refining interest. Thus they obtained conditions more advantageous than anything which had gone before; and this weapon in turn of course ensured the triumph of their pool.

The refiners to be combined under the aegis of the South Improvement Company were to have a rebate of from 40 to 50 per cent on the crude oil they ordered shipped to them and from 25 to 50 per cent on the refined oil they shipped out. The refiners in the Oil Regions were to pay *twice as much* by the new code (though nearer to New York) as the Standard Oil Company at Cleveland. But besides the rebate the members of the pool were to be given also a "drawback" consisting of part of the increased tariff rate which "outsiders" were forced to pay. Half of the freight payments of a rival refiner would in many cases be paid over to the Rockefeller group. Their competitors were simply to be decimated; and to make certain of this the railroads agreed—all being set down in writing, in minutest detail—"to make manifests or way-bills of all petroleum or its product transported over any portion of its lines ... which manifests shall state the name of the consignee, the place of shipment and the place of destination," this information to be furnished faithfully to the officers of the South Improvement Company.

The railroad systems, supposedly public-spirited and impartial, were to open all their knowledge of rival private business to the pool, thus helping to concentrate all the oil trade into the few hands chosen. In return for so much assistance, they were to have their freight "evened," and were enabled at last to enter into a momentous peace pact with each other by which the oil traffic (over which they had quarreled bitterly) was to be fairly allotted among themselves.

By January, 1872, after the first decade of the oil business, John Rockefeller, with the aid of the railroad captains, was busily carrying out a most "elaborate national plan" of his own for the control of his industry—such planned control as the spokesman of the business system asserted ever afterward was impossible. The first pooling of 1872, beautiful as was its economic architecture and laudable its motive, had defects which were soon plainly noticeable. All the political institutions, the whole spirit of American law still favored the amiable, wasteful individualism of business, which in Rockefeller's mind had already become obsolete and must be supplanted by a centralized, one might say almost *collectivist*—certainly coöperative rather than competitive—form of operation. Moreover, these "revolutionists" took little account of the social dislocations their juggernaut would bring. Like the railroad baron, Vanderbilt, working better than they knew, their eyes fixed solely upon the immediate task rather than upon some millennium of the future, they desired simply, as they often said, to be "the biggest refiners in the world...."

To the principal oil firms in Cleveland Rockefeller went one by one, explaining the plan of the South Improvement Company patiently, pointing out how important it was to oppose the creek refiners and save the Cleveland oil trade. He would say:

"You see, this scheme is bound to work. There is no chance for anyone outside. But we are going to give everybody a chance to come in. You are to turn over your refinery to my appraisers, and I will give you Standard Oil Company stock or cash, as you prefer, for the value we put upon it. I advise you to take the stock. It will be for your good."

Then if the men demurred, according to much of the testimony at the Senate Investigation of 1876, he would point out suavely that it was useless to resist; opposition would certainly be crushed. The offers of purchase usually made were for from a third to a half the actual cost of the property.

Now a sort of terror swept silently over the oil trade. In a vague panic, competitors saw the Standard Oil officers come to them and say (as Rockefeller's own brother and rival, Frank, testified in 1876): "If you don't sell your property to us it will be valueless, because we have got the advantage with the railroads."

The railroad rates indeed were suddenly doubled to the outsiders, and those refiners who resisted the pool came and expostulated; then they became frightened and disposed of their property. One of the largest competitors in Cleveland, the firm of Alexander, Scofield & Co., held out for a time, protesting before the railroad officials at the monstrous unfairness of the deal. But these officials when consulted said mysteriously: "*Better sell —better get clear*—better sell out—no help for it." Another powerful refiner, Robert Hanna, uncle of the famous Mark Alonzo, found that the railroads would give him no relief, and also was glad to sell out at 40 or 50 cents on the dollar for his property value. To one of these refiners, Isaac L. Hewitt, who had been his employer in boyhood, Rockefeller himself spoke with intense emotion. He urged Hewitt to take stock. Hewitt related: "He told me that it would be sufficient to take care of my family for all time... and asking for reasons, he made this expression, I remember: '*I have ways of making money that you know nothing of.*'"

All this transpired in secret. For "silence is golden," the rising king of oil believed. Though many were embittered by their loss, others joined gladly. The strongest capitalists in Cleveland, such as the wealthy Colonel Oliver H. Payne, were amazed at the swift progress Rockefeller had made, at the enormous profits he showed them in confidence to invite their coöperation. Payne, among others, as a man of wealth and influence, was taken into the board of directors and made treasurer of the Standard Oil Company. (The officers of the South Improvement Company itself were "dummies.") Within three months by an economic *coup*

d'état the youthful Rockefeller had captured all of Cleveland's oil-refining trade, all twenty-five competitors surrendered to him and yielded him command of one-fifth of America's output of refined oil.

Tomorrow all the population of the Oil Regions, its dismayed refiners, drillers, and workers of oil, might rise against the South Improvement Company ring in a grotesque uproar. The secret, outwardly peaceful campaigns would assume here as elsewhere the character of violence and lawlessness which accompanied the whole program of the industrial revolution. But Rockefeller and his comrades had stolen a long march on their opponents; their tactics shaped themselves already as those of the giant industrialists of the future conquering the pigmies. Entrenched at the "narrows" of the mighty river of petroleum they could no more be dislodged than those other barons who had formerly planted their strong castles along the banks of the Rhine could be dislodged by unarmed peasants and burghers.

NO   Ralph W. Hidy and Muriel E. Hidy

PIONEERING IN BIG BUSINESS, 1882–1911

FROM CHAOS TO COMBINATION

During the years from 1882 to 1911 the leaders of the Standard Oil group
of companies, including the Standard Oil Company (New Jersey), carried
out an extraordinary experiment in the management of a business. John D.
Rockefeller and his associates successfully created and applied a system for
operating a large, integrated industrial enterprise which was one of the earliest representatives of Big Business, to use the phrase popular in the United
States. As executives of the large combination those men contributed greatly
to the rapid development of the American petroleum industry and through
it to the growth of the economy as a whole. Being innovators, however,
they also made numerous mistakes and learned only slowly that large size
and concentrated economic power in a democratic society required conduct
conforming to new rules set by popular demand.

The early life of the Standard Oil Company (New Jersey), generally referred to as Jersey Standard, was marked by rapid growth from infancy to
early parenthood. Organized as one of the units of the Standard Oil Trust
in August, 1882, for its first ten years the corporation existed primarily as
the owner of a refinery and other manufacturing establishments at Bayonne;
late in the decade the company acquired a few wholesaling facilities in the
same northern New Jersey area. As a consequence of a court decision in Ohio
in 1892, Standard Oil executives reorganized their enterprise under twenty
corporations of which Jersey Standard was one of the three largest; top managers vested this company with direct ownership of extensive additional
manufacturing and marketing properties and also made it one of the holding companies within the group of sister corporations. The Jersey Company
continued to perform operating functions after it had become the parent of
the entire combination in 1899.

From Ralph W. Hidy and Muriel E. Hidy, *History of Standard Oil Company (New Jersey), vol. 1:
Pioneering in Big Business, 1882–1911* (Harper & Brothers, 1955). Copyright © 1955, renewed 1983,
by Business History Foundation, Inc. Reprinted by permission of HarperCollins Publishers, Inc.
Notes omitted.

As the apex of a pyramid of companies dominating the American petroleum industry, Jersey Standard naturally became the symbol of the much-distrusted Standard Oil "monopoly" in the public mind. In 1911 the Supreme Court of the United States, affirming that general conviction, broke up the combination by divesting the Standard Oil Company (New Jersey) of thirty-three affiliates, thus bringing to a close one eventful and significant phase of the corporation's history. . . .

THE STANDARD OIL TEAM AND ITS EARLY POLICIES

As an early corporate product of the Standard Oil combination, Jersey Standard fell heir to the policies and practices of the men who created the alliance. In the course of working together before 1882, this group of executives had set precedents for the management of the Standard Oil family of firms which were to influence vitally the life of the new company.

The Men Who Made Standard Oil

The Standard Oil alliance in 1881 was the creation of a team of men. As one man paraphrased John D. Rockefeller's own statement, the "secret of the success of the Standard Oil Company was that there had come together a body of men who from beginning to end worked in single-minded co-operation, who all believed in each other and had perfect confidence in the integrity of each other, who reached all their decisions after fair consideration with magnanimity toward each other" in order to assure "absolute harmony."

As an instrument for carrying out the ideas of those men, the combination necessarily took its character from those who made it and managed it. When they chose to create a new corporation, such as Jersey Standard, it became part of the mechanism for pursuing their policies. Extremely significant, therefore, for understanding the history of the company is acquaintance with the individuals who created and directed both the Standard Oil family of companies and the Jersey Company itself. Scores of men made material contributions to the early development of the combination but only a relatively few ranked as outstanding.

John D. Rockefeller (1839–1937) was captain of the team. By all odds the largest holder of shares, he probably would have been chosen the head for that reason alone. Although not the only person to have the conviction in the 1870's that the petroleum industry should be stabilized, he first formulated the idea that the only satisfactory means was to organize a commonly owned unit on a national scale. Allan Nevins has characterized Rockefeller as careful, patient, cautious, methodical, quick to observe and to learn, grave, pious, aloof, secretive, reticent, inscrutable, and taciturn. Rockefeller considered work a duty, loved simplicity, believed in discipline, and possessed little social warmth except with his family and intimate friends. He had a mind of extraordinary force, great power of concentration, and almost infinite capacity for detail. Although he was willing to make decisions and to act forcefully, he possessed not only remarkable foresight, broad vision, and cool judgment, but also willingness to consider the ideas of others.

In the early 1870's Rockefeller began to delegate most details of management to subordinates and thereafter devoted himself primarily to formulation of broad policy. His greatest contribution, beyond the concept of the Standard Oil combination itself, was the persuasion of strong men to join the alliance and to work together effectively in its management. The remarkable fact was that Rockefeller, while still in his thirties, impressed a group of men, almost all older than himself, with his qualities of leadership. His most arduous task later was to preside over meetings of strongly individualistic, positive executives, while they discussed and determined, usually unanimously, strategy and tactics for the combination as a whole.

During the 1860's and 1870's the closest and strongest associate of John D. Rockefeller was Henry M. Flagler (1830–1913). Of average height, slight build, erect figure, unobtrusive and dignified manner, Flagler was an ambitious, patient, and shrewd man of business. It is difficult to determine where the ideas of Rockefeller stop and those of Flagler begin. They were warm personal friends; they talked over their business before, during, and after office hours. Flagler liked to build new things and possessed a faculty for reducing complex problems to their simplest components. His constructive imagination was as broad and as vivid as Rockefeller's. It was caught by a desire to develop Florida, and into its hotels, railroads, and other enterprises he put some $50,000,000, and more of his energy than into Standard Oil, during the 1880's and later. Yet he left his mark on the combination. Having an aptitude for legal affairs, he was a master in drawing up clear, concise contracts. The incorporation of Ohio Standard appears to have been his brain child, and he helped in the later organization of the Trust. Flagler also participated in many negotiations leading to entry of other firms into the Standard Oil family. His special function was the handling of all affairs concerning transportation of both raw materials and finished products, and he drove hard bargains with railroad managers. Gifted with a keen sense of humor and a feeling of personal responsibilities to employees, he won the warm respect and loyal support of most subordinates. Not the least important of Flagler's executive positions was the presidency of Jersey Standard during eight of its first seventeen years. . . .

Although never an executive, one other man colored the history of Standard Oil as much as many of the men who created and managed the combination. Samuel C. T. Dodd (1836–1907), the general solicitor of the organization from 1881 to 1905, began his practice at Franklin, Pennsylvania, in 1859. Short and rotund, affable and learned, he soon became expert in the legal technicalities of the petroleum business. A Democrat in politics, he actively participated in the Pennsylvania constitutional convention of 1872. Though Dodd thought the material prosperity of the United States was attributable "in a great measure" to large combinations of capital, he was equally convinced that they should be regulated by clearly framed laws. Outspokenly opposed to "unjust" railroad rate discriminations, he accepted the invitation to become counsel for Standard Oil in the Oil Regions in 1879 only on the condition that his employers fully recognize his determination to fight the practice of rebating. When Dodd, a Presbyterian elder, abandoned private practice to become general solicitor for Standard Oil in New York, he humorously explained his decision to become the "least victim of the monopoly" by remarking: "Well, as the ministers say when they get a call to a higher salary, it seems to be the Lord's will." Thereafter Dodd quietly and honestly told top managers what they could and could not do under existing law as he interpreted it and occasionally, as extant correspondence shows, advocated a course of action on moral rather than legal grounds. He had a most difficult assignment in charting a course for a large business in a period when a new public policy toward trusts and combinations was emerging.

The executives advised by Dodd were men of varied abilities and complementary qualities. While several of them had specialized at one time or another in separate functions of the petroleum industry, a number of them had broad experience over a number of years. Some were inventors. Others brought special aptitudes in organization and marketing. Almost all had begun their careers in mercantile enterprises. Before joining the Standard Oil alliance, all had engaged in either regional or national co-operative efforts. By 1882 they had worked together for a number of years; while differing in backgrounds and philosophies, they had evolved policies which were, with some modifications, to guide the Standard Oil combination throughout its early history and to affect the petroleum industry for a longer span of years.

Policies, Practices, and Precedents
Policies and practices pursued by Standard Oil executives during the years prior to 1882 emerged in a variety of ways. Some policies were evidenced by votes of directors of components of the alliance and gradually won more general acceptance among its members. In other instances precedents and practices developed into policies over time; no formalized statement ever indicated the direction in which the leaders were traveling, but in a succession of separate steps they evolved a significant behavior pattern.

Many of the concepts and procedures adopted by executives of the alliance stemmed from their early experience as small businessmen. Probably at no other time during the nineteenth century was economic activity more freely competitive than in the period from 1840 to 1865. The customs and mores of the small individual enterpriser became the accepted pattern for almost all men. Naturally enough, therefore, Rockefeller and his associates learned in their youth to believe in freedom of entry into any occupation, in the sanctity of private property, in the obligation of the owner to manage his own operations, and in the right to keep his business affairs secret, a concept dating from time immemorial. As a corollary of that idea, in courts or legislative investigative chambers a businessman testified to the legal truth, and no more, a practice still honored by general observance in spite of critical charges of evasiveness and ambiguity. Since most markets were local, every businessman could observe his competitors with relative ease, and did. His habit was to use any competitive device not clearly prohibited by law. Bargaining in the market place was almost universal, whether for products or for such services as the transportation of freight. Posted prices were a point of departure for haggling, and price reductions were the most widely utilized of competitive techniques.

In response to the chaotic and depressed years of the 1870's, however, Standard Oil men drastically modified some of their socially inherited concepts about competition. They apparently desired at first to bring all gatherers of crude oil and refiners of light petroleum fractions into one commonly owned unit— to create a monopoly. Late in the decade they added lubricating oil specialists and trunk pipelines to their list of components to be unified. By means of common ownership in an association of specializing firms, Rockefeller and his associates created a great horizontal and vertical combination, which, on the eve of the birth of Jersey Standard, maintained overwhelming dominance in gathering, storing, and processing petroleum and its derivatives.

Either by design or through pressure of circumstances, the Standard Oil group of executives had not achieved monopoly in any function by 1881. Strong minority interests in many domestic marketing companies within the alliance, and limited coverage of the market by them, set definite limits to the influence of top managers in that field of operations. In almost all sales for export foreign merchants bought oil from companies in the Standard Oil family and carried on marketing in foreign lands. The combination owned few producing properties. United Pipe Lines men failed to keep pace with expansion in Bradford production, and competing gathering and storing facilities kept appearing. Tide-Water Pipe had thrown the first trunk pipeline over the mountains toward the sea and remained a belligerent competitor. Under the agreement with the producers in 1880 the price of crude oil was set on the oil exchanges, not by Standard Oil. In manufacturing, the area of initial intent for monopoly, the top managers of the alliance had stopped short of their goal. They had refused to pay the prices asked by owners of some plants. Others had sprung up in response to inducements offered by the Pennsylvania Railroad, and in 1882 the editor of *Mineral Resources* noted that the combination had "for some reason" not renewed leases on a number of refineries, several of which were doing "a good trade" and "assuming considerable im-

portance." Thus, by that year some of the firms classified by H. H. Rogers in 1879 as being "in harmony" with Standard Oil had gone their independent ways.

Standard Oil executives employed a variety of tactics in carrying out the expansionist program during the 1870's. After the consolidation in Cleveland and the disastrous South Improvement episode, Rockefeller and his associates first won the confidence of competitors through comprehensive voluntary association. They then brought into the alliance the strongest men and firms in specific areas or functions, a policy pursued, with some exceptions, until 1911. Exchange of stock in the different companies by individuals and guarantee of equality in management provided the final assurance needed to convince such strong individualists as [Charles] Lockhart, [William G.] Warden, [Charles] Pratt, and [Henry H.] Rogers that combination was to their advantage. All then co-operated eagerly in trying to unify the remaining firms in refining by bringing them into The Central Association, by buying plants whenever feasible, and by leasing other works. If a seller personally chose not to enter the combination, he usually signed an agreement not to engage in the petroleum business for a period of years. In any case, evidence in extant records substantiates the point that Standard Oil men completely and carefully inventoried all properties and paid "good," though not high, prices for them, including compensation for patents, trade-marks, brands, good-will, and volume of business. In many instances prices for properties reflected the desire of Standard Oil officials to enlist the inventive capacities or administrative abilities of the owners in the service of the alliance. The preponderance of the evidence indicates that Rockefeller and his fellow executives preferred to buy out rather than fight out competitors.

At the same time, when Standard Oil men felt it necessary to apply pressure as a means of persuading a rival to lease or sell his plant, they showed no hesitancy in utilizing the usual sharp competitive practices prevailing in the oil industry during the 1870's. On one occasion or another they pre-empted all available staves and barrels, restricted as completely as possible the available tank cars to their own business, and indulged in local price cutting. They meticulously watched and checked on competitive shipments and sales, sometimes in co-operation with railroad men, and diligently negotiated advantageous freight rates on railways, even to the point of receiving rebates or drawbacks on rivals' shipments. All acts were kept secret as long as possible. The size and resources of the alliance gave it overwhelming power, which was sometimes used ruthlessly, though it is worthy of note that numerous oilmen successfully resisted the pressure.

Within the alliance itself executives also retained many of their competitive habits. Although price competition al-most completely disappeared within the combination, men and firms raced with each other in reducing costs, devising new techniques, developing products, improving their quality, and showing profits. Top managers believed in compe-tition but not in the undisciplined variety.

In building the alliance the leaders of Standard Oil adopted a long-range view with emphasis on planning, even before they had achieved an organization to carry such an approach into successful operation. They showed a profound faith in the permanence of the industry, a belief not generally held in years when the petroleum business was characterized by instability, rapid exhaustion of producing fields, and doubts about the appearance of new ones. They wanted to plan and to have reasonable assurance that they were taking no more than calculated risks in pushing toward their objectives. A necessary requirement of planning was centralized policy formulation.

That responsibility devolved not upon one man but on a group of executives. The evolution of Standard Oil's committee system, the hallmark of its administrative methods, started early in the seventies. The original bylaws of Ohio Standard provided for an Executive Committee. Its first membership of two, John D. Rockefeller and Flagler, was increased to three during the consecutive terms of Samuel Andrews and O. H. Payne. [John D.] Archbold replaced the latter in 1879. William Rockefeller, Pratt, Warden, and [Jabez] Bostwick had joined the three Cleveland members the previous year. At that time the Executive Committee absorbed the "Advisory Committee," which had been established as early as 1873 to act in the New York area. William Rockefeller and Bostwick, its first members, had been joined by Pratt and Warden soon after they entered the alliance. The enlarged Executive Committee of 1878 held many of its almost daily meetings at 140 Pearl Street, New York, and two years later made four a quorum because of the geographic split in membership between Cleveland and New York. Members of other committees started consultations before 1882. If the making of decisions as a synthesis of opinion of a group after discussion is a characteristic of modern business, as a recent commentator has implied, then Standard Oil was modern in the 1870's.

In order to have easily available the best data and advice for making decisions, the Rockefellers and their associates built up staffs in Cleveland, New York, and other points. For the use of executives they collected, evaluated, and digested information on crude oil supplies, costs of manufacture, and markets all over the world. The practice of watching and reporting on marketing by competitors everywhere in the United States, not merely locally, was already inaugurated, though not yet systematized. S. C. T. Dodd was engaged as legal navigator; Standard Oil officials desired to operate within the law. A beginning was made in standardizing accounting procedures.

As the emergence of the Executive Committee and the formation of staffs indicated, the creation of the combination permitted a division of labor or specialization within the organization. As Archbold expressed the development in 1888, the grouping of talents within the alliance permitted "various individuals to take up the different features of the business as a specialty and accomplish greater efficiency than can possibly be accomplished by an individual who attempts to cover all in a business."

In the matter of finance, as in other aspects of operations, Ohio Standard set precedents on reporting and central review. In 1877 the directors of that company resolved that all persons responsible for different aspects of the business should make quarterly reports in writing to the board. Two years later, its members unanimously agreed that annual financial statements should be presented. In 1875 the directors had voted that expenditures for new construction in manufacturing exceeding $2,500 should be undertaken only with written consent of seven members of the board, but that resolution

was repealed five years later and the company's Executive Committee was given full charge of all matters relating to repairs and new construction.

Since the goal of the members of the alliance was to maximize profits in the long run, they adopted practices to that end. Emphasis was placed on reducing costs, improving and standardizing the quality of products, and striving for new methods of refining, including the engaging of specialists. Stories about John D. Rockefeller's penchant for eliminating waste and effecting economies have been told and retold. As president of the Acme Oil Company in the Oil Regions, Archbold achieved substantial savings through buying supplies in quantity and by making annual contracts regarding the repairing of boilers and barrels for all plants under his jurisdiction. When he purchased a lubricating oil patent in 1879, Archbold guaranteed the owner, Eli E. Hendrick, a salary of $10,000 per year for ten years in return for the devotion of his inventive talents to Acme. Duplicating pipelines were removed, inefficient plants dismantled, strategically located refineries enlarged, and auxiliary manufacturing units developed, all in the name of economy and reduction of costs. By consistently stressing that practice in every function Standard Oil men moved gradually but inevitably toward mass manufacturing and, more slowly, toward mass marketing.

Gathering information, consultation, planning, and experimentation did not always lead to quick action, but the leaders of Standard Oil early indicated flexibility in adopting new methods and thoroughness in carrying them out. Critics voiced the opinion in the late 1870's that Standard Oil, having invested so much in refineries in the Oil Regions, could not take advantage of the pipeline revolution to establish large manufacturing units at the coast. Almost as soon as others had demonstrated the feasibility of building long trunk pipelines the Standard Oil group took action in 1879. It already possessed a system of gathering lines through the United Pipe Lines. After its organization in 1881, the National Transit Company pushed trunk pipeline building vigorously. By the next year it owned 1,062 miles of trunk lines, only 48 of which had been bought from firms outside the alliance. Its policies... illustrate the fact that Standard Oil was not always the earliest to initiate an innovation, but, once launched on a policy, the combination pushed it with a vigor and fervor made possible by efficient organization and ample financial resources.

Standard Oil's financial policy itself was an important element in the successful life of the combination and its components. Not only were the risks spread by the breadth of the alliance's activities, but profits made in one company or phase of the business flowed into development of another when desired. Early in the history of Standard Oil units short-term loans were often obtained from commercial banks, and temporary aid had to be obtained when the properties of The Empire Transportation Company were purchased. A conservative ratio of dividends to net income, however, was soon to permit the accumulation of funds for self-financing.

Ohio Standard furnished an example for the companies in the alliance on the matter of insurance against fire. On the assumption that loss by fire was a normal expense of the petroleum industry and could be carried by a large unit, the directors of the Ohio Company agreed in January, 1877, to insure property in any one place only on the excess of its valuation above $100,000.

As directors of The Standard Oil Company (Ohio), executives of the alliance also set a precedent regarding the ownership of producing properties. In April, 1878, apparently as a result of a suit by H. L. Taylor & Company against John D. Rockefeller and others for breach of contract in a joint producing operation, the directors unanimously voted not to invest any more money in the purchase of crude oil lands. Six months later they resolved to discontinue all activity in producing petroleum and instructed the Executive Committee to dispose of its properties. This point of view had an influence upon the Standard Oil alliance for a decade.

Quite the contrary was the action adopted in regard to pipelines. By 1881 the Standard Oil group was definitely launched on a program for large-scale expansion of its pipeline facilities and soon exercised a greater measure of control over the function. The combination poured an increasing quantity of capital into building lines; the profits from them provided a cushion for all operations of the alliance. The speculatively minded can ask whether the development of the oil industry would have been more rapid or socially beneficial had parallel pipelines competed with each other during the formative years of the industry, and whether the development would have been as efficient, or more so, had the railroad systems controlled competing lines, as had seemed possible in the 1870's. The point remains that the top managers of Standard Oil determined to keep this function in their own hands to the extent possible....

The roots of Standard Oil's policies went deep into the personalities and early experiences of Rockefeller and his associates. Though few of their practices had been satisfactorily systematized by 1881, precedents had been established for many later policies of Jersey Standard and other members of the combination.

By the end of 1881 the general public was hard put to make an accurate estimate of Standard Oil's behavior. Legislative investigations and several legal cases had already elicited an enormous amount of conflicting testimony as to the relations of the combination with both railroads and competitors. Rockefeller and his associates had heightened uncertainty and speculation about their activities by their secrecy in building the alliance and by their evasive, often ambiguous, consistently legally accurate testimony on the witness stand. The very newness, size, dominance, and efficiency of the combination, not to mention its absorption of small competitors in adversity and its avid search for the lowest possible railroad rates, all tended to arouse antagonism. In 1882 S. H. Stowell closed his comments on Standard Oil in *Mineral Resources* with an unbiased observer's puzzlement: "There seems to be little doubt that the company has done a great work, and that through its instrumentality oil refining has been reduced to a business, and transportation has been greatly simplified; but as to how much evil has been mixed with this good, it is not practicable to make a definite statement." It was certain that through combination managers of Standard Oil had brought a measure of order to a formerly confused industry, though they thought that the administration of the alliance itself needed further systematization.

POSTSCRIPT

Was John D. Rockefeller a "Robber Baron"?

Regardless of how American entrepreneurs are perceived, there is no doubt that they constituted a powerful elite and were responsible for defining the character of society in the Gilded Age. For many Americans, these businessmen represented the logical culmination of the country's attachment to laissez-faire economics and rugged individualism. In fact, it was not unusual at all for the nation's leading industrialists to be depicted as the real-life models for the "rags-to-riches" theme epitomized in the self-help novels of Horatio Alger. Closer examination of the lives of most of these entrepreneurs, however, reveals the mythical dimensions of this American ideal. Simply put, the typical business executive of the late nineteenth century did not rise up from humble circumstances, a product of the American rural tradition or the immigrant experience, as is frequently claimed. Rather, most of these big businessmen were of Anglo-Saxon origin and reared in a city by middle-class parents. According to one survey, over half the leaders had attended college at a time when even the pursuit of a high school education was considered unusual. In other words, instead of having to pull themselves up by their own bootstraps from the bottom of the social heap, these individuals usually started their climb to success at the middle of the ladder or higher.

Earl Latham and Peter d'A. Jones have assembled excellent collections of the major viewpoints on the "robber baron" thesis in their respective edited anthologies *John D. Rockefeller: Robber Baron or Industrial Statesman?* (D. C. Heath, 1949) and *The Robber Barons Revisited* (D. C. Heath, 1968). For a critique of Josephson's work, see Maury Klein, "A Robber Historian," *Forbes* (October 26, 1987). Studies focusing specifically upon Rockefeller include David Freeman Hawke, *John D.: The Founding Father of the Rockefellers* (Harper & Row, 1980) and Ron Chernow, *Titan: The Life of John D. Rockefeller, Sr.* (Random House, 1998). Biographical studies of other late-nineteenth-century businessmen include Harold Livesay, *Andrew Carnegie and the Rise of Big Business* (Little, Brown, 1975) and Maury Klein, *The Life and Legend of Jay Gould* (Johns Hopkins University Press, 1986).

The works of Alfred D. Chandler, Jr., are vital to the understanding of American industrialization. See *The Visible Hand: The Managerial Revolution in American Business* (Harvard University Press, 1977) and *Scale and Scope: The Dynamics of Industrial Capitalism* (Harvard University Press, 1990). Chandler's most important essays are collected in Thomas K. McCraw, ed., *The Essential Alfred Chandler: Essays Toward a Historical Theory of Big Business* (Harvard Business School Press, 1988).

ISSUE 3

Did Nineteenth-Century Women of the West Fail to Overcome the Hardships of Living on the Great Plains?

YES: Christine Stansell, from "Women on the Great Plains 1865–1890," *Women's Studies* (vol. 4, 1976)

NO: Glenda Riley, from *A Place to Grow: Women in the American West* (Harlan Davidson, 1992)

ISSUE SUMMARY

YES: Professor of history Christine Stansell contends that women on the Great Plains were torn from their eastern roots, isolated in their home environment, and separated from friends and relatives. She concludes that they consequently endured lonely lives and loveless marriages.

NO: Professor of history Glenda Riley argues that in spite of enduring harsh environmental, political, and personal conditions on the Great Plains, women created rich and varied social lives through the development of strong support networks.

In 1893 young historian Frederick Jackson Turner (1861–1932) delivered an address before the American Historical Association entitled "The Significance of the Frontier in American History." Turner's essay not only sent him from Wisconsin to Harvard University, it became one of the most important essays ever written in American history. According to Turner's thesis, American civilization was different from European civilization because the continent contained an abundance of land that was settled in four waves of migration from 1607 through 1890. During this process the European heritage was shed and the American characteristics of individualism, mobility, nationalism, and democracy developed.

This frontier theory of American history did not go unchallenged. Some historians argued that Turner's definition of the frontier was too vague and imprecise; he underestimated the cultural forces that came to the West from Europe and the eastern states; he neglected the forces of urbanization and industrialization in opening the West; he placed an undue emphasis on sectional developments and neglected class struggles for power; and, finally, his provincial view of American history prolonged the isolationist views of a nation that had become involved in world affairs in the twentieth century.

By the time Turner died, his thesis had been widely discredited. Historians continued to write about the West, but new fields and new theories were competing for attention.

Younger historians have begun to question the traditional interpretation of western expansion. For example, the older historians believed that growth was good and automatically brought forth progress. New historians William Cronin, Patricia Limerick, and others, however, have questioned this assumption in examining the disastrous ecological effects of American expansionism, such as the elimination of the American buffalo and the depletion of forests.

Until recently, most historians did not consider women part of western history. One scholar who searched 2,000 pages of Turner's work could find only one paragraph devoted to women. Men built the railroads, drove the cattle, led the military expeditions, and governed the territories. "Women," said one writer, "were invisible, few in number, and not important to the taming of the West."

When scholars did acknowledge the presence of women on the frontier, perceptions were usually based on stereotypes that were created by male observers and had become prevalent in American literature. According to professor of history Sandra L. Myres (1933–1991), there were three main images. The first image was that of a frightened, tearful woman who lived in a hostile environment and who was overworked and overbirthed, depressed and lonely, and resigned to a hard life and an early death. The second image, in contrast, was of a helpmate and a civilizer of the frontier who could fight Indians as well as take care of the cooking, cleaning, and rearing of the children. A third image of the westering woman was that of the "bad woman," who was more masculine than feminine in her behavior and who was "hefty, grotesque and mean with a pistol."

The proliferation of primary source materials since the early 1970s—letters, diaries, and memoirs written by frontierswomen—led to a reassessment of the role of westering women. They are no longer what professor of history Joan Hoff-Wilson once referred to as the "orphans of women's history." There are disagreements in interpretation, but they are based upon sound scholarship. One area where scholars disagree is how women were changed by their participation in the westward movements of the nineteenth century.

In the following selection, Christine Stansell, arguing from a feminist perspective, asserts that women on the Great Plains were torn from their eastern roots, isolated in their home environments, and forced to endure lonely lives and loveless marriages because they could not create networks of female friendships.

In the second selection, Glenda Riley argues that in spite of harsh environmental, political, and personal conditions on the Great Plains, women were able to create rich and varied social lives through the development of strong support networks.

YES

Christine Stansell

WOMEN ON THE GREAT PLAINS 1865–1890

In 1841, Catharine Beecher proudly attested to the power of her sex by quoting some of Tocqueville's observations on the position of American women. On his tour of 1831, Tocqueville had found Americans to be remarkably egalitarian in dividing social power between the sexes. In his opinion, their ability to institute democratic equality stemmed from a clearcut division of work and responsibilities: "in no country has such constant care been taken... to trace two clearly distinct lines of action for the two sexes, and to make them keep pace with the other, but in two pathways which are always different." In theory, men and women controlled separate "spheres" of life: women held sway in the home, while men attended to economic and political matters. Women were not unaware of the inequities in a trade-off between ascendancy in the domestic sphere and participation in society as a whole. Attached to the metaphorical bargain struck between the sexes was a clause ensuring that women, through "home influence," could also affect the course of nation-building. For Miss Beecher, domesticity was also imperial power "to American women, more than to any others on earth, is committed the exalted privilege of extending over the world those blessed influences, which are to renovate degraded man, and 'clothe all climes with beauty.' "

Yet despite Beecher's assertions to the contrary, by 1841 one masculine "line of action" was diverging dangerously from female influences. Increasing numbers of men were following a pathway which led them across the Mississippi to a land devoid of American women and American homes. In the twenty-odd years since the Santa Fe trade opened the Far West to American businessmen, only men, seeking profits in furs or trading, had gone beyond the western farmlands of the Mississippi Valley; no women participated in the first stages of American expansion. Consequently, by 1841 the West was in one sense a geographical incarnation of the masculine sphere, altogether untouched by "home influence." Although in theory American development preserved a heterosexually balanced democracy, in actuality, the West, new arena of political and economic growth, had become a man's world.

In 1841, the first Americans intending to settle in the trans-Mississippi region rather than only trap or trade began to migrate over the great overland

From Christine Stansell, "Women on the Great Plains 1865–1890," *Women's Studies*, vol. 4 (1976). Adapted from Christine Stansell, *City of Women: Sex and Class in New York, 1789–1860* (Alfred A. Knopf, 1986). Copyright © 1982, 1986 by Christine Stansell. Reprinted by permission of Alfred A. Knopf, Inc. Notes omitted.

road to the coast. For the first time, women were present in the caravans, and in the next decades, thousands of women in families followed. Their wagon trains generally carried about one-half men, one-half women and children: a population with the capacity to reinstate a heterosexual culture. Only during the Gold Rush years, 1849–1852, were most of the emigrants once again male. Many of the forty-niners, however, chose to return East rather than to settle. In the aftermath of the Rush, the numerical balance of men and women was restored. By 1860, the sex ratio in frontier counties, including those settled on the Great Plains, was no different from the average sex ratio in the East.

Despite the heterosexual demography, however, the West in the years after 1840 still appeared to be masculine terrain. Everywhere, emigrants and travellers saw "such lots of men, but very few ladies and children." In mining camps, "representatives of the gentler sex were so conspicuous by their absence that in one camp a lady's bonnet and boots were exhibited for one dollar a look." Similarly, "the Great Plains in the early period was strictly a man's country." Even later, historians agree that "the Far West had a great preponderance of men over women," and that the absence of "mothers and wives to provide moral anchorage to the large male population" was a primary cause of its social ills. What accounts for the disparity between these observations and the bare facts of demography? In many frontier regions, women failed to reinstitute their own sphere. Without a cultural base of their own, they disappeared behind the masculine preoccupations and social structure which dominated the West. Despite their numbers, women were often invisible, not only in the first two decades of family settlement but in successive phases as well.

In this [selection], I try to sketch out some ways of understanding how the fact of this masculine imperium affected women's experiences in the great trans-Mississippi migrations. The following pages are in no way a monograph but rather a collection of suggestions which I have developed through reading and teaching about the West, and which I hope will encourage others to begin investigating this neglected area. Western migration constituted a critical rite of passage in nineteenth century culture; its impact still reverberates a century later in our own "Western" novels, movies, and television serials. Women's relationship to this key area of the "American experience" has remained submerged and unquestioned. There are only a few secondary books on women in the West, and the two best-known works are simplistic and sentimental. Few writers or scholars have attempted to look at frontier women in the light of the newer interpretations of women's history which have evolved over the last four years. There are a wealth of questions to investigate and a wealth of sources to use. To demonstrate how new analyses can illuminate conventional teaching and lecture material, I have chosen one clearly defined area of "pioneer experience," settlers on the Great Plains from 1865–1890....

Until after the Civil War, emigrants usually travelled over the Great Plains without a thought of stopping. Explorers, farmers, and travellers agreed that the dry grasslands of the "Great American Desert"—the Dakotas, western Kansas, and western Nebraska—were not suitable for lucrative cultivation. In the late

60's, however, western land-grant railroads attempting to boost profits from passenger fares and land sales by promoting settlement in the region launched an advertising campaign in America and Europe which portrayed the Plains as a new Eden of verdant grasslands, rich soil, and plenteous streams. The railroad propaganda influenced a shift in public opinion, but technological advances in wheatgrowing and steadily expanding urban markets for crops were far more significant in attracting settlers from Europe and the Mississippi Valley to the region. Emigrants came to take advantage of opportunities for more land, more crops, and more profits.

Who decided to move to the new lands? In the prevailing American notions of family relations, decisions about breadwinning and family finances were more or less in the hands of the male. Of course, removal to the Plains was a significant matter, and it is doubtful that many husbands and fathers made a unilateral decision to pull up stakes. Unfortunately, no large body of evidence about the choice to migrate to the Plains has been found or, at least, utilized in scholarly studies. I have sampled, however, some of the more than seven hundred diaries of men and women travelling to California and Oregon twenty years earlier. These indicate that the man usually initiated a plan to emigrate, made the final decision, and to a greater or lesser degree imposed it on his family. Men's involvement with self-advancement in the working world provided them with a logical and obvious rationale for going West.

The everyday concerns of "woman's sphere," however, did not provide women with many reasons to move. In the system that Tocqueville praised and Beecher vaunted, women's work, social responsibilities, and very identities were based almost entirely in the home. Domesticity involved professionalized housekeeping, solicitous childrearing, and an assiduous maintenance of a proper moral and religious character in the family. Clearly, women could keep house better, literally and metaphorically, in "civilized" parts, where churches, kinfolk, and women friends supported them. The West held no promise of a happier family life or a more salutary moral atmosphere. On the contrary, it was notoriously destructive to those institutions and values which women held dear.

The Plains region was an especially arid prospect for the transplantation of womanly values. Lonely and crude frontier conditions prevailed into the 90's; in some areas, the sparse population actually declined with time: "following the great boom of the 80's, when the tide of migration began to recede, central Dakota and western Nebraska and Kansas presented anything but a land of occupied farms." The loneliness which women endured "must have been such as to crush the soul," according to one historian of the region. Another asserts that "without a doubt" the burden of the adverse conditions of Plains life— the aridity, treelessness, heat, perpetual wind, and deadening cold—fell upon the women. Almost without exception, others concur: "although the life of the frontier farmer was difficult special sympathy should go to his wife" ... "it is certain that many stayed until the prairie broke them in spirit or body while others fled from the monotonous terror of it." An observer who visited the Plains in the 50's found life there to be "peculiarly severe upon women and oxen." The duration as well as the severity of cultural disruption which Plains women experienced was perhaps without parallel in the history of nineteenth-century frontiers.

First of all, emigrant women did not move into homes like the ones they had left behind, but into sod huts, tarpaper shacks, and dugouts. Seldom as temporary as they planned to be, these crude structures still existed as late as the nineties. Most settlers lived in one room "soddies" for six or seven years: if luck left a little cash, they might move into a wooden shack. Thus a farmer's wife often spent years trying to keep clean a house made of dirt. The effort became especially disheartening in rainstorms, when leaking walls splattered mud over bedclothes and dishes: "in those trying times the mud floors were too swampy to walk upon and wives could cook only with an umbrella held over the stove; after they were over every stitch of clothing must be hung out to dry." Dry weather gave no respite from dirt, since dust and straw incessantly sifted down from the walls. Housekeeping as a profession in the sense that Catharine Beecher promulgated it was impossible under such circumstances. Soddies were so badly insulated that during the winter, water froze away from the stove. In summer, the paucity of light and air could be stifling.

Often there was simply no money available to build a decent house. Drought, grasshoppers, or unseasonable rains destroyed many of the harvests of the 80's and 90's. Even good crops did not necessarily change a family's living conditions, since debts and mortgages which had accrued during hard times could swallow up any profits. But in any case, home improvements were a low priority, and families often remained in soddies or shacks even when there was cash or credit to finance a frame house.

The farmer usually earmarked his profits for reinvestment into the money-making outlay of better seeds, new stock, machinery, and tools. Farm machinery came first, labor-saving devices for women last: "there was a tendency for the new homesteader to buy new machinery to till broad acres and build new barns to house more stock and grain, while his wife went about the drudgery of household life in the old way in a little drab dwelling overshadowed by the splendour of machine farming." Washers and sewing machines graced some farms in the 80's, but "for the most part ... the machine age did not greatly help woman. She continued to operate the churn, carry water, and run the washing machine—if she were fortunate enough to have one—and do her other work without the aid of horse power which her more fortunate husband began to apply in his harvesting, threshing, and planting."

Against such odds, women were unable to recreate the kinds of houses they had left. Nor could they reinstate the home as a venerated institution. A sod house was only a makeshift shelter; no effort of the will or imagination could fashion it into what one of its greatest defenders eulogized as "the fairest garden in the wide field of endeavour and achievement." There were other losses as well. Many feminine social activities in more settled farm communities revolved around the church, but with the exception of the European immigrant enclaves, churches were scarce on the Plains. At best, religious observance was makeshift; at worst, it was non-existent. Although "it is not to be supposed that only the ungodly came west," one historian noted, "there seemed to exist in some parts of the new settlements a spirit of apathy if not actual hostility toward religion." Circuit-riders and evangelical freelancers drew crowds during droughts and depressions, but during normal times, everyday piety was rare. Few families read the Bible, sang hymns, or prayed together: "when people heard that a family was religious, it was thought that the head of the household must be a minister."

Women were also unable to reconstitute the network of female friendships which had been an accustomed and sustaining part of daily life "back home." Long prairie winters kept everyone housebound for much of the year. During summers and warmer weather, however, men travelled to town to buy supplies and negotiate loans, and rode to nearby claims to deliver mail, borrow tools, or share news. "As soon as the storms let up, the men could get away from the isolation," wrote Mari Sandoz, Nebraska writer and daughter of a homesteader: "But not their women. They had only the wind and the cold and the problems of clothing, shelter, food, and fuel." On ordinary days men could escape, at least temporarily, "into the fields, the woods, or perhaps to the nearest saloon where there was warmth and companionship, but women had almost no excuses to leave. Neighbors lived too far apart to make casual visiting practicable; besides, a farmer could seldom spare a wagon team from field work to take a woman calling. Hamlin Garland, who moved to the Plains as a young boy, remembered that women visited less than in Wisconsin, his former home, since "the work on the new farms was neverending": "I doubt if the women—any of them—got out into the fields or meadows long enough to enjoy the birds and the breezes."

In most respects, the patterns of life rarely accommodated women's needs.

Plains society paid little mind to women, yet women were essential, not incidental, to its functioning. Without female labor, cash-crop agriculture could never have developed. A man could not farm alone, and hired help was almost impossible to come by. Ordinarily, a farmer could count only on his wife and children as extra hands. On the homestead, women's responsibilities as a farmhand, not as a home-maker or a mother, were of first priority. Women still cooked, sewed, and washed, but they also herded livestock and toted water for irrigation.

The ambitious farmer's need for the labor power of women and children often lent a utilitarian quality to relations between men and women. For the single settler, marriage was, at least in part, a matter of efficiency. Courtships were typically brief and frank. Molly Dorsey Sanford, a young unmarried homesteader in Nebraska territory, recorded in her diary over half a dozen proposals in a few years. Most of her suitors were strangers. One transient liked her cooking, another heard about a "hull lot of girls" at the Dorsey farm and came to try his luck, and an old man on the steamboat going to Nebraska proposed after an hour's acquaintance. Jules Sandoz, father of Mari Sandoz, married four times. Three wives fled before he found a woman who resigned herself to the emotionless regimen of his farm. Stolid and resilient, the fourth, Mari's mother, lived to a taciturn old age, but her daughter could not forget others of her mother's generation who had not survived their hasty marriages: "after her arrival the wife found that her husband seldom mentioned her in his letters or manuscripts save in connection with calamity. She sickened and left her work undone ... so the pioneer could not plow or build or hunt. If his luck was exceedingly bad, she died and left him his home without a housekeeper until she could be replaced." With characteristic ambivalence, Sandoz added, "at first this seems a calloused, even a brutal attitude, but it was not so intended."

Instrumentality could also characterize other family relations. Jules Sandoz "never spoke well of anyone who might make his words an excuse for less prompt jumping when he commanded. This included his wife and children." Garland described himself and his fellows as "a Spartan lot. We did not believe in letting our wives and children know they were an important part of our contentment." Jules' wife "considered praise of her children as suspect as self praise would be." Preoccupied by her chores, she maintained only minimal relationships with her family and assigned the care of the younger children to Mari, the oldest daughter.

In the domestic ideology of the family, careful and attentive child-rearing was especially important. Unlike the stoic Mrs. Sandoz, the American women who emigrated were often openly disturbed and troubled by a situation in which mothering was only peripheral to a day's work, and keenly felt the absence of cultural support for correct child-rearing. Mrs. Dorsey, the mother of diarist Molly Sanford, continually worried that her children, exiled from civilization, would turn into barbarians. In towns like Indianapolis, the family's home, schools, churches, and mothers worked in concert. In Nebraska, a mother could count on few aids. The day the Dorseys reached their claim, Molly wrote, "Mother hardly enters into ecstasies ... she no doubt realizes what it is to bring a young rising family away from the world ... if the country would only fill up, if there were only

schools or churches or even some society. We do not see women at all. All men, single, or bachelors, and one gets tired of them." Molly occasionally responded to her mother's anxiety by searching herself and her siblings for signs of mental degeneration, but Mrs. Dorsey's fears were never warranted. The children grew up healthy and dutiful: in Molly's words, "the wild outdoor life strengthens our physical faculties, and the privations, our powers of endurance." To her confident appraisal, however, she appended a cautionary note in her mother's mode: "so that we do not degenerate mentally, it is all right; Heaven help us." Mrs. Dorsey, however, could seldom be reassured. When a snake bit one of the children, "Poor Mother was perfectly prostrated ... she sometimes feels wicked to think she is so far away from all help with her family." On her mother's fortieth birthday, Molly wrote, "I fear she is a little blue today. I do try so hard to keep cheerful. I don't know as it is hard work to keep myself so, but it is hard with her. She knows now that the children ought to be in school. We will have to do the teaching ourselves." ...

As Mrs. Dorsey saw her ideas of child-rearing atrophy, she also witnessed a general attenuation of the womanliness which had been central to her own identity and sense of importance in the world. Her daughters particularly taxed her investment in an outmoded conception of womanhood. Molly, for instance, was pleased with her facility in learning traditionally male skills. "So it seems I can put my hand to almost anything," she wrote with pride after helping her father roof the house. Mrs. Dorsey regarded her daughter's expanding capacities in a different light. When Molly disguised herself as a man to do some chores, "it was very funny to all but Mother, who fears I am losing all the dignity I ever possessed." Molly was repentant but defensive: "I know I am getting demoralized, but I should be more so, to mope around and have no fun."

Mrs. Dorsey's partial failure to transmit her own values of womanhood to her daughter is emblematic of many difficulties of the first generation of woman settlers. Women could not keep their daughters out of men's clothes, their children in shoes, their family Bibles in use, or their houses clean; at every step, they failed to make manifest their traditions, values, and collective sensibility. It was perhaps the resistance of the Plains to the slightest feminine modification rather than the land itself which contributed to the legend of woman's fear of the empty prairies: "literature is filled with women's fear and distrust of the Plains... if one may judge by fiction, one must conclude that the Plains exerted a peculiarly appalling effect on women." The heroine of [O. E.] Rolvaag's *Giants in the Earth* echoed the experience of real women in her question to herself: "how will human beings be able to endure this place?... Why, there isn't even a thing that one can *hide behind!*" The desolation even affected women who passed through on their way to the coast. Sarah Royce remembered shrinking from the "chilling prospect" of her first night on the Plains on the Overland Trail: "surely there would be a few trees or a sheltering hillside.... No, only the level prairie.... Nothing indicated a place for us—a cozy nook, in which for the night we might be guarded."

Fright was not a rarity on the Plains. Both men and women knew the fear of droughts, blizzards, and accidental death. Yet the reported frequency of madness and suicide among women is one indication that [Everett] Dick may have been right in his contention that "the real burden... fell upon the wife and mother." Men's responsibilities required them to act upon their fears. If a blizzard hung in the air, they brought the cattle in; if crops failed, they renegotiated the mortgages and planned for the next season. In contrast, women could often do nothing in the face of calamity. "If hardships came," Sandoz wrote, "the women faced it at home. The results were tersely told by the items in the newspapers of the day. Only sheriff sales seem to have been more numerous than the items telling of trips to the insane asylum."

Men made themselves known in the acres of furrows they ploughed up from the grassland. Women, lacking the opportunities of a home, had few ways to make either the land or their neighbors aware of their presence. The inability of women to leave a mark on their surroundings is a persistent theme in Sandoz's memoirs. When Mari was a child, a woman killed herself and her three children with gopher poison and a filed down case knife. The neighbors agreed that "she had been plodding and silent for a long time," and a woman friend added sorrowfully, "If she could 'a had even a geranium, but in that cold shell of a shack...." In Sandoz's memory, the women of her mother's generation are shadows, "silent... always there, in the dark corner near the stove."

I have emphasized only one side of woman's experience on the Plains. For many, the years brought better times, better houses, and even neighbors. A second generation came to maturity: some were daughters like the strong farm women of Willa Cather's novels who managed to reclaim the land that had crushed their mothers. Yet the dark side of the lives of the first women on the Plains cannot be denied. Workers in an enterprise often not of their own making, their labor was essential to the farm, their womanhood irrelevant. Hamlin Garland's *Main Travelled Roads,* written in part as a condemnation of "the futility of woman's life on a farm," elicited this response from his mother: "you might have said more but I'm glad you didn't. Farmer's wives have enough to bear as it is."

NO

Glenda Riley

WOMEN, ADAPTATION, AND CHANGE

Gender norms and expectations affected all types of western women
—African American, Native American, Asian American, Anglo, and
Spanish-speaking—in some way. Yet many women pushed at customary boundaries and tested limits. Sometimes they had feminist
intentions, but other times they sought to fulfill their own needs,
talents, and desires. As a result, women turned up everywhere, and
often in unexpected places: holding jobs, fighting for the right of
suffrage, forming labor organizations, and divorcing their spouses
at a higher rate than women in any other region of the country.

Other women, who are less obvious in the historical record, fought
against other forms of injustice—prejudicial attitudes and discriminatory practices. Although historical accounts often present women
of color only as victims of oppression and exploitation, in reality
they frequently resisted and developed their own ways to live in
an often hostile world. A wide variety of resources gave women
of diverse races and ethnic backgrounds the strength to live in a
West composed of groups of people who persistently belittled and
shunned other groups who differed from them.

WOMEN'S RESPONSES TO THE CHALLENGES OF PLAINS LIVING

The Great Plains region is an especially revealing case study of women's
adaptation and survival in the West. Here, women, as in other western regions, carried the primary responsibility for home and family. Not only wives
and mothers, but all women, young or old, single or married, white or black,
Asian or Hispanic, whether employed outside the home or not, were expected
to attend to, or assist with, domestic duties. In addition, women helped with

From Glenda Riley, *A Place to Grow: Women in the American West* (Harlan Davidson, 1992).
Copyright © 1992 by Harlan Davidson, Inc. Reprinted by permission.

the family enterprise and often held paid employment outside the home. They were also socially, and sometimes even politically, active. In all these realms, women had to deal on a daily basis with the particular limitations imposed upon them by the harsh and demanding Plains environment. This essay examines how the Plains affected women's duties and concerns, and how the majority of women triumphed over these exigencies.

Between the early 1860s and the early 1910s the Great Plains attracted much controversy. It had vehement boosters and equally determined detractors. Land promoters and other supporters were quick to claim that a salubrious climate, rich farming and grazing lands, and unlimited business opportunities awaited newcomers. This "boomer" literature presented an attractive image that did not always seem completely truthful to those men and women who actually tried to profit from the area's purported resources.

Particularly during the early years of settlement, many migrants widely bemoaned the lack of water and relatively arid soil as well as their own inability to grapple effectively with these natural features of the Plains. At times their hardships were so severe that special relief committees and such groups as the Red Cross and the United States Army had to supply food, clothing, and other goods to help them survive.[1] Consequently, twentieth-century historical accounts have often focused on the ongoing struggles of existence. Until recently, only a few of these studies documented or analyzed the special problems that the Plains posed to women. Fortunately, a growing sensitivity to women's roles in history has led to an examination of women's own writings. This analysis of diaries, letters,

and memoirs has clearly and touchingly revealed the details of their lives.[2]

The challenges that confronted women on the Plains can be grouped into three categories: the natural environment; political upheavals over such crucial issues as slavery, racism, and economic policy; and personal conflict with other people, including spouses. Obviously, all these factors also affected men, but they had a particular impact upon women.

The Natural Environment

The physical environment of the Plains created numerous difficulties for women. They showed, for instance, tremendous creativity and energy in obtaining the water that constantly was in such short supply. They carried water in pails attached to neck yokes or in barrels on "water sleds." They melted snow to obtain cooking and wash water. They used sal soda to 'break' the alkali content of water. Women also helped build windmills and dig wells. And in their desperation they even resorted to hiring a 'water-witch' or diviner to help them locate a vein of water.[3]

The aridity of the Plains created another problem for women—horribly destructive prairie fires. Men feared these fires because they endangered the animals, crops, and buildings that were largely their responsibilities, but women thought first of their children and homes as well as their cows, pigs, and chickens. In 1889 a fire in North Dakota destroyed one man's horses and barn and also claimed his wife's precious cows and chickens. Four years later, another fire in Fargo, North Dakota, burned to the ground both the shops where primarily men labored and the homes where primarily women worked. Recalling her childhood, a Kansas woman explained that because most buildings were made of wood, the "greatest danger" they faced was fire. She added that her father immediately turned all stock loose in the face of an oncoming fire because the animals instinctively headed for the safety of the river valley, while her mother placed her in the middle of the garden on the presumption that fire would not "pass into the ploughed land." Other women described the deafening noise and blinding smoke of the fires that threatened their families and homes.[4]

In addition, many women claimed that the Plains climate plagued them and interfered with their work. Destructive storms and blizzards were a constant threat, while summer heat and winter cold were regular annoyances. A Norwegian woman confronted her cold kitchen each winter morning dressed in overshoes, heavy clothing, and a warm headscarf. Another woman simply wrote in her journal, "the snow falls upon my book while I write by the stove."[5]

Ever-present insects and animals also challenged women at every turn. Grasshoppers not only demolished crops, but could destroy homes and household goods as well. The "hoppers" gnawed their way through clothing, bedding, woodwork, furniture, mosquito netting, and stocks of food. Bliss Isely of Kansas claimed that she could remember the grasshopper "catastrophe" of 1874 in vivid detail for many years after its occurrence. As she raced down the road trying to outrun the "glistening white cloud" of grasshoppers thundering down from the sky, she worried about the baby in her arms. When the grasshoppers struck, they ate her garden to the ground, devoured fly netting, and chewed a hole in her black silk shawl. "We set ourselves to live through a hungry winter," she remembered. In the months that followed, she "learned to cook wheat and potatoes in every way possible." She made coffee from roasted wheat and boiled wheat kernels like rice for her children. Another Kansas woman who survived the grasshopper attack bitterly declared that Kansas had been "the state of cyclones, the state of cranks, the state of mortgages—and now grasshopper fame had come!"[6]

Political Upheaval

As if the physical environment wasn't enough to discourage even the hardiest and most determined women, another problem, political conflict, beset them as well. The ongoing argument over slavery especially affected the Kansas Territory when in 1856 an outbreak of violence between free-staters and proslavery factions erupted. "Border ruffians" added to the chaos by crossing frequently into "Bleeding Kansas" from Missouri in an attempt to impose slavery on the territory by force. Sara Robinson of Lawrence felt terrorized by frequent "street broils" and saw her husband imprisoned during what she termed the "reign of terror" in Kansas. Another Kansas woman lamented that there was no respite between this convulsive episode and the Civil War, which plucked men out of homes for military service. Women not only lost the labor and income of their men, but they feared the theft of food and children and the threat of rape for themselves and their daughters at the hands of raiders, thieves, and other outlaws made bold by the absence of men. In addition, the departure of men caused the burden of families, farms, and businesses to fall on the shoulders of already beleaguered women.[7]

The disputes that followed in the wake of the Civil War continued to disrupt women's lives. The period of Reconstruction between 1865 and 1877 included, for example, the chaotic entry of Exodusters (former slaves) into Kansas and other Plains states. In turn, prejudice against Exodusters created difficulties for African American women who had hoped they were migrating to a more hospitable region than the American South. Also during this period, economic unrest and dissatisfaction with federal and state government policies resulted in Populist agitation through the Plains during the 1880s and 1890s. By 1900, it seemed to many women that their lives had been entangled in a long series of political upheavals.

Personal Conflict

Women experienced personal conflict as well. Prejudice against Catholics, Jews, and people of other faiths led to intolerance at best and violence at worst. Ethnic and racial groups also received their share of distressing treatment. African American, Asian, and Mexican women were expected to work in the most menial, low-paid jobs, were barred from shops and other businesses, and were personally treated with disdain by many other migrants. This situation was especially difficult for women because they were frequently told that they were to be the arbitrators of society, yet they felt helpless to right this situation. Women also wanted desperately to shield their children from such treatment.

Some women also faced trouble within their own homes. Anecdotal evidence demonstrates that some husbands were domineering, demanding, and physically or verbally abusive. A young Jewish woman whose father had insisted that his family migrate to North Dakota remembered continual strife between her mother and father. "How can one bring the close, intimate life of the Russian *shtetl* to the vast open wilderness of the prairie?" she asked. But her mother tried. According to her daughter, "she rose early and cooked and baked and washed and scrubbed and sewed. She prayed and observed the fast days and holidays by making special dishes." Yet she also regretted and complained. Unable to understand her sorrow or offer her some much-needed sympathy, her husband argued and remonstrated. One day, much to his daughter's relief, he ran from the house storming and raging. Jumping into a buggy and seizing the reins, he shouted, "Goodbye, goodbye—I am leaving. This is more than human flesh can bear.... This is the end. I can take no more. It is beyond enduring. Goodbye, goodbye." When he soon returned, her joy dissipated: "My father had not kept his promise to go away and leave us in peace. He had returned. We were all trapped."[8]

On the Plains, and throughout the West, thousands of women deserted such husbands or sought relief in divorce courts. Census figures indicate that western women sought and received a higher proportion of divorces than women in other regions of the country. Whether economic opportunities encouraged this proclivity to divorce or whether western women had a spirit that sought independence is as yet unclear.[9]

Given the many difficulties that beset women, a reasonable person might ask why they stayed on the Plains. In fact, many did not stay. They and their families returned to former homes or moved onward to try life in another western region or town. After spending two years in Kansas, Helen Carpenter was delighted to become a new bride about to migrate to California. In 1857, Carpenter began her trail journal by going "back in fancy" over the two years she had spent in Kansas. She recalled the initial "weary journey of three weeks on a river boat" when all the children fell ill. Then, she wrote, it was "the struggle to get a roof over our heads... then followed days of longing for youthful companions... and before the summer waned, the entire community was stricken with fever and ague." Just as she finally made some friends and established something of a social life, "such pleasures were cut short by border troubles and an army of 'Border Ruffians'... who invaded the neighborhood, with no regard for life or property." She admitted that Kansas was "beautiful country" with its tall grass and lush wildflowers, but added that "the violent thunderstorms are enough to wreck the nerves of Hercules and the rattlesnakes are as thick as the leaves on the trees, and lastly 'but not leastly,' the fever and ague are corded up ever ready for use." Given the nature of her memories, it is not surprising that Carpenter concluded, "in consideration of what we have undergone physically and mentally, I can bid Kansas Good Bye without a regret." Another Kansas woman whose family left the region said that her father had taken sick and that her "Auntie wanted to get away from a place always hideous in her eyes."[10]

Fortunately, not all women felt so strongly about the drawbacks of their environment. Many women had already experienced a demanding life and, as Laura Ingalls Wilder put it, they saw the rigors of the Plains as "a natural part of life." They hung on because they had hope for the future, or according to one migrant, because they didn't expect the hard times to last. Often, their optimism was rewarded, and conditions did improve. Innovative technology gradually conquered the arid Plains, and economic booms occasionally appeared. A Nebraska woman of the early 1900s summed up her triumph in a pithy way when she wrote, "we built our frame house and was thru with our old leaky sod house.... We now had churches, schools, Telephones, Rural Mail."[11]

Still we must ask: did the women who remained on the Plains suffer disillusionment and despair, growing old and ill before their time? Did they blame their menfolk who had seen economic opportunity in the Plains for their misfortunes? The answer is "yes": many women who stayed on the Plains did so with resentment and hostility. Their writings tell of crushing work loads, frequent births, illnesses and deaths, recurring depression, loneliness, homesickness, and fear. A common complaint was the absence of other women; Plains women also longed for family members who had stayed at home. A Wyoming woman even claimed that the wind literally drove her crazy and that she could no longer bear to spend long winters on a remote ranch with no other women.[12]

Some women's lamentations were unrelenting, but others gradually included more pleasant observations. They noted that other people, including women, soon moved in and that often members of their own families joined them. Gradually, the depression of many hostile women ebbed and was replaced by a sense of affection for their new homes. Even the Wyoming woman who feared for her own mental stability later maintained that "those years on the Plains were hard years but

I grew to like the West and now I would not like to live any other place."[13]

Numerous women did blame men for their circumstances. But it is often difficult to determine which women had fair cause to lay blame. Because women were hesitant to record personal troubles in journals or letters sent back home, it is not always clear how responsible men were for women's difficulties. Certainly, sad stories do exist of men who verbally or physically abused women or who were alcoholic, lazy, financially inept, or generally irresponsible. In the patriarchal family structure of the time, men were often slow to recognize the importance of women's labor, allow women a voice in family decisions, and extend understanding for women's concerns. As early as 1862, the U.S. Commissioner of Agriculture's annual report suggested that the supposedly prevalent insanity of plainswomen resulted more from the harsh treatment doled out by their own men than from the Plains climate, family finances, or infant mortality. In following years, newspaper reports of wife-beating or journal accounts of alcoholic husbands gave credence to his assertion.[14]

Here again, the negative testimony is balanced by other accounts. Countless women wrote about the energy, responsibility, support, community participation, and kindness of fathers, brothers, husbands, and sons. Women spoke of men's "cheerful spirits," patience, thoughtfulness, sympathy, and companionship. Army wives Ada Vogdes and Elizabeth Custer both felt that the hardships of their lives as women in western forts were greatly offset by the courtesy and consideration of their husbands, other officers, and enlisted men. More important, a considerable number of plucky women faced challenges with creativity,

energy, optimism, and motivation. They battled the circumstances of their environment by confronting the necessities of each day while maintaining hope for a better future. They met political upheaval and violence with religious faith and a commitment to help establish order. And they endured conflict with family members, neighbors, and members of other cultural groups by persevering and seeking the companionship of others, especially other women.

A Kansan of the 1880s, Flora Moorman Heston, is one example of a woman who confronted poverty, hard work, loneliness, and other problems with buoyant spirits. In a letter home, she maintained that "we have the best prospect of prosperity we ever had and believe it was right for us to come here." She added that "I have a great deal more leasure [sic] time than I used to have it dont take near the work to keep one room that it does a big house."[15] Like women in the Midwest, Southwest, and Far West, plainswomen relied on their inner strength and kept a positive outlook. Although these qualities are often forgotten in conventional descriptions of the darker side of Plains living, they did indeed exist.

How Women Adapted

Most women who ventured to the Plains states were highly motivated. They sought wealth, health, a more promising future for their children, lower taxes, and end to slavery, less prejudice or more freedom from governmental control. During the hard times and disasters, their hopes sustained them. When their fathers, brothers, or husbands talked of moving elsewhere, they often reminded the men of the particular dream that had brought them to the Plains in the first place. Others relied upon religious faith, or clung to their belief that they were civilizing a raw region, or some other commitment to keep them strong in the face of adversity.

Many women migrants created rich and varied social lives out of limited opportunities. They relieved their own isolation by writing in cherished journals or penning letters to friends and family. A young Nebraska woman who lamented the lack of women in the neighborhood wrote daily in her journal. "What should I do without my journal!" she exclaimed on one of its pages. Yet, as time passed, her entries became less frequent while her apologies to her neglected journal increased.[16]

Women also turned to the books and newspapers they had brought with them, borrowed from others, or had purchased with hoarded butter-and-egg money. Bliss Isely explained that even when she and her husband could "not afford a shotgun and ammunition to kill rabbits" they subscribed to newspapers and bought books. She made it a personal rule that "no matter how late at night it was or how tired [she] was, never to go to bed without reading a few minutes from the Bible and some other book." Other women wrote of their longing for more books, of feeling settled when their books were unpacked, and of borrowing books from others. Faye Cashatt Lewis poignantly wrote: "Finishing the last book we borrowed from the Smiths, and having it too stormy for several days to walk the mile and a half to return it and get more, was a frequent and painful experience. Seeing the end of my book approaching was like eating the last bite of food on my plate, still hungry, and no more food in sight."[17]

Music also provided solace and sociability. Frequently women insisted upon bringing guitars, pianos, and miniature parlor organs to the Plains. Despite the fact that Ada Vogdes and her husband were transported from fort to fort in army ambulances with limited space, she clung to her guitar. In her journal, she frequently mentioned the pleasure that playing guitar and singing along brought to her and others.[18] Vogdes, like many others, also depended upon mail to keep her amused and sane. When a snowstorm stopped the mail for two long weeks, Vogdes proclaimed that she could not wait much longer. To many women, the arrival of the mail provided a lifeline to home and family and brought news of the larger world through magazines, journals, ethnic and other newspapers, and books.[19]

The coming of the railroad had great social implications. Not only did railroad companies bring additional people, but they sponsored fairs and celebrations and provided ties with other regions of the country. An Indian agent's wife in Montana wrote that "the coming of the Northern Pacific Railroad in 1883 brought us in closer touch with civilization, with kin and friends, with medical and military aid, but put an end to the old idyllic days." In 1907, a Wyoming woman was delighted to see the railroad come into her area and claimed that its very existence alleviated her depression. She explained that with "no trees and few buildings" to hamper her view of passing trains, she felt that she kept "in touch with the outside pretty well."[20]

Women also became effective instigators and organizers of a huge variety of social events including taffy pulls, oyster suppers, quilting bees, dinners, picnics, box suppers, church "socials," weddings and chivarees, spelling bees, dances, theatricals, song fests, puppet shows, and readings. Perhaps most important were the celebration of such special holidays as Thanksgiving, Hanukkah, Christmas, and the Fourth of July. The menus concocted by women on special occasions often confounded other women. After a particularly splendid dinner, one woman wrote, "however she got up such a variety puzzled me, as she cooks by the fireplace and does her baking in a small covered skillet."[21]

A third way in which women adapted was in their belief that they were family and cultural conservators. Women often derived great satisfaction and a sense of significance by establishing "real" homes for their families, preserving traditional values, folkways, and mores, passing on family and ethnic traditions, contributing to local schools and churches, and establishing women's organizations. Many would have probably agreed with the poetic woman who said of them, "Without their gentle touch, the land/Would still be wilderness." Certainly, women spent a good deal of time and energy recording and relating their cultural activities.[22]

In this role, women placed a great deal of emphasis on material goods. They preserved, but also used, family treasures. Some insisted on fabric rather than oilcloth table coverings, served holiday eggnog to cowhands in silver goblets, and used their best silver and chinaware whenever the occasion arose. Years after coming to the Plains, Faye Lewis still proudly displayed her mother's Haviland china. She explained that "Father had urged strongly that this china be sold, but the thought was so heartbreaking to mother that he relented and helped her pack it." Lewis perceptively saw that her mother's china was "more than a set of dishes to her, more than usefulness, or even beauty. They were a tangible link, a reminder, that there are refinements of living difficult to perpetuate... perhaps in danger of being forgotten." Certainly Mary Ronan felt this way. On an isolated Indian reservation in Montana, she still regularly set her dinner table with tablecloths and ivory napkin rings. She explained that "heavy, satiny damask" cloths gave her "exquisite satisfaction" although her children did not like them. She added that she had "one beautiful set of dishes" but used them only on "gala occasions."[23]

Rituals such as the celebration of Christmas were also important. In the early years, the Christmas trees in many Plains homes were scraggly, ornaments few and homemade, and Christmas dinner far from lavish. But as their situations improved financially, women provided more festive trees, elaborate presents, and special foods. They placed trees decorated with nuts, candy, popcorn balls, strings of cranberries, wax candles, and homemade decorations in schools and churches. They then surrounded the trees with gifts for family and friends as well as presents for poor children who might otherwise be deprived of a Christmas celebration. Often music, singing, speeches, and prayers preceded the arrival of a local man dressed as Santa Claus.[24]

It is important to note that women contributed to a diversity of cultural patterns because of their own mixed ethnic and racial stock. European, Native American, African American, Mexican, and Asian women who desired to preserve their own rich heritages subscribed to a variety of newspapers and magazines in their own languages, continued to wear traditional clothing, practiced their customary holiday rituals, and added their own words, foods, and perspectives to the evolving society. A Norwegian woman in Nebraska continued to speak Norwegian in her home, sent her children to parochial school, and cooked Norwegian food. African American women were another group who added their folkways to the cultural blend, especially after the Civil War when significant numbers of them migrated to Plains states as Exodusters.[25]

Jewish women were yet another group who brought their own culture to the Plains. Although many Jewish settlers first came to the Plains as members of agricultural communities, particularly under the auspices of the Jewish Colonization Association and the Hebrew Emigrant Aid Society, they soon relocated in such cities as Omaha, Nebraska, and Grand Forks, North Dakota. Here they established businesses and communities that could support rabbis and supply other religious needs. This relocation was important to many Jewish women who despaired of their inability to provide their children with religious education and keep a kosher home when separated from a sizable Jewish community.[26]

A fourth, and crucial, factor that aided many women in their adaptation to life on the Plains was their ability to bond with other women and to create what we would today call supportive networks. On the Plains, as elsewhere, women turned to each other for company, encouragement, information, and help in times of need. Women's longing for female companionship is clearly revealed by their laments about the lack of other women. One of only three known women migrants in a remote region of North Dakota stated simply, "Naturally I was very lonely for women friends."

Consequently, women frequently overcame barriers of age, ethnicity, social class, and race in forming friendships. Arriving in Oklahoma Territory in the early 1900s, Leola Lehman formed an extremely close friendship with a Native American woman whom she described as "one of the best women" she had known in her lifetime. A Kansas woman similarly characterized an African American woman who was first a domestic, then a confidante and friend, as "devoted, kind-hearted, hard-working." Still other women told how they found a way around language barriers in order to gain companionship from women of other races and cultures.[27]

Typically, women began a friendship with a call or chat. Lehman was hanging out her wash when the Indian woman who became her friend quietly appeared and softly explained, "I came to see you.... I thought you might be lonesome." The company of other women was especially important in male-dominated military forts, where a woman began receiving calls upon arrival. Ada Vogdes recorded her gratitude for being whisked off by another officer's wife the moment she first arrived at Fort Laramie. Her journal overflowed with mention of calls, rides, and other outings with women friends. When her closest friends left the fort, Vogdes described herself as feeling "forsaken and forlorn" and overwhelmed by an aching heart. Some years later, Fanny McGillycuddy at Fort Robinson in South Dakota also logged calls and visits with other women and noted their great importance to her.[28]

Women also established friendships, gave each other information and support and passed on technical information, often through quilting bees and sewing circles. Bliss Isely remembered that as a young woman she was always invited to the "sewings and quiltings" held by the married women in her neighborhood. On one occasion, she invited them in return and was pleased that "they remained throughout the day." Isely felt that these events gave her invaluable training in much-needed domestic skills and that the women had "a good time helping each other" with their work.[29]

Older women lavished new brides with maternal attention and were often very generous in sharing their time, energy, and skills with the novice. In 1869 the *Bozeman Chronicle* quoted a recent bride as saying, "In all there were just fourteen women in the town in 1869, but they all vied with each other to help us and make us welcome." This hospitality even included much-needed cooking lessons for the seventeen-year-old wife. A decade later, another bride arriving in Miles City, Montana, recalled that she met with a similar welcome: "Ladies called. . . . I wasn't at all lonely."[30]

Women were also quick to offer their services to other women in times of childbirth, illness, and death. Such aid in time of need created strong bonds between women that often stretched beyond racial, ethnic, and class lines. In 1871, the *Nebraska Farmer* quoted a settler who claimed that such women acted "without a thought of reward" and that their mutual aid transformed women into "unbreakable friends." During the early 1880s, a Jewish woman in North Dakota explained that when a woman was about to give birth she would send her children "to the neighbors to stay for the time" so that she "could have rest and quiet the first few days, the only rest many of these women ever knew." She added that "the rest of us would take home the washing, bake the bread, make

the butter, etc." Other women said that in time of illness or death they would take turns watching the patient, prepare medicines, bring food, prepare a body with herbs, sew burial clothes, organize a funeral, and supply food.[31] The crucial nature of another woman's assistance in time of physical need was perhaps best expressed by Nannie Alderson, a Montana ranch wife during the 1880s. When she was ill, male family members and ranch hands strongly urged her to call a doctor from Miles City. Her reply: "I don't want a doctor. I want a woman!" When the men surrounding her failed to understand her need, they again pressed her to call a doctor. She sent for a neighbor woman instead. After her recovery, she justified her action by saying, "I simply kept quiet and let her wait on men, and I recovered without any complications whatever."[32]

As the number of women increased in an area, women began to join together in the public arena as well as in private. They formed a myriad of social, education, and reform associations. Women's literary clubs studied books and started libraries. Temperance societies—the most famous of which was the national Women's Christian Temperance Union—attempted to help control the evil of alcoholism that was so damaging to women and children who were economically dependent upon men. And woman suffrage groups fought for the right to vote. Nebraskan Clara Bewick Colby, suffragist and editor of *The Woman's Tribune*, noted again and again that the Plains states were particularly fertile ground for suffrage reform.[33]

Plainswomen split, however, on the issue of suffrage. Nebraskan Luna Kellie explained that she "had been taught that it was unwomanly to concern oneself with politics and that only the worst class of women would ever vote if they had a chance." But when a tax reform proposed to cut the length of the school term, Kellie, a mother of several small children, "saw for the first time that a woman might be interested in politics and want a vote." With her father's and husband's help, she promoted a campaign that resulted in woman suffrage in local school elections. Kellie's husband urged her to continue her efforts to obtain women's right to vote in general elections.[34] In 1888, one Kansas women placed a cap bearing presidential candidate Belva Lockwood's name on her daughter's head. Still, many women opposed the suffrage cause, maintaining that the vote should belong to men only. These women believed that women should focus on their homes and families rather than on making political decisions. Some of these women even organized anti-suffrage associations.[35]

But advocates of woman suffrage were not so easily deterred. After the National Woman Suffrage Association was organized in 1869 (the same year that Wyoming Territory granted women the right to vote), Elizabeth Cady Stanton and Susan B. Anthony traveled through the West promoting suffrage. Stanton thought that Wyoming was a "blessed land ... where woman is the political equal of man." Although Esther Morris is usually given credit for bringing woman suffrage to Wyoming Territory and was later called the Mother of Woman Suffrage, some people dispute the centrality of her role. Evidently, many women worked to convince the Democratic legislature to adopt a Women's Rights Bill in December 1869 and persuaded Republican governor John A. Campbell to sign the bill on December 10, 1869.[36]

In addition to suffrage organizations, thousands of other women's clubs and associations existed, including hospital auxiliaries, housekeepers' societies, current events clubs, musical groups, tourist clubs, world peace groups, Red Cross units, and Women's Relief Corps chapters. By the 1880s, so many organizations existed that one Wyoming woman termed the era "the golden age of women's clubs." One leading Oklahoma clubwoman established or led over forty associations during her life.[37]

Unfortunately, much of the sharing that had existed during the early days of a region now began to dissipate. Many women's clubs were segregated; women of color formed their own groups and fought for suffrage or reforms in their own way. For instance, African American women worked energetically within their own communities to provide medical care, playgrounds, and better educational facilities.

Some men's organizations also invited women (usually only white women, however) to join their membership and support their causes. A few even expanded their platforms to include women's issues. As a result, women joined the Patrons of Husbandry (the Grange), the Farmers' Alliance, and the Populist party. Annie La Porte Diggs of Kansas, for example, was an active Populist speaker and writer known for her religious liberalism. Of course, the most famous Populist woman orator was Mary Elizabeth Lease, a woman who was admitted to the Kansas bar in 1885 and who gave in 1890 over 160 speeches in support of the Populist cause. She became famous for her admonition to farmers to "raise less corn and more hell" and was dubbed by the media "Mary Yellin'." So many other women spoke from wagons and platforms, carried banners, and marched in parades that political humorist Joseph Billings wrote, "Wimmin is everywhere."[38]

Women also began to run for office on the Populist ticket. They had long held elected positions on local, county, and state school boards so the idea was not totally unacceptable to many women and men. In 1892, Ella Knowles, a Montana lawyer who in 1889 successfully lobbied for a statute allowing women to practice law in the state, ran unsuccessfully for attorney general. She was, however, appointed to a four-year term as assistant attorney general, and during the mid 1890s was a delegate to Populist conventions and a member of the Populist National Committee. During this period, Olive Pickering Rankin served as the only woman on the school board in Missoula, Montana. She was also the mother of Jeanette Rankin, the first woman to serve in the U.S. Congress and the person who introduced the "Anthony Amendment" for woman suffrage into the U.S. House of Representatives.[39]

Many men also supported women in other areas of life. Cases of supportive, helpful, sympathetic men who offered a helping hand and a listening ear when needed abounded in all communities. Faye Cashatt Lewis, whose mother so plaintively complained that the great trouble with North Dakota was that "there is nothing to make a shadow," claimed that her father was her mother's "saving support" throughout her various travails. Lewis said that her mother "could never have felt lost while he was by her side."[40] Children too offered assistance, company, and comfort to the older women of a family. While the men were gone in the fields, working in a shop, practicing a profession, or making trips,

children were often women's solace, friends, and helpers. According to Lewis, she and her siblings were not only her mother's assistants, but her friends and confidantes as well.[41]

The ability of many women to concentrate on their hopes and dreams, create and enjoy socializing, serve as cultural conservators, and form strong bonds with others—both female and male—helped them triumph over the innumerable demands of the West. Although the Plains was an especially difficult environment for women, they were not generally disoriented, depressed, or in disarray. Rather, the majority of them managed to maintain homes and families, carry out domestic functions, and perpetuate the many values associated with the home. While depression, insanity, or bitterness characterized some women's lives, many more were able to respond to the challenges and hardships involved in Plains living in ways that insured survival and often brought contentment and satisfaction as well.

NOTES

1. Gilbert C. Fite, "The United States Army and Relief to Pioneer Settlers, 1874–1875," *Journal of the West* 6 (January 1967), 99–107.

2. Louise Pound, *Pioneer Days in the Middle West: Settlement and Racial Stocks* (Lincoln: Nebraska State Historical Society, n.d.); Mary W. M. Hargreaves, "Homesteading and Homemaking on the Plains: A Review," *Agricultural History* 47 (April 1973), 156–63; Lillian Schlissel, "Women's Diaries on the Western Frontier," *American Studies* 18 (Spring 1977), 87–100, and Lillian Schlissel, "Mothers and Daughters on the Western Frontier," *Frontiers* 3 (1979), 29–33; Christine Stansell, "Women on the Great Plains, 1865–1900," *Women's Studies* 4 (1976), 87–98; John Mack Faragher and Christine Stansell, "Women and Their Families on the Overland Trail to California and Oregon, 1842–1867," *Feminist Studies* 2 (1975), 150–66; Glenda Riley, *The Female Frontier: A Comparative View of Women on the Prairie and the Plains* (Lawrence: University Press of Kansas, 1988).

3. See Myra Waterman Bickel, Lydia Burrows Foote, Eleanor Schubert, and Anna Warren Peart, Pioneer Daughters Collection, SDHRC; Abbie Bright, Diary, 1870–1871, KHS; Barbara Levorsen, "Early Years in Dakota," *Norwegian-American Studies* 21 (1961), 167–69; Kathrine Newman Webster, "Memories of a Pioneer," in *Old Times Tales*, Vol. 1, Part 1 (Lincoln: Nebraska State Historical Society, 1971); Bertha Scott Hawley Johns, "Pioneer Memories 1975," WSAMHD; Emma Crinklaw (interview by Mary A. Thon), "One Brave Homesteader of '89," 1989, WSAMHD. Regarding 'witching' for water in Kansas see Bliss Isely, *Sunbonnet Days* (Caldwell, Idaho: Caxton Printers, 1935), 176–79.

4. Ellen Stebbins Emery, letter to "Dear Sister Lizzie," December 31, 1889, from Emerado, SHSND (used by permission); "Prairie Pioneer: Some North Dakota Homesteaders," *North Dakota History* 43 (Spring 1976), 22; Adela E. Orpen, *Memories of the Old Emigrant Days in Kansas, 1862–1865* (New York: Harper & Brothers, 1928) 65–69; Florence Marshall Stote, "Of Such is the Middle West," n.d., KHS; Meri Reha, Pioneer Daughters Collection, SDHRC.

5. Amanda Sayle Walradth, Pioneer Daughters Collection, SDHRC, and Ada Vogdes, Journal, 1868–1872, HL.

6. Isely, *Sunbonnet Days*, 196–201, and Anne E. Bingham, "Sixteen Years on a Kansas Farm,] 1870–1886," Kansas State Historical Society *Collections* 15 (1919/20), 516.

7. Sara Tappan Doolittle Robinson, *Kansas, Its Interior and Exterior Life* (Freeport, New York: Books for Libraries Press, 1856), 85, 249–69; 347; Georgiana Packard, "Leaves from the Life of a Kansas Pioneer," 1914, KHS; Marian Lawton Clayton, "Reminiscences—The Little Family," 1961, KHS.

8. From Sophie Trupin, *Dakota Diaspora: Memoirs of a Jewish Homesteader* (Lincoln: University of Nebraska Press, 1984), 35, 39, 41–42.

9. For a fuller discussion of western divorce see Glenda Riley, *Divorce: An American Tradition* (New York: Oxford University Press, 1991), ch. 4.

10. Helen M. Carpenter, "A Trip Across the Plains in an Ox Wagon," 1857, HL, and Orpen, *Memories of the Old Immigrant Days*, 8.

11. Laura Ingalls Wilder, *The First Four Years* (New York: Harper & Row, 1971), Mollie Dorsey Sanford, *Mollie: The Journal of Mollie Dorsey Sanford in Nebraska and Colorado Territories, 1857–1886* (Lincoln: University of Nebraska Press, 1976), 54; Eva Klepper, "Memories of Pioneer Days," n.d., in May Avery Papers, NHS.

12. Sarah Ettie Armstrong, "Pioneer Days," n.d., WSAMHD.

13. Ibid.

14. U.S. Commissioner of Agriculture, *Annual Report*, 1862, 462–70; *Laramie Sentinel*, October 10, 1885; Martha Farnsworth, Diary, 1882–1922, KHS.

See also John Mack Faragher, "History from the Inside-Out: Writing the History of Women in Rural America," *American Quarterly* 33 (Winter 1981), 537–57, and Melody Graulich, "Violence Against Women in Literature of the Western Family," *Frontiers* 7 (1984), 14–20.

15. Flora Moorman Heston, " 'I think I will Like Kansas': The Letters of Flora Moorman Heston, 1885–1886," *Kansas History* 6 (Summer 1983), 92.

16. Sanford, *Mollie*, 38.

17. Isely, *Sunbonnet Days*, 180, and Lewis, *Nothing to Make a Shadow*, 76.

18. Vogdes, Journal.

19. Ibid.

20. Margaret Ronan, *Frontier Woman: The Story of Mary Ronan* (Helena: University of Montana, 1973), 123, and Mrs. Charles Robinson, "Pioneer Memories," 1975, WSAMHD.

21. Sanford, *Mollie*, 63. Descriptions of social events can be found in Nannie T. Alderson and Helen H. Smith, *A Bride Goes West* (Lincoln: University of Nebraska Press, 1969), 169; Mary and George Baillie, "Recollections in the Form of a Duet," 1939, WSAMHD; Enid Bennets, "Rural Pioneer Life," 1939, WSAMHD; Minnie Doehring, "Kansas One-Room Public School," 1981, KHS; W. H. Elznic, Pioneer Daughters Collection, SDHRC; Lottie Holmberg (recorder), Laura Ingraham Bragg, Recollections, n.d., WSAMHD; Lena Carlile Hurdsman, "Mrs. Lena Hurdsman of Mountain View," 1939, WSAMHD; Levorson, "Early Years in Dakota," 161; Alice Richards McCreery, "Various Happenings in the Life of Alice Richards McCreery," n.d., WSAMHD; Minnie Dubbs Millbrook, ed., "Rebecca Visits Kansas and the Custers: The Diary of Rebecca Richmond," *Kansas Historical Quarterly* 42 (Winter 1976), 366–402; Graphia Mewhirter Wilson, "Pioneer Life," 1939, WAHC.

22. Catherine E. Berry, "Pioneer Memories," 1975, WSAMHD. For discussions of women reconstructing their known lifestyle patterns on the Plains see James I. Fenton, "Critters, Sourdough, and Dugouts: Women and Imitation Theory on the Staked Plains, 1875–1910," in John R. Wunder, ed., *At Home on the Range: Essays on the History of Western Social and Domestic Life* (Westport, Conn.: Greenwood Press, 1985), 19–38; Jacqueline S. Reinier, "Concepts of Domesticity on the Southern Plains Agricultural Frontier," in Wunder, ed., *At Home on the Range*, 55–70.

23. Mrs. G. W. Wales, Reminiscences, 1866–1877, SHSND; Florence McKean Knight, "Anecdotes of Early Days in Box Butte County," *Nebraska History* 14 (April–June 1933), 142; Alderson and Smith, *A Bride Goes West*, 89; Lewis, *Nothing to Make a Shadow*, 71–72; Ronan, *Frontier Woman*, 115.

24. Lorshbough, "Prairie Pioneers," 78–79; Walter F. Peterson, "Christmas on the Plains," *American West* 1 (Fall 1964), 53–57; Anna Warren Peart, Pio-

neer Daughters Collection, SDHRC; Mabel Cheney Moudy, "Through My Life," n.d., WAHC.

25. Hannah, Birkley, "Mrs. Iver O. Birkley," 1957, NHS. For descriptions of Exodusters see Roy Garvin, "Benjamin, or 'Pap' Singleton and His Followers," *Journal of Negro History* 33 (January 1948), 7–8; Glen Schwendemann, "Wyandotte and the First 'Exodusters' of 1879," *Kansas Historical Quarterly* 26 (Autumn 1960), 233–49, and "The 'Exodusters' on the Missouri," *Kansas Historical Quarterly* 29 (Spring 1963), 25–40; Arvarh E. Strickland, "Toward the Promised Land: The Exodus to Kansas and Afterward," *Missouri Historical Review* 69 (July 1975), 405–12; Nell Irvin Painter, *Exodusters: Black Migration to Kansas after Reconstruction* (New York: Alfred A. Knopf, 1977; reprint, Lawrence: University Press of Kansas, 1986), 108–17; George H. Wayne, "Negro Migration and Colonization in Colorado, 1870–1930," *Journal of the West* 15 (January 1976), 102–20; "Washwomen, Maumas, Exodusters, Jubileers," in *We Are Your Sisters: Black Women in the Nineteenth Century,* ed. Dorothy Sterling (New York: Norton, 1984), 355–94.

26. For descriptions of Jewish women and men on the Plains see Lipman Goldman Feld, "New Light on the Lost Jewish Colony of Beersheba, Kansas, 1881–1886," *American Jewish Historical Quarterly* 60 (December 1970), 159, 165–67; Susan Leaphart, ed., "Frieda and Belle Fligelman: A Frontier-City Girlhood in the 1890s," *Montana: The Magazine of Western History* 32 (Summer 1982), 85–92; James A. Rudin, "Beersheba, Kansas: 'God's Pure Air on Government Lands,' " *Kansas Historical Quarterly* 34 (Autumn 1968), 282–98; Elbert L. Sapinsley, "Jewish Agricultural Colonies in the West: The Kansas Example," *Western States Jewish Historical Quarterly* 3 (April 1971), 157–69; Lois Fields Schwartz, "Early Jewish Agricultural Colonies in North Dakota," *North Dakota History* 32 (October 1965), 217, 222–32; William C. Sherman, *Prairie Mosaic: An Ethnic Atlas of Rural North Dakota* (Fargo: North Dakota Institute for Regional Studies, 1983), 19–20, 53–54, 70, 112.

27. Mrs. W. M. Lindsay, "My Pioneer Years in North Dakota," 1933, SHSND; Leola Lehman, "Life in the Territories," *Chronicles of Oklahoma* 41 (Fall 1963), 373; Orpen, *Memories of the Old Emigrant Days,* 219; Lucy Horton Tabor, "An Old Lady's Memories of the Wyoming Territory," n.d., WSAMHD; Emma Vignal Borglum, "The Experience at Crow Creek: A Sioux Indian Reservation at South Dakota," 1899, SDHRC.

28. Lehman, "Life in the Territories," 373; Vogdes, *Journal;* Fanny McGillycuddy, Diary, 1877–78, SDHRC.

29. Isely, *Sunbonnet Days,* 78–79. For other descriptions of the importance of quilting see Mrs. Henry (Anna) Crouse, Reminiscence, January 12, 1939, MSU; Ellen Calder DeLong, "Memories of

Pioneer Days in Cavalier County," n.d., SHSND; Agnes Henberg, Interview, September 6, 1979, WAHC; Olivia Holmes, Diary, 1872, KHS; Sarah Bessey Tracy, Diary, 1869, MSU.

30. *Bozeman Chronicle,* August 10, 1954; unidentified newspaper clipping, "Journey from Missouri to Montana in 1880 Great Adventure According to Mrs. Mary Myer," n.d., MSU.

31. *Nebraska Farmer,* December 8, 1934; Martha Thal, "Early Days: The Story of Sarah Thal, Wife of a Pioneer Farmer of Nelson County, N.D.," *American Jewish Archives* 23 (April 1971), 59; Mary Raymond, "My Experiences as a Pioneer," 1929, 1933, NHS; Allen, Diary; Lindsay, "My Pioneer Years"; Eleanor Schubert and Mary Louise Thomson, Pioneer Daughters Collection, SDHRC.

32. Alderson and Smith, *A Bride Goes West,* 205–06.

33. Clara Bewick Colby, Scrapbook of Clippings from *The Woman's Tribune,* 1883–1891, Clara Colby Collection, HL. See in particular pp. 24, 25, 257.

34. Luna Kellie, "Memoirs," n.d., NHS.

35. Catherine Wiggins Porter, "Sunday School Houses and Normal Institutes: Pupil and Teacher in Northern Kansas, 1886–1895," KHS, and Bingham, "Sixteen Years on a Kansas Farm," 502.

36. Stanton is quoted in Beverly Beeton and G. Thomas Edwards, "Susan B. Anthony's Woman Suffrage Crusade in the American West," *Journal of the West* 21 (April 1982), 5. See also Virginia Scharff, "The Case for Domestic Feminism: Woman Suffrage in Wyoming," *Annals of Wyoming* 56 (Fall 1984), 29–37; Dr. Grace Raymond Hebard, "How Woman Suffrage Came to Wyoming," n.d., WSAMHD; Katharine A. Morton, "How Woman Suffrage Came to Wyoming," n.d., Woman Suffrage Collection, WSAMHD; Staff of the Library of the University of Wyoming, "Esther Hobart Morris and Suffrage," n.d., Woman Suffrage File, WAHC; and Mary Lee Stark, "One of the First Wyoming Women Voters Tells How Franchise Was Granted," n.d., WAHC.

37. Mathilda C. Engstad, "The White Kid Glove Era," n.d., SHSND, and Marilyn Hoder-Salmon, "Myrtle Archer McDougal: Leader of Oklahoma's 'Timid Sisters,' " *Chronicles of Oklahoma* 60 (Fall 1982), 332–43.

38. Marilyn Dell Brady, "Populism and Feminism in a Newspaper by and for Women of the Kansas Farmers' Alliance, 1891–1894," *Kansas History* 7 (Winter 1984/85), 280–90; O. Gene Clanton, "Intolerant Populist? The Disaffection of Mary Elizabeth Lease," *Kansas Historical Quarterly* 34 (Summer 1968), 189–200; Katherine B. Clinton, "What Did You Say, Mrs. Lease?" *Kansas Quarterly* 1 (Fall 1969), 52–59; and Richard Stiller, *Queen of the Populists: The Story of Mary Elizabeth Lease* (New York: Crowell, 1970). See also Elizabeth Cochran, "Hatchets and Hoopskirts: Women in Kansas History," *Midwest Quarterly* 2 (April 1961), 229–49.

39. Richard B. Knowles, "Cross the Gender Line: Ella L. Knowles, Montana's First Woman Lawyer," *Montana: The Magazine of Western History* 32 (Summer 1982), 64–75, and Olive Pickering Rankin, Montana American Mothers Bicentennial Project, MHSA.

40. Stote, "Of Such is the Middle West," KHS; Bingham, "Sixteen Years on a Kansas Farm," 517; Alderson and Smith, *A Bride Goes West*, 206, 233–34, Elizabeth B. Custer, *"Boots and Saddles" Or Life in Dakota With General Custer* (New York: Harper & Brothers, 1885), 126, 145; Vogdes, Journal; Faye Cashatt Lewis, *Nothing to Make a Shadow* (Ames: Iowa State University Press, 1971), 33–34.

41. Lewis, *Nothing to Make a Shadow*, 33–34.

POSTSCRIPT

Did Nineteenth-Century Women of the West Fail to Overcome the Hardships of Living on the Great Plains?

In her study of 700 letters, journals, and diaries, Stansell concludes that nineteenth-century women were forced by their husbands to move to a primitive, isolated environment and to live in sod houses far removed from their families and friends in the more civilized states east of the Mississippi River. In Stansell's view, women regressed from the traditional cult of motherhood adhered to by middle-class eastern women who attended to the moral and physical needs of their homes and their children. Out on the frontier, says Stansell, women were isolated from their support systems of other women, and their marriages were often dominated by males who showed their wives neither love and affection nor respect. In short, Stansell paints a very grim picture of frontier life for women.

Riley grants that women on the Great Plains faced physical hardships, political disputes, and personal family tragedies. But she also shows how women adapted to the new environment and developed close friendships through church services, holiday parties, and quilting bees. In addition, it was in the West that women began to move out of the home through the Prohibition and Populist reform movements and eventually achieved voting rights.

Riley's research indicates the new directions in which western women's history has been moving. First, she has established the multicultural links that women felt toward one another on the frontier, exemplified by the friendships that developed between white and Indian women. Second, Riley has studied the West as a continuum that transcends several generations down to the present time. See *Building and Breaking Families in the American West* (University of New Mexico Press, 1996).

Two major anthologies that sample new western history are William Cronon, George Miles, and Jay Gitlin, eds., *Under an Open Sky: Rethinking America's Western Past* (W. W. Norton, 1992) and Patricia N. Limerick, Charles Rankin, and Clyde A. Milner, Jr., eds., *Trails: Toward a New Western History* (University of Kansas Press, 1991). These readers deal with the environment, industrialization, painting, film, minorities, and women—areas of the West neglected by Frederick Jackson Turner and his followers.

The two best overviews of the new western history are Patricia N. Limerick's *The Legacy of Conquest: The Unbroken Past of the American West* (W. W. Norton, 1988) and Richard White's *"It's Your Misfortune and None of My Own": A New History of the American West* (University of Oklahoma Press, 1992).

ISSUE 4

Were American Workers in the Gilded Age Conservative Capitalists?

YES: Carl N. Degler, from *Out of Our Past: The Forces That Shaped Modern America,* 3rd ed. (Harper & Row, 1984)

NO: Herbert G. Gutman, from *Work, Culture, and Society in Industrializing America: Essays in American Working-Class and Social History* (Alfred A. Knopf, 1976)

ISSUE SUMMARY

YES: Professor of history Carl N. Degler maintains that the American labor movement accepted capitalism and reacted conservatively to the radical organizational changes brought about in the economic system by big business.

NO: Professor of history Herbert G. Gutman argues that from 1843 to 1893, American factory workers attempted to humanize the system through the maintenance of their traditional, artisan, preindustrial work habits.

The two major labor unions that developed in the late nineteenth century were the Knights of Labor and the American Federation of Labor. Because of hostility toward labor unions, the Knights of Labor functioned for 12 years as a secret organization. Between 1879 and 1886 the Knights of Labor grew from 10,000 to 700,000 members. Idealistic in many of its aims, the union supported social reforms such as equal pay for men and women, the prohibition of alcohol, and the abolition of convict and child labor. Economic reforms included the development of workers' cooperatives, public ownership of utilities, and a more moderate, eight-hour workday. The Knights declined after 1886 for several reasons. Although it was opposed to strikes, the union received a black eye (as did the whole labor movement) when it was blamed for the bombs that were thrown at the police during the 1886 Haymarket Square riot in Chicago. According to most historians, other reasons that are usually associated with the decline of the Knights include the failure of some cooperative businesses, conflict between skilled and unskilled workers, and, most important, competition from the American Federation of Labor. By 1890 the Knight's membership had dropped to 100,000. It died in 1917.

A number of skilled unions got together in 1896 and formed the American Federation of Labor (AFL). Samuel Gompers was elected its first president, and his philosophy permeated the AFL during his 37 years in office. He pushed for practical reforms—better hours, wages, and working conditions. Unlike the Knights, the AFL avoided associations with political parties, workers' cooperatives, unskilled workers, immigrants, and women. Decision-making power was in the hands of locals rather than the central board. Gompers was heavily criticized by his contemporaries, and later by historians, for his narrow craft unionism. But despite the depression of the 1890s, membership increased from 190,000 to 500,000 by 1900, to 1,500,000 by 1904, and to 2,000,000 by the eve of World War I.

Gompers's cautiousness is best understood in the context of his times. The national and local governments were in the hands of men who were sympathetic to the rise of big business and hostile to the attempts of labor to organize. Whether it was the railroad strike of 1877, the Homestead steel strike of 1892, or the Pullman car strike of 1894, the pattern of repression was always the same. Companies would cut wages, workers would go out on strike, scab workers would be brought in, fights would break out, companies would receive court injunctions, and the police and state and federal militia would beat up the unionized workers. After a strike was broken, workers would lose their jobs or would accept pay cuts and longer workdays.

On the national level, Theodore Roosevelt became the first president to show any sympathy for the workers. As a police commissioner in New York City and later as governor of New York, Roosevelt observed firsthand the deplorable occupational and living conditions of the workers. Although he avoided recognition of the collective bargaining rights of labor unions, Roosevelt forced the anthracite coal owners in Pennsylvania to mediate before an arbitration board for an equitable settlement of a strike with the mine workers.

In 1905 a coalition of socialists and industrial unionists formed America's most radical labor union: the Industrial Workers of the World (IWW). There were frequent splits within this union and much talk of violence. But in practice, the IWW was more interested in organizing workers into industrial unions than in fighting, as were the earlier Knights of Labor and the later Congress of Industrial Organizations. Strikes were encouraged to improve the daily conditions of the workers through long-range goals, which included reducing the power of the capitalists by increasing the power of the workers.

Were the American workers of the Gilded Age conservative supporters of American capitalism? In the following selection, Carl N. Degler argues in the affirmative. He concludes that, led by the bread-and-butter leader of the American Federation of Labor, Samuel Gompers, the American worker sought a larger slice of the profits in the form of better hours, wages, and benefits. In the second selection, however, Herbert G. Gutman argues that in the Gilded Age, the American worker tried to humanize the factory system through the maintenance of traditional, cultural, artisan, preindustrial work habits.

YES

Carl N. Degler

OUT OF OUR PAST

THE WORKERS' RESPONSE

To say that the labor movement was affected by the industrialization of the postwar years is an understatement; the fact is, industrial capitalism created the labor movement. Not deliberately, to be sure, but in the same way that a blister is the consequence of a rubbing shoe. Unions were labor's protection against the forces of industrialization as the blister is the body's against the irritation of the shoe. The factory and all it implied confronted the workingman with a challenge to his existence as a man, and the worker's response was the labor union.

There were labor unions in America before 1865, but, as industry was only emerging in those years, so the organizations of workers were correspondingly weak. In the course of years after Appomattox, however, when industry began to hit a new and giant stride, the tempo of unionization also stepped up. It was in these decades, after many years of false starts and utopian ambitions, that the American labor movement assumed its modern shape.

Perhaps the outstanding and enduring characteristic of organized labor in the United States has been its elemental conservatism, the fantasies of some employers to the contrary notwithstanding. Indeed, it might be said that all labor unions, at bottom, are conservative by virtue of their being essentially reactions against a developing capitalism. Though an established capitalist society views itself as anything but subversive, in the days of its becoming and seen against the perspective of the previous age, capitalism as an ideology is radically subversive, undermining and destroying many of the cherished institutions of the functioning society. This dissolving process of capitalism is seen more clearly in Europe than in America because there the time span is greater. But, as will appear later, organized labor in the United States was as much a conservative response to the challenge of capitalism as was the European trade union movement.

Viewed very broadly, the history of modern capitalism might be summarized as the freeing of the three factors of production—land, labor, and capital—from the web of tradition in which medieval society held them. If capitalism was to function, it was necessary that this liberating process take place. Only when these basic factors are free to be bought and sold according to the dictates of the profit motive can the immense production which capitalism promises be realized. An employer, for example, had to be free to dismiss labor when the balance sheet required it, without being compelled to retain workers because society or custom demanded it. Serfdom, with its requirement that the peasant could not be taken from the land, was an anachronistic institution if capitalism was to become the economic ideology of society. Conversely, an employer needed to be unrestricted in his freedom to hire labor or else production could not expand in accordance with the market. Guild restrictions which limited apprenticeships were therefore obstacles to the achievement of a free capitalism.

The alienability of the three factors of production was achieved slowly and unevenly after the close of the Middle Ages. By the nineteenth century in most nations of the West, land had become absolutely alienable—it could be bought and sold at will. With the growth of banking, the development of trustworthy monetary standards, and finally the gold standard in the nineteenth century, money or capital also became freely exchangeable. Gradually, over the span of some two centuries, the innovating demands of capitalism stripped from labor the social controls in which medieval and mercantilistic government had clothed it. Serfdom as an obstacle to the free movement of labor was gradually done away with; statutes of laborers and apprenticeships which fixed wages, hours, and terms of employment also fell into disuse or suffered outright repeal. To avoid government interference in the setting of wage rates, the English Poor Law of 1834 made it clear that the dole to the unemployed was always to be lower than the going rate for unskilled labor. Thus supply and demand would be the determinant of wage levels. Both the common law and the Combination Acts in the early nineteenth century in England sought to ensure the operation of a free market in labor by declaring trade unions to be restraints on trade.

Like land and capital, then, labor was being reduced to a commodity, freely accessible, freely alienable, free to flow where demand was high. The classical economists of the nineteenth century analyzed this long historical process, neatly put it together, and called it the natural laws of economics.

To a large extent, this historical development constituted an improvement in the worker's status, since medieval and mercantilist controls over labor had been more onerous than protective. Nevertheless, something was lost by the dissolution of the ancient social ties which fitted the worker into a larger social matrix. Under the old relationship, the worker belonged in society; he enjoyed a definite if not a high status; he had a place. Now he was an individual, alone; his status was up to him to establish; his urge for community with society at large had no definite avenue of expression. Society and labor alike had been atomized in pursuit of an individualist economy. Herein lay the radical character of the capitalist ideology.

That the workingman sensed the radical change and objected to it is evident from what some American labor leaders said about their unions. Without rejecting the new freedom which labor enjoyed, John Mitchell, of the Mine Workers, pointed out that the union "stands for fraternity, complete and absolute." Samuel Gompers' eulogy of the social microcosm which was the trade union has the same ring. "A hundred times we have said it," he wrote, "and we say it again, that trade unionism contains within itself the potentialities of working class regeneration." The union is a training ground for democracy and provides "daily object lessons in ideal justice; it breathes into the working classes the spirit of unity"; but above all, it affords that needed sense of community. The labor union "provides a field for noble comradeship, for deeds of loyalty, for self-sacrifice beneficial to one's fellow-workers." In the trade union, in short, the workers could obtain another variety of that sense of community, of comradeship, as Gompers put it, which the acid of individualistic capitalism had dissolved.

And there was another objection to the transformation of labor into an exchangeable commodity. The theoretical justification for the conversion of the factors of production into commodities is that the maximum amount of goods can be produced under such a regime. The increased production is deemed desirable because it would insure greater amounts of goods for human consumption and therefore a better life for all. Unfortunately for the theory, however, labor cannot be separated from the men who provide it. To make labor a commodity is to make the men who provide labor commodities also. Thus one is left with the absurdity of turning men into commodities in order to give men a better life! ...

Seen in this light, the trade union movement stands out as a truly conservative force. Almost instinctively, the workers joined labor unions in order to preserve their humanity and social character against the excessively individualistic doctrines of industrial capitalism.

Eventually, the workers' organizations succeeded in halting the drive to the atomized society which capitalism demanded, and in doing so, far from destroying the system, compelled it to be humane as well as productive.

The essential conservatism of the labor movement is to be seen in particular as well as in general. The organizations of American labor that triumphed or at least survived in the course of industrialization were conspicuous for their acceptance of the private property, profit-oriented society. They evinced little of the radical, anticapitalist ideology and rhetoric so common among European trade unions. Part of the reason for this was the simple fact that all Americans—including workers—were incipient capitalists waiting for "the break." But at bottom it would seem that the conservatism of American labor in this sense is the result of the same forces which inhibited the growth of socialism and other radical anticapitalist ideologies. ...

"The overshadowing problem of the American labor movement," an eminent labor historian has written, "has always been the problem of staying organized. No other labor movement has ever had to contend with the fragility so characteristic of American labor organizations." So true has this been that even today the United States ranks below Italy and Austria in percentage of workers organized (about 25 per cent as compared, for instance, with Sweden's 90 per cent). In such an atmosphere, the history of organized labor in America has been both painful and conservative. Of the two major national organizations of workers which developed in the latter half of the nineteenth century, only the cautious, restrictive, pragmatic American Federation of Labor [A.F. of L.] lived into the twentieth century. The other, the Knights of Labor, once the more powerful and promising, as well as the less accommodating in goals and aspirations, succumbed to Selig Perlman's disease of fragility.

Founded in 1869, the Noble Order of the Knights of Labor recorded its greatest successes in the 1880's, when its membership rolls carried 700,000 names. As the A.F. of L. was later to define the term for Americans, the Knights did not seem to constitute a legitimate trade union at all. Anyone who worked, except liquor dealers, bankers, lawyers, and physicians, could join, and some thousands of women workers and Negroes were members in good standing of this brotherhood of toilers. But the crucial deviation of the Knights from the more orthodox approach to labor organization was its belief in worker-owned producers' co-operatives, which were intended to make each worker his own employer. In this way, the order felt, the degrading dependence of the worker upon the employer would be eliminated. "There is no good reason," Terence V. Powderly, Grand Master Workman of the order, told his followers, "why labor cannot, through co-operation, own and operate mines, factories and railroads."

In this respect the order repudiated the direction in which the America of its time was moving. It expressed the small-shopkeeper mentality which dominated the thinking of many American workers, despite the obvious trend in the economy toward the big and the impersonal. As the General Assembly of 1884 put it, "our Order contemplates a radical change, while Trades' Unions... accept the industrial system as it is, and endeavor to adapt themselves to it. The attitude of our Order to the existing industrial system is necessarily one of war." Though the order called this attitude "radical," a more accurate term, in view of the times, would have been "conservative" or "reactionary."

In practice, however, the Knights presented no more of a threat to capitalism than any other trade union. Indeed, their avowed opposition to the strike meant that labor's most potent weapon was only reluctantly drawn from the scabbard. The Constitution of 1884 said, "Strikes at best afford only temporary relief"; members should learn to depend on education, co-operation, and political action to attain "the abolition of the wage system."

Though the order officially joined in political activity and Grand Master Workman Powderly was at one time mayor of Scranton, its forays into politics accomplished little. The experience was not lost on shrewd Samuel Gompers, whose American Federation of Labor studiously eschewed any alignments with political parties, practicing instead the more neutral course of "rewarding friends and punishing enemies."

In a farewell letter in 1893, Powderly realistically diagnosed the ills of his moribund order, but offered no cure: "Teacher of important and much-needed reforms, she has been obliged to practice differently from her teachings. Advocating arbitration and conciliation as first steps in labor disputes she has been forced to take upon her shoulders the responsibilities of the aggressor first and, when hope of arbitrating and conciliation failed, to beg of the opposing side to do what we should have applied for in the first instance. Advising against strikes we have been in the midst of them. While not a political party we have been forced into the attitude of taking political action."

For all its fumblings, ineptitude, and excessive idealism, the Knights did organize more workers on a national scale than had ever been done before. At once premature and reactionary, it nonetheless planted the seeds of industrial unionism which, while temporarily overshadowed by the successful craft organization of the A.F. of L., ultimately bore fruit in the C.I.O. [Committee for Industrial Organization]. Moreover, its idealism, symbolized in its admission of Negroes and women, and more in tune with the mid-twentieth century than the late nineteenth, signified its commitment to the ideals of the democratic tradition. For these reasons the Knights were a transitional type of unionism, somewhere between the utopianism of the 1830's and the pragmatism of the A.F. of L. It seemed to take time for labor institutions to fit the American temper.

In the course of his long leadership of the American Federation of Labor, Samuel Gompers welcomed many opportunities to define the purposes of his beloved organization. . . .

"The trade unions are the business organizations of the wage-earners," Gompers explained in 1906, "to attend to the business of the wage-earners." Later he expressed it more tersely: "The trade union is not a Sunday school. It is an organization of wage-earners, dealing with economic, social, political and moral questions." As Gompers' crossing of swords with Hillquit demonstrated, there was no need or place for theories. "I saw," the labor leader wrote years later, in looking back on his early life in the labor movement, "the danger of entangling alliances with intellectuals who did not understand that to experiment with the labor movement was to experiment with human life. . . . I saw that the better-

ment of workingmen must come primarily through workingmen."

In an age of big business, Samuel Gompers made trade unionism a business, and his reward was the survival of his Federation. In a country with a heterogeneous population of unskilled immigrants, reviled and feared Negroes, and native workers, he cautiously confined his fragile organization to the more skilled workers and the more acceptable elements in the population. The result was a narrow but lasting structure.

Though never ceasing to ask for "more," the A.F. of L. presented no threat to capitalism. "Labor Unions are *for* the workingman, but against no one," John Mitchell of the United Mine Workers pointed out. "They are not hostile to employers, not inimical to the interests of the general public. . . . There is no necessary hostility between labor and capital," he concluded. Remorselessly pressed by Morris Hillquit as Gompers was, he still refused to admit that the labor movement was, as Hillquit put it, "conducted against the interests of the employing people." Rather, Gompers insisted, "It is conducted for the interests of the employing people." And the rapid expansion of the American economy bore witness to the fact that the Federation was a friend and not an enemy of industrial capitalism. Its very adaptability to the American scene—its conservative ideology, if it was an ideology at all—as Selig Perlman has observed, contained the key to its success. "The unionism of the American Federation of Labor 'fitted' . . . because it recognized the virtually inalterable conservatism of the American community as regards private property and private initiative in economic life."

This narrow conception of the proper character of trade unionism—job consciousness, craft unionism, lack of interest in organizing the unskilled, the eschewing of political activity—which Gompers and his Federation worked out for the American worker continued to dominate organized labor until the earthquake of the depression cracked the mold and the Committee for Industrial Organization issued forth.

NOBODY HERE BUT US CAPITALISTS

"By any simple interpretation of the Marxist formula," commented Socialist Norman Thomas in 1950, "the United States, by all odds the greatest industrial nation and that in which capitalism is most advanced, should have had long ere this is a very strong socialist movement if not a socialist revolution. Actually," he correctly observed, "in no advanced western nation is organized socialism so weak." Nor was this the first time Socialists had wondered about this. Over eighty years ago, in the high noon of European socialism, Marxist theoretician Werner Sombart impatiently put a similar question: *"Warum gibt es in den Vereinigten Staaten keinen Sozialismus?"*

The failure of the American working class to become seriously interested in socialism in this period or later is one of the prominent signs of the political and economic conservatism of American labor and, by extension, of the American people as a whole. This failure is especially noteworthy when one recalls that in industrialized countries the world over—Japan, Italy, Germany, Belgium, to mention only a few—a Socialist movement has been a "normal" concomitant of industrialization. Even newly opened countries like Australia and New Zealand have Labour parties.

Rather than ask, as Americans are wont to do, why these countries have nurtured such frank repudiators of traditional capitalism, it is the American deviation from the general pattern which demands explanation.

In large part, the explanation lies in the relative weakness of class consciousness among Americans. Historically, socialism is the gospel of the *class-conscious* working class, of the workingmen who feel themselves bound to their status for life and their children after them. It is not accidental, therefore, that the major successes of modern socialism are in Europe, where class lines have been clearly and tightly drawn since time immemorial, and where the possibility of upward social movement has been severely restricted in practice if not in law. Americans may from time to time have exhibited class consciousness and even class hatred, but such attitudes have not persisted, nor have they been typical. As Matthew Arnold observed in 1888, "it is indubitable that rich men are regarded" in America "with less envy and hatred than rich men in Europe." A labor leader like Terence Powderly was convinced that America was without classes. "No matter how much we may say about classes and class distinction, there are no classes in the United States.... I have always refused to admit that we have classes in our country just as I have refused to admit that the labor of a man's hand or brain is a commodity." And there was a long line of commentators on American society, running back at least to Crèvecoeur, to illustrate the prevalence of Powderly's belief.

The weakness of American class consciousness is doubtless to be attributed, at least in part, to the fluidity of the social structure. Matthew Arnold, for example, accounted for the relative absence of class hatred on such grounds, as did such very different foreign observers as Werner Sombart and Lord Bryce. The British union officials of the Mosely Commission, it will be recalled, were convinced of the superior opportunities for success enjoyed by American workers. Stephan Thernstrom in his study of Newburyport gave some measure of the opportunities for economic improvement among the working class when he reported that all but 5 per cent of those unskilled workers who persisted from 1850 to 1900 ended the period with either property or an improvement in occupational status.

Men who are hoping to move upward on the social scale, and for whom there is some chance that they can do so, do not identify themselves with their present class. "In worn-out, king-ridden Europe, men stay where they are born," immigrant Charles O'Conor, who became an ornament of the New York bar, contended in 1869. "But in America a man is accounted a failure, and certainly ought to be, who has not risen about his father's station in life." So long as Horatio Alger means anything to Americans, Karl Marx will be just another German philosopher.

The political history of the United States also contributed to the failure of socialism. In Europe, because the franchise came slowly and late to the worker, he often found himself first an industrial worker and only later a voter. It was perfectly natural, in such a context, for him to vote according to his economic interests and to join a political party avowedly dedicated to those class interests. The situation was quite different in America, however, for political democracy came to America prior to the Industrial Revolution. By the time the industrial transformation was getting under way after 1865, all adult males could vote and, for the most part, they had already chosen their political affiliations without reference to their economic class; they were Republicans or Democrats first and workers only second —a separation between politics and economics which has become traditional in America. "In the main," wrote Lord Bryce about the United States of the 1880's, "political questions proper have held the first place in a voter's mind and questions affecting his class second." Thus, when it came to voting, workers registered their convictions as citizens, not as workingmen. (In our own day, there have been several notable failures of labor leaders to swing their labor vote, such as John L. Lewis' attempt in 1940 and the C.I.O.'s in 1950 against Senator Taft and the inability of union leaders to be sure they could hold their members to support Hubert Humphrey in the Presidential election of 1968.) To most workers, the Socialist party appeared as merely a third party in a country where such parties are political last resorts.

Nor did socialism in America gain much support from the great influx of immigration. It is true that many Germans came to this country as convinced Socialists and thus swelled the party's numbers, but they also served to pin the stigma of "alien" upon the movement. Even more important was the fact that the very heterogeneity of the labor force, as a result of immigration, often made animosities between ethnic groups more important to the worker than class antagonism. It must have seemed to many workers that socialism, with its central concern for class and its denial of ethnic antagonism, was not dealing with the realities of economic life.

In the final reckoning, however, the failure of socialism in America is to be attributed to the success of capitalism. The expanding economy provided opportunities for all, no matter how meager they might appear or actually be at times. Though the rich certainly seemed to get richer at a prodigious rate, the poor, at least, did not get poorer—and often got richer. Studies of real wages between 1865 and 1900 bear this out. Though prices rose, wages generally rose faster, so that there was a net gain in average income for workers during the last decades of the century. The increase in real wages in the first fifteen years of the twentieth century was negligible—but, significantly, there was no decline. The high wages and relatively good standard of living of the American worker were patent as far as the twenty-three British labor leaders of the Mosely Commission were concerned. The American is a "better educated, better housed, better clothed and more energetic man than his British brother," concluded the sponsor, Alfred Mosely, a businessman himself.

But America challenged socialism on other grounds than mere material things. Some years ago an obscure Socialist, Leon Samson, undertook to account for the failure of socialism to win the allegiance of the American working class; his psychological explanation merits attention because it illuminates the influence exercised by the American Dream. Americanism, Samson observes, is not so much a tradition as it is a doctrine; it is "what socialism is to a socialist." Americanism to the American is a body of ideas like "democracy, liberty, opportunity, to all

of which the American adheres rationalistically much as a socialist adheres to his socialism—because it does him good, because it gives him work, because, so he thinks, it guarantees him happiness. America has thus served as a substitute for socialism."

Socialism has been unable to make headway with Americans, Samson goes on, because "every concept in socialism has its substitutive counterconcept in Americanism." As Marxism holds out the prospect of a classless society, so does Americanism. The opportunities for talent and the better material life which socialism promised for the future were already available in America and constituted the image in which America was beheld throughout the world. The freedom and equality which the oppressed proletariat of Europe craved were a reality in America—or at least sufficiently so to blunt the cutting edge of the Socialist appeal. Even the sense of mission, of being in step with the processes of history, which unquestionably was one of the appeals of socialism, was also a part of the American Dream. Have not all Americans cherished their country as a model for the world? Was not this the "last, best hope of earth"? Was not God on the side of America, as history, according to Marx, was on the side of socialism and the proletariat?

Over a century ago, Alexis de Tocqueville predicted a mighty struggle for the minds of men between two giants of Russia and the United States. In the ideologies of socialism and the American Dream, his forecast has been unexpectedly fulfilled.

NO

Herbert G. Gutman

WORK, CULTURE, AND SOCIETY IN INDUSTRIALIZING AMERICA

The traditional imperial boundaries (a function, perhaps, of the professional subdivision of labor) that have fixed the territory open to American labor historians for exploration have closed off to them the study of such important subjects as changing work habits and the culture of work. Neither the questions American labor historians usually ask nor the methods they use encourage such inquiry. With a few significant exceptions, for more than half a century American labor history has continued to reflect both the strengths and the weaknesses of the conceptual scheme sketched by its founding fathers, John R. Commons and others of the so-called Wisconsin school of labor history. Even their most severe critics, including the orthodox "Marxist" labor historians of the 1930s, 1940s, and 1950s and the few New Left historians who have devoted attention to American labor history, rarely questioned that conceptual framework. Commons and his colleagues asked large questions, gathered important source materials, and put forth impressive ideas. Together with able disciples, they studied the development of the trade union as an institution and explained its place in a changing labor market. But they gave attention primarily to those few workers who belonged to trade unions and neglected much else of importance about the American working population. Two flaws especially marred this older labor history. Because so few workers belonged to permanent trade unions before 1940, its overall conceptualization excluded most working people from detailed and serious study. More than this, its methods encouraged labor historians to spin a cocoon around American workers, isolating them from their own particular subcultures and from the larger national culture. An increasingly narrow "economic" analysis caused the study of American working-class history to grow more constricted and become more detached from larger developments in American social and cultural history and from the writing of American social and cultural history itself. After 1945 American working-class history remained imprisoned by self-imposed limitations and therefore fell far behind the more imaginative and innovative British and Continental European work in the field....

[T]he focus in these pages is on free white labor in quite different time periods: 1815–1843, 1843–1893, 1893–1919. The precise years serve only as guideposts to mark the fact that American society differed greatly in each period. Between 1815 and 1843, the United States remained a predominantly preindustrial society and most workers drawn to its few factories were the products of rural and village preindustrial culture. Preindustrial American society was not premodern in the same way that European peasant societies were, but it was, nevertheless, premodern. In the half-century after 1843 industrial development radically transformed the earlier American social structure, and during this Middle Period (an era not framed around the coming and the aftermath of the Civil War) a profound tension existed between the older American preindustrial social structure and the modernizing institutions that accompanied the development of industrial capitalism. After 1893 the United States ranked as a mature industrial society. In each of these distinctive stages of change in American society, a recurrent tension also existed between native and immigrant men and women fresh to the factory and the demands imposed upon them by the regularities and disciplines of factory labor. That state of tension was regularly revitalized by the migration of diverse premodern native and foreign peoples into an industrializing or a fully industrialized society. The British economic historian Sidney Pollard has described well this process whereby "a society of peasants, craftsmen, and versatile labourers became a society of modern industrial workers." "There was more to overcome," Pollard writes of industrializing England,

than the change of employment or the new rhythm of work: there was a whole new culture to be absorbed and an old one to be traduced and spurned, there were new surroundings, often in a different part of the country, new relations with employers, and new uncertainties of livelihood, new friends and neighbors, new marriage patterns and behavior patterns of children within the family and without.

That same process occurred in the United States. Just as in all modernizing countries, the United States faced the difficult task of industrializing whole cultures, but in this country the process was regularly repeated, each stage of American economic growth and development involving different first-generation factory workers. The social transformation Pollard described occurred in England between 1770 and 1850, and in those decades premodern British cultures and the modernizing institutions associated primarily with factory and machine labor collided and interacted. A painful transition occurred, dominated the ethos of an entire era, and then faded in relative importance. After 1850 and until quite recently, the British working class reproduced itself and retained a relative national homogeneity. New tensions emerged but not those of a society continually busy (and worried about) industrializing persons born out of that society and often alien in birth and color and in work habits, customary values, and behavior. "Traditional social habits and customs," J. F. C. Harrison reminds us, "seldom fitted into the patterns of industrial life, and they had . . . to be discredited as hindrances to progress." That happened regularly in the United States after 1815 as the nation absorbed and worked to transform new groups of preindustrial peoples, native whites among them. The result, however, was neither a static tension nor the mere recurrence of similar cycles, because American society itself changed as did the composition of its laboring population. But the source of the tension remained the same, and conflict often resulted. It was neither the conflict emphasized by the older Progressive historians (agrarianism versus capitalism, or sectional disagreement) nor that emphasized by recent critics of that early twentieth-century synthesis (conflict between competing elites). It resulted instead from the fact that the American working class was continually altered in its composition by infusions, from within and without the nation, of peasants, farmers, skilled artisans, and casual day laborers who brought into industrial society ways of work and other habits and values not associated with industrial necessities and the industrial ethos. Some shed these older ways to conform to new imperatives. Others fell victim or fled, moving from place to place. Some sought to extend and adapt older patterns of work and life to a new society. Others challenged the social system through varieties of collective associations. But for all—at different historical moments—the transition to industrial society, as E. P. Thompson has written, "entailed a severe restructuring of working habits— new disciplines, new incentives, and a new human nature upon which these incentives could bite effectively."

Much in the following pages depends upon a particular definition of culture and an analytic distinction between culture and society. Both deserve brief comment. "Culture" as used here has little to do with Oscar Lewis's inadequate "culture of poverty" construct and has even less to do with the currently fashionable but nevertheless quite crude behavioral social history that defines class by mere occupation and culture as some kind of a magical mix between ethnic and religious affiliations. Instead this [selection] has profited from the analytic distinctions between culture and society made by the anthropologists Eric Wolf and Sidney W. Mintz and the exiled Polish sociologist Zygmunt Bauman. Mintz finds in culture "a kind of resource" and in society "a kind of arena," the distinction being "between sets of historically available alternatives or forms on the one hand, and the societal circumstances or settings within which these forms may be employed on the other." "Culture," he writes, "is *used;* and any analysis of its use immediately brings into view the arrangements of persons in societal groups for whom cultural forms confirm, reinforce, maintain, change, or deny particular arrangements of status, power, and identity." ...

Despite the profound economic changes that followed the American Civil War, Gilded Age artisans did not easily shed stubborn and time-honored work habits. Such work habits and the lifestyles and subcultures related to them retained a vitality long into these industrializing decades. Not all artisans worked in factories, but some that did retained traditional craft skills. Mechanization came in different ways and at different times to diverse industries. Samuel Gompers recollected that New York City cigarmakers paid a fellow craftsman to read a newspaper to them while they worked, and Milwaukee cigarmakers struck in 1882 to retain such privileges as keeping (and then selling) damaged cigars and leaving the shop without a foreman's permission. "The difficulty with many cigarmakers," complained a New York City manufacturer in 1877, "is this. They come down to the shop in the morning; roll a few cigars and then go to a beer saloon and play pinnocio or some other game,... working probably only two or three hours a day." Coopers felt new machinery "hard and insensate," not a blessing but an evil that "took a great deal of joy out of life" because machine-made barrels undercut a subculture of work and leisure. Skilled coopers "lounged about" on Saturday (the regular payday), a "lost day" to their employers. A historian of American cooperage explained:

> Early on Saturday morning, the big brewery wagon would drive up to the shop. Several of the coopers would club together, each paying his proper share, and one of them would call out the window to the driver, "Bring me a Goose Egg," meaning a half-barrel of beer. Then others would buy "Goose Eggs," and there would be a merry time all around.... Little groups of jolly fellows would often sit around upturned barrels playing poker, using rivets for chips, until they had received their pay and the "Goose Egg" was dry.
>
> Saturday night was a big night for the old-time cooper. It meant going out, strolling around the town, meeting friends, usually at a favorite saloon, and having a good time generally, after a week of hard work. Usually the good time continued over into Sunday, so that on the following day he usually was not in the best of condition to settle down to the regular day's work.
>
> Many coopers used to spend this day [Monday] sharpening up their tools, carrying in stock, discussing current events, and in getting things in shape for the big day of work on the morrow. Thus, "Blue Monday" was something of a tradition with the coopers, and the day was also more or less lost as far as production was concerned.

"Can't do much today, but I'll give her hell tomorrow," seemed to be the Monday slogan. But bright and early Tuesday morning, "Give her hell" they would, banging away lustily for the rest of the week until Saturday which was pay day again, and its thoughts of the "Goose Eggs."

Such traditions of work and leisure—in this case, a four-day work week and a three-day weekend—angered manufacturers anxious to ship goods as much as it worried Sabbatarians and temperance reformers. Conflicts over life- and work-styles occurred frequently and often involved control over the work process and over time. The immigrant Staffordshire potters in Trenton, New Jersey, worked in "bursts of great activity" and then quit for "several days at a time." "Monday," said a manufacturer, "was given up to debauchery." After the potters lost a bitter lockout in 1877 that included torchlight parades and effigy burnings, the *Crockery and Glass Journal* mockingly advised:

> Run your factories to please the crowd. ... Don't expect work to begin before 9 a.m. or to continue after 3 p.m. Every employee should be served hot coffee and a bouquet at 7 a.m. and allowed the two hours to take a free perfumed bath.... During the summer, ice cream and fruit should be served at 12 p.m. to the accompaniment of witching music.

Hand coopers (and potters and cigarmakers, among others) worked hard but in distinctly preindustrial styles. Machine-made barrels pitted modernizing technology and modern habits against traditional ways. To the owners of competitive firms struggling to improve efficiency and cut labor costs, the Goose Egg and Blue Monday proved the laziness and obstinacy of craftsmen as well as the tyranny of craft unions that upheld venerable traditions. To the skilled cooper, the long weekend symbolized a way of work and life filled with almost ritualistic meanings. Between 1843 and 1893, compromise between such conflicting interests was hardly possible.

Settled premodern work habits existed among others than those employed in nonfactory crafts. Owners of already partially mechanized industries complained of them, too. "Saturday night debauches and Sunday carousels though they be few and far between," lamented the *Age of Steel* in 1882, "are destructive of modest hoardings, and he who indulges in them will in time become a striker for higher wages." In 1880 a British steelworker boasted that native Americans never would match immigrants in their skills: "adn't the 'ops, you know." Manufacturers, when able, did not hesitate to act decisively to end such troubles. In Fall River new technology allowed a print cloth manufacturer to settle a longstanding grievance against his stubborn mule spinners. "On Saturday afternoon after they had gone home," a boastful mill superintendent later recollected, "we started right in and smashed a room full of mules with sledge hammers.... On Monday morning, they were astonished to find that there was not work for them. That room is now full of ring frames run by girls." Woolen manufacturers also displaced handjack spinners with improved machinery and did so because of "the disorderly habits of English workmen. Often on a Monday morning, half of them would be absent from the mill in consequence of the Sunday's dissipation." Blue Monday, however, did not entirely disappear. Paterson artisans and factory hands held a May festival on a Monday each year ("Labor Monday") and that popular

holiday soon became state law, the American Labor Day. It had its roots in earlier premodern work habits.

The persistence of such traditional artisan work habits well into the nineteenth century deserves notice from others besides labor historians, because those work habits did not exist in a cultural or social vacuum. If modernizing technology threatened and even displaced such work patterns, diverse nineteenth-century subcultures sustained and nourished them. "The old nations of the earth creep on at a snail's pace," boasted Andrew Carnegie in *Triumphant Democracy* (1886), "the Republic thunders past with the rush of an express." The articulate steelmaster, however, had missed the point. The very rapidity of the economic changes occurring in Carnegie's lifetime meant that many, unlike him, lacked the time, historically, culturally, and psychologically, to be separated or alienated from settled ways of work and life and from relatively fixed beliefs. Continuity not consensus counted for much in explaining working-class and especially artisan behavior in those decades that witnessed the coming of the factory and the radical transformation of American society. Persistent work habits were one example of that significant continuity. But these elements of continuity were often revealed among nineteenth-century American workers cut off by birth from direct contact with the preindustrial American past, a fact that has been ignored or blurred by the artificial separation between labor history and immigration history. In Gilded Age America (and afterward in the Progressive Era despite the radical change in patterns of immigration), working-class and immigration history regularly intersected, and that intermingling made for powerful continuities. In 1880, for example, 63 of every 100 Londoners were native to that city, 94 coming from England and Wales, and 98 from Great Britain and Ireland. Foreign countries together contributed only 1.6 percent to London's massive population. At that same moment, more than 70 of every 100 persons in San Francisco (78), St. Louis (78), Cleveland (80), New York (80), Detroit (84), Milwaukee (84), and Chicago (87) were immigrants or the children of immigrants, and the percentage was just as high in many smaller American industrial towns and cities. "Not every foreigner is a workingman," noticed the clergyman Samuel Lane Loomis in 1887, "but in the cities, at least, it may almost be said that every workingman is a foreigner." And until the 1890s most immigrants came from Northern and Western Europe, French- and English-speaking Canada, and China. In 1890, only 3 percent of the nation's foreign-born residents —290,000 of 9,200,000 immigrants—had been born in Eastern or Southern Europe. (It is a little recognized fact that most North and West European immigrants migrated to the United States after, not before, the American Civil War.) When so much else changed in the industrializing decades, tenacious traditions flourished among immigrants in ethnic subcultures that varied greatly among particular groups and according to the size, age, and location of different cities and industries. ("The Irish," Henry George insisted, "burn like chips, the English like logs.") Class and occupational distinctions within a particular ethnic group also made for different patterns of cultural adaptation, but powerful subcultures thrived among them all.

Suffering and plain poverty cut deeply into these ethnic working-class worlds.

In reconstructing their everyday texture there is no reason to neglect or idealize such suffering, but it is time to discard the notion that the large-scale uprooting and exploitative processes that accompanied industrialization caused little more than cultural breakdown and social anomie. Family, class, and ethnic ties did not dissolve easily. "Almost as a matter of definition," the sociologist Neil Smelzer has written, "we associate the factory system with the decline of the family and the onset of anonymity." Smelzer criticized such a view of early industrializing England, and it has just as little validity for nineteenth-century industrializing America. Family roles changed in important ways, and strain was widespread, but the immigrant working-class family held together. Examination of household composition in sixteen census enumeration districts in Paterson in 1880 makes that clear for this predominantly working-class immigrant city, and while research on other ethnic working-class communities will reveal significant variations, the overall patterns should not differ greatly. The Paterson immigrant (and native white) communities were predominantly working class, and most families among them were intact in their composition. For this population, at least (and without accounting for age and sex ratio differences between the ethnic groups), a greater percentage of immigrant than native white households included two parents. Ethnic and predominantly working-class communities in industrial towns like Paterson and in larger cities, too, built on these strained but hardly broken familial and kin ties. Migration to another country, life in the city, and labor in cost-conscious and ill-equipped factories and workshops tested but did not shatter what the anthropologist Clifford Geertz has described as primordial (as contrasted to civic) attachments, "the 'assumed' givens... of social existence: immediate contiguity and kin connections mainly, but beyond them, the givenness that stems from being born into a particular religious community, speaking a particular language, and following particular social patterns." Tough familial and kin ties made possible that transmission and adaptation of European working-class cultural patterns and beliefs to industrializing America. As late as 1888, residents in some Rhode Island mill villages figured their wages in British currency. Common rituals and festivals bound together such communities. Paterson silk weavers had their Macclesfield wakes, and Fall River cotton mill workers their Ashton wakes. British immigrants "banded together to uphold the popular culture of the homeland" and celebrated saints' days: St. George's Day, St. Andrew's Day, and St. David's Day. Even funerals retained an archaic flavor. Samuel Sigley, a Chartist house painter, had fled Ashton-under-Lyne in 1848, and built American trade unions. When his wife died in the late 1890s a significant ritual occurred during the funeral: some friends placed a chaff of wheat on her grave. Mythic beliefs also cemented ethnic and class solidarities. The Irish-American press, for example, gave Martin O'Brennan much space to argue that Celtic had been spoken in the Garden of Eden, and in Paterson Irish-born silk, cotton, and iron workers believed in the magical powers of that town's "Dublin Spring." An old resident remembered:

There is a legend that an Irish fairy brought over the water in her apron from the Lakes of Killarney and planted it in the humble part of that town.... There

were dozens of legends connected with the Dublin Spring and if a man drank from its precious depository... he could never leave Paterson [but] only under the fairy influence, and the wand of the nymph would be sure to bring him back again some time or other.

When a "fairy" appeared in Paterson in human form, some believed she walked the streets "as a tottering old woman begging with a cane." Here was a way to assure concern for the elderly and the disabled.

Much remains to be studied about these cross-class but predominantly working-class ethnic subcultures common to industrializing America. Relations within them between skilled and unskilled workers, for example, remain unclear. But the larger shape of these diverse immigrant communities can be sketched. More than mythic beliefs and common work habits sustained them. Such worlds had in them what Thompson has called "working-class intellectual traditions, working-class community patterns, and a working-class structure of feeling," and men with artisan skills powerfully affected the everyday texture of such communities. A model subculture included friendly and benevolent societies as well as friendly local politicians, community-wide holiday celebrations, an occasional library (the Baltimore Journeymen Bricklayer's Union taxed members one dollar a year in the 1880s to sustain a library that included the collected works of William Shakespeare and Sir Walter Scott's Waverley novels), participant sports, churches sometimes headed by a sympathetic clergy, saloons, beer gardens, and concert halls or music halls and, depending upon circumstances, trade unionists, labor reformers, and radicals. The Massachusetts cleric Jonathan Baxter Harrison published in 1880 an unusually detailed description of one such ethnic, working-class institution, a Fall River music hall and saloon. About fifty persons were there when he visited it, nearly one-fourth of them young women. "Most of those present," he noticed, were "persons whom I had met before, in the mills and on the streets. They were nearly all operatives, or had at some time belonged to that class." An Englishman sang first, and then a black whose songs "were of many kinds, comic, sentimental, pathetic, and silly.... When he sang 'I got a mammy in the promised land,' with a strange, wailing refrain, the English waiter-girl, who was sitting at my table, wiped her eyes with her apron, and everybody was very quiet." Harrison said of such places in Fall River:

All the attendants... had worked in the mills. The young man who plays the piano is usually paid four or five dollars per week, besides his board. The young men who sing receive one dollar per night, but most of them board themselves.... The most usual course for a man who for any reason falls out of the ranks of mill workers (if he loses his place by sickness or is discharged) is the opening of a liquor saloon or drinking place.

Ethnic ties with particular class dimensions sometimes stretched far beyond local boundaries and even revealed themselves in the behavior of the most successful practitioners of Gilded Age popular culture. In 1884, for example, the pugilist John L. Sullivan and the music-hall entertainers Harrigan and Hart promised support to striking Irish coal miners in the Ohio Hocking Valley. Local ties, however, counted for much more and had their roots inside and outside of the fac-

tory and workshop. Soon after Cyrus H. McCormick, then twenty-one, took over the management of his father's great Chicago iron machinery factory (which in the early 1880s employed twelve hundred men and boys), a petition signed by "Many Employees" reached his hands:

It only pains us to relate to you... that a good many of our old hands is not here this season and if Mr. Evarts is kept another season a good many more will leave.... We pray for you... to remove this man.... We are treated as though we were dogs.... He has cut wages down so low they are living on nothing but bread.... We can't talk to him about wages if we do he will tell us to go out side the gate.... He discharged old John the other day he has been here seventeen years.... There is Mr. Church who left us last Saturday he went about and shook hands with every old hand in the shop... this brought tears to many men's eyes. He has been here nineteen years and has got along well with them all until he came to Mr. Evarts the present superintendent.

Artisans, themselves among those later displaced by new technology, signed this petition, and self-educated artisans (or professionals and petty enterprisers who had themselves usually risen from the artisan class) often emerged as civic and community leaders. "Intellectually," Jennie Collins noticed in Boston in the early 1870s, "the journeymen tailors... are ever discussing among themselves questions of local and national politics, points of law, philosophy, physics, and religion."

Such life-styles and subcultures adapted and changed over time. In the Gilded Age piece-rates in nearly all manufacturing industries helped reshape traditional work habits. "Two generations ago," said the Connecticut Bureau of Labor Statistics in 1885, "time-work was the universal rule." "Piece-work" had all but replaced it, and the Connecticut Bureau called it "a moral force which corresponds to machinery as a physical force." Additional pressures came in traditional industries such as shoe, cigar, furniture, barrel, and clothing manufacture, which significantly mechanized in these years. Strain also resulted where factories employed large numbers of children and young women (in the 1880 manuscript census 49.3 percent of all Paterson boys and 52.1 percent of all girls aged eleven to fourteen had occupations listed by their names) and was especially common among the as yet little-studied pools of casual male laborers found everywhere. More than this, mobility patterns significantly affected the structure and the behavior of these predominantly working-class communities. A good deal of geographic mobility, property mobility (home ownership), and occupational mobility (skilled status in new industries or in the expanding building trades, petty retail enterprise, the professions, and public employment counted as the most important ways to advance occupationally) reshaped these ethnic communities as Stephan Thernstrom and others have shown. But so little is yet known about the society in which such men and women lived and about the cultures which had produced them that it is entirely premature to infer "consciousness" (beliefs and values) only from mobility rates. Such patterns and rates of mobility, for example, did not entirely shatter working-class capacities for self-protection. The fifty-year period between 1843 and 1893 was not conducive to permanent, stable trade unions, but these decades were a time of frequent strikes and lockouts and other forms of sustained conflict.

Not all strikes and lockouts resulted in the defeat of poorly organized workers. For the years 1881 to 1887, for example, the New Jersey Bureau of Labor Statistics collected information on 890 New Jersey industrial disputes involving mostly workers in the textile, glass, metal, transportation, and building trades: 6 percent ended in compromise settlements; employers gained the advantage in 40 percent; strikers won the rest (54 percent). In four of five disputes concerning higher wages and shorter hours, New Jersey workers, not their employers, were victorious. Large numbers of such workers there and elsewhere were foreign-born or the children of immigrants. More than this, immigrant workers in the mid-1880s joined trade unions in numbers far out of proportion to their place in the labor force. Statistical inquiries by the Bureau of Labor Statistics in Illinois in 1886 and in New Jersey in 1887 make this clear. Even these data may not have fully reflected the proclivity of immigrants to seek self-protection. (Such a distortion would occur if, for example, the children of immigrants apparently counted by the bureaus as native-born had remained a part of the ethnic subcultures into which they had been born and joined trade unions as regularly as the foreign-born). Such information from Illinois and New Jersey suggests the need to treat the meaning of social mobility with some care. So does the sketchy outline of Hugh O'Donnell's career. By 1892, when he was twenty-nine years old, he had already improved his social status a great deal. Before the dispute with Andrew Carnegie and Henry Clay Frick culminated in the bitter Homestead lockout that year, O'Donnell had voted Republican, owned a home, and had in it a Brussels carpet and even a piano. Nevertheless this Irish-American skilled worker led the Homestead workers and was even indicted under a Civil War treason statute never before used. The material improvements O'Donnell had experienced mattered greatly to him and suggested significant mobility, but culture and tradition together with the way in which men like O'Donnell interpreted the transformation of Old America defined the value of those material improvements and their meaning to him.

Other continuities between 1843 and 1893 besides those rooted in artisan work habits and diverse ethnic working-class subcultures deserve brief attention as important considerations in understanding the behavior of artisans and other workers in these decades. I have suggested in other writings that significant patterns of opposition to the ways in which industrial capitalism developed will remain baffling until historians re-examine the relationship between the premodern American political system and the coming of the factory along with the strains in premodern popular American ideology shared by workers and large numbers of successful self-made Americans (policemen, clergymen, politicians, small businessmen, and even some "traditional" manufacturers) that rejected the legitimacy of the modern factory system and its owners. One strain of thought common to the rhetoric of nineteenth-century immigrant and native-born artisans is considered here. It helps explain their recurrent enthusiasm for land and currency reform, cooperatives, and trade unions. It was the fear of dependence, "proletarianization," and centralization, and the worry that industrial capitalism threat-

ened to transform "the Great Republic of the West" into a "European" country. In 1869, the same year that saw the completion of the transcontinental railroad, the chartering of the Standard Oil Company, the founding of the Knights of Labor, and the dedication of a New York City statue to Cornelius Vanderbilt, some London workers from Westbourne Park and Notting Hill petitioned the American ambassador for help to emigrate. "Dependence," they said of Great Britain, "not independence, is inculcated. Hon. Sir, this state of things we wish to fly from... to become citizens of that great Republican country, which has no parallels in the world's history." Such men had a vision of Old America, but it was not a new vision. Industrial transformation between 1840 and 1890 tested and redefined that vision. Seven years after their visit, the New York *Labor Standard*, then edited by an Irish socialist, bemoaned what had come over the country: "There was a time when the United States was the workingman's country,... the land of promise for the workingman.... We are now in an *old country*." This theme recurred frequently as disaffected workers, usually self-educated artisans, described the transformation of premodern America. "America," said the Detroit *Labor Leaf*, "used to be the land of promise to the poor.... The Golden Age is indeed over —the Age of Iron has taken its place. The iron law of necessity has taken the place of the golden rule." We need not join in mythicizing preindustrial American society in order to suggest that this tension between the old and the new helps give a coherence to the decades between 1843 and 1893 that even the trauma of the Civil War does not disturb.

POSTSCRIPT

Were American Workers in the Gilded Age Conservative Capitalists?

Degler agrees with the traditional labor historians that the American worker accepted capitalism and wanted a bigger piece of the pie. But he reverses the radical-conservative dichotomy as applied to the conflict between the worker and the businessman. In his view, the real radicals were the industrialists who created a more mature system of capitalism. Labor merely fashioned a conservative response to the radical changes brought about by big business. The system led to its demise. Its place was taken by the American Federation of Labor, whose long-time leader Samuel Gompers was famous for his acceptance of the wage system and American capitalism. The American Federation of Labor adopted practical goals; it strove to improve the lot of the worker by negotiating for better hours, wages, and working conditions. "In an age of big business," says Degler, "Samuel Gompers made trade unionism a business, and his reward was the survival of his Federation."

In explaining the failure of socialism in America, Degler argues that Americans lacked a working-class consciousness because they believed in real mobility. Also, a labor party failed to emerge because Americans developed their commitment to the two-party system before the issues of the industrial revolution came to the forefront. The influx of immigrants from a variety of countries created the heterogeneous labor force, and animosities between rival ethnic groups appeared more real than class antagonisms. "In the final reckoning," says Degler, "the failure of socialism in America is to be attributed to the success of capitalism."

For the past 25 years historians have been studying the social and cultural environment of the American working class. The approach is modeled after Edward P. Thompson's highly influential and sophisticated Marxist analysis *The Making of the English Working Class* (Vintage Books, 1966), which is the capstone of an earlier generation of British and French social historians. The father of the "new labor history" in the United States is Gutman, who was the first to discuss American workers as a group separate from the organized union movement. Gutman's distinction between preindustrial and industrial values laid the groundwork for a whole generation of scholars who have performed case studies of both union and nonunion workers in both urban and rural areas of America. Such works have proliferated in recent years but should be sampled first in the following collections of articles: Daniel J. Leab and Richard B. Morris, eds., *The Labor History Reader* (University of Illinois Press, 1985); Charles Stephenson and Robert Asher, eds., *Life and Labor: Dimensions of American Working-Class History* (State University of New

York Press, 1986); and Milton Cantor, ed., *American Working Class Culture: Explorations in American Labor and Social History* (Greenwood, 1979).

Gutman's essay differs from Degler's more traditional approach in several ways. Gutman abandons the division of American history at the Civil War/Reconstruction fault line. He proposes a threefold division for free, white workers: (1) the premodern early industrial period from 1815 to 1843; (2) the transition to capitalism, which encompasses the years 1843–1893; and (3) the development of a full-blown industrial system, which took place from the late 1890s through World War I. Gutman's unique periodization enables us to view the evolution of the free, white nonunion worker, whose traditional values withstood the onslaughts of an increasingly large-scale dehumanized factory system that emphasized productivity and efficiency until the depression of 1893.

Gutman also challenges the view that workers were helpless pawns of the owners and that they were forced to cave in every time a strike took place. He shows that on a local level in the 1880s, immigrants workers not only joined unions but also usually won their strikes. This is because small shopkeepers and workers in other industries often supported those who were out on strike. Gutman also argues from census data of the 1880s that immigrant families were more stable and less prone to divorce and desertion than native-born families. Gutman applied many of these insights to slaves in his prizewinning book *The Black Family in Slavery and Freedom* (Pantheon, 1976).

To learn more about the rise and fall of the Knights of Labor, see the case studies in Leon Fink's *Workingmen's Democracy: The Knights of Labor and American Politics* (University of Illinois Press, 1983). See also Fink's collection of articles *In Search of the Working Class* (University of Illinois Press, 1994). Two other noteworthy books on the Knights of Labor are Robert E. Weir, *Beyond Labor's Veil: The Culture of the Knights of Labor* (Penn State University Press, 1996) and Kim Voss, *The Making of American Exceptionalism: The Knights of Labor and Class Formation in the Nineteenth Century* (Cornell University Press, 1993).

Two journals have devoted entire issues to the American labor movement: the fall 1989 issue of *The Public Historian* and the February 1982 issue of *Social Education.* Students who wish to sample the diverse scholarships on the American worker should consult "A Round Table: Labor, Historical Pessimism, and Hegemony," *Journal of American History* (June 1988).

The question of why the United States never developed a major socialist movement or labor party has been the subject of much speculation. A good starting point is John H. Laslett and Seymour Martin Lipset, eds., *Failure of a Dream? Essays in the History of American Socialism* (University of California Press, 1984). Political scientist Theodore J. Lowi argues that the U.S. political system of federalism prevented a socialist movement in "Why Is There No Socialism in the United States?" *Society* (January/February 1985). Finally, see Rick Halpern and Jonathan Morris, eds. *American Exceptionalism? U.S. Working-Class Formation in an International Context* (St. Martin's Press, 1997).

ISSUE 5

Did William M. Tweed Corrupt Post–Civil War New York?

YES: Alexander B. Callow, Jr., from *The Tweed Ring* (Oxford University Press, 1966)

NO: Leo Hershkowitz, from *Tweed's New York: Another Look* (Anchor Press, 1977)

ISSUE SUMMARY

YES: Professor emeritus of history Alexander B. Callow, Jr., insists that by exercising a corrupting influence over the city and state government, as well as over key elements within the business community, William M. "Boss" Tweed and his infamous "ring" extracted enormous sums of ill-gotten money for their own benefit in post–Civil War New York.

NO: Professor of history Leo Hershkowitz portrays Tweed as a devoted public servant who championed New York City's interests during his 20-year career and whose reputation as the symbol for urban political corruption is grossly undeserved.

On the eve of the Civil War, the United States remained primarily a rural, agrarian nation. Of the country's 31 million inhabitants, 80 percent were characterized as "rural" dwellers by the U.S. Bureau of the Census; only 392 "urban" places (incorporated towns with 2,500 or more residents, or unincorporated areas with at least 2,500 people per square mile) dotted the national landscape; a mere nine U.S. cities contained populations in excess of 100,000. By 1920 the population of the United States had more than tripled, and for the first time in American history a majority of those residents lived in cities. The number of places defined as "urban" had increased to 2,722, and 68 cities housed over 100,000 residents each.

After 1865 the growth of urban America was directly linked to the economic and technological changes that produced the country's industrial revolution, as well as to rapid immigration, which filled the nation's cities with what seemed to native-born Americans to be a multitude of foreigners from around the globe. Reflecting many of the characteristics of modern America, these industrial cities produced a number of problems for the people who lived in them—problems associated with fire and police protection, sanitation, utilities, and a wide range of social services. These coincided with increased concerns over employment opportunities and demands for transportation and housing improvements. Typically, municipal governments became the clearinghouses for such demands. They also became the targets for charges of corruption.

Political corruption is virtually synonymous with the post–Civil War era. Whether at the local, state, or national levels of government, and regardless of party affiliation, charges of corruption seemed commonplace. Nowhere did this appear to be more the case than in the realm of New York politics dominated by the Tammany Hall Democratic "machine" and its notorious "boss," William M. Tweed.

Born in New York City in 1823 to Irish immigrant parents, Tweed rose to political prominence by serving as alderman, congressman, and state senator. He developed a power base in local and state politics both during and immediately after the Civil War, and he controlled that base until reform initiatives by the *New York Times* and Samuel J. Tilden brought him down. He died in jail, serving a sentence for failing to audit claims against the city, in 1878.

Undoubtedly, James Lord Bryce had Tweed and the infamous "Tweed Ring" in mind when he depicted city government in the United States as a "conspicuous failure." But does Tweed deserve the charges of wrongdoing that have been heaped upon him? Did his activities run counter to the best interests of his constituents? Is it conceivable that this long-standing symbol of corruption in urban America has been unduly maligned? These questions are addressed in the selections that follow.

According to Alexander B. Callow, Jr., William Tweed's malefic reputation is well deserved. "Boss" Tweed, he says, perfected the art of political corruption by controlling three vital sources of graft: the city, the state, and the business community. Under Tweed's direction, the Tweed Ring extracted wealth from New York's city and state government by controlling the key legislative and financial agencies that awarded charters and franchises and that were responsible for city improvements. The record of bribery and excessive charges for construction, says Callow, are incontrovertible, and Tweed used his political power to benefit personally from the graft collected.

Leo Hershkowitz, on the other hand, defends Tweed's reputation and insists that the "Boss's" image was fabricated by journalists, such as cartoonist Thomas Nast, to sell newspapers in New York. New York's diversity of peoples and interests, says Hershkowitz, made it impossible for one person to control the political realm to the extent that is attributed to Tweed. Hershkowitz points out that Tweed was never convicted on charges of graft or theft. He concludes that, in fact, the Tammany leader effectively represented the interests of New York residents by opening schools, building hospitals, paving streets, and providing a wide variety of other necessary services.

YES

Alexander B. Callow, Jr.

"HONEST" GRAFT

Post-Civil-War New York has been described as being encircled by a host of political rings, rings within rings, each depending on the other. There was the Gravel Ring, the Detective Ring, the Supervisors' Ring, the Courthouse Ring, the Albany Ring, the Street Commissioners' Ring, the Manure Ring, the Market Ring, and, consolidating and hovering above all, the Tweed Ring. And what was a political ring? It was the source of "magic wisdom" that made Tammany Hall a political power, said a big chief of the Tammany braves. Samuel Tilden, who almost became President of the United States on the claim he had smashed a "ring," said:

> The very definition of a "Ring" is that it encircles enough influential men in the organization of each party to control the action of both party machines; men who in public push to extremes the abstract ideas of their respective parties, while they secretly join their hands in schemes for personal power and profit.

Scholars and public alike have generally accepted Tilden's definition of the Tweed Ring. Why was it that later city bosses like [Richard] Croker had a "machine," while Tweed had a "Ring"—a word, as it were, with a more ominous ring, a political synonym for conspiracy, venality, and corruption? If the Tweed Ring's skills at organization have never been rightfully emphasized, its achievements in corruption certainly have, although large-scale graft existed before the emergence of the Tweed Ring, and continued after its downfall.

We shall probably never know exactly how much the Ring stole. Calculations have run as high as $300 million, which was probably too high, even for the Tweed Ring. The *New York Evening Post* estimated it at $59 million; the *Times* thought it was more like $75 million to $80 million....

Years after the fall of the Ring, Matthew J. O'Rourke, who had made a study of the Ring's plunders, estimated that if fraudulent bonds were included, the Ring probably stole about $200 million. Henry J. Taintor made the closest study. For six years he had been employed by the City to determine the amount of the Ring's graft. It cost the City over $73,000 to maintain Taintor's investigation, and for a moment during the Tweed Ring investigation in 1877

From Alexander B. Callow, Jr., *The Tweed Ring* (Oxford University Press, 1966). Copyright © 1966 by Alexander Callow. Reprinted by permission of Oxford University Press, Inc. Notes omitted.

there was the suspicion, later dispelled, that a dreadful irony had occurred: that Taintor, in investigating graft, had been tempted himself, and had padded his bills. At any rate, he testified his research showed that the Ring had stolen at least $60 million, but even this was not an accurate figure, he said, because he did not possess all the records. Whatever the figure, in order to maintain a political machine as well as to increase their personal fortune, the Tweed Ring's operation was on a gigantic scale.

There [were] three primary sources of graft: the city, the state, and the business community. In the city, the Ring's control of the key legislative and financial agencies, from the Supervisors and Aldermen to the Comptroller and Mayor, gave it command of New York's financial machinery and bountiful opportunity for graft. Every warrant, then, charged against the city treasury passed the Ring's scrutiny and was subject to its manipulation. Every scheme for city improvement, be they new streets, new buildings, new city parks, had to be financed from the city treasury, controlled by the Ring. The results were often graft, reflected in excessive charges and needless waste. Every charter and franchise for new businesses had to meet the approval of the city legislature and the Mayor, and many companies, therefore, had to pay the tribute of the bribe to get them passed. All the city's financial affairs, such as bond issues, tax-collecting, rentals on city properties, were vulnerable as sources of graft. In effect, there was a direct relationship between power and graft. The Ring's political influence was so extensive that one roadblock to graft, the check and balance system—pitting the upper house of the City legislature against the lower house, and the Mayor as a check to the combined houses of the legislature—was simply nullified. When this happened, the city's financial operations became an open target.

This was largely true for the State legislature as well. Any check and balance between state and city, governor and legislature, was nullified. The Ring controlled the governor, John Hoffman; it controlled the powerful block of city Democrats in the State legislature. When he was elected State Senator in 1867 (and assumed office in 1868, when the Senate convened), Boss Tweed, as Chairman of the influential State Finance Committee, and as a member of the important Internal Affairs of Towns and Counties, Charitable and Religious, and Municipal Affairs committees, was in a commanding position to influence tax-levies, bond issues, and special projects for the city—all sources of graft. As the leader of the Black Horse Cavalry, a corrupt band of State legislators, he could control legislation leading to graft.

Not all the money came from the City and State treasury. The business community was an important source of profit, both as allies and victims. The Tweed Ring operated as lobby brokers for businessmen seeking to pass or kill legislation vital to their interests. Services rendered for the Erie Railroad, for example, brought in thousands of dollars. Businessmen provided large "kick-backs" in payment for receiving profitable contracts. The "cinch" bill, legislative extortion threatening business firms and individuals, was used extensively by the Ring through both the City and State legislatures.

Unlike the sly, sophisticated tactics of modern-day graft—the highly complicated dummy corporation, the undercover payoff via the "respectable" attorney—the Ring operated in a remarkably open and straightforward fashion. In effect, the shortest distance to the city treasury was a straight line. While the Ring used several methods for plunder, the largest share of the booty was gained by a method simple, direct, brazen, daring—and often sloppy. Every person who received a contract from the city, whether for supplies or for work on the city buildings and public works was instructed to alter his bills before submitting them for payment. At first the tribute was levied somewhat irregularly at 10 per cent, then it was raised to 55 per cent; in July 1869 it jumped to 60 per cent; and from November 1869 on, the tradesmen received 35 per cent and the Ring 65 per cent on all bills and warrants. When bills from contractors and tradesmen did not come in fast enough, Tweed ordered vouchers to be made out to imaginary firms and individuals. On large contracts, Tweed acted directly and got immediately to the point. When he was told that electric fire alarms would cost the city $60,000, he asked the contractor, "If we get you a contract for $450,000 will you give us $225,000?" No time was wasted. The contractor answered with a simple yes and got the contract. Nor did the Boss quibble over small sums. Once a merchant told Tweed that Comptroller [Richard B.] Connolly had refused to pay his bill. Only by "kicking-back" 20 per cent of the bill, would the merchant ever get paid. Tweed wrote Connolly: "For God's sake pay ——'s bill. He tells me you people ask 20 per cent. The whole d——d thing isn't but $1100. If you don't pay it, I will. Thine."

The division of the spoils varied: Tweed received from 10 to 25 per cent; Connolly from 10 to 20 per cent; [Peter B.] Sweeny 10 per cent; [A. Oakey] Hall 5 to 10 per cent. There was a percentage for the "sinking fund," and James Watson and W. E. Woodward shared 5 per cent. These last two, clerks of the gang, did the paper work and forging. "You must do just as Jimmy tells you, and you will get your money," was a well-known saying among Tweed Ring contractors.

James Watson, the Ring's bookkeeper, was City Auditor in Connolly's office. He first demonstrated his talents while a convict. In 1850 Watson was an agent for a prosperous firm which suddenly began to experience severe losses that Watson found inconvenient to explain. He fled to California. He was brought back to New York in irons and clapped in Ludlow Street jail. An active fellow with pleasant manners, he soon won the friendship of the warden. He took charge of the prison records and performed with such admirable efficiency, especially in calculations, that he was released, with the warden's help, and was appointed a collector in the Sheriff's office. He held that position under three Sheriffs. When the Tweed Ring was formed in 1866, he was made City Auditor, a position that paid a small salary. Four years later, he was worth anywhere from two to three million dollars. It was said that he was a simple man and lived in a curious state of "ostentatious modesty." He had only one luxury—fast trotting horses, a passion that later helped to ruin the Tweed Ring.

W. E. Woodward occupied a key post as clerk to the Supervisors; he helped to rig the percentages of the business that came through that office. At the time of the Aldermen's investigation of the Ring in 1877, the Aldermen were curious how a mere clerk could own a $150,000 home, the best home, in fact, in Norwalk, Connecticut. Asked how he could do this on a salary that never exceeded

$5000, Woodward gave a straightforward answer. "I used to take all I could get, and the Board of Supervisors were very liberal to me."

In the Comptroller's Office, Slippery Dick Connolly performed feats that justified his name, as his successor in 1871, the reformer, Andrew Green, confirmed when he found the treasury thoroughly sacked. As Comptroller, Connolly served the Ring three ways. He spent the money collected through the city's regular channels of revenue—taxes, rents from such city properties as markets, docks, armories, etc. While some of the money was spent legitimately, a good deal of it was either embezzled or found its way into fraudulent contracts, excessive rents, or padded payrolls, a percentage of which was "kicked-back" into the Ring's coffers. However, only about a third of the city's money came from taxes or rents; the rest came from securities. Thus when a tax-levy of some $30 or more million was spent, usually at a brisk pace, Connolly's next job was to realize $30 to $50 millions more by issuing stocks and bonds.

Connolly performed this task like a financial conjuror. He created a litter of stocks and bonds raised for every conceivable project, ingenious in wording and intent. There were Accumulated Debt Bonds, Assessment Fund bonds, Croton Aqueduct Bonds, Croton Reservoir Bonds, Central Park Improvement Fund Stocks, City Improvement Stocks, Street Improvement Bonds, Fire Department Stocks, Tax Relief Bonds, Bridge Revenue Bonds, New Court House Stock. Repairs to the County Offices and Building Stocks, Dock Bonds, and bonds for the Soldiers' Relief Fund. The war chest to provide funds for padded payrolls, for example, was raised by the sale of appropriately named Riot Damages Indem-

nity Bonds. As a result of Connolly's various enterprises, the city groaned under a debt which increased by nearly $70 million from 1869 to 1871.

Finally, it was Connolly's responsibility to mask the Ring's fraudulent expenditures by slippery accounting techniques. In this, he was helped by the extensive power of the Ring which nullified an elaborate series of regulations established to prevent fraud. By state law, every warrant and claim drawn against the City must be itemized and accompanied by a signed affidavit certifying its authenticity. Before it could be cashed it must be thoroughly examined and signed by the Comptroller, City Auditor, the Board of Supervisors, and the Mayor. But since the Ring "owned" all these offices, it was relatively simple to rig a phony warrant and get the required signatures. Indeed, the Ring became so powerful that it owned its own bank, the Tenth National, to ensure the safe deposit of its booty. (Tweed, Connolly, Hall, James Ingersoll, and James Fisk, Jr., were the Tenth National's distinguished directors.) ...

Added to all this was another lush source for graft. Connolly and his lieutenant James Watson were in a position to audit and pay off fictitious claims against the city. With logic, the New York City Council of Political Reform said: "In a sound fiscal system one officer *adjusts* claims and another *pays* them. From the weakness of human nature it is not deemed wise or prudent for the government of any great city or county to allow the *same* officer to adjust a claim *who* is to *pay* it; lest he may be tempted by a share of the money to conspire with the claimant and allow an unjust claim. But in our city, in 1868 and 1870, a *single* officer, the Comptroller, *adjusted* and *paid*, by adding so much to the permanent debt, $12,500,000 of claims!"

The Comptroller's office was also a point of frustration for those with legitimate claims against the city. They were kept waiting sometimes for years, before they could get their money. Subsequently, they often sold their claim to one of the Ring's agents for 50 or 60 cents on the dollar. Immediately after the transaction took place, the new owner was promptly paid. A clerk in Connolly's office, named Mike Moloney, was in charge of this branch of business.

> Moloney sits opposite the door by which his victims enter and watches for them with all the avidity that a spider might watch the approach of a fly. The moment an unlucky claimant makes his appearance Moloney jumps on his feet and steps forward to the counter to meet him. Bending forward he listens to the application of the victim, and then by a series of ominous shakes of his head, and "the oft-told tale" repeated in half-smothered whispers, he tries to convince the applicant that there is no prospect of him receiving his money for some time to come, and that, if he really needs it, he had better go over to City Hall and see Mr. Thomas Colligan. (The victim sees Mr. Colligan)... and comes out feeling much the same as if he had lost his pocketbook, while the genial Mr. Colligan pockets the "little difference," invites Moloney to dinner, and quietly divides the spoils while sipping Champagne or smoking a Havana.

It is difficult to know where to begin in dealing with the many specific schemes of the Tweed Ring. Perhaps it is best to begin with what E. L. Godkin once called "one of those neat and profitable little curiosities of fraud which the memory holds after graver things are forgotten."

In 1841, a man named Valentine, a clerk in the Common Council, persuaded the city to finance the publication of a city almanac which he would edit. Initially, it was a small volume of not quite 200 pages, which had a map of the city and a list of all persons associated with the government of New York City and their business and home addresses. Although the City Directory contained the same information, for some obscure reason the almanac seemed valuable. Down through the years, the almanac increased in bulkiness, and, more important, in cost to the taxpayers, until it became "a manual of folly, extravagance, and dishonesty." By 1865, *Valentine's Manual*, as it was called, had become a 879-page monument of costliness and superficiality. Among 141 pictures was a large, folding four-page lithograph, illustrating—"O precious gift to posterity!"—a facsimile of each Alderman's autograph. Expensive lithographs covered a number of vital subjects: a fur store built in 1820; a house that Valentine had once lived in; a grocery and tea store of ancient vintage; Tammany Hall as it looked in 1830; a Fifth Avenue billiard saloon; and a host of "portraits of undistinguished persons." Well over 400 pages were cluttered with extracts from old government documents, newspapers, and "memories." The cost of printing was $57,172.30; the number of copies printed, 10,000. A few copies found their way into secondhand bookstores, which paid two dollars apiece for them, $3.36 less than a copy cost the city. An outraged public opinion forced Mayor Hoffman to veto the resolution authorizing a similar expenditure for 1866. He found that Appleton's or Harper's would have published the same number of copies for $30,000 instead of $53,672. The Aldermen, however, overrode his veto....

The Tweed Ring created several companies which moved in to monopolize every phase of city printing as well as city advertising. One such firm was the New York Printing Company. Its expansion reflected all the gusto of American business enterprises. It began in a shabby little office on Centre Street, but almost at once business became so good that it absorbed three of the largest printing establishments in the city. The New York Printing Company was growing, said a newspaper, "but like other mushrooms it grows in the dark. It is spreading under the cover of night, and running its roots into the Treasury by deep underground passages." On a capital stock of $10,000 it paid a dividend of $50,000 to $75,000 to each of its stockholders. The city apparently liked its work, for during 1870–71 the firm obtained $260,283.81 of its business. All these amounts incorporated a 25 per cent tribute to the Ring. The company became so versatile in printing all kinds of material that the city paid it another $300,000 for printing in book form the records of New York City from 1675 to 1776. Nor did the firm confine its customers to the City and County. Insurance companies and steamboat and ferry companies were extremely vulnerable to a legislative bill which, in the public interest, could hurt them by regulating their activities and profits. Hence, they all received a notice that the New York Printing Company would be happy to do their printing.

The Tweed Ring composed the major stockholders of the Manufacturing Stationers' Company, which sold stationery supplies to city offices and schools. In 1870 the City and County paid it over $3 million. Among its many bills, there was this interesting one: for six reams of note paper, two dozen penholders, four ink bottles, one dozen sponges, and three dozen boxes of rubber bands, the city paid $10,000. James Parton singled out the Manufacturing Stationers' Company for its treachery.

> We have before us a successful bid for supplying the city offices with stationery, in which we find the bidder offering to supply "blue folio post" at one cent per ream; "magnum bonum pens," at one cent per gross; "lead pencils," at one cent per dozen; "English sealing-wax," at one cent per pound; and eighty-three other articles of stationery, at the uniform price of one cent for the usual parcel. This was the "lowest bid," and it was, of course, the one accepted. It appeared, however, when the bill was presented for payment, that the particular kind of paper styled "blue folio post" had never been called for, nor any considerable quantity of the other articles proposed to be supplied for one cent. No one, strange to say, had ever wanted "magnum bonum" pens at one cent a gross, but in all the offices the cry had been for "Perry's extra fine," at three dollars. Scarcely any one had used "envelopes letter-size" at one cent per hundred but there had been countless calls for "envelopes note-size" at one cent each. Between the paper called "blue folio post," at one cent per ream, and paper called "foolscap extra ruled," at *five dollars and a half*, the difference was too slight to be perceived; but every one had used the foolscap. Of what avail are contracts, when the officials who award them, and the other officials who pay the bill, are in league with the contractor to steal the public money?

As the fictional Boss Blossom Brick said, "Official advertising is the Pain Killer of Politics." During the Civil War three men started an insignificant newspaper titled *The Transcript*. They were George Stout, "a journalist unknown to fame," Charles E. Wilbour, a court stenographer and "literary man, somewhat less unknown," and Cornelius Corson, "an employee in the City Hall, and not devoid of influence in that quarter." When Tweed, Connolly, and Sweeny became their partners, business, but not circulation, picked up. The Common Council (the Aldermen and Assistant Aldermen) ordered that a full list of all persons liable to serve in the army, amounting to some 50,000 names, should be printed in the *Transcript*. Later, thirty-five copies of the list were published in book-form, "though the bill was rendered for a large edition." From then on the *Transcript* enjoyed days of high prosperity. It published the major share of all "city advertising," which meant official records of the courts, and official statements and declarations, statistical reports, new ordinances, in effect, the facts and figures of city business. The rates were exorbitant enough to ensure a heady profit; for example, messages from the Mayor cost a dollar a line. A great deal of the advertisements came from Tweed's Department of Public Works, and from the Bureau of Assessments, where Richard Tweed was in control. Although the newspaper never sold more than a hundred copies, the city paid it $801,874 from 1869 to 1871 for publishing its official business and advertisements. The December 3, 1870, issue, for example, consisted of 504 pages. Advertisements were charged at a rate of 25 cents a line, higher than prevailing newspaper rates. It was estimated that the Ring received $68,000 in profits for that issue alone. The Christmas number for that year was a special: a double extra of 1000 pages, all advertisements, for which double rates were charged. It appeared to one newspaper that the Ring paid for its Christmas presents out of the public till. The profits, then, made by the three companies of the Ring which corralled city printing reached a grand total over a three-year period of $2,641,828.30, of which nine-tenths was pure profit.

As Boss Blossom Brick said, "Give the people plenty of taffy and the newspapers plenty of advertising—then help yourself to anything that's lying around loose." Funneling the taxpayers' dollars through the *Transcript* was a way to finance Tweed's mansion on Fifth Avenue and his palatial estate in Greenwich, Connecticut; but there was another method of using city advertising which ensured, for a few years at least, that gracious living could be enjoyed. The Tweed Ring found that the best way to protect itself against newspaper criticism was to distribute city advertising as a token of peace. It became a kind of hush money which bound the press to silence. Until the storm broke, in 1871, probably no New York political regime ever enjoyed less newspaper criticism than the Tweed Ring, and only when the evidence became painfully obvious and practically overwhelming did the press join the crusade against evil begun by the *New York Times* and *Harper's Weekly*. Before the storm, there had been some criticism, but it was spotty and half-hearted. The *Tribune* might thunder for a while, the *Sun* became nasty—as was its style—but a general grant of advertising had the same effect as placing alum on the tongue.

By law, the city corporation was limited to nine daily and eight weekly papers in which to advertise. But the Tweed Ring, with its usual disregard for procedure, extended delicious morsels of city advertising to twenty-six daily and forty-four weekly newspapers in the city alone, and seventeen weekly journals outside the city, making a total of eighty-seven organs. Probably no political regime in the history of New York City had exerted so much influence on the press. . . .

Not content with the method of using advertising, the Ring also won the hearts of City Hall reporters by giving them $200 gifts at Christmas. This practice had started as early as 1862, under the administration of Mayor George Opdyke (who disapproved), but the Ring elaborated on the scheme. It also subsidized six to eight reporters on nearly all the city papers with fees of $2000 to $2500 to exercise the proper discretion when it came to writing about politics. There was the reward of patronage for the especially deserving: Stephen Hayes, on the *Herald* staff during the high days of the Ring, was rewarded with a sinecure in the Marine Court ($2500 a year), and Michael Kelly, also of the *Herald*, received positions in both the Fire Department and the Department of Public Works. Moreover, reporters from various newspapers of the country, from a Cleveland newspaper to the *Mobile Register*, were hired to write favorable notices of the Democratic administration in New York. And if a firm went too far and tried to print a pamphlet exposing the Ring, it might find its offices broken into by the Ring's men and the type altered to present a glowing account of the Ring's activities—as did the printing company of Stone, Jordan and Thomson.

At the time the Ring was breaking up, the City found itself confronted with claims amounting to over a million and a half dollars negotiated between newspapers and the Ring, some fraudulent and some not, for not all journals which received city advertising did so on the basis of a conspiracy with the Ring. But

enough of them did to ensure the complacency and the apathy which seemed to grip many during the Ring's rule.

The Ring needed complacency and apathy when it came to operations behind the opening, widening, and improving of the city streets. With the city's enormous growth came a legitimate demand for new streets and the improvement of old ones. It became one of the Ring's most lucrative forms of graft. It was, indeed, a democratic form of graft—laborers got work; City Hall clerks were able to supplement their incomes; political debts were paid off in commissionerships, judges no longer had to rely entirely on their salaries; Ring members and friends prospered from the assessments involved and the excitement of "gambling" in real estate. As in the case of Recorder and Street Commissioner [John] Hackett, the key factor was the appointment of reliable Commissioners by the Ring judges, upon the suggestion of Corporation Counsel [John] O'Gorman. From then on a pattern emerged: Tammany favorites and members of the Ring's families constantly appeared as Commissioners; awards for damages were exorbitantly high; Commissioners charged "from ten to one hundred times as much as the law allowed" for their services and expenses, despite the fact that the Commissioners as employees of the city were disqualified by law from receiving any pay.

To "open" a new street did not mean to begin construction work. It was a legal term signifying that the land had been bought and was now officially "opened." Announcements of the transaction were published, and those property owners involved were invited to declare any objections to the Commissioners. The clerk drew up a report and the thing was done. Actually it usually amounted to a mere formality.

The cost for this activity under the Tweed Ring, however, would seem to indicate that an enormous amount of work went into it. What usually happened was that the surveyor reproduced a map of the street from maps made in 1811, when Manhattan island, except for a small area at its northern end, was surveyed so well that the maps were still adequate in post-Civil War New York. On the borders of the copy made by the surveyor, the clerk wrote the names of the owners of the lots on both sides of the street, copying his information from the tax books. Then the fun began. "The surveyor charges as though he had made original surveys and drawn original maps. The clerk charges as though his reports were the result of original searchers and researchers. The commissioners charge as though the opening had been the tardy fruit of actual negotiations." For the year ending in June 1866, it was estimated that the cost for "opening" twenty-five streets was $257,192.12. Of this cost, $4433 was charged for rent of an office, which ordinarily rented for $300 a year; "disbursements and postage-stamps" cost $950; and one surveyor's bill alone accounted for an astounding $54,000.

The Broadway widening "job" was a good example of the Ring in action. On May 17, 1869, the State legislature passed an act providing for the widening of Broadway between Thirty-fourth and Fifty-ninth streets, whereupon the Ring seized control of the legal machinery that decided assessments and damages to the property involved. With the friendly judge Albert Cardozo presiding, and two of the three Commissioners good Ring men, the Ring and a selected few began to buy property. Two of them paid $24,500 for a lot for which the Commissioners generously awarded them damages of $25,100. The new front was worth $10,000 more. Another lot sold for $27,500, but this payment was absorbed by a $30,355 award in damages. It was the resale value of the property, however, where the profit was made, and lots on Broadway were worth thousands. With tactics of this sort, the Ring managed to purchase some of the most valuable property in New York City.

With minor variations, the Broadway widening scheme was repeated in the Madison Avenue extension, the Church Street extension, the opening of Lexington Avenue through Stuyvesant Park, the Park Place widening, and the so-called "Fifth Avenue raid," where the Ring profited from the widening, extending, and "improvement" of that street. To one writer, who greatly exaggerated, it seemed that streets were opened "which no mortal had seen, no foot had trod; and they appeared only on the city map as spaces between imaginary lines leading from No-where to No-place." To a New York citizen in 1871 who examined the New York State *Senate Journal* of 1869, it might have seemed that the State legislature had gone No-where. On page 61 was an act entitled, "An act to afford relief against frauds and irregularities in assessments for local improvements in the city of New York."

Whether the source of graft was street openings, real estate speculation, city advertising, padded contractor's bills, juggled city records and bond issues fat with graft, a simple but imaginative profit on the City Directory, or a straightforward attack on the city treasury by supplying printing and stationery goods, the Tweed Ring explored the various paths to civic dishonesty. The roads to graft, however, were paved by the very interests the Ring exploited. The financial community, consumed in its own self-interests, stood to gain from the massive pump-priming in city improvements. The "open door" policy of state and city welfare deadened the voice of religious and philanthropic organizations; the newspapers, split by political partisanship and competitive self-interest, were softened by the morsels of political handouts; and the "people" were indifferent. The Tweed Ring thrived on the lack of civic conscience, and the result was graft.

NO

Leo Hershkowitz

TWEED'S NEW YORK: ANOTHER LOOK

MYTH

William M. Tweed, the notorious "Boss" Tweed, is one of the great myths of American history. His ugly features, small beady eyes, huge banana-like nose, vulturish expression and bloated body are the personification of big-city corruption. Thomas Nast, political propagandist and executioner of *Harper's Weekly*, has made them a triumph of the caricaturist art. Tweed's deeds, or rather misdeeds, as fashioned by historians and the like, are perhaps even better known. They have been told and retold in countless textbooks, monographs, biographies, articles, reminiscences, and have become an American epic whose proportions with each recounting become more fantastic, more shocking. Here are fables of monumental robberies of the New York City treasury, of fraud, deceit, treachery, of monstrous villainies, of carpets, furniture and of courthouses. Like fables, they are largely untrue, but like most legends, they perpetuate themselves and are renewed and enlarged with each telling.

The myth has become so much a part of history and Tweed such a convenient reference for the after-dinner speaker, pulp writer, or simply something to frighten little children with, that if there wasn't a Tweed, he would have to be invented, and he was.

Tweed is a fat, urban Jesse James without any saving graces. James is a western Robin Hood, a sort of criminal St. Francis. Tweed's patron saint is an eastern St. Tammany, refuge for the greedy, vulgar, corrupt—in short, consummate—politician. Tweed is the essence of urban rot, malodorous, the embodiment of all that is evil and cancerous in American municipal and political life. The monster lives. In a recent tax-evasion case, the prosecution charged a defendant with failure to report income allegedly obtained illegally. During the course of the trial, an enlarged Nast cartoon of "Boss Tweed" was produced to illustrate the similarity of crimes. The jury voted for conviction. Interestingly, the United States Court of Appeals reversed the verdict partly because the court felt use of the cartoon had prejudiced the jury. Eternally threatened plans to destroy the "Tweed Courthouse" (the name itself is an example of the myth) still standing behind New York's City Hall caused many New Yorkers to ask that the building be spared as a monument to graft and a reminder of the necessity of rooting out piggish politicians who take their slops at the public trough. Almost miraculously, the building, though supposedly built by corrupt politicians and contractors, is one of the finest examples of Italian Renaissance design in the country. It has not collapsed into a pile of plaster and sawdust, as critics predicted it would.

A popular cast-iron bank depicts an oily-faced tuxedoed figure, supposedly a banker, greedily swallowing the pennies of innocent children. What really "sells" the bank is calling it "Boss Tweed," even if one has nothing to do with the other. The myth is so salable and so deeply rooted that it is as American as "apple pie" or "Mother." A noted TV station produced a "documentary" on Tweed. When told that a mass of evidence exists that questions the "facts," representatives of the station offered an opinion, without pausing even to look at the material, that they wished all such records were destroyed. What price integrity as long as the legend lives, and it does so with abandon.

When political leaders think of New York, the vile image of Tweed taught them with their earliest history lessons returns to mind and appeals on behalf of the city fall on deaf ears. When Congress or the state legislature meet to debate New York's future, Tweed like some ghoulish specter rises up and beckons an end to discussion.

The myth is outrageously simple. Tweed was born in New York. Big, strong, ambitious and ruthless, he climbed out of the streets, and leaped like a snarling "Tammany Tiger" on unsuspecting citizens. Through fraud, deceit and intimidation, he was elected to various city

and state offices, and even served a term in Congress. Tweed yearned for bigger and better things. He met kindred souls whom he placed in strategic places as members of "The Ring" to pillage the city treasury, conquer the state and finally the nation. By using the simple device of padded or fictitious bills for items not delivered or not needed, millions were stolen. The county courthouse, the "Tweed Courthouse," became the symbol and center of the operation. Subservient members of "The Ring" were Peter B. ("Brains") Sweeny, city chamberlain; Richard B. ("Slippery Dick") Connolly, city comptroller; A. Oakey Hall ("The Elegant One"), mayor; and John T. ("Toots") Hoffman, mayor and governor. Hoffman would hopefully become President to serve Tweed better. An army of poor, unwashed and ignorant were also recruited. These were recent Irish and German immigrants, whose largely illegal votes were cheaply bought in return for jobs given away at City Hall or a turkey at Christmas. Judges were necessary to stay the hands of the law, so added to the conspiracy were George G. Barnard, John H. McCunn and Albert Cardozo. Misguided though willing contractors like Andrew Garvey, "Prince of Plasterers"; James H. Ingersoll, the "Chairmaker"; John Keyser, the "Plumber"; and numerous others were awarded contracts, but kicked back up to 75 per cent to Tweed and "The Ring." Tweed received the lion's or rather "Tiger's" share of perhaps 50 to 200 million dollars at a time when an average workman received two to three dollars a day.

The fable continues that this monumental looting was halted by courageous, honest men. There were Democrats like Samuel J. Tilden, who on the strength of his attacks against "The Ring" became governor and presidential candidate. Honest Republicans like George Jones, editor of the *Times*, combined to disgrace "The Ring" with the help of Nast and *Harper's Weekly*. Indictments were handed down against Tweed, who was found guilty and sentenced to the penitentiary. Finally, like most of the others of "The Ring," he fled the country. Recognized in Spain by a sailor, or someone or other who just happened to be an avid reader of *Harper's Weekly*—the myth is never clear on details—and was quite familiar with the Boss's features, he was returned to prison to die a lonely but deserved death, a lesson to evildoers.

With great delight, happy historians, political activists, popularizers, drooled over juicy tidbits like carpets and plumbing and people named Dummy and Cash, never bothering to look at dust-gathering records, or even those quite dust-free. It would seem that research would interfere with exorcising the devil or prevent the development of some interesting theories. One theory concerned the failure of adequate communication in an evolving, increasingly complicated metropolis. It was a lack of such communication as seen in a decentralized and chaotic government which explains the emergence of Tweed and the "Big Pay-off." Others see Tweed emerging from the schismatic web of Tammany politics to seize and consolidate power by "pulling wires," hiring professional toughs and modernizing control within Tammany.

Lord James Bryce, a hostile critic of American urban government, in his classic *American Commonwealth* found Tweed the end product of "rancid dangerous Democracy." The scornful Englishman felt that "The time was ripe, for the lowest class of voters, foreign and native, had now been thoroughly organized and knew themselves able to control the city."

This voting mob was ready to follow Tammany Hall, which he concluded "had become the Acropolis of the city; and he who could capture it might rule as tyrant." Bryce found Tweed's unscrupulousness matched by the crafty talents of others, creating a perfect blend of flagrant corruption. But the essential ingredient was democracy and failure to follow traditional leadership. It was such democracy which allowed a Falstaff-like Tweed to emerge as a hero; a "Portuguese Jew" like Albert Cardozo who was born in New York to "prostitute" his legal talents for party purposes; or a Fernando Wood, Tweed's predecessor in Tammany, to become a major figure from such small beginnings that he was "reported to have entered New York as the leg of an artificial elephant in a travelling show." Bryce thus denounced Tweed and a form of government that had little if any respect for birth or breeding, but rewarded the mean, the base-born for their audacity and treachery.

It all sounds so plausible, but does it help Tweed emerge from behind Thomas Nast's leering cartoons? The problem with Tweed and the myth is that it is all so much vapor and so little substance, and what has been written has not dispelled shadows; only deepened them. So little has been done to obtain even basic information about the man, and what is known is generally wrong. Perhaps never has so much nonsense been written about an individual.

A few questions to start. Was it possible for one man or even a group of men to plan such a vast swindle involving hundreds if not thousands of officials, clerks, laborers, contractors, and hope to succeed? If Tweed plotted such an operation which supposedly involved bribing the state legislature, coercing judges, muzzling the press, aborting the gossip of bank officers and city auditors, he must have been a genius, a Houdini, Machiavelli, Napoleon rolled into one. Such a mind surely would have withstood the trivial intrusion of a hundred brash reformers. Yet he was shaken from his lofty perch, tumbled into prison and hounded to death. All this was done without organized resistance and in literally the twinkling of an eye. Tweed had such "power" that he was thrown out of his party without a word spoken in his behalf, even before he was found guilty of anything. There was, except for counsel, no one to defend him, no congressman, senator, assemblyman, no one in authority. "The Ring" was so strongly forged that it shattered at the slightest pressure, its component parts flying about with no other thought than every man for himself. If "The Ring" was supposed to be a strong political or financial alliance well led and directed, then it like "Boss" Tweed was simply a figment of historical imagination, a pretty bit of caricature.

At no time did such a "Ring" dominate New York City politics, let alone the state or national scene. Supposed "Ring" members rarely had much to do with one another, socially or otherwise. Sweeny was a friend of Victor Hugo's, Hall aspired to make a mark in the theater, Tweed aspired to office, Connolly had Connolly. There was little to bind the so-called "Ring." Except by an accident of history that they served in various city posts at the same time, there is little to relate one with the other.

Even the dreaded "Tammany Tiger" was a paper one. Certainly in Tweed's day Tammany did not dominate New York politics. Perhaps it never did. The city was and is a complex, competitive system of diverse interest. It was then and is now too heterogeneous, too much made up of various groups, classes, outlooks, beliefs for any part or let alone one person to control. New Yorkers' cosmopolitanism and tolerance have a tragic price.

The city cannot send representatives to Washington or to Albany who can express the single-minded view of smaller, simpler communities. Its large immigrant population creates suspicion: is New York an American city? A rural backwater has more political clout than all of the city when it comes to power on national or state levels.

Partly this is in consequence of an age-old struggle between the city and the farm, and eternal tug of war between the city in its search for greater self-government and rural conservative interests who find New York a threat to themselves and their entrenched power. There were some deeply rooted animosities. Cities are not natural. God made the earth, trees, animals and man. Cities are man-made. Natural things are pure, innocent and obedient to order, while man is sinful, evil, disobedient, whose works like cities are suspect. There may be a Garden of Eden, but there is no City of Eden, only Sodom and Gomorrah. This kind of morality underlines economic and political selection. It is served by the Tweed myth, since the horrors of municipal corruption and Tammany bossism plainly demonstrate the impossibility of the city even governing itself. It is in a deeper sense an implied failure of man governing himself apart from some external power. As New York cannot be given greater home rule, it must even be more closely regulated and watched by the state; so too man must observe a higher authority.

To make matters worse, New York also destroys its political talent, its best lost in the heat of murderous combat. It was a rare aspirant indeed who could emerge from his trials to become a national figure of any permanence. Alexander Hamilton and Aaron Burr were testimony to this. De Witt Clinton and Edward Livingston were further examples of early casualties. By mid-nineteenth century, no New York City politician had any voice in national or state affairs. Fernando Wood, potentially a great politician and a champion of the city's interest against the state rural lobby, was destroyed by bitter intra-party fighting. William Tweed might have provided the city with a voice and he too was destroyed, but in such a way that the city too suffered in countless ways—not the least of which forever identified the metropolis as a spawning ground for corruption and filth. Why then pay it any attention? Why spend money on the sewers? Tweed was and is a convenient stick with which to beat the city over the head, preferably at regular intervals. In many ways, the tragedy of New York is that Tweed did not succeed, that a strong unified political force was not created, that the paper tiger was not real.

As for Tweed, there remain the stories. There is no evidence that he created the "Tammany Tiger" or ordered it to be used as his personal symbol. The clawing, snarling, toothed tiger was Nast's idea, part of the image he wished to create. It was plastered on Tweed and Tammany and sold. What politician would use such a symbol to win votes or influence people, except a madman or a cartoonist like Nast?

One of the universally accepted myths is that of Tweed's reactions to the July 1871 disclosures exposing "The Ring." He is supposed to have snarled like his tiger to a group of cowering reporters, reformers and the public at large, "What are you going to do about it?" Again, what politician, especially in this country, would make such an asinine statement, no matter how sure he was of his position? It was certainly not Tweed's style, and if he made "The Ring," he was not that stupid. In truth, the phrase was never used by Tweed, but invented by Nast as a caption for a June 10, 1871, cartoon a month before Tweed and "The Ring" made headlines. Reporters asked Tweed that question after the deluge and his troubles with the law. It was never Tweed's question. It was all "Boss," all Nast and all nonsense.

Tweed was no saint, but he was not the Nast creature. He was more a victim than a scoundrel or thief. Characteristically, Tweed was intensely loyal, warmhearted, outgoing, given to aiding the underdog and the underprivileged. But he was also gullible, naïve and easily fooled. If he were a real "boss," he should have been able, like Sweeny and others, to avoid inundating calamity. He was a good family man, and there simply is no scandal to report so far as his personal habits are concerned. Even his bitterest enemies could find nothing. He was not an intellectual, he was not at home with a Sweeny or an Oakey Hall, but found a close friendship with Jubilee Jim Fisk, the brilliant short-lived Roman candle and bon vivant.

Why then Tweed? First, he was what he was. In his prime, he reportedly weighed close to three hundred pounds. A "slim" Tweed would not be as inviting a target. Point one, for dieters. His features could

NO Leo Hershkowitz / 111

be easily exaggerated by someone like Nast, and he was enough in the public eye for the *Times* and *Harper's*. He was ambitious, but not ruthless. He had money, but not enough to throw a scare into or buy off his opponents. He had power, but not enough to withstand attacks by newspapers, law, rivals and supposed friends.

Further, and much more importantly, he represented the interests of New York. He had established legislative programs which opened schools, hospitals, museums, programs tailored to meet the needs of a rapidly expanding constituency. His identification with the interests of the city was enough for the traditional rural-suburban leadership to seek his destruction. He provided a means for Republicans from President U.S. Grant on down to those in the local level to make people forget the corruptions in Republican circles, like the Whisky Ring, Indian Ring or Crédit Mobilier—all schemes to defraud millions from the government—but see instead the balloon-like figure of Tweed, Tammany and the defeat of Democratic opposition. National Democrats like Horatio Seymour and the inept "Sammy" Tilden could point to Tweed and gain cheers and votes for their efforts to "delouse" the party. If there ever was a scapegoat, its name was Tweed.

The Tweed story does not need exaggeration, lies, half-truths, rumors to make it interesting. It is in itself an incredible story. Debunking the myth is part of it, but there is much more. There are bigots like Nast, George T. Strong and others who saw in Tweed an outsider threatening their position by his supposedly championing the "drunken-ignorant Irish," the overly ambitious German-Jewish immigrants and those seeking to change the status quo. That

he sought to provide answers to the increasing complications of urban life did not help. Tweed never traveled in upper-class society. With all his apparent success, he was never able to wash away the tarnish of the Lower East Side. Moreover, there are some of the most incredible trials and abuses of the judicial process on record. There are hand-picked judges and juries, not as might be expected by Tweed, but by the prosecution. The misuse of grand jury indictments should become legendary.

Tweed was never tried for or found guilty of graft or theft, the crime Tweed stands accused of by history. He was convicted after some strange, improper, even illegal judicial proceedings, which were in many ways worse than anything Tweed supposedly committed, of a misdemeanor—failing to audit claims against the city. Hall was tried three times on the same charge and was not convicted. Connolly and Sweeny were never tried.

Tweed died in prison after having spent some four years there, and he would have remained longer but for his death—only one of these years was he in a penitentiary, on the misdemeanor conviction. The remaining years he spent in the county jail because he could not raise an exorbitant bail in a civil suit. The manipulation of the law by those sworn to uphold the law was a real crime. Then add the threatening, tampering with, and intimidation of witnesses, as well as the use of informers and agent provocateurs. Under these conditions, Snow White would have been hanged for loitering to commit prostitution.

The threat to individual liberty by an unbridled omnipresent legal system is rarely as clear as in the Tweed case. The innocent and guilty are too often given the same even-handed justice.

Couple this with yellow journalism and abuse of power by the press and Nast. Horace Greeley in his bid for the presidency in 1871 complained that he did not know whether he was running for that office or the penitentiary. Tweed was as much a victim of irresponsible journalism. Tweed, too, was "hot copy." He was also tried and convicted by newspapers in a too often repeated process in which rabid reporters and editors became judge and jury and headlines substitute for trial and district attorneys, while editors scratch each other's backs for the sake of publicity—where an indictment is often all that is necessary to make a point, sell papers and win votes....

EPILOGUE

And so Tweed passed into history to become the fabled legend. It was an undeserved fate. Except for Tweed's own very questionable "confession," there was really no evidence of a "Tweed Ring," no direct evidence of Tweed's thievery, no evidence, excepting the testimony of the informer contractors, of "wholesale" plunder by Tweed. What preceded is a story of political profiteering at the expense of Tweed, of vaulting personal ambitions fed on Tweed's carcass, of a conspiracy of self-justification of the corruption of law by the upholders of that law, of a venal irresponsible press and a citizenry delighting in the exorcism of witchery. If Tweed was involved then all those about him were equally guilty. He was never tried for theft. The only criminal trial that was held was for a misdemeanor of failing to audit, and this trial was held before a hand-picked judge and

jury at a time when Tweed-hunting was at its height.

Probably the "truth" about Tweed, "The Ring" and the "stolen" millions will never be known. It is possible to measure the difference between graft and profit? If Keyser charged so much for plastering, perhaps another could do the work for less, but would it be the same work, could it be done on time? How do you compare the cost of one carpet with that of another? Price is only one consideration. At one point, a decision has to be reached on any contract, no matter who is selected; there will always be someone who could have done it cheaper. Surely there were overcharges, but by how much? The throwing about of figures, 10, 30, 50, 200 million, is of no help. Is it possible to decide at what point profit becomes graft? It is difficult to answer these questions or work out an almost insoluble puzzle. In the end, the easiest solution is of course to blame Tweed, rather than examine financial records, vouchers, warrants. These were allowed to lie dormant silently collecting the dust of a century, in the end hopefully to disappear. How much easier to nail the "Elephant" to a wall or listen to the romanticism of history and the excesses of rhetoric created by Godkin, Bryce, Wingate, Lynch and so many others.

Tweed emerges as anything but a master thief. It was the contractors who willingly padded bills, never calling attention to any undue pressure upon them to do so; it was those lower-echelon agents in the city, especially Woodward and Watson, who were in direct liaison with the contractors, not Tweed. And lastly blame should be placed on the city and state. The former because it did not regulate expenditures properly and failed to pay its bills on time, a point brought up time and again by the contractors, and the latter because it interfered in city business; the city's welfare was subverted by state political interests. The Tweed story, or better the contractors' story, is about as good a reason for New York City home rule as can be offered.

Where did the legendary millions go? None of the contractors, with the possible exception of Garvey, had sizable sums of money, and even he wasn't to be compared to the "robber barons" like Morgan or Whitney or Rockefeller. These could sneeze out in a moment what purported to be the total Tweed plunder. What of Hall, Connolly, Sweeny, Hoffman? There is nothing to show they received any princely sums. No one connected with the so-called "Ring" set up a dynasty or retired to luxurious seclusion. Certainly not Tweed. If money was stolen, it held a Pharaoh's curse. Those who touched it did not enjoy it. So many died suddenly, so many died in dishonor and loneliness. None suffered as much as did William Magear Tweed and the City of New York.

Tweed spent some twenty years in public service. In the Fire Department, as alderman, member of the Board of Supervisors and Board of Education, member of Congress, state senator, commissioner of public works—it was a long list and resulted in a great deal of public good. He was instrumental in modernizing governmental and educational institutions, in developing needed reforms in public welfare programs, in incorporating schools, hospitals, establishing public baths, in preserving a site in Central Park for the Metropolitan Museum of Art, in widening Broadway, extending Prospect Park and removing fences from around public parks, establishing

Riverside Park and Drive, annexing the Bronx as a forerunner of the incorporation of Greater New York, in building the Brooklyn Bridge, in founding the Lenox Library. He was of considerable service during the Civil War. Tweed moved the city forward in so many ways and could have been, if he had not been destroyed, a progressive force in shaping the interests and destiny of a great city and its people.

Tweed's concepts about urbanization and accommodation while not philosophically formalized were years beyond their time. Twenty or thirty years later such programs were adopted by reformers and urban planners. Tweed was a pioneer spokesman for an emerging New York, one of the few that spoke for its interests, one of the very few that could have had his voice heard in Albany. Tweed grew with the city, his death was a tragedy for the future metropolis.

His life in the end was wasted, not so much by what he did, but by what was done to him, his work and the city being relegated to the garbage heap, both branded by the same indelible iron. He became a club with which to beat New York, really the ultimate goal of the blessed reformers.

It is time to seek a re-evaluation of Tweed and his time. If Tweed was not so bad, neither was the city. Old legends die hard, old ideas have deep roots, but hopefully some of the old legends will die and the deep roots wither away.

What was learned from the episode? Practically nothing. Politics, politicians, jurists and venal journalists certainly continued to ply their trade, spurred by their success, as in the past, with hardly a glance or hesitation, comforted in the downfall of the "Boss." The devil had been killed; would anyone bother to look at the judges or ask anyone else to do the Lord's work? Every once in a while, a bill is introduced in the Massachusetts legislature to have the Salem witches exonerated and declared non-witches. Some are. It might be time to have the New York state legislature and history provide a similar service for Tweed. Surely, there are other devils around to take his place. And a statue for Tweed? Yes, it would be his city alive and well.

POSTSCRIPT

Did William M. Tweed Corrupt Post–Civil War New York?

The opposing viewpoints of Callow and Hershkowitz regarding "Boss" Tweed's place in history is representative of a long-standing scholarly debate about the consequences of machine politics in the United States. James Bryce, *The American Commonwealth*, 2 vols. (Macmillan, 1888); Moisei Ostrogorski, *Democracy and the Organization of Political Parties* (1902; reprint, Anchor Books, 1964); and Ernest S. Griffith, *A History of American City Government: The Conspicuous Failure, 1870–1900* (National Civic League Press, 1974) present a litany of misdeeds associated with those who controlled municipal government.

Efforts to rehabilitate the sullied reputations of the machine politicians can be dated to the comments of Tammany Hall ward healer George Washington Plunkitt, whose turn-of-the-century observations included a subtle distinction between "honest" and "dishonest" graft.

There are several excellent urban history texts that devote space to the development of municipal government, including discussions of political machines, in the nineteenth century. Among these are David R. Goldfield and Blaine A. Brownell, *Urban America: From Downtown to No Town* (Houghton Mifflin, 1979); Howard P. Chudacoff and Judith E. Smith, *The Evolution of American Urban Society*, 3d ed. (Prentice Hall, 1981); and Charles N. Glaab and A. Theodore Brown, *A History of Urban America*, 3d ed. (Macmillan, 1983). Explorations of the life and work of other political bosses in this period include James A. Kehl, *Boss Rule in the Gilded Age: Matt Quay of Pennsylvania* (University of Pittsburgh Press, 1981); William A. Bullough, *The Blind Boss and His City: Christopher Augustine Buckley and Nineteenth-Century San Francisco* (University of California Press, 1979); and Zane L. Miller, *Boss Cox's Cincinnati: Urban Politics in the Progressive Era* (Oxford University Press, 1968). Scott Greer, ed., *Ethnics, Machines, and the American Future* (Harvard University Press, 1981) and Bruce M. Stave and Sondra Astor Stave, eds., *Urban Bosses, Machines, and Progressive Reformers*, 2d ed. (D. C. Heath, 1984) are excellent collections of essays on urban political machinery. Significant contributions to urban historiography in the late nineteenth century are Stephan Thernstrom, *Poverty and Progress: Social Mobility in the Nineteenth-Century City* (Harvard University Press, 1964) and Gunther Barth, *City People: The Rise of Modern City Culture in Nineteenth-Century America* (Oxford University Press, 1980).

On the Internet . . .

http://www.dushkin.com

The Spanish-American War

This site from the Hispanic Division of the Library of Congress details events leading up to and occurring during the Spanish-American War. Included are links to pages on many of the key players, with a particular emphasis on Cuban patriots.
http://lcweb.loc.gov/rr/hispanic/1898/trask.html

African American History

This site is part of a larger project by the Department of History at the University of California, Riverside. This page contains links to African American history resources on the World Wide Web.
http://www.ucr.edu/h-gig/horuslinks.html

PART 2

The Response to Industrialism: Reform and War

The maturing of the industrial system, a major economic depression, agrarian unrest, and labor violence all came to a head in 1898 with the Spanish-American war. The victory gave overseas territorial possessions to the United States and served notice to the world that the United States was a "great power."

At the end of the nineteenth century, the African American population began fighting for civil rights, political power, and integration into society. Spokespeople for the blacks, such as Booker T. Washington, began to emerge, but their often unclear agendas frequently touched off controversy among both black people and white people.

At the turn of the century, reformers known as the Progressives attempted to ameliorate the worst abuses brought about in the factories and slums of America's cities. Although many of these reformers tried to impose their old-fashioned, Protestant values on the immigrants, they did manage to clean up the city streets, obtain clean drinking water, and build sewers. They also improved housing and factory structures. However, it is argued that the most serious problems of inequality were never addressed by the Progressives.

■ Did Yellow Journalism Cause the Spanish-American War?

■ Did Booker T. Washington's Philosophy and Actions Betray the Interests of African Americans?

■ Did the Progressives Fail?

ISSUE 6

Did Yellow Journalism Cause the Spanish-American War?

YES: W. A. Swanberg, from *Citizen Hearst: A Biography of William Randolph Hearst* (Charles Scribner's Sons, 1961)

NO: Richard Hofstadter, from *The Paranoid Style in American Politics and Other Essays* (Alfred A. Knopf, 1965)

ISSUE SUMMARY

YES: Journalist W. A. Swanberg argues that newspaper mogul William Randolph Hearst used the sensational and exploitative stories in his widely circulated *New York Journal* to stir up public opinion and to force President William McKinley to wage a war against Spain to free Cuba.

NO: Historian Richard Hofstadter maintains that the Spanish-American War was fought as an idealistic humanitarian crusade to liberate Cuba and that it served as an outlet for Americans' aggressive impulses caused by the "psychic crisis" of a changing America in the 1890s.

Although Spanish rule over Cuba dated from 1511, most American presidents from the 1840s through the 1890s assumed that Cuba's strategic location, 90 miles from Florida, made it inevitable that the island would eventually come under some form of American control. American politicians were convinced that Spain was a declining power with limited influence in the Americas. However, repeated attempts to buy the island from Spain failed. Meanwhile, Cuban insurgents unsuccessfully rebelled against the Spanish government from 1868 until 1878. In 1894, in the midst of a depression, the U.S. Congress imposed a tariff on Cuban sugar, which had been entering the United States duty-free. An economic depression also hit the island and encouraged another rebellion against Spanish rule. The Spanish government retaliated by imposing a policy of "reconcentration." Approximately 300,000 Cubans were rounded up into fortified towns and camps to separate the insurgents from their supporters. As the atrocities were played up by sensationalist American newspapers, a new Spanish government came to power in Madrid that modified "reconcentration" and promised Cuba some autonomy.

Three events in the first few months of 1898 sabotaged a peaceful resolution of the Cuban crisis. On February 9 the *New York Journal* published a stolen private letter from Enrique Dupuy de Lome, the Spanish minister in Washington, which cast doubt on the sincerity with which the Spanish government was pursuing a policy of autonomy for Cuba. Even worse, de Lome stated, "McKinley is weak and a bidder for the admiration of the crowd, besides being a would be politician who tries to leave a door open behind himself while keeping on good terms with the jingos of his party."

The second event stirred up public opinion even more than the de Lome letter. Early in January antireform, pro-Spanish loyalists rioted in Havana. In response, President William McKinley ordered the battleship U.S.S. *Maine* to Havana's harbor to protect the lives of American citizens. On February 15 the *Maine* blew up, killing 260 American service personnel. Two separate investigations were made. The Spanish government said that the explosion was caused by internal failures, while the U.S. panel reported that a mine destroyed the *Maine*.

The third factor that pushed McKinley in the direction of a confrontation with Spain were the reports—official and unofficial—that the president received from public officials. In June 1897 William J. Calhoun, a political friend of the president, reported that the principal cause of the war "can be found in the economic conditions that have prevailed there for many years past." Calhoun's picture of the countryside outside of the military posts was particularly gloomy. Events moved rapidly in spring 1898. There were failed attempts at negotiating an end to "reconcentration," establishing an armistice in the Spanish-Cuban war, and setting up a truly autonomous government with a Cuban relationship to Spain similar to that of Canada's to Great Britain.

Why did President McKinley intervene in Cuba? In his address to Congress on April 11, 1898, the president listed four reasons: (1) "To put an end to the barbarities, bloodshed, starvation, and miseries now existing there"; (2) "to afford our citizens in Cuba protection and indemnity for life and property"; (3) to avoid "very serious injury to the commerce, trade, and business of our people, and by the wanton destruction of property and devastation of the island"; and (4) "the present condition of affairs in Cuba is a constant menace to our peace... where our traditional vessels are liable to seizure and are seized at our very door by war ships of a foreign nation, the expenditures of filibustering and the irritating questions and entanglements thus arising."

Implied in the president's message was the goal of independence for Cuba. Congress supported McKinley's request for intervention with a joint resolution that contained one exception: Senator Henry M. Teller of Colorado added an amendment that forbade the United States from annexing Cuba.

Historians continue to debate the reasons for the war. In the following selection, W. A. Swanberg argues that the war was started by propaganda created by the new yellow journalism of newspaper mogul William Randolph Hearst. In the second selection, Richard Hofstadter argues that a convergence of a number of highly charged events in the 1890s created a "psychic crisis" that resulted in a war being fought for humanitarian reasons.

YES

W. A. Swanberg

CITIZEN HEARST

THE CUBAN JOAN OF ARC

The Power of the Press

The two loudest warmongers in the United States, [William Randolph] Hearst and [Joseph] Pulitzer, were both six feet two inches tall, both millionaires who spent money royally while they espoused the causes of the masses. Both were singularly shy. The similarity ended there. Hearst was in a perfect health, placid and courteous. Pulitzer was blind, a nervous wreck who could fly into profane rages. Hearst was at his office daily, exercising personal control. Pulitzer was rarely at his proud, gold-domed skyscraper. He was only occasionally at his New York home on East Fifty-fifth Street, which was equipped with soundproof rooms to shield his quaking nerves. The rest of the time he was either at one of his four other mansions in Maine, New Jersey, Georgia and France, or aboard his palatial ocean-going yacht *Liberty*, keeping in touch with his editors by telegram or cable. Hearst believed in fighting Spain almost from the start of the Cuban trouble. Pulitzer, at first opposed to United States involvement, came around reluctantly for war, as he later candidly admitted, because it meant circulation.

It is safe to say that had not Pulitzer been locked in a bitter circulation struggle with Hearst, and had he not witnessed the added circulation Hearst's frenetic treatment of the Cuban news brought him, Pulitzer and his mighty *World* would have remained on the side of peace. Thus Hearst, in addition to his own potent newspapers, was responsible for dragging the morning and evening *World*, with the largest circulation in the nation, into the pro-war camp.

These two men addressed literally millions of Americans. In 1897, the circulation of Pulitzer's two papers was more than 800,000 daily. Hearst's morning and evening *Journal* were hardly 100,000 behind, and his San Francisco *Examiner* had 80,000. They had on their pro-war side the influential New York *Sun*, with about 150,000. Through the Associated Press and other news-service affiliations, the *Journal*, *World* and *Sun* dispatches were reprinted in many other important papers across the nation.

From W. A. Swanberg, *Citizen Hearst: A Biography of William Randolph Hearst* (Charles Scribner's Sons, 1961). Copyright © 1961 by W. A. Swanberg. Reprinted by permission of Scribner, a division of Simon & Schuster. Notes omitted.

Against them they had the strongly anti-war *Herald* (100,000), the *Evening Post* (25,000), the conservative *Tribune* (75,000) and the high-priced *Times* (three cents, under 25,000 circulation). The remaining several New York papers were even smaller, had no funds for coverage of the Cuban rebellion, and exercised small weight.

The total circulation of New York's pro-war newspapers was about 1,560,000, against the anti-war total of 225,000.

However, all of these papers were of much more than local moment. The prestige of the large New York dailies on either side was a strong and determining influence on hundreds of fresh-water editors throughout the country who knew little of foreign affairs and traditionally had looked to the New York journals for guidance since the days of [Horace] Greeley, [James Gordon] Bennett and [Henry Jarvis] Raymond. Since the newspapers were the greatest mass medium then existing, their influence in shaping public opinion would be decisive. And since the New York newspapers in one way or another swayed most of the rest, it could be said that—given a situation where war or peace hung in almost equal balance—the clacking Underwoods and Remingtons in the grubby warrens around Printing House Square would decide whether it would be the olive branch or the sword.

No one could discount the national influence of the anti-war *Herald, Post, Tribune* and *Times.* Yet the plain fact was that their relatively quiet, sensible columns were dull newswise. They were like reasonable men speaking in normal tones. Naturally they were outshouted by the screams of the *Journal* and *World.* The majority of the public found it more exciting to read about the murder of Cuban babies and the rape of Cuban women by the Spaniards than to read conscientious accounts of complicated political problems and injustices on both sides. The hero-villain concept of the war was simple, easy to grasp and satisfying. In addition to having the loudest voices and the most money, Hearst and Pulitzer had the best writers and illustrators and had many more dispatch boats, jeweled swords and correspondents in Key West and Cuba than all the other papers combined. Hearst alone sent a total of at least thirty-five writers and artists to "cover the war" at various times....

THE FATE OF THE *MAINE*

Hail Thee City Born Today!
... Like Caesar and Napoleon, Hearst enjoyed power. He derived pleasure from controlling masses of people, manipulating them to bring about events of national or international importance. Unlike Caesar and Napoleon, the bashful Hearst did his manipulating from behind the scenes with the aid of cylinder presses and tons of newsprint. By now, most other newspaper proprietors in New York regarded him with aversion as a man who would do anything for sensation, devoid of honesty or principle, a Polyphemus of propaganda who ate his enemies and kept his Cyclops eye on circulation. They misjudged the man by his methods. An incurable romantic, swayed by gusts of sentiment, Hearst was sincerely devoted to the Cuban cause and at the same time felt that American interests demanded the expulsion of Spain from the hemisphere. But he had no scruples against linking these defensible aims with a ruthless and vulgar drive for circulation, so that in the view

of people of taste he had no unselfish impulses at all.

Considerations of taste in journalism did not disturb him. He had long since decided that the great majority of people, the masses, had no time or training for such a luxury as taste and could be reached and molded most effectively by the noise, sensation and repetition which he liked himself. Since these are the ingredients of modern mass advertising, Hearst deserves some dubious recognition as a pioneer.

His megalomania had grown. In San Francisco, his campaigns had been largely local, even his feud with the S.P. being inspired by local grievances. In New York he had started with local sensations—murders, public utility franchises, soup kitchens, bicycle carnivals. Now he was expanding his zone of operations into the nation and the world. His enemies were McKinley, Hanna, Weyler, Spain, France. The liberation of Miss Cisneros had been so successful that Hearst now had Karl Decker mapping an expedition to Devil's Island to free the wronged Captain Dreyfus and humiliate France as Spain had been humiliated.

In Spain, the American newspaper outcry, the continuation of the Cuban rebellion and the uprising in the Philippines caused the fall of the government and the formation of a new cabinet. Spain, with only some 18,000,000 people, grievously in debt, naturally feared the rich United States with its 75,000,000. In its anxiety to retain Cuba, its most treasured possession, it pocketed American insults and took steps to mollify the Yankees as well as the Cuban rebels. The new government under Práxedes Mateo Sagasta almost entirely accepted the United States position on Cuba. It promised the Cubans self-government under Spain. It dismissed

General Weyler, who left Havana to the accompaniment of a valedictory in Hearst's *Journal* calling him "the monster of the century" who should be hanged for his "innumerable murders." It replaced him with General Ramón Blanco y Erenas, a kindly man not yet known as a murderer. It would be General Blanco's job to install the autonomous Cuban government and restore order.

But Hearst demanded independence for Cuba, not mere autonomy. He wrote a letter dated December 1, 1897, addressed to the unrecognized president of an unrecognized republic.

His Excellency Bartolomé Masso,

President of the Republic of Cuba:

Sir:—Will you kindly state through the New York *Journal,* acting for the people of the United States, the position of the Cuban Government on the offer of autonomy for the island by the Government of Spain?....

—Yours truly, W. R. Hearst.

Although some would dispute Hearst's right to act for "the people of the United States," Señor Masso did not. Apparently the letter was smuggled through to Masso, who eventually replied from Camaguey in part:

... We hold ourselves an independent nation, unrecognized though we may be by the civilized world. Autonomy is not for one moment considered by us. We absolutely reject it.

We have no faith left in Spain or her promises....

Along with Hearst, the insurgents with one voice rejected autonomy. Estrada Palma branded the conciliatory measures as ruses to defeat the rebellion by typical Spanish treachery. Rebel army leaders warned that all Cubans who cooperated with the new Spanish schemes would be considered "traitors to the republic," meaning that they would be shot on sight. The militarily feeble rebels could not have taken this intransigent stand had they not seen how American public opinion had already forced the Spaniards to back down. Counting on further American support to drive the Spaniards out entirely, they continued their pillaging of plantations and villages.

The *Journal* agreed that the Cubans "would be fools if they trust Spanish promises," and boasted that "Spain fears the *Journal* and Karl Decker." Not surprisingly, attempts were made to dynamite the *Journal*'s Havana office. But President McKinley, impressed by the conciliatory efforts of the Sagasta government, was disposed to give it every opportunity for success. When Spain agreed to permit American contributions of food and clothing to be distributed to destitute Cubans by the Red Cross, and the relief work got under way, the outlook for peace on the troubled island seemed improved at last....

In Cuba, Consul General Lee kept hearing rumors of an "anti-American plot" in Matanzas. Although this never materialized, he urged protection for American nationals and property in Cuba. It was on Lee's recommendation that the twenty-four-gun battleship *Maine* was moved first to Key West, then to Havana, as a "friendly act of courtesy" to Spain. Spain, not deceived by the polite words, readied its armored cruiser *Vizcaya* to pay a "friendly visit" to New York.

The *Maine*, commanded by solemn, bespectacled Captain Charles D. Sigsbee, passed under the guns of Morro Castle and anchored in Havana harbor on January 25, 1898. The Spanish commander sent a case of fine sherry to Sigsbee and his officers, who later went ashore to dine with General Lee and enjoy a bullfight.

Hearst had hardly been aware of the *Maine* when she was launched in San Francisco in 1890, but now she loomed large. "OUR FLAG IN HAVANA AT LAST," headlined the *Journal,* urging that American vessels occupy all Cuban ports and demand the withdrawal of the Spanish troops, i.e., to make war. Although Captain Sigsbee and his men were enjoying a quiet sojourn in Havana, the *Journal* saw so many war clouds there that it momentarily forgot its *bête noire,* the Spanish minister in Washington, Dupuy de Lome. De Lome, who for three years had conducted himself with dignity in the capital despite painful provocation, chose this moment to commit an error. He wrote a letter critical of President McKinley to a friend in Havana, José Canalejas. A rebel sympathizer, Gustavo Escoto, who worked in Canalejas' office, read the letter, saw its propaganda possibilities, and stole it, boarding the next boat for New York.

The letter brought joy to Estrada Palma and the Peanut Club. Palma was so grateful to the *Journal* for its efforts for Cuba that he translated the letter and took it in person to the *Journal* office, handing it in triumph to Sam Chamberlain. In commenting on McKinley's pacific message to Congress, De Lome wrote:

> The message has undeceived the insurgents, who expected something else, and has paralyzed the action of Congress, but I consider it bad.... Besides the natural and inevitable coarseness with which he [McKinley] repeats all that the press and public opinion of Spain have said of Weyler, it shows once more what McKinley is: weak and catering to the rabble and, besides, a low politician who de-

sires to leave the door open to himself and to stand well with the jingoes of his party....

Although this was a private letter, stolen, and although the *Journal* had leveled far worse insults of its own about McKinley multiplied by some 800,000 circulation, it flew into a front-page rage at De Lome that lasted for five days. The letter was too provocative for the Peanut Club to give it exclusively to the *Journal*. It gave it to all the newspapers, handing the *Journal* a beat, however, in giving it exclusive right to publish a facsimile. The *Journal* used *all of its front page* to publicize the letter, headlining it "THE WORST INSULT TO THE UNITED STATES IN ITS HISTORY" and demanding the minister's instant dismissal. It dredged up a book which De Lome had published twenty-two years earlier, stressing critical remarks he had made about American women. It perpetrated an enormity in doggerel:

Dupuy de Lome, Dupuy de Lome, what's this I hear of you?

Have you been throwing mud again, is what they're saying true?

Get out, I say, get out before I start to fight.

Just pack your few possessions and take a boat for home.

I would not like my boot to use but— oh—get out, De Lome.

It ran a huge Davenport cartoon showing an angry Uncle Sam thumbing away a quaking De Lome, with a one-word caption, "Git." "Now let us have action immediate and decisive," it said. "The flag of Cuba Libre ought to float over Morro Castle within a week." All this went out over the Associated Press.

In Washington, De Lome instantly cabled his resignation to Madrid. This took the sting out of the State Department's demand for his dismissal, for he was already packing. The Spanish government promptly disavowed his letter and apologized for it. In a few days, United States officials realized that what the *Journal* and a few other New York newspapers chose to construe as a gross affront was nothing more than a comic diplomatic blunder. In Cuba, the new autonomous government was beginning to function. The outlook was promising. The De Lome incident would have been forgotten had it not been followed almost immediately by an event of violence and tragedy that still poses one of history's impenetrable mysteries.

The *Maine* had now been in Havana for three weeks. Its usefulness there was questionable, since there were no anti-American demonstrations. Navy Secretary John D. Long had contemplated recalling it early in February, only to desist because of Consul General Lee's advice that it stay. On the sultry night of February 15, as the clear bugle notes of "Taps" pealed across the quiet harbor, Captain Sigsbee was in his cabin writing a letter in some embarrassment to his wife. He explained that in a uniform pocket he had discovered a letter to her from an old friend which he had forgotten for ten months. He had just sealed the envelope at 9:40 when the *Maine* blew up all around him.

Though shaken, Sigsbee was unhurt. The vessel's lights blacked out. Screams came from wounded and dying men. Fire broke out forward, causing small-caliber ammunition to start popping like firecrackers. Survivors jumped into the water as the ship began settling slowly into the mud. Dazed bluejackets put out a boat to pick up the swimmers. Other boats came from the Spanish cruiser *Alfonso XII* and an American vessel nearby. Spaniards and Americans joined gallantly in the dangerous rescue work as ammunition continued to explode. At his palace, Spain's General Blanco burst into tears at the news and sent officers to express regret and organize assistance. Of the *Maine's* 350 officers and men, 260 died in the catastrophe. Sigsbee dispatched a telegram to "Secnav" in Washington, describing it and adding:

> Public opinion should be suspended until further report.... Many Spanish officers including representatives of General Blanco now with me to express sympathy.

Hearst had left the *Journal* earlier than usual that evening, probably to go to the theater. He returned to his apartment in the Worth House quite late without stopping at his office. He found his man Thompson waiting for him.

"There's a telephone from the office," Thompson said. "They say it's important news."

Hearst telephoned the *Journal*. "Hello," he said. "What is the important news?"

"The battleship *Maine* has been blown up in Havana Harbor," the editor replied.

"Good heavens, what have you done with the story?"

"We have put it on the first page, of course."

"Have you put anything else on the front page?"

"Only the other big news," said the editor.

"There is not any other big news," Hearst said. "Please spread the story all over the page. This means war."

There Is No Other News

Hearst's coverage of the *Maine* disaster still stands as the orgasmic acme of ruthless, truthless newspaper jingoism. As always, when he wanted anything he wanted it with passionate intensity. The *Maine* represented the fulfillment not of one want but two—war with Spain and more circulation to beat Pulitzer. He fought for these ends with such abandonment of honesty and incitement of hatred that the stigma of it never quite left him even though he still had fifty-three years to live.

Intelligent Americans realized the preposterousness of the idea that Spain had blown up the *Maine*. Proud Spain had swallowed insult to avoid a war she knew she would lose. Her forbearance had borne fruit until the explosion in Havana caused journalistic insanity in New York. The disaster was the worst blow Spain could have suffered. The *Maine* might have been wrecked by an accidental explosion of her own magazines. If she was sunk by plotters, it was most reasonable to suspect those who stood to gain from the crime—the Cuban rebels, whose cause was flagging and would be lost unless the United States could be dragged into the struggle. There was one other possibility: that a group of Spaniards or Cuban loyalists, working off their hatred unknown to the Spanish government, were responsible.

Even the *Journal* admitted disbelief that Spain had officially ordered the explosion. But this was tucked away in small type and later disavowed. The big type, the headlines, the diagrams, the cartoons, the editorials, laid the blame inferentially or flatly on Spain. For a week afterward, the *Journal* devoted a daily average of eight and one-half pages to the *Maine* and war. In the face of Sigsbee's wise suggestion that "public opinion be suspended," the *Journal* lashed public opinion day after day.

Some idea of the *Journal*'s enormities, though an inadequate one, is given by a day-by-day recapitulation of its headlines and stories.

February 16: "CRUISER MAINE BLOWN UP IN HAVANA HARBOR." This was simple truth, written before the propaganda machine got into motion. It was the last truthful front-page headline for almost two weeks.

February 17: "THE WARSHIP MAINE WAS SPLIT IN TWO BY AN ENEMY'S SECRET INFERNAL MACHINE." The cause, of course, was unknown. This issue had a seven-column drawing of the ship anchored over mines, and a diagram showing wires leading from the mines to a Spanish fortress on shore—a flight of fancy which many readers doubtless took as fact. The hatred of Spaniards for Americans was mentioned. The caption read, "If this [plot] can be proven, the brutal nature of the Spaniards will be shown in that they waited to spring the mine until after all men had retired for the night." The *Journal* said, "Captain Sigsbee Practically Declares that His Ship was Blown Up by a Mine or Torpedo." Sigsbee said no such thing. He later wrote, "A Spanish officer of high rank... showed me a New York paper of February 17 in which was pictured the *Maine* anchored over a mine. On another page was a plan showing wires leading from the *Maine* to shore. The officer asked me what I thought of that. It was explained that we had no censorship in the United States.... Apparently the Spanish officer could not grasp the idea."

February 18: "THE WHOLE COUNTRY THRILLS WITH THE WAR FEVER." This came at a time when Span-

ish and Cuban military, civil and ecclesiastical leaders were giving the victims a solemn state funeral in Havana, with every mark of respect, dedicating the plots used at Colon Cemetery to the United States in perpetuity. On this day, for the first time, the combined circulation of the morning and evening *Journal* passed a million.

February 20 (over a drawing:) "HOW THE MAINE ACTUALLY LOOKS AS IT LIES, WRECKED BY SPANISH TREACHERY, IN HAVANA BAY."

February 21: "HAVANA POPULACE INSULTS THE MEMORY OF THE MAINE VICTIMS." This was over a story alleging that Spanish officers had been overheard to boast that any other American ship visiting Havana would "follow the *Maine*."

February 23: "THE MAINE WAS DESTROYED BY TREACHERY."

Although the *Journal* knew all along who sank the ship, it offered $50,000 reward for the solution of the mystery. It also began a drive for a memorial to be erected to those lost in the explosion, Hearst donating the first $1000. It began as usual by soliciting famous men whose participation could be exploited, among them ex-President Cleveland. Cleveland won some measure of immortality by replying, "I decline to allow my sorrow for those who died on the *Maine* to be perverted to an advertising scheme for the New York *Journal*." Other "big names" were less percipient, General Nelson Miles, Levi Morton, Chauncey Depew and O. H. P. Belmont being among the many who lent their prestige to the drive.

On February 18, at this most inopportune of times, the Spanish cruiser *Vizcaya* arrived in New York harbor from Cartagena on her "courtesy call."

Her commander, Captain Antonio Eulate, shocked when informed of the *Maine* tragedy, ordered his colors half-masted and said he would take no part in any festivities planned in his honor. In view of the public hysteria, the police and naval authorities took strenuous measures to protect the *Vizcaya*, surrounding her with a cordon of patrol boats. The *World*, almost as frenetic in its Hispanophobia as the *Journal*, warned that the *Vizcaya* might have treacherous intentions, saying, "While lying off the Battery, her shells will explode on the Harlem River and in the suburbs of Brooklyn." However, the *Vizcaya* did not fire a shot.

The Spanish authorities, incensed by the *Journal*'s warmongering, retaliated. *Journal* men were forbidden to board the *Vizcaya*. More important, the *Journal* was denied further use of the cables from Havana. It took cognizance of this with an announcement headed, "SPANISH COURTESIES TO AN AMERICAN NEWSPAPER," and boxed on the front page with a flowing American flag. It read:

The *Journal* takes great pride in announcing that on account of its too decided Americanism and its work for the patriots of Cuba this newspaper and its reporters have been forbidden entrance on board the Spanish warship *Vizcaya*; its dispatches are refused transmission over the Government cables from Havana.

These Spanish acts, of course, do not prevent the *Journal* from getting all the news.... The *Journal* is flattered by these delicate attentions from Spain.... It expects to merit still more attention when the United States decides to end Spanish misrule and horrors in America.

The *Journal* also presented its readers with a newly-devised "Game of War With Spain," to be played by four persons with cards. Two contestants would portray the crew of the United States battleship *Texas*, doing their best to "sink" the other two, who manned the *Vizcaya*.

Hearst had rounded up a carefully-selected group of jingoistic legislators who were not averse to a free trip to Cuba. Senators Hernando Money of Mississippi, John W. Thurston of Nebraska and J. H. Gallinger of New Hampshire, and Representatives William Alden Smith of Michigan and Amos Cummings of New York, embarked from Fort Monroe on the Hearst yacht *Anita* as "*Journal* Commissioners" to make a survey of conditions on the island and to write reports for the *Journal*, their expenses being paid by Hearst. Representatives Smith and Cummings were members of the House Foreign Affairs and Naval Affairs committees respectively. The *Journal* meanwhile appealed to its readers to write their Congressmen, and said it had so far relayed 15,000 such letters demanding war.

The *Journal* raged at Senator Mark Hanna for deprecating the war talk. It referred to him frequently as "President Hanna," to indicate how completely McKinley was his puppet. The cowardly peace policy of the administration was dictated by a base desire for profits in Wall Street, which could be depressed by war. "President Hanna... announced that there will be no war," said the *Journal*. "... This attitude is fairly representative of the eminently respectable porcine citizens who—for dollars in the money-grubbing sty, support 'conservative' newspapers and consider the starvation of... inoffensive men, women and children, and the murder of 250 [*sic*] American sailors... of less importance than the fall of two points in a price of stock."

Anyone advocating peace was a traitor or a Wall Street profiteer, probably both. When Navy Secretary Long dared to say that "Spanish official responsibility for the *Maine* explosion might be considered eliminated," Long joined the *Journal*'s list of officials who had sold out the nation's honor to Wall Street. This was all part of a money-making coup engineered by Hanna, said the *Journal*, with Long as his pawn, for Hanna had advised his friends before the announcement to buy stocks which rose several points as a result of Long's words and netted them $20,000,000.

The treasonous President McKinley had already publicly stated his opinion that the *Maine* was wrecked by an accidental explosion of her own magazines. The perfidious Secretary of the Navy had defended Spain. In Havana at the time was sitting a United States naval board of inquiry, sending down divers to examine the *Maine*'s hull and taking testimony from survivors in an effort to determine the cause of the disaster. Spain had asked, and been promised, that no American newspaper correspondents would take part in the investigation. The *Journal*, with the *World* and *Sun* close behind, was whipping public fury to a point where all these official efforts were rendered useless, a trivial shadow play unheard behind the din of the headlines.

The Nearest Approach to Hell
In Cuba, Hearst's junketing group of Senators and Congressmen were finding plenty of destitution, which indeed was so bad that it could scarcely be exaggerated. The *Journal* praised them as "brave congressmen [who] faced death to get at the truth in Cuba." Each of the five legislators wrote articles for the *Journal* describing the suffering they

saw. Mrs. Thurston, wife of the Senator from Nebraska, who had accompanied her husband, wrote an especially stirring appeal to *Journal* mothers:

> Oh! Mothers of the Northland, who tenderly clasp your little ones to your loving hearts! Think of the black despair that filled each [Cuban] mother's heart as she felt her life-blood ebb away, and knew that she had left her little ones to perish from the pain of starvation and disease.

While in the harbor of Matanzas, Mrs. Thurston suffered a heart attack and died aboard the Hearst yacht—a misfortune the *Journal* blamed on the destitution she had seen. The five "*Journal* Commissioners" returned to make speeches in Congress praising the *Journal*'s patriotic motives and declaring that newspaper reports of conditions in Cuba were not exaggerated. For weeks, while the naval court continued its investigation in Havana, American citizens were conducted into a theater world of Cuban horror, Spanish treachery and United States dishonor staged with primitive efficiency by Producer-Director Hearst and aped by the rabble-rousing Pulitzer (now sadly reduced to the role of imitator) and the respected *Sun*. Edwin Godkin vainly tried to stem the tide in his *Evening Post*, with its puny 25,000 circulation.

"... when one of [the yellow journals] offers a yacht voyage," Godkin wrote, "with free wine, rum and cigars, and a good bed, under the guise of philanthropy, or gets up a committee for Holy purposes, and promises to puff it, it can get almost any one it pleases to go on the yacht voyage and serve on the committee—senators, lawyers, divines, scholars, poets, presidents and what not.... Every one who knows anything about 'yellow journals' knows that everything they do and say is intended to promote sales.... No one—absolutely no one—supposes a yellow journal cares five cents about the Cubans, the *Maine* victims, or any one else. A yellow journal is probably the nearest approach to hell, existing in any Christian state."

Theodore Roosevelt, who had displeased the *Journal* as head of the New York police, was now Assistant Secretary of the Navy under Long and a jingo after Hearst's own heart. Roosevelt had decided instantly that the *Maine* was sunk by treacherous Spaniards. He privately referred with contempt to McKinley as having "no more backbone than a chocolate eclair." The *Journal*, always doubly glad when it could praise itself as it rapped its enemies, quoted Roosevelt in a front-page interview as saying: "It is cheering to find a newspaper of the great influence and circulation of the *Journal* tell [sic] the facts as they exist and ignore the suggestions of various kinds that emanate from sources that cannot be described as patriotic or loyal to the flag of this country."

Roosevelt immediately repudiated the statement, saying, "The alleged interview with me in today's New York *Journal* is an invention from beginning to end. It is difficult to understand the kind of infamy that resorts to such methods." Roosevelt later won a reputation for occasional denials of indiscreet things he had said, but perhaps in this instance it is safer to trust him than the *Journal*.

Long before the Navy report on the *Maine* was ready, the *Journal* anticipated it with sheer falsehood, saying, "the Court of Inquiry finds that Spanish government officials blew up the *Maine*," and that the warship "was purposely moved where a Spanish mine exploded by Spanish officers would destroy it." "The *Journal* can stake its reputation as a war prophet on this assertion: There will be a war with Spain as certain as the sun shines unless Spain abases herself in the dust and voluntarily consents to the freedom of Cuba." The Spaniards were universally painted as such cowardly, two-faced wretches that Madrid editors not surprisingly began railing at the "Yankee pigs," which in turn was faithfully reported by the *Journal* and its contemporaries.

Under these daily onslaughts, multiplied by many extra editions and news-service transmission from coast to coast, the nation was seething. The public was deceived, misled and tricked by its only source of information. McKinley, a kindly man of peace, could deal expertly with legislators but lacked the dynamism, the spark of leadership that grips and sways the public mind. The country was getting away from him. The Presidency of the United States was being preempted by batteries of cylinder presses.

On March 28, McKinley handed the report of the naval court to Congress. The court's opinion was that "the *Maine* was destroyed by the explosion of a submarine mine, which caused the partial explosion of two or more of the forward magazines." The court admitted its inability to fix the blame. A Spanish court of inquiry which had made a similar investigation, but which the Americans had denied an opportunity for close inspection, found for an accidental explosion within the ship. This report was ignored. The guilt for the disaster, if guilt there was, was a mystery then as it is today. No one ever collected the *Journal*'s $50,000 reward.

However, public sentiment was so inflamed that the United States court's opinion that the explosion came from outside and thus was not accidental was enough to lay the blame on Spain. The *Journal*, dissatisfied, declared that the truth was being hidden from the public, saying, "the suppressed testimony shows Spain is guilty of blowing up the *Maine*." Even the heavens demonstrated the inevitability of war. On the night of April 4, the moon was surrounded by two pale rings. "Many persons insisted," said the *Journal*, "that the contact of the two rings meant nothing short of war; the smaller ring standing for the pretension of Spain in the Island of Cuba and the larger circle for the United States and its immensely superior power."

This whimsy was lost in the prevailing theme of American dishonor. "Write to your Congressmen at once," the *Journal* urged its readers. "... Give Congress a chance to know what the people think." The same issue featured a cartoon depicting Hanna, with his puppet McKinley stuck in his back pocket, poking a white feather into the star-studded hat of Uncle Sam, and suggested satirically that the stars on the flag be changed to dollar signs and the stripes to rows of dollar bills. It ran a front-page headline in three-inch type: "HANNA VS. HONOR." When some Ohio politicians charged that Hanna was elected to the Senate by fraud, the *Journal*'s cartoon showed him in prison stripes with the caption, "Here is Our 'President-Maker!' How Do You Like Him?" It warned that "Spain's powerful flotilla" was believed to be "stealing toward our shore." Blasting McKinley and his Wall Street bosses for waiting for Spain to strike the first blow, it demanded, in an issue dotted with American flags, "In the name of 266 [*sic*] American seamen, butchered in cold blood by the Spaniards, what is a 'blow' in the McKinley concept of war?" It ran an imaginative drawing showing Spanish soldiers bayoneting helpless Cubans, with the caption, "The wires bring news of the butchery of two hundred more reconcentrados.... Two hundred murders more or fewer is of little importance in Spain's record, and McKinley can hardly be expected to get excited about this."

The *Journal* pointed out how ridiculously easy it would be to crush Spain. It talked of organizing a regiment of giant athletes including Heavyweights Bob Fitzsimmons and James J. Corbett, Ballplayer Cap Anson, Hammer Thrower Jim Mitchell and Indian Footballer Red Water, all of whom agreed to join. "Think of a regiment composed of magnificent men of this ilk!" glowed the *Journal*. "They would overawe any Spanish regiment by their mere appearance. They would scorn Krag-Jorgensen and Mauser bullets."

According to the *Journal*, volunteers were itching to avenge the *Maine*. Frank James, ex-bandit brother of the legendary Jesse, offered to lead a company of cowboys. Six hundred Sioux Indians were ready and willing to scalp Spaniards in Cuba. The *World* improved on this, reporting the statement of "Buffalo Bill" Cody that 30,000 Indian fighters could clear the Spaniards out of Cuba in sixty days. The *Journal* came back with a report of riots in Havana that had "2,000 AMERICANS IN PERIL," presenting a four-column drawing showing exactly how the Navy would bombard Morro Castle and land men around Havana. *Journal* reporters were sent to interview the mothers of sailors who died in the

Maine living in the New York area. All made pathetic appeals for vengeance.

"How would President McKinley have felt, I wonder," said one of them, "if he had a son on the *Maine* murdered as was my little boy? Would he then forget the crime and let it go unpunished while the body of his child was lying as food for the sharks in the Spanish harbor of Havana?" Another mother was quoted as saying in part, "I ask that mine and other mothers' sons be avenged.... I ask it for justice [*sic*] sake and the honor of the flag."

In Madrid, United States Minister Stewart Woodford was working efficiently for peace, although he was ostracized by Spanish society as De Lome previously had been in Washington. Being out of range of the *Journal*, which attacked his peace efforts as "twaddle," he felt that peace could be preserved. It would have been had not his efforts been junked by the administration. He found the Spanish government ready to go the limit to avoid war. "They cannot go further in open concessions to us," Woodford earlier had informed McKinley, "without being overthrown by their own people here in Spain.... They want peace if they can keep peace and save the dynasty. They prefer the chances of war, with the certain loss of Cuba, to the overthrow of the dynasty." On April 9, Woodford cabled that the Queen's government had gone still farther and had surrendered to all the important United States demands, even to the extent of offering to grant an immediate armistice there. Woodford was confident that this last concession meant peace, saying:

I hope that nothing will now be done to humiliate Spain as I am satisfied that the present government is going, and is

loyally ready to go, as fast and as far as it can. With your power of action sufficiently free, you will win the fight on your own lines.

Here was the key to an amicable settlement, if the United States wanted it. But McKinley knew that the majority of the American people, misled by their newspapers, wanted war. He knew that many legislators, influenced by their angry constituents, wanted war. And he knew that his administration and the Republican party would suffer unpopularity and loss of confidence if it made a stand for peace.

Mr. McKinley bowed to Mr. Hearst. He went over to the war party. Without taking any stand, he submitted the whole problem to Congress in a message given on April 11. He dramatized his own abandonment of peace by burying the all-important Spanish concessions in the last two paragraphs of his speech. Everybody knew that this meant war, but the *Journal* was impatient at the delay in making it official, as one of its headlines showed:

SUICIDE

LAMENTED

THE MAINE

Aged Mrs. Mary Wayt Enhaled [*sic*] Gas Through a Tube.

GRIEVED OVER OUR DELAY

"The Government May Live in Dishonor," Said She,

"I Cannot."

Possibly the President was surprised at the peace sentiment still existing when the Senate on April 19 passed a war resolution by the narrow vote of 42 to 35. Only four more Senators on the peace side would have swung the balance, indicating that determined Presidential leadership might have foiled Hearst. But when the House concurred with the Senate in a 310–6 vote for war, it demonstrated that McKinley, had he won peace, would have won unpopularity along with it.

It was an unnecessary war. It was the newspapers' war. Above all, it was Hearst's war. It is safe to say that had not Hearst, with his magnificently tawdry flair for publicity and agitation, enlisted the women of America in a crusade they misunderstood, made a national heroine of the jail-breaking Miss Cisneros, made a national abomination of Dupuy de Lome, made the *Maine* a mistaken symbol of Spanish treachery, caused thousands of citizens to write their Congressmen, and dragged the powerful *World* along with him into journalistic ill-fame, the public would have kept its sanity, McKinley would have shown more spunk, at least four more Senators would have taken counsel with reason, and there would have been no war.

"The outbreak of the Spanish-American war found Mr. Hearst in a state of proud ecstasy," recalled James Creelman, who was working with Hearst daily. "He had won his campaign and the McKinley Administration had been forced into war." Willis Abbot wrote: "Hearst was accustomed to refer to the war, in company with his staff, as 'our war.'"

He rallied the United States with a headline in four-inch type:

"NOW TO AVENGE THE MAINE!"

NO

Richard Hofstadter

CUBA, THE PHILIPPINES, AND MANIFEST DESTINY

The taking of the Philippine Islands from Spain in 1899 marked a major historical departure for the American people, a breach in their traditions and a shock to their established values. To be sure, from their national beginnings they had constantly engaged in expansions, but almost entirely into contiguous territory. Now they were extending themselves to distant extra-hemispheric colonies. They were abandoning a strategy of defense hitherto limited to the continent and its appurtenances, in favor of a major strategic commitment in the Far East. Thus far their expansion had been confined to the spread of a relatively homogeneous population into territories planned from the beginning to develop self-government; now control was to be imposed by force on millions of ethnic aliens. The acquisition of the islands, therefore, was understood by contemporaries on both sides of the debate, as it is readily understood today, to be a turning point in our history.

To discuss the debate in isolation from other events, however, would be to deprive it of its full significance. America's entrance into the Philippine Islands was a by-product of the Spanish-American War. The Philippine crisis is inseparable from the war crisis, and the war crisis itself is inseparable from a larger constellation that might be called "the psychic crisis of the 1890's."

Central in the background of the psychic crisis was the great depression that broke in 1893 and was still very acute when the agitation over the war in Cuba began. Severe depression, by itself, does not always generate an emotional crisis as intense as that of the nineties. In the 1870's the country had been swept by a depression of comparable acuteness and duration which, however, did not give rise to all the phenomena that appeared in the 1890's or to very many of them with comparable intensity and impact. It is often said that the 1890's, unlike the 1870's, form a "watershed" in American history. The difference between the emotional and intellectual impact of these two depressions can be measured, I believe, not by the difference in severity, but rather by reference to a number of singular events that in the 1890's converged with the depression to heighten its impact upon the public mind.

From Richard Hofstadter, *The Paranoid Style in American Politics and Other Essays* (Alfred A. Knopf, 1965). Copyright © 1964, 1965 by Richard Hofstadter. Reprinted by permission of Alfred A. Knopf, Inc. Notes omitted.

First in importance was the Populist movement, the free-silver agitation, the heated campaign of 1896. For the first time in our history a depression had created a protest movement strong enough to capture a major party and raise the specter, however unreal, of drastic social convulsion. Second was the maturation and bureaucratization of American business, the completion of its essential industrial plant, and the development of trusts on a scale sufficient to stir the anxiety that the old order of competitive opportunities was approaching an eclipse. Third, and of immense symbolic importance, was the apparent filling up of the continent and the disappearance of the frontier line. We now know how much land had not yet been taken up and how great were the remaining possibilities for internal expansion both in business and on the land; but to the mind of the 1890's it seemed that the resource that had engaged the energies of the people for three centuries had been used up. The frightening possibility suggested itself that a serious juncture in the nation's history had come. As Frederick Jackson Turner expressed it in his famous paper of 1893: "Now, four centuries from the discovery of America, at the end of one hundred years of life under the Constitution, the frontier has gone, and with its going has closed the first period of American history."

To middle-class citizens who had been brought up to think in terms of the nineteenth-century order, the outlook seemed grim. Farmers in the staple-growing region had gone mad over silver and [William Jennings] Bryan; workers were stirring in bloody struggles like the Homestead and Pullman strikes; the supply of new land seemed at an end; the trust threatened the spirit of business

enterprise; civic corruption was at a high point in the large cities; great waves of seemingly unassimilable immigrants arrived yearly and settled in hideous slums. To many historically conscious writers, the nation appeared overripe, like an empire ready for collapse through a stroke from outside or through internal upheaval. Acute as the situation was for all those who lived by the symbols of national power—for the governing and thinking classes—it was especially poignant for young people, who would have to make their careers in the dark world that seemed to be emerging.

The symptomatology of the crisis would record several tendencies in popular thought and behavior that had previously existed only in pale and tenuous form. These symptoms were manifest in two quite different moods. The key to one of them was an intensification of protest and humanitarian reform. Populism, utopianism, the rise of the Christian Social gospel, the growing intellectual interest in socialism, the social settlement movement that appealed so strongly to the college generation of the nineties, the quickening of protest and social criticism in the realistic novel—all these are expressions of this mood. The other mood was one of national self-assertion, aggression, expansion. The motif of the first was social sympathy; of the second, national power. During the 1890's far more patriotic groups were founded than in any other decade of our history; the naval theories of Captain Mahan were gaining in influence; naval construction was booming; there was an immense quickening of the American cult of Napoleon and a vogue of the virile and martial writings of Rudyard Kipling; young Theodore Roosevelt became the exemplar of the vigorous, masterful, out-of-doors man; the revival of European imperialism stirred speculation over what America's place would be in the world of renewed colonial rivalries, and in some stirred a demand to get into the imperial race to avoid the risk of being overwhelmed by other powers. But most significant was the rising tide of jingoism, a matter of constant comment among observers of American life during the decade.

Jingoism, of course, was not new in American history. But during the 1870's and 1880's the American public had been notably quiescent about foreign relations. There had been expansionist statesmen, but they had been blocked by popular apathy, and our statecraft had been restrained. Grant had failed dismally in his attempt to acquire Santo Domingo; our policy toward troubled Hawaii had been cautious; in 1877 an offer of two Haitian naval harbors had been spurned. In responding to Haiti, Secretary of State Frelinghuysen had remarked that "the policy of this Government... has tended toward avoidance of possessions disconnected from the main continent." Henry Cabot Lodge, in his life of George Washington published in 1889, observed that foreign relations then filled "but a slight place in American politics, and excite generally only a languid interest." Within a few years this comment would have seemed absurd. In 1895, Russell A. Alger reported to Lodge, after reading one of Lodge's own articles to a Cincinnati audience, that he was convinced by the response that foreign policy, "more than anything else, touches the public pulse of today." The history of the 1890's is the history of public agitation over expansionist issues and of quarrels with other nations.

* * *

Three primary incidents fired American jingoism between the spring of 1891 and the close of 1895. First came Secretary of State Blaine's tart and provocative reply to the Italian minister's protest over the lynching of eleven Italians in New Orleans. Then there was friction with Chile over a riot in Valparaíso in which two American sailors were killed and several injured by a Chilean mob. In 1895 occurred the more famous Venezuela boundry dispute with Britain. Discussion of these incidents would take us too far afield, but note that they all had these characteristics in common: in none of them was national security or the natural interest vitally and immediately involved; in all three American diplomacy was extraordinarily and disproportionately aggressive; in all three the possibility of war was contemplated; and in each case the response of the American public and press was enthusiastically nationalist and almost unanimous.

It is hard to read the history of these events without concluding that politicians were persistently using jingoism to restore their prestige, mend their party fences, and divert the public mind from grave internal discontents. It hardly seems an accident that jingoism and populism rose together. Documentary evidence for the political exploitation of foreign crises is not overwhelmingly abundant, in part because such a motive is not necessarily conscious and where it is conscious it is not always confessed or recorded. The persistence of jingoism in every administration from Harrison's to Theodore Roosevelt's, however, is too suggestive to be ignored. During the nineties the press of each party was fond of accusing the other of exploiting foreign conflict. Blaine was not above twisting the British lion's tail for political purposes; and it is hardly likely that he would have exempted Italy from the same treatment. Harrison, on the eve of the Chile affair, for the acuteness of which he was primarily responsible, was being urged by prominent Republican politicians who had the coming presidential campaign in mind to pursue a more aggressive foreign policy because it would "have the... effect of diverting attention from stagnant political discussions." And although some Democratic papers charged that he was planning to run for re-election during hostilities so that he could use the "don't swap horses in the middle of the stream" appeal, many Democrats felt that it was politically necessary for them to back him against Chile so that, as one of their congressmen remarked, the Republicans could not "run away with all the capital there is to be made in an attempt to assert national self-respect."

Grover Cleveland was a man of exceptional integrity whose stand against pressure for the annexation of Hawaii during 1893–4 does him much credit. But precisely for this act of restraint he was accused by Republican jingoes like Lodge and by many in his own party of being indifferent to America's position in the world. And if Cleveland was too high-minded a man to exploit a needless foreign crisis, his Secretary of State, Richard Olney, was not. The Venezuela affair, which came at a low point in the prestige of Cleveland's administration, offered Olney a rich chance to prove to critics in both parties that the administration was, after all, capable of vigorous diplomacy. That the crisis might have partisan value

was not unthinkable to members of Olney's party. He received a letter from a Texas congressman encouraging him to "go ahead," on the ground that the Venezuela issue was a "winner" in every section of the country. "When you come to diagnose the country's internal ills," his correspondent continued, "the possibilities of 'blood and iron' loom up immediately. Why, Mr. Secretary, just think of how angry the anarchistic, socialistic, and populistic boil appears on our political surface and who knows how deep its roots extend or ramify? One cannon shot across the bow of a British boat in defense of this principle will knock more *pus* out of it than would suffice to inoculate and corrupt our people for the next two centuries."

This pattern had been well established when the Cuban crisis broke out anew in 1895. It was quite in keeping that Secretary Olney should get a letter during the 1896 campaign from Fitzhugh Lee, the American consul in Havana, advising that the conservative faction of Gold Democrats become identified with the strong policy of mediation or intervention in Cuba. Thus, he argued, "the 'Sound Democrats' would get, with the Executive, the credit of stopping the wholesale atrocities daily practised here, the acquisition of Cuba by purchase, or by fighting a successful war, if war there be. In the latter case, the enthusiasm, the applications for service, the employment of many of the unemployed, might do much towards directing the minds of the people from imaginary ills, the relief of which is erroneously supposed to be reached by 'Free Silver.'"

When President McKinley took office he was well aware that nationalist enthusiasm had reached a pitch that made war very likely. A few months earlier, he had told Senator Lodge that he might be "obliged" to go to war as soon as he entered the presidency, and had expressed a preference that the Cuban crisis be settled one way or another in the time between his election and inauguration. Although he had promised Carl Schurz that there would be "no jingo nonsense under my administration," he proved not to have quite enough strength to resist the current. He did not himself partake of the hysteria that was mounting throughout the country, and he was concerned that the country was unprepared to wage a war, uncertain even whether war could be confined to a contest with Spain. He soon found himself under incredible pressures for positive action, which he resisted as long as most Presidents would have been able to do. His failure was not in yielding too soon to the war fever but in not taking early initiative to rein it in. Sending the *Maine* to Havana proved to be one of his most vital mistakes, since it gave a hostage to the war party. The act was meant in part to curb the enthusiasm of the jingoes at home, but Cleveland had resisted just such a proposal on the grounds that an inflammatory incident was all too likely. No doubt the actual sinking of the *Maine* on February 16 went even beyond anything that Cleveland or McKinley could have anticipated. From that time onward, the chances of avoiding war seemed slim.

Members of McKinley's own party put a great deal of pressure on him to give the people their war rather than endanger the Republican position. Some of them feared, as an infuriated senator put it to the Secretary of State, that Congress would declare war in spite of him. "He'll get run over and the party with him." For McKinley himself the prospect that Congress might act without him was, by March, a very real fear. It was widely argued that if war was inevitable, as presumably it was, it would be better for the President to lead rather than to be pushed; that resistance to war would be ruinous to the party; that going to war would prevent the Democrats from entering the next presidential campaign with "Free Cuba" and "Free Silver" as their battle cries. After Senator Proctor's moving speech in the Senate on March 17 about conditions in Cuba, the Chicago *Times-Herald*, a McKinley paper, declared that intervention in Cuba, peaceful or forcible, was "immediately inevitable. Our own internal political conditions will not permit its postponement.... Let President McKinley hesitate to rise to the just expectations of the American people, and who can doubt that 'war for Cuban liberty' will be the crown of thorns that Free Silver Democrats and Populists will adopt at the election this fall.... The President would be powerless to stay any legislation, however ruinous to every sober, honest interest of the country." "The people want no disgraceful negotiations with Spain," cried the Chicago *Tribune*. "Should the president plunge his administration into that morass, he and his party would be swept out of power in 1900 by a fine burst of popular indignation. An administration which stains the national honor never will be forgiven." Reporting to McKinley on sentiment in Massachusetts, Henry Cabot Lodge wrote in March: "If the war in Cuba drags on through the summer with nothing done, we shall go down in the greatest defeat ever known.... I know that it is easily and properly said that to bring on or even to threaten war for political reasons is a crime & I quite agree. But to sacrifice a great party & bring free silver upon the country for a wrong policy is hardly less odious."

In the facing of mounting pressure for war, McKinley was unable to sustain his negotiations with Spain long enough to exhaust the possibilities of a diplomatic solution. By the beginning of April some important demands had been conceded —an end to the *reconcentrado* policy and reparations for the *Maine*. But it is doubtful that a diplomatic solution could have been arrived at, since both the Cuban revolutionaries and the United States were insisting upon full Cuban independence, leaving no face-saving formula for the Spanish government. In the opening days of April, McKinley resolved upon war. On April 10, as he was about to send Congress his war message, word came from his ambassador in Spain, Stewart L. Woodford, that the Spaniards had yielded to the American demand for a prompt armistice, and Woodford also thought, rather optimistically, that even the demand for independence might still be met. This news McKinley incorporated anticlimactically at the end of the war message, thus passing up his chance for one final statesmanlike act, an appeal for further delay. That such a step could have avoided war, however, is doubtful. Americans seemed to want not merely the freedom of Cuba but a war for the freedom of Cuba. The Spanish government, insofar as it confronted the realities at all, seemed to think that it was preferable to lose the island "honorably," as the consequence of a war, than to back down. McKinley was caught between the aggressive irrationality of his own people and the decadent irrationality of the ancient Latin power.

Historians often say that the war was brought on by sensational newspapers. The press, spurred by the rivalry between

Pulitzer and Hearst, aroused sympathy with the Cubans and hatred of Spain and catered to the bellicosity of the public. No one seems to have asked: *Why was the public so fatally receptive to war propaganda?* I believe the answer must be sought in the causes of the jingoism that had raged for seven years before the war actually broke out. The events of the nineties had brought frustration and anxiety to civically conscious Americans. On one hand, as Mark Sullivan has commented, the American during this period was disposed "to see himself as an underdog in economic situations and controversies in his own country"; but the civic frustrations of the era created also a restless aggressiveness, a desire to be assured that the power and vitality of the nation were not waning. The capacity for sympathy and the need for power existed side by side. That highly typical American, William Allen White, recalls in his *Autobiography* how during the nineties he was "bound to my idols—Whitman, the great democrat, and Kipling, the imperialist." In varying degrees the democrat and the imperialist existed in the hearts of White's countrymen— the democrat disposed to free Cuba; the imperialist, to vent his spleen in Spain.

I suspect that the readiness of the public to overreact to the Cuban situation can be understood in part through the displacement of feelings of sympathy or social protest generated in domestic affairs; these impulses found a safe and satisfactory discharge in foreign conflict. Spain was portrayed in the press as waging a heartless and inhuman war; the Cubans were portrayed as noble victims of Spanish tyranny, their situation as analogous to that of Americans in 1776. When one examines the sectional and political elements that were most enthusiastic about policies that led to war, one finds them not primarily among the wealthy eastern big-business Republicans who gave McKinley his strongest support and read the dignified conservative newspapers, but in the Bryan sections of the country, in the Democratic party, among western Republicans, and among the readers of the yellow journals. A great many businessmen were known to fear the effects of a war on the prosperity that was just returning, and some thought that a war might strengthen the free-silver movement. During the controversy significant charges were hurled back and forth: conservative peace advocates claimed that many jingoists were hoping for a costly war over Cuba that could be made the occasion of a return to free silver; in reply, the inflammatory press often fell into the pattern of Populist rhetoric, declaiming, for example, about "the eminently respectable porcine citizens who—for dollars in the money-grubbing sty, support 'conservative' newspapers and consider the starvation of . . . inoffensive men, women and children, and the murder of 250 American sailors . . . of less importance than a fall of two points in a price of stocks." As Margaret Leech has remarked, peace "had become a symbol of obedience to avarice." In the case of some of the war enthusiasts it is not clear whether they favored action more because they bled for the sufferings of the Cubans or because they hated the materialism and the flaccid pacifism of the *haute bourgeoisie*. Theodore Roosevelt, who was not in the habit of brooding over the wrongs done to the underdog in the United States, expressed some of this when he cried at Mark Hanna: "We will have this war for the freedom of Cuba in spite of the timidity of the commercial interests."

Although imputations of base motives were made by both sides, it is also significant that the current of sympathy and agitation ran strong where a discontented constituency, chagrined at Bryan's defeat, was most numerous. An opportunity to discharge hatred of "Wall Street interests" that were coolly indifferent to the fate of both Cuban *insurrectos* and staple farmers may have been more important than the more rationalized and abstract linkage between war and free silver. The primary significance of this war in the psychic economy of the 1890's was that it served as an outlet for expressing aggressive impulses while presenting itself, quite truthfully, as an idealistic and humanitarian crusade. It had the advantage of expressing in one issue both the hostilities and the generous moral passions of the public. The American public on the whole showed little interest in such material gains as might accrue from an intervention in Cuba. It never dreamed that the war would lead to the taking of the Philippines, of whose existence it was hardly aware. Starting a war for a high-minded and altruistic purpose and then transmuting it into a war for annexation was unimaginable. That would be, as McKinley put it in a phrase that later came back to haunt him, "criminal aggression."

William James, who deplored the war fever from the beginning, correctly diagnosed the popular mood when he wrote to a friend in France: "The basis of it all is, or rather was, perfectly honest humanitarianism, and an absolutely disinterested desire on the part of our people to set the Cubans free. . . . Congress was entirely mad, supposing that the people was in the same condition, as it probably was, in less degree.... War... was the only possible discharge. We were winning the most extraordinary diplomatic victories, but they were of no use. We were ready (as we supposed) for war and nothing but war must come." Although he reiterated that the American disclaimer of desire for conquest was *"absolutely* sincere" he also shrewdly predicted that once the excitement of military action was aroused, "the ambition and sense of mastery which our nation has will set up new demands," and he accurately forecast that although we would never annex Cuba we might take Puerto Rico and the Philippines.

One might add that inhibitions against going to war were not so strong as they would have been if a major power had been involved. Spain, hardly a formidable foe in a war whose main strategic object was in the Caribbean, had been described by the press as weak, bankrupt, degenerate, and friendless, and her military incompetence was demonstrated by the events in Cuba itself. As T. R. [Theodore Roosevelt] put it to Lodge: "I do not think a war with Spain would be serious enough to cause much strain on this country." Lodge himself had a shrewder estimation than many timid financiers of the bearing of war on the currency question. "If we should have a war," he wrote in March 1898, "we will not hear much of the currency question in the elections."...

* * *

Since Julius W. Pratt published his *Expansionists of 1898* in 1936, it has been obvious that any interpretation of America's entry upon the paths of imperialism in the nineties in terms of rational economic motives would not fit the facts, and that a historian who approached the event with preconceptions no more sup-

ple than those, say, of Lenin's *Imperialism* would be helpless. This is not to say that markets and investments have no bearing; they do, but there are features of the situation that they do not explain at all. Insofar as the economic factor was important, it can be better studied by looking at the relation between the depression, the public mood, and the political system.

The alternative explanation has been the equally simple idea that the war was a newspapers' war. This notion, once again, has some point, but it certainly does not explain the war itself, much less its expansionist result. The New Deal period, when the political successes of F.D.R. were won in the face of overwhelming newspaper opposition, showed that the press is not powerful enough to impose upon the public mind a totally uncongenial view of public events. It must operate roughly within the framework of public predispositions. Moreover, not all the papers of the nineties were yellow journals. We must inquire into the structure of journalistic power and also into the views of the owners and editors to find out what differentiated the sensational editors and publishers from those of the conservative press.

There is still another qualification that must be placed upon the role of the press: the press itself, whatever it can do with opinion, does not have the power to precipitate opinion into action. That is something that takes place within the *political* process, and we cannot tell that part of the story without examining the state of party rivalries, the origin and goals of the political elites, and indeed the entire political context. We must, then, supplement our story about the role of the newspapers with at least two other factors: the state of the public temper upon which the newspapers worked, and the manner in which party rivalries deflected domestic clashes into foreign aggression. Here a perennial problem of politics under the competitive two-party system became manifest again in the 1890's. When there is, for whatever reason, a strong current jingoism running in the channels of public sentiment, party competition tends to speed it along. If the party in power is behaving circumspectly, the opposition tends to beat the drums. For example, in 1896, with Cleveland still in office, the Republican platform was much more exigent on the Cuba issue. When McKinley came into office and began to show reluctance to push toward intervention, the Democratic party became a center of interventionist pressure; this pressure was promptly supplemented by a large number of Republicans who, quite aside from their agreement on the issue, were concerned about its effect on the fate of their party.

When we examine the public temper, we find that the depression, together with such other events as the approaching completion of the settlement of the continent, the growth of trusts, and the intensification of internal social conflict, had brought to large numbers of people intense frustrations in their economic lives and their careers. To others they had brought anxiety that a period of stagnation in national wealth and power had set in. The restlessness of the discontented classes had been heightened by the defeat of Bryan in 1896. The anxieties about the nation's position had been increased among statesmen and publicists by the revival of world imperialism, in particular by the feeling that America was threatened by Germany, Russia, and Japan. The expansionist statesmen themselves were drawn largely from a restless upper-middle-class elite that had been fighting an unrewarding battle for conservative reform in domestic politics and looked with some eagerness toward a more spacious field of action.

Men often respond to frustration with acts of aggression, and allay their anxieties by threatening acts against others. It is revealing that the underdog forces in American society showed a considerably higher responsiveness to the idea of war with Spain than the groups that were satisfied with their economic or political positions. Our entry into the Philippines then aroused the interest of conservative groups that had been indifferent to the quixotism of freeing Cuba but were alert to the possibility of capturing new markets. Imperialism appealed to members of both the business and the political elites as an enlargement of the sphere of American power and profits; many of the underdogs also responded to this new note of national self-assertion. Others, however, looked upon our conduct in the Philippines as a betrayal of national principles. Anti-expansionists attempted to stir a sense of guilt and foreboding in the nation at large. But the circumstances of the period 1898–1900—the return of prosperity and the quick spectacular victories in war—made it difficult for them to impress this feeling upon the majority. The rhetoric of Duty and Destiny carried the day. The anti-expansionists had neither the numbers nor the morale of their opponents. The most conspicuous result of their lack of drive and confidence can be seen in the lamentable strategy of Bryan over the ratification of the treaty.

Clearly this attempt to see the war and expansion in the light of social history has led us onto the high and dangerous ground of social psychology and into the arena of conjecture. But simple rationalistic explanations of national behavior will also leave us dissatisfied. What I have attempted here is merely a preliminary sketch of a possible explanatory model. Further inquiry might make it seem more plausible at some points, more questionable at others.

This study has been narrowly focused on a single incident. Other expansionist crises in our own history would show important differences. I have not tried to compare American imperialism with that of other countries, or to decide how far our behavior is unique to our own country or similar to that which has been found elsewhere. In the history of other nations we can find many parallels to the role of the press and political parties in whipping up foreign crises, and to the role of the administration in committing the nation to a foreign policy before it could be made a matter of public discussion. The rhetoric and ideology of expansion also were not singular to us; duty, destiny, racism, and the other shibboleths were widespread.

I cannot refrain from adding to these notes on the methods of historical understanding another note on the tragicomic procedure of history itself. It may be of some value to us to be reminded how some of the more grandiose expectations of the nineties were realized. Cuba, to be sure, which might have been freed in peace, was freed in the war—insofar as the little country of Batista, Machado, and Castro can be considered free. The sensational newspapers that had boomed the war lost money on expensive extras, costly war-news coverage, and declining advertising. I do not know whether those silverites who wanted the war really expected that it would remonetize silver, but if they did they were rewarded with McKinley's renewed triumph and the Gold Standard Act of 1900. As for business, the gigantic markets of the East never materialized, and the precise value of the Philippines in getting at them is arguable. The islands themselves proved to be a mildly profitable colony that came to absorb a little over 1 per cent of all United States investments abroad. Yet within a generation the United States had committed itself to restoring independence to the Philippines. When this promise was enacted in 1934 many descendants of Aguinaldo's rebels were unenthusiastic about their new economic and strategic position. Finally, the exact estimation that is to be put on our strategic commitment in the Far East, which began with the Philippines, is still a matter of debate. We should, however, make note of the earlier opinion of one of our most brilliant and farsighted statesmen, who declared in 1907 that the Philippines were the Achilles' heel of our strategic position and should be given "nearly complete independence" at the "earliest possible moment." The author of these remarks was Theodore Roosevelt.

POSTSCRIPT

Did Yellow Journalism Cause the Spanish-American War?

In his biography, Swanberg argues that Hearst sent dozens of his first-rate reporters into Cuba to publicize the failure of the Spanish government to maintain control over the last vestiges of its empire in the Caribbean. "You furnish the pictures, and I'll furnish the war," Hearst supposedly said to his ace artist, Frederic Remington, in 1897, when Remington told him not much was happening.

There is little doubt that Hearst's *New York Journal*, with its sensational headlines, artistic sketches, and inflammatory articles, had a great impact on public opinion. But does Swanberg demonstrate a causal link between the yellow press propaganda machine and the decision for war made by President McKinley and Congress? Some recent historians argue in the negative. See Ian Mugridge, *The View from Xanadu: William Randolph Hearst and United States Foreign Policy* (McGill-Queen's University Press, 1995).

Hofstadter takes a much broader view of the events leading to the Spanish-American war than Swanberg. Hofstadter believes that the major events of the 1890s—the depression of 1893 and the maturing and, in some cases, overexpansion of American capitalism, which caused major labor strikes and agrarian protests in a number of southern and midwestern states—brought about a major psychological crisis in the 1890s. The author attempts to answer a question that has puzzled historians for a number of years: Why was the war fought when Spain had acceded to the United States' demands to free Cuba? Hofstadter's answer to this question is that America needed to fight a war for humanitarian reasons, thereby releasing tensions caused by the major changes that took place in the 1890s.

Recent historians argue that the president made the decision to go to war when Spain refused to allow McKinley to mediate the dispute between the Cuban rebels and the Spanish government. Such an allowance would probably have resulted in Cuba's independence, a goal the Spanish government was unwilling to concede. See, for example, John L. Offner, *An Unwanted War: The Diplomacy of the United States and Spain Over Cuba, 1895–1898* (University of North Carolina Press, 1992) and Lewis L. Gould, *The Spanish American War and President McKinley* (University of Kansas Press, 1982).

Three books that detail the military as well as the social and diplomatic aspects of the war are Frank Friedel, *The Splendid Little War* (Little, Brown, 1958); David F. Trask, *The War With Spain in 1898* (Macmillan, 1981); and Ivan Musicant, *Empire by Default: The Spanish-American War and the Dawn of the American Century* (Holt, 1995).

ISSUE 7

Did Booker T. Washington's Philosophy and Actions Betray the Interests of African Americans?

YES: Donald Spivey, from *Schooling for the New Slavery: Black Industrial Education, 1868–1915* (Greenwood Press, 1978)

NO: Louis R. Harlan, from "Booker T. Washington and the Politics of Accommodation," in John Hope Franklin and August Meier, eds., *Black Leaders of the Twentieth Century* (University of Illinois Press, 1982)

ISSUE SUMMARY

YES: Professor of history Donald Spivey contends that Booker T. Washington alienated both students and faculty at Tuskegee Institute by establishing an authoritarian system that failed to provide an adequate academic curriculum to prepare students for the industrial workplace.

NO: Professor emeritus of history Louis R. Harlan portrays Washington as a political realist who had the same long-range goals of progress toward equality as his black critics and whose policies and actions were designed to benefit black society as a whole.

In the late nineteenth and early twentieth centuries, most black Americans' lives were characterized by increased inequality and powerlessness. Although the Thirteenth Amendment had fueled a partial social revolution by emancipating approximately 4 million southern slaves, the efforts of the Fourteenth and Fifteenth Amendments to provide all African Americans with the protections and privileges of full citizenship had been undermined by the United States Supreme Court.

Seventy-five percent of all African Americans resided in rural areas by 1910. Ninety percent lived in the South, where they suffered from abuses associated with the sharecropping and crop-lien systems, political disfranchisement, and antagonistic race relations, which often boiled over into acts of violence, including race riots and lynchings. Black southerners who moved north in the decades preceding World War I to escape the ravages of racism instead discovered a society in which the color line was drawn more rigidly to limit black opportunities. Residential segregation led to the emergence of racial ghettos. Jim Crow also affected northern education, and competition for jobs produced frequent clashes between black and white workers. By the early twentieth century, then, most African Americans endured a second-class citizenship reinforced by segregation laws (both customary and legal) in the "age of Jim Crow."

Prior to 1895 the foremost spokesman for the nation's African American population was former slave and abolitionist Frederick Douglass, whose crusade for blacks emphasized the importance of civil rights, political power, and immediate integration. August Meier has called Douglass "the greatest living symbol of the protest tradition during the 1880s and 1890s." At the time of Douglass's death in 1895, however, this tradition was largely replaced by the emergence of Booker T. Washington. Born into slavery in Virginia in 1856, Washington became the most prominent black spokesman in the United States as a result of a speech delivered in the year of Douglass's death at the Cotton States Exposition in Atlanta, Georgia. Known as the "Atlanta Compromise," this address, with its conciliatory tone, found favor among whites and gave Washington, who was president of the Tuskegee Institute in Alabama, a reputation as a "responsible" spokesman for black America.

What did Booker T. Washington really want for African Americans? Did his programs realistically address the difficulties confronted by blacks in a society where the doctrine of white supremacy was prominent? Is it fair to describe Washington simply as a conservative whose accommodationist philosophy betrayed his own people? Did the "Sage of Tuskegee" consistently adhere to his publicly stated philosophy of patience, self-help, and economic advancement?

One of the earliest and most outspoken critics of Washington's program was his contemporary, W. E. B. Du Bois. In a famous essay in *The Souls of Black Folk* (1903), Du Bois levels an assault upon Washington's narrow educational philosophy for blacks and his apparent acceptance of segregation. By submitting to disfranchisement and segregation, Du Bois charges, Washington had become an apologist for racial injustice in the United States. He also claims that Washington's national prominence was bought at the expense of black interests throughout the nation.

In the first of the following selections, Donald Spivey offers a more recent interpretation that follows the critical assessment of Du Bois. He portrays Booker T. Washington as an authoritarian "overseer" who imposed a militaristic system at Tuskegee and who alienated students and faculty at Tuskegee by insisting upon a program that not only subordinated political, social, and civil rights to economic goals but also failed to provide the training necessary to allow students to become capable, skilled artisans.

In the second selection, Louis R. Harlan argues that Washington understood the reality of southern race relations and knew what he was capable of accomplishing without endangering his leadership position, which was largely controlled by whites. He was, then, a consummate politician—master of the art of the possible in turn-of-the-century race relations—who shared with his black critics most of the same long-range goals for racial equality.

YES

Donald Spivey

SHINE, BOOKER, SHINE: THE BLACK OVERSEER OF TUSKEGEE

Perhaps Paulo Freire had Booker T. Washington in mind when he wrote in his classic study on education, "The oppressed have been destroyed precisely because their situation has reduced them to things. In order to regain their humanity they must cease to be things and fight as men.... They cannot enter the struggle as objects in order later to become men." To Booker T. Washington the sensible thing for blacks to do was to fashion a coalition with whites in power to make themselves indispensable "objects" to the prosperity of the nation. His conception of the proper course for blacks rested upon the blacks' own exploitability. He believed that the profit motive dictated American thought and action. Those who proved themselves antagonistic would remain powerless or be annihilated; those who proved themselves of value would be rewarded. Thus, he contended that social, political, and civil rights were secondary issues for blacks—subordinate to and dependent upon the race's economic importance. This philosophy of uplift through submission drew heated criticism from many black leaders. What is not a familiar story is that in his championing of these ideas, Washington alienated many of his Tuskegee students and faculty members and never gained the full support of the white South....

Like the good overseer, and like his mentor, Samuel Chapman Armstrong, [the founder of Hampton Institute's industrial education program,] Booker T. sought to make his students superb laborers, that is, totally reliable. He criticized Tuskegee students who showed any signs of being unreliable. "Young men come here [Tuskegee Institute] and want to work at this industry or that, for a while, and then get tired and want to change to something else." To be a good worker, Washington professed, one must understand "the Importance of Being Reliable."

Booker Washington worked diligently to please the dominant white society, to make his blacks "the best labor in the world." He watched his students' every move. He was a stickler for precision and detail. The Founder emphasized such things to the Tuskegee student body and teachers as the proper

From Donald Spivey, *Schooling for the New Slavery: Black Industrial Education, 1868–1915* (Greenwood Press, 1978). Copyright © 1978 by Donald Spivey. Reprinted by permission of Greenwood Publishing Group, Inc., Westport, CT. Notes omitted.

positioning of brooms. Washington sent a notice to three department heads: "Will you kindly see that all brooms in your department are kept on their proper end. I notice that this is not done now." One faculty member responded on top of the Founder's memo: "This must be a mistake." It was not. Booker Washington demanded that everyone, including Mrs. Washington, place and store brooms with the brush end up.

The Founder placed every aspect of the student's life at Tuskegee under a strict regime of rules and regulations. Committees were formed that conducted daily examinations of the students' rooms and personal belongings. Careful attention was given to whether or not all had toothbrushes. One committee reported that it had noted some "absence of tooth brushes and tooth mugs." The Founder received other reports on the toothbrush situation. "There is a very large number of students that use the tooth brush only to adorn the washstand," one of Washington's student informers reported.

The slightest trace of dirt or grime was call for alarm and disciplinary action at Tuskegee. A committee appointed to inspect one of the dorms noted, "The wood work needs scrubbing and dusting thoroughly." The committee also reported that beds were not properly made in military fashion and some of the linen needed ironing and was improperly folded. Students who left their beds unmade were often punished by not receiving dinner.

When Tuskegee students did dine, they did so under stringent rules and regulations. Talking during meals was permitted only at precise intervals designated by the ringing of bells. . . .

The list of regulations ended with Rule Number 15: "For the violation of the above rules you will be severely punished."

Naturally, students sometimes fell short of the mark. Captain Austin, a stickler for detail, noted that student discipline during meals needed improvement. And no detail escaped his military eye: "Students continue to eat after bell rings and this together with the noise made by the knives and forks tinkling against the plates make it very difficult to hear the adjutant read the notices." In Austin's report to Booker Washington, which contained dining violations, he stated that the men students had become "careless in dress." He complained also about the behavior of women students in the dining hall. "The girls," Austin reported, "are exceedingly boisterous and rough when rising from their tables."

Search and seizure comprised part of the everyday life at Tuskegee. Men and women alike were searched for liquor, obscene materials, or anything else that in some way might contribute to the breakdown of rules or affect the school's "reputation." Searching of students' rooms and personal belongings became official policy at Tuskegee in 1906, when it was written into the School Code.

Booker Washington gave the students' social life the closest scrutiny. The institute forbade male and female students from associating after classes. The woman students received constant reminders from the Dean of Women to remain "moral and pure." This same advice was given to the men students by the Commandant of Cadets. Separate walkways across campus were designated for male and female to guarantee the two kept separated. Male students were forbidden to walk around or near the girls' dormitory after dusk. This was done, as one school official put it, to "prevent the promiscuous mingling of boys and girls."

Washington was working to make Tuskegee students into the type of blacks that the white South relished. Their training was primarily in "how to behave" rather than in how to become skilled tradesmen. To be a skilled craftsman requires proficiency in mathematical and verbal skills. The school's curriculum, however, was industrial almost to the total exclusion of the academic. What academic studies that did exist were secondary and often optional. That the school would commit itself to this type of program was clear from the staff that Washington employed at the school. Most of the faculty members were Hampton graduates, and they knew more about discipline than trades.

The *Southern Workman* reported that Hampton graduates held most of the key posts at Tuskegee Institute, noting the fact that the school's principal was "Hampton's most distinguished graduate." Washington issued a directive in 1908 to his departmental heads in which he stated that he wanted the school to "employ each year a reasonable number of Hampton graduates." He added that he "did not want the number of Hampton graduates decreased on the teaching force at Tuskegee."

The Founder was not completely close-minded in hiring personnel for teaching positions at Tuskegee, but instructors he hired from academic institutions often failed to fit well into his educational scheme because he subordinated every aspect of Tuskegee's educational program to the industrial schooling idea of producing tractable blacks. Blacks from academic universities like Howard, Fisk,

and Atlanta were employed at the school. Roscoe Conkling Bruce, a product of Harvard University who headed the so-called academic curriculum at Tuskegee, found that the institute's commitment to preparing students as common laborers was total. Bruce thought that perhaps some of the students might be material for professional careers. He complained about educating students "chiefly in accordance with the demands for labor."

Another thorn in Washington's side was a young instructor in the academic department named Leslie P. Hill, who had been hired by Bruce. Hill obviously failed to adjust to the second-class status of academic studies at Tuskegee. He initiated innovative approaches to his teaching of educational theory, history, and philosophy. However, the Founder regarded Hill as hostile to the educational philosophy of the school. Washington, in his explanation for firing Hill, remarked that the young Harvard graduate seemed to feel that the methods employed at Tuskegee were "either wrong or dangerous."

If he had many of the school's instructors in mind, Hill was absolutely right. Higher education at Tuskegee was a sad joke. Hill recognized that the general atmosphere discouraged serious effort among the industrial faculty. He noted that courses lacked outlines, instructors failed to use facilities properly, and that many of them lacked the competence to teach the skills for which they were hired.

Roscoe Bruce found the entire Tuskegee situation quite perplexing. He understood that Tuskegee was an industrial school—a fact, Bruce remarked, that he was "often reminded of." But he said that he failed to see how students who received little to no academic training would be able to carry on up-to-date craft positions. He wrote to the principal, "You see, the truth is that the carpenter is not taught enough mathematics, the machinist enough physics, or the farmer enough chemistry for the purpose of his particular work." Bruce also found it discouraging that there was no distinction made in the school's curriculum between those students who were going to be teachers and the ones "who plan to make horseshoes or to paint houses."

Washington conceded that some difficulties existed with the industrial idea of education, but that he had said so in his book, *Up From Slavery.*

> I told those who doubted the wisdom of the plan [industrial education] that I knew our first buildings would not be so comfortable or so complete in their finish as buildings erected by the experienced hands of outside workmen, but that in the teaching of civilization, self-help, and self-reliance, the erection of the buildings by the students themselves would more than compensate for any lack of comfort or fine finish.

His point, no doubt, was that problems are to be expected but they will be solved in time.

Regardless of what Booker T. said, Tuskegee was not preparing its students to take their place as skilled artisans in the industrial world. The school maintained a general policy of allowing students to graduate without even having finished a trade course. One report indicated that some positions calling for manual skills had become open to blacks in the South and that the opportunities for the Tuskegee graduates were "greater than ever," but that the students were not properly prepared for these jobs.

Roscoe C. Bruce reported to Washington on another separate occasion in which he complained that upon visiting the Girls' Laundry Department he was struck by the lack of any real skills training. Bruce said that the students did not seem to be receiving instruction in the art of the task but in fact simply performed menial chores.

W. T. B. Williams of the General Education Board conducted a survey of Tuskegee in 1906 and concluded that the student who completed the course of studies had what might be equivalent to a ninth grade education in the public school system. He considered there to be a general lack of training and preparation at the school. In addition, said Williams, "the majority of the students are barely able to read the Bible." He said in conclusion, "Considering the elementary nature of much of this work and the maturity of the students, the daily requirements seem pretty light."

The lack of quality in instruction and academic training at Tuskegee drove Roscoe Bruce to resign in 1906. Washington replaced him with J. R. E. Lee, who fit well into the Tuskegee idea. But Lee's own correspondence reveals the lack of serious academic or skills education at the school. Lee noted that the students who had attended one or two years of education at the general education schools, such as Fisk or Atlanta, were able to go immediately to the senior ranks at Tuskegee. Lee admitted that the work required of students at those schools was "far above the work required here [at Tuskegee]."

The lack of a positive, achievement-oriented atmosphere at Tuskegee had a negative effect on students and teachers. In 1912, one Tuskegee instructor openly admitted that the students they produced were ill-equipped to pursue a skilled occupation in industry. He thought that perhaps the problem lay with the teachers. He begged that they "give more time and attention" to their duties.

Instructors, on the other hand, blamed the problem on the students. Teachers in the industrial classes claimed that the students lacked the necessary attitude to become tradesmen, that they took their assignments lightly and performed them poorly. The instructor in basic construction and design accused the students of not following floor plans and of being sloppy and lazy in the performance of their tasks.

However, the teachers seemed more preoccupied with social matters than with correcting their students' deficiencies. "The young women teachers engage in frivolities hardly in keeping with their calling," W. T. B. Williams reported. "They are good women but not seriously concerned about the work in hand. They seem to give far more attention to dress rather than to almost anything else. . . ."

The female instructors were not alone. The men could stand on their own in terms of being frivolous. They repeatedly hosted gala social outings. One example was the going away party for Booker T. Washington, Jr., given in his honor by the faculty men. It was an elaborate and extravagant affair with orchestra, "seating arrangements patterned after that in the Cabinet Room of the White House," and dinner crowned with "Fried Chicken, Booker T. Washington, Jr. Style."

After a visit to Tuskegee in 1904, Robert Curtis Ogden commented on the "peculiar" social attitude of the school's faculty. He and his other white companions had been guests of honor at a faculty-hosted concert of classical music. Ogden, commenting later to Booker Washington about the concert, said that he believed his guests appreciated the entertainment, but that they would have enjoyed seeing more of the teachers and students at work rather than watching their hosts do their "level best to be like white folks and not natural."

Tuskegee's faculty was imitative of whites, but they were black and not the omnipotent authority symbol that, for example, Hampton's all-white staff was to its students. Tuskegee students, justifiably, found faults with the faculty, the education they received, and the conditions of campus life. They voiced their displeasure. The class in agricultural science at Tuskegee was taught by the renowned George Washington Carver, and he could not escape the growing discontent among students. One student complained that he had come to Tuskegee to learn the most advanced techniques in farming from George Washington Carver but found that the professor seemed to be more interested in producing "hired hands." The student remarked that overall he felt that he was "not receiving progressive instruction."

In addition, students challenged the strict discipline of the school in subtle ways. Julio Despaigne, Washington's key informant in the dorms, reported, "The students have the habit of making their beds at the morning good for when the inspector comes that he can find it well, and in the afternoon they disorder them and put clean and dirty clothes on them."

The rebellion of the students against the oppressive social restrictions of the institute manifested itself in different subtle ways. Some students began skipping chapel to meet with members of the opposite sex. Others volunteered for duties that held a high likelihood of putting them in contact with the opposite sex; a favorite assignment among male and female students was night duty at the school's hospital. Those fortunate enough to draw that duty were on their honor not to fraternize. The administration, however, soon found out the hospital was being used as a place for social carousing. Walter McFadden and Katie Paterson received an official reprimand from the administration "for questionable socializing while on night duty together at the hospital."

Some male students placed latches on their doors to keep night inspectors from entering while they, allegedly, broke school rules. This was met with quick action on the part of the administration. The Executive Council decided that because of

> the misconduct, gambling and so forth, which is indulged in on the part of certain young men who place night latches on their doors and lock themselves into their rooms from teachers' and officers' attempts to get into the room and who jump out of the windows before they can be detected in their mischief: because of this it has been found necessary to remove all the night latches from the doors.

The women students of the laundry class asserted themselves against unfair practices. They could not understand why they should be paid less than their labor was worth. They objected to the hard work with low pay. The young women said that they had the work of both students and teachers to do including that of the summer teachers and that on one occasion they had remained until five o'clock on Saturday evening in order to supply the boys with their week's laundry. "We hope you will not think of us as complainers," they closed in their letter to Booker Washington, "but, simply as children striving to perform their duty; and, at the same time receive some recompense in return. We are asking for higher wages. May we have it?" The Founder's answer was to appoint a committee to investigate their complaint, with the quiet result that nothing ever came of it.

The students' discontent gradually gave way to outright hostility against the school. Students stole from the institution, broke windows, wrecked dormitories, defaced walls, and on several occasions debased the school chapel. Some tried to avoid school and work by pretending to be ill. The institute's physician reported to Booker Washington, "I wish you also to bear in mind that a large number of the students who come to the hospital are not calling because they are ill, but are simply giving way to some imaginary ills, or else taking advantage of the easy method of losing an hour or two from work." One student spoke bluntly to Washington about the feeling among many of the students that to be successful at the school it was required to become "slaves of you [Mr. Washington] and Tuskegee." A group of native-born African students, accused of challenging the authority of one of their instructors and later brought before Washington for discipline, criticized the education they were receiving at Tuskegee and the attitude of teachers, including the Founder himself, who they said "acted as a master ordering his slaves." They concluded: "We do not intend no longer to remain in your institution...."

Students openly rebelled against the school's disciplinary practices. Charles H. Washington, a member of the senior class, considered the prying eyes of the faculty into every aspect of the individual student's private life to be too much for him. He told a faculty member point-blank to pass on the word that they "are to cease meddling with his affairs."

During the last ten years of Washington's reign at Tuskegee, from 1905 to his death in 1915, faculty members alluded to a growing student hostility against them. They became fearful for their personal safety, believing that students were carrying weapons and ready to use them. The situation at Tuskegee became more tense with the passing of each day. Students acted discourteously to instructors in and out of class. A group of faculty members reported to Washington that pupils had become so rebellious that they "never felt safe in appearing before the students."

In the tradition of the overseer whose position is dependent upon his ability to keep those under his charge in line, Washington met student discontent each step of the way with a tightening of rules and regulations. But student unrest continued. The result was that discipline at Tuskegee during the latter part of his administration approached absurdity. Students were suspended for talking without permission, failing to dress according to standards, or even for "failing to take a napkin to the dining hall." Young men students were chastised for "putting their hands in their pockets," and failing to obey that rule, the administration sought to offer "such inducements as will make them do so."

That the punishment students received outweighed the offense is clearly indicated in the case of Lewis Smith, whom a fellow student accused of "over indiscrete conduct with Emma Penny of the same class." Smith, a senior and slated to graduate as class salutatorian, was brought before the administration for allegedly attempting to hug and kiss Miss Penny. Although he denied the charges and his testimony was substantiated by a fellow classmate, the administration saw fit to punish Smith. He was denied the distinction of graduating as class salutatorian.

Smith was lucky. He could have been suspended or expelled—favorite disciplinary measures during the latter years of Booker T.'s rule over Tuskegee Institute. A case in point is the 1912 flag incident. A few members of the senior class of that year decided to celebrate by flying their class flag over Tompkins Hall. They made the unpardonable mistake, however, of not obtaining the administration's permission. School officials considered the students' act a conspiracy against the institute's authority, an "organized movement on the part of some of the members of the senior class... and that this was not carried out on the spur of the moment." The accused students begged for mercy and swore that they acted out of no intent to challenge school authority or embarrass the administration. One of the accused vowed they would rather have had their "heads severed from their bodies" than to do anything against Tuskegee. The young men were suspended.

The slightest infraction on the part of the student, or even suspicion of having broken a rule, was reason enough for the Washington administration to notify parents. This had near disastrous results in the case of Charles Bell, a senior who was brought before the administration on the suspicion of having engaged in "sexual misconduct" with a young woman named Varner of the same class. Both denied the charges. There was no eyewitness testimony or other "proof" that Bell and Varner had done anything wrong, except the fact that they were often seen together. The administration, nevertheless, passed its suspicions on to

Miss Varner's father. He showed up later on campus with his gun, saying that he would shoot Bell on sight. Bell was forced to leave the institute until the situation quieted.

When Tuskegee students did pose a real threat to the sovereignty of Booker Washington, he showed no mercy. In 1903, a group of Tuskegee students launched a strike against the school. The material on the strike, and it is extremely sketchy, does indicate that the participants objected to the entire Tuskegee order of things. They wanted more academic training, better instruction, more opportunity to learn trades, and an easing of rules and regulations. Washington's response was undiluted: "No concessions."

In an official but insubstantial report on the strike to the school's white financial backers, Booker T. contended that a few malcontents had occupied one of the school's buildings, thinking that this was the way to be heard. The students were not upset with the institute, he said, "nor were they in opposition to any industrial work," but "objected to being required to devote too much time to both industrial work and studies with too little time for preparation." The strike apparently ended as quickly as it had begun once the administration served notice that all those who failed to return to work immediately would be expelled.

Those who obtained an "education" at Tuskegee did so in accordance with the industrial schooling idea and under the watchful eyes of Booker Taliaferro Washington. Student dissatisfaction did nothing to change the Founder's mind about the rightness of the type of educational philosophy he professed and protected. His administration practiced a stiff brand of discipline that it never backed down from. But students, on occasion, contin-

ued to try and voice their complaints. Perhaps it is understandable, then, why the Washington administration felt it might be necessary to establish a "guard house" for the purpose of confining its student incorrigibles. It did just that in 1912.

Booker T.'s educational practices were based on his desire to please whites and gain their support. The Founder worked to make whites more a part of the school's operations. He invited them to visit the institute on every occasion. He believed that the school's annual commencement exercises afforded an excellent opportunity to win goodwill from the local whites. "I think it would be well for you to spend a week in Montgomery among the white and colored people," Washington advised a fellow faculty member. "I am very anxious that in addition to the colored people we have a large representative class of whites to attend Commencement." In fact, the Founder considered paying the fares of white visitors to the commencement exercises. The school advertised the commencement of 1904 in the *Tuskegee News*.

Washington did everything possible to bring in more local white support. When Washington received advice from a "reliable source" that if he kept the number of Jews down in attendance at commencement, more local whites would probably come, he responded: "Of course I do not want to keep the Jews away, but I think it would be a good plan to increase the number of Gentiles if possible."

The Founder received unsolicited advice on how to gain more local and national support. One Northerner wrote him suggesting that the school would gain more support if it devoted itself exclusively to the production of domestic servants. The writer suggested that the program should stress "cooking, waiting on table, cleaning silver and washing windows, sewing, dusting, washing and ironing."

In his response, Washington made it clear that Tuskegee did this and more:

> At this institution we give training in every line of domestic work, hence any girl who finishes our course should be able to perform any of the usual duties connected with a servant's life, but one of the most important things to be accomplished for the colored people now is the getting of them to have correct ideas concerning labor, that is to get them to feel that all classes of labor, whether of the head or hand, are dignified. This lesson I think Tuskegee, in connection with Hampton, has been successful in teaching the race.

And, like Hampton, Tuskegee aimed to do more than serve as an agency to place individual domestics. Washington in conclusion said that the most economical thing to be done was to send out a set of people not only trained in hand but thoroughly equipped in mind and heart so that they themselves could go out and start smaller centers or training schools.

He believed that it would be of greater service to the whole country "if we can train at Tuskegee one girl who could go out and start a domestic training school in Atlanta, Baltimore, or elsewhere, than we would be doing by trying to put servants directly into individual houses which would be a never ending task." . . .

Booker T. Washington never intentionally did anything to upset or anger Southern whites. He repledged his love for the South and his obedience to its traditions in *My Larger Education,* published four years before his death. The Founder said in that work, "I understand thoroughly the prejudices, the customs, the traditions of the South—and, strange as it may seem to those who do not wholly understand the situation, I love the South." The philosophy of "uplift" for blacks that he preached across the nation and taught at Tuskegee Institute was in accordance with that love and the prevailing racial, economic order. His role was like that of the black overseer during slavery who, given the position of authority over his fellow slaves, worked diligently to keep intact the very system under which they both were enslaved.

NO

Louis R. Harlan

BOOKER T. WASHINGTON AND THE POLITICS OF ACCOMMODATION

It is ironic that Booker T. Washington, the most powerful black American of his time and perhaps of all time, should be the black leader whose claim to the title is most often dismissed by the lay public. Blacks often question his legitimacy because of the role that favor by whites played in Washington's assumption of power, and whites often remember him only as an educator or, confusing him with George Washington Carver, as "that great Negro scientist." This irony is something that Washington will have to live with in history, for he himself deliberately created the ambiguity about his role and purposes that has haunted his image. And yet, Washington was a genuine black leader, with a substantial black following and with virtually the same long-range goals for Afro-Americans as his rivals. This presentation is concerned with Washington's social philosophy, such as it was, but it also addresses his methods of leadership, both his Delphic public utterances that meant one thing to whites and another to blacks and his adroit private movements through the brier patch of American race relations. It does not try to solve the ultimate riddle of his character.

Washington's own view of himself was that he was the Negro of the hour, whose career and racial program epitomized what blacks needed to maintain themselves against white encroachments and to make progress toward equality in America. The facts of his life certainly fitted his self-image. He was the last of the major black leaders to be born in slavery, on a small farm in western Virginia in 1856. Growing up during the Reconstruction era in West Virginia, he believed that one of the lessons he learned was that the Reconstruction experiment in racial democracy failed because it began at the wrong end, emphasizing political means and civil rights acts rather than economic means and self-determination. Washington learned this lesson not so much through experiences as a child worker in the salt works and coal mines as by what he was taught as a houseboy for the leading family of Malden, West Virginia, and later as a student at Hampton Institute in Virginia. Hampton

From Louis R. Harlan, "Booker T. Washington and the Politics of Accommodation," in John Hope Franklin and August Meier, eds., *Black Leaders of the Twentieth Century* (University of Illinois Press, 1982). Copyright © 1982 by the Board of Trustees of the University of Illinois. Reprinted by permission of the author and University of Illinois Press.

applied the missionary method to black education and made its peace with the white South.

After teaching school in his home town, Washington briefly studied in a Baptist seminary and in a lawyer's office. But he soon abandoned these alternative careers, perhaps sensing that disfranchisement and the secularization of society would weaken these occupations as bases for racial leadership. He returned to Hampton Institute as a teacher for two years and then founded Tuskegee Normal and Industrial Institute in Alabama in 1881. Over the next quarter of a century, using Hampton's methods but with greater emphasis on the skilled trades, Washington built up Tuskegee Institute to be an equal of Hampton.

Washington's bid for leadership went beyond education and institution-building, however. Symbolic of his fresh approach to black-white relations was a speech he gave in 1895 before a commercial exposition, known as the Atlanta Compromise Address, and his autobiography, *Up from Slavery* (1901). As Washington saw it, blacks were toiling upward from slavery by their own efforts into the American middle class and needed chiefly social peace to continue in this steady social evolution. Thus, in the Atlanta Compromise he sought to disarm the white South by declaring agitation of the social equality question "the merest folly" and proclaiming that in "purely social" matters "we can be as separate as the fingers, yet one as the hand in all things essential to mutual progress." These concessions came to haunt Washington as southerners used segregation as a means of systematizing discrimination, and northerners followed suit. And they did not stop at the "purely social."

Washington's concessions to the white South, however, were only half of a bargain. In return for downgrading civil and political rights in the black list of priorities, Washington asked whites to place no barriers to black economic advancement and even to become partners of their black neighbors "in all things essential to mutual progress." Washington saw his own role as the axis between the races, the only leader who could negotiate and keep the peace by holding extremists on both sides in check. He was always conscious that his unique influence could be destroyed in an instant of self-indulgent flamboyance.

Washington sought to influence whites, but he never forgot that it was the blacks that he undertook to lead. He offered blacks not the empty promises of the demagogue but a solid program of economic and educational progress through struggle. It was less important "just now," he said, for a black person to seek admission to an opera house than to have the money for the ticket. Mediating diplomacy with whites was only half of Washington's strategy; the other half was black solidarity, mutual aid, and institution-building. He thought outspoken complaint against injustice was necessary but insufficient, and he thought factional dissent among black leaders was self-defeating and should be suppressed.

Washington brought to his role as a black leader the talents and outlook of a machine boss. He made Tuskegee Institute the largest and best-supported black educational institution of his day, and it spawned a large network of other industrial schools. Tuskegee's educational function is an important and debatable subject, of course, but the central concern here is Washington's use of the school as the base of operations of what came to be known as the Tuskegee Machine. It was an all-black school with an all-black faculty at a time when most black colleges were still run by white missionaries. Tuskegee taught self-determination. It also taught trades designed for economic independence in a region dominated by sharecrop agriculture. At the same time, by verbal juggling tricks, Washington convinced the southern whites that Tuskegee was not educating black youth away from the farms. Tuskegee also functioned as a model black community, not only by acquainting its students with a middle-class way of life, but by buying up the surrounding farmland and selling it at low rates of interest to create a community of small landowners and homeowners. The Institute became larger than the town.

Washington built a regional constituency of farmers, artisans, country teachers, and small businessmen; he expanded the Tuskegee Machine nationwide after the Atlanta Compromise seemed acceptable to blacks all over the country, even by many who later denounced it. His first northern black ally was T. Thomas Fortune, editor of the militant and influential New York *Age* and founder of the Afro-American Council, the leading forum of black thought at the time. Washington was not a member, but he usually spoke at the annual meetings, and his lieutenants so tightly controlled the council that it never passed an action or resolution not in Washington's interest. Seeking more direct allies, Washington founded in 1900 the National Negro Business League, of which he was president for life. The league was important not so much for what it did for black business, which was little, but because the local branch of the league was a stronghold of Washington men in every substantial black population center.

Other classes of influential blacks did not agree with Washington's stated philosophy but were beholden to him for the favors he did them or offered to do for them. He was not called the Wizard for nothing. White philanthropists who approved of him for their own reasons gave him the money to help black colleges by providing for a Carnegie library here, a dormitory there. Through Washington Andrew Carnegie alone gave buildings to twenty-nine black schools. Not only college administrators owed him for favors, but so did church leaders, YMCA directors and many others. Though never much of a joiner, he became a power in the Baptist church, and he schemed through lieutenants to control the secret black fraternal orders and make his friends the high potentates of the Pythians, Odd Fellows, and so on. Like any boss, he turned every favor into a bond of obligation.

It was in politics, however, that Washington built the most elaborate tentacle of the octopus-like Tuskegee Machine. In politics as in everything else, Washington cultivated ambiguity. He downgraded politics as a solution of black problems, did not recommend politics to the ambitious young black man, and never held office. But when Theodore Roosevelt became president in 1901 and asked for Washington's advice on black and southern appointments, Washington consented with alacrity. He became the chief black adviser of both Presidents Roosevelt and William Howard Taft. He failed in his efforts to liberalize Republican policy on voting rights, lynching, and racial discrimination, however, and relations between the Republican party and black voters reached a low ebb.

In patronage politics, however, Washington found his opportunity. For a man who minimized the importance of politics, Washington devoted an inordinate amount of his time and tremendous energy to securing federal jobs for his machine lieutenants. These men played a certain role in the politics of the period, but their first obligation was to the Tuskegean. Washington advised the presidents to replace the old venal officeholding class of blacks with men who had proven themselves in the independent world of business, but in practice it took only loyalty to Washington to cleanse miraculously an old-time political hack.

Washington also used high political office in the North to win the loyalty of key figures in the legal profession whose ideology and natural bent were usually in the direction of more outspoken protest. A notable example was William H. Lewis of Boston, a graduate of Amherst College and Harvard University Law School, who had been an outspoken critic of Washington. President Roosevelt had long admired Lewis's all-American prowess on the football field as much as his professional attainments, and when Washington began talking of raising the quality of the black civil service, Roosevelt brought up Lewis. Washington was skeptical, but as soon as possible he met with Lewis and made a deal with him. As Lewis wrote, there were "many things about which we might differ, but that we had the same aims and the same end in view." Lewis became, with Washington's blessing, the assistant U.S. district attorney in Boston, and a few years later Taft appointed him assistant attorney general of the United States, the highest appointive federal post held by a black man up to that time—and for decades afterward.

In another sphere also Washington spread the web of his Tuskegee Machine over the several hundred black weekly newspapers and half-dozen magazines through which the black community communicated with itself. W. E. B. Du Bois tried in 1903 to prove that Washington's "hush money" controlled the black press through subsidies and outright ownership. Challenged, Du Bois could not prove his case, but when Washington's papers were opened forty years later, they revealed the essential accuracy of the charge. The question of how *much* control is complicated, however, by the willing complicity of the editors in this domination. The editors were themselves small businessmen who generally agreed with Washington's economic orientation and the conventional wisdom of a commercial age. Furthermore, Washington's small subsidies, except in a few instances, were only a minor part of the operating funds of these newspapers.

Washington's outright critics and enemies were called "radicals" because they challenged Washington's conservatism and bossism, though their tactics of verbal protest would seem moderate indeed to a later generation of activists. They were the college-educated blacks, engaged in professional pursuits, and proud of their membership in an elite class—what one of them called the Talented Tenth. The strongholds of the radicals were the northern cities and southern black colleges. They stood for full political and civil rights, liberal education, free expression, and aspiration. They dreamed of a better world and believed Booker T. Washington was a menace to its achievement.

The first to challenge Washington and all his works was a young Harvard graduate, William Monroe Trotter, who founded in 1900 a newspaper, the Boston *Guardian*. Trotter not only differed with the Tuskegean on every conceivable subject but engaged in personal abuse. He spoke of Washington's "crime of race ridicule and belittlement." He called him Pope Washington, The Black Boss, the Benedict Arnold of the Negro race, the Exploiter of Exploiters, the Great Traitor, and the Great Divider. In reporting a speech by Washington in Boston in 1902 Trotter described him thus: "His features were harsh in the extreme. His vast leonine jaws into which vast mastiff-like rows of teeth were set clinched together like a vise. His forehead shot up to a great cone; his chin was massive and square; his eyes were dull and absolutely characterless, and with a glance that would leave you uneasy and restless during the night if you had failed to report to the police such a man around before you went to bed." That this yellow journalism was far from an accurate description of Washington's modest and reassuring appearance was beside the point. In Trotter's vendetta against Washington no charge, true or false, was too big or too petty to use.

Trotter seized the chance to confront Washington directly when the black leader spoke at a Boston church in 1903 under sponsorship of the local branch of the National Negro Business League. Trotter stood on a chair to interrupt Washington's speech with nine questions that were actually challenges. Quoting from a Washington speech, for example, Trotter asked: "When you said: 'It was not so important whether the Negro was in the inferior car as whether there was in that car a superior man not a beast,' did you not minimize the outrage of the insulting Jim-crow car discrimination and justify it by the 'bestiality' of the Negro?" The final provocative question was: "Are the rope and the torch all the race is to get under your leadership?"

The police moved through the crowd to arrest Trotter for disorderly conduct, and Washington proceeded with his speech as though nothing had happened, but Trotter had achieved his purpose. The incident appeared next day in all the newspapers as the Boston Riot, penetrating Washington's news screen to show that not all blacks approved of Washington's leadership. Washington publicly ignored the affair, but his Boston lieutenants made a martyr of Trotter by vigorous prosecution of his case, forcing him to serve thirty days in jail.

Perhaps the most important effect of the Boston Riot was that it forced Du Bois, the leading black intellectual and now the leading civil rights champion of his generation, off the fence. A Harvard Ph.D. with German university training, Du Bois was never even considered for tenure in any leading American university, and in 1903 he was a professor at Atlanta University. In *The Souls of Black Folk*, published before the Boston Riot, he had criticized Washington in a searching but moderate way, in no way comparable with Trotter's cry that the emperor had no clothes. Believing that Trotter was being victimized, Du Bois wrote Trotter a private letter of sympathy, which Trotter promptly published, and this started Du Bois's movement out of academe into the arena of racial politics.

Washington had a chance in January 1904 to heal the wounds of dissidence that the Boston Riot had opened. With the consent and cooperation of Du Bois, Washington convened the Carnegie Hall Conference, a three-day secret meeting of about thirty black leaders, excluding Trotter. But Washington with his penchant for bossism torpedoed his own effort at rapprochement by packing the meeting with his own lieutenants to such a degree that Du Bois and his adherents resigned from the organization that was created at the conference.

The following year, Du Bois and Trotter formed their own organization, the Niagara Movement, dedicated to "persistent manly agitation" for civil rights, voting rights, job opportunities, equal educational opportunities, and human rights in general. The Niagara Movement is an important link in the historical development of the civil rights movement, but here we are concerned with its role in the minority-group leadership struggle with Washington. This small band of intellectuals, hurling their manifestos, was no match for the political skill and marshaled power of the Wizard of Tuskegee. They themselves limited their membership to the small black professional class, insisted on an ideological "likemindedness" that few could achieve, and had no white allies. By contrast, Washington had a broader base and a commoner touch. Though Washington proposed the leadership of another elite class, the black businessmen, he kept in close touch with the black masses and directed his program to their immediate needs. Furthermore, he fished for allies wherever he could find them, among whites and even among the professional men who would ordinarily be expected in the Niagara Movement. He cared little about the ideology of a lieutenant, as long as the man did what Washington wanted done.

The Niagara Movement called Washington, in effect, a puppet of the whites, who thrust him into prominence because he did not challenge their wrongdoing. According to the Niagarites, Washington needed to mollify the whites in be-half of his school to such an extent that he was rendered unfit for black leadership, that instead of leadership he gave them cowardice and apology. Furthermore, his critics charged that Washington was a half-educated southerner whose control over black affairs was stifling an emergent black educated elite, the Talented Tenth, the logical leaders. Because of his own class orientation he was trying to change the social position of blacks through the acquisitive propensities and the leadership of businessmen instead of through political and civil rights agitation, which the Niagara men saw as the need of the hour. Extremists among them called Washington an instrument of white indirect rule, like the slave drivers of the old days. Even the moderate Kelly Miller of Howard University observed in 1903 that Washington was "not a leader of the people's own choosing." Though they might accept his gifts, said Miller, "few thoughtful colored men espouse what passes as Mr. Washington's policy without apology or reserve."

Washington dismissed his black critics by questioning their motives, their claim to superior wisdom, and—the politician's ultimate argument—their numbers. Washington understood, if his critics did not, that his leadership of the black community largely depended on his recognition by whites as the black leader. If he did not meet some minimal standards of satisfactoriness to whites, another Washington would be created. He obviously could not lead the whites; he could not even divide the whites. He could only, in a limited way, exploit the class divisions that whites created among themselves. He could work in the cracks of their social structure, move like Brer Rabbit through the brier patch, and thus outwit the more numerous and powerful whites.

While Washington recognized the centrality of black-white relations in his efforts to lead blacks, he was severely restricted by the historical context of his leadership. It was an age of polarization of black and white. The overheated atmosphere of the South at the turn of the century resembled that of a crisis center on the eve of war. Lynching became a more than weekly occurrence; discrimination and humiliation of blacks were constant and pervasive and bred a whole literature and behavioral science of self-justification. Race riots terrorized blacks in many cities, and not only in the South. It would have required not courage but foolhardiness for Washington, standing with both feet in Alabama, to have challenged this raging white aggression openly and directly. Even unqualified verbal protest would have brought him little support from either southern blacks or white well-wishers. Du Bois took higher ground and perhaps a better vision of the future when he urged forthright protest against every white injustice, on the assumption that whites were rational beings and would respond dialectically to black protest. But few white racists of the early twentieth century cared anything for the facts. And when Du Bois in his Atlanta years undertook to implement his protest with action, he was driven to the negative means of refusing to pay his poll tax or refusing to ride segregated streetcars and elevators.

Instead of either confronting all of white America or admitting that his Faustian bargain for leadership had created a systemic weakness in his program, Washington simply met each day as it came, pragmatically, seeking what white allies he could against avowed white enemies. A serious fault of this policy was that Washington usually appealed for white support on a basis of a vaguely conceived mutual interest rather than on ideological agreement. For example, in both the South and the North Washington allied himself with the white upper class against the masses. In the South he joined with the planter class and when possible with the coal barons and railroad officials against the populists and other small white farmer groups who seemed to him to harbor the most virulent anti-black attitudes born of labor competition. Similarly, in the North, Washington admired and bargained with the big business class. The bigger the businessman, the more Washington admired him, as the avatar and arbiter of American society. At the pinnacle in his measure of men were the industrialists Carnegie, John D. Rockefeller, and Henry H. Rogers and the merchant princes Robert C. Ogden and Julius Rosenwald. To be fair to Washington, he appreciated their philanthropic generosity at least as much as he admired their worldly success, but his lips were sealed against criticism of even the more rapacious and ungenerous members of the business elite.

Washington made constructive use of his philanthropic allies to aid not only Tuskegee but black education and black society as a whole. He guided the generous impulse of a Quaker millionairess into the Anna T. Jeanes Foundation to improve the teaching in black public schools. He persuaded the Jewish philanthropist Julius Rosenwald to begin a program that lasted for decades for building more adequate black schoolhouses all over the South. Washington's influence on Carnegie, Rockefeller, Jacob Schiff, and other rich men also transcended immediate Tuskegee interests to endow other black institutions. In short, Washington did play a role in educational statesmanship. There were limits, however, to his power to advance black interests through philanthropy. When his northern benefactors became involved in the Southern Education Board to improve the southern public school systems, for example, he worked repeatedly but without success to get this board to redress the imbalance of public expenditures or even to halt the rapid increase of discrimination against black schools and black children. He had to shrug off his failure and get from these so-called philanthropists whatever they were willing to give.

Having committed himself to the business elite, Washington took a dim view of the leaders of the working class. Immigrants represented to him, as to many blacks, labor competitors; Jews were the exception here, as he held them up to ambitious blacks as models of the work-ethic and group solidarity. He claimed in his autobiography that his disillusionment with labor unions went back to his youthful membership in the Knights of Labor and stemmed from observation of their disruption of the natural laws of economics. In his heyday, however, which was also the age of Samuel Gompers, Washington's anti-union attitudes were explained by the widespread exclusion of blacks from membership in many unions and hence from employment in many trades. There is no evidence that Washington ever actively supported black strikebreaking, but his refusal to intervene in behalf of all-white unions is understandable. It was more often white employees rather than employers who excluded blacks,

or so Washington believed. He worked hard to introduce black labor into the non-union, white-only cotton mills in the South, even to the extent of interesting northern capitalists in investing in black cotton mills and similar enterprises.

Washington was a conservative by just about any measure. Though he flourished in the Progressive era it was not he, but his opponents who were the men of good hope, full of reform proposals and faith in the common man. Washington's vision of the common man included the southern poor white full of rancor against blacks, the foreign-born anarchist ready to pull down the temple of American business, and the black sharecropper unqualified by education or economic freedom for the ballot. Though Washington opposed the grandfather clause and every other southern device to exclude the black man from voting solely on account of his color, Washington did not favor universal suffrage. He believed in literacy and property tests, fairly enforced. He was no democrat. And he did not believe in woman suffrage, either.

In his eagerness to establish common ground with whites, that is, with some whites, Washington overstepped his purpose in public speeches by telling chicken-thief, mule, and other dialect stories intended to appeal to white stereotypes of blacks, and he occasionally spoke of the Afro-American as "a child race." No doubt his intent was to disarm his listeners, and before mixed audiences he often alternately addressed the two groups, reassuring whites that blacks should cooperate with their white neighbors in all constructive efforts, but saying to blacks that in their cooperation there should be "no unmanly cowering or stooping." At the cost of some forcefulness of presentation, Washington did have a remarkable capacity to convince whites as well as blacks that he not only understood them but agreed with them. It is one of Washington's intangible qualities as a black leader that he could influence, if not lead, so many whites. The agreement that whites sensed in him was more in his manner than in his program or goals, which always included human rights as well as material advancement for blacks.

In his constant effort to influence public opinion, Washington relied on the uncertain instruments of the press and the public platform. A flood of books and articles appeared over his name, largely written by his private secretary and a stable of ghostwriters, because he was too busy to do much writing. His ghostwriters were able and faithful, but they could not put new words or new ideas out over his signature, so for the crucial twenty years after 1895, Washington's writings showed no fresh creativity or real response to events, only a steady flood of platitudes. Washington's speeches generally suffered from an opposite handicap, that he was the only one who could deliver them. But he was too busy making two or three speeches a day to write a new one for each occasion, so the audiences rather than the speeches changed. But everywhere he went, North, South, or West, he drew large crowds ready to hear or rehear his platitudes.

Washington did try to change his world by other means. Some forms of racial injustice, such as lynching, disfranchisement, and unequal facilities in education and transportation, Washington dealt with publicly and directly. Early in his career as a leader he tried to sidestep the lynching question by saying that, deplorable though it was, he was too busy working for the education of black youth to divide his energies by dealing with other public questions. Friends and critics alike sharply told him that if he proposed to be a leader of blacks, he was going to have to deal with this subject. So he began an annual letter on lynching that he sent to all the southern white dailies, and he made Tuskegee Institute the center of statistical and news information on lynching. He always took a moderate tone, deplored rape and crime by blacks, but always denied that the crime blacks committed was either the cause of or justification for the crime of lynching. He tried to make up for his moderation by persistence, factual accuracy, and persuasive logic. Disfranchisement of black voters swept through the South from Texas to Virginia during Washington's day. He publicly protested in letters to the constitutional conventions and legislatures in Alabama, Georgia, and Louisiana and aided similar efforts in several other states. He failed to stop lynching, to prevent the loss of voting rights, and to clean up the Jim Crow cars or bring about even minimal standards of fairness in the public schools. But he did try.

As for social segregation, Washington abided by southern customs while in the South but forthrightly declared it unreasonable for white southerners to dictate his behavior outside of the South. His celebrated dinner at the White House in 1901, therefore, though it caused consternation and protest among white southerners, was consistent with his lifetime practice. Tuskegee Institute underwent an elaborate ritual of segregation with every white visitor, but the man who came to dinner at the White House, had tea with the queen of England, and attended hundreds of banquets and private meals with whites outside the South certainly never internalized the attitudes of the segregators.

What Washington could not do publicly to achieve equal rights, he sought to accomplish secretly. He spent four years in cooperation with the Afro-American Council on a court case to test the constitutionality of the Louisiana grandfather clause, providing funds from his own pocket and from northern white liberal friends. In his own state of Alabama, Washington secretly directed the efforts of his personal lawyer to carry two grandfather-clause cases all the way to the U.S. Supreme Court, where they were lost on technicalities. He took the extra precaution of using code names in all the correspondence on the Alabama cases. Through private pressure on railroad officials and congressmen, Washington tried to bring about improvement in the Jim Crow cars and railroad waiting rooms. He had more success in the Dan Rogers case, which overturned a criminal verdict against a black man because blacks were excluded from the jury. He also secretly collaborated with two southern white attorneys to defend Alonzo Bailey, a farm laborer held in peonage for debt; the outcome here was also successful, for the Alabama peonage law was declared unconstitutional. These and other secret actions were certainly not enough to tear down the legal structure of white supremacy, but they show that Washington's role in Afro-American history was not always that of the accommodationist "heavy." He was working, at several levels and in imaginative ways, and always with vigor, toward goals similar to those of his critics. If his methods did not work, the same could be said of theirs. And he did not take these civil rights actions as a means of answering criticism, because he kept his part in the court cases a secret except to a handful of confidants, a secret not revealed until his papers were opened to historians in recent decades.

There was another, uglier side of Washington's secret behavior, however—his ruthless spying and sabotage against his leading black critics. Washington never articulated a justification for these actions, perhaps because, being secret, they did not require defense. And yet Washington and Emmett Scott left the evidence of his secret machinations undestroyed in his papers, apparently in the faith that history would vindicate him when all the facts were known. Then, too, Washington was not given to explaining himself. . . .

Espionage became an important instrument of Washington's black leadership—or bossism—a few days before the Boston Riot in 1903, when he hired a young black man, Melvin J. Chisum, to infiltrate the inner councils of Trotter's anti-Washington organization in Boston. Chisum later spied on the Niagara Movement's Brooklyn branch, arranged to bribe an opposition newspaper editor in Washington, D.C., and reported these and other clandestine actions to the Wizard on a park bench in New York City. Washington also used Pinkerton detectives and other paid and unpaid secret agents on a variety of errands, to infiltrate the inner councils of the Niagara Movement, to repress newspaper reporting of Niagara meetings, to find out if Trotter's wife worked as a domestic, to research the tax records of Atlanta to get evidence that Du Bois, a champion of black political action, had not paid his poll tax. When a young black magazine editor, J. Max Barber, began to criticize him, Washington tried to muzzle Barber through his publisher and advertisers, then hounded Barber not only out of his magazine but out of job after job until Barber retired from race work to become a dentist. Even the white liberals who joined with the Niagara Movement to form the interracial National Association for the Advancement of Colored People in 1909 were not immune from Washington's secret attacks. Washington arranged with the racially biased New York newspaper reporters to cover—in a sensational fashion —a dinner meeting of the Cosmopolitan Club, an interracial social group to which a number of NAACP leaders belonged. Even they never guessed that Washington had done this in collusion with white racists.

The Booker T. Washington who emerges into the light of history from his private papers is a complex, Faustian character quite different from the paragon of self-uplift and Christian forbearance that Washington projected in his autobiography. On the other hand, there is little evidence for and much evidence against the charge of some of his contemporaries that he was simply an accommodationist who bargained away his race's birthright for a mess of pottage. Nor does he fit some historians' single-factor explanations of his career: that he offered "education for the new slavery," that he was a proto-black-nationalist, that he was or must have been psychologically crippled by the constraints and guilt feelings of his social role.

Washington's complexity should not be overstressed, however, for the more we know about anybody the more complex that person seems. And through the complexity of Washington's life, its busyness and its multiple levels, two main themes stand out, his true belief in his program for black progress and his great skill in and appetite for politics,

broadly defined, serving both his goals and his personal power.

First, let us look closely at Washington's industrial education and small business program. It may have been anachronistic preparation for the age of mass production and corporate gigantism then coming into being, but it had considerable social realism for a black population which was, until long after Washington's death, predominantly rural and southern. Furthermore, it was well attuned to the growth and changing character of black business in his day. Increasingly, the nineteenth-century black businesses catering to white clients surrendered predominance to ghetto businesses such as banks, insurance companies, undertakers, and barbers catering to black customers. These new businessmen, with a vested interest in black solidarity, were the backbone of Washington's National Negro Business League. Washington clearly found congenial the prospect of an elite class of self-made businessmen as leaders and models for the struggling masses. There was also room for the Talented Tenth of professional men in the Tuskegee Machine, however. Washington welcomed every college-educated recruit he could secure. Directly or through agents, he was the largest employer in the country of black college graduates.

Second, let us consider Washington as a powerful politician. Though he warned young men away from politics as a dead-end career, what distinguished Washington's career was not his rather conventional goals, which in public or private he shared with almost every other black spokesman, but his consummate political skill, his wheeling and dealing....

Du Bois spent much of his long life puzzling over the phenomenon of

Washington, a man who did not seem to have an abstraction about him. But toward the end of his life, in 1954 in an oral history memoir at Columbia University, Du Bois said of his old rival dead almost forty years: "Oh, Washington was a politician. He was a man who believed that we should get what we could get." Du Bois, who himself found the political part of his race work the least agreeable, went on to say of Washington: "It wasn't a matter of ideals or anything of that sort.... With everybody that Washington met, he evidently had the idea: 'Now, what's your racket? What are you out for?'" Du Bois was a shrewd observer, but what he saw in Washington as a lack—of ideals, of principles, of vision—was his great and almost unique gift as a black political leader. Washington could almost immediately, intuitively, and without formal questioning see through the masks and intellectual superstructure of men to the mainsprings of their behavior. Then he imaginatively sought to bend their purposes to his own. Du Bois said that Washington had no faith in white people but that he was very popular among them because, whenever he met a white man, he listened to him until he figured out what that man wanted him to say, and then as soon as possible he said it. Washington did not always get his way, of course, but he always understood, as his more doctrinaire critics did not, that politics was the art of the possible. What was surprising about Washington was the number and diversity of those he enlisted in his coalition.

Washington's program was not consensus politics, for he always sought change, and there was always vocal opposition to him on both sides that he never tried to mollify. Denounced on the one hand by the Niagara Movement and the NAACP for not protesting enough, he was also distrusted and denounced by white supremacists for bringing the wooden horse within the walls of Troy. All of the racist demagogues of his time—Benjamin Tillman, James Vardaman, Theodore Bilbo, Thomas Dixon, and J. Thomas Heflin, to name a few—called Washington their insidious enemy. One descriptive label for Washington might be centrist coalition politics. The Tuskegee Machine had the middle and undecided majority of white and black people behind it. Washington was a rallying point for the southern moderates, the northern publicists and makers of opinion, and the thousands who read his autobiography or crowded into halls to hear him. Among blacks he had the businessmen solidly behind him, and even, as August Meier has shown, a majority of the Talented Tenth of professional men, so great was his power to reward and punish, to make or break careers. He had access to the wellsprings of philanthropy, political preferment, and other white sources of black opportunity. For blacks at the bottom of the ladder, Washington's program offered education, a self-help formula, and, importantly for a group demoralized by the white aggression of that period, a social philosophy that gave dignity and purpose to lives of daily toil.

It could be said with some justification that the Tuskegee Machine was a stationary machine, that it went nowhere. Because the machine was held together by the glue of self-interest, Washington was frequently disappointed by the inadequate response of his allies. The southern upper class did not effectively resist disfranchisement as he had hoped and never gave blacks the equal economic chance that he considered an integral part of the Atlanta Compromise. Washington's philanthropist-friends never stood up for equal opportunity in public education. Black businessmen frequently found their own vested interest in a captive market rather than a more open society. And Washington himself often took the view that whatever was good for Tuskegee and himself was good for the Negro.

To the charge that he accomplished nothing, it can only be imagined what Washington would have answered, since he did not have the years of hindsight and self-justification that some of his critics enjoyed. He would probably have stressed how much worse the southern racial reaction would have been without his coalition of moderates, his soothing syrup, and his practical message to blacks of self-improvement and progress along the lines of least resistance. Washington's power over his following, and hence his power to bring about change, have probably been exaggerated. It was the breadth rather than the depth of his coalition that was unique. Perhaps one Booker T. Washington was enough. But even today, in a very different society, Washington's autobiography is still in print. It still has some impalpable power to bridge the racial gap, to move new readers to take the first steps across the color line. Many of his ideas of self-help and racial solidarity still have currency in the black community. But he was an important leader because, like Frederick Douglass before him and Martin Luther King after him, he had the program and strategy and skill to influence the behavior of not only the Afro-American one-tenth, but the white nine-tenths of the American people. He was a political realist.

POSTSCRIPT

Did Booker T. Washington's Philosophy and Actions Betray the Interests of African Americans?

Discussions of race relations in the late-nineteenth- and early-twentieth-century United States invariably focus upon the ascendancy of Booker T. Washington, his apparent accommodation to existing patterns of racial segregation, and the conflicting traditions within black thought, epitomized by the clash between Washington and Du Bois. Seldom, however, is attention given to black nationalist thought in the "age of Booker T. Washington."

Black nationalism, centered on the concept of racial solidarity, has been a persistent theme in African American history, and it reached one of its most important stages of development between 1880 and 1920. In the late 1800s Henry McNeal Turner and Edward Wilmot Blyden encouraged greater interest in the repatriation of black Americans to Africa, especially Liberia. This goal continued into the twentieth century and culminated in the "Back-to-Africa" program of Marcus Garvey and his Universal Negro Improvement Association. Interestingly, Booker T. Washington also exhibited nationalist sentiment by encouraging blacks to withdraw from white society, develop their own institutions and businesses, and engage in economic and moral uplift. Washington's nationalism concentrated on economic self-help and manifested itself in 1900 with the establishment of the National Negro Business League.

A thorough assessment of the protest and accommodationist views of black Americans is presented in August Meier, *Negro Thought in America, 1800–1915* (University of Michigan Press, 1963). Rayford Logan, in *The Betrayal of the Negro: From Rutherford B. Hayes to Woodrow Wilson* (Macmillan, 1965), describes the last quarter of the nineteenth century as "the nadir" for black life. By far the best studies of Booker T. Washington are two volumes by Louis R. Harlan: *Booker T. Washington: The Making of a Black Leader, 1856–1901* (Oxford University Press, 1972) and *Booker T. Washington: The Wizard of Tuskegee, 1901–1915* (Oxford University Press, 1983). In addition, Harlan has edited the 13-volume *Booker T. Washington Papers* (University of Illinois Press, 1972–1984). For assessments of two of Booker T. Washington's harshest critics, see David Levering Lewis, *W. E. B. Du Bois: Biography of a Race, 1868–1919* (Henry Holt, 1993), the first of a projected two-volume study, and Stephen R. Fox, *The Guardian of Boston: William Monroe Trotter* (Atheneum, 1970). John H. Bracey, Jr., August Meier, and Elliott Rudwick, in *Black Nationalism in America* (Bobbs-Merrill, 1970), provide an invaluable collection of documents pertaining to black nationalism. See also Edwin S. Redkey, *Black Exodus: Black Nationalist and Back-to-Africa Movements, 1890–1910* (Yale University Press, 1969) and Hollis R. Lynch, *Edward Wilmot Blyden: Pan-Negro Patriot, 1832–1912* (Oxford University Press, 1967). Diverse views of Marcus Garvey, who credited Booker T. Washington with inspiring him to seek a leadership role on behalf of African Americans, are found in Edmund David Cronon, *Black Moses: The Story of Marcus Garvey and the Universal Negro Improvement Association* (University of Wisconsin Press, 1955); Tony Martin, *Race First: The Ideological and Organizational Struggles of Marcus Garvey and the UNIA* (Greenwood Press, 1976); and Judith Stein, *The World of Marcus Garvey: Race and Class in Modern Society* (Louisiana State University Press, 1986). Some of Garvey's own writings are collected in Amy Jacques-Garvey, ed., *Philosophy and Opinions of Marcus Garvey* (1925; reprint, Atheneum, 1969).

Race relations in the late nineteenth century are explored in C. Vann Woodward, *The Strange Career of Jim Crow* (Oxford University Press, 1966), a volume that sparked a lively historiographical debate concerning the origins of segregation. Of the numerous challenges to the Woodward thesis that a full-blown pattern of racial segregation did not emerge until 1890, Howard N. Rabinowitz's *Race Relations in the Urban South, 1865–1890* (Oxford University Press, 1978) is one of the most insightful. In addition, a number of monographs that have appeared over the past three decades explore the development of an African American presence in the nation's major cities. Among the best of these urban studies are Gilbert Osofsky, *Harlem: The Making of a Ghetto: Negro New York, 1890–1930* (Harper & Row, 1966); Allan H. Spear, *Black Chicago: The Making of a Negro Ghetto, 1890–1920* (University of Chicago Press, 1967); Kenneth L. Kusmer, *A Ghetto Takes Shape: Black Cleveland, 1870–1930* (University of Illinois Press, 1976); and George C. Wright, *Life Behind a Veil: Blacks in Louisville, Kentucky, 1865–1930* (Louisiana State University Press, 1985).

ISSUE 8

Did the Progressives Fail?

YES: Richard M. Abrams, from "The Failure of Progressivism," in Richard Abrams and Lawrence Levine, eds., *The Shaping of the Twentieth Century,* 2d ed. (Little, Brown, 1971)

NO: Arthur S. Link and Richard L. McCormick, from *Progressivism* (Harlan Davidson, 1983)

ISSUE SUMMARY

YES: Professor of history Richard M. Abrams maintains that progressivism was a failure because it tried to impose a uniform set of values upon a culturally diverse people and never seriously confronted the inequalities that still exist in American society.

NO: Professors of history Arthur S. Link and Richard L. McCormick argue that the Progressives were a diverse group of reformers who confronted and ameliorated the worst abuses that emerged in urban industrial America during the early 1900s.

Progressivism is a word used by historians to define the reform currents in the years between the end of the Spanish-American War and America's entrance into the Great War in Europe in 1917. The so-called Progressive movement had been in operation for over a decade before the label was first used in the 1919 electoral campaigns. Former president Theodore Roosevelt ran as a third-party candidate in the 1912 election on the Progressive party ticket, but in truth the party had no real organization outside of the imposing figure of Theodore Roosevelt. Therefore, as a label, "progressivism" was rarely used as a term of self-identification for its supporters. Even after 1912, it was more frequently used by journalists and historians to distinguish the reformers of the period from socialists and old-fashioned conservatives.

The 1890s was a crucial decade for many Americans. From 1893 until almost the turn of the century, the nation went through a terrible economic depression. With the forces of industrialization, urbanization, and immigration wreaking havoc upon the traditional political, social, and economic structures of American life, changes were demanded. The reformers responded in a variety of ways. The proponents of good government believed that democracy was threatened because the cities were ruled by corrupt political machines while the state legislatures were dominated by corporate interests. The cure was to purify democracy and place government directly in the hands of the people through such devices as the initiative, referendum, recall, and the direct election of local school board officials, judges, and U.S. senators.

Social justice proponents saw the problem from a different perspective. Settlement workers moved into cities and tried to change the urban environment. They pushed for sanitation improvements, tenement house reforms, factory inspection laws, regulation of the hours and wages of women, and the abolition of child labor.

A third group of reformers considered the major problem to be the trusts. They argued for controls over the power of big business and for the preservation of the free enterprise system. Progressives disagreed on whether the issue was size or conduct and on whether the remedy was trust-busting or the regulation of big business. But none could deny the basic question: How was the relationship between big business and the U.S. government to be defined?

How successful was the Progressive movement? What triggered the reform impulse? Who were its leaders? How much support did it attract? More important, did the laws that resulted from the various movements fulfill the intentions of its leaders and supporters?

In the following selections, Richard M. Abrams distinguishes the Progressives from other reformers of the era, such as the Populists, the Socialists, the mainstream labor unions, and the corporate reorganization movement. He then argues that the Progressive movement failed because it tried to impose a uniform set of middle-class Protestant moral values upon a nation that was growing more culturally diverse, and because the reformers supported movements that brought about no actual changes or only superficial ones at best. The real inequalities in American society, says Abrams, were never addressed.

In contrast, Arthur S. Link and Richard L. McCormick view progressivism from the point of view of the reformers and rank it as a qualified success. They survey the criticisms of the movement made by historians since the 1950s and generally find them unconvincing. They believe that the Progressives made the first real attempts to change the destructive direction in which modern urban-industrial society was moving.

YES

Richard M. Abrams

THE FAILURE OF PROGRESSIVISM

Our first task is definitional, because clearly it would be possible to beg the whole question of "failure" by means of semantical niceties. I have no intention of being caught in that kind of critics' trap. I hope to establish that there was a distinctive major reform movement that took place during most of the first two decades of this century, that it had a mostly coherent set of characteristics and long-term objectives, and that, measured by its own criteria—not criteria I should wish, through hindsight and preference, to impose on it—it fell drastically short of its chief goals.

One can, of course, define a reform movement so broadly that merely to acknowledge that we are where we are and that we enjoy some advantages over where we were would be to prove the "success" of the movement. In many respects, Arthur Link does this sort of thing, both in his and William B. Catton's popular textbook, *American Epoch,* and in his article, "What Happened to the Progressive Movement in the 1920's?" In the latter, Link defines "progressivism" as a movement that "began convulsively in the 1890's and waxed and waned afterward to our own time, to insure the survival of democracy in the United States by the enlargement of governmental power to control and offset the power of private economic groups over the nation's institutions and life." Such a definition may be useful to classify data gathered to show the liberal sources of the enlargement of governmental power since the 1890's; but such data would not be finely classified enough to tell us much about the *non*liberal sources of governmental power (which were numerous and important), about the distinctive styles of different generations of reformers concerned with a liberal society, or even about vital distinctions among divergent reform groups in the era that contemporaries and the conventional historical wisdom have designed as progressive....

Now, without going any further into the problem of historians' definitions which are too broad or too narrow—there is no space here for such an effort —I shall attempt a definition of my own, beginning with the problem that contemporaries set themselves to solve and that gave the era its cognomen, "progressive." That problem was *progress*—or more specifically, how American society was to continue to enjoy the fruits of material progress without

From Richard M. Abrams, "The Failure of Progressivism," in Richard Abrams and Lawrence Levine, eds., *The Shaping of the Twentieth Century,* 2d ed. (Little, Brown, 1971). Copyright © 1971 by Richard M. Abrams. Reprinted by permission of the author.

the accompanying assault upon human dignity and the erosion of the conventional values and moral assumptions on which the social order appeared to rest....

To put it briefly and yet more specifically, a very large body of men and women entered into reform activities at the end of the nineteenth century to translate "the national credo" (as Henry May calls it) into a general program for social action. Their actions, according to Richard Hofstadter, were "founded upon the indigenous Yankee-Protestant political tradition [that] assumed and demanded the constant disinterested activity of the citizen in public affairs, argued that political life ought to be run, to a greater degree than it was, in accordance with general principles and abstract laws apart from and superior to personal needs, and expressed a common feeling that government should be in good part an effort to moralize the lives of individuals while economic life should be intimately related to the stimulation and development of individual character."

The most consistently important reform impulse, among *many* reform impulses, during the progressive era grew directly from these considerations. It is this reform thrust that we should properly call "the progressive movement." We should distinguish it carefully from reform movements in the era committed primarily to other considerations.

The progressive movement drew its strength from the old mugwump reform impulse, civil service reform, female emancipationists, prohibitionists, the social gospel, the settlement-house movement, some national expansionists, some world peace advocates, conservation advocates, technical efficiency experts, and a wide variety of intellectuals

who helped cut through the stifling, obstructionist smokescreen of systematized ignorance. It gained powerful allies from many disadvantaged business interests that appealed to politics to redress unfavorable trade positions; from some ascendant business interests seeking institutional protection; from publishers who discovered the promotional value of exposés; and from politicians-on-the-make who sought issues with which to dislodge long-lived incumbents from their place. Objectively it focused on or expressed (1) a concern for responsive, honest, and efficient government, on the local and state levels especially; (2) recognition of the obligations of society—particularly of an affluent society—to its underprivileged; (3) a desire for more rational use of the nation's resources and economic energies; (4) a rejection, on at least intellectual grounds, of certain social principles that had long obstructed social remedies for what had traditionally been regarded as irremediable evils, such as poverty; and, above all, (5) a concern for the maintenance or restoration of a consensus on what conventionally had been regarded as *fixed moral* principles. "The first and central faith in the national credo," writes Professor May, "was, as it always had been, the reality, certainty, and eternity of moral values.... A few thought and said that ultimate values and goals were unnecessary, but in most cases this meant that they believed so deeply in a consensus on these matters that they could not imagine a serious challenge." Progressives shared this faith with most of the rest of the country, but they also conceived of themselves, with a grand sense of stewardship, as its heralds, and its agents.

The progressive movement was (and is) distinguishable from other contemporary reform movements not only by its devotion to social conditions regarded, by those within it as well as by much of the generality, as *normative*, but also by its definition of what forces threatened that order. More specifically, progressivism directed its shafts at five principal enemies, each in its own way representing reform:

1. The *socialist reform movement*—because, despite socialism's usually praiseworthy concern for human dignity, it represented the subordination of the rights of private property and of individualistic options to objectives that often explicitly threatened common religious beliefs and conventional standards of justice and excellence.

2. The corporate reorganization of American business, which I should call *the corporate reform movement* (its consequence has, after all, been called "the corporate revolution")—because it challenged the traditional relationship of ownership and control of private property, because it represented a shift from production to profits in the entrepreneurial definition of efficiency, because it threatened the proprietary small-business character of the American social structure, because it had already demonstrated a capacity for highly concentrated and socially irresponsible power, and because it sanctioned practices that strained the limits of conventionality and even legality.

3. The *labor union movement*—because despite the virtues of unionized labor as a source of countervailing force against the corporations and as a basis for a more orderly labor force, unionism (like corporate capitalism

and socialism) suggested a reduction of individualistic options (at least for wage-earners and especially for small employers), and a demand for a partnership with business management in the decision-making process by a class that convention excluded from such a role.

4. *Agrarian radicalism,* and populism in particular—because it, too, represented (at least in appearance) the insurgency of a class conventionally believed to be properly excluded from a policy-making role in the society, a class graphically represented by the "Pitchfork" Bens and "Sockless" Jerrys, the "Cyclone" Davises and "Alfalfa" Bills, the wool hat brigade and the rednecks.

5. *The ethnic movement*—the demand for specific political and social recognition of ethnic or ex-national affiliations—because accession to the demand meant acknowledgment of the fragmentation of American society as well as a retreat from official standards of integrity, honesty, and efficiency in government in favor of standards based on personal loyalty, partisanship, and sectarian provincialism.

Probably no two progressives opposed all of these forces with equal animus, and most had a noteworthy sympathy for one or more of them....

So much for what progressivism was not. Let me sum it up by noting that what it rejected and sought to oppose necessarily says much about what it was—perhaps even more than can be ascertained by the more direct approach.

My thesis is that progressivism failed. It failed in what it—or what those who shaped it—conceived to be its principal objective. And that was, over and above everything else, to restore or maintain the conventional consensus on a particular view of the universe, a particular set of values, and a particular constellation of behavioral modes in the country's commerce, its industry, its social relations, and its politics. Such a view, such values, such modes were challenged by the influx of diverse religious and ethnic elements into the nation's social and intellectual stream, by the overwhelming economic success and power of the corporate form of business organization, by the subordination of the work-ethic bound up within the old proprietary and craft enterprise system, and by the increasing centrality of a growing proportion of low-income, unskilled, wage-earning classes in the nation's economy and social structure. Ironically, the *coup de grâce* would be struck by the emergence of a philosophical and scientific rationale for the existence of cultural diversity within a single social system, a rationale that largely grew out of the very intellectual ferment to which progressivism so substantially contributed.

Progressivism sought to save the old view, and the old values and modes, by educating the immigrants and the poor so as to facilitate their acceptance of and absorption into the Anglo-American mode of life, or by excluding the "unassimilable" altogether; by instituting antitrust legislation or, at the least, by imposing regulations upon corporate practices in order to preserve a minimal base for small proprietary business enterprise; by making legislative accommodations to the newly important wage-earning classes —accommodations that might provide some measure of wealth and income redistribution, on-the-job safety, occupational security, and the like—so as to fore-

stall a forcible transfer of policy-making power away from the groups that had conventionally exercised that power; and by broadening the political selection process, through direct elections, direct nominations, and direct legislation, in order to reduce tensions caused unnecessarily by excessively narrow and provincial cliques of policy-makers. When the economic and political reforms failed to restore the consensus by giving the previously unprivileged an ostensible stake in it, progressive energies turned increasingly toward using the force of the state to proscribe or restrict specifically opprobrious modes of social behavior, such as gaming habits, drinking habits, sexual habits, and Sabbatarian habits. In the ultimate resort, with the proliferation of sedition and criminal syndicalist laws, it sought to constrict political discourse itself. And (except perhaps for the disintegration of the socialist movement) *that* failed, too.

One measure of progressivism's failure lies in the xenophobic racism that reappeared on a large scale even by 1910. In many parts of the country, for example, in the far west and the south, racism and nativism had been fully blended with reform movements even at the height of progressive activities there. The alleged threats of "coolie labor" to American living standards, and of "venal" immigrant and Negro voting to republican institutions generally, underlay the alliance of racism and reform in this period. By and large, however, for the early progressive era the alliance was conspicuous only in the south and on the west coast. By 1910, signs of heightening ethnic animosities, most notably anti-Catholicism, began appearing in other areas of the country as well. As John Higham has written, "It is hard to explain the rebirth of anti-

Catholic ferment [at this time] except as an outlet for expectations which progressivism raised and then failed to fulfill." The failure here was in part the inability of reform to deliver a meaningful share of the social surplus to the groups left out of the general national progress, and in part the inability of reform to achieve its objective of assimilation and consensus.

The growing ethnic animus, moreover, operated to compound the difficulty of achieving assimilation. By the second decade of the century, the objects of the antagonism were beginning to adopt a frankly assertive posture. The World War, and the ethnic cleavages it accentuated and aggravated, represented only the final blow to the assimilationist idea; "hyphenate" tendencies had already been growing during the years before 1914. It had only been in 1905 that the Louisville-born and secular-minded Louis Brandeis had branded as "disloyal" all who "keep alive" their differences of origin or religion. By 1912, by now a victim of anti-Semitism and aware of a rising hostility toward Jews in the country, Brandeis had become an active Zionist; before a Jewish audience in 1913, he remarked how "practical experience" had convinced him that "to be good Americans, we must be better Jews, and to be better Jews, we must become Zionists."

Similarly, American Negroes also began to adopt a more aggressive public stance after having been subdued for more than a decade by antiblack violence and the accommodationist tactics suggested in 1895 by Booker T. Washington. As early as 1905, many black leaders had broken with Washington in founding the Niagara Movement for a more vigorous assertion of Negro demands for equality. But most historians seem to agree that it was probably the Springfield race riot of 1908 that ended illusions that black people could gain an equitable share in the rewards of American culture by accommodationist or assimilationist methods. The organization of the NAACP in 1909 gave substantive force for the first time to the three-year-old Niagara Movement. The year 1915 symbolically concluded the demise of accommodationism. That year, the Negro-baiting movie, "The Birth of a Nation," played to massive, enthusiastic audiences that included notably the president of the United States and the chief justice of the Supreme Court; the KKK was revived; and Booker T. Washington died. The next year, black nationalist Marcus Garvey arrived in New York from Jamaica.

Meanwhile, scientific knowledge about race and culture was undergoing a crucial revision. At least in small part stimulated by a keen self-consciousness of his own "outsider" status in American culture, the German-Jewish immigrant Franz Boas was pioneering in the new anthropological concept of "cultures," based on the idea that human behavioral traits are conditioned by historical traditions. The new view of culture was in time to undermine completely the prevailing evolutionary view that ethnic differences must mean racial inequality. The significance of Boas's work after 1910, and that of his students A. L. Kroeber and Clyde Kluckhohn in particular, rests on the fact that the racist thought of the progressive era had founded its intellectual rationale on the monistic, evolutionary view of culture; and indeed much of the progressives' anxiety over the threatened demise of "the American culture" had been founded on that view.

Other intellectual developments as well had for a long time been whittling away at the notion that American society had to stand or fall on the unimpaired coherence of its cultural consensus. Yet the new work in anthropology, law, philosophy, physics, psychology, and literature only unwittingly undermined that assumption. Rather, it was only as the ethnic hostilities grew, and especially as the power of the state came increasingly to be invoked against dissenting groups whose ethnic "peculiarities" provided an excuse for repression, that the new intelligence came to be developed. "The world has thought that it must have its culture and its political unity coincide," wrote Randolph Bourne in 1916 while chauvinism, nativism, and antiradicalism were mounting; now it was seeing that cultural diversity might yet be the salvation of the liberal society—that it might even serve to provide the necessary countervailing force to the power of the state that private property had once served (in the schema of Locke, Harrington, and Smith) before the interests of private property became so highly concentrated and so well blended with the state itself.

The telltale sign of progressivism's failure was the violent crusade against dissent that took place in the closing years of the Wilson administration. It is too easy to ascribe the literal hysteria of the postwar years to the dislocations of the War alone. Incidents of violent repression of labor and radical activities had been growing remarkably, often in step with xenophobic outbreaks, for several years before America's intervention in the War. To quote Professor Higham once more. "The seemingly unpropitious circumstances under which antiradicalism and anti-Catholicism came to life [after 1910] make their renewal a subject of moment." It seems clear that they both arose out of the sources of the reform ferment

itself. When reform failed to enlarge the consensus, or to make it more relevant to the needs of the still disadvantaged and disaffected, and when in fact reform seemed to be encouraging more radical challenges to the social order, the old anxieties of the 1890's returned.

The postwar hysteria represented a reaction to a confluence of anxiety-laden developments, including the high cost of living, the physical and social dislocations of war mobilization and the recruitment of women and Negroes into war production jobs in the big northern cities, the Bolshevik Revolution, a series of labor strikes, and a flood of radical literature that exaggerated the capabilities of radical action. "One Hundred Per Cent Americanism" seemed the only effective way of meeting all these challenges at once. As Stanley Coben has written, making use of recent psychological studies and anthropological work on cultural "revitalization movements": "Citizens who joined the crusade for one hundred per cent Americanism sought, primarily, a unifying force which would halt the apparent disintegration of their culture.... The slight evidence of danger from radical organizations aroused such wild fear only because Americans had already encountered other threats to cultural stability."

Now, certainly during the progressive era a lot of reform legislation was passed, much that contributed genuinely to a more liberal society, though more that contributed to the more absolutistic moral objectives of progressivism. Progressivism indeed had real, lasting effects for the blunting of the sharper edges of self-interest in American life, and for the reduction of the harsher cruelties suffered by the society's underprivileged. These achievements deserve emphasis, not least because they derived directly from the progressive habit of looking to standards of conventional morality and human decency for the solution of diverse social conflicts. But the deeper nature of the problem confronting American society required more than the invocation of conventional standards; the conventions themselves were at stake, especially as they bore upon the allocation of privileges and rewards. Because most of the progressives never confronted that problem, in a way their efforts were doomed to failure.

In sum, the overall effect of the period's legislation is not so impressive. For example, all the popular government measures put together have not conspicuously raised the quality of American political life. Direct nominations and elections have tended to make political campaigns so expensive as to reduce the number of eligible candidates for public office to (1) the independently wealthy; (2) the ideologues, especially on the right, who can raise the needed campaign money from independently wealthy ideologues like themselves, or from the organizations set up to promote a particular ideology; and (3) party hacks who pay off their debt to the party treasury by whistle-stopping and chicken dinner speeches. Direct legislation through the Initiative and Referendum device has made cities and states prey to the best-financed and -organized special-interest group pressures, as have so-called nonpartisan elections. Which is not to say that things are worse than before, but only that they are not conspicuously better. The popular government measures did have the effect of shaking up the established political organizations of the day, and that may well have been their only real purpose.

But as Arthur Link has said, in his text, *The American Epoch*, the popular government measures "were merely instruments to facilitate the capture of political machinery.... They must be judged for what they accomplished or failed to accomplish on the higher level of substantive reform." Without disparaging the long list of reform measures that passed during the progressive era, the question remains whether all the "substantive reforms" together accomplished what the progressives wanted them to accomplish.

Certain social and economic advantages were indeed shuffled about, but this must be regarded as a short-term achievement for special groups at best. Certain commercial interests, for example, achieved greater political leverage in railroad policy-making than they had had in 1900 through measures such as the Hepburn and Mann-Elkins Acts—though it was not until the 1940's that any real change occurred in the general rate structure, as some broad regional interests had been demanding at the beginning of the century. Warehouse, farm credits, and land-bank acts gave the diminishing numbers of farm owners enhanced opportunities to mortgage their property, and some business groups had persuaded the federal government to use national revenues to educate farmers on how to increase their productivity (Smith-Lever Act, 1914); but most farmers remained as dependent as ever upon forces beyond their control—the bankers, the middlemen, the international market. The FTC, and the Tariff Commission established in 1916, extended the principle of using government agencies to adjudicate intra-industrial conflicts ostensibly in the national interest, but these agencies would develop a lamentable tendency of deferring to and even confirming rather than moderating the power of each industry's dominant interests. The

Federal Reserve Act made the currency more flexible, and that certainly made more sense than the old system, as even the bankers agreed. But depositers would be as prey to defaulting banks as they had been in the days of the Pharaoh—bank deposit insurance somehow was "socialism" to even the best of men in this generation. And despite Woodrow Wilson's brave promise to end the banker's stifling hold on innovative small business, one searches in vain for some provision in the FRA designed specifically to encourage small or new businesses. In fact, the only constraints on the bankers' power that emerged from the era came primarily from the ability of the larger corporations to finance their own expansion out of capital surpluses they had accumulated from extortionate profits during the War.

A major change almost occurred during the war years when organized labor and the principle of collective bargaining received official recognition and a handful of labor leaders was taken, temporarily, into policy-making councils (e.g., in the War Labor Board). But actually, as already indicated, such a development, if it had been made permanent, would have represented a defeat, not a triumph, for progressivism. The progressives may have fought for improved labor conditions, but they jealously fought against the enlargement of union power. It was no aberration that once the need for wartime productive efficiency evaporated, leading progressives such as A. Mitchell Palmer, Miles Poindexter, and Woodrow Wilson himself helped civic and employer organizations to bludgeon the labor movement into disunity and docility. (It is possible, I suppose, to argue that such progressives were simply inconsistent, but if we understand progressivism in the terms I have outlined above I think the consistency is more evident.) Nevertheless, a double irony is worth noting with respect to progressivism's objectives and the wartime labor developments. On the one hand, the progressives' hostility to labor unions defeated their own objectives of (1) counterbalancing the power of collectivized capital (i.e., corporations), and (2) enhancing workers' share of the nation's wealth. On the other hand, under wartime duress, the progressives did grant concessions to organized labor (e.g., the Adamson Eight-Hour Railway Labor Act, as well as the WLB) that would later serve as precedents for the very "collectivization" of the economic situation that they were dedicated to oppose.

Meanwhile, the distribution of advantages in the society did not change much at all. In some cases, from the progressive reformers' viewpoint at least, it may even have changed for the worse. According to the figures of the National Industrial Conference Board, even income was as badly distributed at the end of the era as before. In 1921, the highest 10 percent of income recipients received 38 percent of total personal income, and that figure was only 34 percent in 1910. (Since the share of the top 5 percent of income recipients probably declined in the 1910–20 period, the figures for the top 10 percent group suggest a certain improvement in income distribution at the top. But the fact that the share of the lowest 60 percent also declined in that period, from 35 percent to 30 percent, confirms the view that no meaningful improvement can be shown.) Maldistribution was to grow worse until after 1929.

American farmers on the whole and in particular seemed to suffer increasing disadvantages. Farm life was one of the institutional bulwarks of the mode of life the progressives ostensibly cherished. "The farmer who owns his land," averred Gifford Pinchot, "is still the backbone of the Nation; and one of the things we want most is more of him,... [for] he is the first of home-makers." If only in the sense that there were relatively fewer farmers in the total population at the end of the progressive era, one would have to say farm life in the United States had suffered. But, moreover, fewer owned their own farms. The number of farm tenants increased by 21 percent from 1900 to 1920; 38.1 percent of all farm operators in 1921 were tenants; and the figures look even worse when one notices that tenancy *declined* in the most *impoverished* areas during this period, suggesting that the family farm was surviving mostly in the more marginal agricultural areas. Finally, although agriculture had enjoyed some of its most prosperous years in history in the 1910–20 period, the 21 percent of the nation's gainfully employed who were in agriculture in 1919 (a peak year) earned only 16 percent of the national income.

While progressivism failed to restore vitality to American farming, it failed also to stop the vigorous ascendancy of corporate capitalism, the most conspicuous challenge to conventional values and modes that the society faced at the beginning of the era. The corporation had drastically undermined the very basis of the traditional rationale that had supported the nation's freewheeling system of resource allocation and had underwritten the permissiveness of the laws governing economic activities in the nineteenth century. The new capitalism by-passed the privately-owned proprietary firm, it featured a separation of ownership and control, it subordinated the profit motive to varied and variable other objectives such as empire-building, and, in many of the techniques developed by financial brokers and investment bankers, it appeared to create a great gulf between the making of money and the producing of useful goods and services. Through a remarkable series of judicial sophistries, this nonconventional form of business enterprise had become, in law, a *person*, and had won privileges and liberties once entrusted only to men, who were presumed to be conditioned and restrained by the moral qualities that inhere in human nature. Although gaining legal dispensations from an obliging Supreme Court, the corporation could claim no theoretical legitimacy beyond the fact of its power and its apparent inextricable entanglement in the business order that had produced America's seemingly unbounded material success.

Although much has been written about the supposed continuing vitality of small proprietary business enterprise in the United States, there is no gainsaying the continued ascendancy of the big corporation nor the fact that it still lacks legitimation. The fact that in the last sixty years the number of small proprietary businesses has grown at a rate that slightly exceeds the rate of population growth says little about the character of small business enterprise today as compared with that of the era of the American industrial revolution; it does nothing to disparage the apprehensions expressed in the antitrust campaigns of the progressives. To focus on the vast numbers of automobile dealers and gasoline service station owners, for example, is to miss completely their truly humble dependence upon the very few giant automobile and oil companies, a foretold dependence that was the very point of progressives' anticorporation, antitrust sentiments. The progressive movement must indeed be credited with placing real restraints upon monopolistic tendencies in the United States, for most statistics indicate that at least until the 1950's business concentration showed no substantial increase from the turn of the century (though it may be pertinent to note that concentration ratios did increase significantly in the decade immediately following the progressive era). But the statistics of concentration remain impressive—just as they were when John Moody wrote *The Truth About the Trusts* in 1904 and Louis Brandeis followed it with *Other People's Money* in 1914. That two hundred corporations (many of them interrelated) held almost one-quarter of all business assets, and more than 40 percent of all corporate assets in the country in 1948; that the fifty largest manufacturing corporations held 35 percent of all industrial assets in 1948, and 38 percent by 1962; and that a mere twenty-eight corporations or one one-thousandth of a percentage of all nonfinancial firms in 1956 employed 10 percent of all those employed in the nonfinancial industries, should be sufficient statistical support for the apprehensions of the progressive era *—just as it is testimony to the failure of the progressive movement to achieve anything substantial to alter the situation.*

Perhaps the crowning failure of progressivism was the American role in World War I. It is true that many progressives opposed America's intervention, but it is also true that a great many more supported it. The failure in progressivism lies not in the decision to intervene but in the futility of intervention measured by progressive expectations.

NO

Arthur S. Link and
Richard L. McCormick

PROGRESSIVISM IN HISTORY

Convulsive reform movements swept across the American landscape from the 1890s to 1917. Angry farmers demanded better prices for their products, regulation of the railroads, and the destruction of what they thought was the evil power of bankers, middlemen, and corrupt politicians. Urban residents crusaded for better city services and more efficient municipal government. Members of various professions, such as social workers and doctors, tried to improve the dangerous and unhealthy conditions in which many people lived and worked. Businessmen, too, lobbied incessantly for goals which they defined as reform. Never before had the people of the United States engaged in so many diverse movements for the improvement of their political system, economy, and communities. By around 1910, many of these crusading men and women were calling themselves progressives. Ever since, historians have used the term *progressivism* to describe the many reform movements of the early twentieth century.

Yet in the goals they sought and the remedies they tried, the reformers were a varied and contradictory lot. Some progressives wanted to increase the political influence and control of ordinary people, while other progressives wanted to concentrate authority in experts. Many reformers tried to curtail the growth of large corporations; others accepted bigness in industry on account of its supposed economic benefits. Some progressives were genuinely concerned about the welfare of the "new" immigrants from southern and eastern Europe; other progressives sought, sometimes frantically, to "Americanize" the newcomers or to keep them out altogether. In general, progressives sought to improve the conditions of life and labor and to create as much social stability as possible. But each group of progressives had its own definitions of improvement and stability. In the face of such diversity, one historian, Peter G. Filene, has even argued that what has been called the progressive movement never existed as a historical phenomenon ("An Obituary for 'The Progressive Movement,' " *American Quarterly*, 1970).

Certainly there was no *unified* movement, but, like most students of the period, we consider progressivism to have been a real, vital, and significant phenomenon, one which contemporaries recognized and talked and fought about. Properly conceptualized, progressivism provides a useful framework for the history of the United States in the late nineteenth and early twentieth centuries.

One source of confusion and controversy about progressives and progressivism is the words themselves. They are often used judgmentally to describe people and changes which historians have deemed to be "good," "enlightened," and "farsighted." The progressives themselves naturally intended the words to convey such positive qualities, but we should not accept their usage uncritically. It might be better to avoid the terms progressive and progressivism altogether, but they are too deeply embedded in the language of contemporaries and historians to be ignored. Besides, we think that the terms have real meaning. In this book the words will be used neutrally, without any implicit judgment about the value of reform.

In the broadest sense, progressivism was the way in which a whole generation of Americans defined themselves politically and responded to the nation's problems at the turn of the century. The progressives made the first comprehensive efforts to grapple with the ills of a modern urban-industrial society. Hence the record of their achievements and failures has considerable relevance for our own time.

WHO WERE THE PROGRESSIVES?

Ever since the early twentieth century, people have argued about who the progressives were and what they stood for. This may seem to be a strange topic of debate, but it really is not. Progressivism engaged many different groups of

Americans, and each group of progressives naturally considered themselves to be the key reformers and thought that their own programs were the most important ones. Not surprisingly, historians ever since have had trouble agreeing on who really shaped progressivism and its goals. Scholars who have written about the period have variously identified farmers, the old middle classes, professionals, businessmen, and urban immigrants and ethnic groups as the core group of progressives. But these historians have succeeded in identifying *their* reformers only by defining progressivism narrowly, by excluding other reformers and reforms when they do not fall within some specific definition, and by resorting to such vague, catch-all adjectives as "middle class." ...

The advocates of the middle-class view might reply that they intended to study the leaders of reform, not its supporters, to identify and describe the men and women who imparted the dominant character to progressivism, not its mass base. The study of leadership is surely a valid subject in its own right and is particularly useful for an understanding of progressivism. But too much focus on leadership conceals more than it discloses about early twentieth-century reform. The dynamics of progressivism were crucially generated by ordinary people—by the sometimes frenzied mass supporters of progressive leaders, by rank-and-file voters willing to trust a reform candidate. The chronology of progressivism can be traced by events which aroused large numbers of people —a sensational muckraking article, an outrageous political scandal, an eye-opening legislative investigation, or a tragic social calamity. Events such as these gave reform its rhythm and its power.

Progressivism cannot be understood without seeing how the masses of Americans perceived and responded to such events. Widely circulated magazines gave people everywhere the sordid facts of corruption and carried the clamor for reform into every city, village, and county. State and national election campaigns enabled progressive candidates to trumpet their programs. Almost no literate person in the United States in, say, 1906 could have been unaware that ten-year-old children worked through the night in dangerous factories, or that many United States senators served big business. Progressivism was the only reform movement ever experienced by the whole American nation. Its national appeal and mass base vastly exceeded that of Jacksonian reform. And progressivism's dependence on the people for its objectives and timing has no comparison in the executive-dominated New Deal of Franklin D. Roosevelt or the Great Society of Lyndon B. Johnson. Wars and depressions had previously engaged the whole nation, but never reform. And so we are back to the problem of how to explain and define the outpouring of progressive reform which excited and involved so many different kinds of people.

A little more than a decade ago, Buenker and Thelen recognized the immense diversity of progressivism and suggested ways in which to reorient the study of early twentieth-century reform. Buenker observed that divergent groups often came together on one issue and then changed alliances on the next ("The Progressive Era: A Search for a Synthesis," *Mid-America*, 1969). Indeed, different reformers sometimes favored the same measure for distinctive, even opposite, reasons. Progressivism could be understood only in the light of these shifting coalitions. Thelen, in his study of Wisconsin's legislature, also emphasized the importance of cooperation between different reform groups. "The basic riddle in Progressivism," he concluded, "is not what drove groups apart but what made them seek common cause."

There is a great deal of wisdom in these articles, particularly in their recognition of the diversity of progressivism and in the concept of shifting coalitions of reformers. A two-pronged approach is necessary to carry forward this way of looking at early twentieth-century reform. First, we should study, not an imaginary unified progressive movement, but individual reforms and give particular attention to the goals of their diverse supporters, the public rationales given for them, and the results which they achieved. Second, we should try to identify the features which were more or less common to different progressive reforms.

The first task—distinguishing the goals of a reform from its rhetoric and its results—is more difficult than it might appear to be. Older interpretations of progressivism implicitly assumed that the rhetoric explained the goals and that, if a proposed reform became law, the results fulfilled the intentions behind it. Neither assumption is a sound one: purposes, rationale, and results are three different things. Samuel P. Hays' influential article, "The Politics of Reform in Municipal Government in the Progressive Era" (*Pacific Northwest Quarterly*, 1964), exposed the fallacy of automatically equating the democratic rhetoric of the reformers with their true purposes. The two may have coincided, but the historian has to demonstrate that fact, not take it for granted. The unexamined identification of either intentions or rhetoric with results is also invalid, although it is still a common feature of the scholarship on progressivism. Only within the last decade have historians begun to examine the actual achievements of the reformers. To carry out this first task, in the following... we will distinguish between the goals and rhetoric of individual reforms and will discuss the results of reform whenever the current literature permits. To do so is to observe the ironies, complexities, and disappointments of progressivism.

The second task—that of identifying the common characteristics of progressivism—is even more difficult than the first but is an essential base on which to build an understanding of progressivism. The rest of this chapter focuses on identifying such characteristics. The place to begin that effort is the origins of progressivism....

THE CHARACTER AND SPIRIT OF PROGRESSIVISM

Progressivism was characterized, in the first place, by a distinctive set of attitudes toward industrialism. By the turn of the century, the overwhelming majority of Americans had accepted the permanence of large-scale industrial, commercial, and financial enterprises and of the wage and factory systems. The progressives shared this attitude. Most were not socialists, and they undertook reform, not to dismantle modern economic institutions, but rather to ameliorate and improve the conditions of industrial life. Yet progressivism was infused with a deep outrage against the worst consequences of industrialism. Outpourings of anger at corporate wrongdoing and of hatred for industry's callous pursuit of profit

frequently punctuated the course of reform in the early twentieth century. Indeed, antibusiness emotion was a prime mover of progressivism. That the acceptance of industrialism *and* the outrage against it were intrinsic to early twentieth-century reform does not mean that progressivism was mindless or that it has to be considered indefinable. But it does suggest that there was a powerful irony in progressivism: reforms which gained support from a people angry with the oppressive aspects of industrialism also assisted the same persons to accommodate to it, albeit to an industrialism which was to some degree socially responsible.

The progressives' ameliorative reforms also reflected their faith in progress—in mankind's ability, through purposeful action, to improve the environment and the conditions of life. The late nineteenth-century dissidents had not lacked this faith, but their espousal of panaceas bespoke a deep pessimism: "Unless this one great change is made, things will get worse." Progressive reforms were grounded on a broader assumption. In particular, reforms could protect the people hurt by industrialization, and make the environment more humane. For intellectuals of the era, the achievement of such goals meant that they had to meet Herbert Spencer head on and confute his absolute "truths." Progressive thinkers, led by Lester Frank Ward, Richard T. Ely, and, most important, John Dewey, demolished social Darwinism with what Goldman has called "reform Darwinism." They asserted that human adaptation to the environment did not interfere with the evolutionary process, but was, rather, part and parcel of the law of natural change. Progressive intellectuals and their popularizers produced a vast literature to condemn laissez faire and to promote the concept of the active state.

To improve the environment meant, above all, to intervene in economic and social affairs in order to control natural forces and impose a measure of order upon them. This belief in interventionism was a third component of progressivism. It was visible in almost every reform of the era, from the supervision of business to the prohibition of alcohol (John W. Chambers II, *The Tyranny of Change: America in the Progressive Era, 1900–1917*, 1980). Interventionism could be both private and public. Given their choice, most progressives preferred to work noncoercively through voluntary organizations for economic and social changes. However, as time passed, it became evident that most progressive reforms could be achieved only by legislation and public control. Such an extension of public authority made many progressives uneasy, and few of them went so far as Herbert Croly in glorifying the state in his *The Promise of American Life* (1909) and *Progressive Democracy* (1914). Even so, the intervention necessary for their reforms inevitably propelled progressives toward an advocacy of the use of governmental power. A familiar scenario during the period was one in which progressives called upon public authorities to assume responsibility for interventions which voluntary organizations had begun.

The foregoing describes the basic characteristics of progressivism but says little about its ideals. Progressivism was inspired by two bodies of belief and knowledge—evangelical Protestantism and the natural and social sciences. These sources of reform may appear at first glance antagonistic to one another. Actually, they were complementary, and each imparted distinctive qualities to progressivism.

Ever since the religious revivals from about 1820 to 1840, evangelical Protestantism had spurred reform in the United States. Basic to the reform mentality was an all-consuming urge to purge the world of sin, such as the sins of slavery and intemperance, against which nineteenth-century reformers had crusaded. Now the progressives carried the struggle into the modern citadels of sin—the teeming cities of the nation. No one can read their writings and speeches without being struck by the fact that many of them believed that it was their Christian duty to right the wrongs created by the processes of industrialization. Such belief was the motive force behind the Social Gospel, a movement which swept through the Protestant churches in the 1890s and 1900s. Its goal was to align churches, frankly and aggressively, on the side of the downtrodden, the poor, and working people—in other words, to make Christianity relevant to this world, not the next. It is difficult to measure the influence of the Social Gospel, but it seared the consciences of millions of Americans, particularly in urban areas. And it triumphed in the organization in 1908 of the Federal Council of Churches of Christ in America, with its platform which condemned exploitative capitalism and proclaimed the right of workers to organize and to enjoy a decent standard of living. Observers at the Progressive party's national convention of 1912 should not have been surprised to hear the delegates sing, spontaneously and emotionally, the Christian call to arms, "Onward, Christian Solders!"

The faith which inspired the singing of "Onward, Christian Soldiers!" had significant implications for progressive reforms. Progressives used moralistic appeals to make people feel the awful

weight of wrong in the world and to ex-
hort them to accept personal responsibility for its eradication. The resultant reforms could be generous in spirit, but
they could also seem intolerant to the
people who were "reformed." Progressivism sometimes seemed to envision
life in a small town Protestant community or an urban drawing room—a vision
sharply different from that of Catholic or
Jewish immigrants. Not every progressive shared the evangelical ethos, much
less its intolerance, but few of the era's
reforms were untouched by the spirit and
techniques of Protestant revivalism.

Science also had a pervasive impact
on the methods and objectives of progressivism. Many leading reformers were
specialists in the new disciplines of statistics, economics, sociology, and psychology. These new social scientists set out
to gather data on human behavior as it
actually was and to discover the laws
which governed it. Since social scientists
accepted environmentalist and interventionist assumptions implicitly, they believed that knowledge of natural laws
would make it possible to devise and
apply solutions to improve the human
condition. This faith underpinned the optimism of most progressives and prede-
termined the methods used by almost
all reformers of the time: investigation of
the facts and application of social-science
knowledge to their analysis; entrusting
trained experts to decide what should
be done; and, finally, mandating government to execute reform.

These methods may have been rational, but they were also compatible
with progressive moralism. In its formative period, American social science was
heavily infused with ethical concerns. An
essential purpose of statistics, economics,
sociology, and psychology was to im-

prove and uplift. Leading practitioners
of these disciplines, for example, Richard
T. Ely, an economist at the University of
Wisconsin, were often in the vanguard of
the Social Gospel. Progressives blended
science and religion into a view of human behavior which was unique to their
generation, which had grown up in an
age of revivals and come to maturity at
the birth of social science.

All of progressivism's distinctive features found expression in muckraking—
the literary spearhead of early twentieth-
century reform. Through the medium
of such new ten-cent magazines as *Mc-
Clure's*, *Everybody's* and *Cosmopolitan*, the
muckrakers exposed every dark aspect
and corner of American life. Nothing escaped the probe of writers such as Ida
M. Tarbell, Lincoln Steffens, Ray Stan-
nard Baker, and Burton J. Hendrick—
not big business, politics, prostitution,
race relations, or even the churches. Behind the exposés of the muckrakers lay
the progressive attitude toward industrialism: it was here to stay, but many
of its aspects seemed to be deplorable.
These could be improved, however, if
only people became aware of conditions
and determined to ameliorate them. To
bring about such awareness, the muckrakers appealed to their readers' consciences. Steffens' famous series, published in book form as *The Shame of the
Cities* in 1904, was frankly intended to
make people feel guilty for the corruption
which riddled their cities. The muckrakers also used the social scientists' method
of careful and painstaking gathering of
data—and with devastating effects. The
investigative function—which was later
largely taken over by governmental agencies—proved absolutely vital to educating and arousing Americans.

All progressive crusades shared the spirit and used the techniques discussed here, but they did so to different degrees and in different ways. Some voiced a greater willingness to accept industrialism and even to extol its potential benefits; others expressed more strongly the outrage against its darker aspects. Some intervened through voluntary organizations; others relied on government to achieve changes. Each reform reflected a distinctive balance between the claims of Protestant moralism and of scientific rationalism. Progressives fought among themselves over these questions even while they set to the common task of applying their new methods and ideas to the problems of a modern society. . . .

In this analysis we have frequently pointed to the differences between the rhetoric, intentions, and results of progressive reform. The failure of reform always to fulfill the expectations of its advocates was not, of course, unique to the progressive era. Jacksonian reform, Reconstruction, and the New Deal all exhibited similar ironies and disappointments. In each case, the clash between reformers with divergent purposes, the inability to predict how given methods of reform would work in practice, and the ultimate waning of popular zeal for change all contributed to the disjuncture of rationale, purpose, and achievement. Yet the gap between these things seems more obvious in the progressive era because so many diverse movements for reform took place in a brief span of time and were accompanied by resounding rhetoric and by high expectations for the improvement of the American social and political environment. The effort to change so many things all at once, and the grandiose claims made for the moral and material betterment which would result, meant that disappointments were bound to occur.

Yet even the great number of reforms and the uncommonly high expectations for them cannot fully account for the consistent gaps which we have observed between the stated purposes, real intentions, and actual results of progressivism. Several additional factors, intrinsic to the nature of early twentieth-century reform, help to explain the ironies and contradictions.

One of these was the progressives' confident reliance on modern methods of reform. Heirs of recent advances in natural science and social science, they enthusiastically devised and applied new techniques to improve American government and society. Their methods often worked; on the other hand, progressive programs often simply did not prove capable of accomplishing what had been expected of them. This was not necessarily the reformers' fault. They hopefully used untried methods even while they lacked a science of society which was capable of solving all the great problems which they attacked. At the same time, the progressives' scientific methods made it possible to know just how far short of success their programs had sometimes fallen. The evidence of their failures thus was more visible than in any previous era of reform. To the progressives' credit, they usually published that evidence—for contemporaries and historians alike to see.

A second aspect of early twentieth-century reform which helps to account for the gaps between aims and achievements was the deep ambivalence of the progressives about industrialism and its consequences. Individual reformers were divided, and so was their movement as a whole. Compared to many Americans of the late 1800s, the progressives fundamentally accepted an industrial society and sought mainly to control and ameliorate it. Even reformers who were intellectually committed to socialist ideas often acted the part of reformers, not radicals.

Yet progressivism was infused and vitalized, as we have seen, by people truly angry with their industrial society. Few of them wanted to tear down the modern institutions of business and commerce, but their anger was real, their moralism was genuine, and their passions were essential to the reforms of their time.

The reform movement never resolved this ambivalence about industrialism. Much of its rhetoric and popular passion pointed in one direction—toward some form of social democracy—while its leaders and their programs went in another. Often the result was confusion and bitterness. Reforms frequently did not measure up to popular, antibusiness expectations, indeed, never were expected to do so by those who designed and implemented them. Even conservative, ameliorative reformers like Theodore Roosevelt often used radical rhetoric. In doing so, they misled their followers and contributed to the ironies of progressivism.

Perhaps most significant, progressives failed to achieve all their goals because, despite their efforts, they never fully came to terms with the divisions and conflicts in American society. Again and again, they acknowledged the existence of social disharmony more fully and frankly than had nineteenth-century Americans. Nearly every social and economic reform of the era was predicated on the progressive recognition that diverse cultural and occupational groups had conflicting interests, and that the responsibility for mitigating and adjusting those differences lay with the whole society, usually the government. Such

recognition was one of the progressives' most significant achievements. Indeed, it stands among the most important accomplishments of liberal reform in all of American history. For, by frankly acknowledging the existence of social disharmony, the progressives committed the twentieth-century United States to recognizing—and to lessening—the inevitable conflicts of a heterogeneous industrial society.

Yet the significance of the progressives' recognition of diversity was compromised by the methods and institutions which they adopted to diminish or eliminate social and economic conflict. Expert administrative government turned out to be less neutral than the progressives believed that it would be. No scientific reform could be any more impartial than the experts who gathered the data or than the bureaucrats who implemented the programs. In practice, as we have seen, administrative government often succumbed to the domination of special interests.

It would be pointless to blame the progressives for the failure of their new methods and programs to eradicate all the conflicts of an industrial society, but it is perhaps fair to ask why the progressives adopted measures which tended to disguise and obscure economic and social conflict almost as soon as they had uncovered it. For one thing, they honestly believed in the almost unlimited potentialities of science and administration. Our late twentieth-century skepticism of these wonders should not blind us to the faith with which the progressives embraced them and imbued them with what now seem magical properties. For another, the progressives were reformers, not radicals. It was one thing to recognize the existence of economic and social conflict, but quite another thing to admit that it was permanent. By and large, these men and women were personally and ideologically inclined to believe that the American society was, in the final analysis, harmonious, and that such conflicts as did exist could be resolved. Finally, the class and cultural backgrounds of the leading progressives often made them insensitive to lower-class immigrant Americans and their cultures. Attempts to reduce divisions sometimes came down to imposing middle-class Protestant ways on the urban masses. In consequence, the progressives never fulfilled their hope of eliminating social conflict. Reformers of the early twentieth century saw the problem more fully than had their predecessors, but they nonetheless tended to consider conflicts resolved when, in fact, they only had been papered over. Later twentieth-century Americans have also frequently deceived themselves in this way.

Thus progressivism inevitably fell short of its rhetoric and intentions. Lest this seem an unfairly critical evaluation, it is important to recall how terribly ambitious were the stated aims and true goals of the reformers. They missed some of their marks because they sought to do so much. And, despite all their shortcomings, they accomplished an enormous part of what they set out to achieve.

Progressivism brought major innovations to almost every facet of public and private life in the United States. The political and governmental systems particularly felt the effects of reform. Indeed, the nature of political participation and the uses to which it was put went through transitions as momentous as those of any era in American history. These developments were complex, as we have seen, and it is no easy matter to sort out who

was helped and who was hurt by each of them or by the entire body of reforms. At the very least, the political changes of the progressive era significantly accommodated American public life to an urban-industrial society. On balance, the polity probably emerged neither more nor less democratic than before, but it did become better suited to address, or at least recognize, the questions and problems which arose from the cities and factories of the nation. After the progressive era, just as before, wealthier elements in American society had a disproportionate share of political power, but we can hardly conclude that this was the fault of the progressives.

The personal and social life of the American people was also deeply affected by progressivism. Like the era's political changes, the economic and social reforms of the early twentieth century were enormously complicated and are difficult to summarize without doing violence to their diversity. In the broadest sense, the progressives sought to mitigate the injustice and the disorder of a society now dominated by its industries and cities. Usually, as we have observed, the quests for social justice and social control were extricably bound together in the reformers' programs, with each group of progressives having different interpretations of these dual ends. Justice sometimes took second place to control. However, before one judges the reformers too harshly for that, it is well to remember how bad urban social conditions were in the late nineteenth century and the odds against which the reformers fought. It is also well to remember that they often succeeded in mitigating the harshness of urban-industrial life.

The problems with which the progressives struggled have, by and large, continued to challenge Americans ever since. And, although the assumptions and techniques of progressivism no longer command the confidence with early twentieth-century Americans had in them, no equally comprehensive body of reforms has ever been adopted in their place. Throughout this study, we have criticized the progressives for having too much faith in their untried methods. Yet if this was a failing, it was also a source of strength, one now missing from reform in America. For the essence of progressivism lay in the hopefulness and optimism which the reformers brought to the tasks of applying science and administration to the high moral purposes in which they believed. The historical record of their aims and achievements leaves no doubt that there were many men and women in the United States in the early 1900s who were not afraid to confront the problems of a modern industrial society with vigor, imagination, and hope. They of course failed to solve all those problems, but no other generation of Americans has done conspicuously better in addressing the political, economic, and social conditions which it faced.

POSTSCRIPT

Did the Progressives Fail?

In spite of their differences, both Abrams's and Link and McCormick's interpretations make concessions to their respective critics. Link and McCormick, for example, admit that the intended reforms did not necessarily produce the desired results. Furthermore, the authors concede that many reformers were insensitive to the cultural values of the lower classes and attempted to impose middle-class Protestant ways on the urban masses. Nevertheless, Link and McCormick argue that in spite of the failure to curb the growth of big business, the progressive reforms did ameliorate the worst abuses of the new urban industrial society. Although the Progressives failed to solve all the major problems of their times, they did set the agenda that still challenges the reformers of the 1990s.

Abrams also makes a concession to his critics when he admits that "progressivism had real lasting effects for the blunting of the sharper edges of self-interest in American life, and for the reduction of the harsher cruelties suffered by the society's underprivileged." Yet the thrust of his argument is that the progressive reformers accomplished little of value. While Abrams probably agrees with Link and McCormick that the Progressives were the first group to confront the problems of modern America, he considers their intended reforms inadequate by their very nature. Because the reformers never really challenged the inequalities brought about by the rise of the industrial state, maintains Abrams, the same problems have persisted to the present day.

Historians have generally been sympathetic to the aims and achievements of the progressive historians. Many, like Charles Beard and Frederick Jackson Turner, came from the Midwest and lived in model progressive states like Wisconsin. Their view of history was based on a conflict between groups competing for power, so it was easy for them to portray progressivism as a struggle between the people and entrenched interests.

It was not until after World War II that a more complex view of progressivism emerged. Richard Hofstadter's *Age of Reform* (Alfred A. Knopf, 1955) was exceptionally critical of the reformist view of history as well as of the reformers in general. Born of Jewish immigrant parents and raised in cities in New York, the Columbia University professor argued that progressivism was a moral crusade undertaken by WASP families in an effort to restore older Protestant and individualistic values and to regain political power and status. Both Hofstadter's "status revolution" theory of progressivism and his profile of the typical Progressive have been heavily criticized by historians. Nevertheless, he changed the dimensions of the debate and made progressivism appear to be a much more complex issue than had previously been thought.

Most of the writing on progressivism for the past 20 years has centered around the "organizational" model. Writers of this school have stressed the role of the "expert" and the ideals of scientific management as basic to an understanding of the Progressive Era. This fascination with how the city manager plan worked in Dayton or railroad regulation in Wisconsin or the public schools laws in New York City makes sense to a 1990s generation surrounded by bureaucracies on all sides. Two books that deserve careful reading are Robert Wiebe's *The Search for Order, 1877–1920* (Hill & Wang, 1967) and the wonderful collection of essays by Samuel P. Hayes, *American Political History as Social Analysis* (Knoxville, 1980), which brings together two decades' worth of articles from diverse journals that were seminal in exploring ethnocultural approaches to politics within the organizational model.

In a highly influential article written for the *American Quarterly* in spring 1970, Professor Peter G. Filene proclaimed "An Obituary for the 'Progressive Movement.'" After an extensive review of the literature, Filene concluded that since historians cannot agree on its programs, values, geographical location, members, and supporters, there was no such thing as a Progressive movement. Few historians were bold enough to write progressivism out of the pantheon of American reform movements. But Filene put the proponents of the early-twentieth-century reform movement on the defensive. Students who want to see how professional historians directly confronted Filene in their refusal to attend the funeral of the Progressive movement should read the essays by John D. Buenker, John C. Burnham, and Robert M. Crunden in *Progressivism* (Schenkman, 1977).

Three works provide an indispensable review of the literature of progressivism in the 1980s. Link and McCormick's *Progressivism* (Harlan Davidson, 1983) deserves to be read in its entirety for its comprehensive yet concise coverage. More scholarly but still readable are the essays on the new political history in Richard L. McCormick, *The Party Period and Public Policy: American Politics from the Age of Jackson to the Progressive Era* (Oxford University Press, 1986). The more advanced student should consult Daniel T. Rodgers, "In Search of Progressivism," *Reviews in American History* (December 1982). While admitting that Progressives shared no common creed or values, Rodgers nevertheless feels that they were able "to articulate their discontents and their social visions" around three distinct clusters of ideas: "The first was the rhetoric of antimonopolism, the second was an emphasis on social bonds and the social nature of human beings, and the third was the language of social efficiency."

On the Internet . . .

World War II Resources
This site links to primary source materials on the Web related to World War II, including original documents regarding all aspects of the war. From here you can see documents on Nazi-Soviet relations from the archives of the German Foreign Office, speeches of Franklin D. Roosevelt on foreign policy, and much more.
http://metalab.unc.edu/pha/

General History and World War II Resources
This site of the Miami University Libraries provides research links on World War II, including topics specific to the United States' participation and the impact of the war on the country.
http://www.lib.muohio.edu/inet/subj/history/wwii/general.html

New Deal Network
Launched by the Franklin and Eleanor Roosevelt Institute (FERI) in October 1996, the New Deal Network (NDN) is a research and teaching resource on the World Wide Web devoted to the public works and arts projects of the New Deal. At the core of the NDN is a database of photographs, political cartoons, and texts (speeches, letters, and other historic documents from the New Deal period). Currently, there are over 20,000 items in this database.
http://newdeal.feri.org/index.htm

PART 3

From Prosperity Through World War II

The 1920s are often portrayed as a hedonistic interlude for everyone between the Progressive and New Deal reform eras. Tensions arose between the values of the nation's rural past and the new social and moral values of modern America. The onset of a more activist federal government accelerated with the Great Depression. With more than one-quarter of the workforce unemployed, Franklin D. Roosevelt was elected on a promise to give Americans a "new deal." World War II short-circuited these plans and introduced people throughout the world to the anxious realities of the atomic age and the development of a cold war between the United States and the Soviet Union.

■ Were the 1920s an Era of Social and Cultural Rebellion?

■ Was the New Deal an Effective Answer to the Great Depression?

■ Was Franklin Roosevelt a Reluctant Internationalist?

ISSUE 9

Were the 1920s an Era of Social and Cultural Rebellion?

YES: William E. Leuchtenburg, from *The Perils of Prosperity, 1914–32* (University of Chicago Press, 1958)

NO: David A. Shannon, from *Between the Wars: America, 1919–1941* (Houghton Mifflin, 1965)

ISSUE SUMMARY

YES: History professor William E. Leuchtenburg attributes the social and cultural rebellion of the 1920s to the growing secularization of American society, the demands by newly enfranchised women for economic equality and sexual liberation, and the hedonistic mood in the country, which produced a youth rebellion against the symbols of Victorian authority.

NO: Author David A. Shannon asserts that the social and cultural changes described by many as revolutionary were actually superficial elements whose significance to the 1920s has been exaggerated; the real catalysts were the monumental processes that expanded the American economy by ushering in prosperity through the creation of a mass consumer culture.

Americans have never been shy about attaching labels to their history, and frequently they do so to characterize particular years or decades in their distant or recent past. It is doubtful, however, that any period in our nation's history has received as many catchy appellations as has the 1920s. Described at various times as "the Jazz Age," "the Roaring Twenties," "the dry decade," "the prosperity decade," "the age of normalcy," and simply "the New Era," these years have captured the imagination of the American public, including the chroniclers of the nation's past.

In 1920 the Great War (World War I) was over, and President Woodrow Wilson received the Nobel Peace Prize despite his failure to persuade the Senate to adopt the Covenant of the League of Nations. The "Red Scare" culminated in the Palmer raids conducted by the Justice Department, which came to an embarrassingly fruitless halt, and Republican Warren Harding won a landslide victory in his campaign for the presidency. In this election, women, buoyed by the ratification of the Nineteenth Amendment, exercised their suffrage rights for the first time in national politics. In Pittsburgh, Pennsylvania, the advent of the radio age was symbolized by the broadcast of election results by KDKA, the nation's first commercial radio station. F. Scott Fitzgerald and

Sinclair Lewis published their first important novels and thereby helped to usher in the most significant American literary renaissance since the early nineteenth century.

During the next nine years, Americans witnessed a number of amazing events: the rise and fall of the Ku Klux Klan; the trial, conviction, and execution of anarchists Nicola Sacco and Bartolomeo Vanzetti on murder charges and the subsequent legislative restrictions on immigration into the United States; the continuation of Prohibition laws and the emergence of the illicit manufacture and trade of alcohol controlled by mob bosses like Alphonse "Scarface Al" Capone; battles over the teaching of evolution in the schools, epitomized by the rhetorical clashes between William Jennings Bryan and Clarence Darrow during the Scopes trial in Dayton, Tennessee; the Harding scandals; "talking" motion pictures; and, in 1929, the collapse of the New York Stock Exchange, symbolizing the beginning of the Great Depression and bringing a startling end to the euphoric claims of business prosperity that had dominated the decade.

For many historians the 1920s marked an era of change in the United States, from international involvement and war to isolationism and peace, from the feverish reform of the Progressive Era to the conservative political retrenchment of Republican ascendancy, from the entrenched values of Victorian America to the cultural rebellion identified with the proliferation of "flivvers," "flappers," and hip flasks. In 1931 Frederick Lewis Allen focused on these changes in his popular account of the decade, *Only Yesterday*. In a chapter entitled "The Revolution of Morals and Manners," Allen established a widely accepted image of the 1920s as a period of significant social and cultural rebellion. The selections that follow evaluate the validity of these perceptions.

William E. Leuchtenburg subscribes to Allen's view that the morals and manners of Americans underwent a revolutionary change in the 1920s. According to Leuchtenburg, religious sanctions dissolved in the face of growing secularization and reduced stability of the family. The "new woman" of the decade, politically empowered by the Nineteenth Amendment, rebelled against traditional domestic roles ascribed to her and demanded sexual and economic freedom. Young Americans, in particular, participated in a self-indulgent hedonism that challenged the authority of traditional social and cultural institutions.

David A. Shannon insists that the crucial changes for most Americans in the 1920s were economic, not social or cultural. The prosperity of an expanding industrial economy, with its increased productivity, per capita income, and readily available consumer goods, was the most significant change in the post–World War I United States. The emergence of the "mass man," not the "flapper," therefore, was of greatest consequence to most Americans in the decade.

YES
William E. Leuchtenburg

THE REVOLUTION IN MORALS

The disintegration of traditional American values—so sharply recorded by novelists and artists—was reflected in a change in manners and morals that shook American society to its depths. The growing secularization of the country greatly weakened religious sanctions. People lost their fear of Hell and at the same time had less interest in Heaven; they made more demands for material fulfillment on Earth. The "status revolution" of the turn of the century undercut the authority of the men who had set America's moral standards: the professional classes, especially ministers, lawyers, and teachers; the rural gentry; the farmers; the urban patricians. The new urban minorities and *arriviste* businessmen were frequently not equipped—not even aware of the need either to support old standards or to create new ones. Most important, the authority of the family, gradually eroded over several centuries, had been sharply lessened by the rise of the city. "Never in recent generations," wrote Freda Kirchwey, "have human beings so floundered about outside the ropes of social and religious sanctions."

When Nora, the feminist heroine of *A Doll's House* (1879) by the Norwegian playwright Henrik Ibsen, walked out into the night, she launched against male-dominated society a rebellion that has not ended yet. The "new woman" revolted against masculine possessiveness, against "over-evaluation" of women "as love objects," against being treated, at worst, as a species of property. The new woman wanted the same freedom of movement that men had and the same economic and political rights. By the end of the 1920's she had come a long way. Before the war, a lady did not set foot in a saloon; after the war, she entered a speakeasy as thoughtlessly as she would go into a railroad station. In 1904, a woman was arrested for smoking on Fifth Avenue; in 1929, railroads dropped their regulation against women smoking in dining cars. In the business and political worlds, women competed with men; in marriage, they moved toward a contractual role. Once ignorant of financial matters, they moved rapidly toward the point where they would be the chief property-holders of the country. Sexual independence was merely the most sensational aspect of the generally altered status of women.

In 1870, there were only a few women secretaries in the entire country; by the time of World War I, two million women worked in business offices, typing the letters and keeping the records of corporations and countinghouses in every city in the nation. During the war, when mobilization created a shortage of labor, women moved into jobs they had never held before. They made grenades, ran elevators, polished locomotives, collected streetcar fares, and even drilled with rifles. In the years after the war, women flew airplanes, trapped beaver, drove taxis, ran telegraph lines, worked as deep-sea divers and steeplejacks, and hunted tigers in the jungle; women stevedores heaved cargoes on the waterfront, while other women conducted orchestras, ran baseball teams, and drilled oil wells. By 1930, more than ten million women held jobs. Nothing did more to emancipate them. Single women moved into their own apartments, and wives, who now frequently took jobs, gained the freedom of movement and choice that went along with leaving home.

After nearly a century of agitation, women won the suffrage in 1920 with the adoption of the Nineteenth Amendment. The American suffragettes modeled themselves on their British counterparts, who blew up bridges, hurled bombs, and burned churches, activities previously regarded as the exclusive privilege of Irish rebels. Using less violent methods, American women had greater success, and the adoption of the suffrage amendment climaxed a long debate in which suffragettes argued that the advent of the women's vote would initiate a new era of universal peace and benevolence, while their enemies forecast a disintegration of American society. (The chief result of women's suffrage, [H. L.] Mencken predicted, would be that adultery would replace boozing as the favorite pastime of politicians.)

As it turned out, women's suffrage had few consequences, good or evil. Millions of women voted (although never in the same proportion as men), women were elected to public office (several gained seats in Congress by the end of the 1920's), but the new electorate caused scarcely a ripple in American political life. Women like Jane Addams made great contributions, but it would be difficult to demonstrate that they accomplished any more after they had the vote than before. It was widely believed, although never proved, that women cast a "dry" vote for Hoover in 1928 and that women were likely to be more moved than men to cast a "moral-issue" vote. Otherwise, the earth spun around much as it had before.

The extreme feminists argued that women were equal to men, and even more so. "Call on God, my dear," Mrs. Belmont is alleged to have told a despondent young suffragette. "She will help you." Female chauvinists wanted not merely sexual equality but, insofar as possible, to dispense with sexuality altogether, because they conceived of sexual intercourse as essentially humiliating to women. "Man is the only animal using this function out of season," protested Charlotte Perkins Gilman. "Excessive indulgence in sex-waste has imperiled the life of the race." Chanting slogans like "Come out of the kitchen" and "Never darn a sock," feminist leaders rebelled against the age-old household roles of women; before long, even a woman contented with her familiar role felt called on to apologize that she was "just a housewife."

In Dorothy Canfield Fisher's *The Home-Maker* (1924), the process is taken to its logical conclusion: a woman who has been a failure as a mother succeeds in business while her husband, a failure in business, stays at home and makes a success of raising children. The literature of the time reflects the growing male sense of alarm, notably in D. H. Lawrence's morbid fear that he would be absorbed and devoured by woman but even more in a new American character represented by the destructive Nina Leeds of O'Neill's *Strange Interlude* (1928), the husband-exploiting title figure of George Kelly's *Craig's Wife* (1926), and the possessive "son-devouring tigress" of Sidney Howard's *The Silver Cord* (1927).

The new freedom for women greatly increased the instability of the family. By the turn of the century, women were demanding more of marriage than they ever had before and were increasingly unwilling to continue alliances in which they were miserable. For at least a century, the family had been losing many of its original social and economic functions; the state, the factory, the school, and even mass amusements robbed the family of functions it once had. The more that social usefulness was taken away from the family, the more marriage came to depend on the personalities of the individuals involved, and, since many Americans of both sexes entered marriage with unreasonable expectations, this proved a slender reed. In 1914, the number of divorces reached 100,000 for the first time; in 1929, over 205,000 couples were divorced in a single year. The increase in divorce probably meant less an increase in marital unhappiness than a refusal to go on with marriages which would earlier have been tolerated.

As the family lost its other social functions, the chief test of a good family became how well it developed the personalities of the children, and parents, distrustful both of their own instincts and of tribal lore, eagerly sought out expert advice to avoid the opprobrium of having raised unhappy children. Dr. John B. Watson published the first edition of *Behaviorism* in 1914, but it was not until its third edition in 1925 that behaviorism —the idea that man was nothing but a machine responding to stimuli—took the country by storm. Since man was only a machine, environment alone was significant in determining both man's character and the nature of his society. "Give me a dozen healthy infants, well-formed, and my own specified world to bring them up in," declared Watson, "and I'll guarantee to take any one at random and train him to become any specialist I might select —doctor, lawyer, artist, merchant-chief, and yes, even beggarman and thief, regardless of his talents, tendencies, abilities, vocations and race of his ancestor." Watson's theories had the greatest impact on child-rearing; the Department of Labor incorporated behaviorist assumptions in its pamphlet *Infant and Child Care*, which, with emphasis on rigid scheduling of a baby's activities, became the government's leading best seller. Watson predicted that the time would come when it would be just as bad manners to show affection to one's mother or father as to come to the table with dirty hands. To inculcate the proper attitudes at an early age, Watson warned parents, "Never hug and kiss them, never let them sit in your lap."

Great as Watson's influence was, it could not hold a candle to that of Sigmund Freud. Before the war, Freud's name was known, outside of medical circles, only to a coterie of intellectuals. He had been referred to in the United States as early as 1895 by Dr. Robert

Edes, but, a decade later, only a few well-informed medical men knew his name. By 1908, Dr. A. A. Brill, who had studied at Jung's Clinic of Psychiatry in Zurich, was won to Freudian theory and undertook the major task of translating Freud's work. In 1909, when Freud journeyed to the United States to give a series of lectures at Clark University, he was amazed that "even in prudish America" his work was so well known. The following year, Brill published the first of his translations of Freud, *Three Contributions to a Theory of Sex* (previously available only in the German *Drei Adhandlungen zur Sexual-Theorie)*, and in 1913, Brill, at the invitation of the precocious Walter Lippmann, explained Freud to a group of American intellectuals gathered at Mabel Dodge's salon....

In the years after the war, psychology became a national mania. Books appeared on the *Psychology of Golf*, the *Psychology of the Poet Shelley,* and the *Psychology of Selling Life Insurance.* People talked knowingly of "libido," "defense mechanism," and "fixation," confused the subconscious with the unconscious, repression with suppression, and dealt with the tortuously difficult theories of Freud and of psychoanalysis as though they were simple ideas readily grasped after a few moments' explanation. One article explained solemnly that the immense popularity of the song "Yes, We Have No Bananas" was the result of a national inferiority complex. Psychiatrist Karl Menninger found himself badgered at parties to perform analyses of the personalities of guests as though he were a fortune teller. "When I refuse," he explained, "my questioners often show me how the thing is done." Neophytes were able to read books like *Psychoanalysis by Mail* and *Psychoanalysis Self-Applied,*

while the Sears, Roebuck catalogue offered *Ten Thousand Dreams Interpreted* and *Sex Problems Solved.* Like the automobile, Freud was brought within the reach of everyone.

Freud's popularity had an inevitable effect on the "revolution in morals." It was assumed that he was arguing that unless you freely expressed your libido and gave outlet to your sex energy, you would damage your health; by the distortion of his work, a scientific imprimatur was given to self-indulgence. By a similar but more understandable misinterpretation, it was believed that Freud was denying the reality of love; his name was invoked in support of the dehumanization of sex. "I'm hipped on Freud and all that," observed a Scott Fitzgerald heroine, "but it's rotten that every bit of *real* love in the world is ninety-nine percent passion and one little soupçon of jealousy."

What only the initiate understood was that although Freud did emphasize the strong power of unconscious motivation, psychiatry was aimed not at stressing the irrational or at licensing indulgence but at making it possible for man to use his rational powers to control unconscious forces. Freud taught that the most "irrational" act had meaning. Psychiatrists used Freud's theories to enable men to control their emotions through a clearer understanding of their irrational impulses. The vast popularity of Freud in America, which was to move the center of psychiatry from Vienna to Park Avenue, alarmed many psychoanalysts. They realized that the popularity had been achieved less through an understanding of Freud than through a belief that he shared the American conviction that every man had the right not merely to pursue happiness but to possess it.

This distortion had a number of unfortunate results, not least of which was the disappointment patients experienced when they came to realize that progress could be made only when self-indulgent fantasies were surrendered; but its ultimate effect was good. In Europe, psychiatry followed a course of near-fatalism in treating mental illness; in the more optimistic and more expectant American environment, psychiatry made greater gains and received far greater public support.

Freudian theories had a great impact on American writers, in part because they suggested new techniques for the exploration of human motivation, in part because they gave postwar intellectuals an invaluable weapon against the older standards. In some works the use of Freud was explicit; in others, as in the novels of Sherwood Anderson, where the influence of Freud seems obvious, there was apparently no conscious use of Freud at all. Eugene O'Neill turned to Freudian themes in his ambitious *Strange Interlude* (1928) as well as in his *Desire Under the Elms* (1924) and *Mourning Becomes Electra* (1931). Freud's greatest impact on the form of the novel was in the "stream-of-consciousness" technique, although its most important exponent, the Irish novelist James Joyce, was more directly influenced by Jung than by Freud. Stream of consciousness was employed in America most notably in William Faulkner's *The Sound and the Fury* (1929) and in the works of the novelist and poet Conrad Aiken. "I decided very early," Aiken recalled, "that Freud, and his co-workers and rivals and followers, were making the most important contribution of the century to the understanding of man and his consciousness; accordingly I made it my

business to learn as much from them as I could." ...

In the attempt to work out a new standard of relations between men and women, Americans in the 1920's became obsessed with the subject of sex. Some novelists wrote of little else, in particular James Branch Cabell, whose *Jurgen* (1919), actually a curiously unerotic novel despite its absorption with the subject, was praised for its "phallic candour." Radio singers crooned songs like "Hot Lips," "Baby Face," "I Need Lovin'," and "Burning Kisses." Magazines like *Paris Nights, Flapper Experiences,* and *Snappy Stories* covered newsstands. The newspaperman Frank Kent returned from a tour of the country in 1925 with the conviction that "between the magazines and the movies a lot of these little towns seem literally saturated with sex." Advertising, once pristine, began the transition which, as one writer remarked, was to transmute soap from a cleansing agent to an aphrodisiac and to suggest "that every woman buying a pair of stockings is aiming for an assignation, or at the very least for a rescue via a fire-ladder."

Absorption with sex was the life's blood of the newspaper tabloid. Developed by Lord Northcliffe in England, the tabloid first appeared in America with the founding of the New York *Daily News* in 1919. As a picture newspaper like the *Sketch* and the *Mirror* in England, the *News* caught on immediately; within five years it had the largest circulation of any newspaper in New York. Hearst followed with the *New York Daily Mirror,* a slavish imitation of the *News,* and in 1924 Bernarr MacFadden demonstrated how far salacious sensationalism could be carried with the *New York Evening Graphic.* The New York tabloids soon had their imitators in other cities. Although the tabloids won millions of readers, they did not cut into the circulation of the established newspapers; they found a new, semiliterate market.

Not even the tabloids exploited sex with the zeal of Hollywood; it was the movies which created the American love goddess. When the "vamp," Theda Bara, appeared in *The Blue Flame* in 1920, crowds mobbed theaters in eastern cities to get in. Movie producers found that films like *The Sheik* drew large audiences, while *Sentimental Tommy* or epics like *America* played to empty houses. When it was apparent that sex was infinitely more profitable than the prewar sentimental-patriotic fustian, the country got a steady diet of movies like *Up in Mabel's Room, Her Purchase Price,* and *A Shocking Night.* (Cecil B. De Mille changed the title of Sir James Barrie's *The Admirable Crichton* into *Male and Female.*) Clara Bow was featured as the "It" girl, and no one had to be told what "it" was. The only ones in Hollywood with "it," explained the novelist Elinor Glyn, were "Rex, the wild stallion, actor Tony Moreno, the Ambassador Hotel doorman and Clara Bow." Movie ads promised kisses "where heart, and soul, and sense in concert move, and the blood is lava, and the pulse a blaze."

Threatened by censorship bills in thirty-six states, the industry made a gesture toward reforming itself. Following the model of organized baseball, which had made Judge Kenesaw Mountain Landis its "czar" after the Chicago Black Sox scandal of 1919, the movie industry hired Harding's Postmaster-General, Will Hays, to be the "Judge Landis of the movies." All the Hays Office succeeded in doing in the 1920's was to add hypocrisy to sex by insisting on false moralizations and the "moral" ending. Movie ads continued to entice patrons with "brilliant men, beautiful jazz babies, champagne baths, midnight revels, petting parties in the purple dawn, all ending in one terrific smashing climax that makes you gasp."

Taboos about sex discussion were lifted; women talked freely about inhibitions and "sex starvation." Speech became bolder, and men and women told one another off-color stories that a short while before would have been reserved for the Pullman smoker. Novelists and playwrights spoke with a new bluntness; in Hemingway's *The Sun Also Rises* (1926), the word "bitch" recurs frequently. The woman who once was shocked by everything now prided herself, observed a writer in *Harper's*, on the fact that nothing at all shocked her; "immunity to the sensation of 'recoil with painful astonishment' is the mark of our civilization."

Parental control of sex was greatly lessened; the chaperone vanished at dances, and there was no room for a duenna in the rumble seat of an automobile. The bachelor girl had her own latchkey. Girls petted, and when they did not pet, they necked, and no one was certain of the exact difference; Lloyd Morris observed: "The word 'neck' ceased to be a noun; abruptly became a verb; immediately lost all anatomical precision." At one conference in the Midwest, eight hundred college girls met to discuss petting, to deal with searching questions like What do nice girls do? and How far should you go? "Whether or not they pet," said one writer, "they hesitate to have anyone believe that they do not." The consensus of the delegates was: "Learn temperance in petting, not abstinence."

Victorian dance forms like the waltz yielded to the fast-stepping Charleston, the Black Bottom, or slow fox trots in which, to the syncopated rhythms of the jazz band, there was a "maximum of motion in the minimum of space." Jazz made its way northward from the bordellos of New Orleans to the dance halls of Chicago during these years, crossed the ocean to Paris (where it was instantly taken up as a uniquely American contribution to music), and created its own folk heroes in the lyrical Bix Beiderbecke and the dynamic Louis Armstrong who, legend has it, once played two hundred different choruses of "Sweet Sue." The tango and the fox trot hit the country before the war, but it was not until the 1920's that the more voluptuous and the more frenetic dance crazes swept the nation. Moralists like Bishop Cannon protested that the new dances brought "the bodies of men and women in unusual relations to each other"; but by the end of the period the fox trot was as popular and the saxophones wailed as loudly at the high-school dances of the Bishop's Methodist parishioners as in the dance halls of New York and Los Angeles.

What did it all add up to? Lord Birkenhead, the British Lord High Chancellor, observed in 1928: "The proportion of frail to virtuous women is probably constant throughout the ages in any civilization." Perhaps, but the meager evidence suggests otherwise. There appears to have been an increase in promiscuity, especially in sexual experience before marriage for middle-class women; there was probably an increase in extramarital experience as well. With effective contraceptive techniques widely used, the fear of pregnancy was greatly lessened. ("The veriest schoolgirl today knows as much as the midwife of 1885," wrote Mencken.) At the same time, quite

possibly as a consequence, a great many brothels lost their customers and had to close their doors, while itinerant workers in the same field disappeared from the sidewalks. The degree of sexual experimentation in the 1920's has certainly been exaggerated, but there is a good deal to bear out Alexander Pope's aphorism that "every woman is at heart a rake."

Not only the American woman but the American girl was reputed to be freer with her sexual favors than she had ever been before, although serious periodicals published learned debates over whether this was fact or fiction. The flapper had as many defenders as accusers on this score, but no one doubted that every campus had its Jezebels. Smith College girls in New York, noted Malcolm Cowley, modeled themselves on Hemingway's Lady Brett. Certainly, girls were less reticent than they bad been before the war. "One hears it said," lamented a Southern Baptist periodical, "that the girls are actually tempting the boys more than the boys do the girls, by their dress and conversation." They dressed more freely; they wore bathing suits which revealed more than had ever been revealed before. At dances, corsets were checked in cloakrooms; then even this pretense was abandoned. Above all, they were out for a good time. "None of the Victorian mothers," wrote F. Scott Fitzgerald in *This Side of Paradise*, "had any idea how casually their daughters were accustomed to be kissed."

Although Fitzgerald reported that the ideal flapper was "lovely and expensive and about nineteen," the flapper appeared bent on playing down her femininity and emphasizing her boyishness. She used the most ingenious devices to conceal the fact that she had breasts. Even the nudes at the Folies Bergères were flatchested and were picked for that reason, and in England, women wore the "Eton crop" and bound their chests with wide strips of ribbon to achieve a "boyish bust." The flapper wore dresses that suggested she had no hips at all; her waistline moved steadily southward. As one writer recalled, "Women not only lost their waists; they sat on them." She dieted recklessly in an effort to remove unwanted protuberances. Girls, noted Dr. Charles F. Pabst, were attempting to become "pathologically thin." "A strikingly sad example of improper dieting," he said, "was the case of a shapely motion-picture actress, who became a nervous wreck and blasted her career by restricting herself to tomatoes, spinach and orange juice." The flapper bobbed her hair and dyed it raven black. She concealed everything feminine but her matchstick legs. In 1919 her skirt was six inches above the ground; by 1927 it had edged about to her knees. The well-accoutered flapper wore a tight felt hat, two strings of beads, bangles on her wrists, flesh-colored stockings rolled below the knees, and unbuckled galoshes. Ironically, the more she adopted mannish styles, the more she painted her face, daubing her cheeks with two circles of rouge and her lips with "kissproof" lipstick; cosmetics became the chief way of distinguishing feminine members of the race.

The vogue of the flapper was only the most obvious instance of the new American cult of youth. "It is the glory of the present age that in it one can be young," Randolph Bourne wrote in 1913. In every age, youth has a sense of a separate destiny, of experiencing what no one has ever experienced before, but it may be doubted that there was ever a time in American history when youth had such a special sense of

importance as in the years after World War I. There was a break between generations like a geological fault; young men who had fought in the trenches felt that they knew a reality their elders could not even imagine. Young girls no longer consciously modeled themselves on their mothers, whose experience seemed unusable in the 1920's.

Instead of youth modeling itself on age, age imitated youth. Scott Fitzgerald, looking back on the years of which he was the chief chronicler, recalled: "May one offer in exhibit the year 1922! That was the peak of the younger generation, for though the Jazz Age continued, it became less and less an affair of youth. The sequel was a children's party taken over by elders." "Oh, yes, we are collegiate" was the theme song of a generation yearning for the irresponsible, idealized days of youth. Everyone wanted to be young. Mrs. Gertrude Atherton's *Black Oxen* (1923) described how grandmothers might be rejuvenated through a glandular operation and once more stir up young men. It was the young girl who started the flapper ideal; it was her mother who kept it going.

Americans in the 1920's, at least on the surface, were less sinridden and more self-indulgent than they had ever been before. They broke the Sabbath apparently without compunction, missing the morning sermon to play golf, driving into the country in the afternoon instead of sitting stiffly in the parlor. The mood of the country was hedonistic; Omar Khayyam's quatrains took the colleges by storm. The ideal of hedonism was living for the moment, and if one can isolate a single spirit which permeated every segment of society in the postwar years, it was the obliteration of time.

Abandoning the notion of saving income or goods or capital over time, the country insisted on immediate consumption, a demand which became institutionalized in the installment plan. The President's Research Committee on Social Trends noted "the new attitude towards hardship as a thing to be avoided by living in the here and now, utilizing installment credit and other devices to telescope the future into the present." Songs became obsolescent almost as soon as they appeared, and people prided themselves not on remembering the old songs but on knowing the latest. The imitation of youth by age was an effort to telescope the years, while youth itself tried to escape the inexorability of time. One of the younger generation, replying to its critics, observed: "The trouble with them is that they can't seem to realize that we are busy, that what pleasure we snatch must be incidental and feverishly hurried. We have to make the most of our time.... We must gather rose-buds while we may."

In the magazine *Secession*, a group of intellectuals, including Hart Crane, Kay Boyle, and Elliot Paul, signed a "Proclamation" declaring "Time is a tyranny to be abolished." Gertrude Stein's concept of a "continuous present" effaced not merely history and tradition but any sense of "time." "The future," she declared, "is not important any more." In Italy, the Futurists had cast out Petrarch and Dante and rejected harmony and sentiment; their present-mindedness had a direct impact on Ezra Pound, who found their chief spokesman, Marinetti, "thoroughly simpatico." The characters in the novels of the day, particularly those of Scott Fitzgerald, lived only for the moment, while Edna St. Vincent Millay penned the theme of the generation in "My candle burns at both ends." The

spirit of hedonism of the decade, wrote Edmund Wilson, was "letting oneself be carried along by the mad hilarity and heartbreak of jazz, living only for the excitement of the evening."

The obliteration of time carried with it a conscious assault on the authority of history. The Dada movement, which developed in the war years in Zurich, adopted as its motto: "Je ne veux même pas savoir s'il y a eu des hommes avant moi" ("I do not wish even to know whether there have been men before me"). More remarkably, the very men who were the spokesmen for history and tradition led the onslaught; in this, Henry Ford and Charles Beard were one. Ford's interest in history was actually an anti-history. He took cottages in which Noah Webster and Patrick Henry had once lived and moved them to Dearborn, Michigan, where they had no meaning. He sentimentalized and pillaged the past, but he had no respect for it. "History is more or less the bunk," he said. "We want to live in the present, and the only history that is worth a tinker's dam is the history we make today." As early as 1907, the historians Charles Beard and James Harvey Robinson had deliberately attempted to subordinate the past to the present with the aim of enabling the reader "to catch up with his own times; ... to know what was the attitude of Leo XIII toward the Social Democrats even if he has forgotten that of Innocent III toward the Albigenses." Beard's emphasis on current history had its counterpart in Veblen's dislike for dead languages, Holmes's skepticism about the value of learning as a guide in jurisprudence, and Dewey's emphasis on the functional in education.

The revolution in morals routed the worst of Victorian sentimentality and false modesty. It mitigated the harsh moral judgments of rural Protestantism, and it all but wiped out the awful combination of sanctimoniousness and lewdness which enabled Anthony Comstock to defame Bernard Shaw as "this Irish smut-dealer" and which allowed Teddy Roosevelt, with unconscious humor, to denounce the Mexican bandit Villa as a "murderer and a bigamist." It greatly extended the range of choice; "the conduct of life," wrote Joseph Wood Krutch, had been made "more thrillingly difficult." Yet, at the same time, it raised baffling problems of the relations between husband and wife, parent and child, and, in itself, provided no ready guides to conduct. The hedonism of the period was less a solution than a pathological symptom of what Walter Lippmann called a "vast dissolution of ancient habits," and it rarely proved as satisfying as people hoped. "Sons and daughters of the puritans, the artists and writers and utopians who flocked to Greenwich Village to find a frank and free life for the emotions and senses, felt at their backs the icy breath of the monster they were escaping," wrote Joseph Freeman. "Because they could not abandon themselves to pleasure without a sense of guilt, they exaggerated the importance of pleasure, idealized it and even sanctified it."

NO

David A. Shannon

AMERICAN SOCIETY AND
CULTURE IN THE 1920's

Journalists, scenario writers, even professional historians (usually a rather solemn bunch) who normally make a serious effort to deal with the problems that confront society and individuals in their relations with one another are prone to get a little giddy when they approach the social and cultural history of the 1920's and prattle joyously but aimlessly about "the jazz age." To judge from some accounts, Americans did little else from 1920 until 1929 but make millions in the stock market, dance the Charleston and the Black Bottom, dodge gangster bullets, wear raccoon coats, and carry hip flasks. "Flapper," "saxophone," "bathtub gin," and "speakeasy" are the key words in this special genre of popular historical writing, and the interpretation of the era, usually only implied, is that America went on a hedonistic binge for approximately a decade. Obviously, such a characterization of an epoch is shallow and exaggerated once one thinks about it critically and looks into the epoch more searchingly, but that style of social history for the postwar decade persists and thrives.

Probably the great change in the conditions of society and the mood of the people after 1929 is the root cause of this curious historiographical aberration. The grimness, despair, and drabness of America in the 1930's probably prompted writers to look back at the previous decade with a kind of nostalgia for a more carefree existence and led them to look too fondly and too long at what were actually superficialities. An extraordinarily skillful popular historian, Frederick Lewis Allen, set the style with his *Only Yesterday*, which appeared in 1931, a gray year indeed. The book was a delight to read and still is, and Allen's feat was all the more remarkable for having done it so soon after the fact. A careful reading of *Only Yesterday* reveals that Allen was often concerned with more than the superficialities of the 1920's, but he nevertheless put an unusual emphasis upon the bizarre and transitory aspects of the 1920's that contrasted sharply with the 1930's.

The thesis of this [essay] is not to declaim that there were no flappers, no saxophones, no jazz age. The [essay] will suggest that there were other aspects of the 1920's ... that are more useful to examine if we wish to understand the era and the way that it helped to shape our own contemporary society. In other words, the flappers were not a myth, but we will do well to look beyond the flappers, which have already been written about more than sufficiently.

PROSPERITY AND ECONOMIC CHANGE

Prosperity was a basic fact of the 1920's, one that shaped and conditioned many aspects of life outside the economic realm. A generally expanding economy underlay a generally expansive view about life, as happened again in the generation after World War II. To say that the economy was healthy would be to ignore the almost fatal illness that struck it low in 1929, but it was clearly prosperous.

The path of the economy even during its boom years was not entirely smooth, however. Although relatively brief, the postwar depression that hit in mid-1920 was as steep and as sudden as any the American economy had ever experienced. The year 1921 was a hard one. Unemployment went up to 4,750,000, and national income was down 28 per cent from the previous year. Farm prices were far too low to enable most farmers to meet their costs of production. But in 1922 the economy came back strong, and by the end of the year it was buzzing along in better shape than it had been when the depression hit. There were minor dips in the business cycle in 1924 and 1927, but they were not serious.

Besides cyclical fluctuations there were other blemishes on prosperity's record. Some economic activities did not share in the general prosperity. Agriculture never really recovered from the postwar depression, and low farm prices were the root of farmer discontent that manifested itself in McNary-Haugenism. Some industries were in bad shape throughout the period. The world market for textiles declined when women's styles changed. A dress in 1928 required less than one-half the material that a seamstress needed to make a dress in 1918. Furthermore, many clothes in the 1920's were made of synthetic fibers. Rayon became very popular. Consequently the textile industry was unable to pay wages consistent with the rising standard of living. The industry continued its long-range shift of operations from New England to the South, particularly to the southern Appalachians, where wage rates were lower. Coal was another sick industry. As home owners shifted gradually to other fuels for space heating and as automobiles and trucks gradually displaced the railroads, once a major market for coal, the total coal market shrank slightly. There was approximately 10 per cent less coal mined at the end of the decade than there had been at the beginning. New mining technology enabled mine operators to get along with a smaller labor force. Almost one fourth of the nation's coal miners at work in 1923 were out of the pits by 1929, and since most miners lived in isolated communities where there were almost no other employment opportunities, the economic hardship in the mining towns was acute. Even employed miners worked at hourly wage rates that were 14 per cent lower in 1929 than they had been in 1923.

But despite cyclical downswings and generally depressed conditions in agriculture, textiles, and coal, prosperity was strong. One has only to look at the statistics. Real per-capita income increased almost one third from 1919 to 1929. (Real per-capita income is total national income divided by population and adjusted for price changes.) The mythical average person—not worker, but all people, men, women, and children—received $716 in 1929. In 1919 he had received just $543, measured in 1929 dollars. Manufacturing industries increased their output by almost two thirds, but because of a tremendous increase in labor productivity due to technological advances there were actually fewer people engaged in manufacturing in 1929 than there had been in 1919. A large number of these displaced production workers went into service industries, where many of the jobs were "white collar." Furthermore, there was a shift in the nature of industrial production that tended to improve the lot of the consumer. Since the early days of American industry a large part of production had been capital goods, that is, products that were used to produce further wealth rather than be consumed by the people. Much American production, for example, had gone into building a vast railroad network, the biggest and most intricate rail system that any nation in the world had found it necessary to develop. The number of miles of railroad track began actually to decrease slightly after 1920. When any industrial economy matures it reaches a point at which a significantly higher proportion of production may go to consumer goods, and the American economy reached this level in the postwar decade. This is not to say that capital production ceased, which would have been calamitous for long-range growth —indeed, it even increased in absolute terms—but a larger proportion of annual production was in the form of articles that ordinary people could use, such as washing machines, radios, and motor cars. The number of such durable consumer goods in use was small compared to what it would be by midcentury, but

still more people than ever before enjoyed their convenience. In fact, because of increased national production, relatively stable price levels, and increased production of consumer goods, most Americans lived better in the 1920's than ever before.

To a considerable degree the prosperity of the 1920's was due to the vast expansion of a few relatively new industries and to increased construction, much of which was actually due to the new industries. Road building, for example, was a major enterprise during the decade, and the roads were necessary because of the relatively new automobile industry.

In 1915, soon after Henry Ford developed the Model T, there were about 2.5 million cars on the roads of America. By 1920 there were over 9 million and the industry's growth had only started. By 1925 there were nearly 20 million cars registered, and in 1929 there were 26.5 million. In that last year of the boom the industry produced 5,622,000 motor vehicles. Ford had made the big break-through with his mass-produced, inexpensive Model T, but later decisions of the industry similarly broadened the market. In 1923 the major car manufacturers abandoned open cars except for a few sports models and concentrated on closed vehicles. Many a family that had resisted getting one of the older and colder models succumbed to the lure of relatively comfortable transportation. The auto industry also soon discovered that to tap a really mass market it had to develop a credit system. It developed an auto financing system which remains largely the same today. By 1925 over two thirds of the new cars purchased each year were bought on credit. Installment buying, which became general in other fields as well, did not increase the purchasing power of any given family income. In fact, it reduced it by as much as the interest charges amounted to. But it did greatly stimulate new car purchases, and the purchases had a stimulating effect upon the economy in general.

The auto industry statistics were impressive. In 1929 automobiles accounted for over one eighth of the total dollar value of all manufacturing in the nation. Over 7 per cent of all wage earners engaged in manufacturing worked for automobile companies. The industry took 15 per cent of national steel production. When one considers the effect that auto production had on the manufacture and distribution of tires, oil and gasoline, and glass it has been estimated that the industry provided jobs for about 3.7 million workers, roughly one tenth of the nonagricultural labor force.

Motor vehicles were the most spectacular new industry, but chemicals and electric appliances also had a very large growth. Before World War I the American chemical industry had been rather small, unable to compete with German firms for most items. The war shut off German imports and the federal government confiscated German patents and sold them to domestic corporations. By the end of the 1920's the American chemical industry had grown roughly 50 per cent larger than it had been before the outbreak of the war in Europe. The electric appliance industry became economically significant as more and more American homes gained access to electric power. In 1912 roughly one sixth of America's families had electricity in their homes; by 1927 almost two thirds of them had electric power. The first use that families put the new power to was lighting, but they quickly began to use it to lighten their work. By 1925, 80 per cent of the homes with electricity had electric irons, 37 per

cent had vacuum cleaners, and 25 per cent had washing machines. Most families continued to use ice for food storage. Radio was intimately connected with the electric industry, although especially in the early 1920's many of the sets manufactured were operated by storage batteries, big things that weighed over twenty-five pounds and were nothing like the dry cells that power today's transistor radios. The home radio industry was altogether new. The first commercial radio station was KDKA, operated by the Westinghouse Electric Company from East Pittsburgh, in 1920. By 1924 there were over five hundred commercial radio stations. By 1929 sales of radios amounted to over $400 million and roughly two fifths of the families of America owned one. Without these new industries, which were based primarily upon new inventions or improved technology, it is doubtful if the 1920's would have been any more prosperous than the prewar period.

Trade unions usually increase in membership strength during periods of prosperity. More workers are employed, thereby increasing trade-union potential, and employers, optimistic about the prospect of profits, usually want labor stability and are willing to make concessions to unions in order to prevent disruption of production. But trade unions in the 1920's departed from this general rule; they actually decreased in membership and influence during the decade. Total union membership in 1920 was roughly five million; by the end of the decade it had declined to about three and one-half million.

There were three main reasons for failure of trade unions in the 1920's: a strong counterattack against them by employers, in which government cooperated; cautious and complacent union leadership; and widespread lack of interest in unions among unorganized workers. During the postwar depression, an opportune time, many employers engaged in a fierce and somewhat successful anti-union drive. Their campaign was for the open shop, which they called "the American plan" in an effort to associate unionism with un-Americanism. (In an open shop no employee is under any compulsion to join a union. If a union exists in the shop, nonmembers receive whatever wages and hours union members have, which puts the union at a disadvantage in getting new members. In a closed shop the employer agrees to hire only union members. In a union shop the employer hires as he chooses but the employees must join the union.) The open-shop campaign was strong even in some industries where unionism had been well established, such as printing and building construction. Some building contractors were under pressure to break unions. The president of the Bethlehem Steel Company announced in late 1920 that his firm would not sell steel to contractors in New York and Philadelphia who consented to keep their established closed-shop policy. Also in the 1920's employers embarked upon a program to extend what came to be called welfare capitalism. A rather nebulous concept, welfare capitalism ran the gamut from employee stock-purchase plans (usually nonvoting stock) to athletic and social programs for employees and better toilets and locker rooms. Welfare capitalism programs tended to make employees identify their welfare with the company rather than a union and to remove some of the annoyances that sometimes erupt into union-management conflict.

Despite the intensity of the employers' attack it is likely that more vigorous and imaginative union leadership would have enabled the unions to hold their own. Samuel Gompers, the primary founder of the American Federation of Labor and its president for all but one year of its existence during his lifetime, was seventy years old in 1920, hardened in his approach to unionism, and lacking in the vigor which he had displayed at the beginning of the century. William Green, successor to the AFL presidency after Gompers' death in 1924, was depressingly cautious and almost completely without imagination. Whatever forward motion the labor movement made from Green's accession to the AFL presidency in 1924 to his death in the 1950's was made despite Green rather than because of him. The fundamental difficulty in union leadership from World War I until the early 1930's was that the AFL had no real interest in getting the unorganized into unions except for those in skilled trades. Not until labor leaders eager to organize unskilled workers in basic industry came to the fore in the 1930's did the unions get off the ground. There was one major exception that proved the generalization: in the needle trades David Dubinsky and Sidney Hillman adopted new techniques and ideas. Their innovations were successful, and their organizations thrived while the rest of labor stagnated and shriveled.

Many workers in basic industry in the 1920's were apathetic or hostile to unionism, not only because of their employers' attitudes and the failure of union leadership to excite them but because they lived better than ever they had before and because they had formed their social ideas in a preindustrial society. There is no question but that most industrial workers were better off materially in the 1920's than they had been earlier. Real wages (the relationship of money wages to the cost of living) in 1919 were at 105 on a scale in which 1914 was 100. By 1928 the figure stood at 132, a truly significant increase. Many an industrial worker's social ideas and assumptions earned him the unionist's contemptuous term "company man." Especially in the new industries like autos and electric appliances a large part of the labor force was composed of men who had begun their lives in small towns or on the farm, where there had been no big employers and where the terms of work were laid down by the employer on a take-it-or-leave-it basis or settled by each individual employee bargaining with the employer. Individualistic social attitudes formed in a rural society were difficult to shake, even when a man lived the anything but individualistic life of a city worker on a production line, the employee of a vast and complex corporation. It took the depression of the next decade to shock many workers from a rural background into modifying their views about the relationship of capital and labor sufficiently to join a union and make it a countervailing power to the corporation.

There are no statistics that reveal precisely how many industrial workers in the 1920's were originally from urban areas, but the population statistics reveal a vast growth of the cities during the decade. Many rural counties continued to grow, but urban counties grew much more rapidly. The general pattern of migration was from the farm or small town to the small city of the same region and thence to a big city, often out of the region. The biggest growths were in New York City, the industrial cities on or near the Great Lakes, the San Francisco area,

and Los Angeles. California tended to draw its new population from the West and the Midwest. New York's growth came from all over the nation, but the bulk of it came from the East and the Southeast. The burgeoning cities of the Midwest grew from rural-to-urban movement within the region and from migration from the South.

Great numbers of the migrants from the South were Negro. Negro migration to the North first became numerically significant during World War I. In 1910 more than 90 per cent of the Negroes of the United States lived in states that had been slave areas in 1860. The census of that year showed only 850,000 Negroes living outside the South. The census of 1920 showed 1,400,000 in the North and West, most of them having migrated after 1917. The movement continued, even expanded, during the 1920's. In the 1930 census, 2,300,000 Negroes were living outside the South. The day was rapidly coming when the typical American Negro would not be a southern sharecropper but a northern or western urban wage earner.

This movement from rural to urban areas, for both Negroes and whites, came about for essentially economic reasons. Agriculture languished; industry flourished. Economic conditions pushed people off the farms and out of the small towns; better economic conditions in the cities pulled them into population clusters.

THE EFFECTS OF AFFLUENCE

America in the 1920's was a relatively affluent society. Affluence made it possible for Americans to change significantly the way they lived, to buy a car and a radio, to go to movies, to improve their schools and send their children to school for more years than they themselves had attended. These effects of affluence in turn had their own effects, some of them very far-reaching.

Foreign visitors to the United States in the late 1920's who had not seen the nation for a decade or two were impressed most of all by the numbers of automobiles they saw and the changes that the automobile had wrought in society. In 1929 there were between one fifth and one sixth as many cars in the United States as there were people, a far higher proportion than that of any other country except Canada. It was physically possible for everyone in America to be rolling on automobile wheels simultaneously, and in some of the traffic jams of summer weekends it appeared that the nation had actually tried to perform the feat.

Any attempt to enumerate all the effects of widespread automobile ownership would bog down in superficial relationships, but some of the major effects are evident. The very appearance of the country changed. Merchants and manufacturers could not resist trying to profit from the captive audiences that traveled the main highways and erected billboards on the land that only a few generations back had been a wilderness. Short-order restaurants and gasoline stations lined the roads approaching towns and cities. Tourist cabins, the predecessors of motels, clustered around the main points of tourist interest. Towns and cities began their sprawl into the countryside as the automobile enabled workers to live a great distance from their employment. Cities such as Los Angeles, which experienced most of their growth after the coming of the automobile age, tended not to have the central business area traditional in older American and European cities.

The social effects of the automobile have been the subject of a great deal of speculation. Many observers have asserted that the car changed courtship patterns by making young people more mobile and removing them from the supervision of their elders. Certainly every community by the end of the 1920's had a secluded area known as "lovers' lane" where cars parked on summer nights, but this whole theory of changed courtship patterns tends to underestimate the ingenuity of young people of the pre-automobile age. "Lovers' lanes" once had buggies parked beside them, and because of the superiority of horse intelligence to that of an automobile a buggy driver could pay less attention to his driving than could a car driver. Still, there are other, more important, and better documented social effects of the automobile.

By the end of the 1920's thousands of families took long vacation trips by car and quite obviously the American public knew more of its nation's geography at first hand than had earlier and less mobile generations. In 1904 a Chicago lawyer made a trip by auto from New York to San Francisco, and his trip was so unusual that he wrote a book about his experiences. By 1929, however, families that had taken such trips found it difficult even to interest their neighbors in their tales of travel.

Perhaps one of the most far-reaching changes brought by the automobile, or the bus, was the change in rural schools. Before the day of cars each rural township operated a grade school, some of them through grade six, more often through grade eight. Most of these rural schools had one room and one teacher. Despite the sentimental nostalgia of some people in a later age, these schools did not offer good education. The teachers were poorly prepared; most of them had not been to college at all. With a room full of children of various sizes and ages, most teachers were able to do little more than maintain a degree of discipline. The products of these schools were ill equipped for living anywhere but on the farm and were not particularly well educated even for that. The school bus made consolidated rural schools possible, and farm youngsters of high-school age for the first time began to go beyond the eighth grade in significant numbers. Many of the new consolidated rural schools were a long way from being ideal educational institutions, but they were clearly an improvement over the ungraded one-room school. At last, rural children were receiving substantially the same kind of education as urban children.

Indeed, the automobile and the radio tended to blur the distinction between rural and urban life. The farmer went to town for his entertainment (usually the movies) and listened to the same radio programs as the city dweller. His children attended schools like those in urban centers. He read a city newspaper. The farmer frequently even took a job in the city, at least for part of the year, and continued to live on the land. Because of the generally depressed conditions of agriculture during the 1920's and the greater amount of capital necessary to begin profitable farming that came as a result of farm mechanization, most of the farmer's children became wage earners in town or city. There still remained a great difference in the ways of life of the small town and the big city, but no longer, except in the most primitive, poorest, and most isolated parts of the nation, did the

farmer live significantly differently from the small-town dweller.

Affluence changed the education of the city youngster just as it and the automobile had changed rural schooling. The greatest change was in the number of students in high school. High-school enrollments in 1920 totaled 2.2 million; by 1930 almost exactly twice as many students were in the nation's secondary schools. An increase in the population was part of the reason for the increased enrollments, but more important was an increase in the percentage of high-school-age boys and girls who went on past the eighth grade. In 1930 roughly one half of the population between the ages of fourteen and eighteen was in school.

The main reason why more young people stayed in school instead of dropping out to go to work was that their families, for the first time, could afford to continue without the youngsters' wages. Failure to recognize the fact that children's wages were needed at home was the chief flaw in the reasoning of earlier opponents of child labor. In the first Wilson administration reformers had put a law through Congress prohibiting child labor, and the Supreme Court had in 1918 declared the act unconstitutional. The reformers then set about amending the Constitution, getting an amendment through Congress but never getting it ratified by a sufficient number of states. Enforcement of compulsory school-attendance laws in the 1920's (usually to age fifteen or sixteen) succeeded in accomplishing most of what the reformers had desired, but not even the school laws could be enforced well when public opinion opposed them. When employers wanted to hire children, when parents wanted children to go to work to help on the family income, and when the children themselves wanted to leave school—and this was the situation in many of the textile towns of the Appalachian South throughout the decade—truant officers were unable really to enforce the law. But the attendance laws were enforced where public opinion supported them. Affluence rather than law kept children in school and off the labor market. By 1929 most urban young people at least started to high school. Finishing high school became almost universal in the middle classes, and most of the children from working-class homes finished high school if they had at least average academic ability.

The great number of high-school students had a profound effect on the nature of the high school. At one time, secondary education had been primarily preparation for the college and university. Now in the 1920's the high schools were filled with young people who had no intention whatsoever of going on to college. Furthermore, many of the students lacked the intelligence or the desire or both to cope with the conventional high-school curriculum of literature, mathematics, science, and foreign language. A number of educators argued that trigonometry and Latin did not have much relevance for students who were going to stop their formal education after high school to go to work and that the schools should provide these young people with other training. Many schools never solved the problem in a satisfactory manner; most of them watered down the conventional curriculum to accommodate the new kind of student and created vocational courses which often had little more relevance than did Latin. But despite educational deficiencies—and we must not assume that the secondary schools of the era before World War I were paragons of intellectual virtue—increasing numbers of young people insisted upon a high-school education and they probably profited from their high-school years.

Colleges and universities also were swollen during the 1920's, their enrollments increasing from about 600,000 in 1920 (larger than usual with soldiers returning from World War I) to about 1,200,000 in 1930. The greatest increase in college enrollments came in the vocational fields, teacher preparation, engineering, and business administration. Undergraduate schools of business were something new in higher education, but it was not surprising that in the business civilization of the 1920's hundreds of young men studied such vocational subjects as salesmanship and advertising. . . .

By 1929 the typical American had become a mass man. He worked for a huge industrial corporation; he bought mass-produced articles made by the large corporation; he more than likely lived in an apartment house or in a small residence that differed little from thousands of others; he read a mass newspaper; he attended Metro-Goldwyn-Mayer movies and listened to national radio programs; he avidly followed the athletic exploits of Babe Ruth and Red Grange—and, wondrously, he voted for Herbert Hoover because the Great Engineer praised "rugged individualism." He was the new mass man of the New Era and all seemed rosy. But he and the New Era were soon to receive a jolt of unprecedented force and power.

POSTSCRIPT

Were the 1920s an Era of Social and Cultural Rebellion?

The degree to which one views the 1920s as a rebellious decade may very well depend on the extent to which World War I is interpreted as a watershed event in American history. How much did American society in the 1920s differ from its prewar counterpart? The argument for change is widespread. For example, Henry May has characterized the years from 1912 to 1917 as marking "the end of American innocence." Similarly, the literary and artistic members of the "lost generation" were certain that the war had created a much different world from the one they had occupied previously. A different political climate seemed to exist in the 1920s in which a business-oriented conservatism deflated the momentum for reform that had dominated the first two decades of the twentieth century. An excellent collection of essays that explores this issue is John Braeman, Robert H. Bremner, and David Brody, eds., *Change and Continuity in Twentieth Century America: The 1920s* (Ohio State University Press, 1968).

There are a number of important overviews of the 1920s that treat the topics raised by Leuchtenburg and Shannon. Among the more useful ones are John D. Hicks, *Republican Ascendancy, 1921–1933* (Harper & Row, 1960), a volume in The New American Nation series; Roderick Nash, *The Nervous Generation: American Thought, 1917–1930* (Rand McNally, 1970); and Paul Carter, *The Twenties in America*, 2d ed. (Harlan Davidson, 1975).

The economic history of the decade is discussed in George Soule, *Prosperity Decade: From War to Depression, 1917–1929* (Holt, Rinehart & Winston, 1947); Peter Fearon, *War, Prosperity, and Depression* (University of Kansas Press, 1987); and John Kenneth Galbraith, *The Great Crash, 1929*, rev. ed. (Houghton Mifflin, 1989).

The status of women in the decade after suffrage receives general treatment in William H. Chafe, *The Paradox of Change: American Women in the Twentieth Century* (Oxford University Press, 1991) and, more thoroughly, in Dorothy M. Brown, *Setting a Course: American Women in the 1920s* (Twayne, 1987). Discussions of feminism in the 1920s are presented in William L. O'Neill, *Everyone Was Brave: The Rise and Fall of Feminism in America* (University of Illinois Press, 1973).

Race is also the focal point of several studies of the Harlem Renaissance. The best of these works include Nathan Irvin Huggins, *Harlem Renaissance* (Oxford University Press, 1971); David Levering Lewis, *When Harlem Was in Vogue* (Alfred A. Knopf, 1981); and Cary D. Wintz, *Black Culture and the Harlem Renaissance* (Rice University Press, 1988).

ISSUE 10

Was the New Deal an Effective Answer to the Great Depression?

YES: Roger Biles, from *A New Deal for the American People* (Northern Illinois University Press, 1991)

NO: Gary Dean Best, from *Pride, Prejudice, and Politics: Roosevelt Versus Recovery, 1933–1938* (Praeger, 1990)

ISSUE SUMMARY

YES: Professor of history Roger Biles contends that, in spite of its minimal reforms and nonrevolutionary programs, the New Deal created a limited welfare state that implemented economic stabilizers to avert another depression.

NO: Professor of history Gary Dean Best argues that Roosevelt established an antibusiness environment with the creation of the New Deal regulatory programs, which retarded the nation's economic recovery from the Great Depression until World War II.

The catastrophe triggered by the 1929 Wall Street debacle crippled the American economy, deflated the optimistic future most Americans assumed to be their birthright, and ripped apart the values by which the country's businesses, farms, and governments were run. In the 1920s the whirlwind of a boom economy had sucked people into its vortex. During the next decade, the inertia of the Great Depression stifled their attempts to make ends meet.

The world depression of the 1930s began in the United States, which is where some of the most serious effects were felt. The United States had suffered periodic economic setbacks—in 1873, 1893, 1907, and 1920—but those slumps had been limited and temporary. The omnipotence of American productivity, the ebullient American spirit, and the self-deluding thought "it can't happen here" blocked out any consideration of an economic collapse that might devastate the capitalist economy and threaten U.S. democratic government.

All aspects of American society trembled from successive jolts; there were 4 million unemployed people in 1930 and 9 million more by 1932. Those who had not lost their jobs took pay cuts or worked for scrip. Charitable organizations attempted to provide for millions of homeless and hungry people, but their resources were not adequate. There was no security for those whose savings were lost forever when banks failed or stocks declined. Manufacturing halted, industry shut down, and farmers destroyed wheat, corn, and milk rather than sell them at a loss. Worse, there were millions of homeless Americans—refugees from the cities roaming the nation on freight trains, victims of the drought of the Dust Bowl seeking a new life farther west, and hobo children estranged from their parents. Physicians reported increased cases of malnutrition. Some people plundered grocery stores to avoid starvation.

Business and government leaders alike seemed immobilized by the economic giant that had fallen to its knees. "In other periods of depression there has always been hope, but as I look about, I now see nothing to give ground for hope—nothing of man," said former president Calvin Coolidge on New Year's Day 1933. Herbert Hoover, the incumbent president at the start of the Great Depression, attempted some relief programs. However, they were ineffective, considering the magnitude of the unemployment, hunger, and distress. Nor did Hoover's initiatives recognize the need for serious changes in the relationship between the federal government and society or for any modification of its relationship with individual Americans.

As governor of New York, Franklin D. Roosevelt (who was elected president in 1932) had introduced some relief measures, such as industrial welfare and a comprehensive system of unemployment remedies, to alleviate the social and economic problems facing the citizens of the state. Yet his campaign did little to reassure his critics that he was more than a "Little Lord Fauntleroy" rich boy who wanted to be president. In light of later developments, Roosevelt may have been the only presidential candidate to deliver more programs than he actually promised.

In the following selections, Roger Biles argues that in spite of its minimal reforms and nonrevolutionary programs, the New Deal created a limited welfare state that implemented economic stabilizers to avert another depression. Gary Dean Best is highly critical of Roosevelt's pragmatic approach to solving the depression. Roosevelt established an antibusiness environment, maintains Best, when he created a host of New Deal regulatory programs whose long-range effect was to retard the nation's economic recovery until World War II.

YES
Roger Biles

A NEW DEAL FOR THE
AMERICAN PEOPLE

At the close of the Hundred Days, Franklin D. Roosevelt said, "All of the proposals and all of the legislation since the fourth day of March have not been just a collection of haphazard schemes, but rather the orderly component parts of a connected and logical whole." Yet the president later described his approach quite differently. "Take a method and try it. If it fails admit it frankly and try another. But above all, try something." The impetus for New Deal legislation came from a variety of sources, and Roosevelt relied heavily at various times on an ideologically diverse group of aides and allies. His initiatives reflected the contributions of, among others, Robert Wagner, Rexford Tugwell, Raymond Moley, George Norris, Robert LaFollette, Henry Morgenthau, Marriner Eccles, Felix Frankfurter, Henry Wallace, Harry Hopkins, and Eleanor Roosevelt. An initial emphasis on recovery for agriculture and industry gave way within two years to a broader-based program for social reform; entente with the business community yielded to populist rhetoric and a more ambiguous economic program. Roosevelt suffered the opprobrium of both the conservatives, who vilified "that man" in the White House who was leading the country down the sordid road to socialism, and the radicals, who saw the Hyde Park aristocrat as a confidence man peddling piecemeal reform to forestall capitalism's demise. Out of so many contradictory and confusing circumstances, how does one make sense of the five years of legislative reform known as the New Deal? And what has been its impact on a half century of American life?

A better understanding begins with the recognition that little of the New Deal was new, including the use of federal power to effect change. Nor, for all of Roosevelt's famed willingness to experiment, did New Deal programs usually originate from vernal ideas. Governmental aid to increase farmers' income, propounded in the late nineteenth century by the Populists, surfaced in Woodrow Wilson's farm credit acts. The prolonged debates over McNary-Haugenism in the 1920s kept the issue alive, and Herbert Hoover's Agricultural Marketing Act set the stage for further federal involvement. Centralized economic planning, as embodied in the National Industrial Recovery

From Roger Biles, *A New Deal for the American People* (Northern Illinois University Press, 1991). Copyright © 1991 by Northern Illinois University Press. Reprinted by permission. Notes omitted.

220

Act, flowed directly from the experiences of Wilson's War Industries Board; not surprisingly, Roosevelt chose Hugh Johnson, a veteran of the board, to head the National Recovery Administration. Well established in England and Germany before the First World War, social insurance appeared in a handful of states—notably Wisconsin—before the federal government became involved. Similarly, New Deal labor reform took its cues from the path-breaking work of state legislatures. Virtually alone in its originality, compensatory fiscal policy seemed revolutionary in the 1930s. Significantly, however, Roosevelt embraced deficit spending quite late after other disappointing economic policies and never to the extent Keynesian economists advised. Congress and the public supported the New Deal, in part, because of its origins in successful initiatives attempted earlier under different conditions.

Innovative or not, the New Deal clearly failed to restore economic prosperity. As late as 1938 unemployment stood at 19.1 percent and two years later at 14.6 percent. Only the Second World War, which generated massive industrial production, put the majority of the American people back to work. To be sure, partial economic recovery occurred. From a high of 13 million unemployed in 1933, the number under Roosevelt's administration fell to 11.4 million in 1934, 10.6 million in 1935, and 9 million in 1936. Farm income and manufacturing wages also rose, and as limited as these achievements may seem in retrospect, they provided sustenance for millions of people and hope for many more. Yet Roosevelt's resistance to Keynesian formulas for pump priming placed immutable barriers in the way of recovery that only war could demolish. At a time calling for drastic inflationary methods,

Roosevelt introduced programs effecting the opposite result. The NRA restricted production, elevated prices, and reduced purchasing power, all of which were deflationary in effect. The Social Security Act's payroll taxes took money from consumers and out of circulation. The federal government's $4.43 billion deficit in fiscal year 1936, impressive as it seemed, was not so much greater than Hoover's $2.6 billion shortfall during his last year in office. As economist Robert Lekachman noted, "The 'great spender' was in his heart a true descendant of thrifty Dutch Calvinist forebears." It is not certain that the application of Keynesian formulas would have sufficed by the mid-1930s to restore prosperity, but the president's cautious deflationary policies clearly retarded recovery.

Although New Deal economic policies came up short in the 1930s, they implanted several "stabilizers" that have been more successful in averting another such depression. The Securities and Exchange Act of 1934 established government supervision of the stock market, and the Wheeler-Rayburn Act allowed the Securities and Exchange Commission to do the same with public utilities. Severely embroiled in controversy when adopted, these measures have become mainstays of the American financial system. The Glass-Steagall Banking Act forced the separation of commercial and investment banking and broadened the powers of the Federal Reserve Board to change interest rates and limit loans for speculation. The creation of the Federal Deposit Insurance Corporation (FDIC) increased government supervision of state banks and significantly lowered the number of bank failures. Such safeguards restored confidence in the discredited banking system and established a firm economic foundation that performed well for decades thereafter.

The New Deal was also responsible for numerous other notable changes in American life. Section 7(a) of the NIRA, the Wagner Act, and the Fair Labor Standards Act transformed the relationship between workers and business and breathed life into a troubled labor movement on the verge of total extinction. In the space of a decade government laws eliminated sweatshops, severely curtailed child labor, and established enforceable standards for hours, wages, and working conditions. Further, federal action eliminated the vast majority of company towns in such industries as coal mining. Although Robert Wagner and Frances Perkins dragged Roosevelt into labor's corner, the New Deal made the unions a dynamic force in American society. Moreover, as Nelson Lichtenstein has noted, "by giving so much of the working class an institutional voice, the union movement provided one of the main political bulwarks of the Roosevelt Democratic party and became part of the social bedrock in which the New Deal welfare state was anchored."

Roosevelt's avowed goal of "cradle-to-grave" security for the American people proved elusive, but his administration achieved unprecedented advances in the field of social welfare. In 1938 the president told Congress: "Government has a final responsibility for the well-being of its citizenship. If private co-operative endeavor fails to provide work for willing hands and relief for the unfortunate, those suffering hardship from no fault of their own have a right to call upon the Government for aid; and a government worthy of its name must make fitting response." The New Deal's safety net included low-cost housing; old-age pensions; unemployment insurance; and aid for dependent mothers and children, the disabled, the blind, and public health services. Sometimes disappointing because of limiting eligibility requirements and low benefit levels, these social welfare programs nevertheless firmly established the principle that the government had an obligation to assist the needy. As one scholar wrote of the New Deal, "More progress was made in public welfare and relief than in the three hundred years after this country was first settled."

More and more government programs, inevitably resulting in an enlarged administrative apparatus and requiring additional revenue, added up to a much greater role for the national government in American life. Coming at a time when the only Washington bureaucracy most of the people encountered with any frequency was the U.S. Postal Service, the change seemed all the more remarkable. Although many New Deal programs were temporary emergency measures, others lingered long after the return of prosperity. Suddenly, the national government was supporting farmers, monitoring the economy, operating a welfare system, subsidizing housing, adjudicating labor disputes, managing natural resources, and providing electricity to a growing number of consumers. "What Roosevelt did in a period of a little over 12 years was to change the form of government," argued journalist Richard L. Strout. "Washington had been largely run by big business, by Wall Street. He brought the government to Washington." Not surprisingly, popular attitudes toward government also changed. No longer willing to accept economic deprivation and social dislocation as the vagaries of an uncertain existence, Americans tolerated—indeed, came to expect—the national government's involvement in the problems of everyday life. No longer did "government" mean just "city hall."

The operation of the national government changed as well. For one thing, Roosevelt's strong leadership expanded presidential power, contributing to what historian Arthur Schlesinger, Jr., called the "imperial presidency." Whereas Americans had in previous years instinctively looked first to Capitol Hill, after Roosevelt the White House took center stage in Washington. At the same time, Congress and the president looked at the nation differently. Traditionally attentive only to one group (big business), policymakers in Washington began responding to other constituencies such as labor, farmers, the unemployed, the aged, and to a lesser extent, women, blacks, and other disadvantaged groups. This new "broker state" became more accessible and acted on a growing number of problems, but equity did not always result. The ablest, richest, and most experienced groups fared best during the New Deal. NRA codes favored big business, and AAA benefits aided large landholders; blacks received relief and government jobs but not to the extent their circumstances merited. The long-term result, according to historian John Braeman, has been "a balkanized political system in which private interests scramble, largely successfully, to harness governmental authority and/or draw upon the public treasury to advance their private agendas."

Another legacy of the New Deal has been the Roosevelt revolution in politics. Urbanization and immigration changed the American electorate, and a new generation of voters who resided in the cities during the Great Depression opted for Franklin D. Roosevelt and his party. Before the 1930s the Democrats of the northern big-city machines and the solid South uneasily coexisted and surrendered primacy to the unified Republican party. The New Deal coalition that elected Roosevelt united behind common economic interests. Both urban northerners and rural southerners, as well as blacks, women, and ethnic immigrants, found common cause in government action to shield them from an economic system gone haywire. By the end of the decade the increasing importance of the urban North in the Democratic party had already become apparent. After the economy recovered from the disastrous depression, members of the Roosevelt coalition shared fewer compelling interests. Beginning in the 1960s, tensions mounted within the party as such issues as race, patriotism, and abortion loomed larger. Even so, the Roosevelt coalition retained enough commitment to New Deal principles to keep the Democrats the nation's majority party into the 1980s.

Yet for all the alterations in politics, government, and the economy, the New Deal fell far short of a revolution. The two-party system survived intact, and neither fascism, which attracted so many followers in European states suffering from the same international depression, nor communism attracted much of a following in the United States. Vital government institutions functioned without interruption and if the balance of powers shifted, the national branches of government maintained an essential equilibrium. The economy remained capitalistic; free enterprise and private ownership, not socialism, emerged from the 1930s. A limited welfare state changed the meld of the public and private but left them separate. Roosevelt could be likened to the British conservative Edmund Burke, who advocated measured change to offset drastic alterations—"reform to preserve." The New Deal's great achievement was the application of just enough change to preserve the American political economy.

Indications of Roosevelt's restraint emerged from the very beginning of the New Deal. Rather than assume extraordinary executive powers as Abraham Lincoln had done in the 1861 crisis, the president called Congress into special session. Whatever changes ensued would come through normal governmental activity. Roosevelt declined to assume direct control of the economy, leaving the nation's resources in the hands of private enterprise. Resisting the blandishments of radicals calling for the nationalization of the banks, he provided the means for their rehabilitation and ignored the call for national health insurance and federal contributions to Social Security retirement benefits. The creation of such regulatory agencies as the SEC confirmed his intention to revitalize rather than remake economic institutions. Repeatedly during his presidency, Roosevelt responded to congressional pressure to enact bolder reforms, as in the case of the National Labor Relations Act, the Wagner-Steagall Housing Act, and the FDIC. The administration forwarded the NIRA only after Senator Hugo Black's recovery bill mandating 30-hour workweeks seemed on the verge of passage.

As impressive as New Deal relief and social welfare programs were, they never went as far as conditions demanded or many liberals recommended. Fluctuating congressional appropriations, oscillating economic conditions, and Roosevelt's own hesitancy to do too much violence to the federal budget left Harry Hopkins, Harold Ickes, and others only partially equipped to meet the staggering need. The president justified the creation of the costly WPA in 1935 by "ending this business of relief." Unskilled workers, who constituted the greatest number of WPA employees, obtained but 60 to 80 percent of the minimal family income as determined by the government. Roosevelt and Hopkins continued to emphasize work at less than existing wage scales so that the WPA or PWA never competed with free labor, and they allowed local authorities to modify pay rates. They also continued to make the critical distinction between the "deserving" and "undeserving" poor, making sure that government aided only the former. The New Deal never challenged the values underlying this distinction, instead seeking to provide for the growing number of "deserving" poor created by the Great Depression. Government assumed an expanded role in caring for the disadvantaged, but not at variance with existing societal norms regarding social welfare.

The New Deal effected no substantial redistribution of income. The Wealth Tax Act of 1935 (the famous soak-the-rich tax) produced scant revenue and affected very few taxpayers. Tax alterations in 1936 and 1937 imposed no additional burdens on the rich; the 1938 and 1939 tax laws actually removed a few. By the end of the 1930s less than 5 percent of Americans paid income taxes, and the share of taxes taken from personal and corporate income levies fell below the amount raised in the 1920s. The great change in American taxation policy came during World War II, when the number of income tax payers grew to 74 percent of the population. In 1942 Treasury Secretary Henry Morgenthau noted that "for the first time in our history, the income tax is becoming a people's tax." This the New Deal declined to do.

Finally, the increased importance of the national government exerted remarkably little influence on local institutions. The New Deal seldom dictated and almost always deferred to state and local governments—encouraging, cajoling, bargaining, and wheedling to bring parochial interests in line with national objectives. As Harry Hopkins discovered, governors and mayors angled to obtain as many federal dollars as possible for their constituents but with no strings attached. Community control and local autonomy, conditions thought to be central to American democracy, remained strong, and Roosevelt understood the need for firm ties with politicians at all levels. In his study of the New Deal's impact on federalism, James T. Patterson concludes: "For all the supposed power of the New Deal, it was unable to impose all its guidelines on the autonomous forty-eight states.... What could the Roosevelt administration have done to ensure a more profound and lasting impression on state policy and politics? Very little."

Liberal New Dealers longed for more sweeping change and lamented their inability to goad the president into additional action. They envisioned a wholesale purge of the Democratic party and the creation of a new organization embodying fully the principles of liberalism. They could not abide Roosevelt's toleration of the political conservatives and unethical bosses who composed part of the New Deal coalition. They sought racial equality, constraints upon the southern landholding class, and federal intrusion to curb the power of urban real estate interests on behalf of the inveterate poor.

Yet to do these things would be to attempt changes well beyond the desires of most Americans. People pursuing remunerative jobs and the economic security of the middle class approved of government aiding the victims of an unfortunate economic crisis but had no interest in an economic system that would limit opportunity. The fear that the New Deal would lead to such thoroughgoing change explains the seemingly irrational hatred of Roosevelt by the economic elite. But, as historian Barry Karl has noted, "it was characteristic of Roosevelt's presidency that he never went as far as his detractors feared or his followers hoped."

The New Deal achieved much that was good and left much undone. Roosevelt's programs were defined by the confluence of forces that circumscribed his admittedly limited reform agenda—hostile judiciary; powerful congressional opponents, some of whom entered into alliances of convenience with New Dealers and some of whom awaited the opportunity to build on their opposition; the political impotence of much of the populace; the pugnacious independence of local and state authorities; the strength of people's attachment to traditional values and institutions; and the basic conservatism of American culture. Obeisance to local custom and the decision to avoid tampering with the fabric of American society allowed much injustice to survive while shortchanging blacks, women, small farmers, and the "unworthy" poor. Those who criticized Franklin Roosevelt for an unwillingness to challenge racial, economic, and gender inequality misunderstood either the nature of his electoral mandate or the difference between reform and revolution—or both.

If the New Deal preserved more than it changed, that is understandable in a society whose people have consistently chosen freedom over equality. Americans traditionally have eschewed expanded government, no matter how efficiently managed or honestly administered, that imposed restraints on personal success—even though such limitations redressed legitimate grievances or righted imbalances. Parity, most Americans believed, should not be purchased with the loss of liberty. But although the American dream has always entailed individual success with a minimum of state interference, the profound shock of capitalism's near demise in the 1930s undermined numerous previously unquestioned beliefs. The inability of capitalism's "invisible hand" to stabilize the market and the failure of the private sector to restore prosperity enhanced the consideration of stronger executive leadership and centralized planning. Yet with the collapse of democratic governments and their replacement by totalitarian regimes, Americans were keenly sensitive to any threats to liberty. New Deal programs, frequently path breaking in their delivery of federal resources outside normal channels, also retained a strong commitment to local government and community control while promising only temporary disruptions prior to the return of economic stability. Reconciling the necessary authority at the federal level to meet nationwide crises with the local autonomy desirable to safeguard freedom has always been one of the salient challenges to American democracy. Even after New Deal refinements, the search for the proper balance continues.

NO

Gary Dean Best

PRIDE, PREJUDICE AND POLITICS: ROOSEVELT VERSUS RECOVERY, 1933–1938

This book had its genesis in the fact that I have for a long time felt uncomfortable with the standard works written about Franklin Delano Roosevelt and the New Deal, and with the influence those works have exerted on others writing about and teaching U.S. history. Although I approach the subject from a very different perspective, Paul K. Conkin's preface to the second edition of *The New Deal* (1975) expressed many of my own misgivings about writings on the subject. Conkin wrote that "pervading even the most scholarly revelations was a monotonous, often almost reflexive, and in my estimation a very smug or superficial valuative perspective—approval, even glowing approval, of most enduring New Deal policies, or at least of the underlying goals that a sympathetic observer could always find behind policies and programs."

Studies of the New Deal such as Conkin described seemed to me to be examples of a genre relatively rare in U.S. historiography—that of "court histories."...

But, like most historians teaching courses dealing with the Roosevelt period, I was captive to the published works unless I was willing and able to devote the time to pursue extensive research in the period myself. After some years that became possible, and this book is the result.

My principal problem with Roosevelt and the New Deal was not over his specific reforms or his social programs, but with the failure of the United States to recover from the depression during the eight peacetime years that he and his policies governed the nation. I consider that failure tragic, not only for the 14.6 percent of the labor force that remained unemployed as late as 1940, and for the millions of others who subsisted on government welfare because of the prolonged depression, but also because of the image that the depression-plagued United States projected to the world at a crucial time in international affairs. In the late 1930s and early 1940s, when U.S. economic strength might have given pause to potential aggressors in the world, our economic weakness furnished encouragement to them instead.

From Gary Dean Best, *Pride, Prejudice, and Politics: Roosevelt Versus Recovery, 1933–1938* (Praeger, 1990), pp. ix–xv, xvii, 217–223. Copyright © 1990 by Gary Dean Best. Reprinted by permission of Greenwood Publishing Group, Inc., Westport, CT. Notes omitted.

From the standpoint, then, not only of our domestic history, but also of the tragic events and results of World War II, it has seemed to me that Roosevelt's failure to generate economic recovery during this critical period deserved more attention than historians have given it.

Most historians of the New Deal period leave the impression that the failure of the United States to recover during those eight years resulted from Roosevelt's unwillingness to embrace Keynesian spending. According to this thesis, recovery came during World War II because the war at last forced Roosevelt to spend at the level required all along for recovery. This, however, seemed to me more an advocacy of Keynes' theories by the historians involved than an explanation for the U.S. failure to recover during those years. Great Britain, for example, managed to recover by the late 1930s without recourse to deficit spending. By that time the United States was, by contrast, near the bottom of the list of industrial nations as measured in progress toward recovery, with most others having reached the predepression levels and many having exceeded them. The recovered countries represented a variety of economic systems, from state ownership to private enterprise. The common denominator in their success was not a reliance on deficit spending, but rather the stimulus they furnished to industrial enterprise.

What went wrong in the United States? Simplistic answers such as the reference to Keynesianism seemed to me only a means of avoiding a real answer to the question. A wise president, entering the White House in the midst of a crippling depression, should do everything possible to stimulate enterprise. In a free economy, economic recovery means *business*

recovery. It follows, therefore, that a wise chief executive should do everything possible to create the conditions and psychology most conducive to business recovery —to encourage business to expand production, and lenders and investors to furnish the financing and capital that are required. An administration seeking economic recovery will do as little as possible that might inhibit recovery, will weigh all its actions with the necessity for economic recovery in mind, and will consult with competent business and financial leaders, as well as economists, to determine the best policies to follow. Such a president will seek to promote cooperation between the federal government and business, rather than conflict, and will seek to introduce as much consistency and stability as possible into government economic policies so that businessmen and investors can plan ahead. While obviously the destitute must be cared for, ultimately the most humane contribution a liberal government can make to the victims of a depression is the restoration of prosperity and the reemployment of the idle in genuine jobs.

In measuring the Roosevelt policies and programs during the New Deal years against such standards, I was struck by the air of unreality that hung over Washington in general and the White House in particular during this period. Business and financial leaders who questioned the wisdom of New Deal policies were disregarded and deprecated because of their "greed" and "self-interest," while economists and business academicians who persisted in calling attention to the collision between New Deal policies and simple economic realities were dismissed for their "orthodoxy." As one "orthodox" economist pointed out early in the New Deal years,

> economic realism ... insists that policies aiming to promote recovery will, in fact, retard recovery if and where they fail to take into account correctly of stubborn facts in the existing economic situation and of the arithmetic of business as it must be carried out in the economic situation we are trying to revive. The antithesis of this economic realism is the vaguely hopeful or optimistic idealism in the field of economic policy, as such, which feels that good intentions, enough cleverness, and the right appeal to the emotions of the people ought to insure good results in spite of inconvenient facts.

Those "inconvenient facts" dogged the New Deal throughout these years, only to be stubbornly resisted by a president whose pride, prejudices, and politics would rarely permit an accommodation with them.

Most studies of the New Deal years approach the period largely from the perspective of the New Dealers themselves. Critics and opponents of Roosevelt's policies and programs are given scant attention in such works except to point up the "reactionary" and "unenlightened" opposition with which Roosevelt was forced to contend in seeking to provide Americans with "a more abundant life." The few studies that have concentrated on critics and opponents of the New Deal in the business community have been by unsympathetic historians who have tended to distort the opposition to fit the caricature drawn by the New Dealers, so that they offer little to explain the impact of Roosevelt's policies in delaying recovery from the depression.

The issue of *why* businessmen and bankers were so critical of the New Deal has been for too long swept under the rug, together with the question of *how* Roosevelt and his advisers could possibly expect to produce an economic recovery while a state of war existed between his administration and the employers and investors who, alone, could produce such a recovery. Even a Keynesian response to economic depression is ultimately dependent on the positive reactions of businessmen and investors for its success, as Keynes well knew, and those reactions were not likely to be as widespread as necessary under such a state of warfare between government and business. Businessmen, bankers, and investors may have been "greedy" and "self-interested." They may have been guilty of wrong perceptions and unfounded fears. But they are also the ones, in a free economy, upon whose decisions and actions economic recovery must depend. To understand their opposition to the New Deal requires an immersion in the public and private comments of critics of Roosevelt's policies. The degree and nature of business, banking, and investor concern about the direction and consequences of New Deal policies can be gleaned from the hundreds of banking and business periodicals representative of every branch of U.S. business and finance in the 1930s, and from the letters and diaries of the New Deal's business and other critics during the decade.

* * *

Statistics are useful in understanding the history of any period, but particularly periods of economic growth or depression. Statistics for the Roosevelt years may easily be found in *Historical Statistics of the United States* published by the Bureau of the Census, U.S. Department of Commerce (1975). Some of the trauma of the depression years may be inferred from the fact that the population of the United States grew by over 17 million between 1920 and 1930, but by only about half of that (8.9 million) between 1930 and 1940.

Historical Statistics gives the figures... for unemployment, 1929–1940. These figures are, however, only estimates. The federal government did not monitor the number of unemployed during those years. Even so, these figures are shocking, indicating as they do that even after the war had begun in Europe, with the increased orders that it provided for U.S. mines, factories, and farms, unemployment remained at 14.6 percent.

One characteristic of the depression, to which attention was frequently called during the Roosevelt years, was the contrast between its effects on the durable goods and consumer goods industries. Between 1929 and 1933, expenditures on personal durable goods dropped by nearly 50 percent, and in 1938 they were still nearly 25 percent below the 1929 figures. Producers' durable goods suffered even more, failing by nearly two-thirds between 1929 and 1933, and remaining more than 50 percent below the 1929 figure in 1938. At the same time, expenditures on nondurable, or consumer, goods showed much less effect. Between 1929 and 1933 they fell only about 14.5 percent, and by 1938 they exceeded the 1929 level. These figures indicate that the worst effects of the depression, and resultant unemployment, were being felt in the durable goods industries. Roosevelt's policies, however, served mainly to stimulate the consumer goods industries where the depression and unemployment were far less seriously felt.

One consequence of Roosevelt's policies can be seen in the U.S. balance of trade during the New Deal years. By a variety of devices, Roosevelt drove up the prices of U.S. industrial and agricultural products, making it difficult for these goods to compete in the world market, and opening U.S. markets to cheaper foreign products.... With the exception of a $41 million deficit in 1888, these were the only deficits in U.S. trade for a century, from the 1870s to the 1970s.

... [W]hile suicides during the Roosevelt years remained about the same as during the Hoover years, the death rate by "accidental falls" increased significantly. In fact, according to *Historical Statistics*, the death rate by "accidental falls" was higher in the period 1934–1938 than at any other time between 1910 and 1970 (the years for which figures are given).

Interestingly, the number of persons arrested grew steadily during the depression years. In 1938 nearly twice as many (554,000) were arrested as in 1932 (278,000), and the number continued to increase until 1941. And, while the number of telephones declined after 1930 and did not regain the 1930 level until 1939, the number of households with radios increased steadily during the depression years. And Americans continued to travel. Even in the lowest year, 1933, 300,000 Americans visited foreign countries (down from 517,000 in 1929), while the number visiting national parks, monuments, and such, steadily increased during the depression—in 1938 nearly five times as many (16,331,000) did so as in 1929 (3,248,000).

Comparisons of the recovery of the United States with that of other nations may be found in the volumes of the League of Nations' *World Economic Survey* for the depression years. [A] table (from the volume of 1938/39) shows comparisons of unemployment rates. From this it can be seen that in 1929 the United States had the lowest unemployment rate of the countries listed; by 1932 the United States was midway on the list, with seven nations reporting higher unemployment rates and seven reporting lower unemployment. By mid-1938, however, after over five years of the New Deal, only three nations had higher unemployment rates, while twelve had lower unemployment. The United States, then, had lost ground in comparison with the other nations between 1932 and 1938.

The *World Economic Survey* for 1937/38 compared the levels of industrial production for 23 nations in 1937, expressed as a percentage of their industrial production in 1929.... It must be remembered that the figures for the United States reflect the level of industrial production reached just before the collapse of the economy later that year. Of the 22 other nations listed, 19 showed a higher rate of recovery in industrial production than the United States, while only 3 lagged behind. One of these, France, had followed policies similar to those of the New Deal in the United States. As the *World Economic Survey* put it, both the Roosevelt administration and the Blum government in France had "adopted far-reaching social and economic policies which combined recovery measures with measures of social reform." It added: "The consequent doubt regarding the prospects of profit and the uneasy relations between business-men and the Government have in the opinion of many, been an important factor in delaying recovery," and the two countries had, "unlike the United Kingdom and Germany," failed to "regain the 1929 level of employment and production." The *World Economic Survey* the following year (1939) pointed out that industrial production in the United States

had fallen from the 92.2 to 65 by June 1938, and hovered between 77 and 85 throughout 1939. Thus, by the end of 1938 the U.S. record was even sorrier than revealed by the [data].

* * *

Every survey of American historians consistently finds Franklin Delano Roosevelt ranked as one of this nation's greatest presidents. Certainly, exposure to even a sampling of the literature on Roosevelt and the New Deal can lead one to no other conclusion. Conventional wisdom has it that Roosevelt was an opportune choice to lead the United States through the midst of the Great Depression, that his cheerful and buoyant disposition uplifted the American spirit in the midst of despair and perhaps even forestalled a radical change in the direction of American politics toward the right or the left. Roosevelt's landslide reelection victory in 1936, and the congressional successes in 1934, are cited as evidence of the popularity of both the president and the New Deal among the American people. Polls by both Gallup and the Democratic National Committee early in the 1936 campaign, however, give a very different picture, and suggest that the electoral victories can be as accurately accounted for in terms of the vast outpourings of federal money in 1934 and 1936, and the inability or unwillingness of Landon to offer a genuine alternative to the New Deal in the latter year. To this must be added the fact that after early 1936 two of the most unpopular New Deal programs—the NRA and the AAA—had been removed as issues by the Supreme Court.

Conventional wisdom, in fact, suffers many setbacks when the Roosevelt years are examined from any other perspective than through a pro-New Deal Prism

—from the banking crisis of 1933 and the first inaugural address, through the reasons for the renewed downturn in 1937, to the end of the New Deal in 1937–1938. The American present has been ill-served by the inaccurate picture that has too often been presented of this chapter in the American past by biographers and historians. Roosevelt's achievements in alleviating the hardship of the depression are deservedly well known, his responsibility for prolonging the hardship is not. His role in providing long-overdue and sorely needed social and economic legislation is in every high school American history textbook, but the costs for the United States of his eight-year-long war against business recovery are mentioned in none.

Such textbooks (and those in college, too) frequently contain a chapter on the Great Depression, followed by one on the New Deal, the implication being that somewhere early in the second of the chapters the depression was ended by Roosevelt's policies. Only careful reading reveals that despite Roosevelt's immense labors to feed the unemployed, only modest recovery from the lowest depths of the depression was attained before the outbreak of World War II. Roosevelt, readers are told, was too old-fashioned, too conservative, to embrace the massive compensatory spending and unbalanced budgets that might have produced a Keynesian recovery sooner. But World War II, the books tell us, made such spending necessary and the recovery that might have occurred earlier was at last achieved.

Generations of Americans have been brought up on this version of the New Deal years. Other presidential administrations have been reevaluated over the years, and have risen or fallen in grace as a result, but not the Roosevelt administration. The conventional wisdom concerning the Roosevelt administration remains the product of the "court historians," assessments of the New Deal period that could not have been better written by the New Dealers themselves. The facts, however, are considerably at variance with this conventional wisdom concerning the course of the depression, the reasons for the delay of recovery, and the causes of the recovery when it came, finally, during World War II.

From the uncertainty among businessmen and investors about the new president-elect that aborted a promising upturn in the fall of 1932, to the panic over the prospect of inflationary policies that was a major factor in the banking crisis that virtually paralyzed the nation's economy by the date of his inauguration, Roosevelt's entry into the White House was not an auspicious beginning toward recovery. The prejudices that were to guide the policies and programs of the New Deal for the next six years were revealed in Roosevelt's inaugural address, although the message was largely overlooked until it had become more apparent in the actions of the administration later. It was an attitude of hostility toward business and finance, of contempt for the profit motive of capitalism, and of willingness to foment class antagonism for political benefit. This was not an attitude that was conducive to business recovery, and the programs and policies that would flow from those prejudices would prove, in fact, to be destructive of the possibility of recovery.

There followed the "hundred days," when Roosevelt rammed through Congress a variety of legislation that only depressed business confidence more. The new laws were served up on attractive platters, with tempting descriptions —truth in securities, aid for the farmer, industrial self-regulation—but when the covers were removed the contents were neither attractive nor did they match the labels. By broad grants of power to the executive branch of the government, the legislation passed regulation of the U.S. economy into the hands of New Dealers whose aim was not to promote recovery but to carry out their own agendas for radical change of the economic system even at the expense of delaying recovery. Thus, truth in securities turned to paralysis of the securities markets, aid for the farmer became a war against profits by processors of agricultural goods, and industrial self-regulation became government control and labor-management strife. International economic cooperation as a device for ending the depression was abandoned for an isolationist approach, and throughout 1933 the threat of inflation added further uncertainty for businessmen and investors.

The grant of such unprecedented peacetime authority to an American president aroused concern, but these after all were only "emergency" powers, to be given up once recovery was on its way. Or were they? Gradually the evidence accumulated that the Tugwells and the Brandeisians intended to institutionalize the "emergency" powers as permanent features of American economic life. By the end of 1933, opposition to the New Deal was already sizable. Business alternated between the paralysis of uncertainty and a modest "recovery" born of purchases and production inspired by fear of higher costs owing to inflation and the effects of the AAA and NRA. The implementation of the latter two agencies in the fall of 1933 brought a renewed downturn that improved only slightly during the winter and spring. A renewed legislative onslaught by the New Deal in the 1934 congress, combined with labor strife encouraged by the provisions of the NIRA, brought a new collapse of the economy in the fall of 1934, which lowered economic indices once again to near the lowest levels they had reached in the depression.

The pattern had been established. The war against business and finance was under way, and there would be neither retreat nor cessation. Roosevelt's pride and prejudices, and the perceived political advantages to be gained from the war, dictated that his administration must ever be on the offensive and never in retreat. But the administration suffered defeats, nevertheless, and embarrassment. The Supreme Court proved a formidable foe, striking down both the NRA and the AAA. Dire predictions from the administration about the implications for the economy of the loss of the NRA proved embarrassing when the economy began to show gradual improvement after its departure. But defeat did not mean retreat. Under the goading of Felix Frankfurter and his disciples, Roosevelt became even more extreme in his verbal and legislative assault against business. Their attempts to cooperate with the Roosevelt administration having been spurned, businessmen and bankers awakened to the existence of the war being waged upon them and moved into opposition. Roosevelt gloried in their opposition and escalated the war against them in the 1936 reelection campaign.

Reelected in 1936 on a tidal wave of government spending, and against a lackluster Republican campaigner who offered no alternative to the New Deal, Roosevelt appeared at the apogee of his power and prestige. His triumph was, however, to be short-lived, despite an enhanced Democratic majority in Congress. A combination of factors was about to bring the New Deal war against business to a stalemate and eventual retreat. One of these was his ill-advised attempt to pack the Supreme Court with subservient justices, which aroused so much opposition even in his own party that he lost control of the Democrat-controlled Congress. More important, perhaps, was the growing economic crisis that the Roosevelt administration faced in 1937, largely as a result of its own past policies. The massive spending of 1936, including the payment of the veterans' bonus, had generated a speculative recovery during that year from concern about inflationary consequences. Fears of a "boom" were increased as a result of the millions of dollars in dividends, bonuses, and pay raises dispensed by businesses late in 1936 as a result of the undistributed profits tax. The pay raises, especially, were passed on in the form of higher prices, as were the social security taxes that were imposed on businesses beginning with 1937. Labor disturbances, encouraged by the Wagner Labor Act and the Roosevelt alliance with John L. Lewis' Congress of Industrial Organizations in the 1936 campaign, added further to the wage-price spiral that threatened as 1937 unfolded. Massive liquidations of low-interest government bonds, and sagging prices of the bonds, fueled concern among bankers and economists, and within the Treasury, that a "boom" would imperil the credit of the federal government and the solvency of the nation's banks whose portfolios consisted mainly of low-interest government bonds.

In considering the two principal options for cooling the "boom"—raising interest rates or cutting federal spending —the Roosevelt administration chose to move toward a balanced budget. It was a cruel dilemma that the New Dealers faced. All knew that the economy had not yet recovered from the depression, yet they were faced with the necessity to apply brakes to an economy that was becoming overheated as a consequence of their policies. Moreover, the reduction in consumer purchasing power caused by the cuts in federal spending was occurring at the same time that purchasing power was already being eroded as a result of the higher prices that worried the administration. Private industry, it should have been obvious, could not "take up the slack," since the Roosevelt administration had done nothing to prepare for the transition from government to private spending that John Maynard Keynes and others had warned them was necessary. The New Dealers had been far too busy waging war against business to allow it the opportunity to prepare for any such transition.

In fact, far from confronting the emergency of 1937 by making long-overdue attempts to cooperate with business in generating recovery, Roosevelt was busy pressing a new legislative assault against them. Denied passage of his legislative package by Congress during its regular 1937 session, Roosevelt called a special session for November despite evidence that the economy had begun a new downturn. Even the collapse of the stock market, within days after his announcement of the special session, and the growing unemployment that soon followed, did not deter Roosevelt from his determination to drive the legislative assault through it. With the nation in the grips of a full-blown economic collapse, Roosevelt offered nothing to the special session but the package of antibusiness legislation it had turned down in the regular session. Once again he was rebuffed by Congress. The nation drifted, its economic indices falling, with its president unwilling to admit the severity of the situation or unable to come to grips with what it said about the bankruptcy of the New Deal policies and programs.

By early 1938, Roosevelt was faced with problems similar to those he had faced when he first entered the White House five years earlier, but without the political capital he had possessed earlier. In 1933 the Hoover administration could be blamed for the depression. In 1938 the American people blamed the Roosevelt administration for retarding recovery. Five years of failure could not be brushed aside. Five years of warfare against business and disregard of criticism and offers of cooperation had converted supporters of 1933 into cynics or opponents by 1938. Even now, however, pride, prejudice, and politics dominated Roosevelt, making it impossible for him to extend the needed olive branch to business. The best that he could offer in 1938 was a renewal of federal spending and more of the same New Deal that had brought the nation renewed misery. In the 1938 congressional session he continued to press for passage of the antibusiness legislation that had been rejected by both sessions of 1937.

But Congress was no longer the pliant body it had been in 1933, and in the 1938 congressional elections the people's reaction was registered when the Republicans gained 81 new seats in the House and 8 in the Senate—far more than even the most optimistic Republican had predicted. If the message was lost on Roosevelt, it was obvious to some in his administration, notably his new Secretary of Commerce Harry Hopkins and his Secretary of the Treasury Henry Morgenthau. Two of the earliest business-baiters in the circle of Roosevelt advisers, they now recognized the bankruptcy of that course and the necessity for the administration to at last strive for recovery by removing the obstacles to normal and profitable business operation that the New Deal had erected. This was not what Roosevelt wanted to hear, nor was it what his Frankfurter disciples wanted him to hear. These latter knew, as Hopkins and Morgenthau had learned earlier, just which Rooseveltian buttons could be pushed to trigger his antibusiness prejudices and spite. A battle raged within the New Deal between the Frankfurter radicals and the "new conservatives," Hopkins and Morgenthau, amid growing public suspicion that the former were not interested in economic recovery.

It was not a fair battle. Hopkins and Morgenthau knew how to play the game, including use of the press, and had too many allies. They did not hesitate to talk bluntly to Roosevelt, perhaps the bluntest talk he had heard since the death of Louis McHenry Howe. Moreover, Roosevelt could afford the loss of a Corcoran and/or a Cohen, against whom there was already a great deal of congressional opposition, but a break with both Hopkins and Morgenthau would have been devastating for an administration already on the defensive. Gradually the Frankfurter radicals moved into eclipse, along with their policies, to be replaced increasingly by recovery and preparedness advocates, including many from the business and financial world.

Conventional wisdom has it that the massive government spending of World War II finally brought a Keynesian recovery from the depression. Of more significance, in comparisons of the prewar and wartime economic policies of the Roosevelt administration, is the fact that the war against business that characterized the former was abandoned in the latter. Both the attitude and policies of the Roosevelt administration toward business during the New Deal years were reversed when the president found new, foreign enemies to engage his attention and energies. Antibusiness advisers were replaced by businessmen, pro-labor policies became pro-business policies, cooperation replaced confrontation in relations between the federal government and business, and even the increased spending of the war years "trickled down" rather than "bubbling up." Probably no American president since, perhaps, Thomas Jefferson ever so thoroughly repudiated the early policies of his administration as Roosevelt did between 1939 and 1942. This, and not the emphasis on spending alone, is the lesson that needs to be learned from Roosevelt's experience with the depression, and of the legacy of the New Deal economic policies.

The judgment of historians concerning Roosevelt's presidential stature is curiously at odds with that of contemporary observers. One wonders how scholars of the Roosevelt presidency are able so blithely to ignore the negative assessments of journalists, for example, of the stature of Raymond Clapper, Walter Lippmann, Dorothy Thompson, and Arthur Krock, to name only a few. Can their observations concerning Roosevelt's pettiness and spitefulness, their criticism of the obstacles to recovery created by his anticapitalist bias, and their genuine concern over his apparent grasp for dictatorial power be dismissed so cavalierly? Is there any other example in U.S. history of an incumbent president running for reelection against the open op-

position of the two previous nominees of his own party? Will a public opinion poll ever again find 45 percent of its respondents foreseeing the likelihood of dictatorship arising from a president's policies? Will a future president ever act in such a fashion that the question will again even suggest itself to a pollster? One certainly hopes not.

Perhaps the positive assessment of Roosevelt by American historians rests upon a perceived liberalism of his administration. If so, one must wonder at their definition of liberalism. Surely a president who would pit class against class for political purposes, who was fundamentally hostile to the very basis of a free economy, who believed that his ends could justify very illiberal means, who was intolerant of criticism and critics, and who grasped for dictatorial power does not merit description as a liberal. Nor are the results of the Gallup poll mentioned above consistent with the actions of a liberal president. If the perception is based on Roosevelt's support for the less fortunate "one-third" of the nation, and his program of social legislation, then historians need to be reminded that such actions do not, in themselves, add up to liberalism, they having been used by an assortment of political realists and demagogues—of the left and the right—to gain and hold power.

There were certainly positive contributions under the New Deal, but they may not have outweighed the negative aspects of the period. The weight of the negative aspects would, moreover, have been much heavier except for the existence of a free and alert press, and for the actions of the Supreme Court and Congress in nullifying, modifying, and rejecting many of the New Deal measures. When one examines the full range of New Deal proposals and considers the implications of their passage in the original form, the outline emerges of a form of government alien to any definition of liberalism except that of the New Dealers themselves. Historians need to weigh more thoroughly and objectively the implications for the United States if Roosevelt's programs had been fully implemented. They need also to assess the costs in human misery of the delay in recovery, and of reduced U.S. influence abroad at a critical time in world affairs owing to its economic prostration. We can only speculate concerning the possible alteration of events from 1937 onward had the United States faced the world with the economic strength and military potential it might have displayed had wiser economic policies prevailed from 1933 to 1938. There is, in short, much about Roosevelt and the New Deal that historians need to reevaluate.

POSTSCRIPT

Was the New Deal an Effective Answer to the Great Depression?

Both Biles and Best agree that the New Deal concentrated a tremendous amount of power in the executive branch of the government. They also acknowledge that it was World War II—not the New Deal's reform programs —that pulled the United States out of the depression.

But the two historians disagree with each other in their assumptions and assessments of the New Deal. Biles argues that the New Deal was a nonrevolution compared to the economic and political changes that were taking place in communist Russia, fascist Italy, and Nazi Germany. The New Deal, in his view, was not so new. The Wilson administration had imposed strong governmental controls during World War I, and a number of the farm, business, and collective utility projects had been suggested and passed in different versions during the Harding, Coolidge, and Hoover presidencies.

Best's major failing is his inability to view the human side of the New Deal. By concentrating on the strengths and weaknesses of a business recovery, he seems to forget that the New Deal was much more than the sum total of a number of economic statistics. Since that time, people have come to expect the national government to manage the economy responsibly.

The most influential early books by historians on the New Deal were highly sympathetic and written from the perspective of Washington, D.C. A well-written, partisan, and never-to-be-completed history is Arthur M. Schlesinger, Jr.'s volumes in the Age of Roosevelt series, which consists of *The Crisis of the Old Order, 1919–1933* (1957), *The Coming of the New Deal* (1959), and *The Politics of Upheaval* (1960), all published by Houghton Mifflin. The best one-volume history of the New Deal from this perspective remains William E. Leuchtenburg's *Franklin D. Roosevelt and the New Deal* (Harper & Row, 1963). In a retrospective written 50 years later, "The Achievement of the New Deal," Leuchtenburg chides left-wing critics of the New Deal who blame Roosevelt for not ending racial segregation or hard-core poverty. Both Leuchtenburg and Biles remind us of what the New Deal accomplished, not what it failed to do. This essay, along with other important interpretative essays that the author wrote over many years, can be found in Leuchtenburg's *The FDR Years: On Roosevelt and His Legacy* (Columbia University Press, 1995).

John Braeman has written two bibliographical essays that critically analyze some of the major specialized works written in the 1970s and 1980s. See "The New Deal and the Broker State: A Review of the Recent Scholarly Literature," *Business History Review* (vol. 46, 1971) and "The New Deal: The Collapse of the Liberal Consensus," *Canadian Review of American Studies*

(Summer 1989), which reviews a dozen or so books and concludes that, in the long term, the New Deal brought about "a balkanized political system in which private interests scramble, barely successfully, to harass governmental authority and/or draw upon the public treasury to advance their private agendas."

Comprehensive syntheses and bibliographies can be found in Robert S. McElvaine, *The Great Depression: America, 1929–1941* (Times Books, 1984) and Anthony J. Badger, *The New Deal: The Depression Years, 1933–1940* (Farrar, Straus & Giroux, 1989). For a convenient reproduction of approximately 150 of "the most important" articles on all aspects of the New Deal, see *The Great Depression and the New Deal* (Garland, 1990), edited by Melvyn Dubofsky and Stephen Burnwood.

Liberal criticisms of the New Deal can be found in the first volume of James MacGregor Burns's political biography *Roosevelt: The Lion and the Fox* (Harcourt Brace, 1956), a work so elegantly written that 40 years later the many other biographies pale in comparison. Burns believes that Roosevelt retarded the recovery and created a recession in 1937 when he attempted to balance the budget. Alan Brinkley, in *The End of Reform: New Deal Liberalism in Recession and War* (Alfred A. Knopf, 1995), a study of the much-neglected years 1937–1945, argues that Roosevelt and his advisers gave up on trying to redistribute income by centralized planning and concentrated instead on encouraging production in hopes that a rising tide would lift all boats. James Q. Wilson attacks Brinkley with conservative arguments similar to those of Best in "Liberal Ghosts," *The New Republic* (May 22, 1995).

Radical criticisms of the New Deal and its legacy became common in the 1960s. A good starting point is Howard Zinn, ed., *New Deal Thought* (Bobbs-Merrill, 1966). Two of the most sophisticated New Left criticisms are Barton J. Bernstein, *The New Deal: The Conservative Achievements of Liberal Reform* (Pantheon Books, 1967) and Paul K. Conklin, *The New Deal*, 2d ed. (Harlan Davidson, 1975). Steve Fraser and Gary Gerstle edited a series of social and economic essays, which they present in *The Rise and Fall of the New Deal Order, 1930–1980* (Princeton University Press, 1989). A standard work is Alan Brinkley's overview *Voices of Protest: Huey Long, Father Coughlin and the Great Depression* (Alfred A. Knopf, 1982).

The celebration of Roosevelt's 100th birthday in 1982 and the 50th anniversary of the New Deal in 1983 inspired a number of conferences and the subsequent publication of the resulting papers. Among the most important are Harvard Sitkoff, ed., *Fifty Years Later: The New Deal Evaluated* (Alfred A. Knopf, 1985); Wilbur J. Cohen, ed., *The Roosevelt New Deal: A Program Assessment Fifty Years After* (Lyndon B. Johnson School of Public Affairs, 1986); and Herbert D. Rosenbaum and Elizabeth Barteline, eds., *Franklin D. Roosevelt: The Man, the Myth, the Era, 1882–1945* (Greenwood Press, 1987).

ISSUE 11

Was Franklin Roosevelt a Reluctant Internationalist?

YES: Robert A. Divine, from *Roosevelt and World War II* (Johns Hopkins University Press, 1969)

NO: William E. Kinsella, Jr., from "The Prescience of a Statesman: FDR's Assessment of Adolf Hitler Before the World War, 1933–1941," in Herbert D. Rosenbaum and Elizabeth Bartelme, eds., *Franklin D. Roosevelt: The Man, the Myth, the Era, 1882–1945* (Greenwood Press, 1987)

ISSUE SUMMARY

YES: Diplomatic historian Robert A. Divine argues that even after France fell to Nazi Germany in June 1940, Franklin Roosevelt remained a reluctant internationalist who spoke belligerently but acted timidly because he sincerely hated war.

NO: Professor of history William E. Kinsella, Jr., argues that from the time Adolf Hitler came to power in 1933, Roosevelt viewed Hitler as an overbearing, aggressive, warlike German whose long-range goal was to conquer Europe and the United States.

By the end of World War I the United States had become the world's most powerful nation. Because of its loans to the Allies during the war and its growing international trade in agricultural products, manufactured goods, and armaments, the United States became a creditor nation for the first time in its history. Militarily, the United States had become the world's dominant power.

In order to prevent the reoccurrence of another world war, the United States initiated a series of arms limitation conferences. The most successful conference took place in Washington, D.C., in 1921. In spite of its participation in world trade and its attempts to restore financial solvency in Europe, however, the United States followed a policy that Professor Thomas Paterson has called "independent internationalism." For example, the United States refused to ratify the Treaty of Versailles because by doing so it would have to become a member of the League of Nations. In 1928 the United States and France, along with just about every other nation in the world, signed the Kellogg-Briand Pact outlawing war as an instrument of national policy. But none of the agreements signed by the United States in the 1920s had any enforcement provisions that would have bound the nation to share security responsibilities in Europe or Asia or to punish violators.

The Great Depression of the 1930s destroyed the balance of power in Europe and Asia. When Japan attacked China's province of Manchuria in 1931 it violated the Kellogg-Briand Pact and the Nine-Power Treaty signed at the Washington conference. Meanwhile, events took an ugly turn in Europe. Five weeks before Franklin Roosevelt became president, Adolf Hitler was installed as chancellor of Germany. Hitler hated democracy and communism, but most of all he despised Jews. In 1936 his soldiers marched into the Rhineland and continued making annexations until 1939, when he overran Poland. England and France had no recourse but to declare war. A little more than 20 years after World War I ended, World War II began.

How did the United States respond to the aggressive actions of Germany and Japan? Most of the American public agreed that the drive for profits in the arms industry was one (though not the only one) of the major causes of America's entrance into World War I. Therefore, the American public concluded that they should isolate themselves from the political turmoil in the rest of the world.

President Franklin Roosevelt himself took a nationalist approach, preferring to concentrate on his own domestic New Deal solutions. The Johnson Act of 1934 specified that governments that defaulted on war debt payments to the United States were not permitted to borrow from private American citizens or firms. Congress also passed three Neutrality Acts from 1935 to 1937 that were designed to keep the country from repeating the mistakes that dragged the United States into World War I.

When World War II broke out in September 1939, the cash-and-carry provision of the permanent Neutrality Law had expired the previous May. Roosevelt failed to revise the neutrality laws in the spring and summer of 1939, but in November, after the European war began, he convinced Congress to repeal the arms embargo. Now England and France could purchase munitions from the United States—still on a cash-and-carry basis—to aid their fight against the Nazis.

Did Roosevelt acquiesce in neutrality legislation that he did not like during his first six years in office because he had to concentrate on his domestic reforms? Or did he follow a policy of appeasement, like his English and French counterparts did, at the Munich Conference of 1938? Were there other alternatives?

In the following selection, Robert A. Divine argues that until 1938 Roosevelt was a sincere isolationist like most of the American public because he truly hated war. He remained a reluctant internationalist who spoke belligerently but acted timidly until he was reelected for a third term in 1940. In the second selection, William E. Kinsella, Jr., states that Roosevelt took a consistent hard-line policy toward Hitler. From the time the dictator came to power in 1933, Roosevelt viewed Hitler as an overbearing, aggressive, warlike German whose long-range goal was to conquer Europe and the United States.

YES

Robert A. Divine

ROOSEVELT AND WORLD WAR II

[B]y the end of 1938, Roosevelt was no longer the confirmed isolationist he had been earlier in the decade. The brutal conquests by Italy, Japan, and Germany had aroused him to their ultimate threat to the United States. But he was still haunted by the fear of war that he voiced so often and so eloquently. His political opponents and subsequent historians have too readily dismissed his constant reiteration of the horrors of war as a politician's gesture toward public opinion. I contend that he was acting out of a deep and sincere belief when he declared that he hated war, and it was precisely this intense conviction that prevented him from embracing an interventionist foreign policy in the late 1930's. In the Munich crisis, he reveals himself in painful transition from the isolationist of the mid-1930's who wanted peace at almost any price to the reluctant internationalist of the early 1940's who leads his country into war in order to preserve its security.

No aspect of Roosevelt's foreign policy has been more controversial than his role in American entry into World War II. Although much of the discussion centers on the events leading to Pearl Harbor, I do not intend to enter into that labyrinth. The careful and well-researched studies by Herbert Feis, Roberta Wohlstetter, and Paul Schroeder demonstrate that while the administration made many errors in judgment, Roosevelt did not deliberately expose the fleet to a Japanese attack at Pearl Harbor in order to enter the war in Europe by a back door in the Pacific. This revisionist charge has already received far more attention than it deserves and has distracted historians from more significant issues.

What is more intriguing is the nature of Roosevelt's policy toward the war in Europe. There are a number of tantalizing questions that historians have not answered satisfactorily. Why was Roosevelt so devious and indirect in his policy toward the European conflict? When, if ever, did F.D.R. decide that the United States would have to enter the war in Europe to protect its own security? And finally, would Roosevelt have asked Congress for a declaration of war against Germany if Japan had not attacked Pearl Harbor?

In the months that followed the Munich Conference, President Roosevelt gradually realized that appeasement had served only to postpone, not to

From Robert A. Divine, *Roosevelt and World War II* (Johns Hopkins University Press, 1969), pp. 5–11, 20–40, 43–48. Copyright © 1969 by Johns Hopkins University Press. Reprinted by permission.

prevent, a major European war. In January, 1939, he sought to impart this fact in his annual message to Congress. He warned the representatives and senators that "philosophies of force" were loose in the world that threatened "the tenets of faith and humanity" on which the American way of life was founded. "The world has grown so small and weapons of attack so swift," the President declared, "that no nation can be safe" when aggression occurs anywhere on earth. He went on to say that the United States had "rightly" decided not to intervene militarily to prevent acts of aggression abroad and then added, somewhat cryptically, "There are many methods short of war, but stronger and more effective than mere words, of bringing home to aggressor governments the aggregate sentiments of our own people." Roosevelt did not spell out these "methods short of war," but he did criticize the existing neutrality legislation, which be suggested had the effect of encouraging aggressor nations. "We have learned," he continued, "that when we deliberately try to legislate neutrality, our neutrality laws may operate unevenly and unfairly—may actually give aid to an aggressor and deny it to the victim. The instinct of self-preservation should warn us that we ought not to let that happen any more."

Most commentators interpreted the President's speech as a call to Congress to revise the existing neutrality legislation, and in particular the arms embargo. Yet for the next two months, Roosevelt procrastinated. Finally, after Hitler's armies overran the remainder of Czechoslovakia in mid-March, Senator Key Pittman came forward with an administration proposal to repeal the arms embargo and permit American citizens to trade with nations at war on a cash-and-carry basis. The Pittman bill obviously favored England and France, since if these nations were at war with Nazi Germany, they alone would possess the sea power and financial resources to secure arms and supplies from a neutral United States. At the same time, the cash-and-carry restrictions would guard against the loss of American lives and property on the high seas and thus minimize the risk of American involvement.

Although the Pittman bill seemed to be a perfect expression of Roosevelt's desire to bolster the European democracies yet not commit the United States, the President scrupulously avoided any public endorsement in the spring of 1939. His own political stock was at an all-time low as a result of the court-packing dispute, a sharp economic recession, and an unsuccessful effort to purge dissident Democrats in the 1938 primaries. By May, Roosevelt's silence and Pittman's inept handling had led to a deadlock in the Senate. The President then turned to the House of Representatives, meeting with the leaders of the lower chamber on May 19 and telling them that passage of the cash-and-carry measure was necessary to prevent the outbreak of war in Europe. Yet despite this display of concern, Roosevelt refused to take the issue to the people, asking instead that Cordell Hull champion neutrality revision. The presidential silence proved fatal. In late June, a rebellious House of Representatives voted to retain the arms embargo and thus sabotage the administration's effort to align the United States with Britain and France.

Belatedly, Roosevelt decided to intervene. He asked the Senate Foreign Relations Committee to reconsider the Pittman bill, but in early July the Committee rebuffed the President by voting

12 to 11 to postpone action until the next session of Congress. Roosevelt was furious. He prepared a draft of a public statement in which he denounced congressional isolationists "who scream from the housetops that this nation is being led into a world war" as individuals who "deserve only the utmost contempt and pity of the American people." Hull finally persuaded him not to release this inflammatory statement. Instead, Roosevelt invited a small bipartisan group of senators to meet with him and Cordell Hull at the White House. The senators listened politely while the President and Secretary of State warned of the imminence of war in Europe and the urgent need of the United States to do something to prevent it. Senator William Borah, a leading Republican isolationist, then stunned Roosevelt and Hull by announcing categorically that there would be no war in Europe in the near future, that he had access to information from abroad that was far more reliable than the cables arriving daily at the State Department. When the other senators expressed their belief that Congress was not in the mood to revise the Neutrality Act, the meeting broke up. In a press release the next day, Roosevelt stated that the administration would accept the verdict of Congress, but he made it clear that he and Hull still believed that its failure to revise the neutrality legislation "would weaken the leadership of the United States... in the event of a new crisis in Europe." In a press conference three days later, Roosevelt was even blunter, accusing the Republicans of depriving him of the only chance he had to prevent the outbreak of war in Europe.

When the German invasion of Poland on September 1, 1939, touched off World War II, Roosevelt immediately proclaimed American neutrality and put the arms embargo and other restrictions into effect. In a radio talk to the American people on the evening of September 3, he voiced his determination to keep the country out of the conflict. "We seek to keep war from our firesides," he declared, "by keeping war from coming to the Americas." Though he deliberately refrained from asking the people to remain neutral in thought as Wilson had done in 1914, he closed by reiterating his personal hatred of war and pledging that, "as long as it remains within my power to prevent, there will be no blackout of peace in the United States."

President Roosevelt did not give up his quest for revision of the Neutrality Act, however. After a careful telephone canvass indicated that a majority of the Senate would now support repeal of the arms embargo, the President called Congress into special session. On September 21, Roosevelt urged the senators and representatives to repeal the arms embargo and thereby return to the traditional American adherence to international law. Calling Jefferson's embargo and the neutrality legislation of the 1930's the sole exceptions to this historic policy, he argued that the removal of the arms embargo was a way to insure that the United States would not be involved in the European conflict, and he promised that the government would also insist that American citizens and American ships be barred from entering the war zones. Denying that repeal was a step toward war, Roosevelt asserted that his proposal "offers far greater safeguards than we now possess or have ever possessed to protect American lives and property from danger.... There lies the road to peace." He then closed by declaring that America must stand aloof from the conflict so that it could preserve the culture of Western Europe. "Fate seems now to compel us to assume the task of helping to maintain in the western world a citadel wherein that civilization may be kept alive," he concluded.

It was an amazing speech. No less than four times the President declared that his policy was aimed at keeping the United States out of the war. Yet the whole intent of arms embargo repeal was to permit England and France to purchase arms and munitions from the United States. By basing his appeal on a return to international law and a desire to keep out of the war, Roosevelt was deliberately misleading the American people. The result was a long and essentially irrelevant debate in Congress over the administration bill to repeal the arms embargo and to place all trade with belligerents on a cash-and-carry basis. Advocates of the bill followed the President's cue, repeatedly denying that the legislation was aimed at helping Britain and France and insisting that the sole motive was to preserve American neutrality. Isolationist opponents quite logically asked, if the purpose was to insure neutrality, why did not the administration simply retain the arms embargo and add cash-and-carry for all other trade with countries at war. With heavy majorities already lined up in both houses, administration spokesmen refused to answer this query. They infuriated the isolationists by repeating with parrot-like precision the party line that the substitution of cash-and-carry for the arms embargo would keep the nation out of war.

The result was an overwhelming victory for Roosevelt. In late October the Senate, thought to be the center of isolationist strength, voted for the administration bill by more than two

to one; in early November the House concurred after a closer ballot. Now Britain and France could purchase from the United States anything they needed for their war effort, including guns, tanks, and airplanes, provided only that they paid cash and carried away these supplies in their own ships.

Roosevelt expressed his thoughts most clearly in a letter to William Allen White a month later. "Things move with such terrific speed, these days," he wrote, "that it really is essential to us to think in broader terms and, in effect, to warn the American people that they, too, should think of possible ultimate results in Europe.... Therefore, my sage old friend, my problem is to get the American people to think of conceivable consequences without scaring the American people into thinking that they are going to be dragged into this war." In 1939, Roosevelt evidently decided that candor was still too risky, and thus he chose to pursue devious tactics in aligning the United States indirectly on the side of England and France.

The blitzkrieg that Adolf Hitler launched in Europe in the spring of 1940 aroused Americans to their danger in a way that Roosevelt never could. Norway and Denmark fell in April, and then on May 10 Germany launched an offensive thrust through the low countries into northern France that drove Holland and Belgium out of the war in less than a week and forced the British into a humiliating retreat from the continent at Dunkirk before the month was over. The sense of physical security from foreign danger that the United States had enjoyed for over a century was shattered in a matter of days. The debate over policy would continue, but from May, 1940, on, virtually all Americans recognized that the

German victories in Europe imperiled the United States....

In early June, the news from Europe became even worse. As he sat in his White House study one evening reading the latest dispatches, Roosevelt remarked to his wife, "All bad, all bad." He realized that a vigorous defense program was not enough—that American security depended on the successful resistance of England and France to German aggression. As Hitler's armies swept toward Paris and Mussolini moved his troops toward the exposed French frontier on the Mediterranean, Roosevelt sought to throw American influence into the balance. On June 10, he was scheduled to deliver a commencement speech at the University of Virginia in Charlottesville. Going over the State Department draft, he stiffened the language, telling a diplomat who called at the White House that morning that his speech would be a " 'tough' one—one in which the issue between the democracies and the Fascist powers would be drawn as never before." News that Italy had attacked France reached the President just before he boarded the train to Charlottesville and reinforced his determination to speak out boldly.

Addressing the graduates that evening, President Roosevelt condemned the concept of isolationism that he himself had held so strongly only a few years before. He termed the idea that the United States could exist as a lone island of peace in a world of brute force "a delusion." "Such an island," he declared, "represents to me and to the overwhelming majority of Americans today a helpless nightmare of a people without freedom—the nightmare of a people lodged in prison, handcuffed, hungry, and fed through the bars from day to day by the contemptuous, unpitying masters of other continents." In clear and unambiguous words, he declared that his sympathies lay wholly on the side of "those nations that are giving their life blood in combat" against Fascist aggression. Then, in his most significant policy statement, he announced that his administration would follow a twofold course of increasing the American defense effort and extending to England and France "the material resources of this nation."

The Charlottesville speech marks a decisive turn in Roosevelt's policy. At the time, most commentators focused on one dramatic sentence, written in at the last moment, in which he condemned the Italian attack on France by saying, "the hand that held the dagger has struck it into the back of its neighbor." But far more important was the President's pledge to defend American security by giving all-out aid to England and France. By promising to share American supplies with these two belligerents, Roosevelt was gambling that they could successfully contain Germany on the European continent and thus end the threat to American security. Given the German military advantages, the risks were enormous. If Roosevelt diverted a large portion of the nation's limited supply of weapons to England and France and then they surrendered to Hitler, the President would be responsible for leaving this country unprepared to meet a future German onslaught.

At the same time, the President's admirers have read too much into the Charlottesville speech. Basil Rauch argues that the speech ended America's status as a neutral. Robert Sherwood goes even further, claiming that at Charlottesville Roosevelt committed the United States "to the assumption of responsibility for nothing less than the leadership of the world."

Samuel Rosenman is more moderate, labeling this address as "the beginning of all-out aid to the democracies," but noting that it stopped short of war. But is it even accurate to say that the speech signified all-out aid short of war? An examination of Roosevelt's subsequent steps to help France and England reveals that the President was still extremely reluctant to do anything that would directly involve the United States in the European conflict.

The French quickly discovered the limitations of the President's new policy. Heartened by Roosevelt's words at Charlottesville, Paul Reynaud, the French Premier, immediately tried to secure American military intervention to save his country. In a personal appeal to Roosevelt on June 14, Reynaud asked him to send American troops as well as American supplies in France's hour of greatest need. The next day, the President replied. The United States admired the stubborn and heroic French resistance to German aggression, Roosevelt wrote, and he promised to do all he could to increase the flow of arms and munitions to France. But there he drew the line. "I know that you will understand that these statements carry with them no implication of military commitments," the President concluded. "Only the Congress can make such commitments." On June 17, the French, now fully aware that American military involvement was out of the question, surrendered to Germany.

The British, left waging the fight alone against Germany, also discovered that Roosevelt's actions failed to live up to the promise of his words. On May 15, five days after he replaced Neville Chamberlain as Prime Minister, Winston Churchill sent an urgent message to President Roosevelt. Churchill eloquently expressed his determination to fight Hitler to the bit-

ter end, but he warned that Britain had to have extensive aid from the United States. Above all else, England needed forty or fifty American destroyers to protect the Atlantic supply line from German submarine attacks. Churchill pointed out that England had lost thirty-two destroyers since the war began, and she needed most of her remaining sixty-eight in home waters to guard against a German invasion. "We must ask, therefore," Churchill concluded, "as a matter of life or death, to be reinforced with these destroyers."

Despite the urgency of the British request, Roosevelt procrastinated. On June 5, the President told Secretary of the Interior Harold Ickes that it would require an act of Congress to transfer the destroyers to Great Britain. Even pressure from several other cabinet members, including Henry Morgenthau and the two new Republicans Roosevelt appointed in June, Secretary of War Henry Stimson and Secretary of the Navy Frank Knox, failed to move Roosevelt. His reluctance was increased when Congress decreed on June 28 that the President could not transfer any warships to a belligerent until the Chief of Naval Operations certified that they were "not essential to the defense of the United States."

Roosevelt's inaction caused deep concern among members of the Committee to Defend America by Aiding the Allies, the pro-British pressure group headed by William Allen White. A few of the more interventionist members of White's committee developed the idea in mid-July of arranging a trade whereby the United States would give Britain the needed destroyers in return for the right to build naval and air bases on British islands in the Western Hemisphere. On August 1, a three-man delegation called at the

White House to present this idea to the President, who received it noncommittally. Lord Lothian, the British ambassador, had suggested as far back as May 24 that England grant the United States the rights for bases on Newfoundland, Bermuda, and Trinidad, and in July, in talks with Secretary of the Navy Frank Knox, Lothian linked the possibility of these bases with the transfer of destroyers. Knox liked the idea, but he could not act without the President's consent. And Roosevelt remained deaf to all pleas, including one by Churchill on July 21 in which the British Prime Minister said, "Mr. President, with great respect I must tell you that in the long history of the world this is a thing to do NOW."

Churchill's appeal and the possibility of justifying the transfer of the destroyers as a trade for bases evidently persuaded Roosevelt to act. On August 2, when Frank Knox raised the issue in a cabinet meeting, Roosevelt approved the idea of giving Britain the destroyers in return for the right to build bases on British islands in the Atlantic and Caribbean, and, in addition, in return for a British pledge to send its fleet to the New World if Germany defeated England. Roosevelt still believed that the destroyer transfer would require an act of Congress, and the cabinet advised him to secure the support of Wendell Willkie, the Republican candidate for the presidency in the forthcoming campaign, to insure favorable Congressional action. Through William Allen White, who acted as an intermediary, Roosevelt received word that while Willkie refused to work actively to line up Republican support in Congress, he did agree not to make the destroyer deal a campaign issue.

Roosevelt called his advisers together on August 13 to make a final decision.

With the help of Morgenthau, Knox, Stimson, and Undersecretary of State Sumner Welles, Roosevelt drafted a cable to Churchill proposing the transfer of fifty destroyers in return for eight bases and a private pledge in regard to the British fleet. The next day a joyous Churchill cabled back his acceptance of these terms, saying that "each destroyer you can spare to us is measured in rubies." But Churchill realized that the deal meant more than just help at sea. "The moral value of this fresh aid from your Government and your people at this critical time," he cabled the President, "will be very great and widely felt."

It took two more weeks to work out the details of the transaction, and during that period a group of distinguished international lawyers convinced the Attorney General that the administration could transfer the destroyers without the approval of Congress. One final hitch developed when Churchill insisted that the bases be considered free gifts from the British; Roosevelt finally agreed that two of the sites would be gifts, but that the remaining six would have to be considered a *quid pro quo* for the destroyers. On September 3, the President made the transaction public in a message to Congress in which he bore down heavily on the advantages to be gained by the United States. Barely mentioning the transfer of the destroyers, the President called the acquisition of eight naval and air bases stretching in an arc from Newfoundland to British Guiana "an epochal and far-reaching act of preparation for continental defense in the face of grave danger." Searching desperately for a historical precedent, Roosevelt described the trade as "the most important action in the reinforcement of our national defense that has been taken since the Louisiana Purchase."

What is most striking about the destroyer-for-bases deal is the caution and reluctance with which the President acted. In June he announced a policy of all-out aid to Britain, yet he delayed for nearly four months after receiving Churchill's desperate plea for destroyers. He acted only after interventionists had created strong public support, only after the transfer could be disguised as an act in support of the American defense program, only after the leader of the opposition party had agreed not to challenge him politically on this issue, and only after his legal advisers found a way to bypass Congress. What may have appeared on the surface to be a bold and courageous act by the President was in reality a carefully calculated and virtually foolproof maneuver.

It would be easy to dismiss the destroyer-for-bases deal as just another example of Roosevelt's tendency to permit political expediency to dictate his foreign policy. Certainly Roosevelt acted in this case with a careful eye on the political realities. This was an election year, and he was not going to hand Wendell Willkie and the Republicans a ready-made issue. But I believe that Roosevelt's hesitation and caution stem as much from his own uncertainty as from political calculation. He realized that the gift of vessels of war to a belligerent was a serious departure from traditional neutrality, and one that might well give Germany the grounds on which to declare war against the United States. He wanted to give England all-out aid short of war, but he was not at all sure that this step would not be an act of war. Only when he convinced himself that the destroyer-for-bases deal could be

construed as a step to defend the-nation's security did he give his consent. Thus his rather extravagant public defense of his action was not just a political move to quiet isolationist critics; rather it was his own deeply felt rationalization for a policy step of great importance that undoubtedly moved the United States closer to participation in the European conflict.

Perhaps even more significant is the pattern that emerges from this review of Roosevelt's policy in the spring and summer of 1940, for it is one that recurs again and again in his conduct of foreign policy. Confronted by a major crisis, he makes a bold and forthright call at Charlottesville for a policy of all-out aid short of war. But then, having pleased the interventionists with his rhetoric, he immediately retreats, turning down the French appeal for intervention and delaying on the British plea for destroyers, thus reassuring his isolationist critics. Then, as a consensus begins to form, he finally enters into the destroyer-for-bases deal and thus redeems the pledge he had made months before at Charlottesville. Like a child playing a game of giant steps, Roosevelt moved two steps forward and one back before he took the giant step ahead. Movement in a straight and unbroken line seems to have been alien to his nature—he could not go forward until he had tested the ground, studied all the reactions, and weighed all the risks. . . .

After his triumphant election to a third term, Roosevelt relaxed on a Caribbean cruise. But after only a week, a navy seaplane arrived with an urgent dispatch from Winston Churchill. The Prime Minister gave a lengthy and bleak description of the situation in Europe and then informed the President that England was rapidly running out of money for continued purchases of American goods. "The moment approaches when we shall no longer be able to pay cash for shipping and other supplies," Churchill wrote, concluding with the confident assertion that Roosevelt would find "ways and means" to continue the flow of munitions and goods across the Atlantic.

When the President returned to Washington in mid-December, he called in the press, and in his breeziest and most informal manner began to outline the British dilemma and his solution to it. His advisers were working on several plans, he said, but the one that interested him most was simply to lend or lease to England the supplies she needed, in the belief that "the best defense of Great Britain is the best defense of the United States." Saying that he wanted to get rid of the dollar sign, Roosevelt compared his scheme to the idea of lending a garden hose to a neighbor whose house was on fire. When the fire is out, the neighbor either returns the hose or, if it is damaged, replaces it with a new one. So it would be, Roosevelt concluded, with the munitions the United States would provide Britain in the war against Nazi Germany.

In a fireside chat to the American people a few days later, Roosevelt justified this lend-lease concept on grounds of national security. Asserting that Hitler aimed not just at victory in Europe but at world domination, Roosevelt repeated his belief that the United States was in grave peril. If England fell, he declared, "all of us in the Americas would be living at the point of a gun." He admitted that the transfer of arms and munitions to Britain risked American involvement in the conflict, but he argued that "there is far less chance of the United States getting into war if we do all we can now

to support the nations defending themselves against attack by the Axis than if we acquiesce in their defeat, submit tamely to an Axis victory, and wait our turn to be the object of attack in another war later on." He declared that he had no intention of sending American troops to Europe; his sole purpose was to "keep war away from our country and our people." Then, in a famous phrase, he called upon the United States to become "the great arsenal of democracy."

Congress deliberated over the lend-lease bill for the next two months, and a strong consensus soon emerged in favor of the measure. Leading Republicans, including Wendell Willkie, endorsed the bill, and most opponents objected only to the leasing provision, suggesting instead an outright loan to Britain. The House acted quickly, approving lend-lease by nearly 100 votes in February; the Senate took longer but finally gave its approval by a margin of almost two to one in early March. After the President signed the legislation into law, Congress granted an initial appropriation of seven billion dollars to guarantee the continued flow of vital war supplies to Great Britain.

Roosevelt had thus taken another giant step forward, and this time without any hesitation. His election victory made him bolder than usual, and Churchill's candid plea had convinced him that speed was essential. The granting of lend-lease aid was very nearly an act of war, for it gave Britain unrestricted access to America's enormous industrial resources. But the President felt with great sincerity that this policy would lead not to American involvement but to a British victory that alone could keep the nation out of war....

In the six months preceding Pearl Harbor, Franklin Roosevelt moved slowly but steadily toward war with Germany.

On July 7, he announced that he had sent 4,000 American marines to Iceland to prevent that strategic island from falling into German hands. Secretary of War Stimson, though pleased with this action, expressed disappointment over the President's insistence on describing it solely as a measure of hemispheric self-defense. Iceland was the key to defending the supply route across the Atlantic, and Stimson believed that the President should have frankly told Congress that the United States was occupying the island to insure the delivery of goods to Britain.

Once American forces landed in Iceland, Roosevelt authorized the Navy to convoy American ships supplying the marines on the island. In addition, he at first approved a naval operations plan which permitted British ships to join these convoys and thus receive an American escort halfway across the Atlantic, but in late July he reversed himself, ordering the Navy to restrict its convoys to American and Icelandic vessels. In August, at the famous Atlantic Conference with Churchill, Roosevelt once again committed himself to the principle of convoying British ships halfway across the Atlantic, but he failed to give the necessary order to the Navy after his return to Washington.

Roosevelt's hesitancy and indecision finally ended in early September when a German submarine fired a torpedo at the American destroyer *Greer*. Though subsequent reports revealed that the *Greer* had been following the U-boat for more than three hours and had been broadcasting its position to nearby British naval units, Roosevelt interpreted this incident as a clear-cut case of German aggression. In a press release on September 5, he called the attack on the *Greer* deliberate, and on the same day he told Samuel Rosenman to begin drafting a statement that would express his determination "to use any means necessary to get the goods to England." Rosenman and Harry Hopkins prepared a strongly worded speech, and after a few revisions the President delivered it over a worldwide radio network on the evening of September 11.

In biting phrases, Roosevelt lashed out against Hitler and Nazi Germany. He described the attack on the *Greer* as part of a concerted German effort to "acquire absolute control and domination of the seas for themselves." Such control, he warned, would lead inevitably to a Nazi effort to dominate the Western Hemisphere and "create a permanent world system based on force, terror, and murder." The attack on the *Greer* was an act of piracy, Roosevelt declared; German submarines had become the "rattlesnakes of the Atlantic." Then, implying but never openly saying that American ships would shoot German submarines on sight, Roosevelt declared that henceforth the United States Navy would escort "all merchant ships—not only American ships but ships of any flag—engaged in commerce in our defensive waters."

Contemporary observers and many historians labeled this the "shoot-on-sight" speech, seeing its significance primarily in the orders to American naval officers to fire at German submarines in the western Atlantic. "The undeclared war" speech would be a better label, for its real importance was that Roosevelt had finally made a firm decision on the convoy issue on which he had been hedging ever since the passage of lend-lease by Congress. Branding the Germans as "pirates" and their U-boats as "rattlesnakes" distracted the American people from the fact that the President was now putting into practice the policy of convoying British ships halfway across the ocean, and thereby assuming a significant share of the responsibility for the Battle of the Atlantic. The immediate effect was to permit the British to transfer forty destroyers from the western Atlantic to the submarine-infested waters surrounding the British Isles. In the long run, the President's decision meant war with Germany, since from this time forward there would inevitably be more and more U-boat attacks on American destroyers, increasingly heavy loss of life, and a direct challenge to the nation's honor and prestige. Only Hitler's reluctance to engage in war with the United States while he was still absorbed in the assault on Russia prevented an immediate outbreak of hostilities.

With the convoy issue now resolved, Roosevelt moved to revise the Neutrality Act. In mid-October he asked the House to permit the arming of American merchant ships with deck guns, and then later in the month he urged the Senate to remove the "carry" provision of the law so that American merchantmen could take supplies all the way across the Atlantic to British ports. When a German submarine torpedoed the destroyer *Kearney* near Iceland, Roosevelt seized on the incident to speed up action in Congress.

"America has been attacked," the President declared in a speech on October 27. "The U.S.S. *Kearney* is not just a Navy ship. She belongs to every man, woman, and child in this Nation." Describing Nazi efforts at infiltration in South America, the President bluntly charged that Germany was bent on the conquest of "the United States itself." Then, coming very close to a call for war, he asserted,

"The forward march of Hitlerism can be stopped—and it will be stopped. Very simply and very bluntly—we are pledged to pull our own oar in the destruction of Hitlerism." Although he called only for the revision of the Neutrality Act, the tone of the entire address was one of unrelieved belligerency, culminating in the following peroration: "Today in the face of this newest and greatest challenge, we Americans have cleared our decks and taken our battle stations. We stand ready in the defense of our Nation and the faith of our fathers to do what God has given us the power to see as our full duty."

Two weeks later, by quite slim majorities, Congress removed nearly all restrictions on American commerce from the Neutrality Act. For the first time since the war began in 1939, American merchant vessels could carry supplies all the way across the Atlantic to British ports. The significance of this action was obscured by the Japanese attack on Pearl Harbor which triggered American entry into the war in December and gave rise to the subsequent charge that Roosevelt led the nation into the conflict via the back door. Revision of the Neutrality Act was bound to lead to war with Germany within a matter of months. Hitler could be forbearing when it was only a question of American escort vessels operating in the western Atlantic. He could not have permitted American ships to carry a major portion of lend-lease supplies to Britain without giving up the Battle of the Atlantic. With the German offensive halting before Leningrad and Moscow in December, Hitler would have been compelled to order his submarine commanders to torpedo American ships as the only effective way to hold Britain in check. And once Germany began sinking American ships regularly, Roosevelt would have had to ask Congress for a declaration of war.

The crucial question, of course, is why Roosevelt chose such an oblique policy which left the decision for peace or war in the hands of Hitler. His apologists, notably Robert Sherwood and Basil Rauch, insist that he had no choice. The isolationists were so powerful that the President could not lay the issue squarely before Congress and ask for a declaration of war. If he had, writes Basil Rauch, he would have "invited a prolonged, bitter, and divisive debate" and thereby have risked a defeat which would have discredited the administration and turned the nation back to isolationism. Sherwood sadly agrees, saying, "He had no more tricks left. The hat from which he had pulled so many rabbits was empty. The President of the United States was now the creature of circumstance which must be shaped not by his own will or his own ingenuity but by the unpredictable determination of his enemies."

In part this was true, but these sympathetic historians fail to point out that Roosevelt was the prisoner of his own policies. He had told the nation time and time again that it was not necessary for the United States to enter the war. He had propounded the doctrine that America could achieve Hitler's downfall simply by giving all-out aid to England. He had repeatedly denied that his measures would lead the nation to war. In essence, he had foreclosed to himself the possibility of going directly

to the people and bluntly stating that the United States must enter the war as the only way to guarantee the nation's security. All he could do was edge the country closer and closer, leaving the ultimate decision to Germany and Japan.

We will never know at what point Roosevelt decided in his own mind that it was essential that the United States enter the war. His own personal hatred of war was deep and genuine, and it was this conviction that set him apart from men like Stimson and Morgenthau, who decided that American participation was necessary as early as the spring of 1941. William Langer and Everett Gleason believe that Roosevelt realized by the fall of 1941 that there was no other way to defeat Hitler, but they conclude that, even so, he thought the American military contribution could be limited to naval and air support and not include the dispatch of an American army to the European battlefields.

It is quite possible that Roosevelt never fully committed himself to American involvement prior to Pearl Harbor. His hesitancy was not just a catering to isolationist strength but a reflection of his own inner uncertainty. Recognizing that Hitler threatened the security of the United States, he took a series of steps which brought the nation to the brink of war, but his own revulsion at the thought of plunging his country into the most devastating conflict in history held him back until the Japanese attack left him no choice.

NO

William E. Kinsella, Jr.

THE PRESCIENCE OF A STATESMAN

In December 1932, William Bullitt, then special assistant to Secretary of State Cordell Hull, assured Franklin D. Roosevelt [FDR] that Adolf Hitler was finished as a possible dictator and that Germany's president, Paul von Hindenburg, absolutely refused to have Hitler as chancellor. The German government, wrote Bullitt, was no longer afraid of the Nazi movement. On January 30, 1933, Adolf Hitler was appointed chancellor. Ambassador John Cudahy, writing from Warsaw several months later, told President Roosevelt that there was no cause for alarm. Rumors that Germany was preparing for war were described as entirely baseless. The Germans, he noted, simply love display and pageantry. This blatant exhibition of militarism, he continued, was merely an expression of a uniquely German gregarious instinct, much like that of the Elks, Eagles, and Woodmen. Such misconceptions soon would be dispelled as the world watched with growing alarm a nation's march to war.

FDR had no illusions concerning the threat posed by Adolf Hitler's Germany. Rexford Tugwell recalled that the president's initial impressions were marked by detestation, dread, and implacable hostility. Roosevelt viewed the Fuhrer as insensitive, overbearing, gross, and aggressively German. He foresaw, asserts Tugwell, that an encounter with Germany might be inevitable. This description of Roosevelt's views, although written in retrospect, seems credible. The course of future events would confirm FDR's intuitive prescience, and strengthen a statesman's prophetic realization that a war of primitive barbarism soon would confront the proponents of peace and civility.

Perhaps a more accurate phrase to describe Franklin Roosevelt's predictive assessment of the German threat would be an informed prescience. Diplomatic reports to the White House, more often than not, were remarkably correct in their analyses of Germany's intentions. The ambassadors who were particularly expansive in their evaluations of the evolving war situation included William Dodd (Germany); William Bullitt (Soviet Union and France); Breckinridge Long and William Phillips (Italy); Robert Bingham, Joseph Kennedy, and John Winant (United Kingdom); Joseph Davies (Soviet Union and Belgium); Herbert Pell (Portugal and Hungary); Claude Bowers

From William E. Kinsella, Jr., "The Prescience of a Statesman: FDR's Assessment of Adolf Hitler Before the World War, 1933–1941," in Herbert D. Rosenbaum and Elizabeth Bartelme, eds., *Franklin D. Roosevelt: The Man, the Myth, the Era, 1882–1945* (Greenwood Press, 1987). Copyright © 1987 by Hofstra University. Reprinted by permission of Greenwood Publishing Group, Inc., Westport, CT. Notes omitted.

(Spain and Chile); Josephus Daniels (Mexico); Lincoln MacVeagh (Greece); John Cudahy (Poland); George Earle (Austria); and Joseph Grew (Japan). The Departments of State, War and Navy, and the personal acquaintances of FDR reporting on overseas developments provided extensive and accurate coverage of foreign affairs. The focus of their attention was Hitler's Germany.

Initial appraisals of Adolf Hitler's regime in 1933 were not at all sanguine concerning the future. William Dodd, writing from Berlin, repeatedly warned of war. More men had been trained, uniformed, and armed in Germany, wrote the ambassador one year after Hitler's accession to power, than in 1914. He added that this military might was solely for war. George Earle, minister to Austria, depicted the Fuhrer as a paranoiac who had made the militaristic spirit the most intense in German history. Austria, predicted Earle, would be the first nation to fall. Samuel Fuller, president of the American Bemberg Corporation, reported to the president in May 1933 that Hitler was a successful dictator who was fully organized, absolutely self-confident, and in complete power. The Germans view him almost as a god, he continued, and trust him implicitly. His regime, concluded Fuller, feeds on intense nationalism and pride of race. He predicted that war would be the end result. Felix Frankfurter, New Deal economic advisor and personal friend of FDR, wrote to the president stating that the significance of Hitlerism far transcended ferocious anti-Semitism and fanatical racism. The attack against the Jews, he said, was merely an index to the gospel of force espoused by the rulers of Germany. He warned Roosevelt that the violence and chauvinism of the Hitler regime would be intensified,

and that the air was charged with the kind of feeling preceding 1914.

Similar viewpoints were sent to the president from other diplomatic posts, and each conveyed the impression that Germany contemplated aggressive expansion. Franklin Roosevelt's press conference remarks in September 1934 reflect the fear of Germany which his correspondents had expressed to him. The president described the German preparation for war. Factory workers had gas masks at their side. School children were learning the particular smells of poisonous gases. Bomb shelters were being built everywhere, and with the aid of a government deduction. Roosevelt told reporters of the little German boy who prayed each night that God would permit him to die with a French bullet in his heart. The president intimated that this war psychosis was being created deliberately by the German government in anticipation of eventual aggressive action.

Preparations for conflict were made official soon after these remarks. During the month of March 1935, Adolf Hitler announced the formation of the German air force, proclaimed universal military service, called for an increase in the size of the German army, and initiated a program of naval rearmament. Germany's first move had been peaceful. The Saar plebiscite transferred control of that territory to Germany. Breckinridge Long, ambassador to Italy, expressed his belief that this event would serve as a big drink of schnapps to the Germans and that Hitler would be emboldened to pursue his Pan-Germanic ideas. Germany, he confided to the president, was still suspected like a wolf, and her intentions were about as peaceful as were those of Attila [the Hun].

The Attila analogy was shared by other observers of the international scene in 1935. Edward House wrote to Roosevelt saying that war was much more probable now that Germany intended to rearm. Hitler's madness, confessed House, was impossible to understand. Lincoln MacVeagh described the growing anxiety of many in the Balkans, the tinder box of Europe. John Cudahy said that Hitler's military preparations would be complete by 1938, and any eventuality might occur then. General John J. Pershing told the president that Germany would be prepared militarily for any action within the ten-year period in which that nation pledged to keep the peace. Reporter Charles Sherrill, after an interview with Hitler, informed FDR that Germany would march when its army was ready. In the words of Samuel Fuller, Germany was a day-to-day menace to the peace of all nations.

Franklin Roosevelt shared these views, and the collapse of the Geneva Disarmament Conference (in spite of FDR's promise to presidential envoy Norman Davis that he would be accorded burial in Arlington National Cemetery if the talks succeeded) prompted the president to find a means to constrain Germany. During conversations with Henry Morgenthau and Edward House in 1935, Roosevelt proposed a complete blockade of Germany on the Polish, Czecho-Slovak, Austrian, Swiss, French, Belgian, Dutch, and Danish borders. Access to German ports would be closed by the British navy. The United States would participate in what was a blockade of Germany, not a boycott or sanction. Congressional action would not be needed, thought the president, because recognition of a blockade would fall under the executive's power. These proposals of the president remained momentarily private because of domestic political pressures and the appeasement policies of Great Britain and France. They do reveal, however, his serious concern over the future course of German foreign policy under Hitler.

In early February 1936, Norman Davis described for the president the crisis atmosphere prevailing in Europe. All of the political leaders, he wrote, are thinking of how best to prepare for the war which they think Germany is going to force upon them. It was feared that Italy's recent success in Ethiopia would serve as a catalyst for aggressive acts by other nations. Roosevelt, in a letter to Ambassador Long, said that he was watching the daily news from Europe with the feeling each day that the next would bring a major explosion. The president added that he did not share the optimistic view that each recurring crisis would iron itself out and that nothing really serious would happen. This mood of anticipation was heightened when on March 7, 1936, German troops moved into the once demilitarized Rhineland. FDR confided to Ambassador Dodd that in July 1914 the experts had predicted that there would be no war. Today, the president continued, he had his tongue in cheek and, like a fire department, would be ready for any eventuality. William Dodd described the situation as clearly one of dictator Europe against Western Europe. Hitler's plan, he noted, was to extend Germany's power from the Danube to the Black Sea. Germany, in exchange, would support Italy's quest for a renewed Roman Empire. The ambassador's prediction that Germany and Italy would unite in their quest for European dominance appeared to Roosevelt as entirely accurate, especially in view of the developing situation in Spain. The crisis atmosphere of the spring months had barely subsided when on July 17, 1936, civil war erupted in that country.

The U.S. ambassador to Spain, Claude Bowers, provided the president with detailed accounts of what he would describe repeatedly as a war against democracy. His letters to FDR were replete with references to a worldwide fascist conspiracy for which Spain was simply a testing ground. The sublimated gunmen and gangsters of Rome and Berlin, wrote Bowers, had just begun their conquests. He warned the president that with every victory, beginning with China, followed by Ethiopia and then Spain, the fascist powers, with vanity inflamed, would turn without delay to some other country, such as Czechoslovakia, and that with every surrender the prospects of a European war would grow darker. The pitiful policy of retreating before the gesture of bullies, he told Roosevelt, simply would make stronger the fascist internationale. Indeed, Germany, Italy, and Japan had signed formal agreements pledging associative action. Unbridled in their ambitions, they had unharnessed their machines of war. The Spanish interlude was but a prelude to other undeclared wars against the democracies of Europe.

Numerous other reports sent to President Roosevelt by friends and official representatives reflected this atmosphere of impending crisis. Emil Ludwig predicted that Germany's militant character, its longing for revenge, its inferiority complex, and race theory eventually would make a major war inevitable. William Dodd forecast a German thrust toward Austria, Hungary, Rumania, and Czechoslovakia. William Bullitt depicted the Austrian position as that of an apple left hanging on the bough to be plucked

at an appropriate moment by Hitler. Roosevelt hoped that it would have the effect of a green apple. Nigel Law told FDR that it was useless to negotiate for peace with such people as the leaders of Germany. Herbert Pell, ambassador to Portugal, warned Roosevelt in September 1937 that the fascist movement was approaching the status of a new religion that would produce fanatics, hypocrites, martyrs, and human sacrifices.

These are but a few of the many despatches similar in content which persuaded the president to make a major policy statement on foreign affairs. The Chicago quarantine address (October 5, 1937) set forth a possible solution to stop the epidemic of world lawlessness. The 10 percent who were threatening the security of peace-loving nations should be quarantined to protect the health of the civilized community. His words revealed the gravity of the moment. He described the situation as most dangerous, adding that neither isolation nor neutrality assured an escape from future conflict. FDR earnestly hoped that these remarks would serve as a tonic toward a realistic appraisal of the grave threat to the security of free peoples and their governments. Roosevelt realized that, as William Bullitt had said, the deluge was fast approaching.

The storm would break over Austria during the night of March 11, 1938, as German troops marched into that nation. There were few who believed that the violence would subside in the near future. Arthur Sweetzer, director of the United States Information Section at the League of Nations, had an interview with FDR soon after the Anschluss. His alarming report to the chief executive indicated that nothing in Central Europe could stop Hitler. During the conversation, Roosevelt mentioned that he had just received a letter describing Austrian Chancellor Kurt von Schuschnigg's meeting with the Fuhrer at Berchtesgaden. The chancellor, said the president, apparently had never dreamt of anything like it. Hitler had been unbelievable, repeatedly invoking the names of Julius Caesar and Jesus Christ during his long tirades. Sweetzer recounted that Roosevelt seemed to think you could do very little with such a man. John Cudahy told the president succinctly that all states east and south of Germany were living in constant apprehension as to which might be the next victim of Hitler's expansionist program. The intended victim was identified immediately, for reports that Hitler was planning to seize the Sudentenland in Czechoslovakia were numerous throughout the summer months of 1938. Ambassador Hugh Wilson predicted from Berlin that the Fuhrer would not hesitate to use force to achieve his ambitions in Czechoslovakia. FDR, fully cognizant of Hitler's resolve, decided to intervene to prevent what he foresaw as an inevitable military debacle for the democracies in this approaching confrontation with Germany.

The fear of Germany's military superiority over Great Britain and France convinced Franklin Roosevelt of the necessity for action. All incoming correspondence to the White House had been discouraging. Hugh Wilson had testified repeatedly on the strength and readiness of the German army and air force. From Rome, Ambassador William Phillips expressed no doubts about Mussolini's decision to enter the war as a full-fledged Axis partner. Joseph Kennedy, from his vantage point in London, was certain that Great Britain lacked the preparedness necessary to defeat Hitler. "If war comes they are going to get hell," said Kennedy, "but they are now reconciled." William Bullitt's letters from Paris contained predictions of catastrophic destruction in France should Germany decide on an air attack. It was apparent too that the chief executive took very seriously the Fuhrer's statements concerning the willingness to precipitate a major conflict. He urged that plans be made ready to evacuate Americans from Europe, and later renewed his request for more evacuation ships. Roosevelt expressed his concern to the chief of naval operations, William Leahy, about the need to determine the location of all German warships. He fully expected the worst possible consequences. FDR's plea for a negotiated settlement prevented the expected conflict. The leaders of France, Great Britain, Italy, and Germany agreed to a peaceful solution. The Sudentenland was ceded to Germany.

During a discussion with Josephus Daniels the president explained his actions, acknowledging that if he had been in Neville Chamberlain's place he would have felt constrained to have made terms to prevent a war for which Germany was fully prepared. The chief executive was convinced, he told Daniels, of the great military superiority of the totalitarian countries, and was most concerned with a threatened German air attack on London before the Munich meeting. Roosevelt was certain of a German victory over the prospective British and French allies in September 1938, and this was the major consideration in his decision to attempt to delay the inevitable encounter. These thoughts were in the president's mind when he told a reporter, "It was, as we all know, a very definite crisis and though there are many things which are called crisis which are not, this one was."

President Roosevelt saw no lasting value in any agreement of appeasement with Germany. He told Sir Ronald Lindsay, British ambassador in Washington, that in all probability Hitler would overrun all of Czechoslovakia, and German expansion toward Denmark, the Polish Corridor, and Rumania would follow this success. The Western powers, predicted the president, soon would find themselves at war with Germany and Italy. He then offered a possible response to Axis aggression, telling Ambassador Lindsay to keep secret all aspects of his proposal. Roosevelt renewed his call for a blockade of Germany with the participation of the United States. The blockade line, said FDR, should be drawn down the middle of the North Sea, through the English Channel to Gibraltar and the Mediterranean, including closure of the Suez Canal. Lindsay noted that the president realized that the United States might become involved directly in the European war, although he doubted that U.S. troops could be sent to fight unless Britain was invaded by Germany. FDR later informed Neville Chamberlain, through his personal friend Arthur Murray, that Great Britain would have all the industrial resources of the United States behind it in the event of future hostilities.

Diplomatic despatches relayed to the White House, in addition to the numerous letters sent privately to the president, were in agreement with the view that Germany's drive for European hegemony had only been appeased momentarily. Anthony Biddle told Roosevelt that he was inclined to feel that Hitler's voracious appetite had been whetted by his recent gains. Lincoln MacVeagh warned the president that the shadow of Germany was creeping toward the Balkans, and that fear had become the order of the day everywhere. Claude Bowers continued his reporting of German and Italian atrocities in Spain. John Cudahy described the Fuhrer as intent on building not a ramshackle road like Napoleon once constructed, but one which would not crumble. He believed that Germany intended to have no undigested portions along the way toward its eastward goal. Hitler's program, wrote Josephus Daniels, envisaged control of all territory from Berlin to Baghdad. Joseph Davies was of the opinion that the Fuhrer had crossed the Rubicon and could not stop. Germany was guided by a will for conquest, he observed, not a will for peace. Dictators ride bicycles, he concluded, and are unable to stand still. George Messersmith, assistant secretary of state, was certain that Germany would continue to expand, and he claimed that even the Monroe Doctrine was as much an irritant to the present German government as was the presence of the Czechoslovak state. Breckinridge Long's report to the president of observations he made while touring South America tended to support Messersmith's claims during these immediate post-Munich months. In Brazil, Long told Roosevelt, the whole German population of that nation was part of an organized propaganda network; and in Argentina too, Italy and Germany were sending agents to organize their nationality groups for political activities.

In a speech delivered on October 26, 1938, Franklin Roosevelt made clear his personal interpretation of the real meaning of Munich. Peace by fear, he began, could have no higher or more enduring quality than peace by the sword. The recurrent sanctification of sheer force does not mean peace, he admonished. Americans must be prepared to meet with success any application of force against the

United States. It is evident that the president shared the views of his diplomats. The critical point of encounter was fast approaching. He wrote Herbert Pell saying that his British friends must begin to fish or cut bait, and that the dictator threat from Europe was now much closer to the United States.

The international scene after Munich was marked by the triumph of German blitzkrieg aggression. The seizure of Czechoslovakia confirmed Franklin Roosevelt's prophetic understanding of Adolf Hitler's ultimate ambitions. FDR announced during a press conference on March 31, 1939, that the Fuhrer's policy was not limited to bringing contiguous German people into the Reich. There appeared to be no apparent limit to Germany's aims, said Roosevelt. German domination, he explained, could be expected to extend not only to the small nations of Europe, but to other continents. He expressed the general fear that the German nation was attempting to attain world dominance.

The struggle for empire began formally in September 1939, as German forces crushed Poland. Denmark, Norway, Belgium, Luxemburg, the Netherlands, and France fell in rapid succession. Great Britain stood alone, the last of Europe's Western democracies, confronting a triumphant German war machine. The dire assessments of diplomatic observers such as Ambassador John Winant in London portrayed a beleaguered ally whose future existence seemed to be in grave doubt. FDR's frustration in his efforts to provide a means to halt a presumed invincible Axis war machine surfaced in a brief conversation with Henry Morgenthau. The secretary of the treasury recounted that Roosevelt had told him, "If you have to decide along the lines that will not get us into war You decide, but if there is any decision which you think might get us into war, come and see me about it." Morgenthau added in his diary, "He left me with the distinct feeling that he might want to make decisions which might get us into war. I was terribly disappointed and evidently showed it."

Roosevelt's perspective concerning the ultimate ambitions of Hitler was not limited to Europe. Reports that agents of the Axis nations were active in several Latin American countries became more numerous throughout these years. Claude Bowers, then ambassador to Chile, warned that the German population in that country was militantly Nazi. Roosevelt urged Bowers to send him all information of a disquieting character, adding that German agents in many of the Latin American countries would undertake immediate activities with a view of overthrowing existing governments. Edwin Wilson, minister to Uruguay, reported an increase in Nazi activities in that nation with serious possibilities for the future. A memorandum from the chief of naval operations alerted the White House to the possibility of fifth column activities in all the Latin American countries. Argentina, Brazil, Chile, Uruguay, Ecuador, and Costa Rica were considered to have the most numerous espionage groups, and urgent action was suggested in the latter two nations to halt fascist influence. Cornelius Vanderbilt, after a trip through Mexico and the Central and South American countries, told the president that Hitler's agents were preparing for active intervention in Colombia, Costa Rica, and Mexico.

What were Franklin Roosevelt's personal views concerning the fascist threat to the United States? During a press conference on April 18, 1940, Roosevelt offered the following psychological appraisal on the Fuhrer. What would you do, he asked, if your name happened to be Hitler? Victorious Hitlers, he answered, would want to extend their power. Napoleon and Alexander did not think in terms of world domination at first; the thing tended to grow, he said. If the Fuhrer were to achieve control over Europe, why should he wish to leave an entire continent, North, Central, and South America, alone? World domination would be an enticing objective to the mass Hitler mind, asserted Roosevelt. The theme of the compulsive conqueror was reiterated later before an audience of newsmen. Hitler would say to himself, assumed the president, "I have got a third of the world and I have fixed up relations with another third of the world, the Far East. Why should I stop? How about this American third?" Speaking to an American Youth Congress one month later, the chief executive asked his listeners to imagine themselves as victorious Hitlers. Would you go back and paint pictures as some say the Fuhrer will do, he asked them? He may do it, mused Roosevelt, or he might do as other successful conquerors have done and strive for world domination.

The second conviction accepted by Roosevelt was that Germany's planned conquest of the United States would come by invasion and bombing from strategic contiguous territories which would gradually fall under its control either by military occupation or economic blackmail. His geography lessons were numerous and explicit. He urged listeners on many occasions to look at a map and check the proximity of Greenland, Alaska, Canada, Costa Rica, Colombia, Mexico, Venezuela, Brazil, Bermuda, and the West Indies. He replied to those who

had accepted Hitler's pledge that he had no intention of invading America by saying simply that it brought back memories and recollections. Why should we accept assurances that we are immune, he asked? Such assurances had been given previously to other nations. Americans, Roosevelt emphasized, must begin to think about the prospects of war in relation to the United States.

Economic blackmail of the Latin American nations by a victorious Germany, in Franklin Roosevelt's opinion, might also enable that country to prepare for an eventual attack on the United States. Argentina, he speculated, would be told by the Germania Corporation that it could not sell its cattle, mutton, or sheep anywhere except through the Germania Corporation. Similar coerced arrangements would be made with other small countries. Political domination would follow closely on the heels of economic subjection. Roosevelt believed that an actual invasion of America might not be necessary once economic dominance had been attained by Germany. He described imposed economic isolation as the "helpless nightmare of a people without freedom—the nightmare of a people lodged in prison, handcuffed, hungry, and fed through the bars from day-to-day by the contemptuous, unpitying masters of other continents." The advance of Hitlerism had to be checked forcibly or else the Western Hemisphere soon would be within range of Germany's weapons of destruction. Some people, FDR charged, mistakenly believe that we are not attacked until bombs drop in Chicago, New York, San Francisco, or New Orleans. Czechoslovakia began with Austria, he continued, Norway began with Denmark, and Greece began with Albania and Bulgaria. Roosevelt thought that it would be suicide to wait until Germany was in America's front yard. The Bunker Hill of tomorrow might be several thousand miles from Boston.

In numerous public addresses he conveyed a crisis mood of war expectation. He instructed a gathering of magazine and newspaper editors to give to the reading public an accurate presentation of the terrible seriousness of the Axis threat. He told his listeners that America had to quit all this silly business of "business as usual." The nation must be made to realize that if the fascist powers win, the United States would be put in a vice, a straitjacket, from which it would not recover for one hundred years. The media, Roosevelt demanded, must be frank with the public. Aid to Britain was not of itself a wise slogan, for more might be demanded of Americans who must arm themselves for the future. The seriousness of the situation he suggested, should be played up all the time. We've got to buckle down to the determination to fight the war through, said Roosevelt. Against naked force, he reasoned, the only possible defense was naked force. The United States, he emphasized, could not escape its collective responsibility for the kind of life that would emerge from the present ordeal.

The first encounter came on May 21, 1941, when the merchant ship *Robin Moor* was sunk by a German submarine. Roosevelt declared that this brutal act revealed that Germany intended to pursue a policy of intimidation, terror, and cruelty in its effort to drive U.S. commerce from the oceans. The United States destroyer *Greer* was sunk on September 4, 1941, and FDR again assessed the action bluntly, saying that the Nazi design was to acquire absolute control of the oceans surrounding the Western Hemisphere. The next step, asserted Roosevelt, would be to use the German bridgeheads in Uruguay, Argentina, Bolivia, and Colombia for a concerted attack on U.S. possessions. The sinking of the USS *Kearney* on October 17, 1941, and the loss of the *Reuben James* two weeks later served to further dramatize the chief executive's earlier warnings.

America's Bunker Hill proved to be several thousand miles away. Japan's attack on Pearl Harbor brought a united and angry nation into the war against the fascist powers. Germany and Italy, as had been expected by the president, also declared a state of war with the United States. FDR had foreseen clearly the inevitability of this conflict. A man of peace and civility, he watched the war preparations of the fascist triumvirate with agonizing concern. He urged the democratic countries to abandon the enticing, but disastrous, policies of appeasement. They responded negatively, as did the American public, until the struggle became one of self-preservation. Franklin D. Roosevelt was a prescient statesman whose vision of the terrifying apocalypse was proven tragically correct.

POSTSCRIPT

Was Franklin Roosevelt a Reluctant Internationalist?

Divine is a well-known diplomatic historian who has written numerous books on World War II diplomacy and military policies. Divine takes issue with many historians, like Herbert Feis, Basil Rauch, and playwright Robert Sherwood, who believe that Roosevelt was a true internationalist. He makes the case that Roosevelt sincerely abhorred war and held strong isolationist views until the Munich crisis in September 1938.

But Divine may have underestimated the importance of politics in the presidential election year of 1940, when both candidates were strongly courting the isolationist vote in their campaigns. Roosevelt, in particular, was running for an unprecedented third term and was fearful that any hint that American soldiers may be sent to fight overseas could cost him the election.

Kinsella disagrees with Divine's assessment of Roosevelt's policies toward Europe. Kinsella maintains that from 1933, when Hitler first came to power, through World War II, Roosevelt and his ambassadors had no illusions about "the threat posed by Adolf Hitler's Germany." Contrary to the view of Roosevelt as a reluctant internationalist, Kinsella says that Roosevelt proposed "a complete blockade of Germany [by the British Navy] on the Polish, Czecho-Slovak, Austrian, Swiss, French, Belgian, Dutch, and Danish borders" as early as 1935. Roosevelt agreed to the Munich concessions to Germany in September 1938 only because England and France were not prepared to fight Germany. But, says Kinsella, he "saw no lasting value in any agreement of appeasement with Germany."

Warren F. Kimball offers a view of Roosevelt that differs from the interpretations of Divine and Kinsella. Kimball maintains that Roosevelt was a skillful leader, yet at times he muddled through without any consistent thought patterns. However, says Kimball in *The Juggler: Franklin Roosevelt as Wartime Statesman* (Princeton University Press, 1991), by 1941 Roosevelt had a true foreign policy that centered on "the containment of Hitler, the survival of Britain, and the elimination of any need for large-scale intervention."

The bibliography on America's entrance into World War II is enormous. The best and most accessible short text and comprehensive bibliography is Justus D. Doenecke and John E. Wiltz, *From Isolation to War, 1931–1941,* 2d ed. (Harlan Davidson, 1991), a publication in *The American History Series,* which contains 30 volumes written by specialists summarizing the most recent scholarship and interpretations. The most recent and comprehensive bibliographical critical assessment is Justus D. Doenecke, "Historiography: U.S. Policy and the European War, 1939–1941," *Diplomatic History* (Fall 1995).

On the Internet . . .

Cold War Policies 1945–1991
This site presents U.S. government policies during the cold war, listed year by year from 1945 through 1991, as well as links to related sites.
http://ac.acusd.edu/history/20th/coldwar0.html

The American Presidency: Richard M. Nixon Biography
This Grolier Online page provides a detailed biography of Richard Nixon, including his early political career, the "Nixon fund," his foreign and domestic affairs policies, and his resignation from the presidency. Also included are links to Grolier Online pages on related topics, such as the Watergate affair and Spiro Agnew, and suggested sources for further reading.
http://www.grolier.com/presidents/ea/bios/37pnixo.html

Civil Rights: A Status Report
Kevin Hollaway is the author of this detailed history of black civil rights, from the discovery of the New World to the present. In his own words, "It is not my intent to complain about the present state of Black America, nor to provide excuses. My intent is [to] provide an unbiased picture of Black American history; something that is often missing from many classrooms in America."
http://www.ghgcorp.com/hollaway/civil.htm

The Vietnam War History Page
This page is a link to resources from all perspectives on the Vietnam conflicts from 1945 to 1975. It is intended to be useful to students by showing the conflict from various points of view. The page also links to many pertinent sites that house information on the war. Included are State Department documents, memoirs, articles, Vietnamese literature, and other information that would be useful to history students and scholars.
http://www.bev.net/computer/htmlhelp/vietnam.html

PART 4

The Cold War and Beyond

The United States emerged from World War II in a position of global responsibility and power, but the struggle between the United States and the Soviet Union, which began near the end of the war, dominated U.S. foreign policy for more than 40 years. Since the war, many events have brought about numerous changes, both in the United States and in the world. The 1950s ushered in growth and prosperity. The war in Vietnam still influences U.S. policymakers today. The civil rights movement resulted in many positive political and economic changes for middle-class blacks. This section includes an issue on President Nixon, who played a major role in the political life of the country and whose legacy continues to be debated, and concludes with a review of the 1980s.

■ Was the United States Responsible for the Cold War?

■ Were the 1950s America's "Happy Days"?

■ Was America's Escalation of the War in Vietnam Inevitable?

■ Did the Civil Rights Movement Improve Race Relations in the United States?

■ Will History Forgive Richard Nixon?

■ Were the 1980s a Decade of Greed?

ISSUE 12

Was the United States Responsible for the Cold War?

YES: Thomas G. Paterson, from *Meeting the Communist Threat: Truman to Reagan* (Oxford University Press, 1988)

NO: John Lewis Gaddis, from *Russia, the Soviet Union, and the United States: An Interpretive History,* 2d ed. (McGraw-Hill, 1990)

ISSUE SUMMARY

YES: Professor of history Thomas G. Paterson argues that the Truman administration exaggerated the Soviet threat after World War II because the United States had expansionist political and economic global needs.

NO: Professor of history John Lewis Gaddis argues that the power vacuum that existed in Europe at the end of World War II exaggerated and made almost inevitable a clash between the democratic, capitalist United States and the totalitarian, communist USSR.

Historians are unable to agree on exactly when the cold war began. This is because of the rocky relationship that existed between the United States and the Soviet Union since World War I. The Wilson administration became upset when the communist government declared its neutrality in the war and pulled Russia out of the allied coalition. The Russian leader V. I. Lenin resented the allied intervention in Siberia from 1918 to 1920 because he believed that the pretext for rescuing Czech troops was an excuse to undermine Russia's communist government. The relationship between the two countries improved in 1933 after President Franklin D. Roosevelt accorded diplomatic recognition to the communist government. In the late 1930s the relationship soured once again. Russia, unable to negotiate a security treaty with France, signed a nonaggression pact with Germany on August 23, 1939. This allowed Adolf Hitler to attack Poland in early September and Soviet leader Joseph Stalin to attack Finland and take over the Baltic states Latvia, Lithuania, and Estonia. In September 1939, as World War II was breaking out in Europe, the United States—like the USSR—was officially neutral. But the Roosevelt administration pushed modifications of the neutrality laws through Congress, which enabled significant amounts of economic and military assistance to be extended to England and France (until she surrendered to Germany in 1940). In one of history's great ironies, Stalin, who distrusted everyone, ignored British prime minister Winston Churchill's warnings and was caught completely off guard when Hitler occupied the Balkans and then launched his surprise attack against the Russians in June 1941. By November, lend-lease was extended to the Russians, who would receive a total of $11 billion by the end of the war.

The wartime coalition of the United States, Great Britain, and the USSR was an odd combination. Their common goal—defeat Hitler—temporarily submerged political differences. During the war the United States actually sided with Russia against Great Britain over the appropriate military strategy. Russia and the United States wanted a second front established in France.

As the military victory in Europe became clear, political differences began to crack open the alliance. A number of wartime conferences were held to coordinate military strategy; to establish political and economic international agencies, such as the United Nations, the World Bank, and the International Monetary Fund; and to plan the reestablishment of governments in Eastern and Western Europe. Differences developed over the structure of the United Nations; the composition of the Polish and other Eastern European governments; and the boundaries, reparations, and occupational questions surrounding postwar Germany.

The military situation dominated the Yalta Conference in February 1945. Since the atomic bomb had not yet been tested, the United States thought that a landed invasion of the Japanese mainland would be necessary to win the war. At this time Russia and Japan were neutral toward each other. Stalin promised that three months after the war in Europe ended he would invade Japan. In return Roosevelt promised Stalin the territories and sphere of influence Russia held in Asia prior to 1905, which she had lost in a war with Japan.

Sole possession of the atomic bomb by the United States loomed in the background as the two powers failed to settle their differences after the war. Secretary of State James Byrnes hoped that the bomb would make the Russians more "manageable" in Europe, but atomic diplomacy was never really practiced. Nor were attempts at economic coercion successful.

By 1946 the cold war had begun. In February Stalin gave a speech declaring that communism and capitalism were incompatible and that future wars were inevitable. The next month, at a commencement address with President Truman at his side, Churchill declared that an "iron curtain" had descended over Eastern Europe. In May 1946 the allies refused to send any more industrial equipment to the Russian zone in Germany.

Who started the cold war? Was it inevitable, or should one side take more of the blame? In the following selection, Thomas G. Paterson argues that the Truman administration exaggerated the Soviet threat to world peace after World War II because the United States had its own expansionist, political, and economic global needs. In the second selection, John Lewis Gaddis asserts that the power vacuum that existed in Europe at the end of World War II exaggerated ideological, political, and economic differences and made a clash between the United States and the USSR almost inevitable.

YES
Thomas G. Paterson

HARRY S TRUMAN, AMERICAN POWER, AND THE SOVIET THREAT

President Harry S Truman and his Secretary of State Dean Acheson, Henry A. Kissinger once remarked, "ushered in the most creative period in the history of American foreign policy." Presidents from Eisenhower to Reagan have exalted Truman for his decisiveness and success in launching the Truman Doctrine, the Marshall Plan, and NATO [North Atlantic Treaty Organization], and for staring the Soviets down in Berlin during those hair-trigger days of the blockade and airlift. John F. Kennedy and Lyndon B. Johnson invoked memories of Truman and the containment doctrine again and again to explain American intervention in Vietnam. Jimmy Carter has written in his memoirs that Truman had served as his model—that he studied Truman's career more than that of any other president and came to admire greatly his courage, honesty, and willingness "to be unpopular if he believed his actions were the best for the country." Some historians have gone so far as to claim that Truman saved humankind from World War III. On the other hand, he has drawn a diverse set of critics. The diplomat and analyst George F. Kennan, the journalist Walter Lippmann, the political scientist Hans Morgenthau, politicians of the left and right, like Henry A. Wallace and Robert A. Taft, and many historians have questioned Truman's penchant for his quick, simple answer, blunt, careless rhetoric, and facile analogies, his moralism that obscured the complexity of causation, his militarization of American foreign policy, his impatience with diplomacy itself, and his exaggeration of the Soviet threat....

Because of America's unusual postwar power, the Truman Administration could expand the United States sphere of influence beyond the Western Hemisphere and also intervene to protect American interests. But this begs a key question: Why did President Truman think it necessary to project American power abroad, to pursue an activist, global foreign policy unprecedented in United States history? The answer has several parts. First, Americans drew lessons from their experience in the 1930s. While indulging in their so-called "isolationism," they had watched economic depression spawn political extremism, which in turn, produced aggression and war. Never again, they vowed. No more appeasement with totalitarians, no more Munichs. "Red

Fascism" became a popular phrase to express this American idea. The message seemed evident: To prevent a reincarnation of the 1930s, the United Sates would have to use its vast power to fight economic instability abroad. Americans felt compelled to project their power, second, because they feared, in the peace-and-prosperity thinking of the time, economic doom stemming from an economic sickness abroad that might spread to the United States, and from American dependency on overseas supplies of raw materials. To aid Europeans and other people would not only help them, but also sustain a high American standard of living and gain political friends, as in the case of Italy, where American foreign aid and advice influenced national elections and brought defeat to the left. The American fear of postwar shortages of petroleum also encouraged the Truman Administration to penetrate Middle Eastern oil in a major way. In Saudi Arabia, for example, Americans built and operated the strategically important Dhahran Airport and dominated that nation's oil resources.

Another reason why Truman projected American power so boldly derived from new strategic thinking. Because of the advent of the air age, travel across the world was shortened in time. Strategists spoke of the shrinkage of the globe. Places once deemed beyond American curiosity or interest now loomed important. Airplanes could travel great distances to deliver bombs. Powerful as it was, then, the United States also appeared vulnerable, especially to air attack. As General Carl A. Spaatz emphasized: "As top dog, America becomes target No. 1." He went on to argue that fast aircraft left no warning time for the United States. "The Pearl Harbor of a future war might well be Chicago, or Detroit, or even

Washington." To prevent such an occurrence, American leaders worked to acquire overseas bases in both the Pacific and Atlantic, thereby denying a potential enemy an attack route to the Western Hemisphere. Forward bases would also permit the United States to conduct offensive operations more effectively. The American strategic frontier had to be pushed outward. Thus the United States took the former Japanese-controlled Pacific islands of the Carolines, Marshalls, and Marianas, maintained garrisons in Germany and Japan, and sent military missions to Iran, Turkey, Greece, Saudi Arabia, China, and to fourteen Latin American states. The joint Chiefs of Staff and Department of State lists of desired foreign bases, and of sites where air transit rights were sought, included such far-flung spots as Algeria, India, French Indochina, New Zealand, Iceland, and the Azores. When asked where the American Navy would float, Navy Secretary James Forrestal replied: "Wherever there is a sea." Today we may take the presumption of a global American presence for granted, but in Truman's day it was new, even radical thinking, especially after the "isolationist" 1930s.

These several explanations for American globalism suggest that the United States would have been an expansionist power whether or not the obstructionist Soviets were lurking about. That is, America's own needs—ideological, political, economic, strategic—encouraged such a projection of power. As the influential National Security Council Paper No. 68 (NSC-68) noted in April 1950, the "overall policy" of the United States was "designed to foster a world environment in which the American system can survive and flourish." This policy "we would probably pursue even if there were no Soviet threat."

Americans, of course, did perceive a Soviet threat. Thus we turn to yet another explanation for the United States' dramatic extension of power early in the Cold War: to contain the Soviets. The Soviets unsettled Americans in so many ways. Their harsh Communist dogma and propagandistic slogans were not only monotonous; they also seemed threatening because of their call for world revolution and for the demise of capitalism. In the United Nations the Soviets cast vetoes and even on occasion walked out of the organization. At international conferences their *"nyets"* stung American ears. When they negotiated, the Soviets annoyed their interlocuters by repeating the same point over and over again, delaying meetings, or abruptly shifting positions. Truman labeled them "pigheaded," and Dean Acheson thought them so coarse and insulting that he once allowed that they were not "housebroken."

The Soviet Union, moreover, had territorial ambitions, grabbing parts of Poland, Rumania, and Finland, and demanding parts of Turkey. In Eastern Europe, with their Red Army positioned to intimidate, the Soviets quickly manhandled the Poles and Rumanians. Communists in 1947 and 1948 seized power in Hungary and Czechoslovakia. Some Americans predicted that the Soviet military would roll across Western Europe. In general, Truman officials pictured the Soviet Union as an implacable foe to an open world, an opportunistic nation that would probe for weak spots, exploit economic misery, snuff out individual freedom, and thwart self-determination. Americans thought the worst, some claiming that a Soviet-inspired international conspiracy insured perennial hostility and a creeping aggression aimed at American interests. To Truman and his advisers, the Soviets stood as the world's bully, and the very existence of this menacing bear necessitated an activist American foreign policy and an exertion of American power as a "counterforce."

But Truman officials exaggerated the Soviet threat, imagining an adversary that never measured up to the galloping monster so often depicted by alarmist Americans. Even if the Soviets intended to dominate the world, or just Western Europe, they lacked the capabilities to do so. The Soviets had no foreign aid to dispense; outside Russia Communist parties were minorities; the Soviet economy was seriously crippled by the war; and the Soviet military suffered significant weaknesses. The Soviets lacked a modern navy, a strategic air force, the atomic bomb, and air defenses. Their wrecked economy could not support or supply an army in the field for very long, and their technology was antiquated. Their ground forces lacked motorized transportation, adequate equipment, and troop morale. A Soviet *blitzkrieg* invasion of Western Europe had little chance of success and would have proven suicidal for the Soviets, for even if they managed to gain temporary control of Western Europe by a military thrust, they could not strike the United States. So they would have to assume defensive positions and await crushing American attacks, probably including atomic bombings of Soviet Russia itself—plans for which existed.

Other evidence also suggests that a Soviet military threat to Western Europe was more myth than reality. The Soviet Union demobilized its forces after the war, dropping to about 2.9 million personnel in 1948. Many of its

175 divisions were under-strength, and large numbers of them were engaged in occupation duties, resisting challenges to Soviet authority in Eastern Europe. American intelligence sources reported as well that the Soviets could not count on troops of the occupied countries, which were quite unreliable, if not rebellious. At most, the Soviets had 700,000 to 800,000 troops available for an attack against the West. To resist such an attack, the West had about 800,000 troops, or approximate parity. For these reasons, top American leaders did not expect a Soviet onslaught against Western Europe. They and their intelligence sources emphasized Soviet military and economic weaknesses, not strengths, Soviet hesitancy, not boldness.

Why then did Americans so fear the Soviets? Why did the Central Intelligence Agency, the Joint Chiefs of Staff, and the President exaggerate the Soviet threat? The first explanation is that their intelligence estimates were just that —estimates. The American intelligence community was still in a state of infancy, hardly the well-developed system it would become in the 1950s and 1960s. So Americans lacked complete assurance that their figures on Soviet force deployment or armaments were accurate or close to the mark. When leaders do not know, they tend to assume the worst of an adversary's intentions and capabilities, or to think that the Soviets might miscalculate, sparking a war they did not want. In a chaotic world, the conception of a single, inexorably aggressive adversary also brought a comforting sense of knowing and consistency.

Truman officials also exaggerated the Soviet threat in order "to extricate the United States from commitments and restraints that were no longer considered desirable." For example, they loudly chastised the Soviets for violating the Yalta agreements; yet Truman and his advisers knew the Yalta provisions were at best vague and open to differing interpretations. But, more, they purposefully misrepresented the Yalta agreement on the vital question of the composition of the Polish government. In so doing, they hoped to decrease the high degree of Communist participation that the Yalta conferees had insured when they stated that the new Polish regime would be formed by reorganizing the provisional Lublin (Communist) government. Through charges of Soviet malfeasance Washington sought to justify its own retreat from Yalta, such as its abandonment of the $20 billion reparations figure for Germany (half of which was supposed to go to the Soviet Union).

Another reason for the exaggeration: Truman liked things in black and white, as his aide Clark Clifford noted. Nuances, ambiguities, and counterevidence were often discounted to satisfy the President's preference for the simpler answer or his pre-conceived notions of Soviet aggressiveness. In mid-1946, for example, the Joint Chiefs of Staff deleted from a report to Truman a section that stressed Soviet weaknesses. American leaders also exaggerated the Soviet threat because it was useful in galvanizing and unifying American public opinion for an abandonment of recent and still lingering "isolationism" and support for an expansive foreign policy. Kennan quoted a colleague as saying that "if it [Soviet threat] had never existed, we would have had to invent it, to create a sense of urgency we need to bring us to the point of decisive action." The military particularly overplayed the Soviet threat in order to persuade Congress to endorse larger defense budgets. This happened in 1948–49 with the creation of the North Atlantic Treaty Organization. NATO was established not to halt a Soviet military attack, because none was anticipated, but to give Europeans a psychological boost—a "will to resist." American officials believed that the European Recovery Program would falter unless there was a "sense of security" to buttress it. They nurtured apprehension, too, that some European nations might lean toward neutralism unless they were brought together under a security umbrella. NATO also seemed essential to help members resist internal subversion. The exaggerated, popular view that NATO was formed to deter a Soviet invasion of Western Europe by conventional forces stems, in part, from Truman's faulty recollection in his published memoirs.

Still another explanation for why Americans exaggerated the Soviet threat is found in their attention since the Bolshevik Revolution of 1917 to the utopian Communist goal of world revolution, confusing goals with actual behavior. Thus Americans believed that the sinister Soviets and their Communist allies would exploit postwar economic, social, and political disorder, not through a direct military thrust, but rather through covert subversion. The recovery of Germany and Japan became necessary, then, to deny the Communists political opportunities to thwart American plans for the integration of these former enemies into an American system of trade and defense. And because economic instability troubled so much of Eurasia, Communist gains through subversion might deny the United States strategic raw materials.

Why dwell on this question of the American exaggeration of the Soviet threat? Because it over-simplified international realities by under-estimating lo-cal conditions that might thwart Soviet/Communist successes and by over-estimating the Soviet ability to act. Because it encouraged the Soviets to fear encirclement and to enlarge their military establishment, thereby contributing to a dangerous weapons race. Because it led to indiscriminate globalism. Because it put a damper on diplomacy; American officials were hesitant to negotiate with an opponent variously described as malevolent, deceitful, and inhuman. They especially did not warm to negotiations when some critics were ready to cry that diplomacy, which could produce compromises, was evidence in itself of softness toward Communism.

Exaggeration of the threat also led Americans to misinterpret events and in so doing to prompt the Soviets to make decisions contrary to American wishes. For example, the Soviet presence in Eastern Europe, once considered a simple question of the Soviets' building an iron curtain or bloc after the war, is now seen by historians in more complex terms. The Soviets did not seem to have a master plan for the region and followed different policies in different countries. Poland and Rumania were subjugated right away; Yugoslavia, on the other hand, was an independent Communist state led by Josip Tito, who broke dramatically with Stalin in 1948; Hungary conducted elections in the fall of 1945 (the Communists got only 17 percent of the vote) and did not suffer a Communist coup until 1947; in Czechoslovakia, free elections in May 1946 produced a non-Communist government that functioned until 1948; Finland, although under Soviet scrutiny, affirmed its independence. The Soviets did not have a firm grip on Eastern Europe before 1948—a prime reason why many American leaders believed the Soviets harbored weaknesses.

American policies were designed to roll the Soviets back. The United States reconstruction loan policy, encouragement of dissident groups, and appeal for free elections alarmed Moscow, contributing to a Soviet push to secure the area. The issue of free elections illustrates the point. Such a call was consistent with cherished American principle. But in the context of Eastern Europe and the Cold War, problems arose. First, Americans conspicuously followed a double standard which foreigners noted time and again; that is, if the principle of free elections really mattered, why not hold such elections in the United States' sphere of influence in Latin America, where an unsavory lot of dictators ruled? Second, free elections would have produced victories for anti-Soviet groups. Such results could only unsettle the Soviets and invite them to intervene to protect their interests in neighboring states—just as the United States had intervened in Cuba and Mexico in the twentieth century when hostile groups assumed power. In Hungary, for example, it was the non-Communist leader Ferenc Nagy who delayed elections in late 1946 because he knew the Communist Party would lose badly, thereby possibly triggering a repressive Soviet response. And, third, the United States had so little influence in Eastern Europe that it had no way of insuring free elections—no way of backing up its demands with power.

Walter Lippmann, among others, thought that the United States should tame its meddling in the region and make the best out of a bad arrangement of power. "I do believe," he said in 1947, "we shall have to recognize the principle of boundaries of spheres of influence which either side will not cross and have

to proceed on the old principle that a good fence makes good neighbors." Kennan shared this view, as did one State Department official who argued that the United State was incapable of becoming a successful watchdog in Eastern Europe. American "barkings, growlings, snappings, and occasional bitings," Cloyce K. Huston prophesized, would only irritate the Soviets without reducing their power. Better still, argued some analysts, if the United States tempered its ventures into European affairs, then the Soviets, surely less alarmed, might tolerate more openness. But the United States did not stay out. Americans tried to project their power into a region where they had little chance of succeeding, but had substantial opportunity to irritate and alarm the always suspicious Soviets. In this way, it has been suggested, the United States itself helped pull down the iron curtain.

Another example of the exaggeration of the Soviet threat at work is found in the Truman Doctrine of 1947. Greece was beset by civil war, and the British could no longer fund a war against Communist-led insurgents who had a considerable non-Communist following. On March 12, Truman enunciated a universal doctrine: It "must be the policy of the United States to support free peoples who are resisting attempted subjugation by armed minorities or by outside pressures." Although he never mentioned the Soviet Union by name, his juxtaposition of words like "democratic" and "totalitarian" and his references to Eastern Europe made the menace to Greece appear to be the Soviets. But there was and is no evidence of Soviet involvement in the Greek civil war. In fact, the Soviets had urged both the Greek Communists and their allies the Yugoslavs to stop the fighting for fear that the conflict would draw the United States into the Mediterranean. And the Greek Communists were strong nationalists. The United States nonetheless intervened in a major way in Greek affairs, becoming responsible for right-wing repression and a military establishment that plagued Greek politics through much of its postwar history. As for Turkey, official Washington did not expect the Soviet Union to strike militarily against that bordering nation. The Soviets were too weak in 1947 to undertake such a major operation, and they were asking for joint control of the Dardanelles largely for defense, for security. Then why did the President, in the Truman Doctrine speech, suggest that Turkey was imminently threatened? American strategists worried that Russia's long-term objective was the subjugation of its neighbor. But they also wished to exploit an opportunity to enhance the American military position in the Mediterranean region and in a state bordering the Soviet Union. The Greek crisis and the Truman Doctrine speech provided an appropriate environment to build up an American military presence in the Eastern Mediterranean for use against the Soviets should the unwanted war ever come.

Truman's alarmist language further fixed the mistaken idea in the American mind that the Soviets were unrelenting aggressors intent upon undermining peace, and that the United States, almost alone, had to meet them everywhere. Truman's exaggerations and his commitment to the containment doctrine did not go unchallenged. Secretary Marshall himself was startled by the President's muscular anti-communist rhetoric, and he questioned the wisdom of overstating the case. The Soviet specialist Llewellyn Thompson urged "caution" in swinging too far toward "outright opposition to Russia...." Walter Lippmann, in reacting to both Truman's speech and George F. Kennan's now famous "Mr. 'X' " article in the July 1947 issue of the journal *Foreign Affairs*, labeled containment a "strategic monstrosity," because it made no distinctions between important or vital and not-so-important or peripheral areas. Because American power was not omnipresent, Lippmann further argued, the "policy can be implemented only by recruiting, subsidizing and supporting a heterogeneous array of satellites, clients, dependents and puppets." He also criticized the containment doctrine for placing more emphasis on confrontation than on diplomacy.

Truman himself came to see that there were dangers in stating imprecise, universal doctrines. He became boxed by his own rhetoric. When Mao Zedong's forces claimed victory in 1949 over Jiang's regime, conservative Republicans, angry Democrats, and various McCarthyites pilloried the President for letting China "fall." China lost itself, he retorted. But his critics pressed the point: if containment was to be applied everywhere, as the President had said in the Truman Doctrine, why not China? Truman appeared inconsistent, when, in fact, in the case of China, he was ultimately prudent in cutting American losses where the United States proved incapable of reaching its goals. Unable to disarm his detractors on this issue, Truman stood vulnerable in the early 1950s to political demagogues who fueled McCarthyism. The long-term consequences in this example have been grave. Democrats believed they could never lose "another China"—never permit Communists or Marxists, whether or not linked to Moscow, to assume power abroad. President John F. Kennedy later said, for example, that he could not withdraw from Vietnam because that might be perceived as "another China" and spark charges that he was soft on Communism. America, in fact, could not bring itself to open diplomatic relations with the People's Republic of China until 1979.

Jiang's collapse joined the Soviet explosion of an atomic bomb, the formation of the German Democratic Republic (East Germany), and the Sino-Soviet Friendship Treaty to arouse American feeling in late 1949 and early 1950 that the Soviet threat had dramatically escalated. Although Kennan told his State Department colleagues that such feeling was "largely of our own making" rather than an accurate accounting of Soviet actions, the composers of NSC-68 preferred to dwell on a more dangerous Soviet menace in extreme rhetoric not usually found in a secret report. But because the April 1950 document was aimed at President Truman, we can certainly understand why its language was hyperbolic. The fanatical and militant Soviets, concluded NSC-68, were seeking to impose "absolute authority over the rest of the world." America had to frustrate the global "design" of the "evil men" of the Kremlin, who were unrelentingly bent on "piecemeal aggression" against the "free world" through military force, infiltration, and intimidation. The report called for a huge American and allied military build-up and nuclear arms development.

NSC-68, most scholars agree, was a flawed, even amateurish document. It assumed a Communist monolith that did not exist, drew alarmist conclusions based upon vague and inaccurate information about Soviet capabilities, made grand, unsubstantiated claims about Soviet intentions, glossed over the presence of many non-democratic countries in the "free world," and recommended against negotiations with Moscow at the very time the Soviets were advancing toward a policy of "peaceful co-existence." One State Department expert on the Soviet Union, Charles E. Bohlen, although generally happy with the report's conclusions, faulted NSC-68 for assuming a Soviet plot for world conquest—for "oversimplifying the problem." No, he advised, the Soviets sought foremostly to maintain their regime and to extend it abroad "to the degree that is possible without serious risk to the internal regime." In short, there were limits to Soviet behavior. But few were listening to such cautionary voices. NSC-68 became American dogma, especially when the outbreak of the Korean War in June of 1950 sanctified it as a prophetic "we told you so."

The story of Truman's foreign policy is basically an accounting of how the United States, because of its own expansionism and exaggeration of the Soviet threat, became a global power. Truman projected American power after the Second World War to rehabilitate Western Europe, secure new allies, guarantee strategic and economic links, and block Communist or Soviet influence. He firmly implanted the image of the Soviets as relentless, worldwide transgressors with whom it is futile to negotiate. Through his exaggeration of the Soviet threat, Truman made it very likely that the United States would continue to practice global interventionism years after he left the White House.

NO

John Lewis Gaddis

THE ORIGINS OF THE COLD WAR: 1945–1953

It is, of course, a truism that coalitions tend not to survive their enemies' defeat. Certainly during World War II most observers of the international scene had expected differences eventually to arise among the victors. The hope had been, though, that a sufficiently strong framework of common interests—whether the United Nations or some mutually acceptable agreement on spheres of influence—would develop that could keep these differences within reasonable limits. This did not happen. Although both sides sought security, although neither side wanted a new war, disagreements over how to achieve those goals proved too great to overcome. With a rapidity that dismayed policymakers in both Washington and Moscow, allies shortly before united against the Axis found themselves in a confrontation with each other that would determine the shape of the postwar era. Russian-American relations, once a problem of rarely more than peripheral concern for the two countries involved, now became an object of rapt attention and anxiety for the entire world.

*   *   *

It is no simple matter to explain how national leaders in the United States and the Soviet Union came to hold such dissimilar concepts of postwar security. There did exist, in the history of the two countries' encounters with one another, an ample basis for mutual distrust. But there were also strong motives for cooperation, not the least of which was that, had they been able to act in concert, Russians and Americans might have achieved something close to absolute security in an insecure world. Their failure to do so may be attributed, ultimately, to irreconcilable differences in four critical areas: perceptions of history, ideology, technology, and personality.

Clearly the divergent historical experiences of the two countries conditioned their respective views of how best to attain security. The Russians tended to think of security in terms of space—not a surprising attitude, considering the frequency with which their country had been invaded, or the way in which they had used distance to defeat their adversaries. That such a concept might be outmoded in an age of atomic weapons and long-range bombers appears not to have occurred to Stalin; Hitler's defeat brought no alteration in his determination to control as much territory along the periphery of the Soviet Union as possible. "He regarded as sure only whatever he held in his fist," the Yugoslav Communist Milovan Djilas has written. "Everything beyond the control of his police was a potential enemy."

Americans, on the other hand, tended to see security in institutional terms: conditioned by their own atypical historical experience, they assumed that if representative governments could be established as widely as possible, together with a collective security organization capable of resolving differences between them, peace would be assured. That such governments might not always harbor peaceful intentions toward their neighbors, that the United Nations, in the absence of great power agreement, might lack the means of settling disputes, occurred to only a few informed observers. The general public, upon whose support foreign policy ultimately depended, tended to accept Cordell Hull's vision of a postwar world in which "there will no longer be need for spheres of influence, for alliances, for balance of power, or any of the special arrangements through which, in the unhappy past, the nations sought to safeguard their security or to promote their interests."

There was, of course, room for compromising these conflicting viewpoints. Neither the United States nor its British ally had been prepared wholly to abandon spheres of influence as a means of achieving their own postwar security; both accepted the premise that the USSR was entitled to have friendly countries along its borders. The great diffi-

culty was that, unlike the expansion of American and British influence into Western Europe and the Mediterranean, the Soviet Union's gains took place without the approval of most of the governments and most of the people in the areas involved. The Anglo-Americans simply did not find it necessary, in the same measure as did the Russians, to ensure their own security by depriving people within their sphere of influence of the right to self-determination. Given Western convictions that only the diffusion of democratic institutions could guarantee peace, given Hitler's all-too-vivid precedent, Moscow's imposition of influence in Eastern Europe seemed ominous, whatever its motives. Stalin found himself able to implement his vision of security only by appearing to violate that of the West. The result was to create for the Soviet Union new sources of hostility and, ultimately, insecurity in the world.

Ideological differences constituted a second source of antagonism. Stalin had deliberately downplayed the Soviet commitment to communism during the war, even to the point of abolishing the Comintern in 1943. Some Americans concluded that the Russians had abandoned that ideology altogether, if on no other grounds than that a nation that fought Germans so effectively could not be all bad. The European communist movement remained very much the instrument of Soviet policy, however, and the Russians used it to facilitate their projection of influence into Eastern Europe. This development raised fears in the West that Soviet collaboration against the Axis had been nothing but a marriage of convenience and that, victory having been achieved, the Kremlin was now embarking upon a renewed crusade for world revolution.

This was, it now appears, a mistaken view. Stalin had always placed the security of the Soviet state above the interests of international communism; it had been the former, not the latter, that had motivated his expansion into Eastern Europe. Far from encouraging communists outside the Soviet Union to seize power, Stalin initially advised restraint, especially in his dealings with such movements in France, Italy, Greece, and China. But the Soviet leader's caution was not all that clear in the West. Faced with the sudden intrusion of Russian power into Europe, faced with a revival of anticapitalist rhetoric among communists throughout the world, faced with painful evidence from the recent past of what happened when dictators' rhetoric was not taken seriously, observers in both Western Europe and the United States jumped to the conclusion that Stalin, like Hitler, had insatiable ambitions, and would not stop until contained.

Technological differences created a third source of tension. The United States alone emerged from World War II with an industrial plant superior to what it had possessed before that conflict started; the Soviet Union, in turn, had come out of the war with its land ravaged, much of its industry destroyed, and some twenty million of its citizens dead. The resulting disparity of power caused some Americans to exaggerate their ability to influence events in the rest of the world; it simultaneously produced in the Russians deep feelings of inferiority and vulnerability.

This problem manifested itself most obviously with regard to reconstruction. Stalin had hoped to repair war damage with the help of Lend-Lease and a postwar loan from the United States; his conviction that Americans would soon be facing a postwar depression led him to believe—drawing on clear Leninist principles—that Washington would have no choice but to provide such aid as a means of generating foreign markets for surplus products. His surprise was great when the United States passed up the economic benefits it would have derived from granting a loan in favor of the political concessions it hoped to obtain by withholding it. Nor would Washington allow the use of Lend-Lease for reconstruction; to compound the offense, the Truman administration also cut off, in 1946, the flow of reparations from the American zone in Germany. Whether more generous policies on these matters would have produced better relations with the Soviet Union is impossible to prove—certainly the Russians were never in such need of aid as to be willing to make major political concessions in order to get it. There is no doubt, though, that they bitterly resented their exclusion from these "fruits" of Western technology.

Another "fruit" of Western technology that impressed the Russians was, of course, the atomic bomb. Although Soviet leaders carefully avoided signs of concern about this new weapon, they did secretly accelerate their own bomb development project while simultaneously calling for the abolition of all such weapons of mass destruction. After much debate within the government, the United States, in the summer of 1946, proposed the Baruch Plan, which would have transferred control of all fissionable materials to the United Nations. In fact, however, neither the Russians nor the Americans had sufficient faith in the world organization to entrust their security completely to it. Washington at no point was willing to surrender its bombs until the control system had gone into effect, while Moscow was unwilling to accept the inspection provisions which would allow the plan to operate. Both sides had concluded by 1947 that they would find greater security in an arms race than in an unproven system of international control.

Finally, accidents of personality made it more difficult than it might otherwise have been to achieve a mutually agreeable settlement. The Russians perceived in the transition from Roosevelt to Truman an abrupt shift from an attitude of cooperation to one of confrontation. "The policy pursued by the US ruling circles after the death of Franklin D. Roosevelt," the official history of Soviet foreign policy asserts, "amounted to renunciation of dependable and mutually beneficial cooperation with the Soviet Union, a cooperation that was so effective . . . in the period of joint struggle against the nazi aggressors." In fact, though, Roosevelt's policy had been firmer than Stalin realized; Truman's was not as uncompromising as his rhetoric suggested. What was different was style: where Roosevelt had sought to woo the Soviet leader by meeting his demands wherever possible, the new chief executive, like a good poker player, tried to deal from positions of rhetorical, if not actual, strength. His tough talk was designed to facilitate, not impede, negotiations—any appearance of weakness, he thought, would only encourage the Russians to ask for more.

What Truman failed to take into account was the possibility that Stalin might also be bluffing. Given the history of Western intervention to crush Bolshevism, given the Soviet Union's ruined economy and weakened population, and given the atomic bomb's unexpected confirmation of American technological su-periority, it seems likely that the aging Soviet dictator was as frightened of the West as the West was of him. Truman's tough rhetoric, together with Hiroshima's example, may well have reinforced Stalin's conviction that if *he* showed any signs of weakness, all would be lost. Both leaders had learned too well the lesson of the 1930s: that appeasement never pays. Prospects for an amicable resolution of differences suffered accordingly.

There was nothing in this set of circumstances that made the Cold War inevitable—few things ever are inevitable in history. But a situation such as existed in Europe in 1945, with two great powers separated only by a power vacuum, seemed almost predestined to produce hostility, whether either side willed it or not. As a result, the United States, the Soviet Union, and much of the rest of the world as well would have to suffer through that prolonged period of insecurity that observers at the time, and historians since, have called the "Cold War."

* * *

The evolution of United States policy toward the Soviet Union between 1945 and 1947 can be seen as a three-stage process of relating national interests to national capabilities. From V-J Day through early 1946, there existed genuine confusion in Washington as to both Soviet intentions and appropriate methods for dealing with them. Coordination between power and policy was, as a result, minimal. By the spring of 1946, a consensus had developed favoring resistance to further Soviet expansion, but little had been done to determine what resources would be necessary to accomplish that goal or to differentiate between areas of primary and secondary concern. It was not until

1947 that there began to emerge an approach to the Soviet Union that bore some reasonable relationship to American capabilities for projecting influence in the world.

There appeared to be no lack of power available to the United States for the purpose of ordering the postwar environment as it saw fit, but the task of transforming technological superiority into political influence proved frustratingly difficult. Secretary of State James F. Byrnes had hoped to trade reconstruction assistance and a commitment to the international control of atomic energy for Soviet concessions on such outstanding issues as implementation of the Yalta Declaration on Liberated Europe, peace treaties with former German satellites, and, ultimately, a final resolution of the German question itself. But the Russians maintained a posture of ostentatious unconcern about the atomic bomb, nor would they yield on significant issues to obtain reconstruction assistance. Congressional skepticism about Moscow's intentions ensured that any loan would carry a political price far beyond what the Russians would willingly pay, while public opinion pushed Truman into a decision to seek United Nations control of atomic energy before Byrnes had made any attempt to extract Soviet concessions in return. Economic and technological superiority thus won the United States surprisingly few practical benefits in its early postwar dealings with the USSR.

In Washington, moreover, there still existed a substantial number of officials who viewed Soviet hostility as the product of misunderstandings and who expected that, with restraint on both sides, a mutually satisfactory resolution of differences might still occur. It is significant that as late as November,

1945, a State Department representative could rebuke the Joint Chiefs of Staff for confidentially suggesting that the wartime alliance might not survive victory. "We must always bear in mind," a Department memorandum noted the following month, "that because of the differences between the economic and political systems [of the United States and the Soviet Union], the conduct of our relations requires more patience and diligence than with other countries." Despite his tough rhetoric, President Truman shared this view. Disagreements with the Russians were to be expected once the common bond of military necessity had been removed, he told his advisers; in time, they would disappear because "Stalin was a fine man who wanted to do the right thing."

But events made this position increasingly difficult to sustain. The Russians remained adamant in their determination to exclude Western influence from Eastern Europe and the Balkans, while a continued Soviet presence in Iran and Manchuria raised fears that Moscow might try to impose control over those territories as well. Russian interest in the eastern Mediterranean seemed to be growing, with demands for trusteeships over former Italian colonies, boundary rectifications at Turkey's expense, and a revision of the Montreux Convention governing passage through the Dardanelles. And in February, 1946, news of Soviet atomic espionage became public for the first time with the revelation that the Canadian government had arrested a group of Russian agents for trying to steal information about the bomb. That same month, Stalin in his first major postwar foreign policy speech stressed the incompatibility between communism and capitalism, implying that future wars were inevitable until the world economic system was restructured along Soviet lines.

It was at this point that there arrived at the State Department a dispatch from George F. Kennan, now *chargé d'affaires* at the American embassy in Moscow, which did much to clarify official thinking regarding Soviet behavior. Russian hostility toward the West, Kennan argued, stemmed chiefly from the internal necessities of the Stalinist regime: the Soviet dictator required a hostile outside world in order to justify his own autocratic rule. Marxism provided Soviet leaders with

> justification for their instinctive fear of the outside world, for the dictatorship without which they did not know how to rule, for cruelties they did not dare not to inflict, for sacrifices they felt bound to demand.... Today they cannot dispense with it. It is the fig leaf of their moral and intellectual respectability.

It followed that Stalin was, by nature, incapable of being reassured. "Nothing short of complete disarmament, delivery of our air and naval forces to Russia and resigning of the powers of government to American Communists would even dent this problem," Kennan noted in a subsequent dispatch, "and even then Moscow would smell a trap and would continue to harbor the most baleful misgivings." The solution, Kennan suggested, was to strengthen Western institutions in order to render them invulnerable to the Soviet challenge while simultaneously awaiting the eventual mellowing of the Soviet regime.

There was little in Kennan's analysis that he and other career Soviet experts had not been saying for some time. What was new was Washington's receptivity to the message, a condition brought about both by frustration over Soviet behav-

ior and by growing public and Congressional resistance to further concessions. In contrast to its earlier optimism about relations with Moscow, the State Department now endorsed Kennan's analysis as "the most probable explanation of present Soviet policies and attitudes." The United States, it concluded, should demonstrate to the Kremlin, "in the first instance by diplomatic means and in the last analysis by military force if necessary that the present course of its foreign policy can only lead to disaster for the Soviet Union."

The spring and summer of 1946 did see a noticeable toughening of United States policy toward the Soviet Union. In early March, Truman lent public sanction to Winston Churchill's strongly anti-Soviet "iron curtain" speech by appearing on the platform with him at Fulton, Missouri. That same month, Secretary of State Byrnes insisted on placing the issue of Iran before the United Nations, even after the Russians had agreed to withdraw their troops from that country. The termination of German reparations shipments came in May; three months later, Byrnes publicly committed the United States to support German rehabilitation, with or without the Russians. In July, Truman endorsed the continued presence of American troops in southern Korea on the grounds that that country constituted "an ideological battleground upon which our whole success in Asia may depend." Soviet pressure on Turkey for bases produced a decision in August to maintain an American naval force indefinitely in the eastern Mediterranean. In September, White House aide Clark Clifford submitted a report to the president, prepared after consultation with top military and diplomatic advisers, arguing that "this government should be prepared ... to resist vigorously and successfully any efforts of the U.S.S.R. to expand into areas vital to American security."

But these policies were decided upon without precise assessments as to whether the means existed to carry them out. The atomic bomb was of little use for such purposes, given the strong inhibitions American officials felt about brandishing their new weapon in peacetime and given the limited number of bombs and properly equipped bombers available, if war came. Nor could the administration hold out the prospect of economic aid as a means of inducing more cooperative Soviet behavior, in the face of continued Congressional reluctance to appropriate funds for such purposes. Such conventional military power as the United States possessed was rapidly melting away under the pressures of demobilization, and although most Americans supported firmer policies toward the Soviet Union, the election of an economy-minded, Republican-controlled Congress in November suggested that few were prepared to assume the burdens, in the form of high taxes and military manpower levels, such policies would require.

Shortly thereafter a severe economic crisis, the product of remaining wartime dislocations and an unusually harsh winter, hit Western Europe. This development caused the British to announce their intention, in February, 1947, of terminating economic and military aid to Greece and Turkey, countries that had, up to that point, been regarded as within London's sphere of responsibility. It also raised the longer-range but even more frightening prospect that economic conditions in Western Europe generally might deteriorate to the point that communist parties there could seize power through coups or

even free elections. Suddenly the whole European balance of power, which the United States had gone to war to restore, seemed once again in peril.

This situation, which appeared so to threaten European stability, was one the Russians had done little if anything to instigate; it was rather the product primarily of internal conditions within the countries involved. But there was little doubt of Moscow's ability to exploit the European economic crisis if nothing was done to alleviate it. And action was taken, with such energy and dispatch that the fifteen weeks between late February and early June, 1947, have come to be regarded as a great moment in the history of American diplomacy, a rare instance in which "the government of the United States operat[ed] at its very finest, efficiently and effectively."

Such plaudits may be too generous. Certainly the language Truman used to justify aid to Greece and Turkey ("at the present moment in world history nearly every nation must choose between alternative ways of life.... I believe that it must be the policy of the United States to support free peoples who are resisting attempted subjugation by armed minorities or by outside pressures") represented a projection of rhetoric far beyond either the administration's intentions or capabilities. Whatever its usefulness in prying funds out of a parsimonious Congress, the sweeping language of the "Truman Doctrine" would cause problems later on as the president and his foreign policy advisers sought to clarify distinctions between vital and peripheral interests in the world. That such distinctions were important became apparent with the announcement in June, 1947, of the Marshall Plan, an ambitious initiative that reflected, far more than did the Truman

Doctrine, the careful calibration of ends to means characteristic of the administration's policy during this period.

The European Recovery Program, to use its official title, proposed spending some $17 billion for economic assistance to the non-communist nations of Europe over the next four years. (Aid was offered to the Soviet Union and its East European satellites as well, but with the expectation, which proved to be correct, that Moscow would turn it down.) It was a plan directed, not against Soviet military attack, a contingency United States officials considered remote, but against the economic malaise that had sapped self-confidence among European allies, rendering them vulnerable to internal communist takeovers. It involved no direct military commitments; rather, its architects assumed, much as had advocates of the "arsenal of democracy" concept before World War II, that the United States could most efficiently help restore the balance of power in Europe by contributing its technology and raw materials, but not its manpower. It represented a deliberate decision to focus American energies on the recovery of Europe at the expense of commitments elsewhere: it is significant that the spring of 1947 also saw the Truman administration move toward liquidating its remaining responsibilities in China and Korea. What took place in Washington during the famous "fifteen weeks," then, was not so much a proliferation of commitments as a reordering of priorities, executed with a sharp awareness of what the United States would have to accept in the world and what, given limited resources, it could realistically expect to change.

Unfortunately, rhetoric again obscured the point, this time by way of a mysterious article, entitled "The Sources of Soviet Conduct," which appeared in the July, 1947, issue of *Foreign Affairs.* Attributed only to a "Mr. X," it advanced the notion that

> the main element of any United States policy toward the Soviet Union must be that of a long-term, patient but firm and vigilant containment of Russian expansive tendencies.... Soviet pressure against the free institutions of the Western world is something that can be contained by the adroit and vigilant application of counter-force at a series of constantly shifting geographical and political points, corresponding to the shifts and maneuvers of Soviet policy.

Then, as now, nothing remained secret for very long, and word soon leaked out that "Mr. X" had been none other than Kennan, who had recently become head of the State Department's new Policy Planning Staff. This information gave the "X" article something of the character of an official document, and it quickly came to be seen as the definitive expression of administration policy toward the Soviet Union.

In fact, Kennan had not intended his article as a comprehensive prescription for future action; it was, rather, an elaboration of the analysis of Soviet behavior he had submitted in his February, 1946, telegram to the State Department. Such policy recommendations as Kennan did include reflected only in the most approximate and incomplete way the range of his thinking on Soviet-American relations. The article implied an automatic commitment to resist Russian expansionism wherever it occurred; there was in it little sense of the administration's preoccupation with limited means and of the consequent need to distinguish between primary and secondary interests. Nor did the piece make it clear that economic rather than military methods were to be employed as the chief instrument of containment. The safest generalization that can be made about the "X" article is that, like the Truman Doctrine, it was an outstanding demonstration of the obfuscatory potential of imprecise prose. It was not an accurate description of the policies the United States was, at that moment, in the process of implementing.

Kennan provided a much clearer explanation of what he meant by "containment" in a secret review of the world situation prepared for Secretary of State George C. Marshall in November, 1947. Soviet efforts to fill power vacuums left by German and Japanese defeats had largely been halted, Kennan argued, but this accomplishment had dangerously strained American resources: "The program of aid to Europe which we are now proposing to undertake will probably be the last major effort of this nature which our people could, or should, make.... It is clearly unwise for us to continue the attempt to carry alone, or largely singlehanded, the opposition to Soviet expansion." Further dispersal of resources could be avoided only by identifying clearly those parts of the world upon whose defense American security depended. Aside from the Western Hemisphere, Kennan's list included only noncommunist Europe, the Middle East, and Japan. In China there was little the West could do, although there were as well "definite limitations on both the military and economic capabilities of the Russians in that area." Since Korea was "not of decisive strategic importance to us, our main task is to extricate ourselves without too great a loss of prestige." All in all, Kennan concluded, "our best answer is to strengthen in every way local forces of resistance, and persuade others to bear a greater part of the burden of opposing communism."

"Containment," then, involved no indiscriminate projection of commitments around the world: it was, instead, a policy precise in its identification of American interests, specific in its assessment of threats to those interests, frugal in its calculation of means required to ward off those threats, vague only in its public presentation. But this very vagueness would, in time, corrupt the concept, for where gaps between policy and rhetoric exist, it is often easier to bring the former into line with the latter than the other way around. The eventual consequence would be the promulgation of policies under the rubric of "containment" far removed from what that doctrine had been originally intended to mean.

* * *

Despite its limited character, the vigor of the American response to Soviet postwar probes apparently caught Stalin by surprise. His response was to try to strengthen further the security of his own regime; first by increasing safeguards against Western influences inside the Soviet Union; second, by tightening control over Russia's East European satellites; and finally by working to ensure central direction of the international communist movement. By a perverse kind of logic, each of these moves backfired, as did a much earlier Soviet initiative whose existence only came to light at this point —the establishment, in the United States during the 1930s, of a major espionage network directed from Moscow. The result, in each of these cases, was to produce consequences that only made it more difficult for Stalin to obtain the kind of security he sought.

Soviet leaders had always faced a dilemma regarding contacts with the West. Such associations might carry substantial benefits—certainly this had been true of collaboration with Great Britain and the United States during World War II. But there were also costs, not the least of which was the possibility that prolonged exposure to Western ideas and institutions might erode the still vulnerable base of the Soviet regime. It is an indication of the seriousness with which Stalin viewed this problem that he shipped hundreds of thousands of returning prisoners-of-war off to labor camps in 1945, much to the horror of Americans who had forcibly repatriated many of them at the Russians' request. By 1947, Moscow's campaign against Western influence had extended to literature, music, history, economics, and even genetics. As a result, Soviet prestige suffered throughout the world; the effect of these policies on science, and, in turn, on the advancement of Russian military capabilities, can only be guessed at.

Even more striking in its impact on the West, though, was Stalin's harsh effort to consolidate his control over Eastern Europe. Subservience to Moscow, not ideological uniformity, had been the chief Soviet priority in that area until 1947, but in June of that year the Russians imposed a communist-dominated government in Hungary, a country in which relatively free elections had been held in the fall of 1945. "I think it's an outrage," President Truman told a press conference on June 5. "The Hungarian situation is a terrible one." In February, 1948, the Communist Party of Czechoslovakia overthrew the duly-constituted government of that country —an event that produced the death, by

either murder or suicide, of the popular Czech foreign minister, Jan Masaryk. It would be difficult to exaggerate the impact of this development in the West, where guilty consciences still existed over what had been done to the Czechs at Munich ten years before. One immediate effect was to ensure Congressional passage of the Marshall Plan; another was to provoke Britain, France, and the Benelux countries into forming the Western Union, the first step toward a joint defensive alliance among the non-communist nations of Europe. There also followed the stimulation of something approaching a war scare in the United States, an administration request for Universal Military Training and the reinstitution of the draft, and a public condemnation by Truman of the Soviet Union as the "one nation [that] has not only refused to cooperate in the establishment of a just and honorable peace, but—even worse—has actively sought to prevent it."

Meanwhile, attempts to resolve the question of divided Germany had produced no results, despite protracted and tedious negotiations. In February, 1948, the three Western occupying powers, plus the Benelux countries, met in London and decided to move toward formation of an independent West German state. Stalin's response, after initial hesitation, was to impose a blockade on land access to Berlin, which the World War II settlement had left a hundred miles inside the Soviet zone. The Berlin crisis brought the United States and the Soviet Union as close to war as they would come during the early postwar years. Truman was determined that Western forces would stay in the beleaguered city, however untenable their military position there, and to reinforce this policy he ostentatiously transferred to British bases three squadrons of B-29 bombers. No atomic bombs accompanied these planes, nor were they even equipped to carry them. But this visible reminder of American nuclear superiority may well have deterred the Russians from interfering with air access to Berlin, and through this means the United States and its allies were able to keep their sectors of the city supplied for almost a year. Stalin finally agreed to lift the blockade in May, 1949, but not before repeating the dubious distinction he had achieved in the Russo-Finnish War a decade earlier: of appearing to be brutal and incompetent at the same time.

The Berlin blockade had two important consequences, both of which were detrimental from the Soviet point of view. It provided the impetus necessary to transform the Western Union into the North Atlantic Treaty Organization, a defensive alliance linking the United States, Canada, and ten Western European nations, established in April, 1949. Simultaneously, the blockade lessened prospects for a settlement of the German problem in collaboration with the Russians; the result was to accelerate implementation of the London program, a goal accomplished with the formation, in September, 1949, of the Federal Republic of Germany.

POSTSCRIPT

Was the United States Responsible for the Cold War?

Paterson's selection contains most of the arguments advanced by the revisionist critics of America's cold war policies: Truman's diplomatic style was blunt and impetuous, and he tended to oversimplify complex issues into black and white alternatives.

Paterson believes that the Truman administration exaggerated the Russian threat to the balance of power in Europe. It is not clear whether this was a deliberate miscalculation or whether the Truman administration misperceived the motive behind the "iron curtain" that Russia drew around Eastern Europe. The author maintains that Stalin was more concerned with Russia's security needs than with world conquest.

Gaddis is much less critical than Paterson of America's postwar policy. He believes that the United States and Russia would inevitably clash once the common enemy—Hitler—was defeated because the two countries had fundamentally different political and economic systems. Gaddis maintains that for nearly two years there was confusion and uncertainty in the United States' foreign policy in Europe. Truman, he says, did not reverse Roosevelt's policy. His manner was more blunt and, consequently, he showed less patience in dealing with Stalin.

Gaddis acknowledges revisionist criticisms that the Americans misperceived Stalin's attempts to control Eastern Europe. The Soviet premier used expansionist rhetoric when he was primarily concerned about protecting Russia from another invasion. By early 1946 both sides were pursuing policies that would lead to an impasse.

Students who wish to study the cold war in greater detail should consult *Containment: Documents on American Policy and Strategy, 1945–1950* edited by Thomas H. Etzold and John Lewis Gaddis (Columbia University Press, 1978), which remains the best collection of the major policy documents. Another sophisticated but comprehensive work is Melvyn P. Leffler, *A Preponderance of Power: National Security, the Truman Administration, and the Cold War* (Stanford University Press, 1992). The two best readers to excerpt the various viewpoints on the cold war are Thomas G. Paterson and Robert J. McMahon, eds., *The Origins of the Cold War*, 3rd ed. (D. C. Heath, 1991) and Melvyn P. Leffler and David S. Painter, eds., *Origins of the Cold War: An International History* (Routledge, 1994). Finally, David Reynolds has edited a series of essays in *The Origins of the Cold War: International Perspectives* (Yale University Press, 1994).

ISSUE 13

Were the 1950s America's "Happy Days"?

YES: Melvyn Dubofsky and Athan Theoharis, from *Imperial Democracy: The United States Since 1945*, 2d ed. (Prentice Hall, 1988)

NO: Douglas T. Miller and Marion Nowak, from *The Fifties: The Way We Really Were* (Doubleday, 1977)

ISSUE SUMMARY

YES: Professor of history and sociology Melvyn Dubofsky and professor of history Athan Theoharis argue that throughout the 1950s, the U.S. economy dominated much of the globe and created a period of unprecedented growth and prosperity for the percentage of the American population that made it into the middle class.

NO: Professor of history Douglas T. Miller and journalist Marion Nowak argue that the nostalgia craze, which re-creates the 1950s as a sweet, simple, golden age of harmony, masks the fact that the decade was an era of conformity in which Americans feared the bomb, communists, crime, and the loss of a national purpose.

Since the mid-1970s Americans have used the 1950s as the standard by which all future successes and failures are measured. Cable television replays old shows espousing the family values that Americans most admire. But what were the 1950s really like? Was the period truly America's "Happy Days"?

Most people agree that America in the 1950s reflected the title of economist John Kenneth Gailbraith's book *The Affluent Society* (Houghton Mifflin, 1958). Because the United States was physically untouched during World War II, it was instrumental in rebuilding the economies of the major noncommunist countries in Europe and Asia through the use of the Marshall Plan, Point Four Program, and other foreign aid programs.

At home the expected postwar recession and depression never occurred. Controlling inflation while stabilizing employment became the primary concern of the economists. During the war American workers had built up over $140 billion in savings. Hungry for consumer goods they had been unable to acquire from 1942 through the middle of 1945, Americans went on a massive consumer buying spree—one that has continued to the present day.

There were, however, some disturbing economic trends in the 1950s. Poverty was still widespread among many nonwhite groups and the displaced coal miners in Appalachia. Large corporations were buying up smaller ones, and individual farms were coming under the control of agribusinesses. Income inequality also increased: In 1949 the top 1 percent of the population owned 19 percent of the nation's wealth; by 1960 they owned 33 percent.

If the rich got richer, so did millions of other Americans. As Michael W. Schuger points out in his article "The 1950s: A Retrospective View," *Nebraska History* (Spring 1996), "Average family income, which was $3,000 in 1947, increased dramatically to $5,400 in 1959. The gross national product increased from $318 billion in 1950 to $440 billion in 1960. Between 1945 and 1960 the real earning power of the average wage earner increased by 22 percent."

In spite of this pleasant lifestyle, America became an anxiety-ridden society in the 1950s. World War II ended in the defeat of fascism, but a cold war developed against America's former ally the Soviet Union, which seemed bent on spreading communism not only throughout Eastern Europe but also across the entire world. The United States extended economic and military assistance to Greece and Turkey in 1947 and two years later formed the first peacetime alliance in history—the North Atlantic Treaty Organization—in order to contain the spread of communism. Although Western Europe stood fast, leaks sprang up in other parts of the world.

Crime, corruption, and communism seemed rampant in the 1950s. The news was spread by television. In 1946 there were only 7 television sets in the entire country; by 1960 they numbered over 50 million. Politicians filled the void on daytime television with an endless parade of hearings. Juvenile delinquency, it was argued, resulted from a moral breakdown in the home and community. Comic books and rock and roll were held to be the culprits, and the city council of Jersey City solved the problem by banning rock and roll at all school dances. Meanwhile, Senator Joseph McCarthy continued his search for communists in the government but overreached himself when he bullied high-level military officials in his senatorial investigation of the army in 1954. Eisenhower's powerful chief of staff, Sherman Adams, resigned amidst allegations that he received gifts from a contractor. The government panicked when the Russians launched the earth-orbiting *Sputnik I* satellite into space in October 1957. Could Ivan read better than Johnny? Had America lost its moral leadership and prestige in the eyes of the world, as two government reports indicated in 1960?

In the first of the following selections, Melvyn Dubofsky and Athan Theoharis argue that throughout the 1950s, the United States dominated much of the world's economy. At home the country experienced a period of unprecedented growth and prosperity for nearly two-thirds of the population, which made it into the middle class. In the second selection, Douglas T. Miller and Marion Nowak assert that the decade was an era dominated by the need to conform and by feelings of fear about the bomb, communists, crime, and the loss of a national purpose.

YES

Melvyn Dubofsky and
Athan Theoharis

IMPERIAL DEMOCRACY: THE UNITED STATES SINCE 1945

ECONOMIC GROWTH AND A CONSUMER SOCIETY

Throughout the 1950s the United States economy dominated much of the globe. Though less dependent on foreign trade for economic growth than most other industrial nations, the relatively small percentages of United States domestic production and capital that entered international trade had an enormous impact on the economies of smaller, less productive nations. Despite the fact that America's gross national product expanded relatively more slowly than other rapidly industrializing societies, the United States' productive base was so immense that between 1949 and 1960 absolute real GNP increased from $206 billion to over $500 billion, a rise of nearly 150 percent. Such economic power, especially in relation to weaker, less industrialized societies, allowed the United States to set the terms of trade. Thus American corporations during the 1950s purchased raw materials cheaply and sold manufactured goods dearly. As America grew wealthier, raw material-producing nations in Latin America, Africa, and Asia became relatively poorer. . . .

The New Growth Industries

During the 1950s some of the old standbys of industrial America—railroads, coal mining, textiles, and shoe manufacturing—continued a decline that had begun in the 1920s. Railroad freight traffic fell steadily before the inroads of highway trucking, and passengers discarded long-distance trains in favor of more rapid air or cheaper bus transportation. By the end of the 1960s nearly the entire rail network in the Northeast, including the giant Penn-Central, had gone bankrupt. Coal found itself unable to compete with oil, natural gas, nuclear power, and water power; the nearly 600,000 miners employed at the end of World War II had fallen to about 100,000 by 1970. Cotton and woolen manufacture succumbed to synthetic fibers and domestic production to cheaper foreign manufactures. The shoe industry wrote an equally sorry chapter. Endicott-Johnson, the world's largest shoe manufacturer, had

From Melvyn Dubofsky and Athan Theoharis, *Imperial Democracy: The United States Since 1945*, 2d ed. (Prentice Hall, 1988). Copyright © 1988 by Prentice Hall, Inc., Upper Saddle River, NJ. Reprinted by permission. Notes omitted.

employed about 28,000 production workers in its New York Southern Tier factories in the late 1940s; by 1970 the production force had dipped below 4,000, the company began to dismantle its mills, and it even purchased shoes from Rumania for sale in its American retail outlets. Such instances of economic decline caused permanent depression in many New England towns and Appalachian coal patches. Again in the 1950s, as in the 1920s, economic sores festered on a generally healthy economic body.

If parts of New England and Appalachia declined economically, other regions of the nation prospered as never before. Wherever chemicals, business machines, electronics, and computers were manufactured the economy boomed, for these were the postwar growth industries par excellence. They were the new industries fit for survival in a "new society." Their economic growth based on technological and scientific advances, electronic-chemical firms stressed research and development programs (almost half of which were financed by the federal government), hired thousands of new graduates from the nation's universities, and served as the employers for a technocratic-scientific elite.

E. I. DuPont de Nemours & Co., Dow, and Monsanto prospered by manufacturing the synthetic goods that increasingly transformed the United States into a plastic society. Women wore their nylon stockings, people cooked on their Teflon pots and pans, men donned Dacron suits and Orlon shirts, and cars rolled on synthetic tires. Electronics, the child of wartime technological innovations, transistorized the postwar world. As tiny transistors replaced bulky tubes, teenagers walked everywhere holding the ubiquitous portable radio, and home-

bodies carried small TVs from room to room and house to patio. It was a society in which stereophonic sound replaced high fidelity phonographs only to be displaced in turn by quadraphonic sound. The electronics industry promised to turn every home into a private concert hall; indeed, some new houses were built with sound systems wired into every room. And electric eyes now opened and shut garage doors.

Meantime, automation and its associated business machines produced still greater profits and affected the economy more substantially than plastics and electronics. What Ford and General Electric symbolized in the 1920s, IBM and Xerox personified in post-World War II America. Ever since the industrial revolution, machinery had been replacing human labor in manufacturing. But where humans once operated the new machines, in the postwar era of automation such companies as IBM produced machines that controlled themselves as well as other machines. Automation, based on the same simple feedback principle that operated home thermostats, controlled steel strip mills, auto assembly lines, and entire petrochemical complexes. Computers, the next stage in the process of automation and first introduced commercially in 1950, had the ability to remember, sort materials, and make decisions; computers could also write poetry, compose music, play chess, and simulate strategy in a football game. So varied were the computer's uses that they were utilized by hotel chains, insurance companies, banks, airlines, and even universities (by the 1960s college students were identified by their IBM numbers) to simplify increasingly complex paper transactions. Where automation once threatened only blue-collar industrial workers, it now endangered the job security of millions of white-collar clerks. Even politicians, eager to predict beforehand the results of elections, worshipped at the shrine of the high-speed mainframe computer. . . .

One reason for the success of the new growth industries was their close link to the Department of Defense, postwar America's largest single business contractor. The Pentagon supplied a lavish market for electronic and chemical manufacturers, as its deadly nuclear missiles with their elaborate guidance systems relied on synthetics, transistorized modules, and advanced computers. Even the more mundane hardware used by infantry, artillery, and nonnuclear aircraft depended heavily on electronic components and computerized guidance. NASA too provided an economic bonanza for the world of electronics. Without transistors, computers, and chemical fuels, there would have been no flight in space, no man on the moon. Between government contracts and consumer demand for household appliances (household use of electricity tripled in the 1950s), the growth industries prospered enormously.

American agriculture changed as well in the postwar era. Farming became a big business. Agricultural productivity rose more rapidly than demand for foodstuffs for most of the first two postwar decades, forcing millions of smaller farmers off the land; and large farmers prospered as a result of government subsidy programs and their own efficiency. Because production rose so rapidly, prices for agricultural goods declined, and profits could be made only by lowering unit costs of production through intensive application of fertilizers, use of costly new farm machinery, and introduction of sophisticated managerial techniques. Smaller farms simply lacked the resources and the capital to purchase fertilizer, acquire new machinery, and hire costly managerial experts. They also lacked enough land to make the use of expensive new machinery profitable or to join the soil bank, a program intended to promote soil conservation by paying farmers cash subsidies to let some of their land lie fallow. In other words, because most federal farm programs and subsidies were directly proportional to farm size and productivity, large farmers received proportionately more benefits than small farmers. The beneficiaries of federal largesse, the big farmers also possessed the land, capital, and knowledge necessary to grow food and fibers most efficiently. Consequently the percentage of owner-operated farms rose, and the size of the typical farm increased substantially. Cotton production shifted away from the South, where it remained profitable only on the extremely large plantation, to the immense corporate, irrigated farms of Texas, Arizona, and southern California. Farming in such prosperous agricultural states as California, Arizona, and Florida was justly labeled "agribusiness." In some cases industrial corporations, Tenneco among others, purchased large farms. . . .

Affluence and Consumption

The stability of the American political and economic system as well as the absence of working-class discontent and militancy flowed from the successful creation of a mass consumer society. The car in every garage and chicken in every pot which Hoover and the Republicans had promised Americans in 1928 arrived in the 1950s. And now it also included beefsteaks, color television, stereophonic sound, and suburban split-levels.

Mass consumption depended on constantly rising real wage levels, a condition the United States economy sustained between 1945 and 1960. By 1956 the real income of the average American was more than 50 percent greater than it had been in 1929, and by 1960 it was 35 percent higher than it had been in the last year of World War II.

How typical Americans spent their increased earnings was determined as much by external factors as by intrinsic, real personal needs. Indeed, the larger the income an individual earned the more choice he or she had in its disposal. As growing numbers of citizens satisfied their need for food and shelter, the manufacturers of attractive but nonessential goods competed lustily for the consumer's dollar.

To sell the autos, refrigerators, dishwashers, stereo sets, and other appliances that rolled off production lines, manufacturers resorted to Madison Avenue and intensive advertising. Between 1946 and 1957 expenditures on advertising increased by almost 300 percent, rising to over $10 billion annually. Not only did the money devoted to advertising rise significantly, but the lords of Madison Avenue also developed more sophisticated selling tactics. Successful advertising was complicated when consumers had to select from among breakfast cereals and cars that differed neither in price nor utility and also had to be convinced to buy products never before manufactured. Employing all the tools of normal (and abnormal) psychology, advertisers alerted consumers to the psychic benefits of larger cars, sweeter-smelling underarms, striped toothpaste, and Marlboro—the man's cigarette. Brighter teeth, Madison Avenue implied, guaranteed every wallflower a desirable husband, and the cigarillo won every man a buxom and accommodating female. Able to allocate money and talent to the one-minute television spot, advertisers bombarded viewers with irresistible commercials. Madison Avenue sales campaigns got such good results in the marketplace that in time many candidates for public office substituted the one-minute television spot for the half-hour platform speech. By the 1960s, Madison Avenue sold presidents as well as Pontiacs, congressmen as well as Cadillacs.

More than advertising was required to create the postwar consumer society. Regardless of the reality of rising wages, millions of citizens still lacked income sufficient to satisfy their demand for goods. A 1950 Census Bureau survey of over 7,000 families, for example, showed that 60 percent having earnings of $4,000 or less spent more than they earned. Even those workers whose incomes exceeded their current expenses seldom had a margin of savings adequate to sustain the cash purchase of such costly durables as autos and large home appliances. Only by borrowing money on the assumption that higher future earnings would render repayment painless could most citizens satisfy their desire for cars and dishwashers.

As advertising stimulated the demand for consumer goods, the nation's financial institutions financed their purchase. Between 1946 and 1957, private indebtedness increased by 360 percent—in contrast, total public debt rose by only 11 percent and the federal debt actually declined. More remarkable still was the rise in consumer installment indebtedness; the estimated annual installment credit outstanding soared from just over $4 billion in 1946 to over $34 billion in 1957. Automobile installment credit alone rose from under $1 billion to in excess of $15 billion. The propensity to buy now and pay later made the cash registers ring. Detroit produced over five million new cars in 1949 and in the peak year of 1955 sold nearly eight million autos, a record unsurpassed until the late 1960s.

For those individuals whose earnings rose annually, consumer credit and installment buying provided a relatively easy means to achieve rapid material affluence. But for those Americans whose income failed to rise, or rose only haltingly, installment buying became more an economic trap than an avenue to comfort. Unable to save sufficient cash to underwrite their purchases, these unfortunate consumers frequently failed to earn enough to pay the interest as well as the principal on their installment contract. In some cases, credit costs effectively increased the original purchase price by one third or more.

The consumption craze took many shapes in the 1950s. Such economists as Walt W. Rostow suggested that when men and women in America's "high mass consumption society" satisfied their desire for cars and appliances, they invested surplus income in babies. Whatever the precise cause no one could doubt that a population explosion took place from 1945 through the 1950s. Medical science and improved nutrition lengthened life spans, and the multiple (three or more) child household became commonplace. The public philosophy of the 1950s, as proclaimed by psychologists, TV comedians, preachers, and politicians, sanctified the home and woman's place in it. The ideal female married young and well, bore a large brood, and remained home to create the perfect environment for keeping the American family together. The sanctification of the family and the ide-

alization of the woman as mother and homemaker further promoted the growth of a consumer society. Larger families required bigger houses with more appliances to simplify "mom's" work and increased purchases to provide for the children. Before long many one-car families would become two-, three-, and in rare instances even four-car households.

If affluence enabled many Americans to enjoy unsurpassed material comforts, millions of citizens still struggled to make ends meet. If new recruits joined the "jet set" and flew to vacations in Rio, Biarritz, and Monaco, many workers, like the Bronx couple that *New York Times* reporter A. H. Raskin investigated, who lived half an hour by subway from Times Square, saw "less of Great White Way than the average farmer from Pumpkin Corners." John K. Galbraith lamented in *The Affluent Society* the ubiquity of public squalor amidst America's opulence and hinted at the persistence of poverty. Nonetheless, regardless of how unequally and inequitably the fruits of affluence were distributed, many of those Americans who did not share fully still felt themselves more comfortable in the 1950s than they had been in the 1930s and more fortunate than non-Americans. As Raskin's Bronx worker remarked: "We're a lot better off than we would be anywhere else in the world. We may not get everything we want, but at least we can choose what to do with our money. In other countries they don't even have a choice. No matter how bad things are, we're better off than they are."

The Triumph of the Suburbs

The emergence of an affluent mass consumer society saw the reassertion of a pattern of residential mobility and settlement that had been retarded by depression and war. In the 1950s, as also had happened in the 1920s, millions of citizens deserted the cities for the suburbs. Except in the South and Southwest where urban population continued to grow as a result of the annexation of adjacent land, the bulk of metropolitan population growth occurred in the suburbs. By 1960 in most northern metropolises, suburban residents outnumbered central city occupants, and as people fled the urban core, so, too, did businesses, trades, and professions. The "Miracle Mile" in Manhasset on Long Island's North Shore brought Fifth Avenue to the suburbs, just as similar suburban shopping centers elsewhere attracted downtown's most prestigious retailers to new locations with ample parking space and affluent consumers.

Suburban development stimulated a housing boom of unprecedented dimensions. As of 1960, one fourth of all the housing in the nation had been constructed in the previous decade, during which annual new-housing starts regularly exceeded the growth of new households. In the 1950s, for the first time in history, more Americans owned their homes, albeit usually with heavy mortgages, than rented dwelling space.

The reasons for this exodus to suburbia might have remained constant from the 1920s to the 1950s; after 1945, however, the opportunity to flee the city had expanded significantly. The desire for a private home with a lawn and garden in a suburban arcadia had long been an integral aspect of popular culture. The economic costs and occupational impracticality of suburban life, however, had put it beyond the reach of most Americans. All this changed in the postwar world, as federal credit and highway policies, technological innovations, and a mass

consumer society reshaped metropolitan America.

In the postwar world, as automobile ownership became general, Americans had been liberated from dependence on mass public transit. The possession of a private car snapped the link that hitherto had connected the individual's home to his place of work via public transit. Through federal and state highway programs funded by fuel taxes, limited access highways were constructed that linked new suburbs and older central cities. The prospect of smooth, unimpeded traffic flow on safe, modern highways and in private cars led passengers to abandon subways, trolleys, and buses and to move from the city to the suburbs. Americans were now free to reside wherever their incomes allowed, and suburbia was also opening up to a wider range of incomes.

Federal policies enlarged the suburban housing market by providing generous mortgage loans to World War II veterans and by insuring the mortgages marketed by private lending agencies. The self-amortizing mortgage, whereby the homeowner paid back his original loan at a fixed monthly rate (comparable to rent) over a 20- to 30-year-term, became the common means to home ownership. Federal tax policy also stimulated suburban expansion, for citizens received a generous income tax deduction for the interest charges and real estate taxes paid on their homes. The availability of long-term credit and the inducement of tax advantages drew well-to-do middle-class Americans to suburbia. Working-class citizens needed a further inducement, the chance to purchase a home within their means. Here the firm of Arthur Levitt and Sons provided one solution, doing for the housing market what Ford had done for autos. Just as Ford offered a basic car in a single color at a low price, Levitt sold a standardized dwelling unit in one color —white—at a price within the reach of thousands of working-class Americans. His original "little boxes" constructed in the first Levittown in central Long Island soon had counterparts in New Jersey and Pennsylvania.

Suburbia in general and Levittown in particular occasioned a new image of American society, one consonant with the concept of a mass consumer public. Suburbia, in the words of social critic and planner Lewis Mumford, offered the prospect of

> a multitude of uniform, identifiable houses, lined up inflexibly, at uniform distances, on uniform roads, in a treeless communal waste, inhabited by people of the same class, the same income, the same age group, witnessing the same television performances, eating the same tasteless pre-fabricated foods, from the same freezers, conforming in every outward and inward respect to a common mold.

In the "little boxes made of ticky tacky," about which Pete Seeger sang, lived William F. Whyte's "organization men" who in their haste to adjust smoothly to their fellow junior executives became as undifferentiated as the houses in which they dwelled.

Critics of suburbia mounted a contradictory attack against the emerging character of national life. On the one hand, they charged suburban residents with uniformity, dullness, and unthinking accommodation to neighborhood mores. On the other hand, they indicted suburbanites, as did John Keats in *The Crack in the Picture Window*, for alcoholism, adultery (wife-swapping was said to be the fa-

vorite indoor suburban sport), and juvenile delinquency. Whatever the substance of the criticism, it seemed to miss the mark, for suburban growth proceeded unabated.

In fact most social criticism portrayed a fictional suburbia, not its reality. By the late 1950s American suburbs contained as many differences as similarities; there was no single ideal-type suburban community. Communities of upwardly mobile young executives who preferred accommodation to conflict, uniformity to individualism, such as William F. Whyte located in Chicago's environs, did exist. So, too, did communities of wealthy senior executives and rentiers, whose incomes and security enabled them to experiment with architecture and engage in eccentric behavior. At the other end of the suburban spectrum, one could find working-class developments whose residents had moved from the city but had scarcely altered their life style; they still voted Democratic, preferred baseball to ballet, and the company of relatives to that of neighbors. Even the allegedly undifferentiated, standardized world of Levittown contained, as the sociologist Herbert Gans discovered, a universe of strikingly individualized homes. Levittowners wasted no time in applying personal touches and preferences to the standardized homes and creating a society in which, according to Gans, they felt very much at home and comfortable....

MASS CULTURE AND ITS CRITICS

The affluence of the 1950s and 1960s laid the basis for what came to be known as "mass culture." Never before had so much music, drama, and literature been accessible to so many people as a result of fundamental changes in the presentation of entertainment and enlightenment. Television, the long-playing record, improved sound-reproduction equipment, and paperback books brought a plethora of cultural forms within reach of the great mass of Americans.

Once again, as had happened during the 1920s, Americans celebrated their exceptional prosperity. A new hedonism symbolized by oversized, overpowered cars crammed with options and adorned outside with two-tone color patterns, vinyl tops, and fins captivated consumers. Americans relished a culture of consume, enjoy, and dispose. We were, in the words of the historian David Potter, "people of plenty."

Not everyone, to be sure, joined in the American celebration. Some critics raised questions about the quality of life. Whereas once left-wing intellectuals had lamented the ubiquity of poverty and exploitation, they now bewailed a consumer society in which shoppers had become as indistinguishable from each other as the merchandise they purchased.

A few critical voices cried out in the wilderness. The industrial sociologist William F. Whyte portrayed in scholarly detail the culture of the prototypical success story of the 1950s, the rising young corporate executive, the hero of best-selling novelist Sloan Wilson's *The Man in the Gray Flannel Suit*. Whyte showed these young executives as insecure, status-driven people who lived transitorily in suburban developments housing only their own kind, and as "organization men" who molded their personalities to suit the corporate image. The radical and idiosyncratic scholar C. Wright Mills discerned a bleak future in his 1951 book, *White Collar*. He described a society of men and women who worked without autonomy or direction, who strived only

for status, and who lived as dependent beings, not free citizens. In *White Collar*, one glimpsed an American mass potentially susceptible to producing fascism, as their Italian and German likes had in the 1920s and 1930s.

David Riesman, the premier critic of mass society, early on diagnosed the new American disease in *The Lonely Crowd* (1950). Americans once, he wrote, had been an inner-directed people, men and women who could distinguish right from wrong, who could chart their own directions and goals in life. Now, Americans had become an other-directed people, who lacked their own internal moral compasses. The great mass of postwar Americans lost themselves in a "lonely crowd" to which they looked for values and personal decisions. The independent democratic citizen had become a cypher in the clutches on an anonymous mass society.

Such tendencies toward mass society caused a minority of Americans to worry that the nation had lost its sense of purpose amidst a flood of consumer goods. They wondered if mass society could rise above the level of a car dealer's showroom.

But the great mass of Americans shared no such worries. Those who could consumed as never before, and those who could not aspired to do the same. . . .

The Culture of Consensus

The hard edges of the Cold War and the tensions of McCarthyism had been softened in the United Sates of the late 1950s by the smiles, platitudes, and tranquility of the Eisenhower era. It was a time to consume, to achieve, and to celebrate.

Intellectuals and writers who for much of the twentieth century had been at war with a materialistic, bourgeois America now also joined the celebration. *Partisan Review*, a literary intellectual journal which had served at the end of the 1930s as a voice for non-Stalinist Marxists, in the 1950s sponsored a symposium entitled "Our Country and Our Culture." In it one contributor declared, "For the first time in the history of the modern intellectual, America is not to be conceived of as a priori the vulgarest and stupidest nation of the world."

Indeed, the America of the 1950s was a country in which private foundations generously subsidized free-lance intellectuals and many of those same intellectuals gladly served such government agencies as the Central Intelligence Agency through the Congress for Cultural Freedom. Cultural anticommunism united intellectuals, trade unionists, and such socialists as Norman Thomas in a common front with corporate executives and federal officials.

What had happened to American intellectuals and social critics was aptly caught in the substance and title of *Commentary* editor Norman Podhoretz's 1968 autobiography. The son of Jewish-immigrant parents, himself born and bred in the Brownsville, Brooklyn, ghetto, Podhoretz had made his way to Columbia University and from there to the apex of the New York literary intellectual universe. His journey through life was surely, as he titled it, a case of *Making It* in America.

Formal academic works reflected a similar influence. Where once history books stressed have-nots versus haves, farmers versus bankers, section versus section, and city versus country, in the 1950s they spoke of consensus and shared values. David Potter perceived abundance as the single most influential factor in the American experience, and he entitled his interpretive history of America *People of Plenty*. In 1956 Richard Hofstadter won the Pulitzer Prize for a study, *The Age of Reform*, which emphasized the relative absence of class conflict, the priority of status over class, and the basic American commitment to private property, the profit motive, and capitalist institutions.

Economists, too, saw social harmony and material abundance as the new reality. In their view, the Keynesian economic revolution had given them the tools to fine tune the economy in order to maintain full employment and price stability. Students no longer had to look to classical economics or its Marxist repudiation for solutions to contemporary problems.

None celebrated America's success more lustily than political scientists and sociologists. Both academic groups saw democracy, especially in America, as a completed, successful experiment. Full democratic rights were in place, all adults had basic citizenship, and all were formally legal before the law. No single, unified group ruled or dominated society to the detriment of others. Instead, a variety of equally balanced interest groups competed with each other for public favors and influence with the state, which acted as an honest broker among them. This system came to be known as pluralism to distinguish it from authoritarianism and totalitarianism.

According to the political sociologists, pluralism was not a belief system comparable to socialism, communism, or fascism. It was rather a simple practice of balancing harmoniously competing claims and rights in an affluent, democratic society, which had, as the sociologist Seymour Martin Lipset claimed in his book *Political Man*, abolished all class politics based on irreconcilable "isms." Indeed, as Daniel Bell proclaimed in a collection of essays published in 1960, the United States had seen *The End of Ideology*. One essay in the collection analyzed trade unionism as "The Capitalism of the Proletariat," and another, "Crime as an American Way of Life," dissected criminal activities as an ethnic version of "making it." The passions which had generated mass socialist parties, the Bolshevik Revolution, fascism in Italy, and nazism in Germany, Bell proclaimed as dead. The new generation, he wrote, "finds itself... within a framework of political society that has rejected... the old apocalyptic and chiliastic visions."

John F. Kennedy's election as president symbolized the marriage of "new generation" intellectuals to the power of the American state. The new president invited Robert Frost to read a poem at the inauguration. The historian Arthur Schlesinger, Jr., served as White House scholar-in-residence; the economic historian Walt W. Rostow acted as a foreign-policy planner; the economist John Kenneth Galbraith went to India as ambassador; and the historians Samuel Eliot Morison and Henry Steele Commager sang the praises of "Camelot" on the Potomac.

Not that voices of dissent and criticism were silent in the 1950s. Not at all. The *New Republic* and *Nation* magazines maintained their long traditions of left-liberal social and political commentary. In the 1950s a group of anti-Stalinist Social Democrats founded *Dissent*, a journal which tried to keep alive in America the perspectives associated with Western European labor and social democratic parties. For the more orthodox on the left, there was always *Monthly Review*, in which Paul Baran and Paul Sweezy subjected contemporary American and world developments to the scrutiny of Marxist economics and theory. But in the 1950s and early 1960s their audiences were relatively small and their sometimes strident criticism of affluent America no more than tiny voices in the wilderness.

It was this reality that led C. Wright Mills to cry out as early as 1951 that "political expression is banalized, political theory is barren administrative detail, history is made behind men's backs."

In reality, the affluent mass culture of the 1950s that bred a quiet generation of organization men lost in the void of a "lonely crowd" was more ephemeral than it first appeared. Indeed it was shot through with unseen cracks and flaws. John Kenneth Galbraith may have bemoaned the widespread public squalor amidst the private affluence; for more than 30 million Americans even affluence was beyond reach. Rural life decayed apace, urban ghettos spread and festered, nonwhite Americans remained at best second-class citizens and at worst the hapless victims of social and economic discrimination, and most wage workers, regardless of skin color, endured as objects of external authority. Wealth and poverty, the ideal of equality versus the reality of inequality, and authority against freedom remained inextricably at war in affluent America. During the 1960s, the social tinder represented by poverty and racialism ignited in the form of urban race riots and the impassioned militancy of the New Left and the radical feminist movements.

Before then, however, the presidency of Dwight David Eisenhower made affluence and harmony appear to be the rule. Unprecedented economic growth, rising real incomes, and the new mass culture promoted by television laid the foundation for the relative quiescence of the Eisenhower era. Eisenhower's ability to dampen old political feuds, to legitimate the New Deal "revolution" as he castigated overgrown government and "creeping socialism," his success at softening the harsher aspects of the Cold War, and his taming of the worst excesses of McCarthyism reinforced the aura of complacency associated with the 1950s. Ike's mid-American, small-town origins, his wide, winning grin, and his placidity assured most Americans that all was well at home and abroad.

NO

Douglas T. Miller and
Marion Nowak

THE FIFTIES: THE WAY WE REALLY WERE

Hula hoops, bunny hops, 3-D movies. Davy Crockett coonskins, chloro-
phyll toothpaste, 22 collegians stuffed into a phone booth. Edsels and tail-
finned Cadillacs. Greasy duck's-ass hairdos, leather jackets, souped-up hot
rods, dragging, cruising, mooning. Like crazy, man, dig? Kefauver hearings,
Howdy Doody, Kukla, Fran and Ollie, Bridey Murphy, Charles Van Doren,
Francis Gary Powers. *The Catcher in the Rye, The Power of Positive Thinking;
Howl, On the Road.* Patti Page, Pat Boone, Vic Damone; Little Richard, Chuck
Berry, Elvis Presley; The Platters, The Clovers, The Drifters; Bill Haley and the
Comets, Danny and the Juniors. Mantle, Mays, Marciano. Pink shirts, gray
flannels, white bucks. I LIKE IKE.

THE FABULOUS FIFTIES!—or so 1970s nostalgia would lead one to believe. A 1972 issue of *Newsweek*, complete with Marilyn Monroe cover, explored this phenomenon under the heading "Yearning for the Fifties: The
Good Old Days." "It was a simple decade," *Newsweek* writers recalled, "when
hip was hep, good was boss." That same year *Life* magazine reminisced about
"The Nifty Fifties"—"it's been barely a dozen years since the '50s ended and
yet here we are again, awash in the trappings of that sunnier time."

This wistful view of the fifties first became evident about 1971 and 1972. It
quickly exploded into a national craze that still pervades the popular images
of the mid-century era. Numerous examples of fifties nostalgia exist in the
seventies. It was the theme of movies like *American Graffiti, The Last Picture
Show, Let the Good Times Roll,* and *The Way We Were.* Television shows "Happy
Days" and "Laverne and Shirley" recreated an idyllic fifties world of youth
and innocence. The TV show "M*A*S*H" even managed to make people a
little homesick for the Korean War. By February 1976, the fifties rock-and-
roll parody *Grease* began its fifth season. It had become Broadway's longest
running show by far, and this despite the fact that it never had name stars,
hit songs, or a high budget.

Popular music in this post-Beatles period also saw a major revival of
fifties rock. By the mid-seventies Elvis Presley, Chuck Berry, Rick Nelson,
Fats Domino, Little Richard, and Bill Haley again were drawing mass audi-

ences. Record companies were reissuing fifties hits on special golden-oldies LPs, and many radio stations were devoting several hours daily to an oldies format. The fifties musical revival spawned contemporary groups such as Sha-Na-Na, Flash Cadillac and the Continental Kids, and Vince Vance and the Valiants. These groups not only sang the oldies, they also revived the greaser look. Vince Vance even got himself arrested while attempting to steal an Edsel hubcap. Nightclubs too have cashed in on nostalgia. Across the country, clubs have featured old music and special trivia nights with questions such as "Who played James Dean's girlfriend in *Rebel Without a Cause?*"

Another sign of the fifties fad has been in clothing. Leather motorcycle jackets, picture sweaters, pedal pushers, pleated skirts, and strapless evening dresses have been hot items in the last few years. In 1973, Monique, the New York *Daily News* fashion reporter, announced: "the feeling of the fifties that will rule a large part of the fashion next fall is already apparent." A year earlier Cyrinda Foxe, a Marilyn Monroe look-alike modeling a dress from a fifties collection, claimed that "people just go crazy when I walk down the street! The fifties were so much sexier."

What does all this nostalgia mean? Periods of intense longing for an earlier era indicate that people are discontented with the present. Excessive, sentimental nostalgia generally occurs during times of perceived crisis. Such has been the case in the seventies. The rise of the fifties enthusiasm coincided with widespread disillusionment and a growing conservatism. For many people the 1950s came to symbolize a golden age of innocence and simplicity, an era supposedly unruffled by riots, racial violence,

Vietnam, Watergate, assassinations. People numbed by the traumas of the sixties and seventies, desiring to forget the horrors of presidential crime, soaring prices, Cambodian bombings, Kent State, My Lai, the Manson case, the Chicago Convention, the murder of two Kennedy's, Martin Luther King, and Malcolm X, yearned for a quieter time. As a Cleveland oldies-but-goodies disc jockey put it, "my audience wants to forget its problems and return to—or at least recall—those happy high-school times—the prom, no wars, no riots, no protests, the convertibles and the drive-in." Another DJ even saw the fifties music revival as a way to bridge the generation gap. "I get the feeling that through this music some of the kids are finding a back-door way of getting together with their parents." Nostalgia, then, is a pleasant distraction. One imagines the past, and so overlooks the present.

Additionally, since we live in a society that prizes youth over age, there is a natural tendency for nostalgia on the part of the aging generation. For those who grew up in the fifties, the happy images of that decade are a positive reassurance —a reclaiming of fading youth. Then too in the mid-seventies the general realization that energy, prosperity, and growth are not limitless undoubtedly makes Americans a more retrospective, nostalgic people. We may die tomorrow, but we wish to remember it as a good world while it lasted.

But whatever the reasons for the fifties revival, the image of that decade conveyed by current nostalgia is badly distorted. The artifacts of the fifties are still with us. The facts are less clear. Looking back on that period, people today see it as a time of fun and innocence, a soda-shop world with youth as its only participants. They recall Bo Diddley and Buddy Holly, but ignore Joe McCarthy and John Foster Dulles. Nostalgia is highly selective. No one is staging a House Un-American Activities Committee revival, or longing for the good old days of nuclear brinksmanship and the deadly H-bomb tests.

Certainly, there was some fun in the fifties—the Coasters' songs, Lenny Bruce's nightclub routines, Sid Caesar's TV antics. But in retrospect it was essentially a humorless decade, one in which comic Mort Sahl could raise national ire by cracking a single J. Edgar Hoover joke. Much of what strikes observers as quaint now—Nixon's Checkers speech, Norman Vincent Peale's homilies, or tail-finned Cadillacs—were grotesque realities at the time. It was more an era of fear than fun. The bomb, communists, spies, and Sputnik all scared Americans. And fear bred repression both of the blatant McCarthyite type and the more subtle, pervasive, and personal daily pressures to conform.

Astute social critics have found the fifties anything but the good old days. To the late Paul Goodman it was an "extraordinarily senseless and unnatural" time. American society, in his words, was "a Closed Room with a Rat Race as the center of fascination, powerfully energized by fear of being outcasts." To Michael Harrington the decade "was a moral disaster, an amusing waste of life." Norman Mailer bluntly described the fifties as "one of the worst decades in the history of man." ...

"Meet the Typical American," announced a 1954 Reader's Digest article. "The average American male stands five feet nine inches tall, weighs 158 pounds, prefers brunettes, baseball, beefsteak and French fried potatoes, and thinks the abil-

ity to run a home smoothly and efficiently is the most important quality in a wife." The average American woman, the article continued, "is five feet four, weighs 132, can't stand an unshaven face." This typical female preferred marriage to a career. As the average weights of men and women might suggest, many Americans were on the heavy side. The prevalent styles encouraged this. Women in pleated skirts falling a few inches below the knees were expected to be shapely in a plump sort of way. Bikinis were largely limited to the girlie magazines. But big breasts, symbols of motherhood, were definitely in vogue. For men, excess flab was easily concealed beneath baggy pleated pants, suits and shirts that did not follow body lines, boxer shorts and bathing trunks, Bermudas with knee-length socks. So in this decade of suburban prosperity, many people carried paunches as if they were symbols of success.

The goals of these "average" Americans were not radical. What George Meany said of organized labor in the mid-fifties would have applied to most groups: "We do not seek to recast American society. We do seek an ever-rising standard of living by which we mean not only more money but more leisure and a richer cultural life."

Leisure and culture—Americans took to these as never before. About one sixth of all personal income was spent on leisure pursuits. In record force people painted-by-numbers, drank, gardened, watched TV, traveled, listened to music, hunted and fished, read Reader's Digest condensed books. Doing-it-oneself became a national fad. Everything from home permanents to boat building had millions of amateur practitioners. In 1954 it was reported that 70 per cent of all wallpaper bought was hung by novices,

304 / 13. WERE THE 1950s AMERICA'S "HAPPY DAYS"?

while some 11 million weekend carpenters drilled, sawed, and sanded some 180 square miles of plywood with their 25 million power tools. In California, the Pan Pacific Do-It-Yourself Show even exhibited separate pieces of fur that could be assembled into a do-it-yourself mink coat. For persons of a more sedentary nature, American industry produced quantities of amusing junk—cigarette lighters that played "Smoke Gets in Your Eyes," whisky-flavored toothpaste, mink-trimmed clothespins, Venus toothpicks, Jayne Mansfield hot-water bottles.

Americans could do just about anything. Or so at least they were told in hundreds of books purportedly revealing the secrets of how to make love, how to tap one's secret source of strength, how to mix a good martini, how to get thin or fat, how to be popular, powerful, famous, rich.

But it was *Culture* that American boosters boasted of most. "Once in a great while a society explodes in a flood of new ideas, new tastes, new standards," claimed Fenton Turck in a 1952 *Reader's Digest* article. "A fresh and exciting age emerges, alive with expanding opportunities. Today's Americans are living in one of these extraordinary periods." Turck talked of a great flowering of culture. As evidence of this he cited such things as increased attendance at concerts, opera, and theater. Art museums, opera companies, and symphony orchestras all multiplied in the fifties, as did the sale of quality paperbacks and classical records.

Culture had status appeal and an increased portion of the population had both the leisure and money to dabble in it. Perhaps the apogee of the era's culture boom was reached in April 1960, when the Parke-Bernet Galleries held a huge art auction to benefit the Museum of Modern Art. The New York City auction room was linked via closed-circuit TV to similar rooms in Chicago, Dallas, and Los Angeles. The auction was a great success; an Utrillo went to a Dallas millionaire for $20,000, A Cézanne to a New York collector for $200,000. Bidding on a Hans Hartung had reached the $10,000 level before anyone noticed it was hung upside down. "We're ready for our renaissance," claimed poet Louis Untermeyer at mid-decade. "Westward the course of culture!"

In addition to celebrating American culture and living standards, many people saw the United States in the middle of the twentieth century as having a peculiar and providential mission. "We are living in one of the great watershed periods of history," asserted Democratic presidential nominee Adlai Stevenson in the 1952 campaign. This era "may well fix the pattern of civilization for many generations to come. God has set for us an awesome mission: nothing less than the leadership of the free world." The editors of *Fortune* felt the same. "There come times in the history of every people," they wrote, "when destiny knocks on their door with an iron insistence." In American history, as they read it, destiny had so knocked three times: "Once when we faced the seemingly impossible odds of British power to gain our independence: once at Fort Sumter, when we faced the bloody task of preserving our union: and it is knocking today [1951].... Our outlook is the same as it was at the time of the Revolution, and again at the time of the Civil War: the shape of things to come depends on us: our moral decision, our wisdom, our vision, and our will."

That America would succeed in fulfilling its God-given mission few doubted. The future was bright. "Our spiritual road map," predicted philosopher Morris Ernst, "will carry the direction pointers: 1976—This Way—Energy, Leisure, Full Rich Life."

Yet despite the varied and frequent versions of "America the Beautiful," doubts and anxieties were also present. The fifties was a time of tensions and insecurities. Early in the decade the usually optimistic Norman Vincent Peale spoke of an "epidemic of fear and worry" in the United States. "All doctors," he declared, "are having cases of illness which are brought on directly by fear, and aggravated by worry and a feeling of insecurity." For some Americans the greatest anxieties stemmed from the cold war. "Our nation," warned a late-fifties civil defense pamphlet, "is in a grim struggle for national survival and the preservation of freedom in the world." And of course there was the constant threat of nuclear destruction which left people, in the words of one mid-fifties observer, "in a state of suspension, waiting to see whether the Bomb is going to fall or not."

For other people, the speed of social and economic change generated uncertainties and cast doubts on old certitudes. The new prosperity and changing lifestyles, while materially benefiting many, caused insecurities. Traditional ethnic neighborhoods were breaking down as newly prosperous people fled to suburbia. Yet this very mobility created rootlessness. Many people simply discovered that abundance was not enough. In any case Americans became quite self-critical and made best sellers of books telling them of their shortcomings.

In this light, some of the most important social and cultural phenomena of the fifties are more understandable. The overwhelming emphasis on the family gave people a sense of place and personal identity. The massive return to religion provided individuals with a sense of security; it reassured them that the traditional moral verities were still valid. Sustained and successful attacks against progressive education were another manifestation of the search for traditional, absolute values. So too was the intellectual emphasis on consensus. Historians, sociologists, and other social scientists played down conflict and instead stressed the harmonious and enduring nature of American democratic values. Blacks and other nonwhites, who did not share equally in America's bounty, were assured by the white media that they never had it so good. Generally speaking, neither racial nor economic classes were recognized. Critics of this celebrated consensus, whether from right or left, tended to be treated as psychological deviants suffering from such cliché ills as status anxiety or authoritarian personality. Nonconformists and rebels were subject to harsh conformist pressures. No wonder then that bipartisan banality flourished. Both major political parties clung tenaciously to the same center, maintaining the status quo while mouthing provincial Protestant platitudes and preparing for Armageddon....

If one were attempting a precise periodization, the fifties could well be divided into three parts: 1948–53, 1954–57, 1958–60. These three periods might then be labeled "The Age of Fear," "The Era of Conservative Consensus," and "The Time of National Reassessment."

The Age of Fear: The post-World War II era really begins around 1948. By then the nation had essentially adjusted to a peacetime economy; depression had not recurred and people were coming to believe in the possibility of perpetual prosperity. At the same time, the cold war had become a debilitating reality. A chronology of terror began unfolding. In 1948 a communist coup was successful in Czechoslovakia and the Soviets blockaded western access to Berlin. That same year in the United States, talk of treason and communist infiltration became commonplace, especially after a former New Deal State Department official, Alger Hiss, was accused by Whittaker Chambers of having passed secrets to the Russians. The following year, 1949, the Soviets exploded their first atomic bomb and Mao Tse-tung's communist forces were victorious in China. Early in 1950 President Harry S. Truman announced plans to begin development of a hydrogen bomb (it was perfected by 1952); Senator Joseph McCarthy added the loudest voice to the already sizable outcry of anticommunist witch hunters. Nineteen fifty also saw the conviction of Alger Hiss for perjury, the arrest and trial of Ethel and Julius Rosenberg as atomic spies (they were executed in 1953), the outbreak of the Korean War, and Senator Estes Kefauver's televised criminal investigations that dramatically revealed the extent and power of organized crime.

Such events shocked and frightened people, and the last years of Truman's presidency proved a trying time—a period of suspicions, accusations, loyalty oaths, loathings, extreme chauvinistic Americanism. Republicans, attempting to regain power, were not averse to charging the Democrats with being "soft on communism," though in reality both parties were excessively anticommunist. Tensions raised by Korean fighting, supposed communist infiltration, spy trials, loyalty investigations, inflation, crime, and the bomb reached near hysteric proportions in the early fifties. Dissent was suppressed, conformity demanded. With the exception of a few legitimate espionage cases, none of which really endangered national security, *most victims of the anti-red mania were guilty of little more than holding unpopular opinions.* Not only the national government, but thousands of local communities as well felt obliged to search out and destroy suspected subversive views. Teachers, government workers, entertainers, and many others were dismissed. Textbooks were censored and libraries closed.

Yet such fear and repression, plus prosperity, also made Americans seem united under a national faith. Seeing the world in dualistic terms of good versus evil, people celebrated the United States as the bastion of freedom, democracy, and "people's capitalism." Intellectuals defended America and searched for enduring consensual values of the country's past and present. A noncritical conservative consensus emerged offering hope and reassurance during this age of fear. The widespread emphasis on religion and the family gave further solace. The combined anxiety and hope of this period is well illustrated in the title of a 1950 song— "Jesus Is God's Atomic Bomb."

The Era of Conservative Consensus: The conservative consensus and celebration of America continued into the mid-fifties, and fortunately for national nerves the fears and anxieties began to ebb. Several factors contributed to this: the death of Stalin and the end of the Korean War in 1953; the downfall of Senator McCarthy in 1954; The Geneva summit conference with the Soviets in 1955; the lack of new spy sensations after 1950; continued prosperity; and, above all, the election of Eisenhower to the presidency.

When Ike was first elected in 1952, one Pennsylvania housewife remarked: "It's like America has come home." And so it seemed to millions. While politics traditionally means conflict, Ike appeared to people as above politics. He was the heroic general come to unite the nation in peace and prosperity as he had defended it earlier in war. Democratic presidents Roosevelt and Truman had for 20 years emphasized a politics of class strife and crisis. With Eisenhower came the appearance at least of a politics of unity and classlessness. His boyish grin and downhome homely face, his simple sincere platitudes about home, mother, and heaven, his circumlocutions when difficult issues came up, all these things endeared him to millions and made him a symbol, not of party, but of national consensus. Americans, tired of constant crises and the hysteria of the age of fear, found in Ike a symbol of hope and confidence.

And so, by the mid-fifties there came a brief happy moment—the quintessential fifties—prosperous, stable, bland, religious, moral, patriotic, conservative, domestic, buttoned-down. Huge tail-finned cars sold in record numbers, *The Power of Positive Thinking* and *The Man in the Gray Flannel Suit* sat atop the best-seller lists, and the "Spirit of Geneva" seemed to diffuse itself over the globe. Domestically no problem appeared more pressing than the specter of juvenile delinquency, though in reality young people overwhelmingly accepted the values of their elders and dedicated themselves to the bourgeois goals of security, sociabil-

ity, domesticity. They went steady, married young, had lots of children, lived the conforming life of "togetherness."

Crises still existed. Poverty, racism, sexism, and militarism all threatened America. But Eisenhower and most citizens tried to ignore such ills. The sting seemed gone from the times, and a cheerful nation overwhelmingly re-elected Eisenhower in 1956. Just before that election, David Riesman and Stewart Alsop visited a new suburb south of Chicago to poll voters. They found people vague about politics but liking Ike. "Most of the people we spoke to were young housewives, often interrupted in their midday television program...." They were educated but complacent. "As one looked over that flat Illinois prairie at all the signs of prosperity," generalized Riesman, "it was not hard to see why these people were so bland politically and responded to the same qualities in Ike.... These people were not self-made men who remembered their struggles against hardship but, rather, a society-made generation who could not believe society would let them down...." These were the model fifties figures —suburbanized, bureaucratized, smug, secure.

The Time of National Reassessment: Eisenhower's second term quickly revealed how precarious the mid-fifties plateau of repose actually was. Even before that new term began, America's foreign relations suffered major setbacks. Just prior to the 1956 elections, fighting broke out in Egypt and Hungary. In late October, Anglo-French-Israeli forces invaded the Suez region of Egypt in an attempt to regain the canal which Egyptian leader Gamal Abdel Nasser earlier had nationalized. Third World anticolonial resentment and threatened Soviet intervention convinced the Eisenhower administration that the invasion must be ended. America pressured Britain, France, and Israel to withdraw. They did so. However, these nations' humiliation embittered them toward the United States. Western unity seemed seriously weakened. During these same tense days of late October and early November 1956, the Soviet Union, taking advantage of the dissent among the Western powers, harshly crushed an anticommunist uprising in Hungary that had broken out only a week before the Suez war. For a few weeks the world hovered on the brink of nuclear war. And while both crises were over at about the same time as Eisenhower's November re-election, they greatly intensified international tensions. Suez and Hungary clearly revealed the 1955 Geneva summit to be only a temporary thaw in the cold war.

Less than a year later, the domestic tranquillity of the mid-fifties was also disrupted. In September 1957, American racism was shockingly unveiled when the school-integration issue reached crisis proportions in Little Rock. Eisenhower, who was not sympathetic to the civil rights movement, reluctantly was forced to send troops into that city to insure compliance with the Supreme Court's 1954 desegregation decision. But the ugly scenes in front of Central High School laid bare for Americans and the world this nation's deep-seated racial tensions.

Then a month later in October 1957, the Soviets launched Sputnik I, the world's first earth-orbiting satellite. Americans were profoundly shocked. National self-confidence seemed shattered in the light of this demonstrated Soviet superiority in space science. Calls for an expanded arms race accelerated. American afflu-ence, once the nation's pride, now was blamed for enfeebling the populace. Progressive education, which had been on the defensive throughout the decade, was quickly demolished as people demanded intellectual discipline with more emphasis on science, mathematics, and language.

Sputnik clearly struck the major blow against mid-fifties tranquillity. But other developments in the last three years of Eisenhower's presidency added to American doubts and increased the national penchant for soul-searching. At about the same time as the Soviet space successes, the American economy began to slump. By the spring of 1958, a major recession existed; unemployment had climbed to 7.7 per cent of the total labor force, the highest rate since 1941. That same year congressional committees disclosed conflict-of-interest violations by presidential appointees and charges of influence-peddling by Vice-President Nixon's former campaign manager. Even Ike's closest, most trusted and influential adviser, Sherman Adams, was dismissed for taking bribes. Adams, it was revealed, had accepted expensive gifts from Bernard Goldfine, a wealthy businessman with cases pending before the government. On tour in Latin America that year, Nixon was spat upon, jeered, and stoned. A year later, Charles Van Doren, a handsome young instructor from Columbia University, scion of an eminent literary family, revealed to investigators that the brilliance he had displayed in winning vast sums on a TV quiz show was fake. The show had been rigged. At about the same time famed disc jockey Alan Freed, the self-appointed father of rock and roll, became involved in a payola scandal. Among other revelations were exposés of widespread cheating in schools and of a group of New York cops working for a burglary ring.

By May 1960, when the Soviets announced that Francis Gary Powers had been shot down in a U-2 spy plane over Russian territory, the American propensity for critical self-evaluation had become obsessive. A presidential Commission on National Goals, which Eisenhower had established after Sputnik, produced a ponderous report, *Goals for Americans*. The Rockefeller Brothers Fund issued their own version, *Prospect for America*. *Life*, *Look*, the New York *Times* and other mass-circulation publications featured articles and whole issues discussing national purpose and the future role of America. Leading social and political writers began turning out books with titles like *American the Vincible* and *What Ivan Knows and Johnny Doesn't*.

Much of the national debate focused on dissatisfaction with the quality of American life. Conformity and materialism, critics argued, had dulled Americans into a complacent averageness. "Our goal has become a life of amiable sloth," complained *Time* editor Thomas Griffith in 1959. "We are in danger of becoming a vibrating and mediocre people." "Looking at some of the institutions we nourish and defend," Robert Heilbroner noted, early in 1960, "it would not be difficult to maintain that our society is an immense stamping press for the careless production of underdeveloped and malformed human beings, and that, whatever it may claim to be, it is not a society fundamentally concerned with moral issues, with serious purposes, or with human dignity." Such laments swelled into a national chorus of self-reproach as Americans once more showed themselves to be an anxious, self-conscious people.

Yet there remained an underlying note of hope in this intramural abuse. Most doubters viewed their disparagements as enterprises of self-correction. "America the Beautiful" would soar once more if only we could speed up economic growth, put a man on the moon, develop a more flexible military establishment, rekindle a spirit of national self-sacrifice, and so on and so on. John F. Kennedy's 1960 campaign epitomized the schizophrenic national mood of doubt and hope. In this, many others concurred. Walter Lippmann stated in July 1960, "We're at the end of something that is petering out and aging and about finished." He was not unhappy about this; rather he sensed that a new and better day was coming. Arthur Schlesinger, Jr., already active with Kennedy people, also lamented the late fifties but foretold "a new epoch" of "vitality," "identity," and "new values... straining for expression and for release."

The fifties, then, is not a neat single unit. The decade began with terror and affluence uniting a people under a national faith. The mid-fifties, desperately tired of crises, continued that faith in a more casual and relaxed manner. Yet by 1960, that mask of faith was drawn aside to reveal a changing face: regretful, doubting, yet also looking in hope to a rebirth.

POSTSCRIPT

Were the 1950s America's "Happy Days"?

The period after World War II was one of both affluence and anxiety for most Americans. Dubofsky and Theoharis emphasize the affluent side. The American economy not only brought prosperity to its increasing white-collar and stable blue-collar workers at home, but it also revived the economies of the Western European nations and noncommunist Asian countries. The increased wealth of the American worker in the 1950s brought about a consumption craze. Installment buying for automobiles and appliances and single-family homes purchased with long-term mortgages, financed in many cases at low interest rates by the government on behalf of the veterans, were the order of the day.

There were cracks in the economy, to be sure. Dubofsky and Theoharis point out that most nonwhites, especially blacks and Hispanics, did not share in the general prosperity. Some of "the old standbys of industrial America—railroads, coal mining, textiles, and shoe manufacturing—continued a decline that had begun in the 1920s." Labor union membership in general dropped, and individual farms fell into the hands of agribusinesses. Finally, many poor people, especially those with incomes under $4,000 per year, were spending more than they earned.

Miller and Nowak focus on the negative side mentioned in passing by Dubofsky and Theoharis. They point out that in a society "that prizes youth over age," there is a tendency on the part of the older generation to re-create through television, movies, and books a nostalgic past that never really existed. Americans, say Miller and Nowak, lost their motives and became anxious as they moved to their "little boxes" in the suburbs. They became overweight, were obsessed with their status, and were afraid that communists might overthrow the American government.

Both readings can be criticized for giving an unbalanced assessment of the 1950s, although Dubofsky and Theoharis do mention the cracks in the affluent society. However, blacks would push their demands for school desegregation, which the Supreme Court ordered in the *Brown v. Board of Education of Topeka, Kansas,* decisions of 1954 and 1955, and demonstrate successfully for political and legal equality in the 1960s.

There is an enormous bibliography on the 1950s. A sympathetic overview is Michael W. Schuyler, "The 1950s: A Retrospective View," *Nebraska History* (Spring 1996), which summarizes the major social and economic currents of the 1950s. Also supportive of the absence of extremes is Stephen J. Whitfield's "The 1950s: The Era of No Hard Feelings," *South Atlantic Quarterly* (Summer 1975). Alan Ehrenhalt's "Learning from the Fifties," *Wilson Quarterly* (Summer 1995) is a brilliant case study of Chicago, Illinois, that points out the high price some people in the 1950s paid to enjoy the good life. The starting point for the critical cultural studies of television, film, and literature is Guile McGregor, "Domestic Blitz: A Revisionist History of the Fifties," *American Studies* (Spring 1993).

There are a number of excellent monographs on the 1950s. Eric F. Goldman, *The Crucial Decade and After: America, 1945–1960* (Random House, 1960) remains a great read and pushes the view that Americans had developed "a broad concern about the public issues of the day."

In a class by themselves are Paul A. Carter's *Another Part of the Fifties* (Columbia University Press, 1983) and journalist David Halberstam's *The Fifties* (Willard Books, 1993), a book that is eminently readable in its portraits of 1950s heroes, such as Charles Van Doren, Marlon Brando, and Bill Russell. Some of the same material is covered from a more conservative viewpoint by Jeffrey Hart, ed., *When the Going Was Good: Life in the Fifties* (Crown, 1982).

President Dwight D. Eisenhower dominated the politics of the 1950s in the same way that one of his predecessors, Franklin D. Roosevelt, did the depression decade and World War II. In the 1950s the public loved Eisenhower, but the intellectuals did not. Early assessments of him as an ineffectual, old man who let his staff make the decisions can be found in Dean Alberton's collection of articles *Eisenhower as President* (Hill & Wang, 1963). Revisionists who have researched through the private papers and diaries of the president and his staff have concluded that he really was in charge. See Fred I. Greenstein, *The Hidden Hand Presidency* (Johns Hopkins University Press, 1994). Past revisionist arguments that he was in charge but fumbled anyway are assessed in the chapter entitled "Vicissitudes of Presidential Reputations: Eisenhower," in Arthur M. Schlesinger, Jr., *The Cycles of American History* (Houghton Mifflin, 1986). A major biography that is sympathetic to its subject is Stephen A. Ambrose's *Eisenhower: Soldier and President* (Simon & Schuster, 1990).

Other worthy books on a variety of 1950s topics include Thomas C. Reeves, ed., *McCarthyism*, 3rd ed. (Robert E. Krieger, 1989); Harold G. Vatter, *The U.S. Economy in the 1950s* (University of Chicago Press, 1985); James Gilbert, *A Cycle of Outrage: America's Reaction to the Juvenile Age* (Oxford University Press, 1986); and Karal A. Marling, *As Seen on TV: The Visual Culture of Everyday Life in the 1950s* (Harvard University Press, 1994).

ISSUE 14

Was America's Escalation of the War in Vietnam Inevitable?

YES: Brian VanDeMark, from *Into the Quagmire: Lyndon Johnson and the Escalation of the Vietnam War* (Oxford University Press, 1991)

NO: H. R. McMaster, from *Dereliction of Duty: Lyndon Johnson, Robert McNamara, the Joint Chiefs of Staff, and the Lies That Led to Vietnam* (HarperCollins, 1997)

ISSUE SUMMARY

YES: Professor of history Brian VanDeMark argues that President Lyndon Johnson failed to question the viability of increasing U.S. involvement in the Vietnam War because he was a prisoner of America's global containment policy and because he did not want his opponents to accuse him of being soft on communism or endanger support for his Great Society reforms.

NO: H. R. McMaster, an active-duty army tanker, maintains that the Vietnam disaster was not inevitable but a uniquely human failure whose responsibility was shared by President Johnson and his principal military and civilian advisers.

At the end of World War II, imperialism was coming to a close in Asia. Japan's defeat spelled the end of its control over China, Korea, and the countries of Southeast Asia. Attempts by the European nations to reestablish their empires were doomed. Anti-imperialist movements emerged all over Asia and Africa, often producing chaos.

The United States faced a dilemma. America was a nation conceived in revolution and was sympathetic to the struggles of Third World nations. But the United States was afraid that many of the revolutionary leaders were Communists who would place their countries under the control of the expanding empire of the Soviet Union. By the late 1940s the Truman administration decided that it was necessary to stop the spread of communism. The policy that resulted was known as containment.

Vietnam provided a test of the containment doctrine in Asia. Vietnam had been a French protectorate from 1885 until Japan took control of it during World War II. Shortly before the war ended, the Japanese gave Vietnam its independence, but the French were determined to reestablish their influence in the area. Conflicts emerged between the French-led nationalist forces of South Vietnam and the Communist-dominated provisional government of the Democratic Republic of Vietnam (DRV), which was established in Hanoi in August 1945. Ho Chi Minh was the president of the DRV. An avowed Communist since the 1920s, Ho had also become the major nationalist figure in Vietnam. As the leader of the anti-imperialist movement against French and Japanese colonialism for over 30 years, Ho managed to tie together the communist and nationalist movements in Vietnam.

A full-scale war broke out in 1946 between the communist government of North Vietnam and the French-dominated country of South Vietnam. After the Communists defeated the French at the battle of Dien Bien Phu in May 1954, the latter decided to pull out. At the Geneva Conference that summer, Vietnam was divided at the 17th parallel, pending elections.

The United States became directly involved in Vietnam after the French withdrew. In 1955 the Republican president Dwight D. Eisenhower refused to recognize the Geneva Accord but supported the establishment of the South Vietnamese government. In 1956 South Vietnam's leader, Ngo Dinh Diem, with U.S. approval, refused to hold elections, which would have provided a unified government for Vietnam in accordance with the Geneva Agreement. The Communists in the north responded by again taking up the armed struggle. The war continued for another 19 years.

Both President Eisenhower and his successor, John F. Kennedy, were anxious to prevent South Vietnam from being taken over by the Communists, so economic assistance and military aid were provided. Kennedy's successor, Lyndon B. Johnson, changed the character of American policy in Vietnam by escalating the air war and increasing the number of ground forces from 21,000 in 1965 to a full fighting force of 550,000 at its peak in 1968.

The next president, Richard Nixon, adopted a new policy of "Vietnamization" of the war. Military aid to South Vietnam was increased to ensure the defeat of the Communists. At the same time, American troops were gradually withdrawn from Vietnam. South Vietnamese president Thieu recognized the weakness of his own position without the support of U.S. troops. He reluctantly signed the Paris Accords in January 1973 only after being told by Secretary of State Henry Kissinger that the United States would sign them alone. Once U.S. soldiers were withdrawn, Thieu's regime was doomed. In spring 1975 a full-scale war broke out, and the South Vietnamese government collapsed.

In the following selection, Brian VanDeMark argues that President Johnson failed to question the viability of increasing U.S. involvement in Vietnam because he was a prisoner of America's global containment policy and he did not want his opponents to accuse him of being soft on communism. In the second selection, H. R. McMaster argues that the Vietnam disaster was not inevitable but a uniquely human failure whose responsibility was shared by Johnson and his civilian and military advisers.

YES

Brian VanDeMark

INTO THE QUAGMIRE

Vietnam divided America more deeply and painfully than any event since the Civil War. It split political leaders and ordinary people alike in profound and lasting ways. Whatever the conflicting judgments about this controversial war—and there are many—Vietnam undeniably stands as the greatest tragedy of twentieth-century U.S. foreign relations.

America's involvement in Vietnam has, as a result, attracted much critical scrutiny, frequently addressed to the question, "Who was guilty?"—"Who led the United States into this tragedy?" A more enlightening question, it seems, is "How and why did this tragedy occur?" The study of Vietnam should be a search for explanation and understanding, rather than for scapegoats.

Focusing on one important period in this long and complicated story—the brief but critical months from November 1964 to July 1965, when America crossed the threshold from limited to large-scale war in Vietnam—helps to answer that question. For the crucial decisions of this period resulted from the interplay of longstanding ideological attitudes, diplomatic assumptions and political pressures with decisive contemporaneous events in America and Vietnam.

Victory in World War II produced a sea change in America's perception of its role in world affairs. Political leaders of both parties embraced a sweepingly new vision of the United States as the defender against the perceived threat of monolithic communist expansion everywhere in the world. This vision of American power and purpose, shaped at the start of the Cold War, grew increasingly rigid over the years. By 1964–1965, it had become an ironbound and unshakable dogma, a received faith which policymakers unquestionably accepted—even though the circumstances which had fostered its creation had changed dramatically amid diffused authority and power among communist states and nationalist upheaval in the colonial world.

Policymakers' blind devotion to this static Cold War vision led America into misfortune in Vietnam. Lacking the critical perspective and sensibility to reappraise basic tenets of U.S. foreign policy in the light of changed events and local circumstances, policymakers failed to perceive Vietnamese realities accurately and thus to gauge American interests in the area prudently.

From Brian VanDeMark, *Into the Quagmire: Lyndon Johnson and the Escalation of the Vietnam War* (Oxford University Press, 1995). Copyright © 1995 by Brian VanDeMark. Reprinted by permission of Oxford University Press, Inc. Notes omitted.

Policymakers, as a consequence, misread an indigenous, communist-led nationalist movement as part of a larger, centrally directed challenge to world order and stability; tied American fortunes to a noncommunist regime of slim popular legitimacy and effectiveness; and intervened militarily in the region far out of proportion to U.S. security requirements.

An arrogant and stubborn faith in America's power to shape the course of foreign events compounded the dangers sown by ideological rigidity. Policymakers in 1964–1965 shared a common postwar conviction that the United States not only should, but could, control political conditions in South Vietnam, as elsewhere throughout much of the world. This conviction had led Washington to intervene progressively deeper in South Vietnamese affairs over the years. And when—despite Washington's increasing exertions—Saigon's political situation declined precipitously during 1964–1965, this conviction prompted policymakers to escalate the war against Hanoi, in the belief that America could stimulate political order in South Vietnam through the application of military force against North Vietnam.

Domestic political pressures exerted an equally powerful, if less obvious, influence over the course of U.S. involvement in Vietnam. The fall of China in 1949 and the ugly McCarthyism it aroused embittered American foreign policy for a generation. By crippling President Truman's political fortunes, it taught his Democratic successors, John Kennedy and Lyndon Johnson [LBJ], a strong and sobering lesson: that another "loss" to communism in East Asia risked renewed and devastating attacks from the right. This fear of reawakened McCarthyism remained a paramount concern as policymakers pon-

dered what course to follow as conditions in South Vietnam deteriorated rapidly in 1964–1965.

* * *

Enduring traditions of ideological rigidity, diplomatic arrogance, and political vulnerability heavily influenced the way policymakers approached decisions in Vietnam in 1964–1965. Understanding the decisions of this period fully, however, also requires close attention to contemporary developments in America and South Vietnam. These years marked a tumultuous time in both countries, which affected the course of events in subtle but significant ways.

Policymakers in 1964–1965 lived in a period of extraordinary domestic political upheaval sparked by the civil rights movement. It is difficult to overstate the impact of this upheaval on American politics in the mid-1960s. During 1964–1965, the United States—particularly the American South—experienced profound and long overdue change in the economic, political, and social rights of blacks. This change, consciously embraced by the liberal administration of Lyndon Johnson, engendered sharp political hostility among conservative southern whites and their deputies in Congress—hostility which the politically astute Johnson sensed could spill over into the realm of foreign affairs, where angry civil rights opponents could exact their revenge should LBJ stumble and "lose" a crumbling South Vietnam. This danger, reinforced by the memory of McCarthyism, stirred deep political fears in Johnson, together with an abiding aversion to failure in Vietnam.

LBJ feared defeat in South Vietnam, but he craved success and glory at home. A forceful, driving President of boundless ambition, Johnson sought to harness the political momentum created by the civil rights movement to enact a far-reaching domestic reform agenda under the rubric of the Great Society. LBJ would achieve the greatness he sought by leading America toward justice and opportunity for all its citizens, through his historic legislative program.

Johnson's domestic aspirations fundamentally conflicted with his uneasy involvement in Vietnam. An experienced and perceptive politician, LBJ knew his domestic reforms required the sustained focus and cooperation of Congress. He also knew a larger war in Vietnam jeopardized these reforms by drawing away political attention and economic resources. America's increasing military intervention in 1964–1965 cast this tension between Vietnam and the Great Society into sharp relief.

Johnson saw his predicament clearly. But he failed to resolve it for fear that acknowledging the growing extent and cost of the war would thwart his domestic reforms, while pursuing a course of withdrawal risked political ruin. LBJ, instead, chose to obscure the magnitude of his dilemma by obscuring America's deepening involvement as South Vietnam began to fail. That grave compromise of candor opened the way to Johnson's eventual downfall.

Events in South Vietnam during 1964–1965 proved equally fateful. A historically weak and divided land, South Vietnam's deeply rooted ethnic, political, and religious turmoil intensified sharply in the winter of 1964–1965. This mounting turmoil, combined with increased communist military attacks, pushed Saigon to the brink of political collapse.

South Vietnam's accelerating crisis alarmed American policymakers, driving them to deepen U.S. involvement considerably in an effort to arrest Saigon's political failure. Abandoning the concept of stability in the South *before* escalation against the North, policymakers now embraced the concept of stability *through* escalation, in the desperate hope that military action against Hanoi would prompt a stubbornly elusive political order in Saigon.

This shift triggered swift and ominous consequences scarcely anticipated by its architects. Policymakers soon confronted intense military, political, and bureaucratic pressures to widen the war. Unsettled by these largely unforeseen pressures, policymakers reacted confusedly and defensively. Rational men, they struggled to control increasingly irrational forces. But their reaction only clouded their attention to basic assumptions and ultimate costs as the war rapidly spun out of control in the spring and summer of 1965. In their desperation to make Vietnam policy work amid this rising tide of war pressures, they thus failed ever to question whether it could work—or at what ultimate price. Their failure recalls the warning of a prescient political scientist, who years before had cautioned against those policymakers with "an infinite capacity for making ends of [their] means."

The decisions of 1964–1965 bespeak a larger and deeper failure as well. Throughout this period—as, indeed, throughout the course of America's Vietnam involvement—U.S. policymakers strove principally to create a viable non-communist regime in South Vietnam. For many years and at great effort and cost, Washington had endeavored to achieve political stability and competence in Saigon. Despite these efforts, South Vietnam's political disarray persisted and deepened, until, in 1965, America intervened with massive military force to avert its total collapse.

Few policymakers in 1964–1965 paused to mull this telling fact, to ponder its implications about Saigon's viability as a political entity. The failure to re-examine this and other fundamental premises of U.S. policy—chief among them Vietnam's importance to American national interests and Washington's ability to forge political order through military power—proved a costly and tragic lapse of statesmanship....

* * *

The legacy of Vietnam, like the war itself, remains a difficult and painful subject for Americans. As passions subside and time bestows greater perspective, Americans still struggle to understand Vietnam's meaning and lessons for the country. They still wonder how the United States found itself ensnared in an ambiguous, costly, and divisive war, and how it can avoid repeating such an ordeal in the future.

The experience of Lyndon Johnson and his advisers during the decisive years 1964–1965 offers much insight into those questions. For their decisions, which fundamentally transformed U.S. participation in the war, both reflected and defined much of the larger history of America's Vietnam involvement.

Their decisions may also, one hopes, yield kernels of wisdom for the future; the past, after all, can teach us lessons. But history's lessons, as Vietnam showed, are themselves dependent on each generation's knowledge and understanding of the past. So it proved for 1960s policymakers, whose ignorance and misperception of Southeast Asian history, culture, and politics pulled America progres-

sively deeper into the war. LBJ, [Secretary of State Dean] Rusk, [Robert] McNamara, [McGeorge] Bundy, [Ambassador Maxwell] Taylor—most of their generation, in fact—mistakenly viewed Vietnam through the simplistic ideological prism of the Cold War. They perceived a deeply complex and ambiguous regional struggle as a grave challenge to world order and stability, fomented by communist China acting through its local surrogate, North Vietnam.

This perception, given their mixture of memories—the West's capitulation to Hitler at Munich, Stalin's postwar truculence, Mao's belligerent rhetoric—appears altogether understandable in retrospect. But it also proved deeply flawed and oblivious to abiding historical realities. Constrained by their memories and ideology. American policymakers neglected the subtle but enduring force of nationalism in Southeast Asia. Powerful and decisive currents—the deep and historic tension between Vietnam and China; regional friction among the Indochinese states of Vietnam, Laos, and Cambodia; and, above all, Hanoi's fanatical will to unification—went unnoticed or unweighed because they failed to fit Washington's worldview. Although it is true, as Secretary of State Rusk once said, that "one cannot escape one's experience," Rusk and his fellow policymakers seriously erred by falling uncritical prisoners of their experience.

Another shared experience plagued 1960s policymakers like a ghost: the ominous specter of McCarthyism. This frightful political memory haunted LBJ and his Democratic colleagues like a barely suppressed demon in the national psyche. Barely ten years removed from the traumatic "loss" of China and its devastating domestic repercussions, Johnson and his advisers remembered its consequences vividly and shuddered at a similar fate in Vietnam. They talked about this only privately, but then with genuine and palpable fear. Defense Secretary McNamara, in a guarded moment, confided to a newsman in the spring of 1965 that U.S. disengagement from South Vietnam threatened "a disastrous political fight that could... freeze American political debate and even affect political freedom."

Such fears resonated deeply in policymakers' minds. Nothing, it seemed, could be worse than the "loss" of Vietnam—not even an intensifying stalemate secured at increasing military and political risk. For a President determined to fulfill liberalism's postwar agenda, Truman's ordeal in China seemed a powerfully forbidding lesson. It hung over LBJ in Vietnam like a dark shadow he could not shake, an agony he would not repeat.

McCarthyism's long shadow into the mid-1960s underscores a persistent and troubling phenomenon of postwar American politics: the peculiar vulnerability besetting liberal Presidents thrust into the maelstrom of world politics. In America's postwar political climate —dominated by the culture of anticommunism—Democratic leaders from Truman to Kennedy to Johnson remained acutely sensitive to the domestic repercussions of foreign policy failure. This fear of right-wing reaction sharply inhibited liberals like LBJ, narrowing what they considered their range of politically acceptable options, while diminishing their willingness to disengage from untenable foreign commitments. Thus, when Johnson did confront the bitter choice between defeat in Vietnam and fighting a major, inconclusive war, he reluctantly chose the second because he

could not tolerate the domestic consequences of the first. Committed to fulfilling the Great Society, fearful of resurgent McCarthyism, and afraid that disengagement meant sacrificing the former to the latter, LBJ perceived least political danger in holding on.

But if Johnson resigned never to "lose" South Vietnam, he also resigned never to sacrifice his cherished Great Society in the process. LBJ's determination, however understandable, nonetheless led him deliberately and seriously to obscure the nature and cost of America's deepening involvement in the war during 1964–1965. This decision bought Johnson the short-term political maneuverability he wanted, but at a costly long-term political price. As LBJ's credibility on the war subsequently eroded, public confidence in his leadership slowly but irretrievably evaporated. And this, more than any other factor, is what finally drove Johnson from the White House.

It also tarnished the presidency and damaged popular faith in American government for more than a decade. Trapped between deeply conflicting pressures, LBJ never shared his dilemma with the public. Johnson would not, or felt he dare not, trust his problems with the American people. LBJ's decision, however human, tragically undermined the reciprocal faith between President and public indispensable to effective governance in a democracy. Just as tragically, it fostered a pattern of presidential behavior which led his successor, Richard Nixon, to eventual ruin amid even greater popular political alienation.

Time slowly healed most of these wounds to the American political process, while reconfirming the fundamental importance of presidential credibility in a democracy. Johnson's Vietnam travail underscored the necessity of public trust and support to presidential success. Without them, as LBJ painfully discovered, Presidents are doomed to disaster.

Johnson, in retrospect, might have handled his domestic dilemma more forthrightly. An equally serious dilemma, however, remained always beyond his —or Washington's—power to mend: the root problem of political disarray in South Vietnam. The perennial absence of stable and responsive government in Saigon troubled Washington policymakers profoundly; they understood, only too well, its pivotal importance to the war effort and to the social and economic reforms essential to the country's survival. Over and over again, American officials stressed the necessity of political cooperation to their embattled South Vietnamese allies. But to no avail. As one top American in Saigon later lamented, "[Y]ou could tell them all 'you've got to get together [and stop] this haggling and fighting among yourselves,' but how do you make them do it?" he said. "How do you make them do it?"

Washington, alas, could not. As Ambassador Taylor conceded early in the war, "[You] cannot order good government. You can't get it by fiat." This stubborn but telling truth eventually came to haunt Taylor and others. South Vietnam never marshaled the political will necessary to create an effective and enduring government; it never produced leaders addressing the aspirations and thus attracting the allegiance of the South Vietnamese people. Increasing levels of U.S. troops and firepower, moreover, never offset this fundamental debility. America, as a consequence, built its massive military effort on a foundation of political quicksand.

The causes of this elemental flaw lay deeply imbedded in the social and political history of the region. Neither before nor after 1954 was South Vietnam ever really a nation in spirit. Divided by profound ethnic and religious cleavages dating back centuries and perpetuated under French colonial rule, the people of South Vietnam never developed a common political identity. Instead, political factionalism and rivalry always held sway. The result: a chronic and fatal political disorder.

Saigon's fundamental weakness bore anguished witness to the limits of U.S. power. South Vietnam's shortcomings taught a proud and mighty nation that it could not save a people in spite of themselves—that American power, in the last analysis, offered no viable substitute for indigenous political resolve. Without this basic ingredient, as Saigon's turbulent history demonstrated, Washington's most dedicated and strenuous efforts will prove extremely vulnerable, if not futile.

This is not a happy or popular lesson. But it is a wise and prudent one, attuned to the imperfect realities of an imperfect world. One of America's sagest diplomats, George Kennan, understood and articulated this lesson well when he observed: "When it comes to helping people to resist Communist pressures,... no assistance... can be effective unless the people themselves have a very high degree of determination and a willingness to help themselves. The moment they begin to place the bulk of the burden on us," Kennan warned, "the whole situation is lost." This, tragically, is precisely what befell America in South Vietnam during 1964–1965. Hereafter, as perhaps always before—*external* U.S. economic, military, and political support provided the vital elements of stability and strength in South Vietnam. Without that *external* support, as events following America's long-delayed withdrawal in 1973 showed, South Vietnam's government quickly failed.

Washington's effort to forge political order through military power spawned another tragedy as well. It ignited unexpected pressures which quickly overwhelmed U.S. policymakers, and pulled them ever deeper into the war. LBJ and his advisers began bombing North Vietnam in early 1965 in a desperate attempt to spur political resolve in South Vietnam. But their effort boomeranged wildly. Rather than stabilizing the situation, it instead unleashed forces that soon put Johnson at the mercy of circumstances, a hostage to the war's accelerating momentum. LBJ, as a result, began steering with an ever looser hand. By the summer of 1965, President Johnson found himself not the controller of events but largely controlled by them. He had lost the political leader's "continual struggle," in the words of Henry Kissinger, "to rescue an element of choice from the pressure of circumstance."

LBJ's experience speaks powerfully across the years. With each Vietnam decision, Johnson's vulnerability to military pressure and bureaucratic momentum intensified sharply. Each step generated demands for another, even bigger step—which LBJ found increasingly difficult to resist. His predicament confirmed George Ball's admonition that war is a fiercely unpredictable force, often generating its own inexorable momentum.

Johnson sensed this danger almost intuitively. He quickly grasped the dilemma and difficulties confronting him in Vietnam. But LBJ lacked the inner strength—the security and self-confidence—to overrule the counsel of his inherited advisers.

Most of those advisers, on the other hand—especially McGeorge Bundy and Robert McNamara—failed to anticipate such perils. Imbued with an overweening faith in their ability to "manage" crises and "control" escalation, Bundy and McNamara, along with Maxwell Taylor, first pushed military action against the North as a lever to force political improvement in the South. But bombing did not rectify Saigon's political problems; it only exacerbated them, while igniting turbulent military pressures that rapidly overwhelmed these advisers' confident calculations.

These advisers' preoccupation with technique, with the application of power, characterized much of America's approach to the Vietnam War. Bundy and McNamara epitomized a postwar generation confident in the exercise and efficacy of U.S. power. Despite the dark and troubled history of European intervention in Indochina, these men stubbornly refused to equate America's situation in the mid-1960s to France's earlier ordeal. To them, the United States possessed limitless ability, wisdom, and virtue; it would therefore prevail where other western powers had failed.

This arrogance born of power led policymakers to ignore manifest dangers, to persist in the face of ever darkening circumstances. Like figures in Greek tragedy, pride compelled these supremely confident men further into disaster. They succumbed to the affliction common to great powers throughout the ages—the dangerous "self-esteem engendered by power," as the political philosopher Hans Morgenthau once wrote, "which equates power and virtue,

[and] in the process loses all sense of moral and political proportion."

Tradition, as well as personality, nurtured such thinking. For in many ways, America's military intervention in Vietnam represented the logical fulfillment of a policy and outlook axiomatically accepted by U.S. policymakers for nearly two decades—the doctrine of global containment. Fashioned at the outset of the Cold War, global containment extended American interests and obligations across vast new areas of the world in defense against perceived monolithic communist expansion. It remained the lodestar of America foreign policy, moreover, even as the constellation of international forces shifted dramatically amid diffused authority and power among communist states and nationalist upheaval in the post-colonial world.

Vietnam exposed the limitations and contradictions of this static doctrine in a world of flux. It also revealed the dangers and flaws of an undiscriminating, universalist policy which perceptive critics of global containment, such as the eminent journalist Walter Lippmann, had anticipated from the beginning. As Lippmann warned about global containment in 1947:

Satellite states and puppet governments are not good material out of which to construct unassailable barriers [for American defense]. A diplomatic war conducted as this policy demands, that is to say conducted indirectly, means that we must stake our own security and the peace of the world upon satellites, puppets, clients, agents about whom we can know very little. Frequently they will act for their own reasons, and on their own judgments, presenting us with accomplished facts that we did not intend, and with crises for which we are

unready. The "unassailable barriers" will present us with an unending series of insoluble dilemmas. We shall have either to disown our puppets, which would be tantamount to appeasement and defeat and loss of face, or must support them at an incalculable cost....

Here lay the heart of America's Vietnam troubles. Driven by unquestioning allegiance to an ossified and extravagant doctrine, Washington officials plunged deeply into a struggle which itself dramatized the changed realities and complexities of the postwar world. Their action teaches both the importance of re-examining premises as circumstances change and the costly consequences of failing to recognize and adapt to them.

Vietnam represented a failure not just of American foreign policy but also of American statesmanship. For once drawn into the war, LBJ and his advisers quickly sensed Vietnam's immense difficulties and dangers—Saigon's congenital political problems, the war's spiraling military costs, the remote likelihood of victory—and plunged in deeper nonetheless. In their determination to preserve America's international credibility and protect their domestic political standing, they continued down an ever costlier path.

That path proved a distressing, multifaceted paradox. Fearing injury to the perception of American power, diminished faith in U.S. resolve, and a conservative political firestorm, policymakers rigidly pursued a course which ultimately injured the substance of American power by consuming exorbitant lives and resources, shook allied confidence in U.S. strategic judgment, and shattered liberalism's political unity and vigor by polarizing and paralyzing American society.

Herein lies Vietnam's most painful but pressing lesson. Statesmanship requires judgment, sensibility, and, above all, wisdom in foreign affairs—the wisdom to calculate national interests prudently and to balance commitments with effective power. It requires that most difficult task of political leaders: "to distinguish between what is desireable and what is possible,... between what is desireable and what is essential."

This is important in peace; it is indispensable in war. As the great tutor of statesmen, Carl von Clausewitz, wrote, "Since war is not an act of senseless passion but is controlled by its political object, the value of this object must determine the sacrifices to be made for it in *magnitude* and also in *duration*. Once the expenditure of effort exceeds the value of the political object," Clausewitz admonished, "the object must be renounced...." His maxim, in hindsight, seems painfully relevant to a war which, as even America's military commander in Vietnam, General William Westmoreland, concluded, "the vital security of the United States was not and possibly could not be clearly demonstrated and understood...."

LBJ and his advisers failed to heed this fundamental principle of statesmanship. They failed to weigh American costs in Vietnam against Vietnam's relative importance to American national interests and its effect on overall American power. Compelled by events in Vietnam and, especially, coercive political pressures at home, they deepened an unsound, peripheral commitment and pursued manifestly unpromising and immensely costly objectives. Their failure of statesmanship, then, proved a failure of judgment and, above all, of proportion.

NO

H. R. McMaster

DERELICTION OF DUTY

The Americanization of the Vietnam War between 1963 and 1965 was the product of an unusual interaction of personalities and circumstances. The escalation of U.S. military intervention grew out of a complicated chain of events and a complex web of decisions that slowly transformed the conflict in Vietnam into an American war.

Much of the literature on Vietnam has argued that the "Cold War mentality" put such pressure on President Johnson that the Americanization of the war was inevitable. The imperative to contain Communism was an important factor in Vietnam policy, but neither American entry into the war nor the manner in which the war was conducted was inevitable. The United States went to war in Vietnam in a manner unique in American history. Vietnam was not forced on the United States by a tidal wave of Cold War ideology. It slunk in on cat's feet.

Between November 1963 and July 1965, LBJ made the critical decisions that took the United States into war almost without realizing it. The decisions, and the way in which he made them, profoundly affected the way the United States fought in Vietnam. Although impersonal forces, such as the ideological imperative of containing Communism, the bureaucratic structure, and institutional priorities, influenced the president's Vietnam decisions, those decisions depended primarily on his character, his motivations, and his relationships with his principal advisers.

*　*　*

Most investigations of how the United States entered the war have devoted little attention to the crucial developments which shaped LBJ's approach to Vietnam and set conditions for a gradual intervention. The first of several "turning points" in the American escalation comprised the near-contemporaneous assassinations of Ngo Dinh Diem and John F. Kennedy. The legacy of the Kennedy administration included an expanded commitment to South Vietnam as an "experiment" in countering Communist insurgencies and a deep distrust of the military that manifested itself in the appointment of officers who would prove supportive of the administration's policies. After

From H. R. McMaster, *Dereliction of Duty: Lyndon Johnson, Robert McNamara, the Joint Chiefs of Staff, and the Lies That Led to Vietnam* (HarperCollins, 1997). Copyright © 1997 by H. R. McMaster. Reprinted by permission of HarperCollins Publishers, Inc. Notes omitted.

November 1963 the United States confronted what in many ways was a new war in South Vietnam. Having deposed the government of Ngo Dinh Diem and his brother Nhu, and having supported actions that led to their deaths, Washington assumed responsibility for the new South Vietnamese leaders. Intensified Viet Cong activity added impetus to U.S. deliberations, leading Johnson and his advisers to conclude that the situation in South Vietnam demanded action beyond military advice and support. Next, in the spring of 1964, the Johnson administration adopted graduated pressure as its strategic concept for the Vietnam War. Rooted in Maxwell Taylor's national security strategy of flexible response, graduated pressure evolved over the next year, becoming the blueprint for the deepening American commitment to maintaining South Vietnam's independence. Then, in August 1964, in response to the Gulf of Tonkin incident, the United States crossed the threshold of direct American military action against North Vietnam.

The Gulf of Tonkin resolution gave the president carte blanche for escalating the war. During the ostensibly benign "holding period" from September 1964 to February 1965, LBJ was preoccupied with his domestic political agenda, and McNamara built consensus behind graduated pressure. In early 1965 the president raised U.S. intervention to a higher level again, deciding on February 9 to begin a systematic program of limited air strikes on targets in North Vietnam and, on February 26, to commit U.S. ground forces to the South. Last, in March 1965, he quietly gave U.S. ground forces the mission of "killing Viet Cong." That series of decisions, none in itself tantamount to a clearly discernable decision to go to war, nevertheless transformed America's commitment in Vietnam.

* * *

Viewed together, those decisions might create the impression of a deliberate determination on the part of the Johnson administration to go to war. On the contrary, the president did not want to go to war in Vietnam and was not planning to do so. Indeed, as early as May 1964, LBJ seemed to realize that an American war in Vietnam would be a costly failure. He confided to McGeorge Bundy, " . . . looks like to me that we're getting into another Korea. It just worries the hell out of me. I don't see what we can ever hope to get out of this." It was, Johnson observed, "the biggest damn mess that I ever saw. . . . It's damn easy to get into a war, but . . . it's going to be harder to ever extricate yourself if you get in." Despite his recognition that the situation in Vietnam demanded that he consider alternative courses of action and make a difficult decision, LBJ sought to avoid or to postpone indefinitely an explicit choice between war and disengagement from South Vietnam. In the ensuing months, however, each decision he made moved the United States closer to war, although he seemed not to recognize that fact.

The president's fixation on short-term political goals, combined with his character and the personalities of his principal civilian and military advisers, rendered the administration incapable of dealing adequately with the complexities of the situation in Vietnam. LBJ's advisory system was structured to achieve consensus and to prevent potentially damaging leaks. Profoundly insecure and distrustful of anyone but his closest civilian advisers, the president viewed the JCS [Joint Chiefs of Staff] with suspicion. When the situation in Vietnam seemed to demand military action, Johnson did not turn to his military advisers to determine how to solve the problem. He turned instead to his civilian advisers to determine how to postpone a decision. The relationship between the president, the secretary of defense, and the Joint Chiefs led to the curious situation in which the nation went to war without the benefit of effective military advice from the organization having the statutory responsibility to be the nation's "principal military advisers."

* * *

What Johnson feared most in 1964 was losing his chance to win the presidency in his own right. He saw Vietnam principally as a danger to that goal. After the election, he feared that an American military response to the deteriorating situation in Vietnam would jeopardize chances that his Great Society would pass through Congress. The Great Society was to be Lyndon Johnson's great domestic political legacy, and he could not tolerate the risk of its failure. McNamara would help the president first protect his electoral chances and then pass the Great Society by offering a strategy for Vietnam that appeared cheap and could be conducted with minimal public and congressional attention. McNamara's strategy of graduated pressure permitted Johnson to pursue his objective of not losing the war in Vietnam while postponing the "day of reckoning" and keeping the whole question out of public debate all the while.

McNamara was confident in his ability to satisfy the president's needs. He believed fervently that nuclear weapons and the Cold War international political environment had made traditional military experience and thinking not only irrelevant, but often danger-

ous for contemporary policy. Accordingly, McNamara, along with systems analysts and other civilian members of his own department and the Department of State, developed his own strategy for Vietnam. Bolstered by what he regarded as a personal triumph during the Cuban missile crisis, McNamara drew heavily on that experience and applied it to Vietnam. Based on the assumption that carefully controlled and sharply limited military actions were reversible, and therefore could be carried out at minimal risk and cost, graduated pressure allowed McNamara and Johnson to avoid confronting many of the possible consequences of military action.

* * *

Johnson and McNamara succeeded in creating the illusion that the decisions to attack North Vietnam were alternatives to war rather than war itself. Graduated pressure defined military action as a form of communication, the object of which was to affect the enemy's calculation of interests and dissuade him from a particular activity. Because the favored means of communication (bombing fixed installations and economic targets) were not appropriate for the mobile forces of the Viet Cong, who lacked an infrastructure and whose strength in the South was political as well as military, McNamara and his colleagues pointed to the infiltration of men and supplies into South Vietnam as proof that the source and center of the enemy's power in Vietnam lay north of the seventeenth parallel, and specifically in Hanoi. Their definition of the enemy's source of strength was derived from that strategy rather than from a critical examination of the full reality in

South Vietnam—and turned out to be inaccurate.

Graduated pressure was fundamentally flawed in other ways. The strategy ignored the uncertainty of war and the unpredictable psychology of an activity that involves killing, death, and destruction. To the North Vietnamese, military action, involving as it did attacks on their forces and bombing of their territory, was not simply a means of communication. Human sacrifices in war evoke strong emotions, creating a dynamic that defies systems analysis quantification. Once the United States crossed the threshold of war against North Vietnam with covert raids and the Gulf of Tonkin "reprisals," the future course of events depended not only on decisions made in Washington but also on enemy responses and actions that were unpredictable. McNamara, however, viewed the war as another business management problem that, he assumed, would ultimately succumb to his reasoned judgment and others' rational calculations. He and his assistants thought that they could predict with great precision what amount of force applied in Vietnam would achieve the results they desired and they believed that they could control that force with great precision from halfway around the world. There were compelling contemporaneous arguments that graduated pressure would not affect Hanoi's will sufficiently to convince the North to desist from its support of the South, and that such a strategy would probably lead to an escalation of the war. Others expressed doubts about the utility of attacking North Vietnam by air to win a conflict in South Vietnam. Nevertheless, McNamara refused to consider the consequences of his recommendations and forged ahead oblivious of the human and psychological complexities of war.

* * *

Despite their recognition that graduated pressure was fundamentally flawed, the JCS were unable to articulate effectively either their objections or alternatives. Interservice rivalry was a significant impediment. Although differing perspectives were understandable given the Chiefs' long experience in their own services and their need to protect the interests of their services, the president's principal military advisers were obligated by law to render their best advice. The Chiefs' failure to do so, and their willingness to present single-service remedies to a complex military problem, prevented them from developing a comprehensive estimate of the situation or from thinking effectively about strategy.

When it became clear to the Chiefs that they were to have little influence on the policy-making process, they failed to confront the president with their objections to McNamara's approach to the war. Instead they attempted to work within that strategy in order to remove over time the limitations to further action. Unable to develop a strategic alternative to graduated pressure, the Chiefs became fixated on means by which the war could be conducted and pressed for an escalation of the war by degrees. They hoped that graduated pressure would evolve over time into a fundamentally different strategy, more in keeping with their belief in the necessity of greater force and its more resolute application. In so doing, they gave tacit approval to graduated pressure during the critical period in which the president escalated the war. They did not recommend the total force they believed would ultimately be required in Vietnam and accepted a strategy they knew would lead to a large but inadequate commitment of troops, for an extended period of time, with little hope for success.

* * *

McNamara and Lyndon Johnson were far from disappointed with the joint Chiefs' failings. Because his priorities were domestic, Johnson had little use for military advice that recommended actions inconsistent with those priorities. McNamara and his assistants in the Department of Defense, on the other hand, were arrogant. They disparaged military advice because they thought that their intelligence and analytical methods could compensate for their lack of military experience and education. Indeed military experience seemed to them a liability because military officers took too narrow a view and based their advice on antiquated notions of war. Geopolitical and technological changes of the last fifteen years, they believed, had rendered advice based on military experience irrelevant and, in fact, dangerous. McNamara's disregard for military experience and for history left him to draw principally on his staff in the Department of Defense and led him to conclude that his only real experience with the planning and direction of military force, the Cuban missile crisis, was the most relevant analogy to Vietnam.

While they slowly deepened American military involvement in Vietnam, Johnson and McNamara pushed the Chiefs further away from the decision-making process. There was no meaningful structure through which the Chiefs could voice their views—even the chairman was not a reliable conduit. NSC meetings were strictly *pro forma* affairs in which the president endeavored to build consensus for decisions already made. Johnson continued Kennedy's practice of meeting with small groups of his most trusted advisers. Indeed he made his most important decisions at the Tuesday lunch meetings in which Rusk, McGeorge Bundy, and McNamara were the only regular participants. The president and McNamara shifted responsibility for real planning away from the JCS to ad hoc committees composed principally of civilian analysts and attorneys, whose main goal was to obtain a consensus consistent with the president's pursuit of the middle ground between disengagement and war. The products of those efforts carried the undeserved credibility of proposals that had been agreed on by all departments and were therefore hard to oppose. McNamara and Johnson endeavored to get the advice they wanted by placing conditions and qualifications on questions that they asked the Chiefs. When the Chiefs' advice was not consistent with his own recommendations, McNamara, with the aid of the chairman of the Joint Chiefs of Staff, lied in meetings of the National Security Council about the Chiefs' views.

Rather than advice McNamara and Johnson extracted from the JCS acquiescence and silent support for decisions already made. Even as they relegated the Chiefs to a peripheral position in the policy-making process, they were careful to preserve the facade of consultation to prevent the JCS from opposing the administration's policies either openly or behind the scenes. As American involvement in the war escalated, Johnson's vulnerability to disaffected senior military officers increased because he was purposely deceiving the Congress and the public about the nature of the American military effort in Vietnam. The president and the secretary of defense deliberately obscured the nature of decisions made and left undefined the limits that they envisioned on the use of force. They indicated to the Chiefs that they would take actions that they never intended to pursue. McNamara and his assistants, who considered communication the purpose of military action, kept the nature of their objective from the JCS, who viewed "winning" as the only viable goal in war. Finally, Johnson appealed directly to them, referring to himself as the "coach" and them as "his team." To dampen their calls for further action, Lyndon Johnson attempted to generate sympathy from the JCS for the great pressures that he was feeling from those who opposed escalation.

The ultimate test of the Chiefs' loyalty came in July 1965. The administration's lies to the American public had grown in magnitude as the American military effort in Vietnam escalated. The president's plan of deception depended on tacit approval or silence from the JCS. LBJ had misrepresented the mission of U.S. ground forces in Vietnam, distorted the views of the Chiefs to lend credibility to his decision against mobilization, grossly understated the numbers of troops General Westmoreland had requested, and lied to the Congress about the monetary cost of actions already approved and of those awaiting final decision. The Chiefs did not disappoint the president. In the days before the president made his duplicitous public announcement concerning Westmoreland's request, the Chiefs, with the exception of commandant of the Marine Corps Greene, withheld from congressmen their estimates of the amount of force that would be needed in Vietnam. As he

had during the Gulf of Tonkin hearings, Wheeler lent his support to the president's deception of Congress. The "five silent men" on the Joint Chiefs made possible the way the United States went to war in Vietnam.

* * *

Several factors kept the Chiefs from challenging the president's subterfuges. The professional code of the military officer prohibits him or her from engaging in political activity. Actions that could have undermined the administration's credibility and derailed its Vietnam policy could not have been undertaken lightly. The Chiefs felt loyalty to their commander in chief. The Truman-MacArthur controversy during the Korean War had warned the Chiefs about the dangers of overstepping the bounds of civilian control. Loyalty to their services also weighed against opposing the president and the secretary of defense. Harold Johnson, for example, decided against resignation because he thought he had to remain in office to protect the Army's interests as best he could. Admiral McDonald and Marine Corps Commandant Greene compromised their views on Vietnam in exchange for concessions to their respective services. Greene achieved a dramatic expansion of the Marine Corps, and McDonald ensured that the Navy retained control of Pacific Command. None of the Chiefs had sworn an oath to his service, however. They had all sworn, rather, to "support and defend the Constitution of the United States."

General Greene recalled that direct requests by congressmen for his assessment put him in a difficult situation. The president was lying, and he expected the Chiefs to lie as well or, at least, to withhold the whole truth. Although the president should not have placed the Chiefs in that position, the flag officers should not have tolerated it when he had.

Because the Constitution locates civilian control of the military in Congress as well as in the executive branch, the Chiefs could not have been justified in deceiving the peoples' representatives about Vietnam. Wheeler in particular allowed his duty to the president to overwhelm his obligations under the Constitution. As cadets are taught at the United States Military Academy, the JCS relationship with the Congress is challenging and demands that military officers possess a strong character and keen intellect. While the Chiefs must present Congress with their best advice based on their professional experience and education, they must be careful not to undermine their credibility by crossing the line between advice and advocacy of service interests.

Maxwell Taylor had a profound influence on the nature of the civil-military relationship during the escalation of American involvement in Vietnam. In contrast to Army Chief of Staff George C. Marshall, who, at the start of World War II, recognized the need for the JCS to suppress service parochialism to provide advice consistent with national interests, Taylor exacerbated service differences to help McNamara and Johnson keep the Chiefs divided and, thus, marginal to the policy process. Taylor recommended men for appointment to the JCS who were less likely than their predecessors to challenge the direction of the administration's military policy, even when they knew that that policy was fundamentally flawed. Taylor's behavior is perhaps best explained by his close personal friendship with the Kennedy family; McNamara; and, later, Johnson. In contrast again to Marshall, who thought it im-

portant to keep a professional distance from President Franklin Roosevelt, Taylor abandoned an earlier view similar to Marshall's in favor of a belief that the JCS and the president should enjoy "an intimate, easy relationship, born of friendship and mutual regard."

* * *

The way in which the United States went to war in the period between November 1963 and July 1965 had, not surprisingly, a profound influence on the conduct of the war and on its outcome. Because Vietnam policy decisions were made based on domestic political expediency, and because the president was intent on forging a consensus position behind what he believed was a middle policy, the administration deliberately avoided clarifying its policy objectives and postponed discussing the level of force that the president was willing to commit to the effort. Indeed, because the president was seeking domestic political consensus, members of the administration believed that ambiguity in the objectives for fighting in Vietnam was a strength rather than a weakness. Determined to prevent dissent from the JCS, the administration concealed its development of "fall-back" objectives.

Over time the maintenance of U.S. credibility quietly supplanted the stated policy objective of a free and independent South Vietnam. The principal civilian planners had determined that to guarantee American credibility, it was not necessary to win in Vietnam. That conclusion, combined with the belief that the use of force was merely another form of diplomatic communication, directed the military effort in the South at achieving stalemate rather than victory. Those charged with planning the war believed that it would be possible to preserve American credibility even if the United States armed forces withdrew from the South, after a show of force against the North and in the South in which American forces were "bloodied." After the United States became committed to war, however, and more American soldiers, airmen, and Marines had died in the conflict, it would become impossible simply to disengage and declare America's credibility intact, a fact that should have been foreseen. The Chiefs sensed the shift in objectives, but did not challenge directly the views of civilian planners in that connection. McNamara and Johnson recognized that, once committed to war, the JCS would not agree to an objective other than imposing a solution on the enemy consistent with U.S. interests. The JCS deliberately avoided clarifying the objective as well. As a result, when the United States went to war, the JCS pursued objectives different from those of the president. When the Chiefs requested permission to apply force consistent with their conception of U.S. objectives, the president and McNamara, based on their goals and domestic political constraints, rejected JCS requests, or granted them only in part. The result was that the JCS and McNamara became fixated on the means rather than on the ends, and on the manner in which the war was conducted instead of a military strategy that could connect military actions to achievable policy goals.

Because forthright communication between top civilian and military officials in the Johnson administration was never developed, there was no reconciliation of McNamara's intention to limit the American military effort sharply and the Chiefs' assessment that the United States could not possibly win under such conditions. If they had attempted to reconcile those positions, they could not have helped but recognize the futility of the American war effort.

The Joint Chiefs of Staff became accomplices in the president's deception and focused on a tactical task, killing the enemy. General Westmoreland's "strategy" of attrition in South Vietnam, was, in essence, the absence of a strategy. The result was military activity (bombing North Vietnam and killing the enemy in South Vietnam) that did not aim to achieve a clearly defined objective. It was unclear how quantitative measures by which McNamara interpreted the success and failure of the use of military force were contributing to an end of the war. As American casualties mounted and the futility of the strategy became apparent, the American public lost faith in the effort. The Chiefs did not request the number of troops they believed necessary to impose a military solution in South Vietnam until after the Tet offensive in 1968. By that time, however, the president was besieged by opposition to the war and was unable even to consider the request. LBJ, who had gone to such great lengths to ensure a crushing defeat over Barry Goldwater in 1964, declared that he was withdrawing from the race for his party's presidential nomination.

Johnson thought that he would be able to control the U.S. involvement in Vietnam. That belief, based on the strategy of graduated pressure and McNamara's confident assurances, proved in dramatic fashion to be false. If the president was surprised by the consequences of his decisions between November 1963 and July 1965, he should not have been so. He had disregarded the advice he did not want to hear in favor of a policy based on the pursuit of his own political fortunes and his beloved domestic programs.

*   *   *

The war in Vietnam was not lost in the field, nor was it lost on the front pages of the *New York Times* or on the college campuses. It was lost in Washington, D.C., even before Americans assumed sole responsibility for the fighting in 1965 and before they realized the country was at war; indeed, even before the first American units were deployed. The disaster in Vietnam was not the result of impersonal forces but a uniquely human failure, the responsibility for which was shared by President Johnson and his principal military and civilian advisers. The failings were many and reinforcing: arrogance, weakness, lying in the pursuit of self-interest, and, above all, the abdication of responsibility to the American people.

POSTSCRIPT

Was America's Escalation of the War in Vietnam Inevitable?

The book from which VanDeMark's selection was excerpted is a detailed study of the circumstances surrounding the decisions that President Lyndon Johnson made to increase America's presence in Vietnam via the bombing raids of North Vietnam in February 1965 and the introduction of ground troops the following July. VanDeMark agrees with McMaster that Johnson did not consult the Joint Chiefs of Staff about the wisdom of the policy of escalating the war. In fact, Johnson's decisions of "graduated pressure" were made in increments by the civilian advisers surrounding Secretary of Defense Robert McNamara. The policy, if it can be called such, was to prevent the National Liberation Front and its Viet Cong army from taking over South Vietnam. Each service branch fought its own war without coordinating with one another or with the government of South Vietnam. In VanDeMark's view, U.S. intervention was doomed to failure because South Vietnam was an artificial and very corrupt nation-state created by the French and later supported by the Americans. It was unfortunate that the nationalist revolution was tied up with the Communists led by Ho Chi Minh, who had been fighting French colonialism and Japanese imperialism since the 1920s—unlike Korea and Malaysia, which had alternative, noncommunist, nationalist movements.

Why did Johnson plunge "into the quagmire"? For one thing, Johnson remembered how previous democratic presidents Franklin D. Roosevelt and Harry S. Truman had been charged with being soft on communism and accused of losing Eastern Europe to the Russians after the Second World War and China to the Communists in the Chinese Civil War in 1949. In addition, both presidents were charged by Senator Joseph McCarthy and others of harboring Communists in U.S. government agencies. If Johnson was tough in Vietnam, he could stop communist aggression. At the same time, he could ensure that his Great Society social programs of Medicare and job retraining, as well as the impending civil rights legislation, would be passed by Congress.

As an army officer who fought in the Persian Gulf War, McMaster offers a unique perspective on the decision-making processes used by government policymakers. McMaster spares no one in his critique of what he considers the flawed Vietnam policy of "graduated pressure." He says that McNamara, bolstered by the success of America during the Cuban Missile Crisis, believed that the traditional methods of fighting wars were obsolete. Johnson believed in McNamara's approach, and the president's own need for consensus in the decision-making process kept the Joint Chiefs of Staff out of the loop.

Unlike other military historians, who generally absolve the military from responsibility for the strategy employed during the war, McMaster argues that the Joint Chiefs of Staff were responsible for not standing up to Johnson and telling him that his military strategy was seriously flawed. McMaster's views are not as new as some reviewers of his book seem to think. Bruce Palmer, Jr., in *The Twenty-Five Year War: America's Military Role in Vietnam* (University Press of Kentucky, 1984), and Harry G. Summers, Jr., in *On Strategy: A Critical Analysis of the Vietnam War* (Presidio Press, 1982), also see a flawed strategy of war. Summers argues that Johnson should have asked Congress for a declaration of war and fought a conventional war against North Vietnam.

One scholar has claimed that over 7,000 books about the Vietnam War have been published. The starting point for the current issue is Lloyd Gardner and Ted Gittinger, eds., *Vietnam: The Early Decisions* (University of Texas Press, 1997). See also Larry Berman, *Planning a Tragedy: The Americanization of the War in Vietnam* (W. W. Norton, 1982) and *Lyndon Johnson's War* (W. W. Norton, 1989); David Halberstam, *The Best and the Brightest* (Random House, 1972); and Lloyd C. Gardner, *Pay Any Price: Lyndon Johnson and the Wars for Vietnam* (Ivan Dee, 1995). Primary sources can be found in the U.S. Department of State's two-volume *Foreign Relations of the United States, 1964–1968: Vietnam,* (Government Printing Office, 1996) and in the relevant sections of one of the most useful collections of primary sources and essays, *Major Problems in the History of the Vietnam War,* 2d ed., by Robert J. McMahon (Houghton Mifflin, 2000).

The bureaucratic perspective can be found in a series of essays by George C. Herring entitled *LBJ and Vietnam: A Different Kind of War* (University of Texas Press, 1995). Herring is also the author of the widely used text *America's Longest War: the United States and Vietnam* (Alfred A. Knopf, 1986). A brilliant article often found in anthologies is by historian and former policymaker James Thompson, "How Could Vietnam Happen: An Autopsy," *The Atlantic Monthly* (April 1968). An interesting comparison of the 1954 Dien Bien Phu and 1965 U.S. escalation decisions is Fred I. Greenstein and John P. Burke, "The Dynamics of Presidential Reality Testing: Evidence from Two Vietnam Decisions," *Political Science Quarterly* (Winter 1989–1990). A nice review essay on Vietnam's impact on today's military thinking is Michael C. Desch's "Wounded Warriors and the Lessons of Vietnam," *Orbis* (Summer 1998).

ISSUE 15

Did the Civil Rights Movement Improve Race Relations in the United States?

YES: Robert Weisbrot, from *Freedom Bound: A History of America's Civil Rights Movement* (Plume Books, 1990)

NO: Tom Wicker, from *Tragic Failure: Racial Integration in America* (William Morrow, 1996)

ISSUE SUMMARY

YES: Professor of history Robert Weisbrot describes the lasting achievements produced by the civil rights movement in the realm of school desegregation, access to public accommodations, the protection of voting rights for African Americans, and the deepening commitment to racial harmony.

NO: Political journalist Tom Wicker recognizes that legal segregation ended in the South in the 1960s but contends that in the 1970s and 1980s enthusiasm for racial integration waned as white animosity toward African American achievements drained momentum from the movement for true racial equality.

On a steamy August day in 1963, Martin Luther King, Jr., mounted a podium constructed in front of the Lincoln Memorial in Washington, D.C., and, in the studied cadence of a preacher, delivered his famous "I Have a Dream" speech. For many Americans, black and white, King's speech represented the symbolic climax of the civil rights movement. The Civil Rights Act of 1964 and the Voting Rights Act of 1965 were merely denouements.

There were other symbolic events at the March on Washington in addition to King's electrifying oration. The call for the march had been issued by A. Philip Randolph, a long-time civil rights activist, who had threatened in 1941 to stage a similar protest march to bring attention to the economic inequality suffered by African Americans. Randolph's presence at the head of the march reflected a realization of *his* dream. Moreover, several of the speakers that day paid homage to W. E. B. Du Bois, the godfather of the twentieth-century black protest movement in the United States, who had died the previous day (at the age of 95) in Ghana, West Africa, an embittered exile from the land of his birth. For decades, African Americans had endured an enforced second-class citizenship. But in the 1940s and 1950s, following constitutional victories spearheaded by the National Association for the Advancement of Colored People (NAACP) in the areas of housing, voting, and education, black Americans awakened to the possibilities for change in their status. These victories coincided with the rise of independent nations in Africa, led by black leaders such as Kwame Nkrumah, and this fostered pride in the African homeland among many black Americans. Finally, the nonviolent direct action movement, pioneered by interracial organizations such as the Congress of Racial Equality (CORE) and individuals like Randolph, King, Ella Baker, James Farmer, and Fannie Lou Hamer, issued a clarion call to African Americans and their white supporters that full equality was around the corner.

Despite these idealistic predictions of the future, King's vision of a color-blind society, liberated from the harsh realities of prejudice and discrimination, faced serious barriers after the mid-1960s. King's desegregation campaigns had little impact on the economic plight of many African Americans, a point made consistently by Malcolm X prior to his assassination in 1965. The rise of black nationalism produced fissures within the leading civil rights organizations and alienated many whites who had committed their time and money to fostering interracial harmony. Following King's death in 1968, the federal government made efforts to enforce school integration and to legislate affirmative action programs. This fueled controversy that manifested itself in a conservative white backlash against much of the racial progress that had occurred during the previous generation. By the 1990s, in the midst of debates over hiring quotas and the racial implications of the sensationalist media attention devoted to the criminal and civil prosecutions of O. J. Simpson, serious questions could be raised concerning the long-term success of the civil rights movement.

In the first of the following selections, Robert Weisbrot acknowledges the illusory nature of many of the movement's hopes for racial progress and admits that the United States remains a race-conscious society. Nevertheless, he credits the nonviolent direct action campaigns of the 1950s and 1960s with sharply reducing the levels of ignorance, fear, and hate that are the products of the nation's racial heritage. Moreover, he recognizes a substantial record of achievement that includes the desegregation of schools and places of public accommodation, the protection of voting rights, and a severe weakening of the legal and social standing once accorded racism in America.

For Tom Wicker, the civil rights glass is half empty. In the second selection, he argues that, despite legal victories over segregation in the South during the 1960s, recent decades have witnessed a retrenchment campaign abetted by both major political parties and stimulated by white fears that black gains during the civil rights era were achieved at the expense of whites. Consequently, in the long run the civil rights movement failed to bring either racial equality or racial harmony to the United States.

YES

Robert Weisbrot

THE SHIFTING POLITICS OF RACE

Lagging progress toward equality led blacks in the 1970s to propose new, bolder answers to the riddle of "all deliberate speed." Instead of seeking merely to punish overt acts of discrimination, some civil rights spokesmen urged the government to guarantee fair representation of blacks in schools, jobs, and other areas of society. This strategy, pursued mainly through a sympathetic judiciary, broadened the concept of equal opportunity and the frontiers of federal regulation. Yet the idea of race-conscious and at times preferential treatment of blacks, even to remedy past injustice, strained the civil rights coalition and brought further backlash in an age of prolonged liberal eclipse. . . .

THE RECEDING CIVIL RIGHTS VISION

It is now clear that the more expansive hopes for civil rights progress were markedly inflated. Residential segregation, seen in the persistence of inner-city black ghettos and lily-white suburbs, has easily survived federal fiats against housing discrimination. De facto segregation of churches, social centers, and private schools also remains routine, suggesting that in important respects the society's newfound emphasis on interracial harmony has been more rhetorical than real. Wealth, too, is largely segregated along racial lines; the median family income of blacks is barely half that of whites, and blacks are three times as likely to be poor. As for black political power, it is still embryonic with regard to national office holding and access to the circles that make foreign and domestic policy. In all, the roots of racial inequality have proved too deeply embedded in centuries of American history to be washed away by a decade's liberal reform.

Race relations have changed at a glacial pace in much of the rural South, where only the hardiest civil rights activists could weather the repressive social climate. Southern whites understandably regard black militancy as an urban malady, for only in the cities have blacks developed an independent business and professional class able to lead sustained protests. In many outlying towns, where whites monopolize credit and own the farms and textile mills that provide crucial jobs, the etiquette of racial deference persists.

Unwritten rules of segregation in small Southern communities still have the force of law. Harassment and occasional beatings discourage blacks from approaching the polls on election day, whatever the language of federal statutes. Blacks also know to avoid restaurants where they will draw stares instead of service, hotels that will always be "fully booked," and golf courses where management sand traps will foil their bids for access. Even white physicians who treat persons of both races commonly route their patients into separate waiting rooms with pre-1960 firmness. Here progress in race relations often comes in rudimentary concessions to black dignity, as in the recent removal of a chain-link fence dividing black and white plots in a Georgia county cemetery. Until that headline-making decision, black funeral processions had entered the cemetery through a back gate.

Challenges to old racial mores can bring spiraling retaliation. In Ludowici, Georgia, where students picked separate white and black homecoming queens until 1984, an argument in the high school lunchroom over interracial dating degenerated into an interracial brawl. Discipline was swift and selective: several students were expelled, all of them black. After local black leaders protested, hooded Klansmen visited the town, and within hours the home of a civil rights activist was burned to the ground. Fire marshals blamed faulty wiring, but Joseph Lowery of the Southern Christian Leadership Conference thought it absurd to deny the real problem: faulty white racial attitudes. The former SNCC [Student Nonviolent Coordinating Committee] worker Charles Sherrod observed, "Those people who shot at us, and blew up churches and all that 20 years ago, they haven't gone anywhere. The attitudes are still there. Their behavior has changed because we have got a little power. They won't do anything they can't get away with."

Few officials anywhere in the South still defy civil rights laws openly, for events in the 1960s showed the futility of shrill racist posturing. Softer sabotage, however, still limits the impact of federal guarantees. After passage of the Voting Rights Act in 1965, whites generally acquiesced in the registration of blacks but devised ways to undermine the new electorate. Testimony in 1982 before the Senate Judiciary Committee revealed that nearly half the counties of Alabama, Georgia, Louisiana, and South Carolina had disregarded the act's "preclearance" requirement by changing electoral laws—often for transparent racial reasons—without first obtaining federal approval. Cities with large black populations imported white voters by annexing adjacent suburbs, and cities with a few predominantly black areas discarded district elections for at-large voting. Legislators have also excluded black voters from communities through redistricting schemes of rare cartographic cunning. The understaffed Justice Department has trailed such infractions at a discouraging distance. An amendment to the North Carolina constitution, designed to gerrymander away the influence of new black voters, escaped challenge from federal attorneys until 1981, fourteen years after it was illegally implemented.

Outside the South racism treads more softly but still sequesters most blacks in ghettos. Blacks formed 6 percent of the suburban population in 1980 (up from 5 percent in 1970), and even this figure was inflated by spillover into older, industrial suburbs that white flight turned into segregated enclaves. Federal studies show pervasive discrimination by white realtors and residents, resulting in hundreds of census tracts in New York, Cleveland, and other metropolitan areas that contain no nonwhites. Nor is housing bias entirely covert. Obscene phone calls, curses, threats, firebombings, and rocks and bricks crashing through windows are among the dozens of incidents that each year impart a rough frontier quality to black settlement in white neighborhoods. Such experiences confirm that the open-housing legislation of the 1960s has meant little beside the resolve of whites to maintain property values and "ethnic purity" in their communities.

Racial violence and harassment, a central target of civil rights protest, still occurs daily in every region of the country. The Justice Department conservatively recorded a rise in racist attacks from 99 in 1980 to 276 in 1986; the count by individual cities is more extensive. New York City's police department charted an increase in bias-related clashes from four a week to ten a week in early 1987. Chicago reported 240 episodes of racially motivated violence and harassment in 1986, an increase for the third consecutive year. The spark is often no more than the presence of a black person in a store, on the street, in a new home. For dejected white students at the University of Massachusetts at Amherst, the defeat of the Boston Red Sox in the 1986 World Series was enough reason to beat a black New York Mets fan unconscious and injure several others. Several months earlier, at Howard Beach, New York, three black "outsiders" fled an attack by eleven

whites; one of the blacks, twenty-three-year-old Michael Griffith, was killed when he ran onto a parkway of speeding cars in his attempt to escape a beating. Kevin Nesmith, a black student at the Citadel Military School, in Charleston, South Carolina, resigned after whites in Klan robes burst into his room at two in the morning shouting racial slurs and hazing him. Something akin to a freedom ride befell black students returning from Newton North High School to their homes in Boston when whites smashed the bus windows with stones and a tire iron. These and other recent episodes do not approach the systematic, officially sanctioned terror against blacks that once scarred American history. They nonetheless point to the continued difficulty blacks face in securing basic civil rights.

Police each year kill dozens of blacks, including children. Defenders of police conduct stress the extreme danger facing officers in some ghetto neighborhoods, their need to use deadly force on occasion to survive, and their able protection of blacks, notably during civil rights marches that have drawn white hecklers. Still, cases abound of unprovoked, cold-blooded police shootings of ghetto residents that almost invariably go unpunished.

The criminal justice system is less blatantly harsh toward blacks than in the past, but patterns of punishment still appear skewed by racial prejudice. Blacks average longer prison terms than whites for the same offense and are the primary victims of capital punishment. Criminals of any race, moreover, are treated more severely for victimizing whites. In 1987 a case that challenged the death penalty as being tainted, in practice, by racial bias showed that in Georgia, even after accounting for 230 other factors, killers of white persons were four times more likely to be executed than killers of blacks. Despite corroborating evidence of prejudice in meting out capital punishment, the Supreme Court narrowly upheld the death penalty. The majority opinion asserted, in language shades removed from *Plessy v. Ferguson*, that the treatment of black and white prisoners was admittedly different but not discriminatory.

* * *

Failure to include blacks fully in the nation's prosperity is the most glaring limitation of the movement for racial justice. In the South two-thirds of all black workers, compared with one-third of all whites, hold low-income jobs. The national economy today relegates more than half of all black workers to menial jobs, perpetuates a black underclass of deepening antisocial bent, and confines even educated blacks to the margins of wealth and opportunity. These problems can be traced to various causes—racial differences in family structure, education, and job experience among them—but they are also rooted in both past and persistent discrimination.

Title VII of the 1964 Civil Rights Act did not end bias in employment but drove it behind closed office doors. Managers commonly assigned blacks to dead-end jobs, minimized their executive role, scrutinized them more harshly than comparably trained whites, and excluded them from the after-hours fraternizing that can advance careers. In 1982 only one in thirty black men (compared with one in ten whites) filled management or administrative jobs, reflecting a ten-year increase so minute that it was probably a matter of statistical error. No

black headed a corporation in *Fortune* magazine's top 1,000, and few had risen above the level of vice-president in any major firm. Tokenism thus became more intricate in the era of affirmative action, permitting a greater minority presence in the office but seldom in the conference suites where deals, promotions, and salaries are decided.

An aura of the closed medieval guild still surrounds craft unions, which have countered civil rights laws with subtler means of racial exclusion. One AFL-CIO union, representing New York City's electrical contractors, avoided punishment for racist practices by devising an "outreach training program" for minorities in 1971. Over a decade later state investigators charged that the program required black and Hispanic trainees to work eleven years before they could reach class A journeyman status, compared with five years for white apprentices. Nonwhite trainees were also taught a curriculum separate from that of whites, with obsolete textbooks and without the fifth year of classroom instruction needed to pass the union exam and obtain work at journeymen's wages. Many other AFL-CIO locals have also been exposed for turning affirmative action programs into a permanent racial obstacle course for minorities....

A RECORD OF CHANGE

Like other reform movements the crusade for racial justice inevitably fell short of the utopian goals that sustained it. Still, if America's civil rights movement is judged by the distance it traveled rather than by barriers yet to be crossed, a record of substantial achievement unfolds. In communities throughout the South, "whites only" signs that had stood for generations suddenly came down from hotels, rest rooms, theaters, and other facilities. Blacks and whites seldom mingle socially at home, but they are apt to lunch together at fast-food shops that once drew blacks only for sit-ins. Integration extends equally to Southern workers, whether at diner counters or in the high-rise office buildings that now afford every Southern city a skyline.

School desegregation also quickened its pace and by the mid-1970's had become fact as well as law in over 80 percent of all Southern public schools. Swelling private school enrollments have tarnished but not substantially reversed this achievement. A privileged 5 to 10 percent of all Southern white children may find shelter from the *Brown* [*v. Board of Education of Topeka, Kansas* (1954)] verdict at private academies; but the words "massive resistance" have virtually disappeared from the region's political vocabulary.

Hate groups once flourished without strong federal restraint, but the civil rights movement has curbed the Ku Klux Klan and other extremist threats. Beginning in 1964 the FBI infiltrated the Klan so thoroughly that by 1965 perhaps one in five members was an informant. During the 1980s, amid a rise in racial assaults, synagogue bombings, and armed robberies to bankroll fringe groups, the federal government mounted the largest campaign against organized subversion since World War II. In 1987, members of the Florida Realm of the United Klans of America were convicted of illegal paramilitary training exercises, and leaders of the Identity Movement, which preaches a theology of hatred toward Jews and blacks, were indicted for conspiring to overthrow the government. Federal action has encouraged private lawsuits, including one that bankrupted the United Klans of America. After a black teenager in Mobile, Alabama, was murdered by Klansmen and left hanging from a tree in 1981, the boy's family won a $7 million judgment. To pay damages the Klan had to cede its two-story national headquarters, near Tuscaloosa, Alabama, to the black litigants. Reeling from legal and financial adversity, Klan membership declined from 10,000 in 1981 to less than 5,500 in 1987, the lowest since the early seventies.

Protection of voting rights represents the movement's most unalloyed success, more than doubling black voter registration, to 64 percent, in the seven states covered by the 1965 act. Winning the vote literally changed the complexion of government service in the South. When Congress passed the Voting Rights Act, barely 100 blacks held elective office in the country; by 1989 there were more than 7,200, including 24 congressmen and some 300 mayors. Over 4,800 of these officials served in the South, and nearly every Black Belt county in Alabama had a black sheriff. Mississippi experienced the most radical change, registering 74 percent of its voting-age blacks and leading the nation in the number of elected black officials (646).

Black influence in electoral politics acquired a compelling symbol during the 1980s with the emergence of the Reverend Jesse Jackson of Chicago as a presidential contender. As a young aide to Dr. King from 1966 to 1968, Jackson had stood out for his eloquence, élan, and ambition. In the 1970s Jackson won national acclaim for spurring ghetto youths to excel in school, but his denunciations of American society as racist, capitalist, and imperialist kept him on the fringes of public life. Over the next decade, however, as blacks increasingly protested President Reagan's neglect of minorities and the poor, Jackson began to temper his revolutionary message in hopes of forging a revitalized reform coalition.

Jackson campaigned in the 1984 Democratic presidential primaries, drawing large crowds and intense media coverage with his mixture of evangelical fervor, nimble wit, and self-conscious identification with minority hopes. He spoke of a "Rainbow Coalition" that would transcend racial lines, though his campaign chiefly focused on mobilizing black voter registration and turnout with the aid of Negro churches. This strategy enabled Jackson to win nomination contests in South Carolina, Louisiana, and Washington, D.C., and to finish third in delegates at the Democratic National Convention. Partly offsetting this achievement was Jackson's failure to draw even 5 percent of the white voters, whether because of his race, radical image, or suspect character. (Jews in particular recoiled at Jackson's ties with the Black Muslim Louis Farrakhan, who had branded Judaism a "gutter religion.") Despite these weaknesses Jackson's campaign legitimized Black Power to the American people in a way that Stokely Carmichael and others in the 1960s had vainly tried to do from outside the political mainstream.

In 1988 Jackson hewed closer to the political center and reached well beyond his core supporters, in a second bid for the Democratic presidential nomination. The now seasoned candidate trimmed his radical rhetoric, conciliated many who had thought him opportunistic and divisive, and emphasized broadly appealing liberal themes of economic opportunity for all citizens. Jackson's approach, which this time afforded him second place among seven competitors, reflected and fostered a new openness toward blacks in the Democratic party and in the nation. An especially prominent landmark of political change was Jackson's Michigan primary victory, with 54 percent of the vote, just twenty years after that state's Democratic contest had gone to the Alabama segregationist George Wallace. The candidate's progress, as in 1984, remained in key respects exceedingly personal, for it did not appreciably change his party's stand on key issues nor dispel racism as a factor in national politics. Still, more than any black leader since Martin Luther King, Jr., Jackson had inspired Americans with the faith —crucial to every reform movement— that the decisive state of America's democratic odyssey lay just ahead.

* * *

Despite unsettling parallels with the aftermath of Reconstruction, the modern civil rights movement should prove better able to resist the undoing of black gains. A salient difference is the greater reluctance in recent times to risk convulsing society by spurning the ideal of equality. Blacks during Reconstruction had exerted relatively minor influence over the white leadership that instituted—and then abandoned—measures for racial justice. By contrast blacks a century later shook whole cities with mass demonstrations, demanded and secured sweeping changes in federal law, and reshaped the political agenda of two strong-minded chief executives. These protests brought a new respect for Afro-Americans, breaking forever the comfortable myth that blacks were content with a biracial society and proving that they had the rare courage needed to challenge it.

New currents in world affairs have reinforced the consensus to guarantee black civil rights. During the late nineteenth century Americans were largely indifferent to the nonwhite world except for the growing possibilities of colonizing or otherwise controlling it. The European nations that most influenced this country were themselves indulging in imperialism based on racial as well as national interests. Global pressures today are vastly different. Competition for the support of nonwhite nations and the near-universal ostracism of South Africa, which asserts a racist ideology, require American society to pay at least nominal homage to racial equality.

Pluralism is also more firmly rooted in American values than ever before. The black revolution stimulated others, including women, homosexuals, Hispanics, native Americans, and Asians, who frequently modeled their actions on the values and tactics popularized by Martin Luther King, Jr. Each emerging movement, while pursuing a discrete agenda, has bolstered the principle that government must guarantee equal rights and opportunities to all citizens.

Racism lost more than legal standing with the triumph of civil rights campaigns; it lost social standing. Even the Daughters of the American Revolution, an organization known for its racially exclusive character, apologized in 1982 for having spurned the singer Marian Anderson over four decades earlier. The DAR's president general, a native of Beulah, Mississippi, invited Anderson to perform at the organization's ninety-first convention in Constitution Hall. The eighty-year-old singer was by then too frail to attend, but the black soprano Leontyne Price, who treated the DAR to a concert ending with "The Battle Hymn of the Republic," assured her interracial audience that Anderson was "here in spirit."

The deepening interest in racial harmony has encouraged recognition of the black experience as central to American history. The 1977 television drama "Roots," which engaged audiences in the trauma of racial slavery and the struggle for freedom, became the most widely viewed special series in the history of the medium. Six years later Congress created a holiday to honor Martin Luther King, Jr., and by extension the civil rights movement he symbolized. Such a tribute had eluded Thomas Jefferson, Andrew Jackson, both Roosevelts, and other giants of American history. President Reagan, who had originally opposed enacting a holiday for King as an unwise "ethnic" precedent, signed the popular bill into law while standing alongside King's widow, Coretta.

* * *

In the South, as in the rest of the nation, few whites seriously contemplate returning to the state of race relations before 1960. This outlook differs strikingly from Southern intransigence after Reconstruction and reflects the disparate ways in which the two eras of racial change occurred. Reconstruction came as a sudden, violently imposed upheaval in Southern race relations that virtually nothing in the region's history had prepared it to accept. The civil rights movement instead advanced nonviolently, secured small gains over decades, and fostered progress from within the region. The campaigns that ended legalized segregation in the sixties marked the culmination of this gradual change. Many white Southerners had by then reconciled themselves to reforms that seemed inevitable and even, per- haps, beneficial.

Freed from the albatross of defend- ing Jim Crow at the expense of national respect and regional peace, Southerners could focus on tasks of economic and so- cial modernization. Mississippi's leading journal, the *Jackson Clarion-Ledger*, offered a glimpse into this revolution in priori- ties. After the March on Washington in 1963, a front-page story reported that the capital was "clean again with Negro trash removed." Twenty years later the paper won a Pulitzer Prize in public serve for exposing the need for fuller desegrega- tion and better funding of public schools.

Southern memories of black protests have mellowed to the point where both races treat them as parts of their history to be proud of. Montgomery motorists now drive down the Martin Luther King, Jr. Expressway, and the Dexter Baptist Church, where King was pastor, has be- come a national landmark. The prison cell King occupied in Birmingham is set aside as a library for inmates, his "Letter from a Birmingham Jail" framed on the wall. In Georgia's capitol a portrait of King hangs near a bust of Alexander Stephens, the Confederate vice-president. One elderly black tour guide, assigned to interpret these landmarks of the past, ignored the bust of Stephens, and beamed, "Here is Nobel prize winner Martin Luther King, Jr. He was born and bred right here in Atlanta on Auburn Avenue."

Political calculation has sealed this acceptance of racial change. Over a quiet bourbon and branch water in his Senate office, Mississippi's arch-segregationist James Eastland confided, "When [blacks] get the vote, I won't be talking this way anymore." Later Eastland was among the many officials who jettisoned their tested appeals to prejudice, learned to pronounce "Negro" in place of more casual epithets, and prefaced the names of newly valued black constituents with the once forbidden appellation "Mister."

Even the past master of race baiting, Alabama's George Wallace, was struck color-blind on the road to Montgomery in his 1982 gubernatorial campaign. Wal- lace, who like most politicians believed above all in winning elections today, to- morrow, and forever, spent much of his hard-fought contest kissing black babies and humbly supplicating their parents' support, assuring them of his reborn atti- tudes on race matters. (He won the cam- paign with the aid of a forgiving black electorate and welcomed several blacks to positions in his cabinet.) Whatever Wallace's deepest sentiments, his actions were a striking testament to the legacy of the civil rights protests that he once vowed to crush but that instead have left an indelible imprint on the nation's moral landscape.

* * *

The full impact of civil rights campaigns has yet to be felt. The movement could not wholly sweep away old Jim Crow hierarchies, but rather superimposed new patterns of behavior on a still race-conscious society. Cities like Selma, Alabama, where black activists battled white supremacists in the 1960s, today reflect two eras of race relations at once, giving no final sign of which will prevail.

Segregated neighborhoods persist in Selma, along with segregated social patterns. The Selma Country Club has no black members and until 1983 would not allow a black dance band inside. Elks Club members attend separate white and black chapters. Nearly a thousand white students attend two private academies founded with the express purpose of excluding blacks. Racial lines run through the city's economy: the overall jobless rate in Selma in 1985 was 16 percent but nearly twice as high for blacks as for whites. And in politics, residents tend to make racial choices for public office. The black community leader Frederick Reese won 40 percent of the mayoral vote in 1984 but only a handful of white supporters; Joseph Smitherman received 10 to 15 percent of the black vote but stayed in office with nearly 100 percent of the white vote.

Yet race relations in Selma have noticeably changed since the city's landmark civil rights demonstrations in 1965. The onetime "moderate segregationist" Smitherman began to tend an image as a facilitator of black mobility. In 1984 Smitherman observed proudly that 40 percent of the police force was black, including the assistant chief, several lieutenants, captains, and key department heads. The city's personnel board had three blacks and two whites, the eight-person library board was evenly composed of blacks and whites, and the school board had five blacks to four whites. Asphalt pavement, which had often stopped short of black neighbor-hoods, now stretched for miles throughout the town, covering over dirt roads and, with them, an era of flagrant neglect of black residents.

Perhaps most important to Selma's blacks and many whites, the movement reduced ignorance, fear, and hate. The black lawyer and civil rights activist J. L. Chestnut remarked in 1985, on the twentieth anniversary of his city's civil rights marches, that new attitudes were taking root: "My children don't think of white children as devils, and I don't think white children see my kids as watermelon-eating, tap-dancing idiots. If there is hope, it is in the fact that children in Selma today don't have to carry the baggage that Joe Smitherman and J. L. Chestnut carry. And that means they will never be scared the way we used to be scared." Teenagers at Selma's integrated public high school knew about the events of "Bloody Sunday" but viewed them as a mystery from another time. "Kids today, they're used to the way things are," explained Karyn Reddick, a black student. "Try as you can, you can't believe that white people once treated black people that way. It seems like something that happened long, long ago."

NO

Tom Wicker

TRAGIC FAILURE: RACIAL INTEGRATION IN AMERICA

INTRODUCTION

Sharply conflicting white and black reactions to the O.J. Simpson verdict [not guilty of murder] dramatized the tragic fact that neither civil war in the nineteenth century nor the civil rights movement in the twentieth has brought racial equality, much less racial amity, to America.

I believe they can be reached only in the hearts of the people; wars will never achieve either, nor narrow legalities. Perhaps nothing can. Derrick Bell has written that African-Americans, despite surface changes in society, continue to be "the faces at the bottom of the well," the faces upon which whites, no matter how deprived themselves, can look down in the sure and comforting knowledge that at least *they* aren't black.

Having spent the first thirty-four years of my life in what was then the segregated South and the last thirty-five in what's only legally an integrated nation—and not always that—I believe the problem is not least that those black faces in the well are *reassuring* to most whites and *vital* to the self-esteem of the many disadvantaged among us, few of whom really want those faces to disappear.

The continuing separation of whites and blacks into hostile and unequal classes, however, is a fundamental cause of the political deadlock, economic inequity, and social rancor that mark American life. And if "a house divided against itself" could not stand in the era of chattel slavery, can it long endure in today's destructive atmosphere of black disadvantage, white anger, and racial animosity?

Long before O.J. Simpson went on trial, it was obvious that genuine racial equality—despite laws and legal decisions—had not been achieved in America. The high proportion of African-Americans[1] males in U.S. prisons and the low economic status of more than half the black population were evidence enough for anyone willing to see it, but few were. Even as the Simpson trial unfolded, white resentment erupted over affirmative action—an effort to overcome black disadvantages that's now widely seen, despite little evidence, as reverse racism.

When a Los Angeles jury brought in the Simpson verdict, the hard truth finally was too visible to be ignored. Whites denounced what they saw as black racial prejudice by a predominantly black jury in favor of a black hero despite the evidence. African-Americans, on the other hand, hailed black jurors for a courageous stand against white racial prejudice and constitutionally impermissible evidence provided by the racist Los Angeles police.

Throughout the long trial, "the white position [that Simpson was guilty] was treated as the rational, normal, acceptable one," David Shaw of the *Los Angeles Times* said on October 25, 1995, in a panel discussion of media coverage of the Freedom Forum. "The black perception [that Simpson was not guilty] was treated as irrational."

It's almost irrelevant [that] the black or white judgment might be more nearly correct. In my view, what mattered was the demonstration that whites and blacks, though living in the same America, see themselves in different worlds. Similarly conflicting views were evident in the responses of African-American journalists and their mostly white supervisors to a survey question of whether U.S. press organizations are "committed to retaining and promoting black journalists." Of the white supervisors, 94 percent believed newspapers and broadcasters were so committed; 67 percent of the black (mostly middle-class) journalists thought not. Both worked in the same newsrooms; neither saw the same world of work.

The Simpson trial and verdict were followed immediately by the so-called "Million-Man March," in which at least hundreds of thousands of orderly African-American males demonstrated peacefully on the Mall in Washington in October 1995. Despite a demagogic speech by Louis Farrakhan of the Nation of Islam, the marchers espoused what white Americans, watching on television, could readily recognize as middle-class values—thus confounding the recent white view of black men as lawless and shiftless, as well as conveying the message that African-Americans still are far from equal citizenship in a supposedly integrated nation.

The march emphasized the strong growth of the black middle class in the last three decades—to perhaps 40 percent of the African-American population. Even that growth has not banished the faces from the bottom of the well, any more than it has produced real racial equality. Middle-class African-Americans testify copiously to the indignities and embarrassments they still suffer from the white assumption of black inferiority, black income and wealth still are far below white levels, housing remains largely segregated by race, and *all* African-Americans tend to be judged by the unacceptable behavior of the worst off among them.

I consider it the saddest racial development of the last quarter century that as the black middle class expanded, the urban underclass grew even faster. The scary and undisciplined behavior of that largely black underclass—those African-Americans who for lack of jobs and hope and discipline turned in the seventies and eighties to crime and welfare and drugs and were sent to prison in droves —was seen (often graphically, on television) by frightened whites as the behavior of African-Americans generally.

In one panicked and self-destructive result, whites turned against social welfare programs designed to benefit the white as well as the black poor—hence society generally. Worse, African-Americans once seen as bravely facing the police dogs and cattle prods of Bull Connor in the name of freedom came to be regarded, instead, as irresponsible muggers, drug dealers, addicts, rapists, and welfare queens.

The same period exposed the failure of the African-American political empowerment that white and black civil rights leaders of the sixties had hoped would be the remedy for black disadvantages. One of them, Dr. Kenneth Clark, sadly conceded in 1993 that greater numbers of black elected officials had been "unable to increase justice and humanity for those who have been forgotten in the inner cities."

Thirty-five years of failing integration have convinced me that economic as well as political empowerment is needed if African-American disadvantages—particularly those of the underclass—are to be overcome. Only when the faces at the bottom of the well achieve generally higher economic status might they—as well as those talented and energetic blacks in the middle class—reach genuine equality in the hearts of whites, and only through economic gains for all might the threatening underclass become a more constructive element in a more amicable American life.

Such an economic transformation will not be easily or soon accomplished, and it probably never will be if the task is left to today's major political parties. Neither any longer even talks of such ambitious goals; both are less concerned with the truly disadvantaged than with the numerically dominant white middle class, with its plaints about an unfair tax burden and unfair preferences for blacks. The Republicans offer a new home to white defectors from a Democratic party the defectors regarded as too partial to blacks, and the supposedly "liberal" Democrats, alarmed by the loss of white votes, pay scant attention to the interests of African-Americans, whose allegiance causes the white defections.

In their own interest, therefore, but also in that of a racially torn nation, blacks should turn away from the Democrats to form a new party dedicated to economic equality through economic growth for whites and blacks alike. Such a new party could build upon predicted demographic change that in the next century will bring today's minority groups into rough numerical equality with non-Hispanic whites. It might even win the support of those millions of despairing Americans who now take no part in the politics of a prosperous nation they believe ruled by the affluent and for the affluent.

The new party might never win the presidency, but in the historical tradition of third parties, it could have [a] profound effect upon the other two and upon society generally. That's why I've suggested in this book that such a radically conceived party might also have the potential to do what our old, familiar politics-as-usual never can: "To achieve real democracy—to change American life by attacking its inequities—perhaps to save us from ourselves."

THE END OF INTEGRATION

Integration is like Prohibition. If the people don't want it, a whole army can't enforce it.

—Paul Johnson,
governor of Mississippi

The sweeping conservative victory in the elections of 1994 returned control of Congress to Republicans, repudiated what was left of liberal government, and dramatized the tragic failure of racial integration in America.

Race, as it always is in a modern American election, was the underlying issue. In the autumn of 1994 that issue was a prime determinant of the outcome, as white voters everywhere expressed unmistakable yearning for a lost time, before "they" forced themselves into the nation's consciousness.

White animosity toward and fear of African-Americans—seen largely as criminals and welfare cheats—gave emotional edge and added energy to the election's ostensible issues, and the campaign was fought out in code words and symbolism that disclosed rather than disguised its racial character.

- Fierce denunciations of crime and welfare, in white eyes the most prominent products of the black underclass
- Withering blasts at liberals and liberalism as the "social engineers" behind the "big government" that tried to force racial integration and brought higher taxes
- Diatribes against "spending" and "the redistribution of wealth" to the poor, a euphemism for social programs believed primarily to aid African-Americans
- Loud promises to extend the death penalty, from which African-Americans suffer proportionally far more than whites
- Overwrought demands for a return to "family values" (a term of many meanings, one of which is the sexual restraint that blacks are supposed by whites to disdain)

Anyone who might have misunderstood what had happened in the 1994 elections should have been set straight on January 23, 1995. That day, in the ornate hearing room of the House Rules Committee, the victorious Republicans removed a portrait of former Representative Claude Pepper of Florida, a renowned white liberal Democrat. That was understandable, but the new Republican committee chairman, Gerald Solomon of New York, had ordered the Pepper portrait replaced by that of *another Democrat*, the late Howard Smith of Virginia, a last-ditch segregationist and in his many years as Rules Committee chairman one of the most powerful opponents of the civil rights legislation of the sixties.

Blacks clearly believed race was the principal issue in the campaign; the reason, said Robert Smith, a professor of political science at San Francisco State University, was "absolute disgust" with the campaign among blacks of all walks.

"It took us black people so long to get the vote," T. J. Smith of Philadelphia told Richard Berke of *The New York Times* in 1994. "Now they're making us not want to vote" by neglecting black interests. Chris Williams, a Philadelphia ironworker, agreed: "Why do they talk about just building jails? Why don't they talk about building schools?"

The returns, if anything, left African-Americans feeling even more frustrated. Black turnout—perhaps fueled by fear —more than doubled nationally, over the 1990 midterm elections, with black voters going heavily Democratic; yet the Republicans won in a landslide and not a single Republican incumbent was defeated. Clearly, *white* voters had turned to the Republicans.

Fifty-one percent of the whites, moreover, who had responded to an election-year survey by the Times Mirror Center for the People and the Press said openly that they believed "equal rights" had been pushed too far—an increase of nine percentage points since 1992.

California, the nation's most populous state, voted by an overwhelming margin for Proposition 187, a ballot initiative designed to deprive illegal immigrants—mostly Latinos in California—of education, health, and welfare benefits. Governor Pete Wilson, whose reelection made him seem at the time a strong contender for the Republican presidential nomination, derived substantial political profit from his support for this initiative.

California's approval of Prop 187, which Democratic candidates for governor and senator opposed, may well have been symbolic of the 1994 elections as a whole. It was not an "anti-black" measure, nor was it an anti-black election *by definition.* The vote favoring Prop 187, however, clearly reflected the angry and vengeful or at least resentful racial attitudes many white Americans had developed since the high-water mark of the civil rights movement in the sixties. The entire selection reflected such white attitudes.

* * *

If those attitudes reached a political peak in 1994, they had been a long time in the making. Racial integration in America had been failing for years, even though legal segregation in the southern states was ended in the sixties. The elections of 1994 only dramatized a fact that had long existed.

By that year integration had failed nationally because too few white Americans wanted it or were willing to sacrifice for it. Integration had failed too because whites' sterotypical view of blacks had been re-shaped by the violence, idleness, and drug reliance of the urban black underclass. And the kind of political empowerment integration brought to blacks had proved unable to provide most African-Americans the economic and social gains needed for acceptance in white America.

The angry and fearful white reaction to undisciplined ghetto behavior also blinded whites to the concurrent growth of a substantial black middle class. Perhaps worse, that reaction had undermined white support for economic and social programs beneficial not only to the black poor but to millions of impoverished whites as well.

In actual practice, as a result of all this, integration had not been the policy of either Republican or Democratic administrations since the accession of Ronald Reagan to the presidency in 1981. In the decade before that, integration had been pursued only halfheartedly; zeal for enforcement of equal rights in education, housing, and employment had declined as antagonism to African-Americans rose.

Crime, though its victims as well as its perpetrators often were black, and welfare, widely considered a dole and an aid to shiftless blacks' supposed instinct to spawn, had long been favored targets of public and political anger.

Now the primary national approach to the ills of the urban underclass, endorsed in the polling booths of 1994, is to imprison poor blacks—an expensive, ineffective, misdirected, and self-destructive course sustained by white fear, politicians' posturing, and the sensationalism of the white press. More executions, mostly of blacks, an equally punitive and ill-considered response to crimes that already have been committed, are promised in response to the conservative landslide of 1994. Early in 1995 New York's new Republican governor, George Pataki, signed a death penalty law after nearly a quarter century of vetoes by the Democratic governors Hugh Carey and Mario Cuomo.

The inner city does teem with crime, idleness, and anger, spilling dangerously outward. Black family disintegration and welfare dependence are serious concerns. But for better or for worse, the American community necessarily *includes* the black community—African-Americans, some Latinos, many from the Caribbean. The Census Bureau predicts the black community will grow far larger. Its exclusion in anything like a democratic or humane manner would be impossible and would not solve the nation's most pressing problems; rather it would worsen some old problems and create many new ones.

Glaring economic inequities and class distinctions abound, among *both* blacks and whites. Technological or administrative competence, a prerequisite in today's economy, is seldom within the reach of poor and ill-educated Americans, of whom there are more and more of both races. Millions of whites and blacks are out of any kind of work, in the city and on the farm, and more will be in a newly competitive and technological era, with even profitable corporations laying off workers by the thousands. Manufacturing wages have declined for all. The real gap between rich and poor is widening. Unemployment, which strikes blacks first and worst, also hits whites hard—yet is fostered by a government too fearful of inflation to push economic growth strenuously and by a "lean and mean" business sector in which cost cutting has become the new panacea for all problems.

A seventh of the nation lives in poverty: more than forty million people, by no means all of them black, and including more than a fifth of all American children. Families of all races are disintegrating. The economy, measured against population growth and expected living standards, is not adequately expanding. Demographic changes predicted by the Census Bureau for the next fifty years will be of incalculable effect.

What the brash conservatives who triumphed in 1994 may be able to do about any of these troublesome truths remains, at this writing, largely to be seen. But the end of integration more or less subtly marked by their victory will not remove or diminish those ills, each of which, in large part or small, is linked to or affected by race, the continuing, the cancerous, the unconfronted American dilemma.

* * *

In the fifties and the first half of the sixties, owing mostly to effective black demonstrations and demands, the shameful institutions of legally established racial segregation in the South at last were abolished. But this shining hour for the civil rights movement proved to be brief and limited.

In the late sixties and the seventies, efforts to broaden integration into a national, not just a southern, reality caused anxiety and anger in the nonsouthern white majority. Outside the old Confederacy, integration came to be seen as moving too fast and going too far—faster and farther than most whites in the rest of the nation had expected or wanted.

A "backlash" of white resistance to civil rights quickly gathered momentum, importantly furthered by the presidential campaigns of Governor George Wallace of Alabama. The long national retreat from integration was under way within a year or two after its greatest triumphs.

Such a turnabout had hardly seemed possible in the period when antisegregation laws were being passed—slowly but, as it seemed, inevitably—by Congress under pressure from the Eisenhower, Kennedy, and Johnson administrations and over die-hard southern opposition. Even, however, in the Goldwater debacle of 1964—the most smashing Democratic and liberal presidential victory since Franklin Roosevelt's in 1936—the Republicans had carried four southern states.

The old Solid South had been shattered, a development that did not surprise the victorious President Lyndon Johnson, a southerner himself. The night Congress passed the massive Civil Rights Act of 1964, proposed by President Kennedy and pushed through by Johnson, a young White House aide named Bill Moyers called the president to congratulate him on the success of the legislation.

"Bill," Johnson replied, "I think we Democrats just lost the South for the rest of my life."

Inasmuch as LBJ died in 1972, it turned out to be for considerably longer than that. In 1994, thirty years later, the Democratic share of the vote in House races in the South dropped to 13.4 percent of eligible voters.

To most observers in 1964—including Tom Wicker, a *New York Times* political reporter—the southern defections had seemed relatively unimportant. After all, LBJ had defeated Goldwater by 486 to 52 in the electoral college. The Republicans had carried only one state (Goldwater's Arizona) outside the South, had lost 38 seats in the House and retained only

140, their lowest total since 1936. They also had lost 2 Senate seats and held only 32, no more than they had had in 1940. Republican defeats in state and local elections had been so severe as to cause frequent laments that the GOP was no longer an effective national party.

Only two years later, in a vigorous 1966 campaign led by Richard M. Nixon (out of office since 1961 but obviously on the road back), Republicans picked up forty-seven House seats, three in the Senate, and eight governorships, most significantly in California, where the political newcomer and old movie star Ronald Reagan first won political office. The Republican comeback was marked by a superb organizing and fundraising effort in the wake of Goldwater's defeat and by Nixon's leadership. But it benefited above all from *the Democratic party's and Johnson's racial liberalism.*

The president and his party had pushed through the Civil Rights Act of 1964, guaranteeing equal access to public facilities and banning racial discrimination in the workplace. They had achieved the Voting Rights Act of 1965, putting the federal government behind blacks' right to vote. Johnson himself had proclaimed to Congress the battle cry of Martin Luther King and his followers: "We shall overcome!" LBJ and John F. Kennedy rather reluctantly before him had identified their party more closely with African-Americans than any president since Lincoln.

Three decades later, in his 1995 inaugural speech as the new Republican Speaker of the House, Newt Gingrich—magnanimously praising the opposition, or so it appeared—noted that Democrats had been "the greatest leaders in fighting for an integrated America." He added pointedly: "It was the liberal wing of the Democratic party that ended segregation."

These honeyed words, intentionally or not, were political poison. Voters had shown in 1994 and earlier that they were well aware, and not favorably, of the Democrats' racial record. It had been apparent for years that this record was a political liability not just in the South but with the nation's white majority.

In early 1964, the year of Goldwater's defeat, a Gallup poll had found that 72 percent of nonsouthern whites believed the Johnson administration's pace toward civil rights was "about right" or even too slow. But as civil rights legislation began to touch life *outside* the South, although it had been expected generally that only the old Confederacy would be much affected, nonsouthern whites began to fear for property values, job security, local government, neighborhood cohesion—for the old, inherited, comfortable (for them) order of things.

By 1966 opinion surveys were showing a startling reversal: Three quarters of white voters thought blacks were moving ahead too fast, demanding and "being given" too much, at the expense of whites. As white backlash mounted, polls the next year suggested that "the number one concern" of most respondents was fear that black gains would damage the well-being of whites. And as the decade continued, blacks rioting in the cities—fearfully or angrily watched by a nation becoming addicted to television —and blacks raising clenched fists in the black power salute seemed not only threatening but ungrateful for white "concessions" (as whites tended to see changes in the old racial order).

The black separatist and "black is beautiful" movements, the anti-integrationist rhetoric of Malcolm X, the militant stance and demands of organizations like the Black Panthers and the Student Nonviolent Coordinating Committee (SNCC) all stirred white animosity and anxiety. So did aggressive African-Americans like H. Rap Brown, Stokely Carmichael, Huey Newton, and Bobby Seale. The student and anti-Vietnam demonstrations were assumed by many whites to be a predictable consequence of black protests. Crime was increasing, much of it perpetrated by poor blacks, with television dramatizing it in the living room.

In 1967, as a result of the urban riots, President Johnson appointed a bipartisan commission, chaired by Governor Otto Kerner of Illinois, to look into the riots' causes. After extensive inquiry the Kerner Commission dismissed the notion that integration was proceeding too swiftly. Its report contended instead that despite the apparent success of the civil rights movement, black disadvantages still were so overwhelming that "our nation is moving toward two societies, one black, one white—separate but unequal."

Many prominent Americans, white and black, shared and approved this view, but many others resented it. Hadn't enough already been done for blacks? Even Lyndon Johnson, with a presidential election impending and the nation alarmed at what many believed to be insurrection in the cities, disliked the commission's conclusion and might have disavowed it if he could have. The backlash was not reversed; the riots undoubtedly heightened it.

Thus in 1968 fear and resentment of African-Americans underlay the "law and order" issue loudly demagogued by George Wallace and more subtly exploited by Richard Nixon in the "southern strategy" by which he narrowly won the presidency. The national loss of confidence in "Johnson's war" in Vietnam and destructive divisions within the party hurt the Democrats. But primarily, I believe, it was white racial anxieties that brought disaster to the party of Kennedy and Johnson only four year after its greatest victory. And the black community's impressive gains were becoming the cause of alarming losses of white support for Democrats.

Wallace campaigned widely and effectively, using code words and flamboyant oratory to stimulate white fears and to castigate the federal government. He finished a relatively distant third in the 1968 election, receiving votes from Democrats deserting the old civil rights advocate Hubert Humphrey and from Republicans who preferred Wallace's tough talk to Nixon's subtler appeal to white sentiment. In retrospect, however, Wallace's campaign was one of the most consequential of the postwar years. It effectively moved the country to the right, making racial fears seem more legitimate and paving the way for Ronald Reagan to win the presidency twelve years later.

Nixon's election and Wallace's campaign in 1968 sped along the national retreat from integration (though the courts forced President Nixon to push southern school desegregation in 1970). During the seventies affirmative action and "busing" were widely resented, even in Boston, once the seat of abolitionism. Low-income whites who could not afford private schools for their children and who felt their job security threatened by new competition from minority groups and women were especially alienated.

The Democrats and the integration they had pushed and supported were blamed for these perceived threats to the established order. Twenty-four years

of Republican and conservative ascendancy, broken only briefly and feebly by Jimmy Carter's single presidential term (1977–81),[2] followed the election of 1968 with near inevitability.

During the seventies escalating fears of busing, affirmative action, and neighborhood breakdown caused many whites to see integration not as laudable national policy but as "racism in reverse." The deterioration of cities and the increase in crime and violence were largely blamed on blacks. This development of the newly visible underclass, moreover, sharpened white fear and anger.

Whites continued to look down at the black "faces at the bottom of society's well," those "magical faces" of which Derrick Bell has written that "[e]ven the poorest whites, those who must live their lives only a few levels above, gain their self-esteem by gazing down at us." Those black faces had always been there, viewed merely with contempt and complacency by some, with bitter relief by the poor, the disadvantaged, the despised, who had little of value but their white skins. Despite civil rights laws, surely those "faces at the bottom of the well" always would be there.

Their absence would announce to whites not just the end of segregation in the South but the arrival of an all but unimaginable new world, making life less comfortable for some whites, nearly unbearable for others. And those black faces imposed a double imperative on whites: Not only must they be kept at the bottom of the well, but those who would bring them to the top, or nearer to it, must be feared, castigated, opposed.

And then came Reagan.

* * *

On August 3, 1980, looking virile and businesslike, he spoke in shirtsleeves to a cheering crowd of about ten thousand people, nearly all white, at the Neshoba County Fairgrounds near Philadelphia, Mississippi.

"I believe in states' rights," Reagan declared that day in the well-modulated voice that was to become so familiar to Americans. The Republican presidential nominee then promised a restoration to the states and to local governments of "the power that properly belongs to them."

Fresh from his Republican National Convention victory at Detroit, Ronald Reagan was making the first formal appearance of his presidential campaign, and his choice of a site for that opening appearance was powerfully symbolic: Philadelphia, Mississippi, was the place where three volunteer civil rights workers in the Mississippi Summer Project of 1964, two Jews and a black—Andrew Goodman, Michael Schwerner, and James Chaney—had been murdered. The sheriff and deputy sheriff of Neshoba County had been charged with these crimes. Most of the county's white population, by its silence, had been either complicit or oblivious.

No presidential candidate before Reagan had visited remote Neshoba County, in a state that had been the last stronghold of resistance to blacks' civil rights. Reagan was there because a Mississippi member of Congress, Trent Lott (now the [Senate majority leader]), had assured him that a personal visit to the state would carry it for him against President Carter.

The candidate might not fully have grasped the significance of Philadelphia,

as later he would not understand the opposition to his visit to the Bitburg Cemetery in Germany, where members of the Nazi SS were buried. But if Reagan didn't know about Philadelphia, Mississippi, he should have. It could not conceivably have been a routine campaign stop. One week after the bodies of Goodman, Schwerner, and Chaney had been discovered buried in a nearby earthen dam in 1964, Governor Paul Johnson—without a word of sympathy for the dead youths or their families —had told a crowd of six thousand at the Neshoba County fair that no Mississippian, including state officials, had any obligation to obey the Civil Rights Act of 1964.

"Integration," Johnson declaimed, "is like Prohibition. If the people don't want it, a whole army can't enforce it."

In 1964 that was the voice of last-ditch resistance, soon to be overwhelmed by events. But by 1980, as Ronald Reagan stood where the governor had stood, looking out upon much the same sea of white faces, it was possible to see Paul Johnson as a national prophet, no longer as a southern relic. Reagan's mere appearance at Philadelphia—unthinkable for a major-party presidential candidate even a few years earlier—was evidence that times had changed, radically. And when the candidate chose to open his campaign where Schwerner, Chaney, and Goodman had made the last sacrifice to rabid segregationist resistance, he sent the nation a message many Americans *wanted* to hear. That message was far more powerful and far more convincing than the deceptive plausibility with which Reagan was later to call for a "color-blind society" and insist that he was "heart and soul in favor of the things that have been done in the name of civil rights and desegregation. . . ."

Reagan's actual policies exposed those words as lip service, and anyway, much of the nation was watching what he did—visiting Philadelphia, Mississippi, for instance—rather than listening to what he said. Even before his speech at Philadelphia, Reagan had openly opposed the Civil Rights Act of 1964, the Voting Rights Act of 1965, the Opening Housing Act of 1968 and in numerous other ways had demonstrated his fundamental opposition to the *fact*, if not the concept, of integration. And by the time he sought the presidency—nearly winning the Republican nomination in 1976, taking it easily in 1980—neither his clear anti-integration record nor even his appearance in Mississippi was a political liability. It was, in fact, largely *because* of these that Ronald Reagan was elected to the White House.

Reagan did not single-handedly and from his own convictions turn the nation against integration. Rather a national reversal had begun not long after the civil rights triumphs of the sixties and his own entry into public life in California. In those years, as outlined above, national reluctance—neither confined to the South nor always most pronounced there—moved steadily toward opposition to integration. That movement owed more to crime, the underclass, busing, affirmative action, and *fear* (as much of the unknown as of any observable phenomena) than to the words or deeds of any one politician, even George Wallace. Reagan benefited politically from a greatly changed public mood even as he contributed to that mood.

Once he was in the Oval Office, moreover, the anti-civil rights record

Reagan accumulated was so lengthy and substantial that he could not have compiled it without the acquiescence and support of white Americans. "From Philadelphia to the Bitburg cemetery to the veto on sanctions against South Africa," Jesse Jackson observed toward the end of the Reagan years, "it's one unbroken ideological line."

That was true enough, but it was also true that Reagan had read accurately a public mood of disenchantment with racial integration. If even a beloved president thought blacks were being "given too much," as his actions (if not always his words) suggested, then surely ordinary Americans could think so too.

With tacit support from a popular president, it became respectable for whites to express loudly their misgivings about integration and to act on their fearful or hostile instincts about black neighbors or employees or schoolmates or job competitors. Those misgivings were many and fierce, those instincts had been frequently offended; so all too many white Americans were grateful that Reagan seemed to share their views. They took full advantage of what seemed to be approval from the top.

NOTES

1. The author is aware that not all black Americans approve of the designation "African-American," or consider it accurate. The term is used interchangeably with "black" throughout this [selection] and no disrespect is intended in either case.

2. Carter's narrow victory over Gerald Ford derived mostly from reaction against the Watergate scandal of the Nixon years and Ford's pardon of Nixon himself. Without those counterbalancing factors, the Democrats might well have lost the close election of 1976 too, owing to the party's racial record and Carter's relatively liberal stance.

POSTSCRIPT

Did the Civil Rights Movement Improve Race Relations in the United States?

Regardless of how one assesses the civil rights movement, there can be little doubt that the struggle for equality produced an important legacy. First, the movement had a critical impact on the civil rights struggles of groups other than African Americans. Women demanding equality, the American Indian movement, and gay rights protesters have all employed activities and strategies inherited from the civil rights movement. Second, there is an obvious tie between the forms of civil disobedience advocated by African American leaders and those carried out in protests against U.S. involvement in Southeast Asia. In fact, antiwar activists have linked continuing racism at home with their perception of American racism abroad. Third, as both Weisbrot and Wicker point out, the civil rights movement inadvertently produced a serious white backlash, based on the notion that majority rights were being overwhelmed by the will of a minority of the nation's citizens, which stymied further advances toward full equality.

The literature on the civil rights movement is extensive. August Meier, Elliott Rudwick, and Francis L. Broderick, eds., *Black Protest Thought in the Twentieth Century*, 2d ed. (Bobbs-Merrill, 1971) presents a collection of documents that places the activities of the 1950s and 1960s in a larger framework. The reflections of many of the participants of the movement are included in Howell Raines, *My Soul Is Rested: The Story of the Civil Rights Movement in the Deep South* (G. P. Putnam, 1977). Students should also consult Aldon D. Morris, *The Origins of the Civil Rights Movement: Black Communities Organizing for Change* (Free Press, 1984).

August Meier's contemporary assessment "On the Role of Martin Luther King," *Crisis* (1965) in many ways remains the most insightful analysis of King's leadership. More detailed studies include David L. Lewis, *King: A Critical Biography* (Praeger, 1970); Stephen B. Oates, *Let the Trumpet Sound: The Life of Martin Luther King, Jr.* (Harper & Row, 1982); David J. Garrow's Pulitzer Prize–winning *Bearing the Cross: Martin Luther King, Jr., and the Southern Christian Leadership Conference* (William Morrow, 1986); and Adam Fairclough, *To Redeem the Soul of America: The Southern Christian Leadership Conference and Martin Luther King, Jr.* (University of Georgia Press, 1987). Taylor Branch's *Parting the Waters: America in the King Years, 1954–63* (Simon & Schuster, 1988) is interesting. For King's own assessment of his campaigns and the movement in general, see *Stride Toward Freedom: The Montgomery Story* (Harper & Brothers, 1958); *Why We Can't Wait* (Signet, 1964); and *Where Do We Go from Here: Chaos or Community?* (Harper & Row, 1967).

The black nationalist critique of King and the nonviolent direct action campaign is effectively presented in Malcolm X (with Alex Haley), *The Autobiography of Malcolm X* (Grove Press, 1964) and Peter Goldman, *The Death and Life of Malcolm X* (Harper & Row, 1974). Continued interest in Malcolm X is reflected not only in Spike Lee's 1992 motion picture *X* but also in Bruce Perry, *Malcolm: The Life of a Man Who Changed Black America* (Station Hill, 1991). James H. Cone's *Martin and Malcolm and America: A Dream or a Nightmare* (Orbis, 1991) is a valuable analysis that emphasizes the convergence of these two leaders' ideas.

For an understanding of two prominent civil rights organizations, see August Meier and Elliott Rudwick, *CORE: A Study in the Civil Rights Movement, 1942–1968* (Oxford University Press, 1973) and Clayborne Carson, *In Struggle: SNCC and the Black Awakening of the 1960s* (Harvard University Press, 1981). William H. Chafe, in *Civilities and Civil Rights: Greensboro, North Carolina, and the Black Struggle for Freedom* (Oxford University Press, 1980), evaluates the impact of the movement on race relations in a single city. Seth Cagin and Philip Dray, *We Are Not Afraid: The Story of Goodman, Schwerner, and Chaney and the Civil Rights Campaign for Mississippi* (Macmillan, 1988); John Dittmer, *Local People: The Struggle for Civil Rights in Mississippi* (University of Illinois Press, 1994); and Charles M. Payne, *I've Got the Light of Freedom: The Organizing Tradition and the Mississippi Freedom Struggle* (University of California Press, 1995) relive the terror and heroic efforts connected with the civil rights campaigns in the Magnolia State. Finally, the texture of the civil rights movement is captured brilliantly in Henry Hampton's documentary series *Eyes on the Prize*.

A critical assessment of the legacy of the civil rights movement is presented in two books by political scientist Robert C. Smith: *We Have No Leaders: African Americans in the Post–Civil Rights Era* (State University of New York Press, 1994) and *Racism in the Post–Civil Rights Era: Now You See It, Now You Don't* (State University of New York Press, 1996).

ISSUE 16

Will History Forgive Richard Nixon?

YES: Joan Hoff-Wilson, from "Richard M. Nixon: The Corporate Presidency," in Fred I. Greenstein, ed., *Leadership in the Modern Presidency* (Harvard University Press, 1988)

NO: Stanley I. Kutler, from "Et Tu, Bob?" *The Nation* (August 22/29, 1994)

ISSUE SUMMARY

YES: According to professor of history Joan Hoff-Wilson, the Nixon presidency reorganized the executive branch and portions of the federal bureaucracy and implemented domestic reforms in civil rights, welfare, and economic planning, despite its limited foreign policy successes and the Watergate scandal.

NO: Professor and political commentator Stanley I. Kutler argues that President Nixon was a crass, cynical, narrow-minded politician who unnecessarily prolonged the Vietnam War to ensure his reelection and implemented domestic reforms only when he could outflank his liberal opponents.

In late April 1994 former president Richard M. Nixon, age 81, died in a coma in a hospital in New York City. Twenty years before, Nixon became the only U.S. president forced to resign from office.

Richard Milhous Nixon was born in Yorba Linda in Orange County, California, on January 9, 1913, the second of five children. When he was nine his family moved to Whittier, California. His mother encouraged him to attend the local Quaker school, Whittier College, where he excelled at student politics and debating. He earned a tuition-paid scholarship to Duke University Law School and graduated third out of a class of 25 in 1937. He returned to Whittier and for several years worked with the town's oldest law firm.

Nixon had hopes of joining a bigger law firm, but World War II intervened. He worked in the tire rationing section for the Office of Price Administration in Washington, D.C., before joining the navy as a lieutenant, junior grade, where he served in a Naval Transport Unit in the South Pacific for the duration of the war. Before his discharge from active duty, Republicans asked him to run for a seat in California's 12th congressional district in the House of Representatives. He won the primary and defeated Jerry Vorhees, a nationally known, New Deal Democratic incumbent, in the general election of 1946. In that year the Republicans gained control of Congress for the first time since 1930.

During Nixon's campaign against Vorhees, he accused Vorhees of accepting money from a communist-dominated political action committee. This tactic, known as "red-baiting," was effective in the late 1940s and early 1950s because the American public had become frightened of the communist menace. In 1950 Nixon utilized similar tactics in running for the U.S. Senate against Congresswoman Helen Gahagan Douglas. He won easily.

Young, energetic, a vigorous campaign orator, and a senator from the second largest state in the Union with impeccable anticommunist credentials, Nixon was chosen by liberal Republicans to become General Dwight Eisenhower's running mate in the 1952 presidential election. In the election Eisenhower and Nixon overwhelmed the Democrats. Nixon became the second-youngest vice president in U.S. history and actively used the office to further his political ambitions.

The 1960 presidential campaign was one of the closest in modern times. Nixon, who was considered young for high political office at that time, lost to an even younger Democratic senator from Massachusetts, John F. Kennedy. Out of 68 million votes cast, less than 113,000 votes separated the two candidates.

In 1962 Nixon was persuaded to seek the governorship of California on the premise that he needed a power boost to keep his presidential hopes alive for 1964. Apparently, Nixon was out of touch with state politics. Governor Pat Brown defeated him by 300,000 votes.

Nixon then left for New York City and became a partner with a big-time Wall Street legal firm. He continued to speak at Republican dinners, and he supported Barry Goldwater of Arizona for the presidency in 1964. After Goldwater's decisive defeat by Lyndon B. Johnson, Nixon's political fortunes revived yet again. In March 1968 Johnson announced he was not going to run again for the presidency. Nixon took advantage of the opening and won the Republican nomination.

During the 1968 presidential campaign Nixon positioned himself between Democratic vice president Hubert Humphrey, the liberal defender of the Great Society programs, and the conservative, law-and-order third-party challenger Governor George Wallace of Alabama. Nixon stressed a more moderate brand of law and order and stated that he had a secret plan to end the war in Vietnam. He barely edged Humphrey in the popular vote, but Nixon received 301 electoral votes to 191 for Humphrey. Wallace received nearly 10 million popular votes and 46 electoral college votes.

This background brings us to Nixon's presidency. Was Nixon an effective president? In the following selections, Joan Hoff-Wilson argues that Nixon achieved a number of domestic policy successes in the areas of civil rights, welfare, economic planning, and in the reorganization of the executive branch and some federal agencies. Stanley I. Kutler maintains that President Nixon was a crass, cynical, narrow-minded bigot who implemented policy changes for strictly political reasons.

YES

Joan Hoff-Wilson

RICHARD M. NIXON:
THE CORPORATE PRESIDENCY

Richard Milhous Nixon became president of the United States at a critical juncture in American history. Following World War II there was a general agreement between popular and elite opinion on two things: the effectiveness of most New Deal domestic policies and the necessity of most Cold War foreign policies. During the 1960s, however, these two crucial postwar consensual constructs began to break down; and the war in Indochina, with its disruptive impact on the nation's political economy, hastened their disintegration. By 1968 the traditional bipartisan, Cold War approach to the conduct of foreign affairs had been seriously undermined. Similarly, the "bigger and better" New Deal approach to the modern welfare state had reached a point of diminishing returns, even among liberals.

In 1968, when Richard Nixon finally captured the highest office in the land, he inherited not only Lyndon Johnson's Vietnam war but also LBJ's Great Society. This transfer of power occurred at the very moment when both endeavors had lost substantial support among the public at large and, most important, among a significant number of the elite group of decision makers and leaders of opinion across the country. On previous occasions when such a breakdown had occurred within policy- and opinion-making circles—before the Civil and Spanish American Wars and in the early years of the Great Depression—domestic or foreign upheavals had followed. Beginning in the 1960s the country experienced a similar series of failed presidents reminiscent of those in the unstable 1840s and 1850s, 1890s, and 1920s.

In various ways all the presidents in these transitional periods failed as crisis managers, often because they refused to take risks. Nixon, in contrast, "[couldn't] understand people who won't take risks." His proclivity for risk taking was not emphasized by scholars, journalists, and psychologists until after he was forced to resign as president. "I am not necessarily a respecter of the status quo," Nixon told Stuart Alsop in 1958; "I am a chance taker." Although this statement was made primarily in reference to foreign affairs, Nixon's entire political career has been characterized by a series of personal and professional crises and risky political policies. It is therefore not

From Joan Hoff-Wilson, "Richard M. Nixon: The Corporate Presidency," in Fred I. Greenstein, ed., *Leadership in the Modern Presidency* (Harvard University Press, 1988). Copyright © 1988 by the President and Fellows of Harvard College. Reprinted by permission of the publisher. Notes omitted.

surprising that as president he rationalized many of his major foreign and domestic initiatives as crises (or at least as intolerable impasses) that could be resolved only by dramatic and sometimes drastic measures.

A breakdown in either the foreign or domestic policy consensus offers both opportunity and danger to any incumbent president. Nixon had more opportunity for risk-taking changes at home and abroad during his first administration than he would have had if elected in 1960 because of the disruptive impact of war and domestic reforms during the intervening eight years. Also, he inherited a wartime presidency, with all its temporarily enhanced extralegal powers. Although the Cold War in general has permanently increased the potential for constitutional violations by presidents, only those in the midst of a full-scale war (whether declared or undeclared) have exercised with impunity what Garry Wills has called "semi-constitutional" actions. Although Nixon was a wartime president for all but twenty months of his five and one-half years in office, he found that impunity for constitutional violations was not automatically accorded a president engaged in an undeclared, unsatisfying, and seemingly endless war. In fact, he is not usually even thought of, or referred to, as a wartime president.

Periods of war and reform have usually alternated in the United States, but in the 1960s they burgeoned simultaneously, hastening the breakdown of consensus that was so evident by the time of the 1968 election. This unusual situation transformed Nixon's largely unexamined and rather commonplace management views into more rigid and controversial ones. It also reinforced his natural predilection to bring about change through executive fiat. Thus a historical accident accounts in part for many of Nixon's unilateral administrative actions during his first term and for the events leading to his disgrace and resignation during his second.

The first few months in the Oval Office are often intoxicating, and a new president can use them in a variety of ways. But during the socioeconomic confusion and conflict of the late 1960s and early 1970s, some of the newly appointed Republican policy managers (generalists) and the frustrated holdover Democratic policy specialists (experts) in the bureaucracy unexpectedly came together and began to consider dramatic policy changes at home and abroad. Complex interactions between these very different groups produced several significant shifts in domestic and foreign affairs during the spring and summer of 1969. A radical welfare plan and dramatic foreign policy initiatives took shape.

The country had elected only one other Republican president since the onset of FDR's reform administrations thirty-six years earlier. Consequently, Nixon faced not only unprecedented opportunities for changing domestic policy as a result of the breakdown in the New Deal consensus, but also the traditional problems of presidential governance, exacerbated in this instance by bureaucratic pockets of resistance from an unusual number of holdover Democrats. Such resistance was not new, but its magnitude was particularly threatening to a distrusted (and distrustful) Republican president who did not control either house of Congress. Nixon's organizational recommendations for containing the bureaucracy disturbed his political opponents and the liberal press as much as, if not more than, their doubts about the motivation behind many of his substantive

362 / 16. WILL HISTORY FORGIVE RICHARD NIXON?

and innovative suggestions on other domestic issues such as welfare and the environment.

Because much of the press and both houses of Congress were suspicious of him, Nixon naturally viewed administrative action as one way of obtaining significant domestic reform. Moreover, some of his initial accomplishments in administratively redirecting U.S. foreign policy ultimately led him to rely more on administrative actions at home than he might have otherwise. In any case, this approach drew criticism from those who already distrusted his policies and priorities. Nixon's covert and overt expansion and prolongation of the war during this period reinforced existing suspicions about his personality and political ethics. In this sense, liberal paranoia about his domestic programs fueled Nixon's paranoia about liberal opposition to the war, and vice versa. By 1972, Nixon's success in effecting structural and substantive change in foreign policy through the exercise of unilateral executive power increasingly led him to think that he could use the same preemptive administrative approach to resolve remaining domestic problems, especially following his landslide electoral victory....

FOREIGN POLICY SCORECARD

It was clearly in Nixon's psychic and political self-interest to end the war in Vietnam as soon as possible. Although he came to office committed to negotiate a quick settlement, he ended up prolonging the conflict. As a result, he could never build the domestic consensus he needed to continue the escalated air and ground war (even with dramatically reduced U.S. troop involvement) and to ensure passage of some of his domes-

tic programs. For Nixon (and Kissinger) Vietnam became a symbol of influence in the Third World that, in turn, was but one part of their geopolitical approach to international relations. Thus the war in Southeast Asia had to be settled as soon as possible so as not to endanger other elements of Nixonian diplomatic and domestic policy.

Instead, the president allowed his secretary of state to become egocentrically involved in secret negotiations with the North Vietnamese from August 4, 1969, to January 25, 1972 (when they were made public). As a result, the terms finally reached in 1973 were only marginally better than those rejected in 1969. The advantage gained from Hanoi's agreement to allow President Nguyen Van Thieu to remain in power in return for allowing North Vietnamese troops to remain in South Vietnam can hardly offset the additional loss of twenty thousand American lives during this three-year-period—especially given the inherent weaknesses of the Saigon government by 1973. On the tenth anniversary of the peace treaty ending the war in Vietnam, Nixon admitted to me that "Kissinger believed more in the power of negotiation than I did." He also said that he "would not have temporized as long" with the negotiating process had he not been "needlessly" concerned with what the Soviets and Chinese might think if the United States pulled out of Vietnam precipitately. Because Nixon saw no way in 1969 to end the war quickly except through overt massive bombing attacks, which the public demonstrated in 1970 and 1971 it would not tolerate, there was neither peace nor honor in Vietnam by the time that war was finally concluded on January 27, 1973; and in the interim he made matters worse by secretly bombing Cambodia.

The delayed ending to the war in Vietnam not only cast a shadow on all Nixon's other foreign policy efforts but also established secrecy, wiretapping, and capricious personal diplomacy as standard operational procedures in the conduct of foreign policy that ultimately carried over into domestic affairs. Despite often duplicitous and arbitrary actions, even Nixon's strongest critics often credit him with an unusual number of foreign policy successes.

Although fewer of his foreign policy decisions were reached in a crisis atmosphere than his domestic ones, Nixon's diplomatic legacy is weaker than he and many others have maintained. For example, the pursuit of "peace and honor" in Vietnam failed; his Middle Eastern policy because of Kissinger's shuttling ended up more show than substance; his Third World policy (outside of Vietnam and attempts to undermine the government of Allende in Chile) were nearly nonexistent; détente with the USSR soon foundered under his successors; and the Nixon Doctrine has not prevented use of U.S. troops abroad. Only rapprochement with China remains untarnished by time because it laid the foundation for recognition, even though he failed to achieve a "two China" policy in the United Nations. This summary is not meant to discredit Richard Nixon as a foreign policy expert both during and after his presidency. It is a reminder that the lasting and positive results of his diplomacy may be fading faster than some aspects of his domestic policies.

OUTFLANKING LIBERALS ON DOMESTIC REFORM

Presidents traditionally achieve their domestic objectives through legislation,

appeals in the mass media, and administrative actions. During his first administration Nixon offered Congress extensive domestic legislation, most of which aimed at redistributing federal power away from Congress and the bureaucracy. When he encountered difficulty obtaining passage of these programs, he resorted more and more to reform by administrative fiat, especially at the beginning of his second term. All Nixonian domestic reforms were rhetorically linked under the rubric of the New Federalism. Most competed for attention with his well-known interest in foreign affairs. Most involved a degree of the boldness he thought necessary for a successful presidency. Most increased federal regulation of nondistributive public policies. Most were made possible in part because he was a wartime Republican president who took advantage of acting in the Disraeli tradition of enlightened conservatism. Most offended liberals (as well as many conservatives), especially when it came to implementing certain controversial policies with legislation. Many were also undertaken in a crisis atmosphere, which on occasion was manufactured by individual members of Nixon's staff to ensure his attention and action.

In some instances, as political scientist Paul J. Halpern has noted, Nixon's longstanding liberal opponents in Congress "never even bothered to get the facts straight" about these legislative and administrative innovations; the very people who, according to Daniel Moynihan, formed the "natural constituency" for most of Nixon's domestic policies refused to support his programs. It may well have been that many liberals simply could not believe that Nixon would ever do the right thing except for the wrong reason. Thus they seldom took the time to try to determine whether any of his efforts to make the 1970s a decade of reform were legitimate, however politically motivated. Additionally, such partisan opposition made Nixon all the more willing to reorganize the executive branch of government with or without congressional approval.

My own interviews with Nixon and his own (and others') recent attempts to rehabilitate his reputation indicate that Nixon thinks he will outlive the obloquy of Watergate because of his foreign policy initiatives—not because of his domestic policies. Ultimately, however, domestic reform and his attempts at comprehensive reorganization of the executive branch may become the standard by which the Nixon presidency is judged.

Environmental Policy

Although Nixon's aides cite his environmental legislation as one of his major domestic achievements, it was not high on his personal list of federal priorities, despite polls showing its growing importance as a national issue. White House central files released in 1986 clearly reveal that John Ehrlichman was initially instrumental in shaping the president's views on environmental matters and conveying a sense of crisis about them. Most ideas were filtered through him to Nixon. In fact Ehrlichman, whose particular expertise was in land-use policies, has been described by one forest conservation specialist as "the most effective environmentalist since Gifford Pinchot." Ehrlichman and John Whitaker put Nixon ahead of Congress on environmental issues, especially with respect to his use of the permit authority in the Refuse Act of 1899 to begin to clean up water supplies before Congress passed any "comprehensive water pollution enforcement plan."

"Just keep me out of trouble on environmental issues," Nixon reportedly told Ehrlichman. This proved impossible because Congress ignored Nixon's recommended ceilings when it finally passed (over his veto) the Federal Water Pollution Control Act amendments of 1972. Both Ehrlichman and Whitaker agreed then and later that it was "budget-busting" legislation designed to embarrass the president on a popular issue in an election year. Statistics later showed that the money appropriated could not be spent fast enough to achieve the legislation's stated goals. The actual annual expenditures in the first years after passage approximated those originally proposed by Nixon's staff.

Revamping Welfare

Throughout the 1968 presidential campaign Nixon's own views on welfare remained highly unfocused. But once in the Oval Office he set an unexpectedly fast pace on the issue. On January 15, 1969, he demanded an investigation by top aides into a newspaper allegation of corruption in New York City's Human Resources Administration. Nixon's extraordinary welfare legislation originated in a very circuitous fashion with two low-level Democratic holdovers from the Johnson administration, Worth Bateman and James Lyday. These two bureaucrats fortuitously exercised more influence on Robert Finch, Nixon's first secretary of health, education and welfare, than they had been able to on John W. Gardner and Wilbur J. Cohn, Johnson's two appointees. Finch was primarily responsible for obtaining Nixon's approval of what eventually became known as the Family Assistance Program (FAP).

If FAP had succeeded in Congress it would have changed the emphasis of

American welfare from providing services to providing income; thus it would have replaced the Aid to Families with Dependent Children (AFDC) program, whose payments varied widely from state to state. FAP called for anywhere from $1,600 (initially proposed in 1969) to $2,500 (proposed in 1971) for a family of four. States were expected to supplement this amount, and in addition all able-bodied heads of recipient families (except mothers with preschool children) would be required to "accept work or training." However, if a parent refused to accept work or training, only his or her payment would be withheld. In essence, FAP unconditionally guaranteed children an annual income and would have tripled the number of children then being aided by AFDC.

A fundamental switch from services to income payments proved to be too much for congressional liberals and conservatives alike, and they formed a strange alliance to vote it down. Ironically, FAP's final defeat in the Senate led to some very impressive examples of incremental legislation that might not have been passed had it not been for the original boldness of FAP. For example, Supplementary Security Income, approved on October 17, 1972, constituted a guaranteed annual income for the aged, blind, and disabled.

The demise of FAP also led Nixon to support uniform application of the food stamp program across the United States, better health insurance programs for low-income families, and an automatic cost-of-living adjustment for Social Security recipients to help them cope with inflation. In every budget for which his administration was responsible—that is, from fiscal 1971 through fiscal 1975 —spending on all human resource programs exceeded spending for defense for the first time since World War II. A seven-fold increase in funding for social services under Nixon made him (not Johnson) the "last of the big spenders" on domestic programs.

Reluctant Civil Rights Achievements

Perhaps the domestic area in which Watergate has most dimmed or skewed our memories of the Nixon years is civil rights. We naturally tend to remember that during his presidency Nixon deliberately violated the civil rights of some of those who opposed his policies or were suspected of leaking information. Nixon has always correctly denied that he was a conservative on civil rights, and indeed his record on this issue, as on so many others, reveals as much political expediency as it does philosophical commitment. By 1968 there was strong southern support for his candidacy. Consequently, during his campaign he implied that if elected he would slow down enforcement of federal school desegregation policies.

Enforcement had already been painfully sluggish since the 1954 *Brown v. Board of Education* decision. By 1968 only 20 percent of black children in the South attended predominantly white schools, and none of this progress had occurred under Eisenhower or Kennedy. Moreover, the most dramatic improvement under Johnson's administration did not take place until 1968, because HEW deadlines for desegregating southern schools had been postponed four times since the passage of the 1964 Civil Rights Act. By the spring of 1968, however, a few lower court rulings, and finally the Supreme Court decision in *Green v. Board of Education*, no longer allowed any president the luxury of arguing that freedom-of-choice plans were adequate for rooting out racial discrimination, or that de facto segregation caused by residential patterns was not as unconstitutional as *de jure* segregation brought about by state or local laws.

Despite the real national crisis that existed over school desegregation, Nixon was not prepared to go beyond what he thought the decision in *Brown* had mandated, because he believed that de facto segregation could not be ended through busing or cutting off funds from school districts. Nine days after Nixon's inauguration, his administration had to decide whether to honor an HEW-initiated cutoff of funds to five southern school districts, originally scheduled to take place in the fall of 1968 but delayed until January 29, 1969. On that day Secretary Finch confirmed the cutoff but also announced that the school districts could claim funds retroactively if they complied with HEW guidelines within sixty days. This offer represented a change from the most recent set of HEW guidelines, developed in March 1968, which Johnson had never formally endorsed by signing.

At the heart of the debate over various HEW guidelines in the last half of the 1960s were two issues: whether the intent of the Civil Rights Act of 1964 had been simply to provide freedom of choice or actually to compel integration in schools; and whether freedom-of-choice agreements negotiated by HEW or lawsuits brought by the Department of Justice were the most effective ways of achieving desegregation. Under the Johnson administration the HEW approach, based on bringing recalcitrant school districts into compliance by cutting off federal funding, had prevailed. Nixon, on the other hand, argued in his First Inaugural that the "laws have caught up with our consciences" and insisted that

it was now necessary "to give life to what is in the law." Accordingly, he changed the emphasis in the enforcement of school desegregation from HEW compliance agreements to Justice Department actions—a legal procedure that proved very controversial in 1969 and 1970, but one that is standard now.

Nixon has been justifiably criticized by civil rights advocates for employing delaying tactics in the South, and particularly for not endorsing busing to enforce school desegregation in the North after the April 20, 1971, Supreme Court decision in *Swann v. Charlotte-Mecklenburg Board of Education.* Despite the bitter battle in Congress and between Congress and the executive branch after *Swann,* the Nixon administration's statistical record on school desegregation is impressive. In 1968, 68 percent of all black children in the South and 40 percent in the nation as a whole attended all-black schools. By the end of 1972, 8 percent of southern black children attended all-black schools, and a little less than 12 percent nationwide. A comparison of budget outlays is equally revealing. President Nixon spent $911 million on civil rights activities, including $75 million for civil rights enforcement in fiscal 1969. The Nixon administration's budget for fiscal 1973 called for $2.6 billion in total civil rights outlays, of which $602 million was earmarked for enforcement through a substantially strengthened Equal Employment Opportunity Commission. Nixon supported the civil rights goals of American Indians and women with less reluctance than he did school desegregation because these groups did not pose a major political problem for him and he had no similar legal reservations about how the law should be applied to them.

MIXING ECONOMICS
AND POLITICS

Nixon spent an inordinate amount of time on domestic and foreign economic matters. Nowhere did he appear to reverse himself more on views he had held before becoming president (or at least on views others attributed to him), and nowhere was his aprincipled pragmatism more evident. Nixon's failure to obtain more revenue through tax reform legislation in 1969, together with rising unemployment and inflation rates in 1970, precipitated an effort (in response to a perceived crisis) to balance U.S. domestic concerns through wage and price controls and international ones through devaluation of the dollar. This vehicle was the New Economic Policy, dramatically announced on August 15, 1971, at the end of a secret Camp David meeting with sixteen economic advisers. Largely as a result of Treasury Secretary Connally's influence, Nixon agreed that if foreign countries continued to demand ever-increasing amounts of gold for the U.S. dollars they held, the United States would go off the gold standard but would at the same time impose wage and price controls to curb inflation. The NEP perfectly reflected the "grand gesture" Connally thought the president should make on economic problems, and the August 15 television broadcast dramatized economic issues that most Americans, seldom anticipating long-range consequences, found boring.

When he was not trying to preempt Congress on regulatory issues, Nixon proposed deregulation based on free-market assumptions that were more traditionally in keeping with conservative Republicanism. The administration ended the draft in the name of economic

freedom and recommended deregulation of the production of food crops, tariff and other barriers to international trade, and interest rates paid by various financial institutions. Except for wage and price controls and the devaluation of the dollar, none of these actions was justified in the name of crisis management. In general, however, political considerations made Nixon more liberal on domestic economic matters, confounding both his supporters and his opponents.

Nixon attributes his interest in international economics to the encouragement of John Foster Dulles and his desire as vice-president in the 1950s to create a Foreign Economic Council. Failing in this, he has said that his travels abroad in the 1950s only confirmed his belief that foreign leaders understood economics better than did American leaders, and he was determined to remedy this situation as president. Nixon faced two obstacles in this effort: Kissinger (because "international economics was not Henry's bag"), and State Department officials who saw "economic policy as government to government," which limited their diplomatic view of the world and made them so suspicious or cynical (or both) about the private sector that they refused to promote international commerce to the degree that Nixon thought they should. "Unlike the ignoramuses I encountered among economic officers at various embassies in the 1950s and 1960s," Nixon told me, "I wanted to bring economics to the foreign service."

Because of Nixon's own interest in and knowledge of international trade, he attempted as president to rationalize the formulation of foreign economic policy. After 1962, when he was out of public office and practicing law in New York, he had specialized in international economics and multinational corporations —definitely not Henry Kissinger's areas of expertise. In part because they were not a "team" on foreign economic policy and in part because Nixon bypassed the NSC almost entirely in formulating his New Economic Policy, Nixon relied not on his national security adviser but on other free-thinking outsiders when formulating foreign economic policy.

Next to John Connally, Nixon was most impressed with the economic views of Peter G. Peterson, who, after starting out in 1971 as a White House adviser on international economic affairs, became secretary of commerce in January 1972. Although Connally and Peterson appeared to agree on such early foreign economic initiatives as the NEP and the "get tough" policy toward Third World countries that nationalized U.S. companies abroad, as secretary of commerce Peterson ultimately proved much more sophisticated and sensitive than the secretary of the treasury about the United States' changed economic role in the world. In a December 27, 1971, position paper defending Nixon's NEP, Peterson remarked that the new global situation in which the United States found itself demanded "shared leadership, shared responsibility, and shared burdens... The reform of the international monetary systems," he said, must fully recognize and be solidly rooted in "the growing reality of a genuinely interdependent and increasingly competitive world economy whose goal is mutual, shared prosperity —not artificial, temporary advantage." At no point did Peterson believe, as Connally apparently did, that "the simple realignment of exchange rates" would adequately address the economic realignment problems facing the international economy.

In 1971 Nixon succeeded in establishing an entirely new cabinet-level Council on International Economic Policy (CIEP), headed by Peterson. This was not so much a reorganization of functions as it was an alternative to fill an existing void in the federal structure and to provide "clear top-level focus on international economic issues and to achieve consistency between international and domestic economic policy." For a variety of reasons—not the least of which was Kissinger's general lack of interest in, and disdain for, the unglamorous aspects of international economics—the CIEP faltered and finally failed after Nixon left office. Its demise seems to have been hastened by Kissinger's recommendation to the Congressional Commission on Organization of Foreign Policy that it be eliminated, despite the fact that others, including Peterson, testified on its behalf. The CIEP was subsequently merged with the Office of the Special Trade Representative.

* * *

Even with Nixon's impressive foreign and domestic record, it cannot be said that he would have succeeded as a managerial or administrative president had Watergate not occurred. Entrenched federal bureaucracies are not easily controlled or divested of power even with the best policy-oriented management strategies. That his foreign policy management seems more successful is also no surprise: diplomatic bureaucracies are smaller, more responsive, and easier to control than their domestic counterparts. Moreover, public concern (except for Vietnam) remained minimal as usual, and individual presidential foreign policy initiatives are more likely to be remembered and to appear effective than domestic ones. Nonetheless, the real importance of Nixon's presidency may well come to rest not on Watergate or foreign policy, but on his attempts to restructure the executive branch along functional lines, to bring order to the federal bureaucracy, and to achieve lasting domestic reform. The degree to which those Nixonian administrative tactics that were legal and ethical (and most of them were) became consciously or unconsciously the model for his successors in the Oval Office will determine his final place in history.

Although Nixon's corporate presidency remains publicly discredited, much of it has been privately preserved. Perhaps this is an indication that in exceptional cases presidential effectiveness can transcend popular (and scholarly) disapproval. What Nixon lacked in charisma and honesty, he may in the long run make up for with his phoenixlike ability to survive disaster. Nixon has repeatedly said: "No politician is dead until he admits it." It is perhaps an ironic commentary on the state of the modern presidency that Richard Nixon's management style and substantive foreign and domestic achievements look better and better when compared with those of his immediate successors in the Oval Office.

NO

Stanley I. Kutler

ET TU, BOB?

There is nothing quite like H.R. Haldeman's diaries, published recently during the official period of mourning for Richard Nixon. They are repulsive almost beyond belief, yet therein lies their importance. Ostensibly designed to record the doings of a great man, they devastate Nixon's reputation. Truly Haldeman has proved Mark Antony's observation that the good that men do is buried with their bones; the evil they do lives long after them. The diaries appeared three weeks after Nixon's death as a nearly 700-page book, unveiled first on a two-part *Nightline* program, which predictably focused on Nixon's racial and ethnic slurs. Soon thereafter came the CD-ROM, which included a "complete" version of the diaries (60 percent more material than in the book) and some added attractions, including "home" movies (developed at government expense), photos, bios of key and bit players and an amazing apologia in the form of an unsent 40,000-plus-word letter to James Neal, who prosecuted Haldeman. Like Antony, Haldeman had motives other than praising Caesar.

The diaries reflect two men in an "intense one-on-one relationship," men who were not, according to Haldeman's widow, personal friends. Since Nixon had few close friends, this means very little. The two often dined alone on the presidential yacht and then went to the President's sitting room to chat. The President would drink his '57 Lafite-Rothschild and serve Haldeman the California "Beaulieu Vineyard stuff." And Haldeman would have to read aloud Nixon's *Who's Who* entry. Maybe he was supposed to savor that instead.

The tapes revealed Nixon's shabbiness; the diaries underline his shallowness. The recurring themes of the diaries are simple: getting re-elected, getting even. Nixon was consumed with P.R., constantly prodding Haldeman on how to spin stories, how to protect his image and, almost comically, how to deny that the President was interested in such things. Haldeman, the old advertising executive, usually relished the game, yet he must have found it tiresome as well. P.R., he noted, "would work a lot better if he would quit worrying . . . and just be President." Impossible; for Nixon it was all.

Altogether, the picture is not pretty. It is mostly warts and little face, and certainly not the one Nixon had in mind as he took his leave. Shortly after

Haldeman died last fall, Nixon asked Haldeman's family to delay publication, ostensibly so as not to interfere with the promotion of his own book. What a hoot it would have been if Nixon, appearing on the *Today* show, had had to confront some of the juicier items from his trusted aide's diaries. In any event, Haldeman said that he hoped his book—which fleshes out and expands the daily notes that have been available for some time—would "once and for all" put the Nixon years into perspective. It certainly helps, but probably not as he intended.

Nixon always knew that Haldeman's diaries were potential dynamite. Archibald Cox subpoenaed the files on May 25, 1973, but the President had taken control of the diaries and put them with his papers, which eventually went to the National Archives (over his protests, to be sure). In 1980, Haldeman cut a deal with the Archives, deeding the diaries to the public (meaning he always intended for them to be seen, contrary to *Nightline*'s and his wife's assertions) in exchange for the Archives' agreement to keep them closed for a decade, later extended for several more years. Haldeman then promptly filed suit against the government, claiming (falsely) that he had been unlawfully deprived of access to his property in the intervening years. But the court refused to get involved "in the niceties of Fifth Amendment doctrine" since the case revolved around one question: Why did Haldeman leave his diaries in the White House when he was dismissed on April 30, 1973?

The government nailed Haldeman when it introduced Oval Office conversations for May 2 and 9, 1973 (Haldeman had "left" the White House but he returned—to listen to tapes!), in which Nixon and Haldeman typically concocted a scenario for future spin. In brief, Nixon would claim the materials as his own and cloak them with executive privilege: "Your notes belong to the President," Nixon told him. Haldeman finished the thought: "And fortunately, they're . . . in your possession; they're not in mine." In those days, we had few illusions about Nixon and his aide. District Judge John Garrett Penn said that Haldeman could have avoided the dispute had he claimed the diaries as his own at the outset, or had he made photocopies when he viewed the materials. The conflict, the judge ruled, was entirely Haldeman's fault. "He could have obviated this entire conflict; he chose another route solely for his own protection, and should not now be given a forum to complain that he did not choose wisely." He may not have chosen wisely as far as Nixon is concerned—but Haldeman will do well by his heirs.

* * *

Most reactions to the diaries have concentrated on long-familiar Nixon slanders of Jews and blacks. The reluctance to confront the policy and institutional concerns of the diaries is somewhat understandable, for if the mainstream media honestly surveyed this material, they would impeach themselves for their insipid attempts to peddle revisionist views of Nixon in the wake of his death. The diaries clearly reveal the President's extraordinary cynicism, as well as his lack of knowledge of both domestic and foreign policy. No single work so effectively exposes Nixon as a mean, petty, vindictive, insecure—even incompetent—man, and all this from one who professed to admire him; from a man Nixon even said he "loved." Could it have been intentional?

Haldeman himself spent the past two decades portraying himself as a selfless, self-effacing, dedicated servant to the President. But the myth of Haldeman as Stevens the butler in *Remains of the Day* —just a passive vessel for Nixon's commands—is misleading. Haldeman was an old-fashioned Southern California reactionary, weaned on his family's nativist and patriotic views and supported by a plumbing fortune. Nixon correctly perceived him as a "son-of-a-bitch" and used him as a "Lord High Executioner."

Unintentionally, I would guess, Haldeman has provided us with wonderful comic moments. After the Thomas Eagleton nomination fiasco in 1972, Spiro Agnew, either with inspired wit or sheer meanness, asked Dr. Joyce Brothers to second his own nomination—as if to receive psychological certification of his sanity. Nixon issued a presidential order directing Agnew to rescind the invitation. Then there are Great Moments of Protocol: Who would ride in the President's golf cart, Bob Hope or Frank Sinatra? Finally, Nixon wanted a White House reception to honor Duke Ellington and told Haldeman to invite other jazz notables, including Guy Lombardo. "Oh well," the knowing Haldeman sighed.

Haldeman's diaries show that he spent either hours or "all day" with the President. Sometimes Haldeman recorded Nixon's thoughts on substantive policy such as China or the settlement of the Vietnam War. But usually the subjects were relentlessly repetitive, as were the homilies that Nixon dispensed. And yet Haldeman faithfully recorded and preserved the President's words. During the 1972 campaign, Haldeman and John Ehrlichman spent inordinate amounts of time listening to the President repeatedly go over matters such as his

prospects in every state, who would be dismissed, who would be moved and how enemies would be punished. Apparently even "two of the finest public servants," as Nixon characterized them when he dismissed them, could not abide the monotony of it all without sarcasm. "Why did he buzz me?" Haldeman asked Ehrlichman in a note written during one of the President's soliloquies. Like a schoolchild answering a passed message, Ehrlichman sketched several answers:

> "He had an itchy finger."
>
> "Also there was a chair unoccupied."
>
> "Also he has been talking about not just reordering the chaos, and he would like you to understand that point."

Supposedly, Nixon wanted someone to keep the "routine baloney" away from him; it "bores and annoys him," Haldeman noted. Yet Haldeman often wearily complained about the tedium, as when he noted that the "P had the morning clear, unfortunately, and called me ... for over four hours as he wandered through odds and ends...."

Aside from the President's behavior, the most significant revelations surround Henry Kissinger. From the outset, Nixon and Haldeman recognized Kissinger as a devious, emotionally unstable person. The President saw him as a rival for public acclaim, ever anxious to magnify himself for the contemporary and historical record. Nixon did not entirely trust Kissinger's briefings. Most surprising, however, was Haldeman's intimate involvement in the management of foreign policy as the President regularly shared his thoughts and views on Kissinger with his Chief of Staff.

In the pathology of the Nixon White House, perhaps the sickest subject involved what Haldeman repeatedly called the "K-Rogers flap," which he blamed equally on Kissinger's "unbelievable ego" and Secretary of State William Rogers's pique. We long have understood Kissinger's pre-inaugural coup that enabled him and Nixon to bypass the State Department bureaucracy; yet what Kissinger wanted was the place for himself. Haldeman relentlessly portrays Kissinger as a mercurial, temperamental infant, constantly concerned with his standing and status; Nixon considered Kissinger "obsessed beyond reason" with Rogers.

Nixon and Kissinger appear more as adversaries than as allies. In November 1972, miffed at Kissinger's media attempts to grab the lion's share of credit for the China opening, Nixon instructed Haldeman to tell Kissinger that he had tapes of their conversations! Nixon warned Haldeman that *Time* might "needle us [and] go for K as the Man of the Year, which would be very bad, so we should try to swing that around a different way." Students of Vietnam policy have an interesting task in sorting out responsibility for the protracted peace negotiations. Kissinger expressed to Haldeman his fear that Nixon wanted to "bug out" and not carry through on long-term negotiations. Kissinger well knew that message would get back to Nixon and steel him against any appearances of being "soft."

Haldeman's diaries substantially confirm the criticism of Kissinger's detractors, especially Seymour Hersh's biting analysis of the Nixon-Kissinger foreign policies in *The Price of Power*. Appearance was often substituted for substance, and at times, as in the SALT negotiations, Kissinger seemed entirely out of his element. What then does this say

of the President of the United States —who similarly was unconcerned with substance and seemed most bent on preventing Kissinger from getting too much praise? Certainly, Adm. Elmo Zumwalt had it right when he said that two words did not apply to the Vietnam peace accords: peace and honor. Kissinger's frantic search for a Shanghai Communiqué in 1972 would have bordered on the comic had it not been so fraught with obsequiousness toward his new friends and cynicism toward Nixon's longtime Taiwanese patrons.

Everything had a political calculus. In December 1970, Nixon, Kissinger and Haldeman considered a Vietnam trip the next spring in which the President would make "the basic end of the war announcement." Kissinger objected, saying that if we pulled out in 1971 there could be trouble (ostensibly for the Thieu regime) that the Administration would have to answer for in the 1972 elections. Kissinger urged Nixon to commit only to withdrawing all troops by the end of 1972. Another year of casualties seemed a fair exchange for the President's electoral security.

Billy Graham's choicer remarks about Jews and their "total domination of the media" have been prominently reported. Let's take Graham at his word and agree that some of his best friends are Jews. In the guise of God's messenger, Graham was a Nixon political operative, dutifully reporting back to the White House on what Lyndon Johnson had said about George McGovern, George Wallace's intentions on resuming his presidential bid in 1972, Graham's efforts to calm down Martha Mitchell, plans to organize Christian youth for Nixon, his advice to Johnny Carson to be a little biased in Nixon's favor if he wanted to be helpful and the Shah of Iran's remark that the President's re-election had saved civilization. When Nixon's tapes were first revealed in April 1974, a chastened Graham complained about Nixon's "situational ethics" and lamented that he had been "used." Used once, used again, he could not resist the limelight of preaching at Nixon's funeral.

* * *

John Ehrlichman has maintained that Nixon would be remembered as the great domestic policy President of the twentieth century. (Guess who was Nixon's domestic adviser?) That notion, too, is a chapter in the current drive for revisionism. Well, it won't wash, unless one accepts the view that whatever was accomplished happened in spite of Richard Nixon. His Administration publicly advocated policies that the President clearly didn't believe in. Consider:

- School desegregation: Haldeman noted that Nixon was "really concerned... and feels we have to take some leadership to try to reverse Court decisions that have forced integration too far, too fast." Nixon told Attorney General John Mitchell to keep filing cases until they got a reversal. Nixon proposed getting a right-wing demagogue into some tough race and have him campaign against integration—and he "might even win." He fired Leon Panetta, then a mid-level Health, Education and Welfare functionary, who was doing too much in behalf of school desegregation. (Panetta wouldn't quit, so Nixon announced his "resignation.")
- "[Nixon] was very upset that he had been led to approve the IRS ruling about no tax exemption for private schools, feels it will make no votes anywhere and will badly hurt private schools...."
- "About Family Assistance Plan, [President] wants to be sure it's killed by Democrats and that we make big play for it, but don't let it pass, can't afford it."
- "On welfare, we have to support HR 1 until the election. Afterward, we should not send it back to Congress." "On HR 1 there's some concern that if we hang too tight on the passage of it, that it may actually pass and defeat our Machiavellian plot. Our Congressional tactic overall has got to be to screw things up."
- "He's very much concerned about handling of the drug situation; wants the whole thing taken out of HEW. He makes the point that they're all on drugs there anyway."
- Nixon agreed to continue an I.B.M. antitrust action but urged Haldeman "to make something out of it so we can get credit for attacking business."
- "The P was also very upset about the DDT decision. Ruckleshaus has announced a ban on it. He [Nixon] thinks we should get this whole environment thing out of E and [John] Whitaker's hands because they believe in it, and you can't have an advocate dismantle something he believes in. He also wanted [Fred] Malek to check on who Ruckleshaus has on his staff in terms of left-wing liberals."
- Nixon "made the point that he feels deeply troubled that he's getting sucked in too much on welfare and environment and consumerism."

Liberals cringed in 1968 when Nixon promised to appoint judges who would favor the "peace forces" as opposed to the "criminal forces." Nixon, of course, like all Presidents, sought appointments to mirror his (and his constituency's) wishes. After the Senate rejected his nomination of G. Harrold Carswell for the Supreme Court in 1970, Nixon briefly flirted with nominating Senator Robert Byrd, knowing the Senate would be unlikely to reject one of its own. When Hugo Black resigned from the Court in 1971, Nixon, feverishly backed by Pat Buchanan, pushed for Virginia Congressman Richard Poff, once an ardent backer of segregation. Nixon happily recognized that this would only roil the waters again. Poff had the good sense to withdraw, whereupon Nixon raised Byrd's name again. Why not? Byrd was a former Klansman and "more reactionary than [George] Wallace," Nixon said, obviously relishing a chance to embarrass the Senate.

Following this, Nixon warmed to Mitchell's inspired concoction of nonentities: Herschel Friday (a fellow bond lawyer) and Mildred Lilley, an obscure local California judge who was meant only to be a sacrificial lamb. "The theory on the woman is that the ABA is not going to approve her, and therefore, he'll let her pass and blame them for it," Haldeman wrote. (This was the same American Bar Association committee that had endorsed the unqualified Carswell, Haldeman failed to note.) Nixon wanted Lewis Powell, but for the other open seat the White House tendered an offer to Senator Howard Baker, who called in his answer half an hour too late and was displaced by William Rehnquist in a coup led by Richard Moore, friend and aide to John Mitchell. A rare moment as the President caught Haldeman by surprise.

Everyone seemed happy, Nixon said, except his wife, who had been campaigning for a woman. That is the only time Haldeman recorded the President taking Mrs. Nixon seriously. The diaries are filled with Nixon and Haldeman's shared disdain for the First Lady; for example, Nixon could spare but a few moments for her 60th birthday party and then he hid out in his office.

* * *

Almost from the day that Nixon assumed office, he was off and running for 1972. Teddy Kennedy preoccupied him; in 1969, Nixon and his staff saw the battle over the antiballistic missile as the opening salvo of the 1972 campaign against Kennedy. Even after Chappaquiddick, Nixon seriously believed that Kennedy was a threat. He instigated Ehrlichman's own investigation of the incident and repeatedly told Haldeman that they couldn't let the public forget Chappaquiddick. He encouraged Charles Colson, who had agents follow Kennedy in Paris and photograph him with various women.

Vietnam was small potatoes compared with the amount of time the President and his aide plotted strategy and dirty tricks against political enemies. The Boys of '72 knew their way around this territory without much help. In Nixon's 1962 gubernatorial campaign, they had established a bogus Democratic committee to mail cards to registered Democrats expressing concern for the party under Pat Brown. A Republican judge convicted them of campaign law violations and held that the plan had been "reviewed, amended and finally approved by Mr. Nixon personally," and that Haldeman similarly "approved the plan and the project."

In July 1969, Nixon directed Haldeman to establish a "dirty tricks" unit with the likes of Pat Buchanan and Lyn Nofziger. "Hardball politics," Haldeman later called it. Nixon regularly urged that the I.R.S. investigate Democratic contributors and celebrity supporters. He also wanted a review of the tax returns of all Democratic candidates "and start harassment of them, as they have done of us." He wanted full field investigations of Clark Clifford and other doves; he ordered mailings describing Edmund Muskie's liberal views to be sent throughout the South; and one basic line of his Watergate counteroffensive was to expose Democratic Party chairman Larry O'Brien's tax problems and his allegedly unsavory list of clients.

Alas, Haldeman has little new to offer on Watergate. He claims that the diaries are unexpurgated and complete on this score. That may be stretching the truth. The Watergate section contains long, discursive comments about the activities of many principals, but they are merely summaries Haldeman compiled from contemporary documents and his own choice memories. The entries focus on the complicity of just about everyone but H.R. Haldeman. When read together with the lengthy letter that Haldeman allegedly wrote (and did not send) in 1978 to the prosecutor, the implication is that he and Nixon were guilty only of a "political containment"—he was no party to a conspiracy to obstruct justice and he committed no perjury. He knew that the burglars had been given "hush money," but he insisted it was not a cover-up. It is a little late in the day for such a defense; furthermore, his own words demolish it.

The diaries expand on the finger-pointing that emerged from the tape revelations twenty years ago. Now we clearly see how Nixon, Haldeman and Ehrlichman sought to make Mitchell their fall guy, and how they coddled John Dean for so long to keep him in camp. In the letter to prosecutor James Neal, Haldeman turned from Mitchell to establish the outlines of a Dean conspiracy theory, one that has become fashionable among the former President's men in recent years.

From the outset, Haldeman knew the significance of the Watergate break-in. The day after, he called it "the big flap over the weekend," and he immediately knew that the Committee to Re-elect the President was involved. If so, that meant the White House, for John Mitchell and Jeb Magruder reported directly to Haldeman and his aides on campaign activity. Eventually, the True Campaign Chairman—the President himself—knew what happened there. Two days later, Haldeman reported that Nixon "was somewhat interested" in the events. Interested enough that we have eighteen and a half minutes of deliberately erased tape. Later that same day, June 20, Haldeman noted that Watergate "obviously bothered" Nixon and they discussed it "in considerable detail." But he gives us none.

Haldeman is fudging here. Tapes released two years ago, which cover Watergate conversations for June 1972— we previously had only the notorious "smoking gun" tape of June 23—reveal extensive conversations, beginning with the first attempt to concoct a containment or cover-up scenario on June 20. (Once again, the media missed this story as they made much ado about Nixon's remark that Liddy was "a little nuts.") Using the C.I.A. to thwart the F.B.I. was not a one-time occurrence on June 23; the two men repeatedly tried to stifle the investigation under the cover of national security, even after C.I.A. Director Richard Helms ended his cooperation. In these tapes, Haldeman seems to sense the futility of their efforts: "We got a lid on it and it may not stay on," he told the President on June 28. For nearly a year—not just in his last month as Chief of Staff—Haldeman knew that Watergate was trouble.

Significantly, Haldeman omits any mention of the President's offer of cash to him and Ehrlichman in April 1973 —after Ehrlichman ominously said, "I gotta start answering questions." When the President asked if they could use cash, Haldeman reacted with a blend of fury and sarcasm. "That compounds the problem," he said. "That really does." For good reason, Nixon needed their silence. But the President's insensitivity knew no bounds. After he announced Haldeman's resignation, he asked his departing aide to check out reaction to the speech. Probably for the only time, Haldeman refused a direct request. But in fact, he spent several more months listening to tapes to prepare for Nixon's defense.

The thousands of hours of taped conversations that Nixon fought so long to suppress will eventually be made public. Does anyone believe they will exonerate him or enhance his historical reputation? In the meantime, Haldeman's diaries take the lid off the Oval Office for the first four years of Nixon's presidency. What he has shown beyond dispute is that the Nixon of the Watergate years—furtive, manipulative and petty; often weak, sometimes comic and, above all, dishonest—was consistent with the behavior patterns of the earlier years. No Old Nixon; no New Nixon: There was one and only one.

POSTSCRIPT

Will History Forgive Richard Nixon?

Hoff-Wilson is one of the few professional historians to render a positive evaluation of President Nixon. She places him in the context of the late 1960s and early 1970s, when support for big government, New Deal, Great Society programs had dimmed and the bipartisan, anticommunist foreign policy consensus has been shattered by the Vietnam War. She gives him high marks for vertically restructuring the executive branch of the government and for attempting a similar reorganization in the federal bureaucracy.

Unlike most defenders of Nixon, Hoff-Wilson considers Nixon's greatest achievements to be domestic. Although he was a conservative, the welfare state grew during his presidency. In the area of civil rights, between 1968 and 1972, affirmative action programs were implemented, and schools with all black children in the southern states declined from 68 percent to 8 percent. Even on such Democratic staples as welfare, the environment, and economic planning, Nixon had outflanked the liberals.

Hoff-Wilson has fleshed out her ideas in much greater detail in *Nixon Reconsidered* (Basic Books, 1994). British conservative cabinet minister and historian Jonathan Aitken has also written a favorable and more panoramic view of the former president entitled *Nixon: A Life* (Regnery Gateway, 1993).

Historian Stephen E. Ambrose's three-volume biography *Nixon* (Simon & Schuster, 1987, 1989, 1991) also substantiates Hoff-Wilson's emphasis on Nixon's domestic successes. Ambrose's evaluation is even more remarkable because he was a liberal historian who campaigned for George McGovern in 1972 and had to be talked into writing a Nixon biography by his publisher. In domestic policy, Ambrose told the *Washington Post* on November 26, 1989, Nixon "was proposing things in '73 and '74 he couldn't even make the front pages with—national health insurance for all, a greatly expanded student loan operation, and energy and environmental programs." With regard to foreign policy, both Ambrose and Aitken disagree with Hoff-Wilson; they consider Nixon's foreign policy substantial and far-sighted. In the second volume of his biography, *Nixon: The Triumph of a Politician, 1962–1972* (Simon & Schuster, 1989), Ambrose concludes that the president was "without peer in foreign relations where 'profound pragmatic' vision endowed him with the potential to become a great world statesman."

Kutler accepts none of the revisionists' premises. In *The Wars of Watergate: The Last Crisis of Richard Nixon* (Alfred A. Knopf, 1990), Kutler focuses on both the negative side of Nixon's personality and his abuse of presidential power. In his review of *The Haldeman Diaries*, Kutler finds further substantiation for his view that Nixon was a narrow-minded, bigoted, self-calculating individual who took no action in his career that was not politically motivated. Unlike other writers who saw a "new" Nixon emerge as president, Kutler maintains that there was only one Nixon—a man possessed with a "corrosive hatred that decisively shaped" his behavior and career.

Neither Ambrose nor Kutler accept the view that Nixon was a corporate executive who reorganized government to enhance decision making. Both would agree that Nixon loved intrigue, conspiracies, and surprise. At the same time Kutler argues that Nixon went much further than any of his predecessors in abusing presidential power by siccing the Internal Revenue Service (IRS) on potential enemies, impounding funds so that the Democrat-controlled Congress could not implement its legislative programs, and finally covering up and lying for over two years about the Watergate scandal.

Clearly, historians will be disputing the Nixon legacy for a long time. Two works have tried to place Nixon within the context of his times. Liberal historian Herbert S. Parmet, the first to gain access to Nixon's prepresidential papers, published *Richard Nixon and His America* (Little, Brown, 1990). Less thoroughly researched in primary sources but more insightful is *New York Times* reporter Tom Wicker's *One of Us: Richard Nixon and the American Dream* (Random House, 1991).

In order to gain a real feel for the Nixon years, you should consult contemporary or primary accounts. Nixon himself orchestrated his own rehabilitation in *RN: The Memoirs of Richard Nixon* (Grosset & Dunlop, 1978); *The Real War* (Warner Books, 1980); *Real Peace* (Little, Brown, 1984); *No More Vietnams* (Arbor House, 1985); and *In the Arena: A Memoir of Victory, Defeat and Renewal* (Simon & Schuster, 1990). Nixon's own accounts should be compared with former national security adviser Henry Kissinger's memoirs *White House Years* (Little, Brown, 1979). *The Haldeman Diaries: Inside the Nixon White House* (Putnam, 1994), which is the subject of Kutler's review essay, is essential for any undertaking of Nixon. Haldeman's account fleshes out the daily tensions of life in the Nixon White House and adds important details to the Nixon and Kissinger accounts. Other primary accounts include Kenneth W. Thompson, ed., *The Nixon Presidency: Twenty-Two Intimate Perspectives of Richard M. Nixon*, Portraits of American Presidents series, vol. 6 (University Press of America, 1987), which contains a series of discussions with former officials of the Nixon administration conducted by the White Burkett Miller Center for the Study of Public Affairs at the University of Virginia.

Two of the best review essays on the new historiography about our 37th president are "Theodore Draper: Nixon, Haldeman, and History," *The New York Review of Books* (July 14, 1994) and Sidney Blumenthal, "The Longest Campaign," *The New Yorker* (August 8, 1994).

ISSUE 17

Were the 1980s a Decade of Greed?

YES: Kevin Phillips, from *The Politics of Rich and Poor: Wealth and the American Electorate in the Reagan Aftermath* (Random House, 1990)

NO: Alan Reynolds, from "Upstarts and Downstarts," *National Review* (August 31, 1992)

ISSUE SUMMARY

YES: Political analyst Kevin Phillips argues that President Ronald Reagan's tax reform bills in the 1980s widened the income gap by decreasing the tax burden on the rich and increasing the taxes paid by the middle-income and poor classes.

NO: Conservative economist Alan Reynolds asserts that all income groups experienced significant gains in income during the 1980s.

In 1939, after six years of the New Deal, unemployment remained at an unacceptably high rate of 17 percent. World War II bailed America out of the Great Depression. When 20 million workers entered the armed forces, married American women, along with African American and Hispanic males and females, filled the void in the higher-paying factory jobs. Everyone not only made money but poured it into war bonds and traditional savings accounts. Government and business cemented their relationship with "cost plus" profits for the defense industries.

By the end of 1945 Americans had stashed away $134 billion in cash, savings accounts, and government securities. This pent-up demand meant there would be no depression akin to the end of World War I or the 1930s. Following initial shortages before industry completed its conversion to peacetime production, Americans engaged in the greatest spending spree in the country's history. Liberals and conservatives from both political parties had developed a consensus on foreign and domestic policies. Cold war liberals accepted an anticommunist and interventionist foreign policy, which used Marshall plan money to successfully rebuild the economic foundations of Western Europe and foreign aid to develop capitalist economies in southeast Asia and Japan. Conservatives reconciled themselves to the development of the welfare state that the New Dealers created. These conservatives reluctantly accepted the idea implied in the Employment Act of 1946—that government had become the manager of the economy.

The president's Council of Economic Advisers was comprised of Keynesians, who believed that government spending could increase employment even if it meant that budget deficits would be temporarily created. For nearly 25 years they used fiscal and monetary tools to manipulate the economy so that inflation would remain low while employment would reach close to its maximum capacity.

Around 1968 the consensus surrounding domestic and foreign policy broke down for three reasons: (1) the Vietnam embroglio; (2) the oil crises of 1974 and 1979; and (3) the decline of the smokestack industries.

Lyndon Johnson had his presidency ruined by the Vietnam War. He believed that he could escalate the war and his Great Society programs at the same time. His successor, Richard Nixon, attempted to solve the Vietnam dilemma by bringing the American boys home and letting Asians fight Asians. The process of withdrawal was slow and costly. So were many of the Great Society programs, such as Social Security, Aid to Dependent Children, environmental legislation, and school desegregation, which Nixon continued to uphold. In August 1971 Nixon acknowledged that he had become a Keynesian when he imposed a 90-day wage and price control freeze and took the international dollar off the gold standard and allowed it to float. With these bold moves Nixon hoped to stop the dollar from declining in value. He was also faced with a recession that included both high unemployment and high inflation. "Stagflation" resulted, leading to the demise of Keynesian economics.

In early 1974, shortly before Nixon was forced to resign from office, the major oil-producing nations of the world—primarily in the Middle East—agreed to curb oil production and raise oil prices. The OPEC cartel, protesting the pro-Israeli policies of the Western nations, brought these countries to their knees. In the United States gasoline went from $0.40 to $2.00 per gallon in a matter of days. In the early 1980s President Jimmy Carter implored the nation to conserve energy, but he appeared helpless as the unemployment rate approached double digits and as the Federal Reserve Board raised interest rates to 18 percent in a desperate attempt to stem inflation.

The Reagan administration introduced a new economic philosophy: supply-side economics. Its proponents, led by economists Martin Anderson and Arthur Laffer, believed that if taxes are cut and spending on frivolous social programs is reduced—even while military spending increases—businesses will use the excess money to expand. More jobs will result, consumers will increase spending, and the multiplying effect will be a period of sustained growth and prosperity. Did it work?

In the following selections, Kevin Phillips argues that President Reagan's tax reform bills in the 1980s lessened the tax burden on the rich, while the upper-middle, middle, and poor classes had a higher effective tax burden because more of their incomes went toward regressive Social Security and sales taxes. Alan Reynolds maintains that all groups benefited from Reagan's tax reduction program, the economic recession of 1981–1982 notwithstanding.

YES
Kevin Phillips

TAX-BRACKET REDUCTION: THE CENTERPIECE OF THE REAGAN ERA

The reduction or elimination of federal income taxes had been a goal of all three major U.S. capitalist periods, but were ... a personal preoccupation for Ronald Reagan, whose antipathy toward income taxes dated back to World War II, when a top rate of 91 percent made it foolish to work beyond a certain point. Under Reagan, the top personal tax bracket would drop from 70 percent to 28 percent in just seven years. In 1987 the Congressional Budget Office (CBO) showed just who was getting the cream from these reductions: the top 1 to 5 percent of the population.

In 1861 a Republican administration and Congress imposed the first U.S. income tax to finance the Civil War. After two wartime increases, the federal levy was terminated in 1872, abetting the mushrooming fortunes of the Astors, Carnegies, Morgans and Rockefellers.

Later, as postwar laissez-faire collapsed into populism and progressivism, public doubts about excessive wealth resurged, and with them came income tax pressures. In 1894, after the prior year's unnerving stock market panic, Congress passed a tax of 2 percent on incomes over four thousand dollars, which the U.S. Supreme Court declared unconstitutional in 1895. A constitutional amendment solved the problem in 1913. As Europe marched to war in 1914, joined by the United States in 1917, the demand for income tax revenue soon repeated itself. Levies climbed quickly, and by 1920, the top rate was 73 percent.

As a result, postwar federal revenues exceeded peacetime needs and discouraged peacetime enterprise. When the Harding administration took office in 1921, tax rates were quickly reduced, in four stages, to a top bracket of just 25 percent in 1925. As Reaganite theorists would recall six decades later, cutting income taxes amidst gathering commercial prosperity helped create the boom of the 1920s. The prime beneficiaries were the top 5 percent of Americans, people who rode the cutting edge of the new technology of autos, radios and the like, emerging service industries (including new practices like advertising and consumer finance), a booming stock market and unprecedented real estate development. As federal taxation eased, especially on the upper brackets, disposable income soared for the rich—and with it conspicuous consumption and financial speculation.

By the crash of 1929, striking changes had occurred in the distribution of both taxes *and* wealth. The bottom-earning 80 percent of the population, never much affected, had been cut off the income tax rolls entirely. As a result, the top 1 percent of taxpayers were paying about two thirds of what the Treasury took in. Even so, because the top rate had fallen from 73 percent to 25 percent, federal taxation was taking less and less of booming upper-bracket incomes and stock profits. By contrast, many farmers and miners, and some workers, hurt by slumping commodity prices, found themselves with lower real purchasing power than they had enjoyed in the placid decade before World War I. Tax policy was not the only source of upward redistribution, but it contributed greatly to the polarization of U.S. wealth and the inequality of income, which peaked between 1927 and 1929.

But Democrats, soon back in control of Congress and then the White House, preferred to afflict rather than nurture concentrated wealth. Now the direction of redistribution moved *downward*. To achieve that, the top tax rate reached 63 percent by 1932, 79 percent by 1936 and soared to 91 percent during World War II, the incentiveless bracket that so offended Ronald Reagan and his Hollywood friends. Ninety-one percent remained the nominal top rate until 1964, when it fell in two stages to 77 percent and then 70 percent.

If not for the war in Vietnam, there might have been further cuts in the late sixties, but the war was costly, sustaining a high rate structure and even requiring a surtax from 1968 to 1970. More perversely, wartime outlays generated an inflation that lifted more and more middle-class citizens into what had long been *upper-class* brackets. So by the late 1970s, with the war over but with inflation still intensifying, cyclical demand for tax reduction gathered momentum. After nearly fifty years, proposals for deep rate reductions were back on the national agenda. Though Republican politicians aroused little interest in the Kemp-Roth tax cuts in 1978, this lack of support was only temporary.

Over the next two years, a new conservative outlook took shape in Washington, entrenched in 1980 by Reagan's election. The 1981 Economic Recovery Tax Act, passed by a surprisingly willing Congress, offered far more than relief for middle-class bracket creep. Supply-side proponents of individual rate cuts and business-organization lobbyists for capital formation and corporate depreciation allowances shared a half-trillion-dollar victory.[1] For the first time since the New Deal, federal tax policy was fundamentally rearranging its class, sector and income-group loyalties.

Corporate tax rates were reduced and depreciation benefits greatly liberalized. By 1983 the percentage of federal tax receipts represented by corporate income tax revenues would drop to an all-time low of 6.2 percent, down from 32.1 percent in 1952 and 12.5 percent in 1980. For individuals the 1981 act cut taxes across the board—by 5 percent in 1981, then 10 percent in 1982 and another 10 percent in 1983. Another highly significant change trimmed the top bracket from 70 percent to 50 percent. Taxation of *earned* income had been capped at a 50 percent top rate since 1972. Now the same treatment would be extended to *unearned* income, an enormous boon to the small percentage of the population deriving most of its income from rents and interest. Meanwhile, the top rate on capital gains was effectively cut to 20 percent, having earlier been dropped from 49 percent to 28 percent by the Steiger Amendment reductions of 1978. Conservative tax-reduction supporters predicted a surge in savings, venture capitalism and entrepreneurialism. Liberal economists, disheartened, prophesied more inflation and mounting inequality. Both predictions only half proved out. The savings rate didn't grow, and neither did inflation, but enterprise *and* inequality did—an old story.

Critics of emerging income polarization would eventually cite the increasingly benign treatment between 1978 and 1981 of property income (interest, dividends and rents) and capital gains, a benefit that flowed mostly to a small stratum of taxpayers. According to a 1983 Federal Reserve Board survey, families in the top 2 percent owned 30 percent of all liquid assets (from checking accounts to money market funds), 50 percent of the corporate stocks held by individuals, some 39 percent of corporate and government bonds and 71 percent of tax-exempt municipals. And applying a broader measurement of upper-income status, the wealthiest 10 percent owned 51 percent of liquid assets, 72 percent of corporate stocks, 70 percent of bonds and 86 percent of tax-exempts.

The inflation of the late 1970s and then subsequent post-1981 disinflation would affect different economic strata in different ways. At first, under inflation, blue-collar wages stagnated, at least in real terms, but a fair percentage of reasonably well off property owners benefited from increased bank CD interest rates, real estate values, precious metals, jewelry, art and rents. When disinflation took over in 1981–82, the big benefit shifted to the more truly rich. Real interest rates soared, and as that happened, upper-bracket holders of financial assets —mostly stocks and bonds—chalked up the greatest gains. Data compiled by the Economic Policy Institute in 1988 spelled out the much larger 1978–86 gain in property income (up 116.5 percent) compared with wage, salary and other labor income (up 66.6 percent). Lightened levies on capital gain and property income, coming just around the time when those categories were climbing, helped fuel upper-bracket wealth and capital accumulation more or less as conservative tax strategists and entrepreneurial theorists had hoped.

The second big redistributive spur was Washington's decision to let Social Security tax rates climb upward from 6.05 percent in 1978 to 6.70 percent in 1982–83, 7.05 percent in 1985 and 7.51 percent in 1988–89—a schedule originally voted in 1977 under Carter—while income tax rates were coming down. By 1987, however, Maine Democratic senator George Mitchell complained that "as a result, there has been a shift of about $80 billion in annual revenue collections from the progressive income tax to the regressive payroll tax. The Social Security tax increase in 1977 cannot be attributed to the current administration. But the response in the 1980s—to make up for a tax increase disproportionately burdening lower-income households with a tax cut disproportionately benefiting higher-income households—*can* be laid to the policies of this administration." Mitchell was hardly overstating the new reliance on Social Security. Between 1980 and 1988, the FICA tax on $40,000-a-year incomes doubled from $1,500 to nearly $3,000. The portion of total annual federal tax receipts represented by Social Security rose from 31 percent to 36 percent while income tax contributions dropped from 47 percent to under 45 percent. Table 1 shows the consequent 1977–88 realignment of effective tax rates for different groups.

After his reelection in 1984, Reagan moved to replicate the full reduction of the Harding-Coolidge era and succeeded in doing so when the 1986 tax reform cut top individual rates from 70 percent in 1981 to just 28 percent as of 1988 —effectively matching the 1921–25 reduction from 73 percent to 25 percent. Democrats were largely uncritical; as we have seen, their acquiescence in such reversals is typical of capitalist heydays.

Taxpayers would not feel the final effects of the 1986 tax reductions until April 1989, and 1988 tax distribution data couldn't be officially analyzed for several years thereafter, well past the president's departure from office. Yet the debate over who had gained and lost under Reagan intensified. Reaganites and their critics both had a substantial case. Supply-siders and other advocates of bracket reduction could show that the upper-tier rate cuts had not increased the *proportion* of taxes paid by the poor and middle classes. During the Reagan years the percentage of total federal income tax payments made by the top 1 percent of taxpayers actually rose, climbing from 18.05 percent in 1981 to 19.93 percent in 1983, 21.9 percent in 1985 and 26.1 percent in 1986. And this could have been predicted. As we have seen, their share of national income was increasing by similar proportions. When wealth concentrates at the top of the pyramid, lower rates *do* bring larger receipts than the higher rates of the preconcentration period. Coolidge-era precedents, invoked by supply-siders from the first, had been

even more lopsided. Because the upper-bracket rate cuts of the 1920s also removed most lower- and lower-middle-income families from the rolls, the percentage of total taxes paid by the top 1 percent actually climbed from 43 percent in 1921 to 69 percent in 1926. Early supporters of a tax rollback—not least Coolidge—were quick to boast of this, and assigned credit to the rate cuts. The same boasts were made in the 1980s.

The statistical deception, of course, was that the increased ratios of total tax payments by high-income persons were not an increased burden. Overzealous supply-siders were way too insistent that Reagan's tax policy "soaked the rich," promoted "economic justice," and that "the Reagan years have been, contrary to the conventional wisdom, an age of benevolent Robin Hoodism." Claims that the tax cuts had helped promote prosperity under Coolidge and Reagan were plausible, although more plausibly these cuts *overlapped* rather than caused the two capitalist heydays. That the rich were "soaked" during the 1980s was, however, untrue, as anyone walking down Rodeo Drive could see. It was precisely such exaggerations that undermined supply-sider credibility.

Under Reagan, as under Coolidge, the clear evidence is that the net tax burden on rich Americans as a percentage of their total income *shrank* substantially because of the sweeping rate cuts. The surge in actual tax payments was the result of higher upper-bracket incomes. To measure the benefits, imagine a businessman who had made $333,000 in salary, dividends and capital gains in 1980, and paid $120,000 in federal income taxes. As prosperity returned in 1983, his income climbed to $500,000. Yet with the applicable rates reduced, he might well have paid, say,

Table 1

Shifts in Effective Federal Tax Rates by Population Income Decile, 1977–88

Decile	1977	1984	1988	Percentage Point Change in Effective Rate (1977–84)	(1977–88)
First	8.0%	10.5%	9.6%	+2.5%	+1.6
Second	8.7	8.5	8.3	– .2	– .4
Third	12.0	13.2	13.3	+1.2	+1.3
Fourth	16.2	16.3	16.8	+ .1	+ .6
Fifth	19.1	18.5	19.2	– .6	+ .1
Sixth	21.0	20.1	20.9	– .9	– .1
Seventh	23.0	21.5	22.3	–1.5	– .7
Eighth	23.6	23.0	23.6	– .6	±0
Ninth	24.5	23.8	24.7	– .7	+ .2
Tenth	26.7	23.6	25.0	–3.1	–1.7
Top 5%	27.5	23.3	24.9	–4.2	–2.6
Top 1%	30.9	23.1	24.9	–7.8	–6.0

Source: Congressional Budget Office, *The Changing Distribution of Federal Taxes: 1975–1990*, October, 1987, Table 8, p. 48. (Corporate income tax allocated to labor income.) The 1988 figures were estimates.

$150,000 in taxes, *more actual payment*, of course, but *less relative burden*. That many blue-collar and middle-class Americans had lost their jobs in 1981–82 (when unemployment briefly neared 11 percent) also helps explain why the top 1 percent of 1983 taxpayers—disproportionate beneficiaries of a surging stock market—wound up shouldering a higher portion of the overall federal income tax burden. They were gaining while the bottom half of the population was losing. "Soaked" is hardly the term to describe what happened to millionaires paying out lower percentages of sharply rising incomes.

In 1987, to plot the rearrangement of effective *overall* tax rates, the economists at the Congressional Budget Office took *all* federal taxes—individual income, Social Security, corporate income and excise—and calculated the change in their combined impact on different income strata after 1977. Families below the top decile, disproportionately burdened by Social Security and excise increases and rewarded less by any income tax reductions, wound up paying *higher* effective rates. The richest families, meanwhile, paid lower rates, largely because of the sharp reduction applicable to nonsalary income (capital gains, interest, dividends and rents).

These shifts go a long way to explain both the surge in consumption *and* the rising inequality of income. America's richest 5 percent (and richest 1 percent, in particular) were the tax policy's new beneficiaries. Nor did the CBO's 1988 projections anticipate a significant reversal from the 1986 tax reform, with its unusual combination of further rate reductions (down to a 28 percent top bracket) partly balanced by elimination of credits and deductions. Effective tax rates for 1988 *would* fall slightly for the bottom 20 percent relative to 1984, the CBO found, but not by enough to restore 1977's lower combined-impact levels. Middle and upper groups, in turn, would find their effective rates slightly higher in 1988 than in 1984. For these brackets, a part of the 1981 cut was recaptured. As Table 1 notes, however, the *overall* net effect of the 1977–88 tax changes would be different for *middle-class* versus *top-tier* taxpayers. For Mr. and Mrs. Middle America, the changes during Reagan's second term had the effect of canceling out the minor benefits of 1977–84 reductions. Escalating Social Security rates were a principal culprit. *Upper-echelon taxpayers alone were projected to benefit from a large net reduction in effective overall federal tax rates for the entire 1977–88 period.*

Some of the anomalies of the redesigned tax burden were extraordinary, not least the "bubble" that imposed a marginal income tax rate of 33 percent on family incomes of $70,000 to $155,000 in contrast to the 28 percent rate that applied above these levels. In 1988 a $90,000-a-year family with two husband-and-wife breadwinners making $45,000 each found itself in a 40.5 percent marginal federal tax bracket—a 33 percent income tax rate plus a 7.5 percent Social Security levy—in contrast to the 28 percent marginal rate of a millionaire or billionaire.

Policy at the federal level wasn't unique. During 1988 a collateral thesis began to emerge that state-level tax changes during the 1980s were also aggravating the trend to inequality. Citizens for Tax Justice, a group financed by labor unions and various liberal organizations, calculated that rising state sales taxes were falling disproportionately on poor families. And a 1988 study contended that half the states with income taxes had made them less fair for many low- and middle-income residents in 1986–87. The

1986 federal revisions required modification of state tax laws. The complaint was that those modifications were biased. Critics, however, lacked the documentation rapidly proliferating on the federal level, and in any event, *federal fiscal policy was the main issue.*

The irony was that Democratic election-year presidential politicking did not recognize that importance. Opinion polls in April 1988—tax time—revealed public skepticism of tax reform, its fairness and its wisdom. Yet [Democratic candidate Michael S.] Dukakis avoided the subject. Upper-bracket increases were rejected at the Democratic National Convention. Tax issues were ignored in 1988 as they had been in 1928.

What was also ignored—perhaps because of its complexity—were the data, contrary to widespread belief, showing that non–Social Security taxes for all Americans as a percentage of GNP had been significantly cut during the 1980s. Conservative insistence that the overall federal tax burden hadn't been reduced was deceptive. Certain revenue ratios *did* decline. Between 1 and 2 percent of GNP that had been gathered in taxes for *general* public sector purposes under Eisenhower and Nixon—some $40 billion to $80 billion a year in 1988 dollars—was routed back to the private sector under Reagan, enlarging the federal budget deficit, and thereby affecting federal spending and interest rate outlays, also with redistributive effects. It was true, as Table 2 shows, that *total* federal tax receipts remained roughly constant as a percentage of Gross National Product, but Social Security receipts were rising sharply, disguising a relative decline in *other* revenues, reducing Washington's ability to fund non–Social Security programs from schools to highways.

Table 2

Total Federal Receipts/Outlays as a Percentage of GNP

Fiscal Year	Total Social Security Receipts	Total Non–Social Security Receipts	Total Receipts	Total Outlays
1945	1.6%	19.7%	21.3%	43.6%
1960	2.9	15.4	18.3	18.2
1970	4.5	15.0	19.5	19.8
1980	5.9	13.5	19.4	22.2
1981	6.1	14.0	20.1	22.7
1982	6.4	13.3	19.7	23.7
1983	6.3	11.8	18.1	24.3
1984	6.5	11.5	18.0	23.1
1985	6.7	11.9	18.6	23.9
1986	6.8	11.6	18.4	23.7
1987	6.8	12.5	19.3	22.6
1988	7.0	12.0	19.0	22.3

Other postwar Republican administrations had not sought this kind of fundamental reversal in government's role. Under Eisenhower, on average, non–Social Security federal receipts— principally from personal income, corporate income and excise taxes—had represented 15 percent of GNP, enabling the government to run without deficits. By the late 1960s federal deficits were a fact of fiscal life. Ironically, bracket creep in the late 1970s was perversely helpful —non–Social Security receipts expanded to 14 percent of GNP, reducing deficits again, compared with mid-decade figures.

But the 1981 tax cuts, along with rising military outlays, tight Federal Reserve Board policy and the cost of the 1981–82 recession, sent the federal deficit soaring to 5 to 6 percent of GNP, the highest peacetime levels since the Depression. Non–Social Security revenues in the range of 12 percent of GNP simply were not enough to run the U.S. government in the late 1980s, no matter what the stimulus of tax cuts might be. Part of the slack was made up by money borrowed at home and abroad at high cost. But how long could this go on? Tax relief and incentive economics meant not only income polarization but a frightening buildup of debt.

By 1989, the question was no longer whether tax policy would have to change, but when, how much—and to whose benefit?

NOTES

1. That was the estimated cost of the 1981 tax cuts over the next five years.

NO

Alan Reynolds

UPSTARTS AND DOWNSTARTS

The economic policies presided over by Ronald Reagan were stunningly successful—except to informed opinion, as represented by the academy and the major media. The principal charge against Reagan has become almost a chant: The rich got richer, the poor got poorer, and the middle class was squeezed out of existence.

A key player in the campaign to popularize this view has been Sylvia Nasar of the *New York Times,* who relied on statistics concocted by Paul Krugman of MIT, who, in turn, garbled some already disreputable estimates from the Congressional Budget Office (CBO).

The purpose of the crusade was obvious. Mr. Krugman has been advocating that we somehow double tax collections from those earning over $200,000, so as to greatly increase federal spending. Miss Nasar openly boasted about "supplying fresh ammunition for those... searching for new ways to raise government revenue." Governor Clinton immediately seized upon the Krugman–Nasar statistics as the rationale for his economic plan to tax us into prosperity.

Since the question is what happened in the 1980s, after the Carter Administration, it makes no sense to begin with 1977, as Mr. Krugman and Miss Nasar do, or with 1973, as the Children's Defense Fund does. Real incomes fell sharply during the runaway inflations of 1974–75 and 1979–80. Median real income among black families, for example, fell 15 per cent from 1973 to 1980, then rose 16 per cent from 1982 to 1990.

[Table 1] shows the actual real income of households by fifths of the income distribution, for the most commonly cited years. There is no question that *all* income groups experienced significant income gains from 1980 to 1989, despite the 1981–82 recession, and were still well ahead of 1980 even in the 1990 slump. For all U.S. households, the mean average of real income rose by 15.2 per cent from 1980 to 1989 (from $33,409 to $38,493, in 1990 dollars), compared with a 0.8 per cent *decline* from 1970 to 1980.

This table shows that the "income gap" did not widen merely between the bottom fifth and any "top" group, but also between the bottom fifth and the next highest fifth, the middle fifth, and so on.

From Alan Reynolds, "Upstarts and Downstarts," *National Review* (August 31, 1992). Copyright © 1992 by National Review, Inc., 150 East 35th Street, New York, NY 10016. Reprinted by permission.

A common complaint about these figures is that they exclude capital gains, and therefore understate income at the top. However, the figures also exclude *taxes*. Average income taxes and payroll taxes among the top fifth of households amounted to $24,322 in 1990, according to the Census Bureau, but capital gains among the top fifth were only $14,972. To add the capital gains and not subtract the taxes, as some CBO figures do, is indefensible. Indeed, all CBO estimates of income gains are useless, because they include an estimate of capital gains based on a sample of tax returns. Since lower tax rates on capital gains after 1977 induced more people to sell assets more often, the CBO wrongly records this as increased income. It also ignores all capital losses above the deductible $3,000, and fails to adjust capital gains for inflation.

THE MIDDLE-CLASS BOOM

One thing that we know with 100 per cent certainty is that *most* Americans—far more than half—did very well during the long and strong economic expansion from 1982 to 1989. In those fat years, real after-tax income per person rose by 15.5 per cent, and real *median* income of families, before taxes, went up 12.5 per cent. That means half of all families had gains *larger* than 12.5 per cent, while many below the median also had income gains, though not as large. Many families had to have gained even more than 12.5 per cent, since the more familiar *mean* average rose 16.8 per cent from 1982 to 1989. Even if we begin with 1980, rather than 1982, median income was up 8 per cent by 1989, and mean income by 14.9 per cent. And even if we end this comparison with the slump of 1990,

median family income was still up 5.9 per cent from 1980, and mean income was up 12 per cent.

In *U.S. News & World Report* (March 23, 1992), Paul Krugman claimed that "the income of a few very well-off families soared. This raised average family income—but *most* families didn't share in the good times" (emphasis added). Mr. Krugman apparently does not understand what a rising median income means.

The whole idea of dividing people into arbitrary fifths by income ignores the enormous mobility of people in and out of these categories. What was most unusual about the Eighties, though, was that the number moving *up* far exceeded the number moving *down*. A Treasury Department study of 14,351 taxpayers shows that 86 per cent of those in the lowest fifth in 1979, and 60 per cent in the second fifth, had moved up into a higher income category by 1988. Among those in the middle income group, 47 per cent moved up, while fewer than 20 per cent moved down. Indeed, many more families moved up than down in every income group except the top 1 per cent, where 53 per cent fell into a lower category. Similar research by Isabel Sawhill and Mark Condon of the Urban Institute found that real incomes of those who started out in the bottom fifth in 1977 had risen 77 per cent by 1986—more than 15 times as fast as those who started in the top fifth. Miss Sawhill and Mr. Condon concluded that "the rich got a little richer and the poor got much richer."

This remarkable upward mobility is the sole cause of "The Incredible Shrinking Middle Class," featured in the May 1992 issue of *American Demographics*. Measured in constant 1990 dollars, the

Table 1

Average Household Income (In 1990 Dollars)

	Lowest Fifth	Second Fifth	Third Fifth	Fourth Fifth	Highest Fifth	Top 5%
1990	7,195	18,030	29,781	44,901	87,137	138,756
1989	7,372	18,341	30,488	46,177	90,150	145,651
1980	6,836	17,015	28,077	41,364	73,752	110,213
1977	7,193	17,715	29,287	42,911	76,522	117,023

Source: Bureau of the Census, *Money Income of Households, Families & Persons: 1990*, p. 202.

percentage of families earning between $15,000 and $50,000 fell by 5 points, from about 58 per cent to 53 per cent. This is what is meant by a "shrinking" middle class. We know they didn't disappear into poverty, because the percentage of families earning less than $15,000 (in 1990 dollars), dropped a bit, from 17.5 per cent in 1980 to 16.9 per cent in 1990. What instead happened is that the percentage earning more than $50,000, in constant dollars, *rose* by 5 points—from less than 25 per cent to nearly 31 per cent. Several million families "vanished" from the middle class by earning much more money!

It is not possible to reconcile the increase in median incomes with the often-repeated claim that low-wage service jobs ("McJobs") expanded at the expense of high-wage manufacturing jobs. Actually, there were millions more jobs in sectors where wages were rising most briskly, which meant competitive export industries but also services. From 1980 to 1991, average hourly earnings rose by 6.8 per cent a year in services, compared with only 4.8 per cent in manufacturing. The percentage of working-age Americans with jobs, which had never before the 1980s been nearly as high as 60 per cent, rose to 63 per cent by 1989.

THE MYTH OF LOW-WAGE JOBS

An editorial in *Business Week* (May 25) claimed that, "according to a just-released Census Bureau study, the number of working poor rose dramatically from 1979 to 1990." This is completely false. In fact, the report shows that the percentage of low-income workers who are in poverty *fell* dramatically. Among husbands with such low-income jobs, for example, 35.7 per cent were members of poor families in 1979, but only 21.4 per cent in 1990.

Low incomes, in this report, were defined as "less than the poverty level for a four-person family" ($12,195 a year in 1990). Yet very few people with entry-level or part-time jobs are trying to support a family of four. Husbands now account for only a fifth of such low-income jobs, which are instead increasingly held by young singles and by dependent children living with their parents. Wives had 34 per cent of such jobs in 1979, but fewer than 28 per cent in 1990. That reflects the impressive fact that the median income of women rose by 31 per cent in real terms from 1979 to 1990.

It is true that the absolute *number* of low-income jobs increased in all categories, but that increase was not nearly as large as the increase in medium- and high-income jobs. All that the rise in low-income jobs really shows is that students living with their parents and young singles found it much easier to find acceptable work. The only reason fewer young people had low-income jobs back in the glorious Seventies is a larger percentage of them had no jobs at all! Only 51.4 per cent of single males had full-time jobs in 1974, but 61.8 per cent did by 1989. Young people always start out with low earnings, if they get a chance to start out at all.

In his... book, *Head to Head*, Lester Thurow writes that "between 1973 and 1990, real hourly wages for non-supervisory workers... fell 12 per cent, and real weekly wages fell 18 per cent." Yet these averages include part-time workers, which is why *average* wages appeared to be only $355 a week in 1991, even though half of all full-time workers (the *median*) earned more than $430 a week. Because many more students and young mothers were able to find part-time jobs in the Eighties, that diluted both the weekly and the hourly "average" wage. It most definitely did not mean that the wages of the "average worker" went down, but rather that otherwise unemployed part-time and entry-level workers were able to raise their wages above zero. The increase in part-time jobs also does not mean that families are poorer; rather, they are richer. Out of 19.3 million part-time workers in 1991, only 1.2 million were family heads, and only 10 per cent said they were unable to find full-time work.

THE RICH WORK HARDER

Although the vast majority clearly had large income gains in the Eighties, Mr. Krugman and Miss Nasar nonetheless assert that those at the top had even larger gains, and that this is something that ought to provoke resentment or envy. Yet the figures they offer to make this point are grossly misleading. Moreover, the whole static routine of slicing up income into fifths is bound to show the highest percentage increases in average (mean) incomes among the "top" 20 per cent or 1 per cent. *That is because for top groups alone, any and all increases in income are included in the average, rather than in movement to a higher group.*

In his *U.S. News* article, Krugman first claimed that CBO figures show that "Ronald Reagan's tax cuts" boosted after-tax income of the top 1 per cent "by a whopping 102 per cent." That figure, though, is based on a "tax simulation model" which estimates "adjusted" incomes as a multiple of the poverty level. The top 1 per cent supposedly earned less than 22 times the poverty level in 1980, but 44 times the poverty level in 1989—hence the gain of 102 per cent. Yet this is a purely relative measure of affluence, not an absolute gain in real income. As more and more families rose further and further above the unchanged "poverty line" in the Eighties, thus lifting the income needed to be in the "top 1 per cent," the CBO technique had to show a "widening gap."

Furthermore, the share of federal income tax paid by the top 1 per cent soared from 18.2 per cent in 1981 to 28 per cent in 1988, though it slipped to 25.4 per cent in 1990. Indeed, this unexpected revenue from the rich was used to double personal exemptions and triple the earned-income tax credit, which was of enormous benefit to the working poor.

By the time Mr. Krugman's alleged 102 per cent gain at the top had reached the

New York Times, it had shrunk to 60 per cent. However, the CBO wrote a memo disowning this estimate too, noting that "of the total rise in aggregate income… about one-fourth went to families in the top 1 per cent." By fiddling with "adjusted" data, the CBO managed to get that share of the top 1 per cent up to one-third. Whether a fourth or a third, these estimates still begin with 1977, not 1980. Between 1977 and 1980, the CBO shows real incomes falling by 6.6 per cent for the poorest fifth. The top 5 per cent fared *relatively* well before 1980, because everybody else suffered an outright drop in real income.

Even if the Krugman–Nasar figures had been remotely accurate, the whole exercise is conceptually flawed. In every income group except the top, many families can move up from one group to another with little or no effect on the average income of those remaining in the lower group. Above-average increases in income among those in the lower groups simply move them into a higher fifth, rather than raising the average income of the fifth they used to be in. Only the top income groups have no ceiling, as those in such a group cannot possibly move into any higher group. A rap star's first hit record may lift his income from the lowest fifth to the top 1 per cent, with no perceptible effect on the average income of the lowest fifth. But two hit records in the next year would raise the total amount of income counted in the top 1 per cent, and thus raise the average for that category.

Nobody knows exactly how much income is needed to be counted among the top 1 per cent, because the Census Bureau keeps track only of the top 5 per cent. Census officials argue that apparent changes in the small sample

used to estimate a "top 1 per cent" may largely reflect differences in the degree of dishonest reporting. When marginal tax rates fell from 70 per cent to 28 per cent, for example, more people told the truth about what they earned, so "the rich" *appeared* to earn much more.

One thing we do know, though, is that the minimum amount of income needed to be included among the top 1 per cent has to have risen quite sharply since 1980, because of the huge increase in the percentage of families earning more than $50,000, or $100,000. This increased proportion of families with higher incomes pushed up the income ceilings on all middle and higher income groups, and thus raised the floor defining the highest income groups.

While $200,000 may have been enough to make the top 1 per cent in 1980, a family might need over $300,000 to be in that category a decade later. Clearly, any average of all the income above $300,000 is going to yield a much bigger number than an average of income above $200,000. The CBO thus estimates that average pre-tax income among the top 1 per cent rose from $343,610 in 1980 to $566,674 in 1992. But this 65 per cent increase in the average does *not* mean that those specific families that were in the top 1 per cent in 1980 typically experienced a 65 per cent increase in real income. It simply means that the standards for belonging to this exclusive club have gone way up. That is because millions more couples are earning higher incomes today than in 1980, not because only a tiny fraction are earning 65 per cent more.

Sylvia Nasar totally misreported the CBO's complaints with her first article, and audaciously quoted her own discredited assertions in a later *New York Times* piece (April 21). This front-page editorial changed the subject—from income to wealth. It claimed a "Federal Reserve" study had found that the wealthiest 1 per cent had 37 per cent of all net worth in 1989, up from 31 per cent in 1983. Paul Krugman, writing in the *Wall Street Journal*, likewise cited this "careful study by the Federal Reserve." Yet the cited figures are from a mere *footnote* in a rough "working paper" produced by one of hundreds of Fed economists Arthur Kennickell, along with a statistician from the IRS, Louise Woodburn. It comes with a clear warning that "opinions in this paper ... in no way reflect the views of ... the Federal Reserve System."

At that, all of the gain of the top 1 per cent was supposedly at the expense of others within the top 10 per cent, not the middle class or poor. In any case, the figures are little more than a guess. The authors acknowledge that they "cannot offer a formal statistical test of the significance of the change."

"The 1983 and 1989 sample designs and the weights developed are quite different," they write. "The effect of this difference is unknown." Their estimated range of error does not account for "error attributable to imputation or to other data problems." Yet it is nonetheless within that range of error for the share of net worth held by the top 1 per cent to have risen imperceptibly, from 34.5 to 34.6 per cent. This is why Kennickell and Woodburn say their estimates merely "suggest that there may have been an increase in the share of wealth held by this top group in 1989." Or maybe not.

The actual, official Federal Reserve study tells a quite different story. It shows that real net worth rose by 28 per cent among 40 per cent of families earning between $20,000 and $50,000, but by only 6.6 per cent for the top 20 per cent,

earning more than $50,000. Since this huge increase in net worth among those with modest incomes means their assets grew much faster than their debts, this also puts to rest the myth that the Eighties was built upon "a mountain of debt." It was, instead, built upon a mountain of assets, particularly small businesses.

CHILDREN WITHOUT FATHERS

What about the poor? There is no question that there has been a stubbornly large increase of people with very low incomes. However, annual "money income" turns out to be a surprisingly bad measure of ability to buy goods and services. In 1988, average consumer spending among, the lowest fifth of the population was $10,893 a year—more than double their apparent income of $4,942. That huge gap occurs partly because annual incomes are highly variable in many occupations, and many people have temporary spells of low income, due to illness or job loss. People can and do draw upon savings during periods when their income dips below normal.

Another reason why those in the bottom fifth are able to spend twice their earnings is that many in-kind government transfers (such as food stamps) are not counted as "money income." Census surveys also acknowledge that a fourth of the cash income from welfare and pensions is unreported. And, of course, very little income from illegal activities is reported. In CBO figures, incomes of low-income families are further understated by counting singles as separate families, as though young people stopped getting checks from home the minute they get their first apartment.

Despite such flaws in measured income, nearly all of the income differences between the bottom fifth and the top fifth can nonetheless be explained by the number of people per family with full-time jobs, their age, and their schooling. Among household heads in the lowest fifth, for example, only 21 per cent worked full-time all year in 1990, and half had no job all year. In the top fifth, by contrast, the average number of full-time workers was more than two.

The May 25 *Business Week* editorial noted that "the percentage of Americans below the poverty line rose from 11.7 per cent in 1979 to 13.5 per cent in 1990." Yet this poverty rate is exaggerated, because it is based on an obsolete consumer price index that mismeasured housing inflation before 1983. Using the corrected inflation measure, the poverty rate was 11.5 per cent in 1980 and 11.4 in 1989, before rising to 12.1 per cent in 1990. That 12.1 per cent figure, though, is only one of 14 different Census Bureau measures of poverty, and not the most credible. Like income for the "bottom fifth," the usual measure of poverty excludes many in-kind transfer payments, as well as cash from the earned-income tax credit. By instead including such benefits, and also subtracting taxes, the Census Bureau brings the actual poverty rate down to 9.5 per cent for 1990, or to 8.5 per cent if homeownership is considered (those who own homes need less cash because they don't pay rent).

Even by the conventional measure, the poverty rate among married-couple families dropped slightly, from 5.2 per cent in 1980 to 4.9 per cent in 1990, and poverty rates among those above age 65 have fallen quite substantially. On the other hand, among female household heads with children under the age of 18 and "no husband present," poverty rose from 37.1 per cent in 1979 to 39.9 per cent in 1980, and then to 41.6 per cent by 1990.

The poverty rate among fatherless families, then, is slightly higher now than it was in the previous decade, and is lower if these young women work. (Among female householders with children under the age of 6, the poverty rate among those with jobs dropped from 20.2 per cent in 1979 to 17.9 per cent in 1989, and the percentage of such mothers who worked full-time rose from 24.9 to 30.6 per cent.) But there are so many more female-headed households, and so few of these women work, that the net effect is nonetheless to keep the overall poverty rate from falling. The number of female-headed households with children under age 18 rose from 5.8 million in 1979 to 7.2 million in 1989. In too many cases, these mothers are so young that child-labor laws would not allow them to work in any case.

In March 1991, the average money income of female-headed families with children was only $17,500, and most of that money (plus food stamps, housing allowance, and Medicaid) came from taxpayers. For married couples who both worked full-time, average income was $55,700 before taxes—about enough to put the *average* two-earner family in the top fifth. Taxing hardworking two-earner families to subsidize broken, no-earner families can only discourage the former, encourage the latter, and thus exacerbate the problems it pretends to solve.

To summarize what actually happened in the 1980s, the "middle class," and the vast majority by any measure, unquestionably experienced substantial gains in real income and wealth. With millions more families earning much higher incomes, it required much higher incomes to make it into the top 5 per cent or top 1 per cent, which largely accounts for the illusion that such "top" groups experienced disproportionate gains. The rising tide lifted at least 90 per cent of all boats. About 9 to 12 per cent continued to be poor, but this group increasingly consisted of female-headed households with young children. More and better jobs cannot help those who do not work, improved investment opportunities cannot help those who do not save, and increased incomes cannot help families whose fathers refuse to support their own children.

POSTSCRIPT

Were the 1980s a Decade of Greed?

Phillips is a well-known political analyst who, at the age of 29, predicted that the Republican Party would become America's major party in the 1970s and 1980s. He contended that blue-collar, urban Catholics and traditional, southern whites would flee the Democratic Party, which became associated with the counterculture values of the 1960s. His book *The Emerging Republican Majority* (Arlington House, 1969) became the bible of the Nixon administration and paved the way for the southern strategy used to reelect Richard Nixon and his successors, Ronald Reagan and George Bush.

A self-proclaimed conservative populist, Phillips became disillusioned with the policies of the Reagan administration, whose tax bills in 1981 and 1986 favored the economic interests of the wealthy classes over the middle and poorer classes, drastically widening the income gap between the rich and the rest of the American people.

Reynolds, a well-known conservative economist with the Hudson Institute, disagrees with the conventional wisdom that the 1980s primarily benefited the wealthy classes at the expense of everyone else. Marshaling an array of figures compiled at the Census Bureau, Reynolds finds that incomes rose for all classes, including the poor.

Historians will debate the meaning of the 1980s for a long time. Support for Phillips's view comes from Frederick Strobel, a former senior business economist at the Federal Reserve Bank of Atlanta, in *Upward Dreams, Downward Mobility: The Economic Decline of the American Middle Class* (Rowman & Littlefield, 1993). The reasons that Strobel gives for the economic decline include an increased supply of workers (baby boomers, housewives, and immigrants), a decline in union membership, a strong dollar, and an open import dollar that destroyed many U.S. manufacturing jobs, corporate merger mania, declining government jobs, energy inflation, high interest rates, and the corporate escape from federal, state, and local taxes.

Unexpected criticism also comes from President Reagan's own director of the Office of Management and Budget, David A. Stockman. His *Triumph of Politics: Why the Revolution Failed* (Harper & Row, 1986) details the "idealogical hubris" that surrounded Reagan's advisers, who, in conjunction with a spendthrift Congress beholden to outside interest groups, ran up massive budget deficits by implementing a theory known as supply-side economics. More critical from the left are a series of academic articles in *Understanding America's Economic Decline* edited by Michael A. Bernstein and David E. Adler (Cambridge University Press, 1994).

CONTRIBUTORS
TO THIS VOLUME

EDITORS

LARRY MADARAS is a professor of history and political science at Howard Community College in Columbia, Maryland. He received a B.A. from the College of the Holy Cross in 1959 and an M.A. and a Ph.D. from New York University in 1961 and 1964, respectively. He has also taught at Spring Hill College, the University of South Alabama, and the University of Maryland at College Park. He has been a Fulbright Fellow and has held two fellowships from the National Endowment for the Humanities. He is the author of dozens of journal articles and book reviews.

JAMES M. SoRELLE is a professor of history in and chair of the Department of History at Baylor University in Waco, Texas. He received a B.A. and an M.A. from the University of Houston in 1972 and 1974, respectively, and a Ph.D. from Kent State University in 1980. In addition to introductory courses in American history, he teaches upper-level sections in African American, urban, and late-nineteenth- and twentieth-century U.S. history. His scholarly articles have appeared in the *Houston Review, Southwestern Historical Quarterly,* and *Black Dixie: Essays in Afro-Texan History and Culture in Houston* edited by Howard Beeth and Cary D. Wintz (Texas A&M University Press, 1992). He has also contributed entries to *The Handbook of Texas, The Oxford Companion to Politics of the World,* and *Encyclopedia of the Confederacy.*

STAFF

Theodore Knight   List Manager
David Brackley   Senior Developmental Editor
Juliana Poggio   Associate Developmental Editor
Rose Gleich   Administrative Assistant
Brenda S. Filley   Production Manager
Juliana Arbo   Typesetting Supervisor
Diane Barker   Proofreader
Lara Johnson   Design/Advertising Coordinator
Richard Tietjen   Publishing Systems Manager

AUTHORS

RICHARD M. ABRAMS is a professor of history at the University of California, Berkeley, where he has been teaching since 1961. He has been a Fulbright professor in both London and Moscow and has taught and lectured in many countries throughout the world, including China, Austria, Norway, Italy, Japan, Germany, and Australia. He has published numerous articles in history, business, and law journals, and he is the editor of *The Shaping of Twentieth Century America: Interpretative Essays* (Little, Brown, 1965) and the author of *The Burdens of Progress* (Scott, Foresman, 1978).

GARY DEAN BEST is a professor of history at the University of Hawaii in Hilo, Hawaii. He is a former fellow of the American Historical Association and of the National Endowment for the Humanities, and he was a Fulbright Scholar in Japan from 1974 to 1975. His publications include *The Nickel and Dime Decade: American Popular Culture During the 1930s* (Praeger, 1993).

ROGER BILES is a professor in and chair of the history department at East Carolina University in Greenville, North Carolina. He is the author of *The South and the New Deal* (University Press of Kentucky, 1994) and *Richard J. Daly: Politics, Race, and the Governing of Chicago* (Northern Illinois Press, 1995).

IRVING BRANT was an editorial writer for several major newspapers, including the *St. Louis Star-Times* and the *Chicago Sun*. He is the author of over a dozen books, including the six-volume biography *James Madison* (Bobbs-Merrill, 1941–1961) and *The Bill of Rights: Its Origin and Meaning* (Bobbs-Merrill, 1965).

ALEXANDER B. CALLOW, JR., is a professor emeritus of history at the University of California, Santa Barbara. He is the editor of *The City Boss in America: An Interpretive Reader* (Oxford University Press, 1976) and *American Urban History: An Interpretive Reader*, 3rd ed. (Oxford University Press, 1982).

CARL N. DEGLER is the Margaret Byrne Professor Emeritus of American History at Stanford University in Stanford, California. He is a member of the editorial board for the Plantation Society, and he is a member and former president of the American History Society and the Organization of American Historians. His book *Neither Black nor White: Slavery and Race Relations in Brazil and the United States* (University of Wisconsin Press, 1972) won the 1972 Pulitzer Prize for history.

ROBERT A. DIVINE is a professor of history at the University of Texas at Austin. He has written several books, including *Eisenhower and the Cold War* (Oxford University Press, 1981) and *Since 1945: Politics and Diplomacy in Recent American History*, 3rd ed. (Alfred A. Knopf, 1985).

MELVYN DUBOFSKY is the Distinguished Professor of History and Sociology at the State University of New York at Binghamton. Since 1978 he has been a State University of New York Faculty Exchange Scholar, and he is a member of the Organization of Americans and the American Historical Association. He received his Ph.D. from the University of Rochester in 1960. He is the author of *The State and Labor in Modern America* (University of North Carolina Press, 1994).

JOHN LEWIS GADDIS is the Robert A. Lovett Professor of History at Yale University in New Haven, Connecticut. He has also been the Distinguished Professor of History at Ohio University, where he founded the Contemporary History Institute, and he has held visiting appointments at the United States Naval War College, the University of Helsinki, Princeton University, and Oxford University. He is the author of many books, including *The Long Peace: Inquiries into the History of the Cold War* (Oxford University Press, 1987) and *The United States and the End of the Cold War: Implications, Reconsiderations, Provocations* (Oxford University Press, 1992).

HERBERT G. GUTMAN (1928–1985) was internationally recognized as America's leading labor and social historian. He taught at many colleges and universities, including Stanford University, William and Mary College, and the Graduate Center of the City University of New York, where he founded the American Working Class History Project.

LOUIS R. HARLAN is the Distinguished Professor of History Emeritus at the University of Maryland in College Park, Maryland. His publications include *Separate and Unequal: Public School Campaigns and Racism in the Southern Seaboard States, 1901–1915* (University of North Carolina Press, 1958) and *Booker T. Washington: The Wizard of Tuskegee* (Oxford University Press, 1983), which won the 1984 Pulitzer Prize for biography, the Bancroft Prize, and the Beveridge Prize.

LEO HERSHKOWITZ is a professor of history at Queens College, City University of New York.

MURIEL E. HIDY taught at the Harvard Business School for many years and was a pioneer in the field of business history. She is the author of *George Peabody,*
Merchant and Financier: 1829–1854 (Ayer, 1979) and coauthor, with Ralph W. Hidy and Roy V. Scott, of *The Great Northern Railway* (Harvard Business School Press, 1988).

RALPH W. HIDY taught at the Harvard Business School for many years and was a pioneer in the field of business history. He is the author of *House of Baring in American Trade and Finance: English Merchant Bankers at Work, 1763–1861* (Russell & Russell) and coauthor, with Muriel E. Hidy and Roy V. Scott, of *The Great Northern Railway* (Harvard Business School Press, 1988).

JOAN HOFF-WILSON is a professor of history at Indiana University in Bloomington, Indiana, and coeditor of the *Journal of Women's History*. She is a specialist in twentieth-century American foreign policy and politics and in the legal status of American women. She has received numerous awards, including the Berkshire Conference of Women Historians' Article Prize and the Stuart L. Bernath Prize for the best book on American diplomacy. She has published several books, including *Herbert Hoover: The Forgotten Progressive* (Little, Brown, 1975) and *Without Precedent: The Life and Career of Eleanor Roosevelt* (Indiana University Press, 1984), coedited with Marjorie Lightman.

RICHARD HOFSTADTER (1916–1970) was a professor of history at Columbia University and has been called the greatest American historian of the post–World War II generation. His book *The American Political Tradition and the Men Who Made It* (Alfred A. Knopf, 1948) is considered a classic.

HAROLD M. HYMAN was the William P. Hobby Professor of History at Rice University from 1968 to 1996. He has also taught at Arizona State University, the University of California, and the University of Illinois. His scholarly concerns center on U.S. constitutional and legal history and on the U.S. Civil War and Reconstruction. He is the author of many books, including *To Try Men's Souls: Loyalty Tests in American History*, which won the Sidney Hillman Award in 1960, and *A History of the Vinson and Elkins Law Firm of Houston, 1917–1997* (University of Georgia Press, 1998).

MATTHEW JOSEPHSON, who figured among the literary expatriots in France in the 1920s, is the author of numerous critical biographies and histories of the Gilded Age, including *Edison: A Biography* and *The President Makers: The Culture of Politics in an Age of Enlightenment.*

WILLIAM E. KINSELLA, JR., is a professor of history at Northern Virginia Community College in Annandale, Virginia. He has also taught at John Carroll University and Georgetown University. He is the author of *Leadership in Isolation: FDR and the Origins of the Second World War* (Schenkman Books, 1970).

STANLEY I. KUTLER is the E. Gordon Fox Professor of American Institutions at the University of Wisconsin–Madison and editor of *Reviews in American History.* He is the author of *Wars of Watergate: The Last Crisis of Richard Nixon* (Alfred A. Knopf, 1990) and the editor of *American Retrospectives: Historians on Historians* (Johns Hopkins University Press, 1995).

WILLIAM E. LEUCHTENBURG is the William Rand Kennan Professor of History at the University of North Carolina at Chapel Hill and a former president of the American Historical Association and of the Organization of American Historians. He received his Ph.D. from Columbia University. His publications include *Franklin D. Roosevelt and the New Deal, 1932–1940* (Harper & Row, 1963), which won the Bancroft Prize and the Francis Parkman Prize, and *In the Shadow of FDR: From Harry Truman to Bill Clinton,* 2d ed. (Cornell University Press, 1993).

ARTHUR S. LINK was a professor of history at Princeton University. He is coeditor of the Woodrow Wilson papers and the author of the definitive multivolume biography of President Wilson.

RICHARD L. McCORMICK is president of the University of Washington in Seattle, Washington. Prior to that he served as provost and vice chancellor for academic affairs at the University of North Carolina at Chapel Hill. He received his Ph.D. in history from Yale University in 1976. He is the author of *The Party Period and Public Policy: American Politics from the Age of Jackson to the Progressive Era* (Oxford University Press, 1986).

H. R. McMASTER is a 1984 graduate of the U.S. Military Academy at West Point. He has held numerous command and staff positions in the military, and during the Persian Gulf War he commanded Eagle Troop, 2d Armored Cavalry Regiment in combat. He is the author of *A Distant Thunder* (HarperCollins, 1997).

DOUGLAS T. MILLER is the Distinguished Professor of History at Michigan State University in East Lansing, Michigan. He is the author of 10 books, including *On Our Own: Americans in the Sixties* (D. C. Heath, 1996).

MARION NOWAK is a journalist living in Chicago, Illinois.

THOMAS G. PATERSON is a professor of history at the University of Connecticut in Storrs, Connecticut. His articles have appeared in *Journal of American History* and *Diplomatic History*, the editorial boards of which he has served on, and the *American Historical Review*. A past president of the Society for Historians of American Foreign Relations, he has authored, coauthored, or edited many books, including *Contesting Castro* (Oxford University Press, 1994) and *On Every Front*, 2d ed. (W. W. Norton, 1993).

KEVIN PHILLIPS is editor and publisher of *The American Political Report*. He is the author of several books on politics and government, including *Arrogant Capital: Washington, Wall Street, and the Frustration of American Politics* (Little, Brown, 1994).

ALAN REYNOLDS is a senior fellow and director of economic research at the Hudson Institute in Indianapolis. He is also the research director with the National Commission on Economic Growth and Tax Reform and the economics editor of *National Review*.

GLENDA RILEY is a professor of history at Ball State University in Muncie, Indiana. She has written numerous articles and books on women in western history, including *Women and Nature: Saving the "Wild" West* (University of Nebraska Press, 1999) and *Diaries and Letters from the Western Trails, 1852: The California Trail* (University of Nebraska Press, 1997).

DAVID A. SHANNON is the author of *Twentieth Century America*, 4th ed. (Rand McNally, 1977) and the editor of *Southern Business: The Decades Ahead* (MacMillan, 1981).

DONALD SPIVEY is a professor in and chair of the history department at the University of Miami. He received his Ph.D. from the University of California, Davis, in 1976. He is the editor of *Sport in America: New Historical Perspectives* (Greenwood Press, 1985) and the author of *The Politics of Miseducation: The Booker Washington Institute of Liberia, 1929–1984* (University Press of Kentucky, 1986).

CHRISTINE STANSELL is a professor of history at Princeton University in Princeton, New Jersey. She is the author of *City of Women: Sex and Class in New York, 1790–1860* (Random House, 1986) and *American Bohemia: Art, Politics, and Modern Love* (Henry Holt, 1996).

W. A. SWANBERG was a freelance journalist and story writer who also had experience working on a railway. He studied English literature at the University of Minnesota, and during World War II he worked for a year and a half in the Office of War Information. He has written a number of biographies, including *Pulitzer* (Scribner, 1967).

ATHAN THEOHARIS is a professor of history at Marquette University in Milwaukee, Wisconsin. A noted historian of the FBI files and records, he is a member of the Academy of Political Science and the Organization of American Historians. He has written several books, including *J. Edgar Hoover, Sex, and Crime: An Historical Antidote* (Ivan R. Dee, 1995). He received his Ph.D. from the University of Chicago.

BRIAN VANDEMARK teaches history at the United States Naval Academy at Annapolis. He served as research assistant on Clark Clifford's autobiography, *Counsel to the President: A Memoir* (Random House, 1991) and as collaborator on former secretary of defense Robert S. Mc-Namara's Vietnam memoir, *In Retrospect: The Tragedy and Lessons of Vietnam* (Times Books, 1995).

ROBERT WEISBROT is a professor of history at Colby College in Waterville, Maine. He is also on the advisory committee for the African American studies program at Colby. He is the author of *From the Founding of the Southern Christian Leadership Conference to* *the Assassination of Malcolm X (1957–65)* (Chelsea House, 1994).

TOM WICKER, one-time chief of the Washington bureau of the *New York Times,* was a political columnist for the *New York Times* for 25 years, until he retired in 1991. His publications include *A Time to Die: The Attica Prison Revolt* (University of Nebraska Press, 1994) and *One of Us: Richard Nixon and the American Dream* (Random House, 1995).

INDEX

7645

DATE DUE

NO 27 '01			

GAYLORD   PRINTED IN U.S.A.